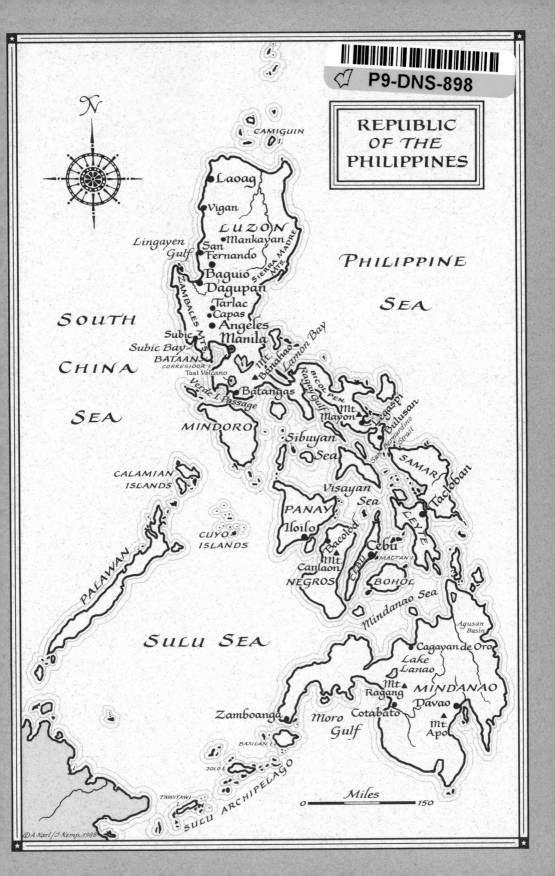

REPUBLIC
OF THE
PHILIPPINES

P9-DNS-898

N

Laoag

Vigan

LUZON

Mankayan

Lingayen
Gulf

San
Fernando

Baguio

Dagupan

Tarlac

Capas

Angeles

Manila

Subic

Subic Bay

BATAAN

CORREGIDOR I.

Taal Volcano

Batangas

Verde I. Passage

MINDORO

Z A M B A L E S   M T S .

S I E R R A   M A D R E   M T S .

PHILIPPINE

SEA

SOUTH

CHINA

SEA

CAMIGUIN I.

MT. Banahao

Lamon Bay

BICOL PEN.

Ragay Gulf

Mt. Mayon

Legaspi

Bulusan

San Bernardino Strait

Sibuyan
Sea

SAMAR

CALAMIAN
ISLANDS

CUYO
ISLANDS

Visayan
Sea

Tacloban

PANAY

Iloilo

Bacolod

Cebu

MACTAN I.

LEYTE

Mt.
Canlaon

CEBU

BOHOL

NEGROS

PALAWAN

Mindanao Sea

Agusan
Basin

SULU SEA

Cagayan de Oro

Lake
Lanao

MINDANAO

Mt.
Ragang

Davao

Zamboanga

Moro
Gulf

Cotabato

Mt.
Apo

BASILAN I.

JOLO I.

TAWITAWI I.

S U L U   A R C H I P E L A G O

Miles

0   150

©A.Karl/J.Kemp,1988

ALSO BY STANLEY KARNOW

Vietnam: A History

Mao and China: From Revolution to Revolution

Southeast Asia

IN OUR IMAGE

IN OUR IMAGE

IMAGE

AMERICA'S EMPIRE IN THE PHILIPPINES

★ ★ ★

STANLEY KARNOW

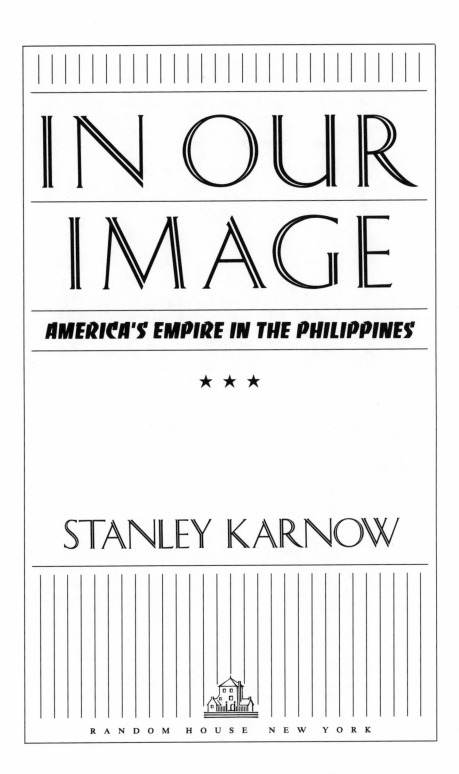

RANDOM HOUSE NEW YORK

Library of Congress Cataloging-in-Publication Data
Karnow, Stanley.
In our image.
Bibliography: p.
Includes index.
1. Philippines—History—1898–1946.   2. Philippines—History.
I. Title.
DS685.K38   1989   959.9   88-42676
ISBN 0-394-54975-9

Manufactured in the United States of America
Typography and binding design by J. K. Lambert
2 4 6 8 9 7 5 3
First Edition

FOR

Curtis and Marilyn,

Catherine, Michael and Benjamin

Facing west from California's shores,

Inquiring, tireless, seeking what is yet unfound,

I, a child, very old, over waves, toward the house

  of maternity, the land of migrations, look afar,

Look off the shore of my Western sea, the circle

  almost encircled. . . .

WALT WHITMAN
"Facing West from California's Shores"

PREFACE

The origins of this book date back thirty years, when as a foreign correspondent I first began to report from Asia. My vast territory included the Philippines, a country that for me differed drastically from any other in the region—or, indeed, from any I had previously covered in Europe, Africa or the Middle East. Here I was, in a former U.S. possession, immediately familiar to an American. Most of the people I initially met spoke Americanized English, and many had been educated in the United States or in American schools. They knew far more about the United States than I knew about the Philippines, as if they were some kind of lost American tribe that had somehow become detached from the U.S. mainland and floated across the Pacific. But with each successive visit I perceived that their values and traditions, though frequently concealed under an American veneer, were their own—and often antithetical to the American model. My observations eventually led to this book, which essentially addresses three questions: What propelled the Americans into the Philippines? What did they do there? And what has been the legacy of their rule? So this is not a history of the Philippines as much as it is the story of America's only major colonial experience.

If journalism is history written under pressure, as Macauley said, this is history written by a journalist at a more leisurely pace. But though I was spared the deadlines that dictated my schedule as a correspondent, I have nevertheless tried to narrate events as they unfolded in an effort to give them a fresh, kinetic quality. The reader will, I hope, note the transition as I shift from the accounts of others to my own recollections in my descriptions and analyses of the characters and their conduct. In any case, I have attempted to tell the story through individuals as they behaved at the time, avoiding the revisionist tendency to impose today's ethics on yesterday's norms. I have not dodged judgments, yet my general attitude, if I can sum it up succinctly, has been one of humility in the face of an enormously complicated subject. One of the lessons I learned as a reporter was that the more I knew the less I knew.

I cannot adequately express my gratitude to Claude Buss, emeritus professor of history at Stanford University, who carefully read the manuscript and generously shared with me the encyclopedic knowledge and profound wisdom he accumulated from more than fifty years in Asia. I am also grateful to Jill Brett for her comments on the manuscript, and my thanks as well to Carmen Nakpil Guerrero, F. Sionil Jose, Virginia Benítez Licuanan, Nicholas Platt, Sheila Platt, Sixto Roxas and Kwoh Yu-pei. Blaine Baggett deserves special mention for proposing the title.

I relied heavily on research assistance from Jenny Springer until, captivated by the subject, she went off to the Philippines as a Peace Corps volunteer. My thanks to her successors: Anne Chamberlin, Susan Cooper, Betty Fisher, Brian

Nienhaus, Jacqueline Sheehan and Jane Shorall. Louis Plummer performed ably as picture researcher.

Peter Osnos, my editor at Random House, and Mitchell Ivers, chief copy editor, furnished me with valuable help. My friend and agent, Ronald Goldfarb, was as usual a source of support and sound advice.

This book is linked with *In Our Image,* a series of television programs conceived with my colleague Andrew Pearson. A veteran television producer and correspondent, Mr. Pearson spent years in Asia, acquiring in the process a rare ability to understand and empathize with its customs and culture. I am deeply indebted to him for his collaboration. My gratitude as well to other members of the television project: Eric Neudel, Alison Smith, Catherine Tse, Jeanne Hallacy, Frank Coakley and Mark Gunning.

Finally, I depended more than she realizes on my wife, Annette, for her extraordinary patience, forbearance and encouragement.

S.K.
Potomac, Maryland
November 1988

CONTENTS

LIST OF MAPS

IN OUR IMAGE

1. ALL IN THE FAMILY

★ ★ ★

By September 1986, after four years as secretary of state, George Shultz had grown accustomed to presiding over official dinners for foreign dignitaries visiting Washington: the rigorous protocol, the solemn oratory, the contrived cordiality. But he could not recall an occasion equal to this night. He was honoring Corazon Cojuangco Aquino, the new president of the Philippines, and a spontaneous charge of emotion electrified the affair. Americans and Filipinos had shared history, tragedy, triumph, ideals—experiences that had left them with a sense of kinship. Shultz captured that spirit exactly: A "Cory" doll pinned to his lapel, his Buddha-like face beamed and his nasal voice lilted with rare elation. Breaking with routine, he delivered his toast before the banquet—in effect telling the guests to relax and enjoy. "This," he said, "is a family evening."

Cory's appeal transcended her American connections. Seven months earlier, she had toppled Ferdinand Marcos in an episode almost too melodramatic to be true—a morality play, a reenactment of the Passion: The pious widow of Marcos's chief opponent, the martyred Benigno "Ninoy" Aquino, she had risen from his death to rally her people against the corrupt despot, his egregious wife and their wicked regime. Throughout the world she became an instant celebrity, a household icon: the saintly Cory who, perhaps through divine intervention, had emerged from obscurity to exorcise evil. Elsewhere in Asia, in Taiwan and in South Korea, demonstrators invoked her name in their protests against autocracy.

Most Americans may have forgotten, perhaps never even knew, that the Philippines had been a U.S. possession; for those who remembered, Cory symbolized anew that special relationship. During its half-century of colonial tutelage, America had endowed the Filipinos with universal education, a common language, public hygiene, roads, bridges and, above all, republican

institutions. Americans and Filipinos had fought and died side by side at
Bataan and Corregidor and perished together on the ghastly Death March.
The United States was still in the Philippines, the site of its two largest overseas
bases, and more than a million Filipinos lived in America. By backing Marcos,
even as an expedient, the United States had betrayed its protégés and its own
principles, but, as if by miracle, Cory Aquino had redeemed her nation—and
redeemed America as well.

Shultz's role in her achievement, though belated, had been decisive. He was
frustrated by unresolved challenges: Central America, the Middle East,
negotiations with the Soviet Union. Not the least of his problems were his
rivals in President Ronald Reagan's entourage, constantly nibbling at his
authority. Here he had scored a visible victory: He had finally won the Washington debate over dumping Marcos—despite recollections of the disasters
that had followed past U.S. maneuvers against such unwanted clients as South
Vietnamese President Ngo Dinh Diem and the shah of Iran. At his urgent
behest, Reagan begrudgingly consented to discard Marcos and hustle him off
to Honolulu. A bloodbath had been narrowly averted in Manila, and Cory had
restored democracy to the Philippines. Now, on this autumn evening, Cory
beside him, Shultz savored her success, his success. In what for him was an
explosion of enthusiasm, he remarked that the occasion had "a real good feel
to it."

Even the chronically foul Washington weather felt good. The summer heat
had faded, leaving the air as soft as satin. From the terrace outside the State
Department's top-floor dining room, the capital resembled a tourist poster.
Lights flooded the Washington Monument and the majestic dome of the
Capitol and between them, like a giant lantern, hung a full harvest moon as
yellow as butter. Aquino, while enduring her husband's imprisonment under
Marcos, had borrowed yellow as her signature color from the poignant Civil
War ballad: "Tie a Yellow Ribbon Around the Old Oak Tree." When a guest
noted the felicitous coincidence, Shultz's spokesman, Bernard Kalb, quipped,
"The CIA can do anything."

Cory desperately needed economic aid and investment, and Shultz had
carefully reviewed the guest list, inviting a heavyweight contingent from Congress along with some of America's major bankers and corporate executives.
Present, too, were the handful of State Department officials who had lobbied
for her against Reagan's reticence and the opposition of his staff. Diplomats,
publishers, journalists, scholars and lawyers were also there, and a group of
influential Filipino businessmen had flown in from Manila. The place was
"loaded," Shultz said proudly, with "important people who make things hap-
pen."

By seven-thirty, the guests were filing through the reception chambers furnished with elegant American antiques, their walls adorned with vintage portraits of America's founders: Washington, Jefferson, Hamilton, John Quincy
Adams. With Shultz towering above her in the receiving line, Cory wore a pink
gown with butterfly sleeves, reserving yellow for her address to Congress the
next day. Nobody who knew her, as I had for twenty years, could have foreseen
this magic moment. Nor could she, for all her belief in providence, have ever
thought it possible. I imagined her reply had I, possessed of some superhuman
faculty, predicted this occasion even a couple of years before. "Golly, Stan,"

she would have remonstrated, "you must be crazy." Yet here she was, a woman of fifty-three, a grandmother, serene and poised, shaking hands, bussing an old friend, her broad smile and amazing grace radiating a natural incandescence. And, as we dined in the spacious Benjamin Franklin Room, a euphoric glow kindled the gathering. Guests table-hopped to exchange nostalgic anecdotes. One effusive congressman was appareled in a lustrous yellow matched set of bow tie, cummerbund and handkerchief, and another sported a yellow badge proclaiming: "I ♥ Cory." As entertainment, Shultz had brought in a loony washboard combo from San Francisco—a frivolous touch described by one of his assistants as "real American."

Vice President George Bush, acting as official greeter, had paid a call on Aquino the previous day at her hotel suite. As they posed for the photo opportunity, she smiled stiffly. Of course she would not spoil the occasion by dredging up old grievances, but Bush was anathema to her for his effulgent praise of Marcos during a visit to Manila in 1981. The Marcoses, masters at lavishing attention on important guests, had laid on an opulent dinner for him at the Malacañang, the presidential palace. Scripted by the State Department to reassure Marcos of the Reagan administration's "friendship," Bush toasted Marcos's "adherence to democratic principles and to the democratic processes." The inane remark had clung to him for years, and he knew that Cory remembered it. Now, however, he sought to reassure her. There was "no resistance of any kind to you" within the administration, he told her, predicting that she and Reagan would "get along very well . . . in terms of chemistry."

He was wrong. A man who prized loyalty, Reagan stuck by those who had been faithful to him—a trait he displayed in his reluctance to dismiss unethical subordinates. Nor did he easily shed illusions, as in his tendency to confuse movies with reality. Whatever Marcos's faults, he still esteemed him an "old friend and ally," an intrepid anti-Japanese guerrilla during World War II and a veteran "freedom fighter" in the struggle against communism. Besides, he had never forgotten his first trip to Manila in 1969, when he was governor of California. President Richard Nixon had sent him and Nancy there to represent the United States at the opening of a cultural center, and the Marcoses had treated them like royalty. By contrast, he instinctively distrusted Cory. On one occasion he had proposed that she compromise with Marcos, which to her was tantamount to a pact with the devil, and despite massive evidence of chicanery by Marcos's followers during the election, he publicly suggested that her supporters had been equally fraudulent. He was angry when she banished Marcos from the Philippines rather than permit him to retire to his native province.

Not until April, a full two months after her victory, did he personally congratulate her by telephone. She interpreted the delay as an indirect reproach—and, a few days later, he exacerbated it with a gesture that she could justifiably consider an insult. En route to Asia, he had stopped for a few days in Hawaii and actually contemplated driving over to see Marcos, who was now living there in splendid exile. Shultz had all he could do to dissuade him, and Reagan telephoned Marcos instead. Marcos, his voice slurred, carried on almost endlessly, insisting that he was still the rightful president of the Philippines, denouncing Cory as incompetent and soft on communism and complaining about his confiscated property. His wife, Imelda, pouring out her heart to Nancy, blubbered that the press had maligned her with exaggerated reports of the thousands of shoes and sundry glitz she had left behind in Manila. The maudlin performance embarrassed the Reagans—all the more so because Imelda, to show that the Marcos connection with the United States was intact, had violated the privacy of the conversation by arranging for a Honolulu television station to broadcast a silent segment. Administration spokesmen, fearing that Reagan's contact with Marcos might alarm Cory, hastily expressed his endorsement of her, but she was unconvinced. She continued to believe that Reagan still yearned for Marcos's restoration to power. And now, five months afterward, as her motorcade sped to the White House, she was rankled as well by Reagan's refusal to elevate her journey to Washington to the full panoply of a "state visit"—an honor that he had accorded the Marcoses in September 1982, which in diplomatic semiotics signified unqualified recognition as a chief of state.

Her intuition was not misplaced. Though Reagan had by now reconciled himself to her ascension to office, he still harbored misgivings about her abilities. But he was a courtly host. After an amiable luncheon with Cory, he listened to her account of the "economic devastation" caused by Marcos's excesses. He was "bullish" on the Philippines, he said, and vowed to "do all we can" to help in its recovery. His real concern, however, was the Communist insurrection nagging the country. Aquino, who had recently begun discussions with the rebels under a cease-fire, explained to him that she was seeking a political solution while keeping open her "military option." The strategy struck him as naïve, even dangerous. After all, he was dedicated to the effort of the *contras* to topple the left-wing Sandinista regime in Nicaragua and, he implied, she had to act tough. Emphasizing the importance of force, he cautioned her to watch herself. "I've had experience dealing with communists," he said.

But the climax of her Washington visit, Cory realized, would be her appearance before a joint session of Congress—where the money was. She delegated the task of drafting her speech to Mark Malloch Brown, a former British journalist employed by a New York public relations firm, and Teodoro Locsin, Jr., a Filipino graduate of the Harvard Law School. Both had worked on her election campaign, enabling her to claim, as a shield again possible nationalist criticism, that she had not relied on American advisers. The address, designed to appeal to liberals and conservatives alike, omitted mention of America's bases in the Philippines—a divisive issue among Filipinos and one Cory preferred to shelve for the time being. She added a passage about her assassinated husband. The words, however, were less dynamic than the picture she would portray of herself. As Cory, the plucky little housewife who had crushed the malevolent Marcos, her conquest of Capitol Hill was virtually guaranteed.

She wore a tailored yellow suit, and the packed chamber was a dazzle of yellow. Senators and congressmen, cabinet members, diplomats and spectators reveled in yellow shirts, blouses, ties, handkerchiefs. The House majority leader, Jim Wright, had shipped in two hundred yellow roses from his home state of Texas, the flowers bedecking her path as she walked down the aisle to the podium—the chant of "Cory, Cory, Cory" rising in cadence to the rhythm of her steps. No longer the model of self-effacement, she was convinced of her mission. She spoke earnestly and confidently for half an hour, pausing

only for the dozen bursts of applause—her eloquent English a further reminder
to the assembly, if it were necessary, that she was the product of America's
tutelage of the Philippines, educated in American schools.

Their "three happiest years" had been her family's exile in Boston. Out of
honest gratitude she said, "Thank you, America, for the haven from oppression." Then, striking a sincerely religious chord, she invoked the "brazen"
murder of her husband in Manila in August 1983, presumably at Marcos's
doing, intoning: "His death was my country's resurrection." Filipinos "threw
aside their passivity and fear" to propel her drive against Marcos. "And so
began the revolution that has brought me to democracy's most famous home,
the Congress of the United States."

But now an insurrection that thrived on poverty and injustice threatened
democracy in the Philippines. Her goal, Cory said, was to lure the Communist
rebels out of the hills, and win them over "by economic progress and justice
. . . for which the best intentioned among them fight." Only by exploring "the
path of peace" would she have "the moral basis" for "picking up the sword
of war" if her effort faltered. She believed in Lincoln's dictum—"with malice
toward none, with charity for all." Like him, she understood that "force may
be necessary before mercy."

In any case, American aid was indispensable. Marcos's profligate rule had
left the Philippines with a foreign debt of $26 billion; the interest alone cost
half its annual export earnings. Congress failed to ease the burden—even
though, Cory chided, "ours must have been the cheapest revolution ever."
Nevertheless, Filipinos had backed her campaign to clamor for democracy,
however abstract the concept may have been to them. "Slum or impoverished
village," she said, "they came to me with one cry: Democracy! Not food,
though they clearly needed it, not work, though they surely wanted it—but
democracy." So her question for Congress—and for America—was plain:
"Has there been a greater test of national commitment to the ideals you hold
dear than what my people have gone through? You have spent many lives and
much treasure to bring freedom to many lands that were reluctant to receive
it. And here you have a people who won it by themselves and need only help
to preserve it."

A volcanic ovation erupted. Engulfing Cory as she descended from the
podium, legislators cheered, applauded and jostled one another as they reached
to grasp her hand. "That was the finest speech I've heard in my thirty-four
years in Congress," exclaimed Thomas P. "Tip" O'Neill, who from his perch
as House speaker had been looking down with avuncular benevolence during
her address. The chamber again chanted "Cory, Cory, Cory" as she walked
up the aisle, escorted by Senator Robert Dole, the leader of the Republican
majority. "You hit a home run," he remarked to her—to which she snapped
back without hesitation, "I hope the bases were loaded."

Similar accolades awaited her elsewhere on her whirlwind schedule. Governor Mario Cuomo and Mayor Edward Koch greeted her on the steps of New
York's City Hall. Fordham University, a Jesuit institution, awarded her an
honorary doctorate, an appropriate tribute to her piety, and she revisited
Mount Saint Vincent, the small Catholic college for women in the Bronx where
she had studied thirty years before. A high school band serenaded her at the
Boston airport with her husband's favorite song, "The Impossible Dream."

She returned to her large brick house in suburban Newton, Massachusetts, now a shrine, then spoke at Harvard, where Ninoy had been a fellow for part of his exile. Boston University gave her an honorary degree at a ceremony attended by Governor Michael Dukakis and Senator John Kerry, a yellow rose in his lapel. Her speechwriters had done their homework; she cited John Winthrop, the first governor of Massachusetts in 1630, when she compared the Philippines to his "city upon a hill, with the eyes of the world upon us." Kerry, the distant cousin of a pioneer U.S. governor of the Philippines, commented that her address to Congress two days earlier had "moved even the most hardened politicians to tears . . . because of the simple truth of her ideas."

But if Cory had belted the ball, as Senator Dole had cracked, the game was being played on a soggy field. Within five hours of her speech, the House of Representatives increased aid to the Philippines by two hundred million dollars above the half-billion dollars already appropriated, but the measure passed by only six votes. "We voted with our hearts, not our heads," said one member regretfully, explaining that foreign aid was poison at this time of budgetary constraints. Ten days later, the Senate rejected the package. Dole was responsible for the rebuff despite his encomium for Cory. Her silence on the U.S. bases in the Philippines had vexed him, as it had several other Republican senators. He was also determined to prove that he would not be suckered by sentimentality. The House decision, he said sardonically, had given Cory "the biggest honorarium in history"; it was "not very good policy" that "because someone came here and made a speech, they get two hundred million dollars." Only through a "mushy compromise," as one congressman phrased it, were the extra funds subsequently approved.

Future aid proposals sparked fresh debates on Capitol Hill, leaving Filipinos wondering whether Cory's stirring performance in Washington would translate into consistent U.S. support. Even Secretary of State Shultz, his affection for the Philippines notwithstanding, put a limit on American help. Cory's vice president, Salvador Laurel, once begged him for urgent economic assistance, saying, "Our needs are infinite." "That may be," Shultz replied, "but our resources are not."

Revisiting Manila over the next few years, I found Cory to be increasingly comfortable with power. Despite her family fortune, she had never flaunted her wealth. Besides, she wanted to project an image of austerity after the outrageous ostentation of the Marcoses. She chose to live in a modest house rather than move into the Malacañang, the ornate presidential palace, studiously avoiding flamboyance of the kind that had become Imelda's trademark. But, no longer shy and self-effacing, she was not afraid to assert her authority over the veteran politicians to whom, as Ninoy's dutiful wife, she had once served coffee. She also seemed to be learning the difference between the poetry of revolution and the prose of government. Rallies and rhetoric, she realized, were not going to solve unemployment or defeat insurgents. Nor did she address every challenge by asking herself what Ninoy would do. "I reached the point," she told me, "when I knew that I was president, not Ninoy, and that I had to make the decisions."

Ninoy had once remarked, she recalled, that the successor to Marcos would face such tremendous problems that he would collapse in six months. Of course Ninoy had never imagined that she would become president, much less foreseen her fortitude. She survived five coup attempts during her first year and a half in office. Some of her cabinet members plotted her ouster, and her inner circle was roiled by rivalries. Nevertheless, she promulgated a new constitution that was ratified by an overwhelming majority of the voters, and she had held the first fully free legislative and local elections since Marcos declared martial law in 1972. Certainly, she conceded, she had not done enough. But, as she phrased it, "there is no school for presidents." She was accumulating experience as she went along, and dealing "step by step" with the insurgencies and economic stagnation. "After all," she said, "we had a dictator for fourteen years. We can't change everything overnight."

After three years in office, though still popular, her reputation had eroded—largely because she could not have conceivably lived up to the image of miracle worker that her own supporters had originally pinned on her. The Marcos legacy was a daunting enough burden for her to bear. But she had inherited a sprawling archipelago of disparate languages and cultures that owed its semblance of unity mainly to the legal definition of Filipino citizenship and an allegiance to the Catholic Church. Despite its modern trappings, it was still a feudal society dominated by an oligarchy of rich dynasties, which had evolved from one of the world's longest continuous spans of Western imperial rule.

★   ★   ★

First came Spain and then the United States—or, as the neat summation of Philippine history goes: "Three centuries in a Catholic convent and fifty years in Hollywood."

Ferdinand Magellan, a Portuguese explorer flying the flag of Spain, stumbled onto the islands in 1521 in his search for the lucrative spices of the Indies. He died there, a victim of his own imprudence, and his ships sailed on—one of them to complete the first circumnavigation of the globe. Other Spaniards returned and remained, even though the archipelago was not the El Dorado of their dreams. Manila was convenient for trade with nearby China, and the provinces offered the Catholic Church a fertile field for saving souls. So, under Spain, the Philippines became the only Christian country of Asia—and, through Christianity, the West's first foothold in the region. Spain left another heritage, in the form of land grants to Spanish settlers—which, passed on to rich Filipino *mestizo* families, created the oligarchy that wields power today. Coupled with her American education, Cory Aquino personifies the legacy of the Spanish era. Her intense piety stems from an almost medieval brand of Spanish Catholicism, and she owes her private fortune to a Chinese great-grandfather who acquired large properties a century ago.

Spain, itself in a cocoon, sealed off the Philippines from the outside world until the nineteenth century, when liberal Spanish kings opened the islands to foreign trade. The landed gentry prospered from the global demand for sugar and other commodities stimulated by the industrial revolution. Seeking recognition to match their wealth, they began to defy their imperial Spanish masters long before the elite of other European possessions in Asia challenged their rulers. The Filipino clergy agitated for equality with Spanish priests. Affluent young Filipinos, sent by their fathers to study in Europe, returned home from the heady atmosphere of Madrid, Paris and Berlin with enlightened ideas that, to the Spanish administration in Manila, seemed subversive.

The most brilliant of them, José Rizal y Mercado, oculist, poet, painter and writer, fueled the ferment with his polemical novels. Cautious and conservative, he championed integration with Spain rather than independence. But reactionary Spanish priests and officials in Manila, resistant to even the mildest change, railroaded him to execution in 1896. Filipinos, for whom the Passion is a reality, perceived in his martyrdom an imitation of Christ's agony, and they have revered him since as a quasireligious national hero—a status they have also begun to confer on Ninoy Aquino.

Rizal's death ignited a rebellion against Spain led by Emilio Aguinaldo y Famy, a dashing if naïve young Filipino whose objective was independence. Most Americans had never heard of the Philippines, but they were soon to become embroiled in the conflict as the United States reached across the Pacific for the first time in its history.

America was then going through a stupendous transition as dynamic entrepreneurs and a restive immigrant population transformed its vast resources into an industrial powerhouse. But Americans were split over the issue of whether to project their new power overseas or to concentrate their energies at home. With nuanced differences, essentially the same debate over global priorities has preoccupied the nation since.

The imperialists, advocates of a strong American presence abroad, included figures like the young assistant secretary of the navy Theodore Roosevelt, Senator Henry Cabot Lodge of Massachusetts and Captain Alfred Mahan, the scholarly naval strategist. Only as a world power, they affirmed, could the United States trade, prosper and protect itself against its potential enemies. This role, they maintained, was America's "manifest destiny"—a phrase originally coined to promote the settlement of the West. William Randolph Hearst, lord of the yellow press, was their publicist. Though mostly Republicans, they were backed by the Populists, poor farmers of the Middle West who blamed their economic problems on foreign bankers, and so thrilled to the idea of fighting any foreigners. They had no plans at that stage to grab territory, as the Europeans were doing in Asia and Africa. Their vague objective was to make America a voice on the international scene. For Teddy Roosevelt, war itself was the highest form of human endeavor.

Various motives inspired the anti-imperialists. Tycoons like Andrew Carnegie asserted that costly foreign ventures would divert America from the development of its domestic economy. An older generation of Americans, recalling the horrors of the Civil War, flinched at the thought of another conflict. The northern factory workers and southern farmers who supported the Democratic party tended to be isolationist. Grover Cleveland, the former president and a Democrat, delayed the annexation of Hawaii as long as he could, and William Jennings Bryan, the party standard-bearer, was equivocal on the issue.

The imperialists prevailed in 1898. The United States went to war with Spain—the first war waged by America beyond its continental boundaries. An inexorable force drove the nation into war, but like all wars, it was not inevitable.

It began over Cuba, where rebels were struggling against Spanish tyranny. Skilled Cuban propagandists in the United States, abetted by Hearst and other sensationalists, had won America's sympathy. American investors in Cuba favored an end to Spanish rule. For the Spanish, whose Latin American empire had crumbled, Cuba was a last vestige of past grandeur—and its potential loss had already ignited political passions in Spain. The queen, traumatized by the threat to her tottering throne, had nevertheless edged toward compromise, and a strong U.S. president might have given her time. But, though the prospect of war alarmed him, William McKinley was weak and indecisive. He waffled for nearly two months following the mysterious sinking of the *Maine* in Havana harbor on February 15, 1898, while hawks whipped up the fervor. Finally, still befuddled, he allowed Congress to push him into a conflict he neither wanted nor understood. Least of all did he grasp the purpose of the offensive against the Philippines.

Congress had affirmed at the outset that America intended to free, not acquire, Cuba. But America's ultimate goal for the Philippines, a sideshow to the main Cuban arena, was left undefined. There, on secret orders from Roosevelt, a U.S. fleet commanded by Commodore George Dewey had sunk a decrepit Spanish armada in Manila Bay in a few hours on the morning of May 1, 1898. McKinley pondered the problem of what to do with the archipelago—which he could not find on the map.

He complied with Dewey's request for forces to secure his victory, and in another historical first, U.S. troops crossed the Pacific. They occupied Manila shortly afterward under an arrangement with the Spanish while McKinley continued to contemplate the future of the Philippines. Eventually, he later revealed to a group of clergymen, God told him to annex the islands and "do the best we could for them."

Unlike presidents today, McKinley rarely committed himself to paper, and the scant record contains no clues to the thinking that went into his decision. So historians have conjectured that, given his malleable character, he was carried along by a momentum that he either would not or could not control—just as he had been propelled into the war with Spain.

Even ardent imperialists initially spurned the notion of retaining the Philippines. At most, they reckoned, the United States might keep a naval base or trading station in Manila. But the dream of empire gradually germinated in the minds of Americans. Some envisioned the archipelago as the pivot of a booming commerce with China. Christian missionaries hoped to convert pagans, and ideologues saw America as the master of "inferior races." Strategists warned that another foreign power—most likely Japan or Germany—would grab the islands if the United States withdrew. Rudyard Kipling, the literary apostle of British imperialism, also exerted influence. He deliberately wrote his famous poem "The White Man's Burden" as an exhortation to Americans to bestow the blessings of their civilization on the Philippines—though, he warned, it would be a thankless task.

The acquisition of the archipelago appalled New York and Boston patricians, many of them old abolitionists who equated the subjugation of people overseas with slavery. Their objections were echoed by such eminent figures as Mark Twain, then at the peak of his fame, and the philosopher William James. Distinguished jurists cautioned that colonialism breached the constitutional principle of "government by consent of the governed." But not all the anti-imperialists were high-minded moralists. Bigots among them feared that

America, by assuming responsibilities in Asia, would be contaminated by "Mongoloid barbarians."

The Senate debate over annexation of the Philippines in early 1899 was both eloquent and bitter—and symptomatic of the nation's schism over the issue of imperialism. Meanwhile, tensions gripped Manila as U.S. troops blocked the Filipino nationalist forces from entering the city. On the night of February 4, a Nebraska volunteer named Willie Grayson shot a Filipino soldier, and fighting broke out. Two days later, the Senate narrowly voted to keep the islands. But a new war had erupted between the United States and Aguinaldo's army. It is one of the forgotten wars of American history.

Though he had declared independence, Aguinaldo would probably have been amenable to an arrangement that granted autonomy to the Philippines under an American protectorate. But the U.S. commanders on the spot, Dewey and Major General Elwell Otis, were fatuous and arrogant men with neither the inclination nor the sensitivity to explore Filipino aspirations. Nor was McKinley, who by now had opted for annexation, in a mood to consider concessions. American history books refer to the war that followed as the "insurrection," as if the Filipinos were rebelling against legitimate U.S. authority. In reality it was an unalloyed American conquest of territory and among the cruelest conflicts in the annals of Western imperialism. At its peak, 70,000 U.S. soldiers were involved, and by its end in 1901, at least 200,000 Filipino civilians had been killed.

Aguinaldo blundered from the start by engaging America's superior forces in large battles. Realizing his mistake, he soon switched to guerrilla tactics, but as a conservative nationalist rather than a social reformer, he failed to promote the changes necessary to win his partisans the support of the peasantry. Isolated, his ranks enfeebled by dissension and defections, he retreated to a remote village in northern Luzon. There he was captured in a bold maneuver by the swashbuckling Colonel Frederick Funston. The Americans pursued the remnant Filipino troops in brutal operations, one so severe that it led to the court-martial of a U.S. general, Jacob Smith.

It was not a living-room war visible to Americans on television, as Vietnam would be two generations later. Unlike in Vietnam, the United States won. Yet there were similarities: Accounts of American atrocities, aired in the U.S. press and in Senate hearings, soured the public at home on the conflict—which in any case dragged on too long. What had started as a glorious mission became a torment. Americans lost their enthusiasm for foreign ventures—just as, in the aftermath of Vietnam, they shunned the role of global policeman. The United States continued to practice forms of economic and political imperialism in the years ahead, but territorial conquest began and ended in the Philippines.

★ ★ ★

Lacking a colonial vocation, the Americans experimented in the Philippines. Judged in retrospect, the performance was neither as brilliant as their publicists claimed nor as bleak as their critics contended. They never quite fulfilled their hope of transforming the Filipinos into facsimile Americans. But in contrast to the Europeans, they were uniquely benign, almost sentimental imperialists. As a result, Filipinos today feel a closer affinity for America than, say, Indians do for Britain or Vietnamese for France. The million or so Filipinos living in the United States are the largest Asian minority in terms of their country's population—and, given their high birthrate, they will be the biggest by the end of this century. Thousands of Filipinos have "green cards"—permits to reside in America. Nearly three hundred thousand Filipinos request authorization to visit the United States every year, and the waiting list for immigration visas is forty-two years long. I once asked a Filipino on the long line at the American consulate in Manila why he wanted to go to the United States. Surprised by such an obvious question, he replied, "America is my other home."

Different economic impulses distinguished European from American imperialism. The British, French and Dutch, with their limited domestic economies, perceived colonial markets and sources of raw materials to be vital to their prosperity. British firms developed tin mines and rubber plantations in Malaya, employing coolie labor under horrendous conditions, and French companies in Vietnam owned rice estates the size of provinces. On the other hand, Americans saw their fortunes at home, in tapping seemingly limitless coal, oil and mineral deposits, building steel mills and railroads, manufacturing and selling consumer products to an immense population and financing all these projects. So Congress could afford to appear ethical—as it did by barring American individuals and corporations from acquiring large land holdings in the Philippines. Filipinos were thus spared exploitation of the kind practiced by the Europeans.

But they were not saved from a classical colonial trade bind. American business was given a virtual import monopoly in the Philippines, for which Filipinos received tariff-free access to the United States for their commodities. Though apparently reciprocal, the arrangement actually stunted the growth of Philippine industry and preserved the archipelago as an agricultural society reliant on the American market. It also perpetuated the power of the Filipino upper class, which derived its wealth from the land. The United States forced the same pattern on the Filipinos after independence, thereby making a mockery of their sovereignty.

Compared to the Europeans, the Americans were far more liberal politically. Though they restricted the vote to the educated class, they nevertheless encouraged elections soon after their arrival, so that the Filipinos had a national legislature, the first in Asia, as early as 1907. Nine years later, in an unprecedented gesture for an imperial power, they pledged eventual freedom for the Philippines. This was a time when the British, despite their own democratic creed, were detaining Indian dissidents without trial and the French, for all their dedication to the principles of liberty, equality and fraternity, were summarily executing Vietnamese nationalists.

But the Americans neglected to establish an effective and impartial administration in the Philippines—as the British did in the creation of the Indian Civil Service, still a model of efficiency. So Filipinos turned to politicians instead of the bureaucracy for assistance, a practice that fostered patronage and corruption. Nor were the Americans, with all their professions of righteousness, as racially tolerant as the French or the Dutch. Prior to World War II, an

American who married a Filipino woman was banished from the American community in Manila.

In many ways, the Filipinos were easier to co-opt than other Asians. The Indians, Vietnamese and Indonesians had a sense of their national character. They could gaze with pride at stone temples that symbolized their past grandeur. Their myths told of victories over alien invaders, of distant divine emperors and legendary warriors whose spirits evoked their nationhood. Western imperialism had violated their ancient culture, and many resisted it by recalling their history. By contrast, the history of the Philippines was colonial history. The Filipinos lacked fabled kings and heroes; the saints they worshiped were Western rather than Filipino. Before Spain arrived, they had been an assortment of tribes, without a central authority, a single language or a common religion. Untrammeled by strong feelings of national exclusivity, they were more receptive than other Asians to foreign influence. Their elite, Westernized long before the upper classes in Europe's colonies, welcomed the United States as a salutary force for modernization, not as a threat to tradition. Numbers of educated Filipinos abandoned Aguinaldo's movement, preferring instead the benison of U.S. rule. Spain had brought them Christianity; now they awaited adoption by the Americans.

Secular missionaries, the Americans zealously went forth with the conviction that the United States was the greatest society ever created, and they hoped to infuse less privileged peoples with their ideals. In the wake of the conquest of the Philippines, they did strive to accomplish that goal. "Benevolent assimilation," McKinley termed the concept, and his secretary of war, Elihu Root, refined it. The U.S. colonial administration, Root prescribed, must promote the "happiness, peace and prosperity" of the Filipinos, but its measures should "conform to their customs, their habits and even their prejudices." Underlying the policy was the theory that the Filipinos, converted by the virtues of their American masters, would submit to their own transformation. The policy proved to be remarkably effective—up to a point.

William Howard Taft, a corpulent Ohio judge, landed in Manila in June 1900 as the first U.S. civilian governor. He went on to become secretary of war and later president and, more than any other American, he shaped the contours of U.S. rule in the Philippines during its first decade.

Reflecting the racist attitudes of his time, he was not particularly fond of the Filipinos. But obedient to Root's instructions, he undertook to Americanize "our little brown brothers," as he condescendingly called them. He built ports and roads to unify the Philippines and develop its economy. To instill in Filipinos the fundamentals of democracy, he assigned young American teachers to schools throughout the archipelago. Finally, he launched a program of political tutelage to prepare the Filipinos to govern themselves, and helped them to found a political party, the *Federalistas,* whose platform advocated statehood for the Philippines. The foundations Taft laid remained largely unshaken during the entire period of U.S. rule—and they have not been completely dismantled. A statehood party exists to this day.

The Taft era ended in 1913 with the inauguration of Woodrow Wilson, the first Democratic president in sixteen years, who assigned Francis Burton Harrison as Manila's new governor. A progressive, Harrison purged the colonial bureaucracy of its Americans and supplanted them with Filipinos. The process, called "Filipinization," effectively put the Filipinos in charge of their own affairs for the next three decades of American rule. In 1935, true to its promise, the United States granted the Philippines internal autonomy under a commonwealth government—with total independence scheduled for ten years later.

But U.S. policies, though liberal by colonial standards, were flawed. American education endowed the Philippines for the first time in its history with a lingua franca, English, which discouraged the development of a national language. The United States introduced the Filipinos to democratic institutions without requiring them to respect the substance of democracy. On the contrary, Taft had vested authority in the *ilustrados,* the rich intelligentsia, whose conservative beliefs he shared, and his successors endorsed their power on the theory that the Filipinos deserved to govern themselves. The landowners and entrepreneurial classes naturally recoiled from economic and social reforms that would have curbed their prerogatives, preferring instead to preserve a feudal system—even though it perpetuated and even widened the shocking gap between wealth and poverty. American officials, long aware of these inequities, only began to suggest improvements in the 1930s, when President Franklin D. Roosevelt's New Deal made it stylish to recommend radical change. By then, however, it was too late. The Filipinos were virtually sovereign; besides, interference in their internal affairs would have smelled of wicked imperialism.

Filipinos, however, yearned for American patronage. Just as Spanish sponsorship had assured them wealth and prestige in the nineteenth century, so American endorsement was the key to success. The two most prominent Filipino political figures of the U.S. colonial period, Sergio Osmeña and Manuel Luis Quezon y Molina, owed their careers to American mentors. As president of the commonwealth, Quezon entrusted the formation of a national Philippine army to General Douglas MacArthur, his ritual brother. Even the Philippine Communist party was founded under the auspices of clandestine American Communist comrades. American officers commanded Filipino troops during World War II, and the pattern persisted after independence. MacArthur, restoring the old oligarchy following the war, engineered the election of Manuel Roxas y Acuña as first president of the sovereign Philippine republic. The most popular postwar president, Ramón Magsaysay, was virtually invented by Colonel Edward Lansdale, a secret American operative. Marcos was delighted when President Lyndon Johnson called him "my right arm in Asia," and he reveled in being termed Ronald Reagan's "old friend." Aquino attributed her election in early 1986 to God and public revulsion against Marcos—an unbeatable alchemy. But Marcos, who also claimed victory, might not have stepped down without a shove from Washington.

Many Filipinos, assuming that every political event in the Philippines is due to U.S. intervention, credit Americans and especially the Central Intelligence Agency with superhuman powers. They suspect American correspondents, businessmen and professors as well as Peace Corps volunteers of working for the CIA, and the suspicion is understandable. The CIA has in fact been a formidable influence over the years. Aside from Magsaysay, several top Filipino politicians were financed by the CIA, among them President Diosdado Macapagal and his vice president, Emmanuel Pelaez, later Cory Aquino's ambassador to Washington. Ninoy was proud to have had a connection with the CIA, contending however that he had worked "with" rather than "for" the agency. The affiliation represented a link to the United States—a badge of distinction.

But Filipinos also recoil from tarnishing their nationalist image by too close an association with the Americans. They seem to be trapped in a tangle of contradictions.

History is responsible. Despite their own vague past, the Filipinos might have forged their national personality had they been compelled to fight for freedom—as they were indeed doing in their conflict against Spain. By acceding to their aspirations for sovereignty so soon after conquest, the United States spared them a long struggle for independence. But, in a sense, their hopes were fulfilled too easily. America's acquiescence to their ambitions deflated the élan of their early nationalism, leaving them confused and ambivalent. From then on, their attitudes toward the United States vacillated between imitation and resentment, subservience and defiance, adulation and contempt, love and hate. The same dichotomy continues to trouble them, as it did Manuel Quezon back in the 1920s. Once, in a fit of nationalist passion, he asserted: "I would prefer a government run like hell by Filipinos to one run like heaven by Americans." On another occasion, incensed that the benevolence of the United States was puncturing his nationalist pretensions, he exploded: "Damn the Americans! Why don't they tyrannize us more?"

★   ★   ★

The impact of the West is still engraved on its former colonies around the world. Apart from the Casbah, Algiers is a southern French city, and Nairobi bears the traces of an English town. Djakarta, with its canals and step-roofed brick houses, faintly recalls its onetime Dutch masters, and Macao, the vest-pocket Portuguese enclave on the rim of China, might be an Iberian port except for the junks riding off its shore. I have watched Jamaicans play cricket, heard Vietnamese recite Molière and listened to Indian army colonels who sounded like British army colonels. But in no place is the imperial legacy more alive than in Manila, where America's presence is almost as dynamic now as it was during the days of U.S. rule.

A shock of recognition immediately accosts an American visiting that city. The public buildings, with their stately Greek columns, were copied from those in Washington by Daniel Burnham, a celebrated American city planner of the turn of the century. He also conceived Baguio, the mountain resort decreed by Taft to emulate an Adirondacks vacation spot. The Manila Hotel, designed in 1912 by William Parsons, one of Burnham's students, is a favorite venue for Rotary luncheons, Shriner conventions, big-ten alumni dinners and June weddings. The Army and Navy Club, another Parsons design, could have been imported from Florida.

The suburbs, a blight of fast-food franchises and used-car lots, stretch endlessly to nowhere, like the outskirts of Los Angeles. Aside from the armed security guards at their gates, testimony to Manila's staggering crime rate, affluent residential districts resemble Beverly Hills. The fanciest of them, Forbes Park, is named for a vintage American governor. Taft Avenue and Harrison Plaza also remember American colonial governors. Streets honor presidents McKinley, Wilson and the two Roosevelts, as well as John D. Rockefeller, Henry Ford, Thomas Edison and Alexander Graham Bell. Bridges commemorate General MacArthur and William Atkinson Jones, an obscure Virginia congressman who in 1916 sponsored the legislation that pledged eventual independence for the Philippines.

The writer Carmen Nakpil Guerrero has observed that chic Filipino families, to emulate Americans, incongruously furnish their living rooms with wool rugs, fur pillows and leather sofas protected against the fierce humidity by plastic covers. Those who can afford it decorate their homes at Christmas with artificial Christmas trees, and spray the windows with fake snow. "As children," a Filipino woman once told me, "we always wondered how Santa Claus would deliver our presents, since we didn't have a chimney."

In a land lush with tropical fruit, snobbish matrons serve their guests canned American fruit salad. "We are eternally grateful to America for peanut butter," jokes Alejandro Roces, a Filipino historian. Kraft cheese and Hellmann's mayonnaise are manufactured under license in the Philippines. But Filipinos drive for hours to Angeles or Olongapo, the towns adjacent to Clark Field and Subic Bay, the U.S. air and naval bases, to buy the same American-made products purloined from the PX. Doreen Fernandez, a cultural anthropologist, explains the distinction: "The prestige is in the label 'Made in the U.S.A.'" Filipinos, who satirize their own foibles, joke about an injured man whose doctor prescribes a local anesthetic. "Please, doc," the patient pleads, "can't I have an imported one?"

Men with names like cigar labels—Benedicto, Benito and Bernardo—are known as Benny, Butch and Bernie. One of Cory Aquino's close aides, Teodoro Locsin, Jr., is "Teddy Boy" to his friends. Upper-crust women, "socialites," in the quaint American vocabulary of Manila, discard their baptismal saints, Perpetua and Victoria, to style themselves Popsy and Vicky. MacArthur's beautiful mistress, whom he secretly installed in a Washington love nest during the early 1930s, was Dimples. Marcos's cronies call him Andy.

The aforementioned statehood party claims five million members. Nearly every Filipino seems to have a relative in California, Illinois or New Jersey. One hundred thousand candidates apply every year for the four hundred slots open to Filipinos in the U.S. Navy. A captured Communist rebel escapes from jail and flees abroad—to San Francisco rather than Hanoi, Beijing or Moscow. In a reverse psychological twist, a young insurgent on the island of Negros explained to me through an interpreter how America's pervasive influence had prompted him to join the insurrection. "My ambition as a kid was to be like an American. We'd been taught in school that the Americans were our saviors, that they brought us democracy. When I saw cowboy-and-Indian movies, I always rooted for the cowboys. I preferred American-style clothes. Americans were rich, handsome and superior. Jesus Christ and the Virgin Mary looked like Americans, with their white skins and long noses. I degraded Filipinos because they were ugly, with flat noses and brown skins. But I was also ugly. I wasn't a good student, and could not speak English well. Then I began to realize that I would never become like an American, and I started to hate America."

Every young Filipino dreams of attending college, and diploma mills grind out worthless degrees in law, accountancy and public relations. But Ivy League credentials are coveted, especially in business administration—the passport to a fat job in Makati, Manila's financial district. In the summer of 1980, Ninoy telephoned me from a Texas hospital, where he was recovering from heart surgery. Marcos had released him from prison for the operation on condition that he return home afterward. Having agreed, Ninoy was now contemplating ways to stay in America without violating his pledge. "Marcos can't resist if I go to Harvard," he mused, figuring that the prestige of Cambridge would melt even his implacable enemy—who himself claimed to have been once accepted at Harvard. Ninoy proved to be correct. A fellowship was arranged, and he spent the next three years in Boston.

Nothing illustrates America's impact as vividly as the widespread use of American English. Candidates campaign in English, delivering florid orations in a rhetoric reminiscent of vintage American politicians. English is employed in the courts and in government agencies. Even Communist insurgents rely on English versions of Marx and Mao Zedong to denounce America. The government has been striving for decades to promote Tagalog, renamed "Pilipino," as the national language. But only thirty percent of Filipinos speak Tagalog, mainly in Luzon. About the same proportion speaks Cebuano, the language of the Visayas, the islands that sprawl across the center of the archipelago. Tagalog is actually "Taglish"; the word for "toothpaste," for example, is *colgate*. A nationalist militant called Cookie Diokno, whose English is as fluent as mine, told me that she had decided to strike a blow for cultural freedom by speaking only Tagalog to her family and friends. One day, however, I overheard her scolding her small son—in English. As she admitted sheepishly, she was doing what came naturally.

Spanish priests, fearing that the natives might become "uppity" if taught Spanish, themselves learned local languages and dialects. But the pioneer American teachers considered it their mission to make English the common tongue, and their students cooperated eagerly. Proficiency in English soon became a mark of distinction among Filipinos, many of whom looked back with veneration on their American education. The journalist and diplomat Carlos Romulo accepted the Pulitzer Prize in 1942 for a newspaper series on Asia with the words: "The real winner is . . . Hattie Grove, who taught a small Filipino pupil to value the beauty of the English language." Essayists, novelists and poets switched from Spanish to English. Under the guidance of American editors, reporters replaced the elegance of Castilian with the razzle-dazzle of Chicago. The Manila press to this day identifies senators as "solons," municipal officials as "city dads" and the president as "the prexy."

American teachers introduced baseball as an antidote to cockfighting, the national Filipino addiction. The *Manila Times*, an American newspaper, wrote early in the century that baseball was "more than a game, a regenerating influence and power for good." The effort partly succeeded. Filipinos became avid fans, and their media detail major league action in the United States, but cockfighting remains the countrywide diversion.

America transmuted the pop culture of the Philippines. By the 1920s, the vernacular press was carrying *komiks*, their Filipino characters modeled on Alley Oop and Happy Hooligan. The intrepid Trece was none other Dick Tracy in Tagalog. Ersatz American soap operas, directed at housewives as in the United States, became a regular afternoon *radyo* feature—and now, complete with detergent commercials, they continue to be a staple of daytime television.

Superb entertainers, Filipinos adapted to the arrival of the Americans by dropping the *zarzuela,* a Spanish music hall, in favor of vaudeville, or *bodabil*—its performers billed as the "Filipino Sophie Tucker," the "Filipino Al Jolson" or the "Filipino Fred Astaire." Subsequent years spawned "Filipino" Bing Crosbys, Glenn Millers, Guy Lombardos, Elvis Presleys, Barbra Streisands. Rock groups with names like Hot Dog and the Boyfriends appeared as clones of the Grateful Dead and Led Zeppelin—though they slowed their beat to a tropical tempo. John Philip Sousa was discovered and canonized early by the Filipinos, and at town fiestas throughout the country, high school bands led by nubile drum majorettes in miniskirts still blare "The Washington Post" and "The Stars and Stripes Forever" with gusto. A talented singer, Imelda Marcos was proud of her knowledge of the lyrics of nearly every Broadway hit—and she could go on into the wee hours. One of Manila's liveliest amateur jazz bands is the Executive Combo, comprised of a half-dozen businessmen, lawyers and government officials. Their hero is Duke Ellington, their theme song is "Take the A Train" and their leader, who doubles on the piano and drums, is Raul Manglapus, the foreign secretary in Cory Aquino's cabinet. His reverence for American jazz notwithstanding, he also composed a satirical musical entitled *Yankee Panky* as an assault against U.S. policy toward the Philippines.

★ ★ ★

While the United States left a more durable imprint on the Philippines than the Europeans did on their colonies, the impact was only superficial. Nevertheless, both Americans and Filipinos have diligently clung to the illusion that they share a common public philosophy—when, in reality, their values are dramatically dissimilar.

America's imperial effort started out as an exercise in "self-duplication," as the historian Glenn May has put it. Taft went to Manila with the preconceived notion that the Filipinos were unsuited to govern themselves, and his first impressions only confirmed his prejudice. "The great mass of the people are ignorant and superstitious," he observed, while the few men "who have any education that deserves the name" were mostly "intriguing politicians, without the slightest moral stamina, and nothing but personal interests to gratify." They were "oriental in their duplicity" and, he estimated, it might take a century of training "before they shall ever realize what Anglo-Saxon liberty is." However, he declared, the United States had a "sacred duty" to Americanize them. With that, he launched his program to instill in them the values that had made America the greatest society on earth: integrity, civic responsibility and respect for impersonal institutions. No matter that the United States at the time was itself riddled with corruption, racism and appalling economic disparities. America's mission was to export its virtues, not its sins. Through patient political tutelage, Taft said, the Filipinos could be taught "the possibility of honest administration." Over time, realizing the limitations of their influence, U.S. officials reluctantly accommodated to Filipino traditions. Yet they continued to claim that America was transforming the Philippines into a "showcase of democracy" rather than admit that their effort had fallen short of expectations.

Their task was daunting from the outset. They found in the Philippines a society based on a complicated and often baffling web of real and ritual kinship ties—the antithesis of the American ideal of a nation of citizens united in their devotion to the welfare of all.

Again history explains the phenomenon: Before the arrival of the Spanish, the Filipinos belonged to no social group larger than the village, which was in fact their family. Catholic priests spread through the countryside, further sanctifying the family by exhorting the Filipinos to identify with the Holy Family—God the powerful father, the compassionate Virgin mother and Christ, whose suffering and humiliation matched their own misery. The friars also introduced the Catholic custom of godparenthood, which fused with the pre-Hispanic practice of blood convenants with tribal allies to create a network of *compadres,* or ritual relatives. The sponsors of a child's baptism, for example, became the ceremonial kin of its parents, and the ritual family could expand to astonishing dimensions as well through weddings, funerals and confirmations. Calculating the possible permutations, Filipinos outdo Chaucer's man from St. Ives. Historian Theodore Friend has reckoned that a father with five children who enlists four sponsors, each with a family of four, can theoretically weave a fabric of nearly five hundred kin. The system has lost its original religious character as Filipinos, out of expediency, forge secular links with professional partners, army comrades, schoolmates.

Filipinos are absorbed into these alliances from infancy. Children, always invited to celebrations attended by real and fictive relatives, learn to feel comfortable at an early age in the warm fold of parents, brothers, sisters, uncles, aunts, cousins and ritual kinfolk. But they also learn as they grow up that these ties impose reciprocal responsibilities that must be observed to avoid the worst of all fates: exclusion from the extended family.

Personal rather than institutional relationships guide Filipinos, making them less sensitive to the rules of society than to the opinions of their real or ritual kin, whose esteem they must win and retain. Hence their obsession with *hiya,* a Tagalog term that conveys the supremely important concept of "face." To behave decorously toward family and friends, to display respect for an elder, kindness toward an underling, deference toward a superior—all show exemplary *hiya* and are ways to gain face. Failure to exhibit these qualities is *walang hiya,* to act shamelessly and thus lose face in the eyes of others. Equally vital is *utang na loob,* the "debt of gratitude" that Filipinos are ethically expected to repay in return for favors, lest they be guilty of *walang hiya.* A Filipino who renders services piles up credit for the future, since those he has assisted become indebted to him.

At its best, this mutual obligation pattern is an ideal social security mechanism. Filipinos help to raise their siblings and later care for their aged parents. If they become wealthy or rise to high office, they are required to support their relatives or find them government jobs. Even the poorest scrape to aid their more indigent kin, and no house is so humble that it lacks a spot for an unfortunate relative. Thousands of Filipinos rely on remittances from their children in the United States. Four hundred thousand Filipinos are employed abroad, mostly in lonely places like Saudi Arabia, Bahrein and Kuwait. Working on contract for two or three years as technicians, nurses, drivers and clerks, they send an estimated $1 billion a year home—a sum equal to one fourth of the country's earnings from exports. Numbers of women serve as domestics in Singapore and Hong Kong, many ending up as prostitutes. Guaranteed the hospitality of cousins and in-laws, Filipinos travel around the islands for only the cost of air fare. They take cheap charter flights to America, then sponge off an uncle in San Diego, a sister in Chicago or a nephew in Boston. The *compradrazgo* system also protects Filipinos, who out of suspicion and fear divide their relationships into "we" and "they." A *compradre* is supposedly trustworthy because he has ritually sworn an oath of eternal fidelity. But the system is not foolproof. The fact that Ninoy Aquino belonged to Marcos's college fraternity—and was by definition a *compadre* whom he privately called "brother"—did not prevent the dictator from imprisoning him for eight years.

The Philippines also owes its worst abuses to the strong blood and ceremonial alliances, whose mutual obligations spawn pervasive corruption. Greed alone is not the motive. Public figures rely on their real and ritual kin to win elected or appointed office, and once in authority, they then must reimburse their supporters with government contracts, tax breaks, import and export licenses and other favors, both legal and illicit. The recipients in turn kick back a proportion of their profits to the cooperative officials, and so the cycle of graft and fraud becomes normal practice.

Reflecting on his career as a mayor, province governor and senator, Ninoy once reckoned that he had amassed some ten thousand *compadres* who would recruit their *compadres* and the *compadres* of their *compadres* to work for him during elections. In exchange, he expedited their business deals, found them jobs, even paid to send their children to private schools. "An American politician kisses babies, but here we finance their education," he quipped— leaving it to me to guess that he had occult sources of money. For all her own integrity, Cory Aquino has not been able to restrain one of her brothers and his wife from engaging in shady transactions. Marcos, himself personally abstemious, pillaged the country partly in hopes of founding a dynasty for his indolent son Bong Bong. He also granted his cronies and army generals lucrative monopolies to recompense them for helping his rise to power. Filipinos, accustomed to venal leaders, might have forgiven him had not his profligacy plunged the nation into bankruptcy. President Carlos García hardly caused a ripple in 1960 when he defended a fraudulent aide on the grounds that he was simply "providing for the future of his family." Not long before, José Avelino, a prominent legislator, dared to state openly what most of his colleagues believed privately. One of the rare politicians ever censured for corruption, he urged the president at the time, Elpidio Quirino, not to press the charge against him. "What are we in power for? We are not hypocrites. Why should we pretend to be saints when in reality we are not? When Jesus Christ died on the cross, he made a distinction between good crooks and bad crooks. We can be good crooks."

The elaborate kinship system accounts as well for the social rigidity of the Philippines. Bishop Francisco Claver, a professor of sociology at the Ateneo de Manila, a Jesuit university, maintains that the country's values have hardly changed since pre-Spanish times. Families, he explained to me, are really ancient tribes in modern disguise, with the father the uncontested chief and everyone else occupying a designated niche in the pyramidal structure. "So Filipinos have been taught since childhood to respect authority, not to rebel or to question, and they are passive, even fatalistic. The poor believe that they are destined to be poor, and the rich assume that their wealth was ordained. Climbing from the lower classes to the peak of the pyramid is impossible. An Abraham Lincoln, a man of humble origin, could never become president of the Philippines." A Filipino journalist phrased it more succinctly: "It's not what you are and what you can do, but who you are, your name and your connections."

The calcified structure approaches feudalism in the rural areas. Plantations have belonged to the same dynasties for generations, and tenants can trace their roots on the property back to their grandfathers and great-grandfathers. Besides furnishing the sharecroppers with loans, seeds and tools in return for a percentage of the harvest, the landowners preside at their baptisms, weddings and funerals—thereby indebting the peasants both financially and morally. The local lords invariably control the mayor, police chief and regional army commander, and many maintain private security forces equipped with modern weapons and trained by foreign mercenaries. Many also subsidize vigilante groups, partly as a defense against insurgents but also to fight their vendettas. I once spent an evening with a banana planter at his house near the city of Davao, on the southern island of Mindanao. We drove out from town in a bullet-proof van and into a floodlit compound, its walls and watchtowers manned by guards with machine guns. "Normal precautions," he said of the setup.

A single statistic is illustrative: The top one fifth of the Philippine population receives half the country's income. An American Jesuit scholar, Father John Doherty, has estimated that sixty families control the Philippine economy. They have also dominated the political scene from the start of the U.S. colonial era to the Aquino government. Despite their Americanized hoopla, elections are actually contests between rival clans, and the "showcase of democracy" is a façade that only transparently conceals the rule of an elite that has consistently refused to surrender its privileges. The latest agrarian reform legislation, like numbers of apparently progressive land tenure laws already on the books, is a tissue of loopholes.

No wonder, then, that a Communist insurgency that began with a handful of rebels in the early 1970s has since spread throughout the archipelago. Cory Aquino, whose ordeal during her husband's imprisonment by Marcos had earned her the sympathy of human rights groups like Amnesty International, has ironically become their target by sanctioning anticommunist vigilantes and failing to prosecute alleged Philippine army abuses. The charges against her military establishment, she has retorted, have "shown up to be total lies." But even if she did attempt to try offenders, it is doubtful that she could rotate the wheels of justice. Clogged by incompetence and corruption, the courts function slowly or not at all. Defendants rely on their families or *compadres* to hire thugs to harass, abduct and even murder witnesses. Frustrated by the paralyzed legal system, Filipinos regularly resort to violence as a means of arbitration, knowing that the chances of being arrested, much less punished, are slim. Mayors and municipal officials live in constant fear, and no political candidate would campaign without a squad of bodyguards. Not a single soldier or policeman was convicted of a human rights violation committed after Cory took office—or, for that matter, during the Marcos regime. Years of hearings and investigations failed to apprehend Ninoy's assassins.

Traditional values have meanwhile shaded the attitudes of Filipinos toward the United States in complex and subtle ways. Many Filipinos, recalling America's schools, liberal political tutelage and early pledge of independence, were motivated by feelings of gratitude toward the United States. And, loyal to the concept of *utang na loob,* they fulfilled the debt of honor by fighting alongside Americans at Bataan and Corregidor, and by joining guerrilla movements to resist the Japanese during World War II. The shared agony ingrained in them the idea of a family tie between the United States and the Philippines. As Quezon's *compadre,* MacArthur perceived as few Americans did their personal approach to the relationship. But the United States, its foreign policy predicated on self-interest rather than sentimentality, ignored their view. As a result, the Filipinos were disappointed and dismayed when, following the war, the Americans gave them far less economic aid than they granted Japan, the common enemy.

Filipinos, in recurrent surges of nationalism, focused their resentment against the U.S. bases in the Philippines, the most visible sign of America's residual presence in the archipelago. And the issue promised to test their ties to the United States for years to come.

The Subic Bay navy yard and Clark air field, America's two largest overseas military installations, had long been of mutual value to both the Philippines and the United States. The "rent" paid for the bases, disguised as various forms of American aid, represented only a part of their importance to the Philippine economy—which, in the aftermath of Marcos's profligacy, desperately needed all the help it could muster. By 1988, the bases employed some seventy thousand Filipinos, more than the nation's ten leading corporations combined, contributing more than a billion dollars a year in revenues, double the total amount of foreign investment in the country. The bases also earned the Philippines more income than any single one of its exports. But the United States was getting its money's worth. Clark Field was no longer as vital as it had been during the decades following World War II as missiles supplanted aircraft as intercontinental weapons, and planes themselves developed long-range capabilities. By contrast, the U.S. Navy cherished Subic Bay for its enormous storage facilities as well as its loyal, skilled and relatively inexpensive Filipino labor force, many of whose fathers and grandfathers had worked there before them, and to relocate the base would have been costly. For American strategists, however, a crucial consideration was the presence of the installations as the symbol of a continued U.S. role in the Pacific—particularly in the wake of the defeat in Vietnam. It was a perception shared by China, Japan and the nations of Southeast Asia, all of whom regarded the American fleet to be a counterweight to growing Soviet strength in the region. The Japanese, almost totally dependent on imported oil, saw the Philippine bases as indispensable to the security of their sea lanes to the Indian Ocean and the Middle East.

Surveys have repeatedly shown a majority of Filipinos to be in favor of the U.S. bases. The attitude has reflected their awareness of the economic value of the bases, combined with the pro-American sentiment that has long pervaded the society. I had been prepared to believe the conventional wisdom that held that sympathy for the United States was concentrated mainly in the older generation of Filipinos who nostalgically remembered America's benevolent colonial rule and liberation of the Philippines from the Japanese during World War II. But a poll conducted in 1986 indicated that 76 percent of Filipino high school editors supported the U.S. bases. The statistic seemed to contradict the mounting clamor against the bases then consuming Manila's vocal elite—and which swelled into strident chorus during the years that followed. In fact, it illustrated once more that a few Manila politicians and newspaper columnists exert disproportionate influence over the Philippine government compared to the opinion of the population.

Spasms of nationalist passions directed against the United States had always served Filipinos as a convenient distraction from their internal problems. Marcos had kept the fervor in check, reserving for himself the right to juggle the bases issue as a device to extract concessions from the United States. By dismantling his regime, however, Cory Aquino restored Manila politics to its rough-and-tumble style—and, in the process, the bases question became fair game for every public figure. She remained silent except to say that she intended to keep her "options open" until 1991, when the lease on the installations expired. But discussions aimed at reaching an interim agreement opened in the summer of 1987, and it quickly appeared to U.S. diplomats involved in the talks that their Filipino counterparts, eager to demonstrate their nationalism, might be swept by their own rhetoric into a position that precluded compromise. Or as one of the American negotiators told me, "They may be painting themselves into a corner." Stealing the initiative from Cory, the Philippine senate voted to ban nuclear weapons from the country. The decision, if upheld by the entire legislature, would render the bases inoperative.

Inconsistencies predictably clouded the subject. Raul Manglapus, foreign secretary and chief Filipino negotiator, asserted from the start that "we must slay the father image"—the metaphor signifying that the Philippines could not mature as a nation as long as the bases remained as a reminder of the American colonial era. On the other hand, he hinted that he might concede if the United States raised its aid package to $1.2 billion a year from the $180 million it was then paying. "If the Americans can't afford it," he said, "they should go." But Father Joaquín Bernas, a Jesuit commentator, remarked that "you don't put a dollar tag on dignity" and others, echoing the same theme, called for "cutting the umbilical cord" and severing "the rope that strangles our growth as a nation." Some Filipinos also contended that a "mini-Marshall plan" of $10 billion in aid for the Philippines, proposed by a group of U.S. congressmen, was actually a trap designed to secure the bases. Amando Doronila, the scholarly editor of the *Manila Chronicle,* who had earlier forecast a settlement, finally concluded in June 1987 that "at some stage—maybe sooner than later—the bases must go." The "special relationship" between America and the Philippines was finished, he wrote: "Of all the nations with which the United States has close ties, there is nothing special about us, no matter whether many of us think otherwise."

His fondness for Cory Aquino notwithstanding, Secretary of State Shultz entered the debate with a virtual ultimatum. Unless the Filipinos toned down their demands, he cautioned, "we'll have to find some other place to have our ships and planes, because we only want to be at a place where we have an ally that wants us there." Admiral William Crowe, Chairman of the Joint Chiefs of Staff, was equally adamant, telling me in an interview: "We don't want to be where we're not wanted." The warnings were not entirely a bluff. Pentagon planners had indeed been weighing alternatives, among them the Pacific islands of Guam, Tinian and Saipan, all U.S. possessions untrameled by the question of sovereignty.

An agreement, ultimately signed in Washington on October 17, 1988, granted the Philippines an annual aid package of $481 million pending the conclusion of a new accord in 1991. But the bases issue, whatever its long-range solution, threatened to confront the Filipinos with a dilemma that transcended the problem of the bases themselves. Despite their nationalist rhetoric, an American withdrawal would symbolize a family schism for most Filipinos. Should the United States remain, their effort to reinforce their national identity would be retarded—as it has been since the Americans first landed in 1898.

A far more critical challenge facing the Filipinos, though, was the renovation of their society. In July 1968, Ninoy Aquino depicted his nation's plight in *Foreign Affairs,* and the portrait still rings true. "The Philippines is a land of traumatic contrasts," he wrote. "Here is a land in which a few are spectacularly rich while the masses remain abjectly poor. Here is a land where freedom and its blessings are a reality for the minority and an illusion for the many. Here is a land consecrated to democracy but run by an entrenched plutocracy. Here is a land of privilege and rank—a republic dedicated to equality but mired in an archaic system of caste." Its government was "financially almost bankrupt," its state agencies "ridden by debts and honeycombed with graft," its industries "in pathetic distress." There was "no organized, no methodical overall economic planning," but only "haphazard attempts to modernize" confused by a "multiplicity of cravings and concerns." So Filipinos were "depressed and dispirited . . . without purpose and without discipline . . . sapped of confidence, hope and will." The fault was mainly theirs. "They profess love of country, but love themselves—individually—more."

Like today's nationalists, Ninoy also blamed Spain and the United States for remolding the Filipinos "in their own image" and depriving them of their "soul"—an experience that had left them "bewildered" about their identity. "They were an Asian people not Asian in the eyes of their fellow Asians, not Western in the eyes of the West." Only by "bold efforts to break away from the fetters of the past," he urged, could they develop a distinct national character.

Few countries, however, have been more heavily shackled by the past than the Philippines. And, after one of the longest continuous periods of Western imperial rule in world history, Filipinos are still freighted with what they lament as their "colonial mentality." But they are doubly dependent: on their own oligarchy and on America. Like much else in history, it all began by accident.

2. IN SEARCH OF SPICES AND SOULS

★ ★ ★

On that torrid Sunday morning in April 1521, Ferdinand Magellan had no idea where he was. A few weeks before, he had sighted an island after his three ships, their crews ravaged by disease and starvation, had sailed for four months across a vast ocean he had called the Pacific. He cruised through the island chain, finally selecting a spot where the natives seemed to be friendly. Somehow sensing the importance of the occasion, he donned a white doublet and went ashore at the head of a hundred men, two in full armor bearing the royal Spanish standard. His cannon sounded a salute as a Catholic chaplain, intoning Latin incantations, baptized the local chief and his followers. Then he planted a wooden cross to proclaim the triumph of Christianity in this unknown, faraway, faithless place—which, twenty years later, another Spanish explorer named the Philippines.

Fragments of the cross are preserved today in a shabby pavilion located on a noisy street in downtown Cebu—the site of Magellan's landing—now, after Manila, the second largest city of the Philippines. The neglected relic, real or bogus, attracts only a few hardy tourists, but it symbolizes a great moment in history. For there in the Visayas, the islands that sprawl across the center of the archipelago, Spain embarked on a mission that, over a span of more than three centuries, was to make the Philippines the only Christian nation of Asia—and, subsequently reinforced by America's influence, the most Westernized society in the region.

★ ★ ★

The Age of Discovery, which propelled the Spanish and other Europeans around the world, resembled in its scope and intensity the modern exploration of outer space. It was an era of illusions and action, promise and failure, zeal, greed, conviction, courage, cruelty and benevolence, whose impact is still being felt. And it owed its origins to a millennium of study and speculation that paralleled human evolution itself.

The philosophers, mathematicians and astronomers of ancient Greece had long before concluded that the earth was a sphere—the geographer Eratosthenes having even calculated its circumference to within a hundred miles. But apart from the Mediterranean basin and the Middle East, which they knew in detail, their familiarity with other areas was limited to notions of northern Europe and Africa south of the Sahara and the parts of India conquered by Alexander the Great. Their learning filtered down to cosmographers of the early Christian era—most notable among them Claudius Ptolemaeus, or Ptolemy, the Alexandrian Greek who drafted an astonishingly accurate map of the world. The Arabs added to this lore, which by the twelfth century had reached Spain and Portugal, then struggling against Moorish domination. Shielded from the turmoil, Christian, Muslim and Jewish scholars worked together at research centers like the University of Toledo, south of Madrid, distilling new ideas out of the flow of information, and similar groups appeared in Italy to fuel that dynamic intellectual and artistic revival the Renaissance.

Europeans were tantalized by tales of remote places—some genuine, others fanciful. The legend of Atlantis, the island paradise of the sixth-century Irish monk Saint Brendan, so captivated the Portuguese that they sent out a series of fruitless expeditions to locate it. Equally seductive was the myth of Prester John, the presumed ruler of a Christian realm supposedly situated in India, beyond the Muslim barrier that blocked Europe's access to East Asia. But more than the lure of adventure now began to fascinate the Europeans. Still distressed by the failure of the Crusades, they dreamed of carrying the gospel to Asia. They were also excited by such accounts as the memoirs of Marco Polo, a Venetian merchant who returned from two decades in the Orient with fabulous and distorted descriptions of Burmese temples "covered with gold a full finger thick" and Indian shores where the "sands sparkled and glittered with gems and precious ores." Electrified by a heady combination of spiritual passion and commercial enterprise, they vaulted into the unknown, their lust for profit justified by their drive to redeem souls.

The European aristocracy had always been able to acquire expensive Chinese silks, costly Persian carpets and other exotic items that came overland from the East. But by the late fourteenth century, as the darkness of the Middle Ages lifted, new consumers gradually emerged in the burgeoning cities of Europe. For them, the coveted Asian treasures were pepper, nutmeg, cloves, cinnamon, ginger, sesame and other spices—former luxuries now essential for the preservation of food. The demand for spices soared, and soon they yielded profits of a thousandfold or more on European markets.

The shrewd merchants of Venice, Genoa, Pisa and lesser Italian city-states had cornered the spice trade through deals with the Muslim potentates who controlled the caravan routes to and from Asia. The Muslims allowed them as far as Aleppo and Alexandria, the great bazaars of the Levantine, but no farther. Rival European powers, resolved on smashing the Italian commercial monopoly, conceived of reaching the East Indies, the world's principal source of spices, either by sailing west across the Atlantic or east around the horn of

Africa. Thus they hoped to outflank the Muslim hold over the Near East and spread Christianity to the Orient.

No European of his generation perceived this vision more vividly or pursued it more vigorously than Prince Henry, the third of six sons of John I, who had crowned himself king in 1385 after liberating Portugal from Spanish rule. The Muslims were by then losing their grip over the Iberian peninsula and Henry, a Catholic mystic, regarded their total destruction to be his holy duty. He was only nineteen when, on his father's orders, he built a fleet to attack the Muslim stronghold of Ceuta, across the Strait of Gibraltar in Morocco. Fighting valiantly, he stormed the fallen fortress and stared in awe at its gold, silver, jewels, tapestries and stores of spices, all from Africa and Asia. His purpose was now clear: to circumvent the continents and sail directly to the fountains of such wealth, converting or killing heathens along the way.

Portugal, facing the uncharted Atlantic, was a natural springboard for his outward thrust, and Henry founded the first European maritime academy at Sagres, a lonely promontory on its stormy coast. There he remained for the next forty years, surrounded by a polyglot staff of cartographers, navigators, ship captains and pilots, engineers, carpenters, metalworkers and makers of sails, among them Italians, Greeks, Germans, Frenchmen, Britons, Scandinavians, Arabs from as far away as the Persian Gulf and Jews from nearly everywhere. Their dual assignment was to perfect his theories of seafaring and to plan actual voyages.

Under his aegis, they redefined latitude and longitude, invented such instruments as the quadrant and, above all, constructed the caravel, a light vessel designed to carry explorers. Soon Portuguese crews were ranging the African littoral below Cape Verde, its westernmost tip, probing rivers, classifying odd animals, plants and tribal customs, and collecting slaves. An ascetic recluse vowed to chastity, Henry never traveled himself, but his bold concepts and organizational genius earned him a sobriquet: the Navigator. He died in 1460, six years after Pope Nicholas V endorsed his enterprise by granting Portugal the exclusive franchise to "bring under submission . . . the pagans of the countries not yet inflicted with the plague of Islam and give them knowledge of the name of Christ."

The need to open a sea-lane to Asia became imperative during the years following Henry's death. The Turks, after capturing Constantinople, imposed their authority throughout the Middle East. Implacably hostile to Christianity, they cut off trade to the West, and the value of spices skyrocketed as supplies to European markets shrank. John II, who had been crowned king of Portugal in 1481, pressed his mariners to sail farther down the African coast, where pepper grew in profusion. One of them, Bartolomeu Dias de Novaes, set forth in August 1487 with two caravels and a cargo ship, planning to bring back spices. But storms drove him south until, to his astonishment, he had rounded the African continent. He had stumbled into the passage to India and would have pressed on had not his crew, weary and terrified, forced his retreat. Just as he landed in Lisbon, an obscure Genoese by the name of Christopher Columbus arrived in the city in search of support for his plan to reach the Indies by sailing westward across the Atlantic. King John rebuffed him, having concluded from the Dias experience and other intelligence that the route lay to the east. So it was that Columbus went to Ferdinand and Isabella, the Spanish monarchs, in quest of patronage.

Columbus's discovery of the western hemisphere, then presumed to be the Indies, infuriated the Portuguese, who claimed sole possession of the holy writ to exploration. Pope Alexander VI intervened to judge the dispute on the grounds that, as God's representative, he was responsible for all creation. In fact, he was a Spaniard who had been induced by Queen Isabella to render a verdict partial to Spain. On May 4, 1493, he issued a series of ambiguous and arrogant bulls collectively entitled *Inter Cetera,* which sliced the earth in two, granting Spain the right to lands west of Europe and Portugal those to the east. Their "saintly and praiseworthy" ventures aboard, the edicts intoned, would "result in the utmost success to the happiness and glory of all Christendom." Anyone trading in the designated areas, except under Spanish or Portuguese authorization, faced excommunication.

The Portuguese finally acquiesced to the compromise in the treaty of Tordesillas, which fixed the dividing line at roughly a thousand miles west of the Cape Verde islands. The pact, signed with papal blessings in 1495, then averted a war between Spain and Portugal, but it contributed to their future quarrels by vainly trying to limit boundaries in a spherical world. It later spurred the rise of Protestantism as the new commercial interests of northern Europe defied the pope's power to exclude them from overseas exploitation.

A new Portuguese king, Manuel I, hastened to benefit from his papal prerogatives and the maritime data gathered by his predecessors. He designated a thirty-five-year-old courtier, Vasco da Gama, to lead an expedition around the horn of Africa to India. The fleet of four ships left Lisbon in July 1497, landing ten months later at Calicut, on the southwestern coast of India. The voyage, an achievement of unprecedented magnitude, confirmed Portugal's assertion to preeminence in the area—a claim that da Gama enforced with brutality. He plundered and killed Muslims who crossed his path, and once even slaughtered a boatload of four hundred pilgrims, among them women and children, returning home from Mecca. Freedom of the seas, he said, "does not extend outside Europe."

During the next decade, the Portuguese exploded out of Europe with spectacular vitality. They consolidated Goa as the capital of their Indian dominions, then pushed east to capture Malacca, fanning out from that pivotal Malayan port to the remotest corners of Asia. They journeyed in search of spices to Sumatra and the distant Moluccas, won commercial concessions in Burma and Siam, and even sailed to forbidden Japan. Portuguese were probably the first Europeans to gaze at Angkor, the fantastic ruins of the Cambodian empire, and they may have visited the great temple of Borobudur, in Java. In 1557, they built a base at Macao, on the southern rim of China, and that colonial cameo has remained in their hands to this day—the oldest imperial possession on earth. Thus Portugal, one of Europe's smallest nations, was a global colossus by the sixteenth century.

Lisbon quickly surpassed Venice as Europe's hub of trade with Asia. But the Portuguese, while splendid sailors, were indifferent businessmen. Their kings, chronically in hock from foreign wars and wasteful domestic expenditures, relied on the revenues from the expeditions to repay their debts to the expanding investment bankers of Germany, Holland and Italy, who financed the ventures and siphoned off the bulk of the profits. As a contemporary English commentator put it: "The Portingall, like a good simple man, sayled every year full hungrily, about three parts of the earth, for spices. When he brought them home, the great rich pursars of the Antwerpians engrossed them all into their own hands . . . making thereof a plaine monopoly."

The seafarers were a hardy breed. Their voyages, sometimes lasting for years, seemed endless aboard their frail ships, with nothing to sustain them except religious faith and the prospect of pillage. They braved storms, wrecks, savages, pirates and disease—at least a third of every crew perishing of scurvy alone. "Where wouldn't they go for pepper!" wrote Joseph Conrad in evocation of their memory. "For a bag of pepper they could cut each other's throats without hesitation, and would forswear their souls. . . . The bizarre obstinacy of that desire made them defy death in a thousand shapes . . . wounds, captivity, hunger, pestilence and despair. It made them great! By heavens! it made them heroic; and it made them pathetic, too, in their craving for trade with the inflexible death levying its toll on young and old."

★ ★ ★

The mysterious lands of Asia, Africa or America then infused imaginative boys with the same ardor that had tempted bold youths during the Middle Ages to join the Crusades—and, in the space age, induces daring young men and women to become astronauts. So Fernão de Magalhães must have dreamed from childhood of unraveling the secrets of the seas. A Portuguese known to history as Ferdinand Magellan, the anglicized version of his name, he eventually attained immortality in the employ of Spain, his own nation's rival in the race to faraway places.

Born in 1480 in a barren mountain region of northern Portugal, the son of a rural squire, he was apprenticed as a page to Queen Leonora, the wife of John II, and later became an attendant at the court of King Manuel. The details of his early life are meager, but he was no doubt stirred by the excitement that greeted Vasco da Gama and other Portuguese mariners as they returned from their audacious voyages. He studied mathematics and navigation and, in March 1505, at the age of twenty-five, sailed with a squadron bound for India under the command of Francisco de Almeida.

Portugal's grand design was to secure bases in India by dominating the Indian Ocean, controlled by the Muslims, then push east to tap the wealth of Asia. The only Portuguese presence in India at the time was a fortress at Cochin, a town on the southwestern Malabar coast, built in 1503 by Afonso de Albuquerque to consolidate da Gama's discovery. King Manuel, elevating this precarious perch to the status of "empire," named Almeida his viceroy, with orders to assure Portuguese supremacy throughout the area. Almeida routed a Muslim fleet deployed to block his advance, thereby enabling Portugal to gain a solid foothold in the Indian port of Goa—which remained in Portuguese hands for five centuries.

Magellan, who had distinguished himself in the fighting, now prepared for more ambitious challenges. He joined an expedition of four ships to reconnoiter the Malayan port of Malacca, the largest market of Southeast Asia.

Arriving in September 1509, they were the first European vessels to reach the entrepôt, a vibrant emporium bustling with Chinese, Malays, Arabs, Indians, Japanese and Siamese gathered to buy spices imported from the Moluccas, Java and Sumatra.

Magellan showed uncommon courage in a disastrous episode. The Muslim ruler, after inviting the Portuguese to tour the town, deviously directed his men to attack them. Leaping into the fray, Magellan suffered a wound as he held off the assailants until his comrades could scramble back to their ships. The clash cost the Portuguese sixty sailors and one of their vessels, and they retreated to India. A dozen years later, Magellan was to die in an almost exact repetition of that performance.

Determined to capture Malacca, the Portuguese returned there during the summer of 1511 with a formidable armada of nineteen ships under the command of Albuquerque, the new viceroy of India. They finally defeated the Muslims after a battle that seesawed for six weeks. Now a captain, Magellan again fought valiantly, and the victory put the Portuguese in a pivotal position at the center of the busy trade routes of East Asia.

Magellan volunteered soon afterward for an expedition to explore the Moluccas, the so-called spice islands, which stretch like a necklace along the easternmost end of the Indonesian archipelago. The ships cruised the unfathomed Java Sea as far as Amboina and Banda, sailing past native canoes and catamarans, and stopping at coastal villages, where the local people gaped in bewilderment at the bearded strangers. The crews, after loading up nutmeg, cloves and other spices, elected to take their valuable cargo back to Malacca rather than investigate the region further. Had they circled only a couple of hundred miles to the north, they would have reached the Philippines, later approached by Magellan from the opposite direction.

Returning to Portugal after seven years abroad, he was anointed a *fidalgo escudeiro,* a minor grade of nobility reserved for army and navy officers. But at thirty-one he was too restless to settle down. He joined yet another expedition—this time an amphibious assault against the Muslim bastion of Azamor, in Morocco. Again wounded in action, now in the leg, he limped for the rest of his life.

Back home, Magellan was assigned to supervise captured enemy booty, a job that made him an easy target for charges of corruption. An official commission of inquiry found him innocent, but rival courtiers at home continued to denounce him to King Manuel, whom he had meanwhile antagonized with demands for larger rewards for his services. Late in 1517, feeling spurned and alienated, he renounced his allegiance to Portugal, and emigrated to Spain.

Geographers were then intrigued by the hypothesis of a southwest passage through America to Asia, preferable to the stormy route around Africa. The concept gained credibility when the news reached Europe that Vasco Nuñez de Balboa, the Spanish explorer, had seen another "ocean sea" from atop a mountain in the Isthmus of Darien, in Central America. An eccentric Portuguese scholar, Ruy Faleiro, who had long shared the notion, convinced Magellan of its possibilities. They went to Spain together to tout the idea to the Spanish, who were constrained under their treaty with Portugal to acquire territories lying only to the west of the pope's demarcation line. At best, Faleiro and Balboa appeared to be visionaries—at worst, a pair of crackpots.

They headed for Seville, then Spain's most affluent city. The maritime center of the Mediterranean, it was the site of the *Casa de Contratación,* the official Spanish bureau for the promotion of trade with the Indies. Ships hugged its wharves, their masts flying the pennants of a dozen nations. Products from around the world packed its warehouses, and merchants from throughout Europe maintained offices within sight of its docks. Its streets were crowded with Castilians, Navarrese, Basques, Catalonians and other Spaniards as well as Greeks, Italians, Germans, French and Portuguese, all competing for a piece of the commerce. Magellan carefully cultivated the influential dignitaries who might help him to find sponsors for his westward approach to the East.

He expediently married the daughter of a prominent Portuguese expatriate, Diogo Barbosa, who introduced him to Juan Rodriguez de Fonesca, the powerful bishop of Burgos and chairman of the Council of the Indies, the government agency responsible for Spain's ventures abroad. Fonesca had casually dismissed Columbus as a "crazy Italian" twenty-five years before, an error that had made him the laughingstock of the court. Fearful of repeating the blunder, he listened intently as Magellan outlined his proposed course on a painted globe. The ambitious project enthused him, and he was also impressed by Magellan's record as an experienced and intrepid seaman who had actually sailed to the Moluccas, the "spice islands." He arranged an audience for Magellan with Charles, the new king of Spain.

At first glance, Magellan did not inspire confidence. He was lame, short and inarticulate—a figure "without much personality," as a contemporary Spanish official noted. But his deep dark eyes seemed to reflect his passionate drive, and his plan fit Spain's aspirations.

The Spanish were then tightening their hold over the western hemisphere. Juan Ponce de León, after establishing a base in Puerto Rico, had landed in Florida. Hernando Cortés was preparing to conquer Mexico, and Francisco Pizarro would soon occupy Peru. New horizons lay beyond the Pacific since Balboa had grandly laid claim for Spain to "all that sea and the countries bordering on it." Magellan further promised to enrich King Charles V with the fabled wealth of the Orient.

Charles desperately needed money. He had just arrived in Spain, a naïve youth of seventeen, following a typically arcane dynastic tangle of the period. Born in Ghent of mixed Spanish and Austrian heritage, he spoke no Spanish and relied for advice on an alien circle of imported French and Dutch favorites. He had inherited the enormous liabilities of his reckless Hapsburg grandfather, Maximilian, whose debts even included unpaid grocery bills. Eager to bid for the hollow title of Holy Roman Emperor in an election that required bribing the religious and political notables of Europe, he had borrowed heavily from Jakob Fugger, the powerful German financier, to whom his family already owed enormous sums. Fugger, who knew of Magellan's project from his agents in Seville, was a pioneer venture capitalist: He would provide financing in exchange for a hefty slice of the profits.

Early in 1518, on the eve of his coronation, Charles approved Magellan's expedition. Their contract, drafted by Bishop Fonesca, was an intricate document worthy of a Wall Street lawyer. Charles would provide five ships and cover all expenses—in return for which Magellan and Ruy Faleiro, cocaptains, pledged to deliver a lucrative cargo of spices. They were to receive one twentieth of the profits, and they and their heirs could govern the lands they discovered in perpetuity. To symbolize his patronage, Charles dubbed them knights of the Order of Santiago, a prized award.

The Portuguese, worried by this threat to their claims in Asia, tried to sabotage the voyage and even contemplated assassinating Magellan. He, meanwhile, was being nagged by Spanish bureaucratic directives on everything from trade practices and accounting procedures to the rules of conduct for his crews. They were prohibited from gambling, using blasphemous language, molesting native women and, under the pain of death, practicing homosexuality. Another order, which Magellan was to violate at the cost of his life, forbade him from going ashore under any circumstances.

On the morning of September 20, 1519, after a year and a half of preparations, Magellan stood on the bridge of his flagship, the *Trinidad,* and shouted the traditional departure command: *"¡Larguen en el nombre de Dios!"*—"Let us go in the name of God!" The flotilla then sailed from the port of San Lucar de Barrameda, twenty-five miles downriver from Seville.

The heavily armed vessels, ranging from 75 to 125 tons in size, carried the usual items for barter such as mirrors, bells, beads and other cheap gimcrackery for ordinary natives and fancier gifts like satin cloth and fine glassware for princes and chiefs. Most of the cargo, however, consisted of food and drink: hardtack biscuits, salt pork, dried fish, anchovies, cheese, garlic, cooking oil, orange marmalade to prevent scurvy, and casks of wine and water. The crew of two hundred and sixty included Spaniards, Portuguese, Italians, Greeks, Germans and a Malay slave whom Magellan had acquired in Malacca and intended to use as an interpreter. At the last minute, Magellan had dropped Faleiro as untrustworthy, but a young Venetian aristocrat, Antonio Pigafetta, volunteered to serve as his personal aide. One of its eighteen survivors, he chronicled the voyage in remarkable vivid detail in *Primo Viaggio Intorno al Mondo,* his published journal. He revered and later eulogized Magellan: "He was more constant than anyone else in greatest adversity. He endured hunger better than all others, and more accurately than any man did he understand sea charts and navigation. . . . No other had such natural talent nor the boldness to circle the world, which he nearly did."

Magellan deserved high praise. Along with his superb skill as a seaman, he was guided by a single-minded conviction in his mission. He was aloof and frequently arrogant, but he commanded his crew with an artful mixture of firmness and compassion. He displayed his abilities in a grave crisis that nearly ruined the expedition.

After more than two grueling months at sea, the fleet reached the coast of Brazil, then headed south in search of a westward passage. Magellan probed almost every inlet and cove, the crew becoming increasingly restive as each proved to be a dead end. By late March 1520, he had gone as far as Patagonia, and the southern winter neared. He decided to sit out the cold weather in beautiful San Julian Bay, sheltered from the storms sweeping up from the Antarctic, and ordered half rations to conserve food. When the men objected, he appealed to their pride, patriotism and religious fervor. He brought most of them around, but four of his senior officers began to conspire against him.

They resented his imperious manner and, as Spaniards, had never reconciled themselves to a Portuguese commander. On the night of Palm Sunday, the captains of two ships seized a third vessel, murdered its master and threatened to sail home. His enterprise in jeopardy, Magellan resorted to a ruse. He sent emissaries to the rebels, ostensibly to negotiate, but instead they killed the chief mutineer, and the others surrendered. Magellan executed only the one responsible for the murder. He marooned another on the desolate Patagonian coast, sparing him because of his kinship to Bishop Fonesca, a patron of the project. He pardoned forty others—among them Juan Sebastian del Cano, a Basque officer who, two years later, was to lead the survivors back to Spain.

Late in August 1520, as winter waned, he resumed the journey south with four seaworthy ships. Now he confronted the rigorous test of locating and navigating the presumed southwest passage to the sea on the other side. To aggravate his plight, he suddenly found that the suppliers in Spain had faked the records and furnished him with inadequate food rations. He assembled his officers, swearing them to keep the shortages a secret. The trip would continue, he declared, even if they had to "eat the cowhide off the yard-arms"—as they eventually did.

The Strait of Magellan, as it was later named, is one of the world's most treacherous waterways—a maze of concealed islands, sandbars and rocks stretching for three hundred and seventy miles through the southernmost tip of South America. Magellan plunged blindly into the tortuous channel in late October. His vessels, buffeted by gales and spun by swirling currents, zigzagged and backtracked as they groped for an opening. When the largest ship disappeared, Magellan scoured the area, only to learn to his dismay that its captain had deserted with most of the fleet's few provisions.

Finally, after nearly seven horrendous weeks, the three remaining vessels debouched into the ocean. Already at sea for more than a year, they still faced the biggest expanse of water on earth. Deceived by its unusual calmness, Magellan christened it the Pacific. But another ghastly experience awaited him and his men. "In truth, the like of this voyage will never be made again," Pigafetta wrote later.

As their sparse food supply dwindled, they subsisted on crumbs of biscuits infested with worms and stinking of rat urine. The rats themselves were a rare delicacy that sold for half a ducat each. They ate sawdust—and, then as Magellan had predicted, the cowhide off the yard-arms, softened in sea water and grilled over braziers. Their water turned yellow from putrefaction, but they drank it nevertheless. Nineteen men succumbed to starvation, and only benign weather favored the ships, permitting them to cover as many as seventy leagues a day. Had it not been for that blessing, Pigafetta recalled, "we would all have died of hunger."

They were close to disaster by early March, when they ran into an island chain. Dropping anchor at one of them—later named Guam—they were greeted by a swarm of cheerful natives who climbed aboard the ships and proceeded to steal everything from cups and saucers to a lifeboat. Magellan, claiming the islands for Spain, appropriately dubbed them the *Ladrones,* the "Thieves." After stocking up on rice, fruit and fresh water, he left hastily, certain that he was near the Moluccas, his goal.

At dawn on March 16, 1521, a week later, he spied distant peaks above the morning mist. He had spotted the island of Leyte, as it was called by the natives. For the first time in history, Europeans gazed on the Philippines—as a subsequent Spanish explorer named the land. Convinced that a miracle had brought him and his crew back from the dead, Magellan christened it the archipelago of San Lázaro, in honor of Lazarus, whom Jesus had resurrected.

The ships sailed toward Leyte and soon came within sight of two other large islands—Samar to the north and Mindanao to the south. Anchoring at an uninhabited atoll, they were approached by a boatload of inquisitive natives bringing rice and coconuts. They looked blank when Magellan, speaking through his Malay interpreter, asked about spices. Impatient, he pushed on to another tiny island, Limasawa, its coast of rocks and sandy coves framed by groves of palms. A faint breeze relieved the oppressive heat and humidity.

Though under orders to stay aboard ship, Magellan was too restless to remain confined, especially on this day, Easter Sunday. He went ashore with fifty men to celebrate mass and to erect a cross atop a hill, explaining to the friendly but puzzled natives that the symbol would protect them against evil. Faithful to protocol, he also intended the ritual to confirm Spain's sovereignty over the area. Two local chiefs, oblivious to its significance, joined in the ceremony, then piloted his fleet to the most populous island in the region. There, from the deck of his ship, he observed a village of about three hundred bamboo huts on stilts. It was the site on which the city of Cebu stands today.

Scanning its fine natural harbor, he imagined a base for trade with the Moluccas, which he still believed to be close. From here, he reckoned, Spain could acquire spices without transgressing Portugal's claims in the vicinity. The longer he pondered the idea, the more he was mesmerized by the vision of converting the people to Christianity and ruling the spot himself as Spain's viceroy. The local chief, Humabon, feigned receptivity to the plan—to advance his own interests.

He welcomed Magellan amicably by sending him a delegation of dignitaries bearing rice, pigs and chickens. Impressed by the gesture, Magellan assumed that the notables were ready to embrace Christianity then and there, and he launched into an emotional speech extolling God and Christ. Though baffled by the cascade of words, which the Malay interpreter spastically translated into their dialect, the natives nevertheless agreed to convert—if Humabon approved. Magellan broke into tears. Henceforth, he pledged, they would enjoy the perpetual love of Spain and immunity from Satan. Pigafetta, who witnessed the spectacle, ecstatically wrote, "We all wept for joy!"

Observing etiquette, Magellan reciprocated by sending presents to Humabon, among them a gaudy Turkish-style yellow and purple silk gown, a red cap and a pair of gilt cups. He assigned Pigafetta and a group of the crew to deliver the gifts. Conducted to Humabon's palace, they found him seated cross-legged on a palm mat, his fat tattooed body garbed only in a cotton loincloth and his ears glittering with gold pendants inlaid with precious gems. He was nibbling turtle eggs from porcelain dishes and sipping aromatic palm wine through a reed straw as his courtiers, whom Pigafetta had briefed, outlined the benefits of Christianity.

Before Pigafetta and his comrades returned to their ship, one of Humabon's nephews treated them to a diversion. He took them to his house to be entertained by an ensemble of young women, some topless and others totally nude, playing musical instruments and dancing. The performers were "very beautiful and almost as white as our girls," Pigafetta recalled—and there, out of discretion, his account of the evening ends.

For a moment Magellan suspected the burst of piety by the natives to be duplicitous, but he overcame his doubts when Humabon himself asked to convert to Christianity. He went ashore on April 21, 1521, his retinue in resplendent regalia, and the two men sealed a blood pact. Then, after raising the cross, his chaplain baptized Humabon, naming him Charles for the Spanish king, and repeated the ritual for the chief's male relatives and courtiers. Humabon's wife and her attendants insisted on being included, and they were followed by lesser folk eager to emulate their ruler. Within a week, some two thousand inhabitants of Cebu and its environs had entered the Catholic fold, several minor chiefs among them. Magellan, elated, now saw his dream of a Spanish empire in the East within grasp. In reality, his influence barely extended beyond a handful of villages; at best, it was ephemeral.

He directed the local tribes to pledge allegiance to Humabon, who as his surrogate would represent the crown of Spain. But Lapu Lapu, a chief on the nearby island of Mactan and Humabon's traditional enemy, resisted. Humabon implored Magellan to punish his rival, and despite the pleas of his officers, who warned him that he was walking into a trap, Magellan agreed. After all, Humabon had been converted to Christianity under his auspices—and, as he put it, "a good shepherd cannot abandon his flock."

Hardly had Magellan decided to launch the strike than word of it leaked. Overnight, Lapu Lapu mobilized fifteen hundred warriors from among the other clans of the region, telling them that foreign intruders had smashed their idols and imposed a strange religion. But Magellan was confident that Europeans, armed with guns, lances and swords, could easily overpower naked natives wielding knives, bamboo spears and bows and arrows—an error that Westerners were to make in Asia repeatedly during the years ahead. Mobilizing only sixty men for the mission, he mistakenly permitted them to discard their cumbersome leg armor and wear only breast plates and cloche helmets. Lusting for action, Humabon had come along with an army of six hundred. Magellan confined him to the sidelines. His crew could handle the job alone.

Setting out in the early hours of April 27, 1521, three boatloads of Magellan's men rowed across the narrow strait from Cebu, reaching Mactan at dawn. Soon they realized that the amphibious operation against the island would be harder than they had expected. With the tide low, the boats could only be brought to within two hundred yards of the beach, where their mounted cannon were out of range of the adversary. They waded ashore, only to face an enemy yelling defiant war cries and poised to charge. Braced back to back, they fired their muskets and crossbows, to no avail. The defenders rushed forward, unleashing a hail of spears and arrows, one piercing Magellan's bare leg. He ordered his men to withdraw slowly, but most fled in panic, leaving him with only Pigafetta and seven others. Pulling back into the surf up to their knees, they waged a rearguard action as they attempted to scramble to their boats. Magellan, sword in hand, stood his ground, covering their retreat.

The assailants had by now singled him out as a target. One lunged at him with a spear, wounding his shoulder. Unable to raise his sword, he could no longer fight back. A native slashed him with a knife, and others hacked his body as he fell. Pigafetta recalled his final moments: "While they were assaulting him, he looked back many times to see if we were all in the boats. . . . Had it not been for our unfortunate captain sacrificing himself, not one of us would have lived. For, as he held out, we were able to reach safety." Magellan, he added in a tribute, had been "our mirror, our comfort and our true guide."

But their ordeal was not over. Humabon, disappointed by their failure to subdue Lapu Lapu, turned against them. He invited twenty-four of their senior officers to a banquet, plied them with wine and women, and slaughtered all except two or three, who managed to flee. Those still aboard the ships swiftly put out to sea.

Death had dwindled their strength to about one hundred and twenty men, fewer than half the number who had departed Seville nearly two years earlier. Scuttling one of their three vessels for the sake of efficiency, they sailed the other two to the Moluccas, their initial goal. One, the dilapidated *Trinidad,* formerly Magellan's flagship, remained there for overhauling and never made it back. The *Vittoria,* the sole remnant, limped westward across the Indian Ocean and around the horn of Africa under the command of Juan Sebastian del Cano, the mutineer pardoned by Magellan. Nearly half its complement of sixty Europeans and assorted natives died of hunger, thirst, disease or exposure before the tattered ship stopped for food and water at the Cape Verde islands, a Portuguese possession. There the Portuguese authorities, hostile to Spain, jailed most of the survivors. The others escaped to reach home.

On September 8, 1522, eighteen of an original crew of two hundred and seventy headed up the sluggish Guadalquivir, proudly firing a salute from their rusty cannon as they anchored at Seville. They had been away twelve days short of their departure three years before. According to Pigafetta, who was aboard, they had covered forty-three thousand nautical miles in the first circumnavigation of the world. The day after their arrival, in gratitude for their deliverance, they marched barefoot, clad only in shirts, carrying candles to the cathedral shrines of Santa Maria de la Victoria and Santa Maria de l'Antigua. King Charles, jubilant, lavished them with rewards—ignoring Magellan in the celebration.

Years passed before Magellan received the recognition he deserved, perhaps because Spain was reluctant to acknowledge the accomplishment of a Portuguese in its employ. Today he ranks with Columbus and Vasco da Gama as a towering figure of the age of discovery. Lapu Lapu, the man responsible for his death, is now honored by the Philippines in statues and postage stamps, and the principal town on the island of Mactan bears his name. But he too was forgotten for centuries, until contemporary Filipino nationalists revived his memory in an effort to endow the Philippines with a historical continuity that never quite existed.

★   ★   ★

Subsequent Spanish settlers, and the Americans who came centuries later, were awed by the beauty of the Philippines. Their wonderment was not misplaced. The archipelago, one of nature's glories, is indeed a brilliant tapestry of land, sea and sky, fields, forests, mountains, wildlife and peoples—all so dazzling and diverse as to seem unreal.

The seven thousand islands sprawl for a thousand miles from north to south like pieces broken off the mainland of Asia—probably their geological origin. Only a thousand are inhabited, and fewer than five hundred are larger than one square mile. Their topography is a quilt of contrasts. Lush green plains and verdant hills stretch out against a horizon of jungle-clad peaks that soar as high as ten thousand feet, some active volcanos. Placid lagoons enclosed by coral reefs bathe beaches of fine white sand, and elsewhere the surf dashes against rugged cliffs. With a coastline longer than that of the United States, everyplace is near the sea, itself a study in extremes. Shallow channels separate the islands, while the ocean off Mindanao plunges down six miles, the deepest spot on earth. Monsoon rains fall with biblical intensity, bringing fertility and decay.

The Philippines is ablaze with flora and fauna. Rich growths of mahogany, rattan, bamboo and palms of a dozen varieties blanket its landscape. Flowers, including nearly a thousand kinds of orchids, bloom everywhere. Forests abound in monkeys, deer, boar, savage buffalo and giant bats, cobras, pythons, iguanas and other reptiles; specialists have not yet fully classified its vast assortment of exotic birds and species of multicolored butterflies. The smallest known fish, the *pondoka pygmaea,* inhabits its surrounding waters along with tuna, sharks, huge green turtles, oysters the size of soup bowls and clams as big as bathtubs. Its prized shells fetch fancy prices on global markets.

Dissimilarity also characterizes the Philippine people. They speak eight different languages and some seventy dialects, and the linguistic jumble is only one clue to their variety. The Ilocanos of northwestern Luzon, a relatively arid area, are reputedly austere and venturesome, and make up many of the emigrants to Hawaii and California. The Tagalogs, from the center of the island, are prototypical Filipinos because of their political, professional and cultural preeminence. But Tagalogs differ among themselves according to region, and all the peoples of Luzon consider themselves to be distinct from those of the Visayas, who have spread out from their central islands to exploit Mindanao and the Sulu archipelago—the terrain of the almost perpetually dissident Muslim Moros. Meanwhile, aboriginal tribes like the Ifugaos, Bontocs, Aetas and Ilongots, former headhunters, roam the highland jungles as they have for millennia. They have long been the victims of repression or, at best, neglect.

Striving to assert their unique origins, some Filipinos contend that the islands rose out of the sea in a prehistoric geological convulsion—thus challenging Western scholars who hold that the archipelago was once connected to the Asian continent by "land bridges" that submerged some two hundred thousand years ago. A Filipino anthropologist, F. Landa Jocano, also disputes the theory that the ancestors of the aborigines initially crossed over from the Asian mainland. He has suggested instead that human traces in the Philippines date back nearly two million years, to the time of Java man, thereby making the archipelago "coequal" to the rest of Southeast Asia. Whatever the truth, successive migrations did populate the islands through the centuries.

One of the earliest, some fifteen thousand years ago, consisted of Mongoloid tribes driven south from the interior of China by the Han Chinese. Nomadic hunters, they brought the rudiments of agriculture to supplement their diet of game and fish. Following them came groups from southern China and Vietnam, skilled in the use of stone and bronze tools and weapons. Settling along protected bays and riverbanks, they built houses on stilts as a safeguard against floods. They introduced the delicate art of cultivating rice in irrigated fields and domesticated for that purpose the ubiquitous beast of burden of Southeast Asia, the *carabao,* or water buffalo. The Ifugaos, who arrived in that influx, drifted into northern Luzon, where they constructed an engineering wonder of the world: the rice terraces of Banaue, painstakingly carved out of hillsides, like giant steps climbing a steep incline.

Malays from Indonesia and the Malay peninsula streamed into the islands more than two thousand years ago to become the predominant ethnic component in the population. Defying storms and hijackers, they sailed along the coast of Borneo and through the Sulu archipelago, first settling mainly in the Visayan Islands and southwestern Luzon. Their outrigger praus, equipped with lateen sails, each carried a family or clans led by a chief. Once ashore, they remained together as *barangays,* as the boats themselves were called. President Marcos, in an effort to revive the past, later changed the formal designation of Philippine villages from *barrios,* as the Spanish had called them, to *barangays.*

The settlements, mostly located on the sea or along accessible rivers, had long lured Chinese merchants. With the rise of the Sung dynasty in the tenth century, however, China forged permanent trade ties with the islands. Hardy Chinese entrepreneurs established headquarters in coastal villages, as they did throughout Southeast Asia. In 1405, the dynamic Ming emperor Yung Lo sought to impose China's supremacy over the Philippines by arbitrarily appointing a "governor" of Luzon—the name of the island having earlier been derived from the Chinese characters *Liu Sung,* a transliteration from Tagalog roughly meaning "land of rice mortars." To enforce his rule, he sent a fleet of sixty armed junks on a tour of the islands under the command of the celebrated eunuch admiral Cheng Ho, renowned for his daring expeditions to Africa and the southwest Pacific. The project crumbled with Yung Lo's death, but the Chinese continued to deal with the Philippines. In the late sixteenth century, when the Spanish first reached the village that was to become Manila, they found a small community of Chinese merchants already functioning there.

An early Chinese trade expert, Chao Yu-kua, described the commerce with the Philippines, presumably as a guide for his compatriots. Chinese ships, carrying cargoes of glass, porcelain, ceramics, iron needles and other products made in China, would sail into the Luzon ports, where their captains promptly presented gifts to the local chiefs to grease the gears of business—just as a bribe to a Filipino official today opens doors. Native brokers were then dispatched by boat to other islands to obtain resin, hemp, pearls, tortoise shells and other goods for barter with the Chinese, who often waited as long as eight or nine months for their return. To save time, Chinese junks occasionally cruised from island to island, anchoring offshore and announcing their arrival by beating drums and clanging gongs. After the villagers had approached in canoes to display their wares, the Chinese traveling salesmen would disembark to bargain under the eye of a local dignitary, who naturally took a commission on the transactions. Chinese seafarers disliked the voyages to the Philippines, whose waters were filled with rocks, shoals and dangerous reefs and infested with pirates. But the profits were worth the risks. A treasure trove of Chinese antiques now being excavated in the Philippines dramatizes the vitality of a trade with China that dates back centuries.

The Chinese taught the Filipinos to mine and work metals, to manufacture gunpowder and, among other quaint practices, to use parasols. Their vocabulary infiltrated Tagalog and other native languages. Above all, they remained. Motivated primarily by money, many converted to Catholicism, married Filipino women and spawned the country's most powerful families. Everybody who is anybody in the Philippines today, except for a few Spanish *mestizos,* has Chinese ancestors.

By the middle of the fourteenth century, Java, Sumatra, Malaya, Cambodia, Siam and the Indochina states of Annam and Tonkin had entered the trade, and they also left an imprint on the Philippines. Traces of Buddhist and Hindu culture, possibly transmitted through the Siamese and Cambodians, found their way into the local idiom in the form of Sanskrit words, and Brahmanic ritual has syncretized with Catholicism in Filipino religious ceremonies.

Islam, which had slowly spread across the world from the Middle East, deeply changed Malaya, Java and Sumatra in the thirteenth century. By offering to end the caste system of Hinduism, the state religion in those areas, it promised equality. By the fifteenth century, Muslim missionaries had arrived in the southernmost islands of the Philippines, where they pursued a familiar pattern. They would convert a local chief, wed his daughter and bring the entire clan into the fold. The most famous of them, Sherif Mohammed Kabungsuwan, traveled from the Malay state of Johore to Mindanao, married a tribal princess named Putri Tunoma, and proclaimed himself sultan of the region after proselytizing her family.

By the sixteenth century the Muslims had crept north to Luzon, where one of their chiefs, Suleiman, ruled Manila. There their advance was halted by the Spanish, who dubbed them Moros, after the Moors they had expelled from Spain. But the Muslims were never completely crushed. Three hundred years later the Americans defeated them in a fierce campaign, yet they continued to resist—and Muslim factions continue to fight the Philippine government.

Most of the natives had meanwhile clung to beliefs that suited their environment. In the Visayas, for instance, they venerated a supreme divinity, Bathala, who presided over a pantheon of functional gods of agriculture, fire, war, death, love and the like. Everywhere they practiced animism, praying to idols representing the spirits of their households, fields and streams, staging ceremonies to propitiate the demons, ghosts, nymphs or elves residing in the plants, trees, birds and beasts around them. Swayed by auguries and magic charms, they held elaborate rituals to worship the souls of the dead, considered to be immortal. Even those drawn to Islam accepted the new faith without discarding their old customs, thereby fusing apparently contradictory creeds—as later converts to Christianity also did. Marcos cherished his *anting-anting,* an amulet that supposedly shielded him against his enemies—though it plainly did not save him from Cory Aquino.

Early Spanish chroniclers compiled meticulous notes on nearly every aspect of Philippine life. Given the diversity of the islands, their accounts are only pertinent to the areas they observed. Still, they portrayed a complicated culture despite customs that seemed primitive to European eyes.

Manila and Cebu, the only "towns," contained no more than a few hundred households, and villages were mostly composed of a single clan. A dozen or so thatch-roofed bamboo huts stood on stilts, families crowded into two or three rooms above as their poultry, goats and pigs scratched the ground underneath. Men wore loincloths woven from tree bark, and women were clad in miniskirts of the same material. Except for gold earrings and bracelets, village chiefs dressed no differently. They all smeared their tattooed bodies with coconut oil to guard against the wind and sun and chewed betel mixed with lime—which, as Pigafetta observed, made their mouths "very red." They tended to be chronically tipsy from too much palm wine.

Class stratified the villages. The chief held absolute authority, and his relatives, who ranked as aristocrats, were exempt from menial tasks. His free subjects paid him tribute in the form of crops and corvée labor, in exchange for his leadership, protection and benevolence. At the bottom of the scale were slaves, usually debtors, captives or criminals, serving their masters as field workers or domestic servants. The structure was not inflexible, however; classes sometimes intermarried, and chiefs often legitimized their children by female slaves. The bilateral kinship system, which gave equal importance to the maternal and paternal lines, accorded women enormous power within the clan. They were entitled to own property, engage in trade, divorce and even become village chiefs in the absence of a male heir. The Spanish, in Latin fashion, later relegated them to a secondary position—but at the same time, by glorifying the Virgin Mary as a model, indirectly buttressed their status inside the family. And, to this day, women play a decisive role in Filipino families. They handle the money, act as religious mentors and, among their other responsibilities, arrange the marriages of sons and daughters—striving always to improve the family's dynastic connections. The emergence of Imelda Marcos and Cory Aquino as public figures shows that Philippine society, for all its male chauvinism, respects women. Still, they were catapulted into prominence only as surrogates of their husbands—proof that they owed their rise primarily to the influence of their political families.

The early village chiefs abided by a legal code, enacted with the advice of a committee of elders. A town crier, bell in hand, announced new laws that covered the kinds of cases that confront any society: larceny, murder, incest, marital squabbles, disputes over inheritances. Trials were public, but not adversarial. The chief sat as judge and the elders as jury, and without lawyers to complicate the proceedings, justice was swift and brutal. Defendants were put through rigorous ordeals on the theory that the gods protected the innocent; to refuse to retrieve a stone from boiling water, for example, was an admission of guilt. Such merciless tests, however, were no harsher than the tortures and punishments then inflicted on convicts and even suspects in Europe. To be hacked to death for adultery, to cite one tribal penalty, was no crueler than the European practice of flaying offenders alive. Similarly, perjurers were flogged and witches burned at the stake. The father of a beautiful girl who denied his chief the *droit du seigneur* could be banished for life, as vassals were in feudal Britain or France.

Feuds were chronic, often interminable. Villages went to war over real or imagined insults, to capture slaves or to abduct women, to resolve water disputes or rival claims to rice fields. Without the arbitration of a higher authority, like the impartial magistrate that functioned at the time in China, conflicts were seldom adjudicated. The winners would impose their will on the losers, who awaited the chance for revenge, and the vendettas could drag on for generations. Clans often formed alliances to fight a common enemy, their chiefs sealing blood compacts that prefigured the *compadre* relationships that today link factions in the Philippines, where violent family feuds continue to torment the society.

Despite their professions of piety, the early Spaniards were avid voyeurs who took a prurient interest in the sex life of the natives, and their journals cover the topic in clinical detail. Antonio Pigafetta interviewed and examined couples at length, with the diligence of Masters and Johnson. "Both young and old males pierce their penises with a gold or tin rod the size of a goose quill, its ends either pointed like a spur or shaped like the head of a nail. . . . When a man wishes to have intercourse with a woman, she takes his penis not in the normal way, but gently introduces first the top spur and then the bottom one into her vagina. Once inside, the penis becomes erect and cannot be withdrawn until it is limp." Pigafetta asserted that the women hated this mode of fornication, which lacerated their organs. "They very much preferred our men to their own," he noted with the hint of a boast. He was wrong. Later Spaniards found the painful posture to be the rage, especially in the Visayas. Juan de Medina, an Augustinian friar, wrote that women there would copulate only that way and were "grief stricken" when Catholic missionaries compelled them to reform.

The first Jesuits to reach Luzon in the late sixteenth century discovered the natives to be "of a happy disposition . . . candid, loyal, simple and sociable"—a portrait that would fit Filipinos today. Then, as now, they reveled in festivals replete with banquets, sports and especially cockfights—still the national addiction. They were no match for the contemporary architects and artists of Cambodia and Java, who constructed great stone temples or sculpted exquisite bronze statues. But they excelled at handicrafts like basketry weaving and wood carving, and they continue to be skilled artisans. They were also gifted musicians, another talent alive in their present-day folk troupes, dance orchestras and flashy marching bands. Their literature, or what little is known of it, blended music with poetry in sagas that dealt with love, nature or the legends of heroic warriors, often digressing into parables, proverbs, social commentaries or gossip. These epics rambled on for nights, fueling an oral tradition that may account for the current Filipino penchant for marathon oratory. They wrote on bamboo and tree bark, specimens of which have since rotted in the decay of the tropics, or were burned by the Spanish in an effort to efface the pagan culture. Their ability to read, however, reassured the early Catholic missionaries, who translated the catechism into various indigenous alphabets. Or as one of them put it: "They have a lively wit, and easily learn Christian doctrine."

★ ★ ★

King Charles of Spain was far from committed to keeping the territory discovered by Magellan. For him the real prize were the Moluccas, the spice islands, which Portugal claimed under the pope's vague partition of the world. Only after sending out three expeditions in a futile effort to seize them did he finally concede to the Portuguese claim. His only alternative now was to extend Spain's hold over the area that Magellan had found. On his orders, six ships commanded by Ruy Lopez de Villalobos sailed in November 1542 from the port of Navidad, in New Spain, as the Spanish then called their new colony in Mexico. Again the venture failed. Villalobos, instructed to secure a trading post on Mindanao, ran short of food and encountered hostile natives, and his men threatened to mutiny. Before turning back, however, he left an indelible mark on the islands. He named them the *Felipinas,* the Philippines, in honor of Philip, the Spanish crown prince—whom Charles, weary of ruling, had just appointed as his regent.

Charles had by then governed Spain for nearly three decades. He had thrust his influence through Europe to the borders of Turkey and across the Mediterranean into North Africa. But his elastic ambitions had sapped his energy and drained his treasury. In 1556, he abdicated in favor of his son, who as Philip II reigned for the next forty-two years, propelling Spain to the summit of its glory—and to the brink of its decline.

Philip reinforced his power at home by introducing social and political reforms. Like his father, though, he incurred huge debts waging wars against France, Turkey and Lutheran dissidents in the Netherlands, then under Spanish control; even vast imports of silver from Mexico could not rescue him from bankruptcy. His private life was also plagued by his stormy marriage to Mary, the Tudor queen of England, known to history as the infamous "Bloody Mary" for her persecution of English Protestants. Besides, he was by nature cautious—a trait that had earned him the nickname of *El Prudente.* So he flinched at financing new and expensive voyages to Asia. But he shared his father's obsession with the Portuguese, and he was determined to smash their trade with the Orient.

The Portuguese were profiting handsomely. They had a monopoly on commerce with China from their base at Macao and were even dealing with Japan, a forbidden land to foreigners. Spanish officials in Mexico, who saw trade with Asia as a boon to their own interests, advised Philip that Spain's presence in the Philippines would subvert Portuguese ambitions in the region. After considerable hesitation, Philip finally ordered his viceroy in Mexico to prepare for yet another expedition across the Pacific. So, for the next three hundred years, the Spanish authorities in Mexico were to manage the Philippines as an imperial subsidiary, in effect making the archipelago a colony of a colony.

The man selected to lead the new venture, Miguel Lopez de Legazpi, a minor Basque aristocrat, was an improbable choice for the hazardous assignment. A grandfather in his fifties, he had spent nearly thirty sedentary years as a bureaucrat in Mexico City, rising to the top by flattering his superiors and becoming rich through astute real estate investments. Nor was his pompous, pious style suited to command the ruffians who volunteered for such voyages. Spanish officials derided his appointment as a bad joke, one of them remarking that he suffered from "advanced senility." Legazpi reacted to the taunts with characteristic humility: "There are many men more qualified than I, yet none more willing to serve the king." But he proved to be wise, honest and tough.

He owed his appointment and later success to a cousin, Andrés de Urdaneta, an Augustinian friar and one of the great geographers of the age, who masterminded the expedition. A few years younger than Legazpi, he looked like a picture-book monk with his tonsured head, a large pectoral cross adorning his wool cassock. In fact, he was rugged, tenacious and sophisticated. He had quit school to join the army, and distinguished himself fighting in Italy and Germany before retiring to study mathematics and astronomy. After traveling to the Moluccas on an earlier Spanish voyage, he settled in Mexico City, where he joined the Augustinian order and soon won recognition as a navigational expert. He foresaw a lucrative trade between the Orient and Mexico's west coast port of Acapulco, from where Asian products could be transported overland to Vera Cruz, then sent via the Atlantic to Spain. Most significantly, he charted the eastward route across the Pacific, thereby enabling ships to carry their cargoes back from Asia directly to the western hemisphere instead of circling the world. The discovery shaped the destiny of the Philippines—and America's future relations with Asia.

Preparations for the expedition, kept secret as a precaution against Portuguese spies, dragged on for three years. Finally, before sunrise on November 21, 1564, four vessels led by Legazpi's flagship, the *San Pedro,* left the Mexican port of Navidad, cruised down the Bay of Melasa and set forth across the Pacific. The complement of three hundred and sixty men included sailors, soldiers, lawyers, accountants and royal officials in addition to five Augustinian priests headed by Urdaneta, their mission to "bring to the natives . . . a knowledge of the holy Catholic faith." It was a uniquely American enterprise, comprised of men who lived in America traveling aboard ships built and equipped in America to bring the wealth of Asia back to America.

Legazpi stopped briefly at Guam to reaffirm Spanish sovereignty over the island, and on February 15, 1565, his fleet reached the Philippines. The ships anchored off the island of Samar, not far from the site of Magellan's first landing forty-four years earlier. Food there was scarce, and they scoured the nearby islands for supplies. Despite Legazpi's gestures of courtesy, many natives were hostile—confusing the Spaniards with a Portuguese expedition that had ravaged the area two years earlier. On April 27, the flotilla sailed into the bay at Cebu, the scene of Magellan's unhappy encounter with Humabon. To Legazpi's disappointment, all traces of the population's mass conversion to Christianity had evaporated and the present chief, Tupas, refused to acknowledge Spain's hegemony over the area—or even talk.

Legazpi tried persuasion, then resorted to force. His cannon bombarded the town, setting its flimsy huts aflame, as two hundred Spanish troops staged an amphibious landing. The inhabitants had fled, taking their rice and livestock with them. Amid the rubble, Legazpi's men stumbled onto a tiny statue of the Infant Jesus, dressed in a linen blouse and velvet hat and encased in a small pine box. Presumably given by Magellan to Humabon's wife after her baptism, it had remained intact. Legazpi hailed the discovery as a miraculous sign of Christianity's survival and built a wooden shrine to house the image. Pilgrims still venerate the relic, which sits in the stone church of Santo Niño, constructed on the spot in the seventeenth century.

Legazpi chose Cebu to be the first Spanish settlement in the Philippines, calling it *Santisimo Nombre de Jesus,* the Holy Name of Jesus. Tupas returned to the town out of curiosity, and they sealed the traditional bond of friendship in blood.

Taking advantage of the armistice, Legazpi sent the *San Pedro* back to

Mexico—the first eastward crossing of the Pacific in recorded history. He entrusted command to his seventeen-year-old grandson, Felipe de Salcedo, in the belief that the class-conscious sailors would respect a youth of noble birth regardless of his age. But the men really put their confidence in Urdaneta, who was also aboard. He had reckoned against all conventional logic that a northeastern route was feasible, and the voyage justified his calculations. Despite fierce headwinds and tricky currents, the ship sailed into the harbor of Acapulco on October 8, 1565, four months after leaving Cebu. It had cruised during the last lap down the coast of an unexplored wilderness known as California—then thought to be islands inhabited by black Amazons.

The exploit elated King Philip, who was doubly pleased by a glowing report from Legazpi on the great success of the Philippine venture. He approved Legazpi's request for more men and equipment—but, pressed by more urgent problems, he delayed the actual appropriations. The archipelago appeared to lack spices, gold or, for that matter, anything else of value. And he had not yet decided whether he wanted to make it a permanent Spanish possession.

In Cebu, meanwhile, Legazpi had run into trouble. Food shortages were riling his men, some of whom plotted a mutiny that narrowly aborted. The Portuguese, claiming the region, had briefly deployed ships against the island, reminding the small Spanish garrison of its weakness. The natives were also menacing, perhaps at the instigation of Tupas, who may have been vexed by an incident that reflected a clash of cultural values. As a friendly gesture he had sent Legazpi a young girl, described as a niece, whose function needed no explanation. Legazpi piously rejected her and had her instead baptized and married to one of his crew. Offended, Tupas vowed never to embrace Christianity, and his relations with Legazpi deteriorated. Legazpi left a classic comment that foreshadowed the exasperation of Westerners with Asians for centuries to come: "Face to face, they agree to anything—never saying 'no' to any proposal. The moment they turn their backs, however, they never keep a promise nor have they any concept of honesty or sincerity. Accordingly, it will be difficult to make durable arrangements with them on the basis of friendship, rather than through coercion and fear."

Legazpi intuitively understood a characteristic of the Philippines that earlier Spaniards had failed to perceive. Magellan, for one, had forfeited his life in the illusion that he had won the fidelity of an entire region after sealing his pact with Humabon—when, in fact, the chief's mandate barely extended beyond his minuscule community. Shortly after his arrival, however, Legazpi sensed the fragmented quality of the archipelago and its advantages. He could subjugate the natives with a minimum of force, he observed, because "they have no leaders and are so divided among themselves . . . that they can never join together in a demonstration of strength." So the Spanish easily subdued and governed the Philippines. Similarly, the United States conquered the islands by splitting an indigenous resistance movement fractured by internecine rivalries. Regionalism has continued to this day to bedevil the country's rulers.

The uncertainties of Cebu prompted Legazpi to shift his headquarters to Panay, at the westernmost fringe of the Visayas, where food was plentiful and the natives friendlier. King Philip eventually fulfilled his pledge to furnish help, and Spanish pioneers from Mexico, attracted by generous land grants, began to move to the Philippines—the women and children among them an indication that Spain intended to retain its precarious possession. As he entered his twilight years, however, Legazpi continued to look for a more solid base. One of his captains had caught a glimpse of Manila, a port on the northern island of Luzon, which was reputed to be in Muslim hands. Legazpi ordered a fuller investigation.

On May 3, 1570, two frigates commanded by Martin de Goiti, an army officer, sailed north with a force composed of a hundred Spanish soldiers and two or three hundred native auxiliaries in canoes. The flotilla entered spacious Manila Bay, passing the site of a future American tragedy: a tiny island that subsequent Spaniards named Corregidor, the "corrector," because it guided traffic into the harbor. The men were impressed by the neatly cultivated landscape around the bay, a contrast from the jungles of the southern islands. As have tourists over the centuries since, they stared with stupefaction at the spectacular sunset.

De Goiti anchored off Cavite, on the southeastern rim of the bay, and soon received an invitation to meet the local Muslim chief, Suleiman. Spanish accounts, predictably biased, portray Suleiman as sullen and arrogant, claiming that he threatened to rebuff any attempts to usurp his authority. Nor would he, at first, even permit the visitors to enter the fortified town. By contrast, de Goiti is depicted as gentle and tactful. Whatever the truth, the two men did conduct an amicable conversation and ended up by concluding the usual blood covenant. Suleiman allowed the Spanish to establish a settlement in exchange for their promise to protect him against his enemies. But the agreement broke down.

The Spanish maintained that Muslim artillery bombarded their ships after their cannon had innocently fired a salute. In any case, de Goiti landed troops and burned Manila to the ground as its inhabitants fled the town. Rather than risk further action, he returned to Panay, reaching there just as a flotilla arrived from Mexico carrying money, supplies and mail from Spain—including a letter from Philip to Legazpi. The king, after years of wavering, finally put it in writing: Spain, he said, was in the Philippines to stay. He appointed Legazpi governor at an annual salary of two thousand ducats—a handsome sum, except it would have to come out of local taxes that were difficult to collect.

Legazpi now decided to appraise Manila as a possible capital. Departing his base at Panay in April 1571, he sailed north for a month at the head of a convoy of Spanish soldiers and native auxiliaries. He sent emissaries ahead to tell the population that he sought peace, and the tactic worked. Two local Muslim chiefs, arriving by boat, climbed aboard his galleon, prepared to parley. They had witnessed de Goiti's devastating raid of the previous year and, fearful of another Spanish attack, agreed to submit. But, they warned, Suleiman was still sulking from the earlier assault and might fight. Legazpi enlisted them to take a Homeric message to Suleiman: "Let him come to me in complete safety, provided he is willing to be a loyal subject and true friend." Without waiting for a reply, he and his troops disembarked in Manila on May 17, 1571, and Suleiman yielded shortly afterward. Try as he did, he could not organize a unified resistance to the Spanish. The reason, as he explained it to one of Legazpi's men, still describes the Philippines: "You must understand that there is no sole authority in this land. Everyone has his own opinions and does what he likes."

Legazpi formally founded the city of Manila on June 24, the feast of Saint John the Baptist. A veteran bureaucrat, he quickly created a municipal administration and, inevitably, ordered the construction of a cathedral. Fourteen months later, at the age of sixty-seven, he died of a stroke after scolding an aide.

The Philippines, originally perceived as a springboard for more lucrative ventures elsewhere, was now a permanent Spanish colony—and, as a crucible of Christianity, destined to become the most Westernized country of Asia.

3. THE SPANISH BOND

★ ★ ★

Under three centuries of Spanish rule the Philippines suffered as much from neglect as from tyranny. Spain itself during that span was an anachronism, its political, social, economic, cultural and religious institutions languishing in a medieval cocoon. Its officials, soldiers and priests brought to the archipelago the archaic, parochial dogmas of their sectarian society—demanding total obedience to their absolute authority as they sought to reap profits and save souls. They were at least consistent; just as their kings and cardinals, appalled by modern trends, secluded Spain from the rest of Europe, so they shielded the Philippines against the contaminating impact of the outside world. The islands, consequently, remained throughout most of the Spanish colonial period in a state of suspended animation, an isolated sprawl of specks on the map.

American imperialists at the turn of the twentieth century, clamoring for the seizure of the Philippines, circulated lurid accounts of Spain's "barbarism" in an effort to justify their cause. Filipino nationalists then struggling for independence echoed the same theme. But Spanish rule, while far from benevolent, was not entirely inhumane.

Nearly all the Spaniards sent to the Philippines came from Mexico, where thousands of peons had been enslaved and slaughtered. Here they found different conditions. Unlike Mexico, the Philippines had no silver mines that required a massive force of indentured labor. Its people, divided among themselves, were less difficult to control than the Mexicans, whose Aztec empire had left their elite with a memory of past grandeur and a sense of national identity. Thus Spanish officials could govern the Philippines with a lighter hand than they laid on Mexico. Their primary preoccupation was to protect the prestige of Spain—and, of course, to promote Christianity. Spanish monarchs usually endorsed the policy. Half a world away, they were principally concerned with the swaying pendulum of power in Europe. The Philippines became a priority mainly when it figured in their global rivalries.

The Spanish governor, his bureaucrats and his military commanders sat in Manila as representatives of the king's viceroy in Mexico. His officials and soldiers were mostly confined to scattered towns, and their tours of duty rotated. Hence the masters of the country were the Catholic monastic orders, virtually autonomous organizations, which answered to their separate hierarchies in Rome. Perceiving their role to be spiritual rather than temporal, they hoped to foster in the *indios,* as they called the Filipinos, a passivity that would serve their own evangelical aims. They favored an indirect administration under which the natives could retain their traditional social and economic system as long as they converted to Christianity and respected Spain's sovereignty. Their purpose, in short, was to preserve the Philippines in a time warp, isolated from alien influences that might subvert their paternal theocracy. Soon entrenched throughout the provinces, they alone personified the Spanish presence. "Between the Philippines and Spain," observed Sinibaldo de Mas, a nineteenth-century Spanish commentator, "there is no other bond of union than the Christian religion."

But Christianity, the cement of Spanish rule, was more pervasive than profound. The friars devoted their lives to their missions, propagating the faith with extraordinary dedication and remarkable success. Yet they barely altered the indigenous tribal structure and its values. Nor could they adjust to change. Jealous of their prerogatives, they opposed the ordination of Filipino priests, thereby splitting the Catholic establishment. The opening of the Philippines to foreign trade and investment in the nineteenth century spawned a new class of rich young Filipinos, many of them schooled in Spain, who demanded equality commensurate with their wealth and education. The reactionary monastic orders, increasingly desperate to maintain the status quo, lobbied through their pressure groups in Manila and Madrid to resist reforms. Their intransigence eventually contributed to the emergence of the Filipino revolutionary movement that launched a war for independence from Spain. It was during a lull in that conflict that America, with an almost naïve inadvertence, first intervened in the Philippines.

★ ★ ★

Within a decade after Legazpi founded Manila, the Spanish controlled the Philippines except for pockets of northern Luzon and the Muslim regions of Mindanao. The conquest had been relatively bloodless. Weak and fragmented, the Filipinos usually submitted without a fight, and those who fled could not long survive in the mountain jungles. The main challenges to Spain came from without. The Dutch and Portuguese, rivals for power in the area, were a constant nuisance, and the celebrated British marauders, Sir Francis Drake and Thomas Cavendish, raided coastal towns. In 1574, a formidable Chinese pirate, Limahong, attacked Manila with an army of two thousand men, almost capturing the city. Peasant revolts recurred periodically over the centuries ahead, many sparked by local mystics, but most of the natives were too docile to defy the Spanish.

Though they spared the Filipinos the worst horrors of their exploitation of

Latin America, early Spanish officials did bring with them from Mexico such harsh practices as the *repartimiento* system—a draft of labor to build and repair roads or to cut and transport timber for the construction of ships. They would form brigades of seven or eight thousand men, whom they fed badly, paid poorly and sometimes flogged to death for indiscipline or indolence. Natives often bribed their way out of the conscription, sinking into endless debt by borrowing money at exorbitant rates from local usurers. Others escaped to remote areas to lead fugitive lives—a terrible fate for people closely linked to their families and clans. Village chiefs, pressed to furnish taxes to sustain the projects, squeezed their impoverished communities into ruin. The Spanish clergy, as protector of the natives, tried to stop the corvée. In 1620, a Franciscan friar, Pedro de San Pablo, warned the king that the *indios* were being "enslaved, exhausted and killed" instead of being encouraged "to love Spain and to attend better . . . to the worship of God." But the practice persisted throughout the Spanish era—ironically, in subsequent years, under the aegis of the friars.

Equally onerous was the *encomienda* system, also borrowed from Mexico. A land grant arrangement, it had been contrived to attract Spanish immigrants to the archipelago. They could tax the areas they settled—on condition that they assumed responsibility for the natives. The so-called royal bounty entitled "well-deserving persons . . . to receive and enjoy the tribute of natives assigned to them, with the obligation of providing for [their] spiritual and temporal welfare, especially in maintaining peace in the locality where they resided." Consonant with Spain's medieval mentality, the concept presaged a feudal utopia, with masters and vassals harmoniously fulfilling their respective duties. But in practice it was egregiously abusive.

Inept Spanish bureaucrats distributed land haphazardly. Worse yet, Spanish officers and troops, unpaid for years, grabbed property with cavalier disregard for the rights of the natives. Deploring the depredations, Diego de Herrera, an Augustinian prelate, termed the system "evil" and begged King Philip II of Spain to renounce it. Spaniards in the Philippines, he wrote in 1570, were persecuting Christian converts and pagans alike, committing "acts of violence against people in their own homes, and against their wives, daughters and property." Like modern racketeers, they even murdered natives who balked at paying "protection" money. During a raid on one village, Herrera reported, a native cried out from atop a palm tree, "Spaniards, what did my ancestors do to you that you should pillage us?"

Another priest, Francisco de Ortega, vividly described the brutality of Spanish troops as they entered villages: "They first send in an interpreter, not with gifts or to speak of God, but to demand tribute. The people, never having been subjects of a king or a lord, are puzzled and shocked when forced to hand over their necklaces or bracelets, their only property. . . . Some refuse, others submit reluctantly and still others flee to the hills, terrified by this strange new race of armed men. The Spaniards pursue them, firing their arquebuses and killing without mercy, then return to the village to slaughter all the pigs and poultry, carry off all the rice and burn all the houses." Estimating that they had destroyed more than four thousand houses and killed some five hundred people in the the region of Ilocos alone, Ortega concluded: "This ruined land will not recover in six years, some say never."

To present the king with a few jewels extorted from the natives was sense-less, Ortega continued, when Spain had squandered two million pesos in the Philippines since it first colonized the islands fifteen years before. "How much more would God our Lord and his Majesty be served if the gold sent to him were left on the arms of the women of Ilocos, to whom it belongs, instead of adorning the necks of the ladies at the court of our queen." The Spanish were also violating their sacred trust. "Rather than promoting friendship and good will in the souls of the natives, they create hatred and disgust against us and against the name of Jesus Christ crucified, whose teachings they are supposed to spread."

Spanish bureaucrats naturally denied the allegations. Judging from all their gold trinkets, fine porcelains and expensive fabrics, one contended, the natives could afford to pay tribute. Besides, they were wastrels who "spend their time feasting, drinking and worshipping idols." They had been killing each other for years and would readily kill outsiders. Spain had to rule with a "mailed fist," and the priests were naïve zealots whose criticism threatened to "harm the community and hinder progress."

King Philip upheld the friars. In a circular issued in 1583, he attacked the *encomienda* system, disclosing that its excesses had caused so many deaths that the population in some areas of the archipelago had declined by more than a third. The people were "treated worse than slaves," some dying "under the lash," and "mothers even kill their infants to spare them from the suffering that they themselves are subject." As a result, Philip concluded, "the natives have conceived such great hatred of the Christian name, looking upon the Spaniards as deceivers who do not practice what they preach, that whatever they do is only out of compulsion."

With that, he decreed reforms. The only Spaniards apart from friars permit-ted to enter native villages would be tax collectors and inspectors. Provincial Spanish officials would be rotated to prevent their becoming too intimately attached to any one district, and even the governor was to exercise only limited authority outside Manila. The monastic orders, triumphant, had been vin-dicated, and henceforth their reign over the rural areas would be uncontested. But as motivated by moral fervor as they had been in their desire to defend the natives, they swiftly degenerated into a vested interest determined to safeguard their own privileges.

By the early seventeenth century, five religious orders had each carved out its distinct sphere of influence. The Augustinians, Franciscans and Domini-cans took over Luzon, leaving the Visayas and Mindanao to the Jesuits and the Recollects, an austere offshoot of the Augustinians. Their criticism of the *encomienda* system notwithstanding, they acquired large estates, which they leased to managers who enlisted tenants to farm the fields. To tighten their grip over the natives, whose scattered villages were autonomous, they built *pueblos,* or townships. Their centerpiece in the town, located in the main square, was a large stone church named for a favorite saint, which dwarfed the homes of the few local officials and landowners, and a sprawl of bamboo huts that housed artisans and servants. Thus, as the phrase went, they brought the population *"debajo de las campanas"*—"under the bells."

In theory, the natives were to rule themselves under Spain's guidance.

Councils of elders would select *cabezas,* village chiefs, to collect taxes and recruit labor for public projects. The chiefs in turn comprised the *principalía,* an elite corps, which chose a *gobernadorcillo* to enforce the law, judge petty disputes and generally run the community. In fact, the friars ran the show. "Their despotism is absolute," lamented an eighteenth-century Manila official. "They command these islands, governing at their own will."

They derived their power from the enormous influence of the monastic orders: independent institutions, worldwide in scope, much like present-day multinational corporations. The Council of Trent, which revamped the Catholic Church in the sixteenth century, had directed diocesan bishops to supervise missions abroad. But the friars counted on their superiors to shield them against episcopal intrusion. Above all, they owed their authority to their dedication, tenacity, tenure and familiarity with their parishes.

Secular officials came and went, but the clergy stayed. Over a twenty-five-year period in the nineteenth century, sixteen Spanish governors served in Manila—compared to only two archbishops. The rural friars never numbered more than a thousand at any one time, yet the *padre,* true to the term, was the father figure throughout the countryside. "Travel around the provinces," observed a seventeenth-century Spanish official, "and you will see populations of five, ten or twenty thousand *indios* ruled in peace by one old man who, with his doors open at all hours, sleeps secure in his dwelling."

Wedded to their vocation, the priests learned the local languages and adapted to local customs. Some abandoned their vows of celibacy and sired children by native women. Many upper-class Filipinos today, for whom Spanish blood is a mark of distinction, proudly evoke a clerical ancestor. Sinabaldo de Mas contemplated such trespasses with Latin indulgence: "Though it may appear evil, the offense is most excusable, especially in young and healthy men set down in a torrid climate. Duty continually struggles against nature. The garb of the native women is very seductive and girls, far from being unattainable, regard themselves as lucky to attract the attention of the curate, and their mothers and fathers share that sentiment. What virtue and stoicism does not the friar need to possess!"

The friar exercised power through a staggering panoply of functions. He audited the parish budget, conducted the census, registered the residents, directed the tax board, managed health and public-works projects, screened recruits for military service, presided over the police and reviewed conditions at the local jail. As censor he could ban any publication or play he deemed politically or morally reprehensible. He could banish people without trial and veto the decisions of the cosmetic native administration, which in any case would not act without his assent. Most of all, he oversaw education and religion.

Shortly after their arrival, the monastic orders founded universities and colleges in Manila—among them Santo Tomas, which dates back to 1601 and still operates. For centuries these institutions admitted only young Spaniards training for the clergy. Rural schools for the natives, by contrast, were usually simple affairs run by friars, themselves simple men of peasant origin versed in only a few sacred subjects. They taught the catechism and the lives of the saints, submitting their pupils to inane interrogations, recited in unison and heavily dosed with discipline.

Teacher: What is the reward for diligence?
Pupils: Sugar and molasses.
Teacher: And what is the reward for sloth?
Pupils: One hundred lashes.

The friars conducted the classes in local tongues on the principle that fluency in Spanish would make the *indios* uppity and arrogant. "Experience has taught us," asserted a Spanish official, "that those who know our language are almost always the most headstrong . . . the ones who talk behind our back, criticize and rebel." Hence the Filipinos, unlike Latin Americans, never became a Spanish-speaking people. Nor were large numbers truly educated under Spain's rule. A survey taken by U.S. specialists in 1903 found more than half the population to be illiterate, even in regional dialects.

For three hundred years, young natives repeated the same religious routine that Juan Francisco de San Antonio, a Franciscan, described in the sixteenth century:

Daily without exception, at the sound of the bell, all the children promptly assemble in the church. The little choristers led by the choir master intone the *Te Deum* with solemn devotion, ending with the versicle and prayer to the Most Holy Trinity, then sing prime of the Little Office of the Blessed Mother. There follows the conventional mass, after which the boys recite the rosary along with those who have remained for this exercise. Then they file out behind a small processional cross to attend school, while the choristers retire to practice. Two strokes of the bell signal the end of classes, and everyone goes home for lunch. At two o'clock, the bell sounds for vespers and the children, back in church, again chant the Little Office of the Blessed Mother in the manner described. They then go to their assigned duties until five o'clock, when a very devotional procession forms in the church and winds through town, reciting the rosary. This concludes in the church with litanies, the antiphon of the Immaculate Conception of the Mother of God, and a responsory for the blessed souls in Purgatory.

Weekends were more rigorous. On Saturdays, the children prayed and chanted steadily from morning until night so that, San Antonio noted with approval, they "would not forget what they had learned by rote." The entire town would join in on Sunday to celebrate mass and to hear the priest deliver his sermon, invariably an admonition to obey God and the word of Christ. The holiday stretched beyond religion, becoming a communal event that brought the people together in a carnival mood—the church square crowded with gamblers, musicians, itinerant actors, fortune-tellers and, of course, swindlers, beggars and pickpockets. Even today in Philippine towns the reverent Sunday observance is frequently followed by a band concert—and, if the priest is liberal, a beauty pageant.

The friars, realizing that however much zeal they might display in church, the natives had not forsaken their ancient beliefs, accommodated to a syncretic compound of Catholic doctrine and animistic practices. In some places, they baptized babies with pig blood, and nearly everywhere they blessed fields during planting and harvesting seasons to coincide with native rites that propitiated the spirits of nature. Adapting their prayers to pagan incantations, they tolerated fake shrines, spurious sanctuaries and the widespread use of rosaries, icons and medallions as amulets, talismans and charms—worn even by bandits who believed that their magical powers warded off bullets. For these curates to encourage or abide superstition was understandable; their sole purpose being to proselytize, they relied on any expedient. Besides, they were Spanish Catholics, themselves suffused with obscure mysticism.

The Spanish were often baffled by the Filipinos. To one early Spanish observer they were easygoing, uncorrupted, enviably simple. "The native is the freest man in the world," he wrote. "Undisturbed by ambition, or social or political passions, his life is his rice field, his banana trees, his church, his rituals, his pilgrimages, his fighting cocks, his fiestas and his tribute to the king. If he feels victimized by some oppression, the curate consoles him. If he commits a sin, he resigns himself to the punishment." But Gaspar de San Agustín, an Augustinian prelate, differed. After forty years in the archipelago, he admitted, "It would be easier for me to square the circle or discover a way to measure the longitude of the earth . . . than to define the nature, customs and vices of the natives." Juan Manuel de la Matta, a nineteenth-century Spanish official, found it equally difficult to "draw a moral picture" of the Filipino. "He is a mixture of abjectness and ferocity, timidity and wonderful courage, indolent laziness and slovenliness, industry and avaricious self-interest . . . superstitious, peaceful, respectful, heedless, distrustful and deceitful."

Aside from reflecting the diversity of the Philippines, the kaleidoscope of contradictory views also revealed the extent to which the Spanish never quite grasped what they had wrought in the archipelago: They unified the islands under their crown and religion, but failed to eliminate its tribal texture. Even though they pacified the country, they were repeatedly surprised to discover that the natives, beneath a passive exterior, simmered with resentments that could erupt in fiery, futile uprisings—often inspired, paradoxically, by their own religious teachings.

The Filipinos derived a particular significance from Christian functions— especially the gaudy Easter rituals that reenacted the suffering, death and resurrection of Jesus. The Passion of Christ, first translated into Tagalog in the eighteenth century under official Catholic auspices, spread among rural folk until the friars, perceiving its potentially seditious message, sought in vain to stop its circulation. Peasants, poor and humiliated, identified their plight with Christ's ordeal, convinced that by emulating him they could transform their misery into salvation, their darkness into light, their ignorance into knowledge, their dishonor into purity, their despair into hope. In their desperate quest for salvation, they recurrently rallied behind dissident leaders who, imitating Christ, promised redemption. The history of the Philippines, from the Spanish era through the American colonial period and on into the present, has been punctuated by revolts triggered by messianic figures claiming to be divinely guided.

Apolinario de la Cruz, to cite an example, commanded an outlawed religious movement that fought for ten days in October 1841 against a Spanish force on the slopes of Mount San Cristobal, in the Luzon province of Tayabas. A pious youth who had been refused membership in a Spanish monastic order because of his native origins, he founded the *Hermandad de la Archicofradía del Glorioso Señor San José y de la Virgen del Rosario*—the Brotherhood of the Great Sodality of the Glorious Lord Saint Joseph and of the Virgin of the Rosary—a lay confraternity dedicated to spreading the gospel and healing the sick. He preached with a mystical twist picked up from Spanish medieval literature, and peasants frustrated by high taxes and forced labor soon hailed him as their "king of the Tagalogs." His sermons were innocent pleas for love and charity, but the Catholic authorities excommunicated him as a heretic. Spanish troops besieged his followers, who fought suicidally in the belief that angels would rescue them. Finally captured, he was summarily shot, and his head displayed in a cage as a warning to others. He "died serenely, showing unusual greatness of spirit," wrote a Spanish priest who witnessed his death. Two hundred of his disciples faced execution with equal composure. Asked why they had revolted, they replied: "To pray."

To this day, many Filipinos worship martyred heroes as the reincarnation of Christ. The cult of José Rizal, the national messiah executed by the Spanish in 1896, is centered in his hometown of Calamba, south of Manila. There a mural above the altar in a ramshackle church depicts Christ in his guise, a dapper little man in a dark suit and black tie, the twelve apostles portrayed as other noted militants in the struggle for freedom from Spain. In imitation of Christ, indeed, martyrdom seems to be a prerequisite for glory in the Philippines, as if only those who have been executed, assassinated, killed in battle or otherwise have met violent ends merit immortality. Faith, suffering, sacrifice, death, resurrection and salvation are the charges that suffuse the history of the Philippines.

General Douglas MacArthur appreciated the vitality of these themes when he led the American forces back to the Philippines in October 1944. After dramatically wading through the surf at Leyte, he proclaimed in a remarkable radio broadcast to the population that "the hour of your redemption is here." Similarly, the struggle of the Aquinos against the Marcos regime contained all the ingredients of a religious crusade.

Ninoy Aquino, jailed by Marcos, later revealed that a vision of the Virgin Mary during his imprisonment had renewed his morale. Cory, whose intense piety fueled her drive to oust Marcos, also disclosed that she and her family "were able to accept suffering as part of our life with Christ." The Catholic Church campaigned on her behalf as she evoked the spirit of her murdered husband: Holy Ghost and Holy Mother, martyr and madonna, sharing the ticket. With total sincerity, she attributed her victory to "divine providence."

★ ★ ★

The Spanish explorers who followed Magellan were quickly disappointed by the new dominion. Its only spice was an inferior brand of cinnamon, and neither gold nor silver seemed to be present in large quantities. China, with its fabled wares, was nearby—a tempting target for trade. But China, closed to foreign merchants, permitted only the Portuguese to maintain a tiny commercial post at Macao. Soon, however, the Spanish in Manila saw fortunes to be made by reexporting to Mexico the kinds of Chinese products that had been entering the islands for centuries. These goods were so common that the Filipinos used splendid Sung celadon bowls as everyday dishes, superb Soochow silks as sarongs, exquisite Ming porcelains to store unhusked rice. Thus unfolded the lucrative "galleon trade," through which precious Chinese commodities were imported into Manila, then transshipped to Mexico, either to be marketed there or sent on to Spain.

The enterprise owed its origin to Legazpi's companion, the Augustinian priest Andrés de Urdaneta, whose chart of the eastward course across the Pacific enabled vessels to ply the route from Manila to Acapulco. The early galleons had transported officials, soldiers and settlers as well as a voluminous correspondence between the Spanish colonial regime and the viceroy of Mexico. At first the merchants of Seville objected when the ships went commercial, partly because they could not compete with Chinese silks in Latin America and partly because China's insistence on payment in silver imperiled Spain's reserves. But, in a compromise, the Seville entrepreneurs were granted an exclusive market in Peru, and the trade out of Manila was tightly regulated.

Only one galleon, limited in size to three hundred tons, was permitted to make the annual round trip. Its Manila-bound cargo was legally limited in value to 250,000 pesos, twice that sum on the return to Mexico. But, given the huge profits to be earned, the regulations were violated from the start. The *San Francisco Xavier,* for example, sailed into Manila in 1698 with some 2 million pesos in silver aboard. Heavy silver coins minted in Mexico, later known as "dollars Mex," eventually became the coveted currency of the China coast—until the rise of the American greenback following World War II.

Fleets of sixty or seventy seagoing Chinese junks riding high above the waves, resembling large flying fish with their latticed sails, would swarm into Manila Bay in late December or early January to unload their freight, returning in March to pick up the silver payments. Coming from coastal Fukien province, their cargoes included pearls, porcelains, paper, lacquers, thread and parasols. But their prized treasures were damasks, velvets and taffetas of many designs and colors and white silk of a purity unmatched in Europe. Chinese agents stored the wares in Manila godowns to await their purchase by lucky Spanish merchants entitled to export the goods aboard the annual galleon to Mexico.

The Spanish governor and a panel of twelve dignitaries granted the export rights in the form of *boletas,* tickets that gave each holder cargo space aboard the galleon. The system worked like a raffle in which all the players won: The governor and his board received kickbacks from allocating the *boletas* to their cronies and surreptitiously grabbed tickets for themselves. Speculators bid handsomely in hopes of doubling or tripling their investment, spurring a brisk black market in tickets. The affluent monastic orders participated directly in the trade or lent money at usurious interest rates to merchants in need of capital. Ship captains, appointed by the governor, were rewarded with hefty commissions. Even ordinary sailors received generous bonuses.

The risks were immense: The journey from Manila to Acapulco took four or five months; the ships often becalmed in the doldrums or wrecked in storms. They were frequently plundered by freebooters of every nationality, and their crews faced death from diseases like beriberi and dysentery, or from scarcities of food and fresh water. The voyage, noted seventeenth-century Italian traveler Gemelli Careri, was "enough to destroy a man, or make him unfit for anything as long as he lives." Yet, out of greed, many "went through it four, six, even ten times." But while the galleon trade generated fat profits for a few, the narrow tie to Mexico left the Philippines isolated from the rest of the world and also stunted its domestic economy.

The wealth from the galleon trade had, by the eighteenth century, transformed Manila into a metropolis of "equal rank with the greatest and most celebrated cities of the world," as a Spanish official proudly wrote at the time. Modeled on Mexico City, a grid of spacious boulevards and plazas, it stretched out from a grand cathedral and array of imposing stone buildings contained within the Intramuros—the walled enclave that still stands, incongruously flanked by a golf course. The population, nearly ninety thousand in 1780, had doubled over the past century and was to triple during the century ahead. Only three or four thousand were Spaniards; the rest, natives who served as menials, were packed into a jumble of bamboo shacks sprawled amid the nearby streams and swamps of the suburbs, where they suffered from recurrent floods, fires and epidemics of cholera and smallpox.

Prosperity corrupted the city's Spanish residents, who hung on the vagaries of the galleon trade, many making and losing fortunes from one year to the next. Francisco Leandro de Viana, a member of the *Audiencia,* the colonial high court, deplored the crass concern with money that confined the Spanish to the capital. "They consider unworthy any pursuit other than commerce, preferring to live in utter idleness rather than work in the provinces. They loiter about, gambling and indulging in other vices . . . and so Manila is a most abominable place, with its gangs, its malicious rumors and slanders, its sloth and licentiousness. Even the richest and busiest citizen spends ten months of the year with nothing to do."

The rural areas meanwhile slumbered in seclusion and neglect as the peasants cultivated their rice fields, raised livestock and fished the waters. The friars, dreading change, did nothing to improve the subsistence economy. For centuries, the Philippine provinces were as remote from Manila as Manila was from the outside world.

Late in the eighteenth century, however, a series of shocks began to stimulate an inexorable economic, social and political evolution that had dramatic consequences.

The first jolt hit in 1762, when a British expedition captured Manila in a sideshow skirmish to the Seven Years' War, then being waged by Britain against France and Spain in Europe and America. The easy British victory underlined both Spain's disregard for its faraway dominion and the fragility of its colonial administration.

The joint post of governor and military commander had been vacant since its occupant had died eight years before, and the archbishop, Manuel Antonio Roja, was in charge. Even though Britain and Spain had been at war for nine months, he knew nothing of the conflict until the afternoon of September 23, 1762, when to his astonishment he saw a fleet of fifteen British ships sailing into Manila Bay. He was neither qualified nor prepared to cope with the enemy force of two thousand British and Indian troops. The Spanish garrison, numbering fewer than six hundred regulars in addition to native auxiliaries armed with spears and bows and arrows, fell back as the British stormed the city. The hapless Roja surrendered in violation of Spain's chivalric code of conduct. A senior Spanish official generously forgave him, concluding that he was "an imbecile rather than a traitor . . . who unfortunately had been assigned responsibilities for which he lacked both the intelligence and the valor."

At the end of the Seven Years' War in 1764, the British withdrew from Manila, having barely stepped outside the city during their occupation. But their exposure of the weakness of the Spanish regime sparked peasant revolts in parts of Luzon. The perennially dissident Moros also went on the warpath against lonely Spanish outposts in Mindanao and Sulu, even advancing as far north as the Visayas. The Spanish easily crushed the uprisings, yet the resistance simmered.

Britain's disruption of the galleon trade also revealed the frailties of the mercantile monopoly. The British had seized both outgoing and incoming galleons during their attack against Manila. They soon halted the trade altogether and, as they departed, confiscated every Spanish ship in the harbor. Manila's economy collapsed, ruining the speculators and the monastic orders. The city's commercial rhythm had been abating in any event. Europe, then beginning to deal directly with Asia, no longer needed the Manila entrepôt. New policies introduced in Madrid entitled exporters in Spain to compete in the Mexican market, which had been the exclusive preserve of the Manila merchants. Fashions were evolving as well during that embryonic era of the industrial revolution as manufactured Spanish textiles replaced the taste for Chinese silks, once the rage in Latin America. The crippled galleon trade limped along for another fifty years before its demise. The final galleon from Manila sailed in 1811, and the last voyage from Acapulco took place four years later.

The British had opened Manila to foreign entrepreneurs for the first time, and the brief introduction to free trade gradually convinced a few farsighted Spaniards that Spain's hold over the islands was doomed without reforms. They were opposed by Spanish reactionaries, primarily the friars and their confederates. The latter half of the nineteenth century became a period of constant and bitter debate, both in Manila and in Madrid, over the shape of Spain's strategy toward the Philippines.

Not all the Spanish clergy spurned innovation. Pedro Murillo Velarde, a perceptive Jesuit, had warned as early as the beginning of the eighteenth century that the galleon trade augured disaster. The Spanish in Manila, he said, were like "visitors to an inn," who come and go without leaving anything durable in their wake. He recommended the establishment of government-chartered companies to spur agriculture, industry and domestic and foreign commerce. His proposed program gathered dust until Charles III, a Bourbon who ascended the throne of Spain in 1759. Then forty-three, he had served a long apprenticeship to his father, Ferdinand VI, a scholarly and conscientious king, and he formulated plans to modernize his realm and its overseas possessions.

The salons of Europe were then agog with the ideas of the Enlightenment, an intellectual cataclysm whose most articulate advocates included Voltaire, Rousseau and the French *encyclopédistes*. Rejecting the divinity of kings, they preached an approach to government based on reason. Charles fell under their spell, and they praised him as their ideal "benevolent despot." He curbed the Catholic Church's monopoly over education, reformed its ecclesiastical courts, gave land to peasants, promoted industry and built roads and canals. Finally, focusing on Spain's overseas territories, he sent a new governor to the Philippines with instructions to renovate its economy.

José de Basco y Vargas was a career naval officer with no economic experience. But he was intelligent, energetic, confident and, in the spirit of the times, devoted to that panacea progress. Soon after landing in Manila in 1778, he founded the *Sociedad Económica de los Amigos del País*—the Economic Society of the Friends of the Country—to revive the Philippine economy through rational planning and scientific research. He envisioned the large-scale cultivation of silk, tobacco, spices and sugarcane as well as the exploitation of the colony's mineral resources, timber reserves and ocean deposits as part of a grand scheme designed to boost trade. Decrying Spain's neglect of the archipelago until then, he promised in one public speech: "The sun will rise over our islands after more than two hundred years of darkness."

Some of his projects failed, but the state-owned tobacco industry was a huge success. Tobacco, a cash crop, brought hitherto fallow land under cultivation, and its export put the Philippines on a firm financial footing for the first time in centuries. But the conversion of rice fields into tobacco plantations caused food shortages in parts of northern Luzon. Natives resented recruitment into brigades to grow tobacco, and smuggling and cheating also riddled the business.

Basco set up the *Real Compañía de las Filipinas,* the Royal Company of the Philippines, which for the first time allowed foreign ships to land in Manila. They could legally carry only cargo from China and India, a restriction devised to protect Manila's Spanish merchants, who had a monopoly on the import of Western goods. But European and American entrepreneurs, skirting the regulations, began to arrive soon afterward with their own products, among them wine and hats.

The Philippines was first mentioned officially in the United States in 1786, when the Continental Congress meeting in Philadelphia pondered the notion of urging Spain to grant Americans trading privileges in Manila. The idea faded, but tramp freighters flying the Stars and Stripes had already been stopping there as they plied Asian waters. An American ship finally made Manila a scheduled port of call in October 1796, when the *Astrea* arrived under the command of Nathaniel Bowditch of Salem, Massachusetts. Then only twenty-three, Bowditch was a genius who had taught himself six languages, mathematics and astronomy and other sciences, and over his lifetime published two dozen technical books, including a classic on navigation. During his seventy days in Manila, he enlisted the help of John Stuart Kerr, a local businessman and probably the first permanent American resident of the Philippines, who had settled there after marrying a Spanish woman. Bowditch also met William Bowles, an American Tory from Maryland whom the Spanish had banished to the archipelago for organizing a liberation movement among the Muskogee Indians of Florida, then a dominion of Spain.

Bowditch's Yankee dynamism bridled at Manila's sluggish pace, as he confided to his diary. Spanish merchants rose at six or seven in the morning, sipped a cup of chocolate and lounged around until nine, when they might dictate a couple of letters before breakfast. They then went out in their carriages to transact business, returning home at twelve or one for a copious lunch, their main meal of the day, followed by a siesta that lasted until four in the afternoon. After a stroll along the esplanade facing the bay, perhaps to watch the blazing sunset, they would receive visitors or call on friends. They dined at ten or eleven and were asleep by midnight—unless they attended parties, at which men and women smoked heavily, gambled avidly and flirted shamelessly. Bowditch omits mention of it, but his prudish sensibilities may have been ruffled by their wickedness. A contemporary British traveler, repelled by Manila's Spaniards, wrote: "There exists among them a want of moral discrimination. This is no country for an honest man."

Bowditch nevertheless loaded his ship with nearly four hundred tons of sugar destined for the rum distilleries of New England, whose regular imports of molasses from the West Indies were then being interrupted by Britain's blockade of its rebellious American colonies.

Cane sugar, then becoming a worldwide staple, was alien to the Philippines until Basco spurred its cultivation as part of his economic plan. It was a bittersweet contribution to the islands—yielding immense profits for a few plantation owners at the expense of workers who labored under conditions close to bondage. The sugar-producing areas of central Luzon and the Visayas remain to this day a landscape of stark gaps between wealth and poverty, a fertile breeding ground for Communist insurgents promising radical change. But during the nineteenth century sugar was a crucial element in the compound that drastically altered the economic, social and political chemistry of the Philippines.

The transformation largely stemmed from a combination of two impulses: the soaring demand for commodities stimulated by the industrial revolution in the West and the liberal economic policies promoted by the Spanish administration in the Philippines in an effort to meet that demand.

As factories spread throughout Europe and America, their appetite for raw materials grew with staggering speed and intensity. The Philippines could furnish their ravenous diet with such products as hemp, copra and sugar, and Spanish colonial officials, with approval from Madrid, spurred the export drive. Foreign firms, authorized to establish offices in Manila, Cebu and other towns at successive stages during the nineteenth century, became active in trade, insurance, banking and currency exchange. A pioneer American company, Russell and Sturgis, reported as early as 1830 that it was deluged with orders to "purchase all that can be got" in the way of commodities. The economic velocity accelerated with the advent of the steamship, followed in 1869 by the opening of the Suez Canal—both of which shortened the voyage between Europe and Asia from months to weeks. From the beginning of the 1820s until the end of the century, the total annual value of Philippine exports soared thirty-six times.

The boom took a heavy human toll. The concentration on cash crops shrank the acreage devoted to rice, so that food had to be imported, at high prices for the average Filipino. The islands also fell prey to the uncertainties of the global market and, like developing countries today, periodically slid into recession. Landless peasants became a rural proletariat of tenants and hired laborers dependent on the *caciques,* big property owners who dominated the provinces along with the monastic orders, themselves the proprietors of large estates.

Even though Spain encouraged the economic growth, most Spaniards in Manila continued to disregard the hinterlands, as they had in centuries past.

Convinced of the eternal durability of the old order, they never saw the potential for change. Colonial privilege had also endowed them with the equivalent of aristocratic status, and they recoiled from soiling their hands in agriculture or even trade. So they ceded the rural Philippines to foreigners, who by default played a significant role in its development.

★ ★ ★

The evolution of the Visayan island Negros exemplifies the phenomenon. A sparsely inhabited backwater of jungles and scrub vegetation before the middle of the nineteenth century, its only European residents, except for a few Spanish friars, were an Englishman, Frenchman and a Spaniard who had settled there to experiment in sugarcane cultivation. The sugar industry advanced slowly until the Spanish colonial regime opened the island to foreign investors. By 1864 twenty-five Europeans had moved to Negros to carve out large plantations and build modern sugar mills. They generated a momentum of stupendous proportions: Over the next three decades, the island's sugar exports multiplied six hundred times and its population increased tenfold.

Sugar became a pillar of economic and political power—as it is to this day. The sugar barons reached out from their estates to acquire shipping lines, banks, newspapers and other enterprises, using their fortunes to buy and sell bureaucrats and elected officials alike. Their wealth grew geometrically during the Spanish era and, with lapses, continued to expand under American rule, when they enjoyed a duty-free market in the United States. The "sugar bloc," one of those clichés beloved by muckrakers, was in reality a redoubtable force in Manila. Through lobbyists, its tentacles stretched across the Pacific to Washington.

One of the distinguished sugar clans of Negros traces its origins back to Yves Leopold Germain Gaston, a Frenchman who settled there in 1840. An adventurous youth, he left his native Normandy for Mauritius, an island in the Indian Ocean taken over from France by Britain after the Napoleonic wars where he learned the rudiments of the young sugar industry. He pushed on to the Philippines at the age of thirty to become foreman of a Spanish-owned estate in the Luzon province of Batangas. Determined to start his own plantation, he moved to Negros and won the right to buy land, until then forbidden to foreigners. He consorted with a local woman, spawning a clan that proliferated to include many prominent Filipinos, among them a former governor of Negros. John Maisto, a family member through marriage, was one of the handful of State Department officials to warn against the excesses of the Marcos regime early in the 1980s.

When I revisited Negros in the 1980s, the original Gaston plantation, divided among his heirs, was still being managed by a great-granddaughter, Margarita Locsin. A vigorous woman in her fifties, she had a keen sense of history. As we bounced around in a jeep, she recalled that in her childhood the estate had been "right out of *Gone With the Wind.*" It had not improved since. The workers lived in shacks without electricity or running water, laboring for the equivalent of a dollar or two a day during planting and harvesting seasons—a total of six months a year. Margarita's husband, José María, a cheerful fat man with the look of a jovial Buddha, was a local trucker and political gadfly with a condo in Los Angeles and other investments in the United States. His family in the Philippines began with a poor Chinese immigrant who landed in Manila from Fukien province in 1750. The Gastons and Locsins hold regular reunions and have published complex genealogical trees delineating their hybrid ancestry.

Neither would have felt uncomfortable during the Spanish era. At the peak of the pyramid then were the *peninsulares,* Spaniards from Spain. Then came *criollos,* creoles, Spaniards born in the Philippines, Latin America or other colonies. Spanish *mestizos* ranked next, followed by Chinese of mixed blood, with *indios* at the bottom. But the Spanish, themselves an amalgam of the various races that had crisscrossed their own country over centuries, were permissive. They tolerated and even engaged in intermarriage, their yardstick wealth and color. Rich Filipinos with the lighter hues of Spain and China were preferable to the brown-skinned peasants of Malay origin—and the same standard prevails today.

Of all the races in the Philippines, the Chinese were the most potent economically; later, as *mestizos,* they became influential politically. Originally they were called *sangleys,* a word derived from *xang lai,* aptly meaning "trade and barter" in the Hokkien dialect of southern China. A few had immigrated to the islands as merchants long before the Spanish arrived. Their numbers swelled with the galleon trade, which they served as agents and brokers. By the eighteenth century, some fifteen thousand inhabited Manila and the provinces—outnumbering the Spanish by four to one. They supplied the Spanish community with food and were skilled cobblers, tailors and furniture makers. They were also the carpenters, masons and stone cutters who constructed cathedrals, churches, forts and public buildings. They sculpted, gilded and painted religious statues, images and icons of marble and wood, and the first printer in the country was Chinese. Above all, they traveled tirelessly to the remotest islands as peddlers and brokers, dominating domestic business— much as Jews had cornered the commerce of medieval Europe.

Like the Jews, they were both needed and feared, alternately tolerated and persecuted. Spanish officials and priests alike, feigning observance of the Catholic injunction against dealing with money, depended on them as financiers and middlemen. But, out of jealousy or racial zeal, they would periodically submit them to discriminatory taxes, confinement to ghettos or arbitrary deportation. At least thirty thousand Chinese were massacred in Manila during the seventeenth century, when twice they staged uprisings to protest against oppression—including a regulation that they cut off their pigtails. Yet they remained, accommodated and prospered despite recurrent harassment and chronic insecurity. In contrast to the Jews, however, they had fewer compunctions about forsaking their identity.

The Spanish gradually relaxed the restrictions to permit Chinese to reside in the provinces—on condition that they marry a Filipino woman or convert to Christianity. Many did both, and the number of Chinese *mestizos* spread, becoming indispensable to the economy. Mobile and energetic, they collected and transported sugar, hemp, copra and other commodities for foreign export firms situated in the port cities and distributed such imports as textiles and rice to the rural areas. They were often enlisted by the monastic orders to manage their plantations, and later they themselves leased or bought estates. The big landowning families in the provinces today are largely of part-Chinese origin.

As the economy grew, the Spanish eased the residence requirements for pure Chinese, and they also fanned out around the country. Chinese shopkeepers became a feature of nearly every town and village, as they are still. Operating out of a small bamboo hut, they sell the peasants salt, kerosene, yard goods, cheap plastic articles and other basics, mostly on credit. They seem to be as poor as the farmers themselves, but they lend them money to buy seeds and fertilizer or to finance weddings and baptisms, and most rural folk are in their debt—often constantly. With predictable regularity, Filipino demagogues in need of a scapegoat have vowed in ambiguous terms to crack down on the Chinese. The irate politicians, almost always, are of Chinese ancestry.

"Scratch a Filipino banker and you will find a Chinese grandfather," notes Virginia Benítez Licuanan, a Filipino historian of the country's financial institutions. The Tuasons, founders of the Banco Español Filipino, trace their descent to a poor Chinese boy, Son Tua, who came from the Fukien province port of Amoy. Carlos Palanca, head of the China Banking Corporation, also from Amoy, converted to Christianity and obtained his Hispanic name from a relative who had been adopted by a Spanish army officer, Carlos Palanca y Gutierrez. The fabulously wealthy Lopez family, proprietors of banks, newspapers, plantations and public utilities, is of Chinese extraction despite the Hispanic sound of its name—which was derived from Lo, one of the commonest names in China.

Just as the sons of rich businessmen in America and Europe embraced idealistic causes, so during the nineteenth century the scions of many affluent Chinese *mestizo* families in the Philippines joined nationalist movements opposed to Spanish rule. José Rizal and Emilio Aguinaldo were both Chinese *mestizos*. Subsequent Filipino political dynasties like the Osmeñas and Laurels had Chinese forebears. Marcos is part Chinese, and Cory Aquino's great-grandfather José Cojuangco was a penniless Chinese immigrant whose statue now stands on the ancestral sugar estate in Tarlac province—one of the largest plantations in Luzon.

During the nineteenth century, too, the growth of the Philippine economy blurred racial distinctions, and different ethnic groups began to consider themselves to be Filipinos—a symptom of their incipient sense of nationality. The Spanish colonial regime indirectly recognized this trend in 1884, when it rescinded the requirement that ethnic origin be stated on compulsory identity cards. The newly enriched also started to travel abroad, or sent their sons to study in Europe, where they inhaled freedom and absorbed contemporary ideas. The fresher climate produced an important species known as the *ilustrados*—an intelligentsia of lawyers, doctors, scholars, artists, journalists and other professionals with no stake in the preservation of an antiquated Spanish imperial structure. Elite conservatives, seeking to be treated as Spaniards, they agitated at first for assimilation rather than independence. Their hopes periodically rose as liberal Spanish governors, reflecting political shifts in Spain, proposed rerforms. But the monastic orders—the "friarocracy," as its critics dubbed it—systematically subverted progressive measures.

The friars might have accepted, even espoused, reform. After all, the Vatican was then evolving under Pope Leo XIII, whose famous encyclical *Rerum novarum,* published in 1891, championed economic and social justice. But they had become accustomed to absolute authority over the centuries, and they feared that even modest concessions would jeopardize their immediate power and ultimately destroy their organizations. In short, they equated compromise with suicide. They found support among the numbers of Spaniards who had drifted into Manila from Mexico, Colombia and the other countries of Latin America that had recently won their freedom from Spain. These dislocated expatriates, many of them carpetbaggers and raffish adventurers striving to retrieve their lost colonial privileges, naturally advocated rigidity. In Madrid, too, ultraconservative factions were always looking for a pretext to advance their own interests by siding with reactionary allies, whatever their cause. Inexorably, the forces for and against change collided. They first clashed in a complicated ecclesiastical controversy that kindled nationalist passions, and eventually flared into a political conflict.

★   ★   ★

The roots of the dispute dated back to the fifteenth century, when the pope granted the king of Spain control over the Catholic establishment in the Philippines in exchange for his commitment to subsidize its missionaries. Though they welcomed the money, the autonomous monastic orders recoiled at any intrusion onto their turf. Papal edicts notwithstanding, they refused diocesan bishops the right to supervise or even visit their fiefdoms. They also opposed plans then being contemplated to admit Filipinos into the clergy and assign them to parishes. Writing in 1725, the Augustinian prelate Gaspar de San Agustín disparaged the idea in bluntly racist terms: "The native who seeks priesthood does so not because he has a call to a more perfect state of life, but because of the great and infinite advantages that accrue to him. What a difference between paying tribute and being paid a stipend! Between being drafted to cut timber and being waited on hand and foot! Between rowing a galley and being conveyed in one! . . . What reverence will the *indios* themselves show toward him, when he is of their color and race? Especially when they realize that they are perhaps the equals or better of one who managed to get himself ordained, when his proper station should be that of a convict or a slave?"

Charles III, the "benevolent despot" of Spain, sought to subdue the monastic orders as part of an effort to bring the Spanish Catholic hierarchy under his control. Launching the campaign in 1767, he expelled the Jesuits from every Spanish colony, including the Philippines. He allowed the Dominicans, Augustinians and others to remain—on condition that they relinquish several of their provincial parishes to Filipino priests. The outbreak of the Napoleonic wars in the early nineteenth century disrupted Spain, halted the flow of young Spanish friars to the Philippines and created additional vacancies for the Filipino clergy, but with the restoration of peace in Europe in 1815 Spanish policy went into reverse.

Mexican, Peruvian and other Latin American clergymen had played an active role in the emancipation of their countries from Spain during the early years of the nineteenth century. In 1826, suspecting that Filipino priests might be infected by the liberation fever, the ultraconservative Spanish king, Ferdinand VII, removed them from their parishes. Nor did the Filipinos fare better when the Liberals briefly held power in Madrid soon afterward. Though anticlerical, the Liberals were too weak to defy the Catholic Church and its confederates, particularly in the armed forces. They banned the monastic orders in Spain, but balked at curbing their activities in the Philippines. By now only the Philippines, Cuba and Puerto Rico remained of Spain's once glorious empire, and as a new generation of Spanish friars reached the archipelago to reassert their power, the Filipinos braced for trouble.

The Recollects fired the first salvo in 1849, winning back parishes from Filipinos in Cavite province, south of Manila. Tensions gradually mounted during the decade ahead as the Jesuits returned. New decrees prohibited native curates from serving except as assistants to the Spanish clergy, and they protested that racial discrimination not only transgressed the Christian principle of equality under God but assaulted their growing sense of national identity.

Many Spanish clergymen born in the Philippines shared this faint nationalist feeling—just as Englishmen born in the American colonies began to regard themselves as Americans in reaction against British oppression—and they initially directed the struggle against the monastic orders.

Their first leader, Pedro Palaez, was the son of a senior Spanish official. A brilliant theologian, he had risen to the rank of vicar capitular, or ecclesiastical governor, of the Manila archdiocese—the highest position ever attained by a *criollo* priest. He decried the friars, both in Manila and through surrogates in Madrid, insisting that their claim to Philippine parishes violated canon law as prescribed by the Council of Trent. On June 3, 1863, just as his campaign was accelerating, an earthquake struck Manila and buried him in the ruins of the main cathedral. His enemies, alleging that he had been struck down by divine providence, now focused on another dissident priest, José Burgos, charging him with conspiring against Spain.

Burgos, like Palaez a full-blooded Spaniard, was born in 1837 in Vigan, a charming port town in northern Luzon, the son of an army officer. As a student at a Dominican seminary in Manila, he had demonstrated in favor of equality for Filipino novices. Catholic officials marked him as a troublemaker, but they were impressed by his theological scholarship. He was ordained at the age of twenty-seven, just as the controversy over the future of the native clergy began to escalate. A contemporary photograph shows him in a white clerical collar and black soutane, his deep-set dark eyes and pinched lips the picture of fervor.

In 1864, on the eve of his ordination, Burgos denounced the friars for portraying Filipinos as unfit to be priests because "their intelligence is unequal to the lofty office of pastor of souls." Citing scientific texts, a radical move for a clergyman at the time, he argued that "preeminence stems from education rather than any innate superiority." If the Filipinos lacked skills, the monastic orders were at fault for keeping them in "ignorance and rusticity" in an effort to deprive the Philippines of "civilization and prosperity." But Burgos was no partisan of independence—or perhaps he felt constrained to disavow any hint of disloyalty. "Emancipation from the magnanimous Spanish nation," he wrote, "would deliver us to complete anarchy or harsh enslavement by foreigners greedily awaiting the moment to sink their claws into our coveted soil. We must maintain Spanish rule, sheltering ourselves under its great shadow, protection and high culture."

In Spain, liberals and reactionaries were again locked in a recurrent battle that had been going on since 1833, when Queen Isabella II inherited the crown as a child under her mother's regency. Her supporters had blocked a bid for power by the ultraconservative Carlists, mobilized by her uncle, Don Carlos, but she became rigidly autocratic after ascending the throne on her own. In 1868, seeking a more enlightened monarch, an army group staged a coup and replaced her with Amadeo, a genial Italian prince, who abdicated three years later, appalled by the confusion. During this hectic period, the junta selected one of its officers, General Carlos María de la Torre, to be governor of the Philippines.

De la Torre was warmly greeted by Filipino lawyers, merchants, priests and writers on his arrival in Manila in 1869, and initially he fulfilled their hopes for a new deal. To the dismay of the Spanish community, he introduced legal reforms, opened the universities to natives and pledged freedom of the press. He seemed to side with the dissident clergy by calling Burgos a "great Filipino." At a banquet, he stunned the old by pronouncing a toast never before made by a Spanish official: *"¡Las Filipinas para los Filipinos!"*—"The Philippines for the Filipinos!" But the rosy glow darkened as quickly as a tropical sunset.

Coming under the spell of the reactionaries, de la Torre began to suspect his most ardent Filipino sympathizers of seditious tendencies. "With very rare exceptions," he reported to Madrid, "every priest and lawyer born in this country, now as always, has been using his education and his influence to create aspirations for independence." He assumed that the native clergy was behind the disaffection. "Those who are ill-disposed to the friars are the same as those who are ill-disposed toward Spain. . . . They are attempting to destroy one of the strongest pillars of our radiant rule."

Amadeo, then trying to cover his conservative flank in Madrid, nevertheless concluded that de la Torre was too moderate. In 1871, he named a new governor, General Rafael de Izquierdo, an unabashed hard-liner who warned as he stepped ashore in Manila that he would rule "by the sword and the cross." An episode soon gave him a pretext to wield both instruments with a vengeance.

Izquierdo reckoned that *criollos,* Spaniards born in the Philippines, must logically be of divided loyalties—and were thus untrustworthy. He annulled the privileges of several *criollo* army officers and noncoms, and replaced them with *peninsulares.* Rankled, a *criollo* sergeant named Lamadrid planned a revolt at an arsenal in Cavite, where he commanded two hundred native troops. Only official Spanish accounts of the incident survive, and they inflate a minor mutiny into a major roil for the purpose of implicating Filipino dissidents—in particular Burgos.

Launched on the night of January 20, 1872, the uprising went wrong from the start. A native woman, learning of the plot from her *criollo* lover during an amorous siesta that afternoon, had informed the Spanish officer in charge of the garrison, who put his men on alert. The conspirators, mistaking a fireworks display at a nearby town fiesta as a signal, acted prematurely. Breaking out of their barracks, they raced through the narrow streets of Cavite, killing Spanish soldiers and civilians alike, then occupied a fort in the area. Two Spanish regiments, landing by boat from Manila, stormed the fort and slaughtered the insurgents, including Sergeant Lamadrid. Other rebels were summarily executed during the ensuing days, and the authorities disarmed most native troops. Panic paralyzed Manila as offices, shops and markets closed, and citizens fled into the walled city for safety.

Presuming their complicity in the affair, Izquierdo ordered the arrest of thirty prominent Filipino lawyers, writers and priests and either jailed or banished them to faraway islands. But a stiffer penalty awaited Burgos and two other clergymen, Mariano Gómez and Jacinto Zamora. Then in his seventies, Gómez had long been a vigorous proponent of reform. Zamora, by contrast, was an easygoing curate addicted to cards and cockfights, caught in the drag-net only because he worked with Burgos at the Manila cathedral. Their court-martial and punishment recalled the Inquisition.

The official transcript of the trial has never been published—as if Spanish governments to this day have feared that it might damage Spain's reputation. From what is known, however, the proceedings were a travesty. A key witness for the prosecution was Francisco Saldúa, an eccentric government employee who oddly claimed descent from Charlotte Corday, the assassin of Jean-Paul Marat. Saldúa was probably involved in the plot, but in an attempt to win leniency, he preposterously alleged that Burgos was in league with the United States to oust Spain from the Philippines. Other witnesses, many of them captured mutineers, were tortured into denouncing the defendants. An oath of fidelity to Spain signed by Burgos years before was peculiarly offered as proof of his disloyalty.

Predictably, the judges condemned the priests to death along with Saldúa, whose effort to save himself failed. The evidence was so dubious that Izquierdo withheld it from the archbishop of Manila, who despite his own orthodoxy refused to defrock the doomed priests as a gesture of disapproval. Izquierdo also rejected the archbishop's appeal to commute the sentence to imprisonment or exile.

The execution was another reminder of Spanish medieval mentality. By dawn on February 17, 1872, some forty thousand Spaniards and Filipinos, many from the nearby countryside, had assembled at the Bagumbayan field, Manila's central park, now called the Luneta. The victims were to be slowly strangled by a hideous garrote, turned by a large iron screw. The aged Gómez, proud, erect and dignified, died first. Zamora, dazed, followed. Then came Burgos, in tears, angrily protesting his innocence. The crowd fell to its knees, completing the litany for the dead in less time than it took the ghastly device to break his neck. The three priests have since been enshrined as heroes in an acronym—*Gomburza*—which for Filipino patriots later became a magic incantation. That morning, as Filipino historian Nick Joaquin afterward wrote, marked "the beginning of a nationalist consciousness."

★ ★ ★

At the time, José Rizal y Mercado was eleven years old—too young to have been affected by the deaths of the three priests. But, inspired by their martyrdom, he later dedicated one of his novels to their sacred memory. Their sacrifice, he wrote, "awakened my imagination, and I vowed to devote myself to avenge such victims some day."

Rizal hoped to show, through his own attainments, that Filipinos were potentially the equal of Westerners. He avoided native dress in favor of European garb—looking, in his black suit, spotless white shirt and bowler hat, like the groom on the wedding cake. A reformer rather than a revolutionary, he maintained that elites of his kind would determine the future. "A common misfortune and a common abasement have united the people of the islands," he observed, but their destiny lay in the hands of the educated class. "If it is nothing more today than the brains of the nation, it will become in a few years its whole nervous system. Then we shall see what it will do."

One of eleven children, Rizal was born in June 1861 in the busy market town of Calamba, located in a fertile rice and sugar belt about forty miles south of Manila. His father, an ambitious Chinese *mestizo,* leased land from the Dominicans that he farmed through sharecroppers. Rizal worshiped his mother, an unusual woman for her time, who had graduated from college and first tutored him in mathematics and literature. The rich family, typical of provincial *ilustrados* of the time, owned one of the town's few stone houses and ranked high among the gentry. Local Spanish officials often dined at their table, lingering late over music and conversation. But they were also distrusted by the authorities—despite, or perhaps because of, their wealth and prominence. The police had once humiliated Señora Rizal deliberately by detaining her on vague charges of plotting to poison a cousin. Rizal's older brother Paciano, a student in Manila, was suspect in their eyes because of his relations with the dissident clergy. As young José departed to continue his education in Manila, his mother ominously objected: "He already knows enough. If he learns more, he will only end up on the scaffold."

Rizal graduated from the Ateneo, a Jesuit high school, then entered Santo Tomas, the university run by Dominicans. A polymath, he majored in medicine and swept the gamut of literary awards, defeating a Spaniard for the best essay in Spanish. One night, while strolling through a dark alley in the Intramuros, he accidentally brushed against a Spanish policeman, who struck him. He raced to the governor's palace to lodge a complaint, only to be snubbed. The incident wounded his pride, and he related it over and over again in subsequent years to illustrate the injustice of colonialism. He interrupted his studies and left for Madrid, later claiming that he went there in search of help for the Filipino cause. But like many other elite young Filipinos of the period, he may also have been attracted by the lure of Europe.

Arriving in 1882 at the age of twenty-one, he embarked on a formidable schedule. He matriculated at the University of Madrid, working for degrees in medicine, philosophy and literature. In addition, he hired private tutors in French, English, Italian and German, studied painting and sculpture at an art school, practiced fencing and shooting and did daily calisthenics. But above all, he observed the political scene. Power in Spain was oscillating between conservatives and liberals, and republicans, monarchists, socialists, anarchists, atheists and clergymen seemed to be continually embroiled in boisterous debates at meetings, dinners, in cafés, on street corners and especially in the press. Amazed and exhilarated by the giddy atmosphere, Rizal pondered an obvious question: Why did Spain forbid such freedom in the Philippines?

His prescription was integration: to grant Filipinos the same rights as Spaniards. "We do not desire separation from Spain," he declared, proposing instead such reforms for the Philippines as equal opportunity, improved schools, social benefits, honest officials, impartial justice and representation in the *Cortés,* the Spanish parliament. He did not preclude a Filipino identity. The relationship, in his vision, would be filial: the Philippines the child of a solicitous and protective "Mother Spain." But, in their obstinacy, the Spanish reactionaries spurred the rise of revolutionaries who later made Rizal seem tame by comparison.

The Filipino experience prefigured the shape of things to come, with variations, in nearly every European colony. Mohandas Gandhi appealed to Britain for reforms until, his demands rebuffed, he perceived no other alternative for India except independence. His successor, Jawaharlal Nehru, wrote from prison in 1933 that "national movements everywhere begin moderately, and inevitably become more extreme" unless their aspirations are satisfied. And Ho Chi Minh, the Vietnamese Communist leader, who had spent his formative years in Paris, rebelled against France after being denied the status of a Frenchman. The colonizers, moreover, unwittingly drove the colonized to frustration and violence by instilling in them the principles of justice and equality, then rejecting their pleas to make those ideals a reality. Long before the age of modern imperialism, Shakespeare illustrated the phenomenon in *The Tempest* as Caliban ripostes to Prospero:

> You taught me language, and my profit on't
> Is, I know how to curse.

Just as Nehru had studied at Harrow and Cambridge, and Ho Chi Minh had been a dandy in Paris, so the young Filipino expatriates in Madrid and Barcelona during the late nineteenth century adapted comfortably to the Spanish cities. They were mostly gilded youths, sustained by wealthy families at home. Captivated by *la vie de bohème,* they shed their provincial inhibitions, lavishing their nights on casinos, cabarets and costume balls, often surrounded by pretty girls. Even Rizal, at first an earnest prude, soon succumbed to love affairs.

But they were committed to their cause. By the 1880s, before the term had acquired a pejorative connotation, they called themselves the Propagandists. They published tracts, pamphlets, newspapers and a magazine, *La Solidaridad,* and lobbied Spanish politicians when they were not distracted by their own frothy debates. Fulfilling Rizal's dream, some proved to be the match of Spaniards. Trinidad Hermenegildo Pardo de Tavera, a Spanish *mestizo* doctor, linguist, botanist, and ethnologist, won election to the Royal Academy of Science. Juan Luna and Felix Resurrección Hidalgo took the top prizes in an official contest for Spanish artists. Rizal, honoring them in a florid banquet speech, pictured the Philippines and Spain as "two extremes of the globe, the Orient and the Occident . . . two peoples blended by the sympathy of a common origin, united by eternal bonds."

Rizal hardly fit the image of a militant: Short, slim and pale, with thick black hair and a distant look in his narrow eyes, he lisped. He would probably have preferred a life of scholarly introspection, but his passions prevailed.

Influenced by Eugène Sue's popular anticlerical classic *The Wandering Jew,* he chose fiction as the vehicle for his views. In 1887, while studying medicine in Heidelberg and Paris, he completed his first novel and published it in Berlin.

He entitled it *Noli Me Tangere,* or *Touch Me Not,* the phrase lifted from the Vulgate version of the New Testament. The melodramatic story involves a young Filipino, clearly a fantasy of Rizal himself, who returns home from Europe to be killed after inciting the wrath of a Spanish friar. Despite its purple prose, banal plot and preachy quality, the book accurately depicts conditions in the Philippines at the time with unsparing candor. Its Spanish characters, venal priests and officials are as reprehensible as the ignorant, servile and corrupt natives, and its message is simple: Without reforms, a revolution will erupt, and "the defenseless and the innocent will suffer most."

The book, smuggled into Manila, swiftly became the Philippine equivalent of *Uncle Tom's Cabin.* Excoriated by the Catholic hierarchy as "heretical, impious, scandalous [and] an offense to public order," its success was assured. Literate Filipinos snapped up covert copies, turning Rizal into an instant celebrity. His sequel, *El Filibusterismo,* roughly *The Subversive,* portrayed the friars and their sympathizers even more starkly, and again cautioned that only reforms could prevent disaster. It too was banned by the Spanish regime, which about that time had dispossessed Rizal's father for defying the Dominicans in a property dispute.

Rizal, weary of Europe, had by now moved to Hong Kong, where his family had been exiled as punishment for his activities. He practiced medicine there briefly, then returned to Manila in June 1892, expecting the political climate to be relaxed under a new liberal governor, Eulogio Despujol. Haunted by the martyrdom of Burgos twenty years before, he divulged to a friend a premonition of his own execution. "No one knows how he will conduct himself at that supreme moment. Life is pleasant, and it is so repugnant to die by hanging, young and filled with ideas."

Back in Manila, he founded the *Liga Filipina,* the Philippine League, to promote moderate reforms. Its members, in customary Asian style, were inducted with blood oaths and sworn to secrecy. Innocuous though the movement was, the friars smelled sedition. They leaned on Despujol, who was too weak to withstand the pressure. He outlawed the society and banished Rizal to the town of Dapitan, on the island of Mindanao. Rizal remained there for the next four years.

Dapitan was a lovely little place, with its quaint stone church and main square shaded by acacia trees, palms fringing its nearby beaches, ribbons of fine coral sand washed by the cobalt sea. At first it seemed to Rizal to be the end of the world but, typically, he plunged into projects. He set up a school for children and taught fishermen to use modern fishing nets. Importing technical manuals and farm tools from America, he experimented with fruit, coffee and cacao on land bought with his winnings from a lottery. He built a clinic, treating the natives for everything from colds to toothaches, and his reputation as an oculist brought him patients from throughout the archipelago. He also found the time to paint, sculpt and send rare plant and insect specimens to naturalists in Europe. Improbably, he met Josephine Bracken, the eighteen-year-old adopted daughter of a blind American resident of Hong Kong, who was visiting the area. Denied a religious marriage unless he renounced his iconoclasm, he cohabited with her without benefit of clergy, thus compounding his sins in the eyes of the friars.

In 1896 yellow fever was sweeping through Cuba, where a rebellion against

Spain had broken out. Rizal, replying to a Spanish government appeal for doctors, volunteered. Another liberal Spanish governor, General Ramón Blanco y Erenas, approved his request to rescue him from the friars, who still hoped to punish him. Rizal sailed for Cuba, spurning as dishonorable the advice of friends that he jump ship at a port along the way. But he was arrested en route and extradited to Manila to be accused of treason for involvement in a revolt that had just erupted.

The uprising had been triggered by Andrés Bonifacio, an extreme national-ist. Months earlier, he had sent an emissary to Rizal, urging him to participate, but Rizal had rejected the idea. Now the Spanish authorities charged him with being its mastermind. They threw him into a dungeon in Fort Santiago, a Manila military camp, to await a court-martial as their torture chambers worked overtime, coercing some fifteen witnesses to testify against him.

The investigating magistrate, a senior Spanish army officer, had already concluded that Rizal was "the principal organizer and living soul of the insurrection." But Governor Blanco, reckoning that Rizal's martyrdom would only touch off further rebellions, had decided in advance to veto a death sentence. Out for blood, the Dominicans secretly persuaded the ultraconserva-tive Spanish queen, María Cristina, then acting as regent for her young son, to relieve Blanco—who in addition to his liberalism had failed to check the growing insurgency. Blanco went home, and Rizal was doomed.

Denying the indictment, Rizal pledged loyalty to Spain and publicly repu-diated Bonifacio's uprising as an "absurd and savage" adventure that "dishon-ors us before the Filipinos and discredits us with those who otherwise would argue in our behalf." General Camilo García de Polavieja, the new governor, was intractable. Cued by the Dominicans, who had secured his appointment, he dismissed Rizal's declaration as a devious maneuver, called him a traitor and scheduled his trial for the day after Christmas. The Manila correspondent of *El Imparcial,* a Madrid newspaper, reported the obvious: "Rizal is trying by all means to save himself, but he will certainly be condemned to die."

The trial, conducted before seven military judges in a barracks located inside Manila's walled city, lasted less than a day. The improvised courtroom had been packed since early morning, mostly with Spaniards. On a bench, alone, sat Rizal's common-law wife, Josephine. Impeccably attired as always, Rizal entered, escorted by two guards, his wrists bound behind him. He listened serenely as the proceedings droned on. Summing up the case against him, the prosecutor, an officer, remarked that "the fact that the criminal is a native must be considered as an aggravating circumstance." Rizal's lawyer, a court-appointed army lieutenant, argued that his client's guilt had not been estab-lished. Rizal finally rose to defend himself. His arms untied, he read from notes in a low voice, refuting the indictment of treason. "I have sought political liberty," he said, "but never the freedom to rebel."

At daybreak on December 30, 1896, two hours before his execution, Rizal married Josephine in an austere religious rite performed by a Jesuit priest who claimed to have brought him back into the Catholic fold. Rizal bequeathed her one of his few remaining books, appropriately Thomas à Kempis's *On the Imitation of Christ.* Then, again in a black suit, white shirt and derby hat, his elbows bound behind him, he marched the mile from Fort Santiago past the cathedral and beneath the walls of the Intramuros to the Luneta, where

Burgos, Gómez and Zamora had been garroted. It was a beautifully bright morning, the air crisp and the blue sky cloudless, Manila's best season. The city had been festooned with flags and bunting, and thousands packed the field, many of them Spaniards in holiday garb, laughing and chatting and flirting. Rizal, preceded by a drummer and flanked by two priests, reached his destination. Against his protest, the Spanish officer in charge ordered him to face the bay, his back to the firing squad, the stance reserved for traitors. *"Consummatum est!"*—"It is over,"—he said audibly as the Spanish soldiers and Filipino auxiliaries fired. His body spun as it fell, hitting the ground with his lifeless eyes gazing upward at the sun. The crowd shouted, *"¡Viva España!"*

Rizal foreshadowed the Westernized elite that later inspired, organized and led Asian nationalism. He was born in the same decade as two other Asian nationalists who became more famous: Gandhi and Sun Yat Sen, founder of the Chinese republic. But he was dead long before their emergence. His martyrdom notwithstanding, he might have been relegated to minor sainthood, perhaps obscurity, had not the Americans revived his memory after their arrival in the Philippines. In contrast to the revolutionaries then resisting their conquest, he had been a moderate, a reformer, the kind of Filipino who would have welcomed their presence. He was the country's "greatest genius and most revered patriot," said President Theodore Roosevelt in 1904, and the United States would "carry out exactly what he steadfastly advocated."

On the eve of his death, at the age of thirty-five, Rizal had composed a long poem, *Ultimos Adiós,* his final farewell, concealing it in an alcohol stove in his dungeon. A dozen translations of the verse now hang on the wall of the cell, preserved as a museum. Morbidly romantic in the Spanish tradition, its unalloyed sentimentality continues to move Filipinos—the national testament of their national hero. In 1916, during a debate in Congress over a bill to pledge future independence to the Philippines, a speaker read the stanzas aloud. The members, their eyes moistened, passed the legislation, convinced that the United States, to its eternal credit, had emancipated the archipelago from the iniquities of Spanish rule.

> Farewell, land that I love, beloved of the sun,
> Pearl of the Orient Sea, our Eden lost! . . .
> I go where there are no slaves, no tyrants reign,
> Where faith does not slay, where God is most high.

★ ★ ★

Though Rizal died for a revolt he had disavowed, news of his martyrdom spread swiftly, inflaming the uprising ignited by Andrés Bonifacio—a figure drastically different from the sophisticated young *ilustrados* of the time.

Two years Rizal's junior, Bonifacio had been born of poor parents in the Tondo, then as now a squalid Manila slum, whose alleys were said to be "as crooked as the Spanish administration and as dirty as the conscience of its officials." One of six children, he quit school to support his family. He learned to make canes and paper fans, which he peddled in the street, and held such jobs as messenger, broker in rattan, and warehouse watchman. Aspiring to rise into the middle classes, he would read late at night: law texts, the novels of

Hugo and Dumas, the biographies of American presidents and, of course, the works of Rizal, which he copied in his exquisite handwriting.

Attracted by nationalistic ideas, Bonifacio had attended the only meeting of Rizal's aborted *Liga Filipina* in July 1892. Immediately after Rizal's banishment, he founded his own movement, giving it the tongue-twisting title of the *Kataastaasang Kagalanggalang Katipunan ng mga Anak ng Bayan,* The Exalted and Most Honorable Society of the Sons of the People, soon to be known simply as the *Katipunan* or sometimes the *KKK.* Its charter members, like Bonifacio himself, were clerks or workers, and they borrowed slogans and symbols from the Catholic Church, the Freemasons and the Triads, clandestine Chinese brotherhoods. They held mystical rituals, sealed blood pacts, used covert names, exchanged arcane passwords, wore colored masks and sashes, invented secret codes and ciphers, and memorized aphorisms as trite as fortune-cookie sayings, such as "Time lost will never be recovered" and "The noble man prefers honor to personal gain." The cabal consumed their personal lives. When Bonifacio remarried following his first wife's death from leprosy, he wed his new bride in church—and later in an extravagant *Katipunan* ceremony.

Spanish officials deluded themselves, dismissing the unrest as the work of a few "troublemakers." But in central and southern Luzon, slumping sugar and hemp prices, aggravated by rice shortages, were driving masses of peasants to desperation. They rallied to self-styled messiahs, who in turn perceived the *Katipunan* to be an instrument of redemption. Bonifacio shrewdly co-opted local cults. During Holy Week of 1895, he trekked into the San Mateo mountains southeast of Manila to honor a mythical Tagalog savior, Bernardo Carpio, whose ghost supposedly inhabited a cave. He scrawled a slogan on the wall of the cave demanding independence.

Violence, he had now decided, was the only option. "It is a waste of time to wait for promises of felicity that will never come," he wrote. "We can only expect suffering upon suffering, treachery upon treachery, tyranny upon tyranny." He asked Rizal, then in Mindanao, to help him to raise funds from rich Filipinos. Rizal refused, cautioning against a premature uprising. Thrown back on their own resources, Bonifacio's men stole guns from Spanish arsenals, and honed their spears and *bolos,* single-edged machetes. The Spanish, aware of the mounting tension, strengthened their army in the Philippines from eighteen thousand to twenty-two thousand troops—an additional burden to their costly war in Cuba.

As a precaution, Governor Blanco banished four hundred native suspects. But he rebuffed the friars, who demanded the arrest of thousands. "The danger exists only in your minds," he told them.

One day in August 1896, an Augustinian friar learned from an informer that the *Katipunan* was printing tracts on the presses of a Manila newspaper and steered the police to the evidence. The Spanish community, in panic, urged Blanco to jail every Filipino even vaguely considered seditious. He remained calm, but Spaniards ran amok.

Exhorted by the archbishop, Spanish vigilantes fanned out across the city, wantonly slaughtering or rounding up natives. Hundreds of prisoners, jammed into cells inside Fort Santiago, suffocated when a Spanish soldier blocked the only ventilating shaft with a rug. In Cavite, the hysterical wife of the absent

Spanish governor ordered an army firing squad to execute thirteen prominent Filipinos, among them two rich merchants and the local doctor—"Christ and the twelve apostles," as a Spanish eyewitness sneered. Standing on a Manila wharf, a British observer watched as a ship discharged a human cargo of Filipinos seized in the northern Luzon town of Vigan. "Bound hand and foot, and carried like packages of merchandise," he wrote, they were unloaded from the hold of the steamer "with chains and hooks to haul up and swing out the bodies like bales of hemp."

Bonifacio resorted to a classic scheme to co-opt rich Filipinos who had spurned him as too radical. He forged their signatures on his movement's membership rolls, then secretly passed them to the Spanish police. The Spaniards had a field day. Underpaid, lower-class expatriates, they had long been resentful of upper-class Filipinos, and they took a perverse satisfaction in arresting, humiliating and even killing them. Francisco Roxas, a distinguished factory and plantation owner, was executed after a farcical trial despite desperate efforts by his conservative Spanish friends in Madrid to save him. Thus the *ilustrados* found themselves with no choice except to rally behind Bonifacio.

The wholesale repression furnished him with an opportunity to escalate his rebellion. He declared war on August 29, 1896, and thousands of Filipinos heeded his call, but he soon proved to be an inept soldier. Attacking a Spanish warehouse in the Manila suburbs, he was repulsed with heavy losses, and the reverse made clear his delinquency. By contrast, one of his lieutenants, Emilio Aguinaldo y Famy, was fighting brilliantly in his native Cavite, the center of the insurrection. Then only twenty-seven, Aguinaldo quickly emerged as the national leader.

A slight figure, his boyish faced scarred by smallpox, Aguinaldo was infused with an overweening sense of his own destiny—a trait that stirred him to grandiloquent rhetoric. But he was an effective commander, whose dedication, compassion and sincerity inspired his men to follow him unflinchingly.

He was the sixth of eight children of a well-to-do Chinese *mestizo* family. His father, who died when he was nine, had been a lawyer and mayor of Kawit, one of the main Cavite towns. He quit school to help his mother run the family farm and sugar mill, and later joined his brothers in business, dealing in cattle, salt and tallow. Prospering, he took over his father's former position as mayor of Kawit. The job brought him into contact with Bonifacio, who was recruiting local politicians for the *Katipunan.* Aguinaldo volunteered, and adopted the code name of Magdolo, after Mary Magdalene, the patron saint of Kawit. He proceeded to enlist many of the town notables, who were attracted by the mystery and mysticism of the *Katipunan,* just as they had been lured into the Freemasonry, then a popular organization. They probably never expected a war, but Aguinaldo, who yearned to flee the tedium of trade, was elated by the hostilities.

He became an overnight hero. Cavite, with its dense growth, deep ravines, swamps and maze of rivers and streams, was ideal terrain for his guerrillas— most of them peasants armed only with knives, staves and homemade rifles. Within days after the revolt broke out, he controlled three towns. He then scored a major victory at the town of Imus, where one group of his men smoked out Spanish soldiers besieged in a monastery by setting fire to an adjacent grain silo, while another ambushed a relief column. The Filipinos hid at the approaches to a bridge and, at dawn on September 3, surprised five hundred Spanish troops as they attempted to cross. Routed, the Spaniards plunged into the river or waded into flooded rice fields as the pursuing rebels cut them to shreds. Aguinaldo seized seventy Remington rifles, along with a sword dropped by the retreating Spanish commander. The blade was inscribed *Made in Toledo—1869,* the year of his birth. Seeing the coincidence as an omen, Aguinaldo wore it proudly until the Americans captured and disarmed him in 1901. Charles Bohlen, the U.S. ambassador in Manila, returned it to him at a nostalgic ceremony in 1960—when Aguinaldo was ninety-two.

In October 1896 Aguinaldo announced his intention to create a government like "that of the United States"—its motto, borrowed from the French Revolution, to be "liberty, equality and fraternity." By now the insurgents dominated the region around Manila. Lacing Cavite with trenches, barricades and parapets of earth and plaited bamboo, they improvised cannons made of water pipes and iron hoops, which shot scrap iron and bits of telegraph wire. They mobilized the local peasantry to provide them with food, and Aguinaldo, maintaining strict discipline, decreed death for looters and levied taxes fairly. He also treated the Spanish humanely, once asking forgiveness of a dying friar who had been hit by a stray rebel bullet.

Blanco, in an attempt to regain Cavite, personally led a Spanish amphibious force of two thousand men in landings along the coast. The rebels drew them deep into the area, then burst out of the mangrove thickets, brandishing spears and knives. By dusk, they had killed or wounded five hundred Spaniards, and the rest fled. Beaten by a Filipino novice half his age, Blanco fell prey to the friars, who hated him for his leniency toward Rizal. When, at their instigation, he was replaced by General Polavieja, the new governor directed his troops to "wash all offences in blood." A Spanish officer amplified the order in a banquet toast to a newly arrived regiment: "The cannibals are still in the forests. The wild beasts are hiding in their lairs. The hour has come to exterminate the savages. Destroy! Kill! Show no mercy!"

Polavieja launched a reign of terror. A veteran of the war in Cuba, he imported the severe measures employed there, such as herding peasants into controlled areas. He relieved congested jails by executing prisoners after drumhead trials, as he did Rizal, or simply had them shot. Reinforced from Spain with fresh troops, he also stepped up the campaign against the insurgents in Cavite during the spring of 1897, recapturing most of the province.

But realizing that despite his success he lacked the resources to crush the Filipinos completely, he proposed to Queen María Cristina either negotiations or escalation of the war; she would have neither. As defender of the faith, she dared not offend the Spanish clergy by bargaining with the rebels. Nor, with the Cuban war draining her coffers, could she afford Polavieja's request to add forty thousand men to the twenty-five thousand already under his command. Nevertheless she wanted results, and she considered Polavieja's recommendations a sign of weakness. She replaced him with General Fernando Primo de Rivera, the governor of the Philippines thirteen years before, who had departed under a cloud of corruption.

Naïvely anticipating an imminent Spanish collapse, the Filipino leaders were already jockeying for power. Aguinaldo, in a dream of grandeur, had arrogated for himself the rank of "generalissimo," thereby infuriating Bonifacio, and tensions between them rose. In March 1897, their lieutenants met at an abandoned estate in Cavite to resolve the quarrel. Aguinaldo's supporters maneuvered the group into agreeing to form a republic with him as president. Angrily rejecting the decision, Bonifacio planned a rival regime. He also ceded several areas under his control to the Spanish troops, who in one undefended spot killed Aguinaldo's brother Crispulo.

Aguinaldo tracked down Bonifacio and had a kangaroo court condemn him to death. He then commuted the sentence to "indefinite exile . . . in an isolated place"—but, he lamely claimed afterward, the pardon reached the executioners too late. Bonifacio had been wounded in the chase and, on a rainy morning in May 1897, they carried him by hammock to a forest clearing and shot him and his brother Procopio. Aguinaldo's command was now secure. The dispute had enfeebled his ranks, however, strengthening the Spanish as a result. His position was particularly precarious in Cavite, his former stronghold.

If retreat is the most difficult military maneuver, Aguinaldo demonstrated remarkable skill as a soldier by extracting his troops from Cavite. They traveled with their families, camp followers and cattle—and he led them all, more than a thousand men, women and children, around the Spanish cordon. They marched across streams, through jungles and into the mountains of Bulacan province, sixty miles northeast of Manila. There, at the site of an old iron mine in the Biacnabato valley, he found an impregnable sanctuary. The only road, which cut through precipitous cliffs, could be blocked with boulders and defended from the surrounding slopes. Aguinaldo set up his headquarters in a cave.

First he offered to recognize Spanish rule on condition that the friars be expelled from the archipelago and, among other things, that the Philippines be represented in Spain's parliament. When the Spanish rebuffed him, he proclaimed a republic with himself as president. "To arms, noble hearts, to arms!" he intoned. "Enough of suffering!"

The fiery pronouncement did nothing for his predicament. He was locked into his bastion, which now resembled a refugee camp rather than an army camp. Pressed by Spanish attacks, five thousand more rebels and their families swelled the area. They lacked food and water, sanitation was primitive and smallpox and leprosy appeared. But Aguinaldo was determined to hold out for Spanish concessions.

Primo de Rivera's repeated attempts to storm the redoubt had failed, and his men were stalled by torrential rains and rebel assaults. He advised Queen María Cristina, as Polavieja had, that the deadlock could only be broken either by all-out war or by compromise. She opted for a settlement. The Cuban revolt was depleting her treasury, and the political balance in Madrid had also changed. In August 1897 an anarchist had assassinated Antonio Canovas del Castillo, the conservative prime minister and, despite her reactionary views, she named Práxedes Mateo Sagasta, a liberal, to succeed him. A champion of conciliation, he ordered Primo de Rivera to discuss peace.

A Filipino fixer with a foot in each camp volunteered to mediate. Pedro Alejandro Paterno, a Spanish *mestizo,* was a lawyer and sometime scholar who had hobnobbed with the Filipino reformists in Madrid, where he had also known Primo de Rivera. A dubious opportunist, he later requested a dukedom in Spain and a million dollars for his services, receiving neither. But he performed creditably.

Primo de Rivera instructed him to inform Aguinaldo that Spain wanted an honorable agreement, and Paterno began the arduous process. Borne in a hammock by porters, he shuttled for seven months between Biacnabato and Manila, an agonizing trek along muddy roads, down turbid rivers and over mountain trails. The main issue was money. Finally, late in 1897, the two sides reached an accord: Spain would pay the rebels 800,000 pesos—half immediately, a quarter when they laid down their arms and the rest after a Te Deum marking the armistice was chanted in the Manila cathedral. In exchange, Aguinaldo agreed to go abroad. A check in his pocket, he sailed for the British colony of Hong Kong along with a group of aides. His escort was the governor's nephew, Colonel Miguel Primo de Rivera, who was to become dictator of Spain twenty-five years later. As he departed, Aguinaldo disavowed his rebellion, declaring "our loyalty to Spain . . . and to the government and laws of the fatherland."

Manila celebrated with fireworks, balls and the Te Deum, and with good reason. The Spanish had decapitated the revolt and banished its leader—without committing themselves to real reforms. Aguinaldo was also satisfied. He had gained time while amassing the funds to purchase weapons for the next outbreak. Soon after landing in Hong Kong, he disavowed his disavowal of the insurrection.

Felipe Agoncillo, his agent in Hong Kong, had already dangled a proposal before the American consul, Rounseville Wildman. Foreseeing a future war between the United States and Spain, he suggested that the Americans and Filipinos join forces. The Filipinos would buy twenty thousand guns and two hundred thousand rounds of ammunition from the United States on credit, paying when they won independence. Aguinaldo's republic, which only existed on paper, would meanwhile pledge two Philippine provinces and the receipts from the Manila customs bureau as collateral. Wildman was enthusiastic. Agoncillo was "not particular about the price," he reported to Washington, calculating that the United States could reap a profit of twenty-five or thirty percent on the transaction. As it turned out, he anticipated a healthy commission from the deal. The State Department snubbed the offer. Wildman subsequently developed an admiration for Aguinaldo and, though he was a veteran diplomat, he later snarled the ties between the Americans and Filipinos.

As both Aguinaldo and the Spanish expected, peace proved to be only a truce. The Filipinos had not abandoned their dream of independence and Spain could not face the prospect of a lost empire, and their war resumed shortly thereafter. But the Filipinos soon discovered that a new and stronger power had come to supplant their decrepit Spanish masters as the United States arrived to taste the glories and the perils of imperialism for the first time in its history.

4. AMERICA GOES GLOBAL

★ ★ ★

At about half past eleven on the night of April 30, 1898, Commodore George Dewey's squadron of nine ships slipped through the Boca Grande channel and past the island of Corregidor, entering Manila Bay. Squalls occasionally relieved the heat and humidity. Clouds concealed the moon and, in the distance, streaks of lightning illuminated the dark sky. Dewey's flagship, the *Olympia,* led the American vessels in column formation as they advanced slowly, waiting for daybreak to show them the deployment of the Spanish armada. Dawn came quickly, as it does in the tropics, and shells from Spanish shore batteries began to lob overhead, falling wide. Dewey, preserving ammunition, gave no reply. Dressed in a white uniform and golf cap, he sat calmly in a wicker armchair on the bridge, fingering his lucky rabbit's foot, rising from time to time to train a telescope on the scene as his fleet headed toward Sangley Point, at the tip of Cavite. There the entire Spanish force of twelve ships, lined up in a row, faced the approaching Americans. Their cannons flashed, again without effect, and still the American guns held back. Finally, at a quarter to six on the morning of May 1, within two and half miles of the enemy, Dewey issued the command that was to become his escutcheon. He leaned over the rail and gently called down to Captain Charles V. Gridley, the *Olympia*'s skipper: "You may fire when you are ready, Gridley."

Seven hours later, only a single Spanish ship remained afloat, tattered beyond recognition. Not one American vessel had been damaged, and only one American had died, of heat prostration. Nearly two hundred Spaniards had perished.

Americans at home, elated by the victory, celebrated Dewey with hysterical enthusiasm. Cities across the country honored him with prayers, parades, fireworks and other ceremonies, one in Manhattan's Madison Square drawing a crowd of more than a hundred thousand. He was extolled in jingles, songs and poems. Public buildings and private homes alike displayed his portrait, the red face, white mustache and blue naval uniform tinted to personify the national colors. His name suddenly adorned everything from avenues, hotels, yachts and racehorses to souvenir dishes, silverware, paperweights, canes, shaving mugs, watch charms and teething rings for the hundred of babies who, by accident of birth, were to go through life named Dewey. Young women sported nautical Dewey blouses and jaunty Dewey sailor hats, while their boyfriends wore Dewey neckties, Dewey stickpins and Dewey cufflinks. A candy company labeled a new brand of gum "Dewey Chewies," and a pharmaceutical firm advertised a laxative featuring Dewey's picture above the slogan "The Salt of Salts." By special act, Congress promoted Dewey to rear admiral, and soon afterward elevated him to full admiral—awarding him a Tiffany sword almost as big as himself, its gold-plated hilt set in jewels. Dewey, no model of modesty, accepted the acclaim as his due. Rather than return home promptly, he was to remain at the scene of his glory for another year, a distant idol, holding court aboard his flagship for the correspondents who came to validate his immortality. "The Battle of Manila Bay," he wrote to his son, "is one of the most remarkable naval battles of the ages."

The exultation over Dewey's triumph reflected more than the flush of victory. Americans, having conquered their own continent, were now being driven by a new dynamism toward a global role. The annihilation of the Spanish fleet was not only a remarkable battle, but a rite of passage. The United States, at times reluctantly, would henceforth rise into the ranks of the world powers.

The war with Spain—a "splendid little war" as the future secretary of state John Hay flippantly dubbed it—began as a pious endeavor to liberate Cuba from Spanish oppression. But an inexorable momentum propelled the United States into ejecting Spain from the Philippines and then, in a confused series of events, into a conflict to crush the Filipino independence movement. The episode marked a pivotal point in the American experience. For the first time, U.S. soldiers fought overseas. And, for the first time, America was to acquire territory beyond its shores—the former colony itself becoming colonialist.

The prospect of war with Spain had polarized America's politicians, editors, businessmen, clergy and other makers of opinion. Their controversy, however, revived a question that had been debated with increasing intensity for years: Should the United States reach outside its natural frontiers to seek the benefits, yet risk the burdens, of international status? In various guises and over different issues, isolationalists and interventionists have recurrently debated essentially the same question ever since.

The champions of expansion prevailed in 1898. A cabal of willful men, notably Theodore Roosevelt, Henry Cabot Lodge and Alfred Thayer Mahan, they largely owed their success to their ability to manipulate President William McKinley, whose sincerity and virtuous innocence were exceeded only by his ignorance and almost paralytic indecisiveness. But the expansionists were also attuned to the mood of the American public.

Regional concerns sharply divided the United States at the time. The preoccupations of New England factory workers bore little resemblance to the problems of Middle West farmers, and both were remote from the difficulties facing the Deep South. Meanwhile, waves of immigrants from Europe were pouring into the country, their exotic traits reshaping the profile of the population. Amid this diversity, though, the nation was searching for unity to efface the nightmare of the Civil War, still a traumatic memory after a generation.

The quest for cohesion found expression in patriotism, intuitive or contrived. Their imagination stimulated by a jingoistic press, Americans conjured up a heady vision of the United States: flags flying, drums beating and troops marching, soaring like its emblematic eagle to heights of imperial grandeur. They were intoxicated by stirring parades, martial music and flamboyant oratory—all flushed with a sense of high moral purpose. In contrast to the Europeans, who merely lusted for power, Americans would mobilize their might to spread the blessings of their exceptional civilization to the world. McKinley was swept up by these sentiments, which he had neither the courage to curb nor the skill to direct, and he stumbled into a war with Spain whose purpose he neither fully believed nor understood.

Ironically, the most fervent imperialists of the era later disavowed their original purpose. Henry Cabot Lodge emerged as the apostle of isolationism following World War I, when he blocked U.S. membership in the League of Nations. Theodore Roosevelt, the romantic warrior, had already turned prudent after Japan's defeat of Russia in 1905, anticipating the rise of Japanese power in the Pacific. Forecasting the Japanese invasion during World War II with uncanny accuracy, he warned that America's continued rule of the Philippines would make them "our heel of Achilles if we are attacked by a foreign power." He favored their independence "at an early date, and without any guarantee that might . . . commit us to staying on the Asiatic coast." But as U.S. obligations abroad deepened, Asia in particular became America's new frontier.

History is often a series of expedients that grow into dogmas—today's pragmatism becoming tomorrow's doctrines; thus the American presence in Asia evolved. The U.S. foray into the Philippines, a diversion to the war in Cuba, implanted America in the Far East. John Hay soon articulated the Open Door, a pledge to preserve the "territorial and administrative entity" of China against the encroachments of the European and Japanese imperialists—in reality, it was to protect American interests there. Hence the United States assumed a special responsibility for China that was to be, for decades, both the object of emotional solicitude for the American public and an article of faith of American foreign policy. American missionaries, educators and advisers flocked to China, hoping to teach its masses to pray and brush their teeth. President Franklin D. Roosevelt, out of sentimental motives, insisted on including China among the major Allied powers during World War II. The Communist takeover of China in 1949, exacerbated by the outbreak of the Korean war a year later, spotlighted Asia as never before as vital to U.S. security. Vietnam eventually came into focus as an illusory barrier against Chinese Communism, with tragic consequences. Though the United States withdrew from the Asian mainland in the aftermath of the Vietnam tragedy, it remains preeminent in the Pacific, still hostage to the place where its thrust began, the site of its two largest overseas bases—the Philippines.

★ ★ ★

During the first half of the nineteenth century, electrified by their own independence, Americans displayed an adolescent cockiness. They seized territory
from Mexico, contemplated grabbing Cuba and Santo Domingo, and talked
of aiding republican revolutionaries in Hungary. Lincoln's secretary of state,
William Seward, even pondered the idea of provoking a conflict in Europe to
avert the Civil War. But the ghastly struggle between the states, followed by
the ordeal of Reconstruction, shifted the gaze of Americans inward, and
Europeans dismissed the United States as a player in the world arena. Compared to London, Paris, Vienna, Berlin or St. Petersburg, Washington was a
provincial capital where the European powers maintained minor legations—or
often none at all. In 1881, Britain banished Sir Lionel Sackville-West there as
ambassador to spare his noble family the embarrassment of his notorious
liaison with a Spanish flamenco dancer, by whom he had six illegitimate
children.

But as the century waned a phenomenal economic boom transformed America into the biggest granary on earth, a foremost manufacturer of consumer
goods and a major producer of coal, iron and steel. Railroads and telegraph
lines linked the continent's far-flung areas, and massive immigration made it
the world's most populous industrial country except for Russia. The growth
generated in Americans an ebullient, almost rash sense of national pride. "The
pulse of the people is becoming quick, nervous, feverish," wrote a contemporary editor, and Finley Peter Dunne's irrepressible Mr. Dooley caught the
mood precisely. "We're a great people. We ar-re that. An' the' best iv it is, we
know we ar-re."

The term "manifest destiny" was coined in 1845 to promote the annexation
of Texas. It had been the slogan of reformers like the sponsors of the Home-
stead Act, who sought to distribute land in the West to small farmers, primarily Irish and German immigrants, as a means of giving them freedom and
dignity. Now the phrase became freighted with fresh significance as the assertion of America's duty, through either conversion or conquest, to bring the
benefits of its civilization to the ignorant and misguided abroad.

Proponents of this ambitious version of manifest destiny found in Charles
Darwin's theory of "survival of the fittest" a pseudoscientific basis to affirm
the racial superiority of Americans. John Fiske, a popular essayist and lecturer, predicted to audiences around the country that the dimensions of the
United States would one day reach from "pole to pole," surpassing "any
empire that has yet existed." To Josiah Strong, a Congregationalist minister
and spokesman for the American Evangelical Alliance, the Anglo-Saxon, with
his "unequalled energy" and "genius for colonizing," was "divinely commissioned to be . . . his brother's keeper." So the United States, heir to Britain's
leadership of the Anglo-Saxon race, would "impress its institutions upon
mankind" and "spread itself over the earth." Even Walt Whitman, the shaggy
idealist, urged America to carry its "happiness and liberty" across the Pacific
to the ancient cultures of Asia:

> Facing west from California's shores,
> Inquiring, tireless, seeking what is yet unfound,

> I, a child, very old, over waves, towards the house
> of maternity, look afar,
> Look off the shores of my Western sea, the circle
> almost encircled. . . .

The imperialists also advanced practical arguments. They recognized that the American continent, its vast riches far from tapped, remained the central field of development. But special interests, such as the oil, mining and trading companies, equated expansion abroad with profits—just as the myth of El Dorado had hypnotized the Spanish. "New outlets for American capital and new opportunities for American enterprises" were vital, said the economist Charles Conant, warning that the U.S. economy would crumble without foreign markets and sources of raw material. American diplomats lobbied in their assigned countries on behalf of U.S. firms—and many, in those days of ambiguous ethics, were paid handsomely by the companies for their efforts.

The anti-imperialists mobilized an impressive array of spokesmen, such as former President Grover Cleveland and Mark Twain, by then a living legend. Among other points, they held that the subjugation of foreign peoples violated the basic American constitutional precept of government by consent of the governed. Marxist analysis to the contrary, they were supported by many big capitalists, most notably steel magnate Andrew Carnegie, who worried that foreign ventures would dissipate the nation's wealth. Union leaders like Samuel Gompers feared the importation of Asian "slave labor," and racists inveighed against America's contamination by the "yellow peril."

Not all clergymen portrayed expansionism as providential. Charles H. Parkhurst, a noted Presbyterian minister, scorned "the novel idea that the reign of Jesus is to be widened under the protection of shells and dynamite." The issue inevitably became political. When the Republican campaign platform of 1892 called for the "achievement" of manifest destiny in "its broadest sense," Champ Clark of Kentucky, an eloquent Democrat and later speaker of the House of Representatives, ridiculed the concept as "the specious plea of every robber and freebooter" since genesis. A contemporary commentator, Frederick W. Gookin, voiced doubts that still trouble Americans as they contemplate the impact of U.S. power abroad on their own values. "The serious question," he wrote, "is what effect the imperial policy will have upon ourselves."

★　★　★

In January 1893 the expansionists tested their influence over the issue of Hawaii, then an independent monarchy. A group of American sugar planters, bankers and clergymen deposed the gracious and enlightened queen, Liliuokalani, and asked to join the United States. Acting on his own, the U.S. diplomatic representative on the spot, John L. Stevens, brought in marines from the cruiser *Boston* to aid them, hoisted the Stars and Stripes over public buildings and declared the territory an American protectorate, cabling Washington: THE HAWAIIAN PEAR IS FULLY RIPE, AND THIS IS THE HOUR . . . TO PLUCK IT. He cautioned that Britain might otherwise grab the islands—which, after all, had been discovered by Captain Cook. His warning exemplified what George Kennan, in a study of U.S. foreign policy, has called "contingent necessity," a favorite device of later expansionists, who contended that Japan or a European power would take over the Philippines if the United States procrastinated.

The American public was almost ready to support the seizure of Hawaii, but Grover Cleveland, returning to the White House for a second term in March 1893, shelved a proposed annexation treaty. The Hawaiian fruit, like the imperialist cause, dangled for another five years.

As they do after all wars, Americans had become almost pacifist following the Civil War. It was one of those "never again" interludes, when nations regret their folly, mourn their dead and swear to avoid another such bloodbath at any cost. The United States not only dismantled its army, but scrapped its combat ships, making no attempt to compete with the Europeans in the construction of modern ironclads. The remnant U.S. fleet was a collection of antiques, some of which had been in service for more than twenty years. An American admiral, David Dixon Porter, compared it to a flimsy Chinese fort painted with dragons to scare the enemy, and a London publication termed it "a hapless, broken-down, forlorn apology for a navy." In 1885, when Dewey took command of the *Pensacola,* an old steam sloop, he said that any fourth-rate British cruiser could "easily have kept out of range of her battery, torn her to pieces and set her on fire." Neglect of the navy was visible in its absurd surplus of officers, numbers of whom had not been promoted for ten or fifteen years for lack of new ships. Many lieutenants over the age of fifty had held the same rank for more than a decade.

But the country's attitude gradually changed as its recollections of the Civil War dimmed. By 1890, partly under pressure from New England shipbuilders, Congress had voted funds for fifteen up-to-date cruisers and six battleships, three of them unrivaled in firepower—thereby making the U.S. Navy a match for that of Germany, which itself was rapidly constructing new vessels. The top echelons of the navy were meanwhile renovating the service. Young officers were studying modern ordnance and electricity and being assigned to U.S. legations abroad, where they could observe the European fleets. In 1884, Rear Admiral Stephen B. Luce founded the Naval War College in Newport, Rhode Island, as a pulpit for his bellicose sermons. War, he declared, was "one of the great agencies by which human progress is effected," the experience that "arouses all the latent energies of a people, stimulates them to the highest exertion and develops their mental and material resources."

Luce's successor at the naval college, Captain Alfred Thayer Mahan, turned Newport into the center of America's strategic thinking—and himself into a leading strategist. Born in 1840 at West Point, where his father taught military engineering, Mahan graduated from the naval academy in time to serve in the Civil War. Along with other naval officers of his generation, he faded into obscurity afterward, until Luce invited him to teach naval history at Newport in 1884. He devoted a year to studying the subject beforehand, bringing to it his prodigious memory and language skills. Six years later, he published *The Influence of Sea Power on History,* a complex historical, political, social, economic, military, geographic and technological tapestry that concluded that genuine national security and international supremacy depended on the deployment of a strong navy. The thesis had an immediate impact. "Your book must be our textbook," Luce told him, and soon Mahan was drafting America's contingency plans for war. The book also became the bible of the British, German and Japanese navies, earning Mahan an impressive reputation and array of awards.

Theodore Roosevelt, then thirty-two, devoured Mahan's volume in a weekend, and the two men quickly became close. Their personalities contrasted—Mahan, remote and professorial with his white spade beard, and Roosevelt, eighteen years his junior, the gesticulating and grimacing extrovert. But both believed in translating theory into action. Despite his flashy manner, Roosevelt was himself a noteworthy scholar whose history, *The Naval War of 1812,* written at the age of twenty-three, had pleaded for military readiness and served as one of Mahan's sources.

Biographers, historians and political scientists as well as his contemporaries have described and diagnosed Teddy Roosevelt exhaustively. Out of the huge bibliography emerges a complex, contradictory and sometimes confusing figure who even today still inspires respect and ridicule, praise and censure, adulation and disdain. He was, and he remains in memory, a colossus, disproportionately larger than life. He could be theatrical, charismatic, cunning, tender, ambitious, cautious and reckless, sophisticated and childish. He was, in short, the prototype of that era of America's unbounded energy and limitless aspirations, which he both reflected and shaped. The British king, Edward VII, hailed him as "the greatest moral force of the age," while to Woodrow Wilson he was "the most dangerous man of the age," and Mark Twain, after two encounters, qualified him as "clearly insane."

Delighting in controversy, Roosevelt confected venomous phrases to blast his foes. He dismissed a group of critics as "a bunch of shrill eunuchs" and denounced a senator as "a well-meaning, pin-headed, anarchistic crank, of hirsute and slabsided aspect." He loved the "fun of hating," as the writer Booth Tarkington put it, his gigantic ego reveling in the tempests he stirred up around himself. "If a man has a very decided character, has a strongly accentuated career," Roosevelt explained, "it is normally the case . . . that he makes ardent friends and bitter enemies."

Born into a patrician New York clan, Roosevelt went from Groton and Harvard into public life, swiftly becoming a precocious and potent Republican reformer. He was elected to the New York state legislature at the age of twenty-five, interrupted his career to spend three years on a ranch in the Dakotas, then gained a seat on the U.S. civil service commission, where he struggled against the spoils system. Back in New York City as police commissioner, he incurred the hostility of the politicians and won the admiration of the cops by battling corruption and basing promotions on merit. His contentious reputation nearly deterred McKinley, who hated controversy, from appointing him to his administration.

Roosevelt was predictably inconsistent. He had traveled in Europe and the Middle East as a youth, studied in Germany and hobnobbed with Britain's upper crust, yet he professed an America-right-or-wrong patriotism that bordered on crude xenophobia. Outraged by racial bias, he was to be the first president to invite a black to dine at the White House and praised the Japanese as a "wonderful people" who would become a "formidable" factor in the world. But he also believed in Anglo-Saxon preeminence, attributed the "unexampled spread of civilized mankind" to white superiority and lobbied to bar

Asian immigrants, including Japanese, from the United States as "dangerous" aliens. He spouted belligerent bromides, like "no man who is not willing to bear arms and to fight for his rights . . . should be entitled to the privilege of living in a free community." Nevertheless, he was the first American to win the Nobel Peace Prize, for mediating the war between Russia and Japan.

On one point, however, he never wavered: Obsessed with making the United States "the mightiest republic on which the sun ever shone," he exulted in the dream of America's global predominance. "Our people are neither cravens nor weaklings, and we face the future high of heart and confident of soul, eager to do the great work of a great power." In a speech before the Naval War College in Newport, Rhode Island, Roosevelt clearly articulated the imperialist theme, repeating the word *war* sixty-two times in as many minutes. "All the great masterful races have been fighting races," he blared. "No triumph of peace is quite so great as the triumphs of war."

★   ★   ★

A president need not be more intelligent or better informed than his advisers. But, to govern effectively, he must have policy goals and the decisiveness to pursue them. William McKinley had neither—at least in international affairs. So, unable to lead, he was fated to follow.

His portrait—the heavily handsome Roman profile, wing collar and frock coat, gazing firmly at some undefinable goal—still occupies a place of honor in the towns of his native Ohio, and understandably so. He is a nostalgic reminder of what was once the nation's heartland, now condescendingly called Middle America by big-city commentators. He plunged into politics as a release from an epileptic wife, a local banker's daughter, whom he treated with tender devotion. Serious and sober, he climbed to the top through luck and pluck, like the hero of a Horatio Alger novel, then the inspiration for the youth of America. Like an Alger hero, he spoke in pious platitudes, his warmth and sincerity a reassurance to voters, demonstrating that virtue rather than character, combined with party loyalty, could propel a man into the presidency.

The seventh of nine children, William McKinley was born in January 1843 in Niles, Ohio, the son of a small manufacturer of ironware. He was, by his own account, "a simple country boy" who, years later, would reminisce on the joys of a rural childhood. He inherited his mother's profound religious nature and never lost the faith. She hoped to steer him into the Methodist ministry, a vocation that seemed to suit his natural gift for public speaking. But the family's financial ruin cut short his brief college career. Then came the Civil War, which set him in a new direction.

He enlisted as a private in an Ohio regiment and at first fought against rebel irregulars in Virginia's lovely Monongahela valley. His indifference to danger caught the attention of Rutherford B. Hayes, a kindly Cincinnati lawyer serving as a lieutenant colonel in the outfit. McKinley had found a patron, whose expectations he fulfilled. Hayes named him supply sergeant as the unit advanced into Maryland to protect Washington. On September 17, 1862, the Union and Confederate forces clashed amid the rolling landscape of Antietam. Some thirty thousand Americans on both sides died in a single day in one of the bloodiest battles of history. McKinley distinguished himself by driving a mule train through the shells and bullets to provide the troops with hot food and coffee. Hayes, now regimental commander, awarded him a commission and appointment as his aide-de-camp, calling him "one of the bravest and finest officers in the army." McKinley performed gallantly in other engagements and, at twenty-two, ended the war as a brevet major. The carnage of the conflict remained engraved in his memory.

Demobilized, he attended law school and hung out his shingle in Canton, Ohio, becoming a typical small-town attorney. He joined the Masons and Knights of Pythias, took part in Methodist affairs and helped the county Republican committee, which eventually made him chairman. The German and Irish factory workers and coal miners of the district were solidly Democratic, but they came to esteem McKinley. A true conservative, he believed in fairness—a conviction that prompted him to defend a group of strikers indicted for rioting during a mine dispute. He won their acquittal and refused to accept a fee, and henceforth had labor on his side. The support was decisive in 1867, when he achieved his first election victory as county prosecutor.

The election also swept Hayes into the governorship. McKinley swung his county behind his former commander, who remembered the help. He promoted McKinley in state Republican circles and in 1876, when he became president, propelled him into the House of Representatives. But personal sorrow soured the triumph. McKinley's only child, a four-year-old daughter, died. His wife, once beautiful and animated, was now a nervous invalid, vulnerable to sudden seizures. Intensely loyal, he reserved his few leisure hours for her care and comfort.

The impenetrable veneer of a sunny disposition concealed McKinley's anxieties. He consoled himself in religion—and above all in work. During his fourteen years in Congress, he labored long and hard to master the complexities of trade issues. He would sit up late into the night in his office, chain-smoking cigars or chewing tobacco as he studied reports and schedules, and he rose early in the morning for meetings with visiting businessmen or colleagues. His diligence paid off. He was soon regarded as a foremost expert on tariffs, championing high barriers to protect America's burgeoning manufacturing interests. Perhaps as solace, he also enjoyed the congenial masculinity of Capitol Hill. He was not an effusive backslapper. Nor could he match his articulate associates as they spun out yarns in the haze of smoke after stag dinners, preferring instead to smile gently at their wit. They in turn admired his sweet style, even his touch. He was, as his biographer Margaret Leech has put it, beloved rather than merely popular.

The Democratic landslide of 1890 crushed his attempt at reelection. But he easily won the race for governor of Ohio a year later, and soon became Republican party chairman. He was now a logical choice for the Republican presidential nomination: His reputation was spotless, and he had no personal enemies. The campaign was to be managed by Mark Hanna, the millionaire kingmaker, whom he had naïvely allowed to pay his debts. Handily winning the Republican bid at the 1896 convention, he went on to defeat the Democratic candidate, William Jennings Bryan, who had alienated his party's southern conservatives by opposing the gold standard.

Their effort to annex Hawaii stalled, the imperialists discovered a fresh cause in Cuba. Rebels there, beginning to fight for freedom from Spain, were clamoring for U.S. assistance. Mark Hanna was wary of ventures abroad that might divert America from its economy, then just coming out of a depression. "The United States must not have any damn trouble with anybody," he advised McKinley on the eve of the inauguration. The new president agreed. "We want no wars of conquest," McKinley pledged in his inaugural address. "Peace is preferable to war in almost every contingency."

McKinley's lame State Department appointments reflected his indifference to foreign policy. To vacate a Senate seat for Hanna, he named as secretary of state John Sherman, the senile Ohio senator of seventy-four who was best known for the antitrust statute that bears his name. He propped up Sherman by picking as first assistant secretary Judge William R. Day, another Ohioan, who despite his wisdom and dedication was unfamiliar with international affairs. Direction of the department thus fell to the second assistant secretary, Alvey A. Adee, a remarkable bureaucrat whose career had begun in the U.S. legation in Madrid in 1874, and was to span fifty years. An eccentric bachelor with a squeaky voice and a hearing defect, he would cycle every morning to the gingerbread building adjoining the White House, where the State Department was then housed. He analyzed foreign government statements, wrote diplomatic notes, decoded ciphers, drafted speeches and arranged ceremonies—his spidery signature A.A.A. the imprimatur of authority.

America's diplomatic corps was then largely composed of amateurs who owed their jobs to political patronage. Early in McKinley's term, the influential Senator Joseph Foraker of Ohio appeared at the White House to seek a consular post for a friend, Professor Oscar F. Williams. The only place open, McKinley apologized amiably, was an undesirable spot called Manila. It was "somewhere away around on the other side of the world," he said, but he "did not know exactly where" since he "had not had time to look it up." Williams took the job.

McKinley, preoccupied with domestic matters, sloughed off the War Department on Russell A. Alger. A rich timber tycoon and cousin of Horatio Alger, he was later to become embroiled in a scandal over meat procurements for the army. McKinley chose as secretary of navy a cherished political colleague, John D. Long, former governor of Massachusetts and member of Congress, a rotund little Pickwickian character with no qualifications for the assignment—nor indeed any interests other than writing poetry and puttering around his seaside cottage. McKinley gave Theodore Roosevelt the post of Long's assistant secretary—but only begrudgingly.

Roosevelt enlisted influential allies to secure the job. Henry Cabot Lodge composed a lobby of such senior Republicans as Garret Hobart, the vice president, and Thomas Brackett Reed, the speaker of the House of Representatives. Thomas Platt, the Republican boss of New York, detested Roosevelt but backed his appointment in hopes of removing him from the state. McKinley at first balked. He wanted peace, and Roosevelt was "too pugnacious" and "always in such a state of mind," he protested to a friend. Unable to resist the pressure, McKinley finally capitulated in April 1897. Roosevelt joyfully wired Lodge: SINBAD HAS EVIDENTLY LANDED THE OLD MAN OF THE SEA.

Once in Washington Roosevelt gathered together a coterie of expansionists like himself. They included Lodge, Alfred Thayer Mahan and Commander Charles Davis, chief of naval intelligence, as well as Dewey, now head of the navy's bureau of inspection. They were periodically joined by Charles Dana, editor of the *New York Sun,* and they could rely from afar on John Hay, the U.S. envoy to London and future secretary of state. They lunched or dined regularly under the splendid chandeliers and imposing portraits of the old Metropolitan Club—today in another building but still a gathering place for the capital's elite. Respectable gentlemen, they would have bristled at the word, but they were conspirators.

Cuba was a priority. Spain's war against the rebels there resembled its fight against the Filipino insurgents—with one major difference. Like McKinley, most Americans could not locate the Philippines on a map, nor had they even heard of the archipelago. Cuba, by contrast, was only ninety miles from Florida, and U.S. investments in its sugar and mining industries totaled $50 million. Even more important was American trade with the island, which by 1893 had exceeded $100 million a year—in addition to ancillary profits for shipping, banking and other business interests. The Cuban revolt directly affected American pocketbooks.

The Cuban rebels ran a smooth propaganda machine in the United States under the direction of José Julián Martí y Perez, a Cuban poet and essayist, who had founded the movement in a dingy Manhattan loft in 1892 and organized twenty thousand Cuban émigré lawyers, doctors, journalists and workers in America. Martí rallied U.S. opinion behind his crusade, winning over politicians, business and labor leaders, the press and a large segment of the public with *"¡Cuba libre!"* as his popular slogan. His U.S. sympathizers evoked the Monroe Doctrine, and even though the Cubans were Catholic, several Protestant evangelists assailed the Spanish for insinuating the "papist" peril into the western hemisphere. In 1895, at the age of forty-two, Martí returned to Cuba and was killed in a skirmish with Spanish troops.

The United States ironically contributed to the Cuban revolution in 1895, after Congress imposed a tariff of up to forty percent on sugar imports and knocked the bottom out of the market. The price of sugar, which had been eight cents a pound a few years before, slumped to two cents. Cuban plantations closed and workers, deprived of their jobs, joined the uprising against Spain.

Americans blamed the misery on Spanish repression. Their support for the Cubans soared in 1896, after General Valeriano Weyler y Nicolau, a veteran of the Philippines, arrived in Havana as the Spanish governor. A short, muscular soldier of German origin, he had served as Spanish military attaché in Washington during the Civil War and observed General William Tecumseh Sherman's devastation of Georgia. He brought to Cuba such brutal methods as the *reconcentrado* program, regrouping peasants in camps to deny food and intelligence to the insurgents. Fields fell fallow, and an estimated four hundred thousand perished of famine, earning him the nickname of "Butcher Weyler." Lurid accounts of his measures reached the United States through newspapers like William Randolph Hearst's *New York Journal,* which referred to him as a "fiendish despot" and an "exterminator of men." The paper's editorial writer declaimed: "There is nothing to prevent his carnal animal brain from running riot with itself in inventing tortures and infamies of bloody debauchery."

Republican party imperialists passionately denounced Spain, and the Democrats followed, fearful of forfeiting a a potentially popular issue. In April 1896,

Congress passed a bipartisan resolution urging President Cleveland to press Spain to relinquish Cuba. The vote, while not binding, posed a dilemma for Cleveland. He was no coward. A year earlier, he had faced down Britain over a boundary dispute between its South American colony of Guiana and Venezuela, asserting that the western hemisphere was a U.S. sphere of influence. But now he recoiled from the hysterical demands of war with Spain. He and his secretary of state, Richard Olney, recommended as a compromise that Spain grant limited autonomy to Cuba while retaining sovereignty over the island.

The proposal went nowhere. The conservative Spanish prime minister, Antonio Cánovas del Castillo, afraid to alienate his army, spurned it. Republican expansionists also refused to lose a hot political issue. Henry Cabot Lodge exaggerated the the economic benefits of Cuban independence to ludicrous extremes. "The splendid little island," he said, was "one of the richest spots on the face of the earth," predicting that "free Cuba would mean a great market for the United States [and] an opportunity for American capital."

Roosevelt, impatient with "mere money-getters," was unmoved by Cuba's purported economic value. He championed U.S. intervention "to retain our self-respect as a nation." America could no longer abide the "hideous welter of misery" that Spain had laid "at our doorstep." But he really wanted a war that would lift the United States into the ranks of the world powers. "In strict confidence," he told a friend, "I should welcome any war, for I think this country needs one."

No sooner did he reach Washington than Roosevelt began to worry his boss, Secretary of the Navy John Long, who noted with some trepidation in his diary that Roosevelt "will dominate the department within six months." The forecast proved to be short of the mark. Roosevelt, going to work with whirlwind speed, handed Long an ambitious timetable for doubling the size of the navy to make it second only to the British fleet, arguing that a powerful force was "the cheapest kind of insurance" against war. Long, at first flabbergasted by his assistant's aggressiveness, eventually agreed to request some new ships. On his own initiative, Roosevelt had meanwhile ordered a complete renovation and consolidation of the navy's war plans.

Various plans had been drafted during Cleveland's term, one more complex than the other. They ranged from a naval blockade of Cuba to a direct threat against Spain. One proposed that a small American squadron "capture and reduce" Manila and seize the trade lanes to Cebu and Iloilo to enable the United States to press for an indemnity from Spain. The various schemes so confused Long's predecessor, Hillary A. Herbert, that he buried them in the files, where they lay when Long and Roosevelt took over the department.

Long invariably retreated to cool New England at the first whiff of Washington's summer heat. Roosevelt, left in charge, supervised his own study during June 1897. It bore the imprint of Mahan's global thinking. In the event of a Caribbean war with Spain, the U.S. Navy would encircle Cuba as a small American infantry force landed on the island. The U.S. naval squadron in Asia would meanwhile "show itself in the neighborhood of the Philippines"—possibly attacking Manila "for the purpose of further engaging the attention of the Spanish navy" and also "to improve our position when the time comes for negotiations with a view to peace."

Roosevelt omitted any mention of a permanent American occupation of

Cuba following the defeat of Spain, but he hinted at a different scenario for the Philippines. There, he said, "we could probably have a controlling voice when a final settlement was made" with the Filipino rebels. What he meant is unclear. At that stage, however, he was almost certainly not considering the acquisition of the archipelago. He was enthused only by the prospect of fighting on both sides of the world, and he awaited approval for his ambitious plan from McKinley, who observed events apprehensively.

On a balmy fall evening in 1897, McKinley invited him to dinner at the White House, then proposed a carriage ride around Washington. Roosevelt, garrulous as usual, rambled on about global strategy, his staccato voice counterpointing the clip-clop of the horses' hooves. A war with Spain, he assured McKinley, would not last more than six weeks. The president, still hoping for peace, listened mutely. But Roosevelt did not hear the silence. Certain that McKinley would ultimately acquiesce, he was already contemplating his next move.

The commander of the Asiatic squadron was due to retire soon, and Roosevelt wanted a man responsive to his dictates. The short list comprised two candidates, Commodore John A. Howell and George Dewey.

Howell was a corpulent veteran with bushy burnsides who then commanded the Philadelphia navy yard. He was unpopular with his fellow officers, but much else favored him. A recognized ordnance expert, he had invented a new torpedo. He was also senior to Dewey and had the blessing of a top member of the Senate naval affairs committee and former secretary of the navy, William E. Chandler of New Hampshire, to whose son Howell had promised a staff position if the job materialized. Roosevelt, however, considered him weak, indecisive and unfriendly. Now he faced the challenge, as a lowly assistant secretary, of securing Dewey's appointment over the influence of a powerful politician.

The son of a prosperous Vermont physician and insurance company executive, Dewey was a trim little widower of sixty with silvery hair and matching mustache, his vanity a clue to his exaggerated sense of self-importance. Forever on parade, he would strut about in an immaculate uniform and polished boots, especially at the Metropolitan Club, where over lunch and dinner he could pompously discuss the issues of the day with cabinet members, congressmen, diplomats and other dignitaries. He did not equal truly creative officers like Mahan, yet he was neither better nor worse than his rival, John Howell. He had last heard the sound of serious gunfire more than thirty-five years earlier, when he fought in the Civil War under Farragut, his hero. Since then, except for a brief tour at sea, he had been beached at desks, including his present assignment as the navy's chief inspector—jobs that he performed competently. But he was patient, recalling that Farragut did not achieve distinction until the age of sixty-one. Like every officer at the time, yearning to rise from obscurity, he also knew the story of Ulysses S. Grant, who in 1860 was still working in his father's leather store in Galena, Illinois.

Roosevelt admired his vigor. Dewey had lobbied Congress for fresh funds for coal to keep the navy's ships on the alert and had pushed for equipping them with such modern devices as electric searchlights and internal telephones. Roosevelt also appreciated Dewey's expansionist leanings. He figured as well that Dewey, if chosen, would be eternally indebted to him—thus easy to manipulate.

Long, perennially away from Washington, had decided to extend his vacation until the end of September 1897. One morning during his absence, Roosevelt intercepted a letter to him from Senator Chandler, recommending Howell. A day before Long's return, Roosevelt sent an urgent message to Chandler. He bluntly criticized Howell as "irresolute and . . . extremely afraid of responsibility" and implied that Chandler would do well to change his mind. Chandler remained steadfast. Roosevelt thereupon summoned Dewey, advising him to recruit a senator to plead his case. Though the impropriety of patronage disturbed Dewey, after some prodding he suggested Redfield Proctor of Vermont, a family friend and solid Republican close to McKinley. Delighted to help, Proctor drove that very afternoon from Capitol Hill to the White House, where McKinley, unaware of Howell's candidacy, cheerfully accommodated his request. Long came back to learn of Roosevelt's ruse. Momentarily irritated, he ventilated his annoyance by denying Dewey promotion to rear admiral, the rank that went with the command. But Long, a gentle soul, did not reverse Dewey's appointment. Nor could he continue to bear a grudge against Roosevelt, who charged forward, uncontrolled and uncontrollable.

"I am having immense fun running the navy," Roosevelt told a friend, as if he were in charge of the department. He was, in all but title. Indefatigable, he labored around the clock, purchasing new weapons, procuring ammunition, ordering coal, reassigning ship captains and crews, recruiting men and reviewing deployments. He created one board to modernize navy yards and another to shred bureaucratic red tape. The docile Long, dazed by his deputy's zeal, watched helplessly, almost regretting that he had unshackled a "bull in a china shop," as he confided to his diary. There was a method in Roosevelt's apparent mania, however. Mixing his metaphors, he feared "difficulties . . . if we drift into war butt end forward, and go at it higgledy-piggledy fashion."

The bombastic Roosevelt often used words imprecisely. But *drift* aptly described America's advance toward war.

★ ★ ★

William McKinley was "one of the most enigmatic figures ever to occupy the White House," as Ernest R. May of Harvard has observed in *Imperial Democracy.* Little in his personal papers reveals his real sentiments, and his public statements were masterpieces of ambiguity that sound like deliberate satires. Queried on the Cuba issue as early as 1895, for example, he declined "most politely" to reply on the record, further obfuscating his response with: "At this time I do not care to speak about it. In my position it were better that I say nothing now. Perhaps later I may have something to say."

Loyal to the Horatio Alger myth, McKinley esteemed the "robber barons" of the period—men like John D. Rockefeller of Standard Oil, banker J. P. Morgan and Pennsylvania Railroad boss Frank Thomson. He was also grateful to them as financiers of the Republican party, who bought and sold politicians as effectively as they dealt in coal and steel. Cool to overseas ventures that might stunt domestic development, they communicated their caution to McKinley through Mark Hanna, a major industrialist who shared their reservations. McKinley, mindful of their concerns, would either repeat his desire to avert war or, more often, simply avoid the subject.

But the U.S. business community was no more a monolith then than it is today, and some of its members championed a war against the Spanish in Cuba to advance their interests. The sugar bloc, understandably anxious to retrieve its investments on the island, clamored for intervention through Republican surrogates like Senator Nelson Aldrich of Rhode Island. McKinley tried to fend them off with patronage. He had reluctantly appointed Roosevelt to assuage Henry Cabot Lodge, and distributed lesser federal jobs to quiet other jingoists. To deflect the expansionists, he also endorsed the Hawaii annexation treaty shelved by Cleveland, knowing that it could not win Senate approval. Appeasement worked—for a while. Roosevelt, who lusted for "firm action," admitted to Lodge that McKinley had "done so much that I don't feel like being discontented."

McKinley's game, insofar as he operated on more than sheer instinct, was to buy the time to resolve the Cuban dilemma peacefully. But the longer he stalled, the greater the clamor for war grew.

Despite his unfamiliarity with foreign affairs, he realized that the path to a Cuban compromise passed through Madrid. Dealing with Spain, however, was a formidable task. Cuba and Puerto Rico were the last vestiges of Spain's lost American empire. And despite their cost to the bankrupt Spanish government, they represented a symbol of past grandeur that rival political factions in Madrid could evoke in their arcane struggles for power.

María Cristina, the queen regent, was a solemn Austrian widow who had married the late king two decades earlier. Her only concern was to preserve the throne for the heir, twelve-year-old Alfonso XIII. The liberals seized on the Cuban issue to menace the crown. Concessions, they figured, would enfeeble the monarchy, and eventually lead to a restoration of the republic that had ruled briefly twenty years before. She feared them no less than she did the ultraconservative Carlists, partisans of the pretender Don Carlos, her husband's brother. The Carlists were looking for the slightest hint of weakness on Cuba as a pretext to replace the queen regent with a more reactionary regime. Other groups were also jockeying for power, and into this tangle McKinley sent an envoy, Stewart L. Woodford, a judicious Brooklyn lawyer of sixty-two. A former lieutenant governor of New York and Civil War general, he accepted the thankless mission after four other men had turned it down.

Woodford arrived in Madrid in September 1897 and, on McKinley's instructions, warned the Spanish that America's patience was wearing out. He offered to mediate an "honorable" settlement, perhaps dominion status for Cuba under Spanish sovereignty, setting a deadline. If Spain failed to reply positively by November, the United States would "take such steps as its government should deem necessary" to safeguard "our interests and the general tranquility." By implication, America would back the Cuban rebel bid for full independence—even at the risk of war.

Antonio Cánovas, the conservative prime minister, had just been assassinated by an anarchist, bringing into office Práxedes Mateo Sagasta, a liberal. Sagasta advocated reforms in Cuba, but national pride prevented him from acceding too openly to Woodford's pressure. Within a month, however, he replaced General Weyler, the "butcher," with General Ramón Blanco y Erenas, who as governor of the Philippines had attempted to ease tensions there. He also pledged to end the harsh *reconcentrado* program, and announced plans for limited Cuban self-government.

Logically, McKinley should have now delivered one of his mellifluous orations claiming that, under divine guidance, he had averted war and advanced the cause of humanity. He also could have exhorted America to focus on its own economy, and lift the nation to greater peaks of prosperity. Such a speech would have checked the imperialists and, if nothing more, given him time to ponder a solution. Instead he juggled. Addressing Congress in early 1898, he sought to soothe the doves by voicing hope for a "righteous peace," and tried to satisfy the hawks by promising action "in the near future" should another crisis develop. As a result, he left both sides with the impression that he supported their view.

The situation, meanwhile, was deteriorating. Sagasta's program provoked protests in both Cuba and Spain. On January 12, 1898, angry Spanish mobs led by soldiers loyal to Weyler streamed into the streets of Havana, breaking shop windows and smashing the presses of liberal newspapers. Weyler had by then returned home to crystallize a motley collection of opposition elements that even included republicans and socialists with grievances against the regime. Woodford, in Madrid, confided his concern to María Cristina. The riots in Havana and plots in Spain, he cautioned, might foil a Cuba settlement. With regal aplomb, she assured him that she could handle matters as long as the United States refrained from helping the Cuban insurgents until Sagasta's reforms had been given a "fair chance." The queen was trapped, Woodford concluded. If Sagasta failed and America intervened, he reported to McKinley, she "will have to choose between losing her throne, or losing Cuba at the risk of a war with us." For the present, he added, the best course was to keep cool. But Fitzhugh Lee, the U.S. consul in Havana, was an amateur who further complicated the muddle.

A burly Virginia politician and nephew of Robert E. Lee, he was a former Confederate cavalry general who had been given the sinecure in Havana by Cleveland as a reward for his loyalty to the Democratic party. Some of Cleveland's aides had opposed the assignment out of fear that, as a southerner, he might antagonize dusky Cubans. However, he soon hated the Spanish and adored the Cuban rebels and became a vigorous proponent of U.S. intervention. Though his passions made him unreliable, McKinley regarded his intelligence to be credible and, despite his Democratic affiliations, commended him as a dedicated American.

Lee had warned McKinley weeks in advance that Spanish agitators were planning riots, advising that a U.S. warship be sent to Havana to protect American lives and property. McKinley met the proposal halfway. He ordered the cruiser *Maine* to Key West, five hours from Cuba, and authorized Lee to summon the ship in case of danger. But Lee panicked when the eruption actually occurred. First he telegraphed Captain Charles D. Sigsbee, the *Maine*'s skipper, urging him to come. When the unrest quickly subsided, Lee was uncertain what to do. Finally he asked the Navy Department in Washington to decide. Officials there, however, had no information except distorted tales of horror from newspaper correspondents in Havana.

Roosevelt, uninterested in the truth, exploded. Though his wife was critically ill, he volunteered to fight in Cuba with the New York National Guard.

He pressed Long for more men, ammunition and coal and outlined new naval deployments in the Caribbean, Asia and off Spain. "When the war comes," he told him in a marathon memorandum, "it should come finally on our initiative, and after we have had time to prepare." Long wearily noted in his diary that Roosevelt was a "crank" who "bores me with plans of naval and military movement" and "emergency" attack schemes. Even so, swayed by Roosevelt's frenzy, Long advised McKinley to send the *Maine* to Havana.

As usual, McKinley waffled. He refused to concede to the warmongers, but the Havana riots evoked in him the ghastly vision of Americans being slaughtered by Spanish gangs. The same specter haunted Congress, where both parties had until then shown restraint in deference to the president. Now, however, they were veering toward a debate on Cuba—a prospect that rattled McKinley. As a veteran of Capitol Hill, he knew that a debate could quickly degenerate into demagoguery, thereby usurping his initiative. Perhaps, by putting the *Maine* in Havana, he might defuse the extremists. He endorsed Long's proposal to send the vessel there on a "courtesy" trip. The United States and Spain, after all, were still seeking peace in Cuba.

State Department officials formally requested Spain's permission for the visit through Enrique Dupuy de Lôme, the Spanish envoy in Washington. After consulting Madrid, he told the assistant secretary, Judge William Rufus Day, that the voyage had been approved as a "gesture of friendship"—but he frostily cautioned against "provocative" American moves. McKinley ordered the *Maine* to depart immediately.

At nine o'clock on the morning of January 25, 1898, the ship steamed into Havana harbor. Over the next three weeks, Spanish officials treated its officers with courtesy, inviting them to a reception and a bullfight. Senator Lodge, back on Capitol Hill, casually dropped a portentous remark. "There may be an explosion any day in Cuba," he said, that would "settle many things."

McKinley, pleased that tensions had abated, fêted Dupuy de Lôme at his administration's first diplomatic dinner. The Spanish envoy, his uniform sparkling with gold braid and decorations, was given precedence over nine senior confreres and seated in the company of the British, French and German ambassadors. When the ladies retired, the president invited him to his own table for coffee and cigars. The guests were impressed by the honor accorded the Spaniard, who must have been touched by McKinley's solicitude. But the crisis was about to be rekindled.

Dupuy de Lôme, a blue-blooded conservative with a sad fleshy face, had served in Washington for three years. He had stuck to his post despite an aversion to the liberal Sagasta cabinet, which he disdained for buckling to U.S. demands to introduce reforms in Cuba. Even more, he loathed the uncouth American yokels and their tirades against Spain. He particularly despised McKinley, who to him embodied the lowest democratic denominator. Committing an unpardonable sin for a career diplomat, he put his opinions on paper in a personal letter to a Spanish friend in Havana.

The letter, purloined by a Cuban agent, made its way to the offices of Hearst's *New York Journal.* On February 9—with the *Maine* sitting in Havana harbor—the text appeared in translation on the front page, under the sensational headline WORST INSULT TO THE UNITED STATES IN ITS HISTORY. Dupuy de Lôme had maligned McKinley as "weak and a bidder for the admiration of the rabble . . . a cheap politician who leaves the door open behind himself while keeping on good terms with the jingoes of his party." He also disclosed in the letter that his own conciliatory posture was merely a pose. What he needed, he wrote, was more help to lobby "senators and others" against the Cuban rebels.

Dupuy de Lôme promptly resigned and left town. The Spanish government apologized for the breach of etiquette—and that should have ended the episode. Played up in newspapers across America, however, the letter refueled the flames of patriotic indignation. Hearst's *Journal,* milking its scoop to the last drop, flayed the unfortunate Dupuy de Lôme on the front page for five days in a row—one issue featuring a huge cartoon of a furious Uncle Sam ordering him out of the country, its caption reading NOW LET US HAVE ACTION IMMEDIATE AND DECISIVE.

McKinley felt the heat rising inside the Republican party, whose jingoists began to criticize his moderation. The Republican League massively voted for official U.S. recognition of the Cuban insurgents. Both chambers of Congress passed resolutions calling for publication of the American consular reports in Cuba, which detailed Spanish brutality and Cuban suffering and would set U.S. opinion ablaze. Then came a real conflagration.

At nine-forty on the night of February 15, in Havana harbor, a sudden explosion ripped through the forecastle of the *Maine,* killing two hundred and fifty-four men instantly. Another eight, crushed or burned, died in hospitals during the days that followed. The hull of the ship sank into the mud, forty feet down, its torn and charred superstructure protruding through the water like a tombstone.

"Dirty treachery on the part of the Spaniards," shouted Roosevelt, and the yellow press echoed the cry, Hearst in the forefront. Hearst, who displayed a portrait of Napoleon over his desk, had been lusting for war for a year. He had sent the celebrated artist Frederic Remington to Cuba six months before to illustrate the conflict. When Remington reported, "There will be no war," and asked to come home, Hearst wired his famous reply PLEASE REMAIN. YOU FURNISH THE PICTURES AND I'LL FURNISH THE WAR. Hearst, now vindicated, told his editors that, finally, "this means war." The *Journal* ran a "scientific" study of the alleged Spanish sabotage to show, as its headline declared: DESTRUCTION OF THE WARSHIP MAINE WAS THE WORK OF AN ENEMY. The newspaper featured reheated versions for weeks, along with editorials deriding McKinley's caution. Joseph Pulitzer's rival *New York World* also prized the story, selling a record five million copies in a week.

The *Maine* debacle, despite historical legend, was not a Pearl Harbor that thrust America into war overnight. Seven weeks were to pass before the outbreak of hostilities. The conflict might have been prevented had domestic pressures both in the United States and Spain given diplomacy a chance.

Dismayed, María Cristina and her prime minister moved swiftly to deflect the invective they expected against Spain. They sent messages of regrets and sympathy to McKinley and ordered General Blanco, their man in Havana, to "gather every fact" to prove that the incident "cannot be attributed to us." At the same time, in the United States, several distinguished business and church figures called for calm. Myron T. Herrick, the Cleveland industrialist, told McKinley that he detected no excitement over the *Maine* in his city, and the

Omaha railroad lawyer Charles F. Manderson seconded the view. An Episcopalian minister in Washington decried the "wild clamor for blood, blood, blood," while Congregationalist, Methodist, Baptist and Jewish clergymen delivered similar sermons in other cities. The excesses of the yellow press incensed even many proexpansionist newspapers. Whitelaw Reid, publisher of the *New York Tribune* and an avowed imperialist, speculated that the catastrophe could be "a blessing in disguise" that "might sober up . . . our jingoes a little."

McKinley reacted with restraint. "I don't propose to be swept off my feet. . . . The country can afford to withhold its judgment and not strike an avenging blow until the truth is known. The administration will go on preparing for war, but hoping to avert it." Secretary of the Navy Long commented privately that he believed the Spanish to be innocent.

But the public outcry for reprisals against Spain intensified. Protestant fundamentalists stoked "antipapist" fervor in small towns and farm areas, accusing Catholics of being secretly sympathetic to the Spanish. A Missourian reported from his state that "patriotism is oozing out of every boy who is old enough to pack feed to the pigs," and a Nevada editor wrote that "the clamor for war is heard everywhere . . . without a well-defined idea of the why or wherefor." *The Washington Post* summed up the national mood in an editorial: "A new consciousness seems to have come upon us—the consciousness of strength—and with it a new appetite, the yearning to show our . . . ambition, interest, land hunger, pride, the mere joy of fighting, whatever it may be, we are animated by a new sensation. . . . The taste of empire is in the mouth of the people even as the taste of blood in the jungle. It means an imperial policy."

McKinley continued to temporize. Late in February, he hinted that he might settle for a large cash indemnity from the Spanish if they proved to be at fault for the *Maine* calamity. When Congress rebuffed the idea, he suggested buying Cuba for, say, $300 million. Again Congress spurned him. So did the Spanish queen, who vowed to abdicate rather than sell the island. McKinley then floated another plan. Spain could retain nominal sovereignty over Cuba, with the Cubans ruling themselves under U.S. guidance. That notion also foundered, and now he was confronted by a growing domestic political challenge.

With congressional elections scheduled for the fall, many Democrats sensed that throwing down the gauntlet to Spain was a way to win votes. Their standard bearer, William Jennings Bryan, who until then had been silent, declared that "the time for intervention has arrived." The Populists, who had backed him for president in 1896, swelled the prowar chorus. Their party largely represented discontented farmers who blamed their woes, in part at least, on British and other foreign creditors. Only vaguely aware of world affairs, they saw a blow against Spain as a blow against Europe.

Soon McKinley became a target of the mounting delirium. He was hanged in effigy in Colorado, audiences booed his portrait in New York theaters and many of the businessmen who favored peace began to waver. His political counselors, fearing disaster at the polls, pressed him to act tough—or else, as Lodge said, "We shall go down in the greatest defeat ever known." Elihu Root, the eminent New York lawyer, rang the same alarm. "If the administration does not . . . lead instead of being pushed," he wrote to Roosevelt, "it will be rolled over and crushed, and the Republican party with it."

McKinley knew by late winter that the official inquiry into the *Maine* explosion would indict Spain. Expecting a howl from the warmongers, he devised a tactic to avert the worst. On March 6, he astounded the members of the House of Representatives Appropriations Committee by requesting $50 million in military funds. Despite his efforts to avoid war, he said, "it must come and we are not prepared," and he needed the funds to "get ready." The request, he hoped, would quiet the hawks in Washington, while scaring the Spanish into granting broad concessions to the Cubans. The so-called fifty-million bill passed unanimously, but his maneuver went awry.

The warmongers now reckoned that McKinley would finally fight—a premature assumption that delighted nobody more than Roosevelt. On March 26, Roosevelt addressed the annual banquet of the Gridiron Club, the peerage of the Washington press corps. Facing the hall foggy with cigar smoke, he clenched his fist and bared his teeth as his raspy voice rose in a feverish crescendo. "We will have this war for the freedom of Cuba despite the timidity of the business world and of financiers." The wild applause flushed him with renewed confidence. He looked along the dais to Mark Hanna, one of the last holdouts for peace, taunting him: "Now, senator, may we please have war?"

A research team headed by Rear Admiral Hyman G. Rickover concluded in 1976 that the explosion aboard the *Maine* had been caused by a spontaneous fire in a coal bunker next to a reserve magazine—a frequent mishap aboard steam-driven warships of the period. So the explosion could have occurred elsewhere than Havana. Many experts at the time, including the *Maine*'s skipper, Captain Sigsbee, suspected something of the sort. But a U.S. Navy board of inquiry rushed to judgment despite slim evidence, and blamed an external device, presumably a submerged mine, obviously Spanish. The verdict, published late in March, set Americans to waving flags and a new ditty:

> Remember the *Maine*!
> To hell with Spain!

McKinley sought to muffle the panel's findings in yet another attempt to avert war. Figuring that only swift concessions by the Spanish could prevent U.S. intervention, he sent them an ultimatum demanding an armistice in Cuba and an end to the *reconcentrado* program—scheduling March 31, forty-eight hours away, as the deadline for a reply.

McKinley's ultimatum put Spain in the quandary that General Woodford, the perceptive U.S. envoy in Madrid, had foreseen. Queen María Cristina and her cabinet now realized that, should war with America break out, Spain was sure to be beaten by a superior U.S. force. The chief of the Spanish navy, Rear Admiral Pascual Cervera y Topete, bore no illusions on that score. A conflict with the Americans, he noted privately, "would be disastrous . . . since we are reduced, absolutely penniless, and they are rich." But as much as the prospect of a humiliating defeat appalled them, the queen and her advisers knew that compromise would almost certainly expose her regime to retribution from its domestic opponents. Their only alternative, therefore, was conciliation that did not seem to be submission. To make it work at that late stage—if it could work at all—would require skill and subtlety, both in Madrid and in Washington.

The Spanish tried to retain the initiative to appear as if they were not acting under pressure. They had halted the *reconcentrado* program even before receiving McKinley's ultimatum. But pride, protocol and politics prevented them from agreeing to a truce until the Cuban rebels declared a cease-fire first. With lives hanging in the balance, the issue seemed absurdly trivial, even arrogant. Woodford understood the Spanish despite his short sojourn in Madrid. Their recalcitrance, he explained in a cable to Washington, was a "question of punctilio" integral to their code of conduct. With patience, they could be brought around.

The Spanish foreign minister, Pio Gullón, implored him to "indulge us" until summer, when the rainy season in Cuba would halt hostilities naturally—thus sparing Spain the ignominy of proffering peace to the insurgents. María Cristina, desperate to save her dynasty, appealed in vain for help from her cousin, Queen Victoria, and various European luminaries pondered solutions, among them Pope Leo XIII. These efforts buoyed McKinley, but he could not resist the hawks, who were now bent on war. To placate them, he stiffened his ultimatum. As a precondition to a settlement, Spain would have to pledge Cuba "full self-government, with reasonable indemnity"—in short, total independence.

McKinley was near to cracking under the strain. Haggard and jumpy, his face had become lined and his eyes sunken, and he had taken to sedatives. He would recall to rare visitors his memories of the Civil War, stressing his determination to prevent the recurrence of such horror. One evening in late March, he slipped away from a White House concert with an old friend, Chicago newspaper proprietor H. H. Kohlsaat. They retired to a parlor, where McKinley burst into tears as he poured out his troubles: his wife's failing health, his sleepless nights, his fear of war. After the cathartic confession he checked himself; he could not afford to collapse in this crisis.

In early April, he resorted to another maneuver, requesting Congress to authorize "neutral" American intervention in Cuba to stop the fighting. With that vague mandate, he figured, he could deflect the warmongers and thereby regain control of the situation. Other presidents have used the same ploy for similar aims. In August 1964, Lyndon Johnson asked Congress for the power to commit U.S. forces to Southeast Asia—his objective at the time being to deflate Barry Goldwater, his hawkish rival in that year's presidential campaign, who was accusing him of weakness.

McKinley's resolution was set to go to Congress on April 6, and crowds jammed the Capitol corridors and galleries in anticipation. At the last minute, however, he deferred its delivery—partly to evacuate Americans from Cuba, and also to give diplomacy a reprieve. Woodford had cabled from Madrid that the Spanish had declared an armistice in Cuba; he cautioned against humiliating them at a time when they were going "as fast and far" as they could. There was one hitch. They had not agreed to McKinley's demand that they pledge independence to the island. Woodford again urged patience. At the present pace of events, he forecast, Cuba would be free by August. McKinley stalled. Fuming with frustration, Roosevelt declared: "McKinley has no more backbone than a chocolate eclair."

McKinley would have preferred to keep stalling. But he knew that he could not plausibly persuade Congress, now on a war binge, to accept Woodford's uncertain forecast. On Monday, April 11, he sent his resolution to Capitol Hill.

He proposed U.S. support neither for the Cuban rebels nor for their claim to independence. He simply asked Congress to permit him "to take measures to secure a full and final termination of the hostilities" on the island, along with the power to deploy U.S. ground and naval forces "as may be necessary." The ambiguous request, he reckoned, would leave the door ajar for peace.

During that era of white Protestant supremacy, the two legislative chambers could not conceive of granting U.S. citizenship to Cubans, most of them Catholic and many partly Negro. Nor did they want to convey the impression that America crassly sought territory. Hence they passed an amendment, introduced by Senator Henry M. Teller of Colorado, disavowing any intent to annex Cuba. Then they proceeded to emasculate McKinley's text. They endorsed the Cuban rebel claim to independence and demanded an end to Spanish rule of the island, directing McKinley to use the U.S. armed forces to fulfill those goals. McKinley signed it into law. By ceding his initiative to the legislature, he had abdicated his executive authority. But he was relieved to have had the burden lifted from his shoulders.

CONSIDER WAR AS DECLARED, Madrid cabled General Blanco in Havana. The American fleet in the Atlantic steamed south to blockade Cuba as McKinley appealed for 125,000 volunteers. Roosevelt, commissioned a lieutenant colonel, rushed off as deputy to Colonel Leonard Wood, commander of the First U.S. Volunteer Cavalry—known then and since as Roosevelt's Rough Riders.

The House of Representatives, a faithful barometer of public opinion, had voted massively for war. But the Senate, a more autonomous body, passed the resolution by a margin of only seven votes, and it continued, in the months ahead, to be sharply divided over the issue of America's world role. The Senate split suggested that, with courage, McKinley might have preserved peace. Instead of attempting to guide events, however, he allowed events to sweep him away. "I think, possibly, the president could have worked out the business without war," said Senator John Spooner of Wisconsin, a loyal Republican, "but the current was too strong, the demagogues too numerous, the fall elections too near." A year later, McKinley noted that he could have avoided war had he been "left alone."

It was the only time in history that Congress voted for war without a direct request from the president. Since then, as in Korea, Vietnam and smaller engagements, presidents have steered the nation into military actions overseas without the specific consent of the legislature—even without its knowledge, as in the case of Richard Nixon's secret bombing of Cambodia after 1969. The McKinley period, in contrast to the so-called imperial presidency of recent decades, was a low point of executive influence. Bowing to a mindless public, McKinley reluctantly led America into a conflict that, as Ernest May has put it, "he did not want for a cause in which he did not believe."

★ ★ ★

Rescued from the scrap heap by admirers, the *Olympia* is now berthed at a Philadelphia pier. A quaint naval shrine, it resembles a large private yacht alongside today's gargantuan battlewagons. But at its launching in 1895, it was one of America's most powerful vessels—a swift cruiser of more than five thousand tons, the emblem of the Stars and Stripes proudly emblazoned on its prow. Steel plating clad its hull, and it bristled with such modern weapons as torpedo tubes, six-pounder rapid-firing cannons and guns ranging in size from five to eight inches set in barbettes and turrets. Especially designed to be the flagship of the Asiatic squadron, it rode at anchor in the Japanese port of Nagasaki on New Year's Day of 1898 as Commodore George Dewey, the squadron's new commander, was piped aboard.

Dewey's small force was stretched thin along the vast rim of Asia, its principal function to protect Americans. He had only two cruisers, the *Olympia* and the *Boston,* and awaited three others. American power in the area was insignificant compared to that of the British, French, Russians, Germans and Japanese, who were grabbing territory from Manchuria in the north to Vietnam in the south. Dewey, expecting them to devour each other out of imperialistic greed, wrote to his son: "Things look decidedly squally out here, and I should not be surprised to see a general war at any time."

But the only potential conflict that then preoccupied Washington was the one that loomed between the United States and Spain. Dewey was familiar with the navy's secret plan: His assignment in the event of such a war was to "show" his squadron "in the neighborhood of the Philippines . . . for the purpose of further engaging the attention" of the Spanish in a diversion to the action in Cuba. As he prepared for that contingency, one of his greatest needs was intelligence.

When McKinley vaguely located the Philippines as a place "somewhere away around on the other side of the world," he might have been speaking for most Americans. A few U.S. officials based abroad tried to track events there, but their information was fuzzy. The American naval attaché in Madrid, appointed to the post the year before, monitored the Spanish fleet in the Pacific, half a world away, by scanning the newspapers and picking up gossip at parties. Rounsevelle Wildman, the U.S. consul in Hong Kong, kept in touch with Emilio Aguinaldo, the Filipino insurgent leader then in the British colony. Dewey's most credible source was Oscar Williams, the elderly Ohio professor whom McKinley had agreeably named American consul in Manila as a favor to Senator Joseph Foraker. Though Williams tended to let his opinions color the facts, he worked hard. After arriving in January 1898, he established contacts with Spanish officials and formed a network of Filipino agents to gather details on Manila's defenses. He also observed the growth of the Filipino rebel movement. The insurgents were being armed and trained; they were becoming more efficient and might soon rise up, "Conditions here and in Cuba are practically alike," Williams concluded. "War exists, and battles are of almost daily occurrence."

Anticipating action in the Philippines, Dewey sailed the *Olympia* to Hong Kong to be closer to the scene, leaving the rest of his fleet scattered along the Asia coast. But on February 25, ten days after the *Maine* calamity, he received new instructions from Washington.

Secretary of the Navy Long had walked out of his office early that day to visit an osteopath who was treating him for pains aggravated by insomnia— possibly the result of nervous tension. Hardly had he departed than Roosevelt went into one of his gyrations. Directing U.S. Navy commanders around the world to stock fuel and ammunition, he designated rendezvous points in the event of war. He asked Congress to authorize him to recruit more men, and he cabled Dewey to assemble his ships in Hong Kong promptly: IN THE EVENT OF DECLARATION OF WAR WITH SPAIN, YOUR DUTY WILL BE TO SEE THAT THE SPANISH SQUADRON DOES NOT LEAVE THE ASIATIC COAST, AND THEN OFFENSIVE OPERATIONS IN THE PHILIPPINE ISLANDS. That, Dewey later recalled, was America's "first step" toward the Philippines.

The next day, back at work, Long was stupefied. "The very devil seemed to possess him yesterday afternoon," he wrote of Roosevelt in his diary. But he did not rescind Roosevelt's initiatives, and only rebuked him mildly. "I am not away from town," he said, "and my intention was to have you look after the routine of the office while I got a day off." Henceforth, Long added, Roosevelt was not to make any moves "affecting the policy of the administration without consulting the president or me."

Long's real concern was that the newspapers might learn of Roosevelt's war preparations—and, he noted fretfully, cause a "sensation" that would rush events. But neither he nor McKinley could control Roosevelt. Nor, by now, could they control events, which were hurtling America into war.

By early March, most of Dewey's squadron had gathered in Hong Kong's harbor—then, as today, a spectacular jumble of sampans and junks and freighters flying the ensigns of a dozen nations. Dewey commandeered the *McCulloch,* a U.S. revenue cutter fortuitously there on a shakedown cruise. He also bought a British collier and a small freighter, and registered them both as unarmed American merchantmen—a device to permit their entry into neutral ports in time of conflict. Dry-docking all the vessels, he had them scraped and repainted from peacetime white to drab gray, the color of war.

Oscar Williams had meanwhile taken to espionage with exuberance. Eluding Spanish surveillance, he deluged Dewey with information: The Filipino rebels, despite shortages of guns and ammunition, were growing "stronger than ever" as native auxiliaries serving in the Spanish army defected to their ranks. The Spanish defenses in Manila were "too antiquated to merit consideration in modern war," and he suggested that a bastion at the mouth of the Pasig River could be demolished with "one shot." The coastal artillery was fully manned, if short of shells, while the Spanish warships seemed to be adequately supplied. But most useful to Dewey was the intelligence that the channels into Manila Bay, as well as the bay itself, were "both free from mines and torpedoes."

Security in Washington was notably lax, and Spain's naval attaché had advised his government as early as January 1898 that America's secret war plans included an offensive against the Philippines. But the Spanish navy, though forewarned, nevertheless faced a grave problem.

Its experts had concluded long before that Manila Bay was undefendable. A superior enemy fleet could easily enter the broad body of water and destroy its shore batteries. The alternative was for Spain's ships to retire to Subic Bay, a narrow harbor about thirty miles to the north. There they would be safer from assault yet able to counterattack. But Subic was poorly fortified, since Spanish naval officers preferred the social life of Manila to dreary isolation in the boondocks. Only after the sinking of the *Maine* augured war did they abruptly awake to the need for action. By then, however, the lethargic Spanish bureaucracy could not begin to deliver the guns, mines and other equipment vital to brace Subic. Admiral Patricio Montojo y Pasarón, the Spanish naval commander in Manila, a melancholy-looking man with flaring white mustaches, appealed to Madrid: "I am without resources or time." Show "zeal and activity," he was told.

On April 22, three days after Congress approved its war resolution, the U.S. fleet began to blockade Cuba. McKinley, however, delayed sending Dewey to the Philippines. But Dewey could not stay in Hong Kong as a belligerent, since Britain had declared neutrality. The British governor reluctantly ordered him out of the colony, and Dewey cabled Washington for instructions. Long, with McKinley's approval, responded: PROCEED AT ONCE TO THE PHILIPPINES. COMMENCE OPERATIONS AGAINST THE SPANISH SQUADRON. YOU MUST CAPTURE OR DESTROY. USE UTMOST ENDEAVORS.

As Dewey left for the Philippines, *The New York Times* perceptively observed that the Cuban crisis was expanding to global dimensions. There was a "strange probability," the newspaper wrote, "that the first engagement of a conflict that pertains to the possession of an island off the eastern coast of North America may be fought in the waters of a group of islands off the eastern coast of Asia, half the world away from the origin of the war."

Dewey, never a model of consistency, contemplated the coming clash with contradictory sentiments. "I don't see what we have to gain by a war with Spain," he told his son in one letter while explaining to him in another that a victory in the Philippines would improve America's bargaining posture in eventual peace negotiations. He assured Washington that crushing the Spanish would be "short work for us." But in 1902 he told a different story to a Senate committee reviewing U.S. policy in the Philippines. He had expected to face overwhelming odds, he said: "The enemy's force was unquestionably superior to ours," since the Spanish shore guns could "disable all our ships." In reality, most of the forty Spanish naval vessels in the Manila area were gunboats and other small craft of no consequence.

Like any seasoned commander, Dewey at first opted for prudence until he could assess the situation. Despite orders to "proceed at once" to the Philippines, he sailed to Mirs Bay, an inlet located in Chinese territory a few miles north of Hong Kong, disregarding the fact that China had also asserted its neutrality. His men waited restlessly in the heat and humidity until Oscar Williams arrived from Manila. Dewey had summoned him to get the latest intelligence, and Williams brought disappointing news. The main Spanish fleet had sailed from Manila to Subic Bay. Dewey, recalling the "damn the torpedoes" dictum of his hero, Admiral Farragut, decided to go anyway. As the *Olympia* led the U.S. squadron southeast across the South China Sea, its band serenaded the crew with the tune that became the hit of the war: "There'll Be a Hot Time in the Old Town Tonight!"

Admiral Montojo had moved to Subic Bay despite its deficiencies. Apart from his flagship, the *Reina Cristina,* his armada comprised six vessels, some of which had not seen sea duty in years. The decrepit wooden cruiser *Castilla,* for one, had to be towed after a leak flooded its propeller shaft housing. A glance at Subic's derelict defenses convinced Montojo that he could not fight there. On April 28, as he pondered his alternatives, news from Hong Kong alarmed him. The Spanish consul reported that Dewey was on his way.

In the opinion of naval historians, Montojo should have ranged his ships among the coast's many islands and inlets, from which they could have harried the Americans. But the Spanish governor, General Basilio Augustín Dávila, fearing a U.S. attack against the capital, ordered him back to Manila Bay. To spare the city from becoming a target, however, Montojo aligned his fleet along the Cavite littoral, the southwestern edge of the bay—too far away to benefit from the covering fire of the only modern Spanish shore guns, located on Manila's seaside. Montojo, a compassionate man if hardly a skilled tactician, also saw another advantage in the deployment off Cavite. Its waters were shallow, and his crews could clamber to safety up the masts of their sunken ships in case of defeat.

As Dewey approached, Filipino rebels intensified their attacks against Spanish garrisons near Manila. Augustín, assuming the offensive to be coordinated, panicked. His plight, he cabled Madrid, was "critical." He was "completely defenseless," with "no ships, no forces, no resources to resist two such powerful enemies acting together." Still, he pledged, he would "sternly defend both country and honor." But the government in Madrid, focused on Cuba, ignored him. He issued a stirring call to arms to the Spanish population of the Philippines. "The Americans . . . have exhausted our patience and provoked war with their perfidious machinations, their acts of treachery, their outrages against the law of nations and international conventions. . . . Vain designs! Ridiculous boasts! . . . The aggressors shall not profane the tombs of your fathers, gratify their lustful passions at the cost of your wives and daughters, appropriate the property that our industry has accumulated to provide for your old age. . . . Prepare for the struggle! Let us resist with Christian resolve and the patriotic cry of Viva España!"

At nearly three o'clock in the morning of April 30, Dewey's lookouts spotted the shadowy shape of Luzon island in the distance. Later that day, two of his ships sent out to reconnoiter Subic Bay returned to report it empty. "Now we have them!" exclaimed Dewey. He informed his captains that he would enter Manila Bay that night through Boca Grande, the channel to the south of Corregidor. One officer suggested sending a supply ship ahead of the column to detonate mines in the path. Dewey would have none of it. "I've waited for sixty years for this opportunity. Mines or no mines, I am leading the squadron in myself."

Montojo had increased his flotilla inside the bay to twelve vessels, three more than Dewey possessed. But Dewey was superior in tonnage, firepower and skill. "One of the most remarkable naval battles of the ages," as he later termed it, was opening. It would be a rout.

Shortly after midnight on May 1, the American craft entered Manila Bay after threading through the narrow Boca Grande channel. The Spanish, for some inexplicable reason, failed to fire their heavy guns on Corregidor as the squadron passed the island. Dewey steered his fleet toward Manila, expecting the Spanish vessels to be guarding the city. But suddenly, in the dim light of dawn, he discerned them along the Cavite coast. He switched direction, and headed toward the enemy, himself in the lead.

A Spanish shell burst over the bridge of the Olympia; the crew shouted,

"Remember the *Maine!*"; and Dewey issued his famous order for Gridley to fire when ready. The U.S. ships went into a racetrack pattern, maintaining a slow speed of six knots as they circled Sangley Point, at the tip of Cavite, blasting the Spanish flotilla. Their engine rooms were an inferno, the hissing steam nearly scalding the stokers as they shoveled coal into the furnaces, the ships shaking and vibrating each time their cannons fired. Above, the heat was barely more bearable. The men were stripped to the waist, their torsos slick with sweat and heads wrapped in damp towels. They worked at top speed, flinging shell after shell and charge after charge into the guns. Dewey, pacing the bridge of the *Olympia,* deliberately concealed the strain of battle. This was his rendezvous with immortality.

By seven-thirty in the morning, hardly two hours after the battle began, Montojo had lost his flagship. Dewey withdrew briefly and ordered his men to eat breakfast, a gesture that earned him a reputation for nonchalance. In fact, he had stopped to count his ammunition, having been mistakenly told that it was running low.

The lull lasted for three and a half hours; then the Americans resumed firing. The cruiser *Baltimore* boldly drove into a shower of enemy shells to destroy a Cavite battery. By twelve-thirty, when the Spanish hoisted a white flag, only one of Montojo's ships remained afloat. Their guns in Manila continued sniping for a few hours, then Dewey warned Augustín that he would level the city unless they ceased. The shooting stopped.

Late that afternoon, silhouetted against the spectacular Manila sunset, the U.S. ships steamed closer to the city's waterfront. The *Olympia*'s band played "La Paloma" and other Spanish melodies for the Spaniards, and Filipinos draped over the silent shore guns, curious to see the conquerors. As the music wafted across the harbor, a Spanish artillery colonel, his honor stained by defeat, put a bullet through his head.

Dewey had cut the cable between Manila and Hong Kong to deny its use to the Spanish and could not communicate his victory to Washington. The U.S. press ran various reports from European capitals, but nothing official from Dewey in Manila. As days passed without word from him, Americans nervously began to believe Spanish accounts that the U.S. squadron had sustained "considerable loss of life."

At three o'clock in the morning of May 7, however, the truth interrupted a poker game in the newsroom of the *New York Herald.* It was a dispatch from the newspaper's correspondent, Edwin Harden, reporting a "great American triumph at Manila." Harden had reached Hong Kong aboard the *McCulloch,* which also carried Dewey's account of the battle. Refused the press tariff by the Hong Kong telegraph office, he had filed his story at the commercial rate of $9.90 a word. He scored a beat on the official version, which bureaucrats had encoded, deciphered, checked and double-checked—and which arrived in Washington five hours later.

McKinley, jubilant, turned to a map to locate the Philippines, later confessing to a friend that he "could not have told where those darned islands were within two thousand miles." But five days before, he had assigned Major General Wesley Merritt to lead a U.S. army expedition there, reckoning that

Dewey, whose circumstances were then unknown, would need additional men and ships. Merritt posed a logical question as he accepted the command. Did McKinley intend "to subdue and hold all of the Spanish territory in the islands, or merely to seize and hold the capital?"

At that stage, McKinley had no idea.

5. IMPERIAL DEMOCRACY

★ ★ ★

The American public euphorically assumed that Commodore George Dewey's victory had shattered Spain's rule in the Philippines. But despite their defeat at sea, the Spanish still held Manila as a growing Filipino insurgency spread throughout the islands. The United States stumbled into a long, difficult and divisive ordeal, both in the archipelago and at home. Later regretting the involvement, President McKinley confided to a friend: "If old Dewey had just sailed away when he smashed that Spanish fleet, what a lot of trouble he would have saved us."

In the wake of his triumph, however, Dewey was supremely confident. He reported to Washington that he dominated Manila Bay and controlled the Spanish naval base at Cavite. With five thousand men, he said, he could seize and hold Manila "at any time." Oscar Williams, the U.S. consul who had returned with the American fleet, promised that the Filipino rebels would help. After going ashore to consult their leaders, he informed Dewey that thirty thousand insurgents would "cheerfully follow our flag" in an offensive against the ten thousand Spanish troops defending Manila. The Filipinos, he said, were "brave, submissive and cheaply provided for," and in concert with a U.S. force they could wipe out the Spanish "in a day."

The Philippines was *terra incognita* to Major General Wesley Merritt, whom McKinley had already chosen to command the U.S. Army there. His maps of the archipelago were obsolete and rudimentary. He had no idea if he could procure adequate food and water, if horses were available or if the terrain suited his artillery. His knowledge of health conditions in the islands was sketchy, except that he had heard that diseases there included malaria and leprosy. He was vaguely aware that the climate could be oppressively hot and humid. And apart from the few details collected by Williams, he lacked intelligence on the strength and deployment of the Spanish forces. But worst of all, America's soldiers were unprepared to fight, in the Philippines or anywhere else, as the United States poised for the first overseas war in its history.

The navy had been modernized and strengthened, thanks to Mahan, Roosevelt and others. But the army's 2,000 officers and 26,000 men had experienced combat only in skirmishes with Indians. McKinley appealed for 125,000 volunteers, but organizing them augured nightmarish training, supply and transportation problems. The War Department was a bloated bureaucracy that, with little else to do during the decades of peace since the Civil War, spent much of its time in internecine rivalries. Russell Alger, the secretary of war, set the tone. Bored and ailing, he devoted his feeble energies to hectoring Major General Nelson Appleton Miles, the army chief, who in turn took a perverse pleasure in conniving against his colleagues. Miles was now squabbling with Merritt over the scope of the war to be waged against Spain, and their quarrel baffled the already befuddled McKinley.

A handsome New Englander of sixty-two, Miles, with his silver mustache and chestful of decorations, looked every inch the "brave peacock," as Roosevelt had dubbed him. He had been a fine soldier during the Civil War, when he earned the Congressional Medal of Honor. He later won distinction as an Indian fighter, capturing Chief Joseph and his Nez Percé warriors, and orchestrating the defeat of Geronimo's Apaches. His present post, which he assumed in 1895, had been invented by President Grant as a sinecure for the nation's senior military man, but the tedium of ceremonial prominence made Miles peevish and disputatious. He had also become cautious, perhaps out of recognition of the army's inadequacies. His prudence annoyed Miles, and their squabble was as much a personal clash as a difference over strategy.

Miles favored the occupation of Manila, but he regarded Dewey's request for five thousand men as too small and urged McKinley to triple that number. With regulars scarce, they would be mainly volunteers. Miles argued for confining the action to the seizure of the city; an attempt to take over the entire country would strain America's meager resources.

Merritt disagreed. A West Pointer with a solid Civil War record, he was sixty-one and vegetating on Governor's Island, New York, his headquarters as chief of the eastern military region of the United States. Seeking a last shot at glory, he envisioned nothing less than the complete conquest of the Philippines—with regulars, not raw recruits—and the war would not stop with the defeat of the Spanish. Rejecting Oscar Williams's claim that the natives were "eager to be organized and led" by U.S. officers, he predicted that they would also resist the Americans "with the intense hatred born of race and religion." So, he told McKinley, "it seems more than probable that we will have the so-called insurgents to fight as well as the Spaniards."

Unless he was assigned regulars, Merritt threatened, he would resign the command. McKinley, who admired his vigor, gave him some crack units that had been designated for Cuba. With that, Merritt prepared to plunge into the unknown—his venture complicated by McKinley's failure to define an objective for the expedition.

McKinley at this stage ought to have been pondering America's future role in the Philippines. Assuming that U.S. troops and ships captured Manila, what next? Should they subdue Luzon and the other islands? Or should they back the Filipino bid for independence, as Congress had recognized Cuba's right to freedom? Could Spain retain the archipelago, perhaps in exchange for concessions on Cuba and Puerto Rico? Might the islands be ceded to a foreign power or divided into zones of influence? In short, what was America's ultimate goal?

These were crucial questions, on which hinged not only America's fate in the Philippines, but its broader policy for the Pacific. Today, in Washington, task forces and special committees would be conferring around the clock to churn out piles of studies and recommendations. In the spring of 1898, however, amid the blooming azaleas and dogwoods that annually color the capital, nobody was seriously probing for answers, least of all McKinley. Indeed, he only clouded the confusion when, on May 19, seventeen days after Merritt had asked him to clarify the U.S. mission in the Philippines, he produced a typically amorphous directive.

America's "twofold purpose" was "the reduction of Spanish power in that quarter" and the introduction of "order and security to the islands while in the possession of the United States." Left undefined, though, was whether the "possession" would be permanent or temporary. The United States, after ending the "former political relations" between Spain and the Filipinos, intended to create a "new political power." Again, it was unclear whether America would exercise this authority—and, if so, for how long. Merritt was to announce on his arrival in Manila that the United States had come "not to make war upon the people . . . but to protect them in their homes, in their employments and in their personal and religious rights." A State Department memorandum added, however, that the natives would be required to show the U.S. Army the "obedience that will be lawfully due from them"—an indication that martial law was to be imposed.

Discovered many years following McKinley's death was a rare handwritten note that he had scribbled just after Dewey demolished the Spanish fleet: "While we are conducting war and until its conclusion, we must keep all we can get. When the war is over, we must keep what we want." But he never once articulated what he thought he could get, or what he wanted.

Shortly after his inauguration McKinley had pledged to oppose "all acquisitions of territory" beyond the continental limits of the United States; the promise was soon forgotten. The Teller amendment to the act of war voted by Congress barred America from annexing Cuba, and McKinley could have applied the ban to the Philippines; he made no mention of it. Nor would he confirm or deny talk by members of his cabinet that he might only secure a U.S. naval base and trading station in the islands. Perhaps he kept silent because he regarded the disposition of the archipelago to be a bargaining chip in eventual peace negotiations with Spain. More likely, he simply lacked ideas.

The only clue to his thinking was a report in the *New York Tribune* leaked by the White House. The president believed, said the newspaper, that there would be "time enough to discuss the sale, barter or retention of the islands when Spain has been driven to abandon Cuba and sue for conditions of a general peace." As usual, McKinley was trailing rather than shaping events.

The U.S. public at that juncture was equally hazy. Most Americans opposed the continuation of Spanish rule in the Philippines. The anti-imperialist Springfield (Massachusetts) *Republican* denounced as immoral the return of the islands to "a dominion hated, crushed and regenerate." Roosevelt, at the other end of the spectrum, also said that they should be "taken away" from Spain. But there was no clamor for U.S. acquisition of the archipelago, even from the expansionists. A survey of Congress revealed overwhelming resistance to its retention. Even the jingoist Hearst press warned against annexation of the territory on the grounds that it had been "a source of corruption and weakness to Spain" and might poison America as well. Aboard his flagship in Manila Bay, Dewey voiced the same view to a visitor: "Our government is not fitted for colonies. We have ample room for development at home. The colonies of European nations are vital to their economic life, ours could not be."

But opinions changed as the summer of 1898 approached, and a bitter dispute soon polarized the champions and foes of annexing the Philippines. McKinley, in the crossfire, increasingly faced hard choices.

Henry Cabot Lodge, the archimperialist, did not raise the issue of keeping the Philippines until after Dewey's victory. Then, almost overnight, he concluded: "We must on no account let the islands go. . . . We hold the other side of the Pacific, and the value to this country is almost beyond imagination." Others, for their own motives, began to repeat a similar theme. Evangelists perceived the faraway land to be fertile soil for their aims—a "garden of the universe" to be filled with "school houses and missionaries," as a Baptist minister intoned. A statement by the Daughters of the American Revolution foresaw the islands offering America "a new career . . . grander and more imposing than anything" in the past, and an influential California businessman portrayed Manila as a base for trade with China. Addressing Republican stalwarts on May 17, Chauncey Depew, the New York Central railroad tycoon, warned against bucking the tide. "A strong feeling spreading over the land in favor of colonial exansion [is] getting so strong that it will mean the political death of any man to oppose it pretty soon."

Few imperialists were more eloquent than Albert Jeremiah Beveridge, a young scholar and lawyer, later to be elected senator from Indiana. A passionate progressive in domestic affairs who battled to regulate cartels and child labor, he subsequently became a fierce isolationist, joining Lodge to block U.S. entry into the League of Nations. When war with Spain broke out in April 1898, however, he designated the Philippines as "logically our first target" and the Pacific "the true field of our earliest operations." His speech to a Boston audience marked a milestone in xenophobia: "We are a conquering race. . . . American law, American order, American civilization and the American flag will plant themselves on shores hitherto bloody and benighted, but by those agencies of God henceforth to be made beautiful and bright."

The enemies of expansionism, then organizing, were equally impassioned. Their militants included the prolific Carl Schurz, who in 1856, at the age of twenty-seven, had fled to Wisconsin from political persecution in his native Germany. He became an ardent abolitionist and Republican party activist. After serving as Lincoln's envoy to Spain, he rose to the rank of major general in the Union Army, later won election as senator from Missouri and joined Rutherford B. Hayes's cabinet as secretary of interior. Dour, irascible and brilliant, he wielded enormous sway among the German immigrants of the Middle West and afterward exerted national influence writing for *Harper's Weekly*. A peculiar blend of idealism and racism permeated his resistance to imperialism. To annex the Philippines, he argued, would not only violate

America's principles of "right, justice and liberty," but also bring an influx of "more or less barbarous Asiatics" into the United States. He was, along with Andrew Carnegie and others, a founder of the Anti-Imperialist League.

In the spring of 1898 McKinley still lacked a plan for dealing with the Spanish in the Philippines; and he was paying even less attention to the Filipino insurgents. The evidence suggests, indeed, that he was oblivious to their existence. The absence of guidance from Washington licensed Dewey, Merritt and other American officials to improvise. Their only preoccupation at that juncture was to defeat the Spanish. To achieve that goal, they sought the help of the Filipinos, indulging them with pledges that had no foundation in reality. The Filipinos naïvely believed the promises until they discovered, to their dismay, that they had been manipulated. Within less than a year, tensions were to spark a tragic war between the Americans and Filipinos that almost surely could have been averted had McKinley, at the outset, proceeded into the Philippines with a policy.

★ ★ ★

During the war against the Filipino insurgents U.S. propagandists maligned Emilio Aguinaldo with many charges, including venality. In fact, he behaved with singular probity after reaching Hong Kong late in December 1897. The Spanish had given him a check for four hundred thousand pesos as a first payment for quitting the Philippines, and he deposited the money in a British bank. He siphoned off the interest to feed, lodge and clothe his comrades and himself, leaving the principal intact to buy weapons in hopes of reviving his revolution. Scrupulously pinching pennies, he and his followers languished in poverty. Without their families and friends, and unable to speak either English or Chinese, they also felt sad, lonely and estranged in the British colony. They bickered among themselves as they watched events back home, awaiting the chance to rekindle their struggle against Spain.

Rounsevelle Wildman, the American consul in Hong Kong, had earlier rebuffed a Filipino request for U.S. cooperation. As war with Spain loomed, however, he and other American officials in Asia perceived the insurgents to be possible allies after all, and conceded to talk with them. Their dialogue, conducted in a fog of misunderstanding, was to cloud rather than clarify their relations. The Filipinos assumed that the Americans reflected U.S. policy, but the Americans, without instructions from Washington, represented only themselves.

Soon after Dewey's squadron had assembled in Hong Kong in March 1898, Lieutenant R. V. Hall of the gunboat *Petrel* sought out the Filipinos in the colony to collect intelligence on Manila's defenses. He ducked the issue when they pressed him for U.S. endorsement of their bid for independence, but he assured them, with Dewey's approval, that the Americans would arm and transport their troops back to the Philippines if they agreed to "help fight the Spanish." They concluded that an alliance with the United States was in the works.

Aquinaldo personally pursued the subject on April 6 with Captain Edward P. Wood, the skipper of the *Petrel,* whom Dewey had ordered to continue the talks. Aguinaldo asked him to define America's intentions toward the Philippines. The United States, replied Wood, was "very great and rich, and did not need colonies"—and, he added, Dewey would put such a statement in writing. Aguinaldo, deluded by his hopes, inferred from the elliptical remark that the Americans would back his cause. He and Wood planned to discuss the matter further, but an incident aborted their next session.

The Spanish, striving to subvert the nationalists, sent one of their Filipino agents, a rebel defector, to Hong Kong. He filed suit against Aguinaldo in a British colonial court, demanding a slice of the Spanish indemnity. His game was to raise doubts about Aguinaldo's use of the funds and, in so doing, smear the insurgent leader's image. Though Aguinaldo kept careful ledgers, he recoiled from publicly disclosing his movement's finances in court. He sailed for Singapore, traveling incognito with two aides. He landed there two weeks later, just as war between the United States and Spain broke out. His fortunes were now to take a new twist.

Howard Bray was one of those Western "fixers" who pervade Asia to this day. A former British colonial official in India, he had been a planter in the Philippines until the Spanish expropriated his property in a dispute. He moved to Singapore, where he occasionally wrote on the Philippines for a local newspaper. Lately, too, he had been feeding information on the archipelago to E. Spencer Pratt, the U.S. consul, who forwarded the reports to Dewey. Bray, both out of hatred for the Spanish and to serve his own interests, sympathized with the Filipino rebels. Calculating that they would benefit from American support, he introduced Aguinaldo to Pratt and acted as interpreter.

The U.S. consular service then consisted largely of expatriate merchants, scholars, writers and other amateurs, who for assorted motives chose to live abroad. Many owed their appointment to political patronage and, as diplomats, were dilettantes with only a hazy knowledge of foreign affairs. Their duties tended to be ritual. They flew the flag, hosted social functions and attended receptions. Some promoted trade, even using their positions for personal gain. They often operated without word from Washington, which suited them fine. After all, they were not bureaucrats.

Pratt typified the breed. He had no authority to make commitments on behalf of the United States. Nevertheless, he urged Aguinaldo to return to Hong Kong and join Dewey in the war with Spain. Pratt would not explicitly guarantee U.S. recognition of Philippine independence, but he implied that Aguinaldo could expect America, which had promised freedom to Cuba, to do the same for the Philippines. "As in Cuba, so in the Philippines. Even more so, if possible. Cuba is at our door, while the Philippines is ten thousand miles away."

Aguinaldo agreed to collaborate, but he asked that Dewey send him a formal request along with a written pledge of U.S. support for his cause. Pratt dissimulated. He cabled Dewey that Aguinaldo was prepared to join him in Hong Kong, omitting any mention of conditions. Dewey answered promptly: TELL AGUINALDO COME SOON AS POSSIBLE.

Perplexed by Dewey's terse response, Aguinaldo asked about the written pledge. Pratt again pretended. Dewey, he told Aguinaldo, had assured him in a separate private message the United States would "at least recognize the independence of the Philippines under an American naval protectorate." Both Dewey and he himself could be trusted, Pratt went on, somewhat irritated, as if Aguinaldo's request for a formal promise was disrespectful. "The words of a United States navy officer and an American consul represent a solemn pledge," he said. "The United States government is a very honorable, very just and very powerful government."

Eager for personal profit and self-promotion, Pratt also skirted propriety. He offered to procure guns for the rebels, at a commission, and proposed to serve as their agent in Washington after they won independence.

The Filipino community in Singapore honored Pratt as a benefactor at a noisy party in which he touted his friendship with Aguinaldo and tipsily toasted the Philippine "republic." Proud of his popularity, he sent press reports of the evening to Washington along with newspaper accounts of his talks with Aguinaldo. Secretary of State William Day replied frostily: AVOID UNAUTHORIZED NEGOTIATIONS WITH PHILIPPINE INSURGENTS. Pratt lamely denied that he had even discussed U.S. policy with Aguinaldo. Day, unconvinced, again scolded him for taking steps of a "significance that this government would feel compelled to regret." Pratt, who had expected to be rewarded, was subsequently dismissed. Aguinaldo, however, had been sorely misled by his attention.

The prospect of fighting alongside the Americans elated Aguinaldo as he reached Hong Kong. But he learned, to his chagrin, that Dewey had departed for the Philippines without him. A few days later, he heard of Dewey's victory in Manila Bay. After all the pressure exerted on him to cooperate with the United States, he had been rejected.

Dewey had "attached so little importance" to Aguinaldo, he told a Senate committee nearly four years later, that he had left him behind. Besides, Dewey added, the Filipinos had become a nuisance. "They were bothering me. I was very busy getting my squadron ready for battle, and these little men were . . . taking a good deal of my time." One of them, invited to go along, backed out at the last minute because he had misplaced his toothbrush. But if Dewey had held Aguinaldo in such low esteem, why did he summon him to Hong Kong? "More to get rid of him than anything else."

Aguinaldo was again stranded in the British colony—a warrior without a war. He now began to pester Wildman, who privately described him as a "childish figure of petty moods . . . far more interested in the kind of cane he will carry or the breastplate he will wear than in the figure he will make in history." But Wildman, like Pratt, could not resist a business deal. He contracted to purchase rifles, ammunition and other equipment for the Filipinos for a commission, and accepted a down payment of 117,000 pesos. Most of the matériel was never delivered, nor did Wildman ever account for the missing money. He disappeared in a shipwreck on his way home in 1901, and is honored today in a commemorative plaque for U.S. foreign service heroes in a State Department lobby.

Dewey finally summoned Aguinaldo, who reached Manila Bay aboard an American vessel on May 19, and the two men met for the first time. Aguinaldo, dressed in khaki, proudly wore his captured Spanish sword as he climbed onto the deck of Dewey's flagship, the *Olympia*. Resplendent in a white uniform, the new epaulets of a rear admiral gracing his shoulders, Dewey greeted him with condescending warmth. They repaired to a comfortable salon to converse,

A romanticized version of Filipino peasants before the Spanish discovery of the Philippines in 1521.

Ferdinand Magellan erects a cross on Cebu in April 1521, claiming the archipelago for Spain.
He was killed in a skirmish with the natives soon afterward.

A nineteenth-century photograph of Spanish colonial officials, a priest among them. The Catholic hierarchy heavily influenced the colonial regime.

The execution in 1896 of José Rizal, the Philippine national hero, by Spanish troops. Rizal favored assimilation with Spain rather than independence.

Theodore Roosevelt as a Rough Rider in Cuba during the Spanish-American War of 1898. Roosevelt was instrumental in pushing the United States into the war.

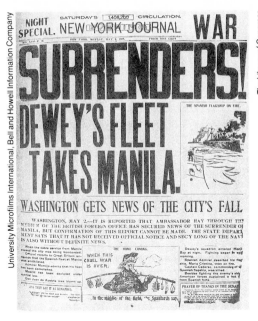

Unofficial news of Commodore George Dewey's defeat of the Spanish fleet in Manila Bay on May 1, 1898.

An icon of Dewey, whose victory turned him into one of America's great heroes.

President William McKinley *(left)* and his cabinet; Secretary of War Elihu Root is second from his left. Root was an architect of U.S. colonial policy for the Philippines.

America ponders whether to keep the Philippines following the defeat of Spain.

The United States as a global power, as seen by a Minneapolis newspaper.

General Arthur MacArthur, an early U.S. commander in the Philippines, father of Douglas MacArthur.

Willy Grayson, a Nebraska volunteer, who fired the first shot in
the war against the Philippine nationalist movement.

Dead Filipino soldiers after fighting broke out in the suburbs of Manila on February 4, 1899.

Kansas volunteers in action outside Manila. Most of the American troops in the Philippines came from states west of the Mississippi.

Wounded Kansas volunteer during the U.S. war against the Filipinos. An estimated 200,000 Filipinos, mostly civilians, died in the war.

Emilio Aguinaldo, chief of
Filipino nationalists, declared
Philippine independence in 1898.

Filipinos celebrate the formation of an independent government
in 1899 in the town of Malolos, north of Manila.

Gregorio del Pilar, the "boy general" of the Philippine nationalist army, was killed in the war
against the Americans. He has since been enshrined as a romantic hero.

Colonel Frederick Funston *(seated)* and the team that captured Aguinaldo in one of the boldest actions of the U.S. war against the Filipinos.

American atrocities against Filipinos eventually appalled the U.S. public, which had earlier supported the war as a manifestation of American power.

Dewey in English and Aguinaldo in Spanish, with one of Aguinaldo's aides haltingly interpreting.

From the blurred perspective of Washington, meanwhile, McKinley anxiously observed the cadence of events. American expeditions were then preparing to embark for Cuba and the Philippines, and the specter of a long and costly war alarmed him. If only Spain would agree to a compromise, perhaps the worst might be avoided. As usual, however, he was bereft of ideas. On the advice of John Hay, his envoy to London, he authorized British diplomats to explore peace possibilities. But a new complication arose when Secretary of State Day informed him of Pratt's talks with Aguinaldo. For the first time, he realized, the Filipinos would have to be part of the equation.

They deserved "just consideration," he told an aide—but how? He could not endorse their claim to independence without jeopardizing a potential deal with the Spanish, who were determined to retain the Philippines even though they had reconciled themselves to losing Cuba. The Filipinos would have to wait for their independence. The problem was confused, however, by McKinley's inability to control his representatives abroad. Pratt had raised Aguinaldo's hopes with promises of support. Now, McKinley discovered, Dewey had also met with Aguinaldo. If Dewey had pledged to back the Filipinos, the Spanish would certainly refuse to negotiate a settlement; an intensified war was virtually inevitable.

It was difficult to communicate with Dewey, who had cut the cable from Manila and could be contacted only through Hong Kong—a tortuous procedure that required his sending a ship to the British colony to collect messages. Dewey was reluctant to spare a boat for the round trip across the South China Sea, a journey of three or four days. Besides, he now viewed himself as a kind of viceroy, capable of managing his private domain without interference from Washington. He had not furnished McKinley with the substance of his conversation with Aguinaldo—nor even reported that the meeting had taken place. McKinley only learned of the encounter in the middle of June, probably from the newspapers. He queried Dewey for details, cautioning him to avoid "a political alliance with the insurgents or any faction in the islands that would incur liability to maintain their cause in the future." Dewey either failed to receive word immediately or felt under no constraint to respond quickly. Finally on June 27 he confirmed in a dispatch to the Navy Department that he had in fact met with Aguinaldo—five weeks earlier.

By then, Dewey had seen Aguinaldo several times. But he flatly denied in his belated reply that he had pledged to "assist the insurgents by any act or promise," or had voiced sympathy for their cause. He had refused Aguinaldo's request for help, telling him that he regarded the insurgents to be nothing more than "friends . . . opposed to a common enemy." Nor did he gather from Aguinaldo that the rebels were "committed to assist us." Some four years later, in testimony before a Senate committee, Dewey insisted that he had never intended to develop close ties with the Filipino leader, even after bringing him back to Manila aboard a U.S. ship. As Dewey put it, he routinely sent boats to pick up mail and supplies from Hong Kong, and one of them fetched Aguinaldo as well. It had merely been, he said, an "act of courtesy."

Aguinaldo related a different story in his memoirs: Dewey had assured him that the United States was "rich in territory and money, and needed no colonies." So the Filipinos ought "have no doubt whatsoever" about American support. When Aguinaldo expressed a fear of hostilities between the U.S. and Filipino forces if the promise were violated, Dewey reacted sharply. An American officer's "word of honor" would never be transgressed, Aguinaldo claimed to have heard him say.

Dewey had become fond of the Filipinos. Several hundred of them had gone to work for him in the former Spanish navy yard at Cavite and, he later recalled, they were "docile, amiable, intelligent [and] most kindly disposed toward us," regarding the Americans as "their liberators." But he was too experienced and disciplined to have given Aguinaldo a firm guarantee of U.S. support for Philippine independence—particularly after McKinley had instructed him to steer clear of the rebels. So Aguinaldo's expectations must have colored his memory of their talks. He also may have confused the pledges of Pratt and Wildman with whatever Dewey told him, since their statements were virtually identical. His hopes were probably buoyed as well by comrades who had stayed behind in Hong Kong to function as his movement's diplomatic service. They monitored American press reports, and concluded from selective reading that U.S. public opinion opposed the annexation of the Philippines.

But Dewey was a study in inconsistency, either tailoring his recollections to suit circumstances or simply forgetting his earlier statements. He tended to babble, casually ventilating his thoughts without paying attention to their repercussions. But his comments carried immense weight at the time. As the hero of Manila Bay, he was for Americans at home the uncontested expert on the Philippines. To the Filipino insurgents, he personified the power and the purpose of the United States. In fact, he was operating in a policy vacuum.

Whatever he actually said, Dewey probably planted in Aguinaldo's head, perhaps inadvertently, the notion that America would not seek to control the Philippines. Without directions from McKinley, he relied for guidance on the U.S. Navy's war plans, which made no mention of territorial acquisition beyond the capture of Manila and a few other towns in order to exert leverage on Spain at a peace conference. His request for only five thousand men to occupy Manila also indicated that he envisioned a limited campaign in the archipelago. He knew as well that Congress had voted to uphold independence for Cuba, an island ninety miles from Florida with major U.S. investments, and he must have assumed that America would not want a property on the other side of the world, where its stake was nil. Indeed, he implicitly recommended in his dispatch to Washington in June 1898 that the same law be applied to the Filipinos. "In my opinion," he wrote, "these people are far superior in intelligence and more capable of self-government than the natives of Cuba."

Dewey later revised his views. The Filipinos "expect independence," he reported with apparent approval in an early message to the Navy Department. But in January 1902, after the United States had gone to war against them, he disclaimed before the Senate committee reviewing Philippine policy that they had aspired to freedom. "You may believe me, gentlemen," he affirmed, "they did not at first. They did not."

Young and naïve, Aguinaldo filtered Dewey's remarks through the prism of his own dreams. He also construed American attention to mean that he was now a U.S. ally in the struggle against Spain. After all, Dewey had given him the equivalent of an order following their talks: "Go ashore and start your army."

Aguinaldo obeyed. Disembarking in his native Cavite, he showed local Filipinos a few Mauser rifles that Dewey had allowed him to take from a captured Spanish arsenal, claiming that he expected more when he was fully mobilized. He also announced the creation of a "provisional dictatorship," with himself at its head, and issued a series of typically verbose proclamations emphasizing American support for his crusade. The U.S. fleet would soon bombard Manila to open the way for his "march into the capital." The Americans, "my friends," had "promised me all that I have asked for, more than we had ever hoped to obtain, and are going to aid me in all things." The United States, "the cradle of genuine liberty," the savior of "our people oppressed and enslaved by tyranny and despotism," had pledged him and his movement "protection as decisive as it is undoubtedly disinterested . . . considering us as sufficiently civilized and capable of governing for ourselves our unfortunate country."

Numbers of Filipinos had already quit the Spanish army to join the insurgents, one of them saying that he would fight Spain's "foreign enemies but not my own compatriots." Aguinaldo's return quickened the trend. By the middle of June, nearly all the native auxiliaries had defected, and the rebels could attack depleted Spanish detachments throughout the country with relative ease. Mariano Noriel, an insurgent general with the build of a heavyweight boxer, overran almost every Spanish garrison in Cavite within weeks, taking three thousand prisoners. His victories stimulated Filipinos to rise up elsewhere in Luzon. Many were dispossessed peasants, inspired as much by the opportunity to grab lands owned by the Spanish monastic orders as by nationalist sentiment.

The Filipinos amassed thousands of rifles and rounds of ammunition, either captured from defeated Spanish outposts or purchased from Chinese smugglers. By early summer, thirty thousand of their troops, commanded by General Antonio Luna, had dug fourteen miles of trenches around Manila. Jammed behind the walls of the inner city, the Spanish were blocked from escaping by sea by Dewey's squadron. The rebels seized the capital's only pumping station, shut off the water supply and gradually began to strangle the beleaguered Spanish.

On June 16, Spanish warships departed Spain to lift the siege. But they abruptly altered course for Cuba, where the U.S. Navy imperiled a Spanish fleet. General Basilio Augustín Dávila, the Spanish governor in Manila, panicked. He communicated with Madrid through circuitous routes, his messages a mounting crescendo of woe. His plight, at first "very grave," soon became "unparalleled in history." He could not cope with the hysterical population that packed the city as his defense force dwindled from injuries, death and desertions. Cavite had "risen in mass," isolating him from the provinces, and the American army would soon land, leaving him no choice "than to succumb"—with "consequences fatal" for Spain. An aide, exasperated by the repetitious pleas of desperation, dubbed him "the undertaker."

With only some two thousand men at his disposal, Dewey awaited Merritt's troops for the offensive against Manila. He praised the Filipinos encircling the city as "our friends, assisting us [and] doing our work," and later likened them to the Negroes who had rallied to the Union side in the Civil War. But while he understood that the slaves had fought for freedom, his notions of Aguinaldo's aims were fuzzy.

He largely relied for information on Oscar Williams, the U.S. consul who had accompanied him to Manila. Williams, who saw Aguinaldo frequently in Cavite, assured Dewey that the rebels "hope that the Philippines will be held as a colony of the United States." Wildman, the consul in Hong Kong, agreed. Their "statements to the contrary," he said, the Filipinos in the British colony wanted to become Americans, and constantly beseeched him for guarantees of eventual U.S. citizenship. Dewey found yet another source of intelligence in Edouard André, the Belgian consul in Manila, who also told him that the Filipinos "do not desire independence." None of this advice concurred with what he had heard from Aguinaldo himself. But these were white men, and Dewey believed them. Aguinaldo, he concluded, merely sought to end Spanish rule, and "did not look much beyond that."

Dewey underestimated Aguinaldo, who was thinking ahead. Aguinaldo had stepped up his campaign in an effort to occupy as much territory as possible before the U.S. ground forces arrived. Thus, he calculated, he could improve his bargaining stance with the Americans. For the same reason, he decided to declare the independence of the Philippines.

Chief among his advisers was Apolinario Mabini, the most cerebral of the rebels. Then thirty-four, Mabini came from a humble Chinese *mestizo* family. He had educated himself, and ultimately earned a law degree from the University of Santo Tomás. Poliomyelitis had crippled his legs, but not his zeal. A member of José Rizal's aborted *Liga Filipina,* he was jailed and quickly released by the Spanish, who could not imagine an invalid to be dangerous. Aguinaldo, hearing of his legal skills, had him carried in a hammock to Cavite by porters. Aguinaldo was repelled by the sight of a cripple, until Mabini's intellect and fervor erased his doubts.

Admirers called Mabini the "brains of the revolution," but his rivals labeled him Aguinaldo's "dark chamber." Lean, dour and frequently tactless, he was a theorist often unable to deal with practicalities. He had derived from his studies of the American and French revolutions the conviction that the first duty of government was "to interpret faithfully the popular will." The thesis, banal today, alienated the rich nationalists, who maintained that *ilustrados* like themselves ought to run the country. To Mabini, however, they were only out to safeguard their own interests. Aguinaldo tried to juggle the two sides. He courted the wealthy elite, whose support lent him social status and respectability. At the same time, he needed Mabini's talents. He never succeeded in harmonizing the irreconcilable differences that, in the end, split and doomed him—perhaps because he failed to define an ideology more profound than the attainment of independence.

Mabini drafted a "constitutional program" that granted full power to Aguinaldo for the duration of the war. But the document envisioned democratic institutions then unique in Asia, like a national legislature and elected officials. Freedom of religion, speech and the press were guaranteed, and women could vote, attend all educational institutions and hold certain offices. Capital punishment was outlawed except for such wartime offenses as "military insubordination in the face of the enemy."

Mabini warned Aguinaldo against proclaiming independence prematurely. The Filipinos, he argued, should organize their government first in areas liberated from the Spanish and demonstrate to the world their ability to rule themselves. He also feared that, without a formal pledge of U.S. support, they risked a two-front war against the Americans and the Spanish. Aguinaldo ignored him. He commissioned a national anthem and a flag as well as a declaration of independence that turgidly related the history of the Filipino struggle since Magellan. One passage, testimony to his persistent faith in the Americans, affirmed Philippine freedom "under the protection of the mighty and humane" United States.

On the afternoon of June 12, 1898, Aguinaldo read the marathon declaration from the balcony of his family house in Cavite el Viejo, now known as Kawit, his hometown in Cavite. The ceremony appears to have been subdued, judging from a faded photograph. Only about a hundred people gathered in front of the ornate mansion, today a ramshackle museum located on a busy road. The *ilustrados,* in top hats and frock coats, seem solemn—perhaps out of concern for the future, maybe from sheer boredom with the tedious proceedings. The sole American present was a Colonel L. M. Johnson, an obscure retired officer then in business in Shanghai, who had come to Manila to exhibit a newfangled contraption known as the cinematograph. Aguinaldo, eager to have an American on hand to symbolize U.S. recognition of his endeavor, had persuaded him to participate. Johnson signed the declaration of independence, his name incongruously standing out in the list of ninety-seven Filipino witnesses.

Aguinaldo had hoped for Dewey's signature. Dewey ignored the invitation to the ceremony, later explaining that it was "mail day" and he had been too busy. Nor had he bothered to read the document, a copy of which Aguinaldo sent to his flagship. In one of his contradictory recollections, Dewey told a Senate committee in 1902 that he had simply been oblivious to the Filipino aspirations. "I attached so little importance to this proclamation that I did not even cable its contents to Washington, but forwarded it through the mails. I never dreamed that they wanted independence."

★ ★ ★

Major General Wesley Merritt welcomed his assignment to the Philippines as a fitting climax to a distinguished career. A dashing cavalry officer during the Civil War, cited six times for gallantry, he had accompanied Grant to Appomattox and later fought with Custer against the Indians. He was still handsome at sixty-two, with silver hair and cold gray eyes, but he had grown stout and snappish at desk jobs, and yearned for action. As his expedition assembled in San Francisco in the middle of May, however, he began to regret the appointment.

The Philippines, he sensed, would be a sideshow to the Cuban theater, which was closer to home and attracted greater public attention, and he feared that his ambitions might go unfulfilled. As it was, he faced the daunting task of training and supplying fifteen thousand men and moving them across an ocean to an unfamiliar battleground. Not the least of his problems was to charter transports from private companies, since neither the army nor the navy owned troopships; America had never before waged a war overseas.

Merritt observed his soldiers with misgivings. Mostly volunteers from west of the Mississippi, they typified the motley civilian mass that America traditionally mobilizes in moments of war: farmers, students, store clerks, office employees, factory workers, adventurers, drifters and roustabouts. The Colorado regiment included one Damon Runyan, a newspaper reporter, decades away from the guys and dolls of Broadway. Merritt had more confidence in his senior officers and sergeants, among them Civil War veterans like himself who had remained in the army to fight Indians. They would discover the Philippines to be a terrain alien to their experience; many, once there, were to act as if they were still pursuing Apaches.

Young Americans had rallied to McKinley's appeal for volunteers with enthusiasm. Time had effaced the horrible memories of the Civil War, and they had only heard tales of its heroics, which they were now eager to emulate. The excitement that pulsated through Nebraska exemplified the frenetic mood of the country.

Hardly had Congress voted its war resolution in early April than Governor Silas Holcomb wired McKinley, pledging Nebraska's two National Guard regiments to the effort. Towns across the state organized enlistments drives, and youths stampeded to join up.

Within three weeks, more than two thousand troops packed a makeshift camp sprawled over the fairgrounds outside Lincoln, the state capital. A parade at the site on the afternoon of May 7 drew twenty-five thousand spectators, a third of them arriving in town aboard special excursion trains. Hotels were booked solid, and restaurants soon ran out of food. Carts, carriages, bicycles and pedestrians clogged the road to the camp, where the crowd was so dense that the soldiers barely had room to march. All he could see, wrote a reporter for the *State Journal,* were "white tents and dark forms" in the distance.

The two state regiments had hoped to serve together. But one was sent to Georgia to prepare for Cuba and the other, bound for the Philippines, went to San Francisco. The rail journey to California enthralled the young Nebraskans in the unit headed for the Philippines, and the *Journal* reporter was caught up in the excitement. "Farmers stopped their plowing and wildly waved, women and girls stood in farm doors and fluttered handkerchiefs and aprons, the country schools turned out to a kidlet and jubilantly demonstrated their patriotism. In every town along the way, people . . . lined the tracks, waving flags and cheering with all their lung power, assisted by brass bands and drum corps."

The volunteers converged on San Francisco to encamp at the Presidio, overlooking Golden Gate Bay, still a U.S. Army installation. Built as a garrison in the late eighteenth century by the Spanish, who were then masters of California, it had scarcely been improved since. Winds constantly swept across the hillside, covering tents with dirt and dust, and the seasonal rain muddied company streets. The new camp, named for Merritt, resembled a confused, raucous carnival. Mothers, wives and sweethearts had accompanied the troops, and they roamed around freely, poking into the field kitchens to bake cakes and cookies for their boys. San Francisco had also been invaded by prostitutes from throughout the country, and the venereal-disease rate was soaring. The city's saloons overflowed with the novice warriors escaping from the daily drudgery of close-order drill and marches. Hardly a night passed without a brawl.

Maintaining discipline and hygiene were not the only problems. The army was unequipped to fight. The regulars had been armed with Krag-Jorgensens, new repeating rifles manufactured in Norway. But volunteers had to make do with single-shot Springfields, which used detectable charcoal powder and often misfired—prompting one rookie to remark, "It's more dangerous to be behind it than in front of it." Canteens and blankets were scarce, and troops had been issued blue-flannel uniforms unsuitable for the tropics. Meanwhile, McKinley's vague orders puzzled Merritt. He wired Russell Alger, the secretary of war, to complain that he was "at a loss to understand" his objective in the Philippines. Alger, equally baffled, could not help.

The expedition was due to depart piecemeal from late May through August. Brigadier General Thomas H. Anderson, a leathery Civil War veteran who had last served in Alaska, commanded the first contingent. Brigadier generals Francis V. Greene and Arthur MacArthur would follow with their units, and Major General Elwell S. Otis was to bring the last detachment. Merritt and his headquarters staff, traveling separately, were to leave at the end of June.

On May 25 Anderson and his 2,500 men steamed out of San Francisco harbor aboard three ships to a cacophony of cheers, songs and whistles coming from a cluster of tugs, barges, ferries and yachts.

For the first time in history, U.S. troops were going to war outside America's continental limits. They began the campaign with a comic-opera overture.

Anderson's convoy was escorted by the cruiser *Charleston,* whose skipper, Captain Henry Glass, read sealed orders after he reached the open sea. He was to detour to seize Guam, a Spanish colony since its discovery by Magellan nearly four centuries before. Early on June 20, leaving the transports at anchor in the distance, Glass entered the port of San Luis d'Apra, the island's capital, and shelled its ancient fort. The fire evoked no response. Glass edged closer in the eerie silence, nervously scanning the coast through his binoculars. Eventually a boat approached, carrying a Spanish officer. He apologized politely. "You will pardon our not immediately replying to your salute, *mi capitán,* but we are unaccustomed to receiving salutes here and are not supplied with proper guns for returning them." "What salute?" riposted Glass. "Those were hostile shots. Our countries are at war."

The island lacked a cable link to the outside world, and the news astounded the Spaniard. Glass ordered him to return with the governor for a surrender ceremony on the *Charleston.* The governor sent regrets. Protocol forbade him from boarding foreign naval craft, but he graciously proposed an audience in his office instead. Glass, without further ado, sent five soldiers ashore to arrest him. Next day, the U.S. convoy resumed its voyage to Manila, now with sixty-four Spanish prisoners, including the melancholy governor. Glass had left a few men behind. They unfurled the Stars and Stripes over Guam—and Spain's first possession in the Pacific became America's first possession in the Pacific.

Late in June, as American troops disembarked in Cuba, the Anderson contingent waded through the surf at Cavite. The soldiers, relieved to be ashore after nearly a month at sea, erected tents and bought fruit and tobacco from native peddlers. They also ventured into the narrow streets of the nearby town, where Aguinaldo's senior officers had taken over the best Spanish mansions. They attracted little attention from the rebels, small men in white cotton pajamas and broad-brimmed straw hats who were busily cleaning and distributing weapons, manufacturing ammunition, training and grinding out manifestos and proclamations.

Soon the burgeoning U.S. force moved to a peanut field closer to Manila, naming it Camp Dewey. Dysentery, malaria and cholera ravaged the troops, and they also suffered from chronic nausea caused by army rations of canned salmon derisively called "goldfish." Rain fell steadily, flooding their trenches and dampening their morale. "It beats all creation how it can rain out here," reported an American correspondent. The soldiers, he observed, had discarded their drenched uniforms to drill in underwear.

The American war correspondents promptly went forth to look at the Filipino deployments around Manila. They bore passes signed by Aguinaldo, as one of them wrote, ordering his men to "permit us to go where we pleased, to guard us well from harm, and, if we were hungry, to feed us."

The *primera zona,* nearest Manila, was commanded by General Noriel and his part-French deputy, Lieutenant Colonel Juan Cailles, a suave soldier with a silky mustache. They welcomed the journalists with customary Filipino hospitality, treating them to a cockfight followed by a dinner of meat, chicken, liver and rice afloat in garlic and coconut sauce. Faintly dyspeptic, the journalists were then bounced by pony cart over a muddy road to the honeycomb of insurgent trenches ringing the city. There, crouched under slapdash shelters between downpours, the rebels smoked cigarettes and chewed sugarcane—periodically rising above the parapets to show their disdain for danger as they exchanged wild shots with the Spanish. Impressed, Oscar King Davis of *Harper's Weekly* commented that the Filipinos had succeeded in driving the Spanish back through "a thick jungle of thorny bamboo and heavy scrub practically impossible" for American soldiers to penetrate. "Whatever the outcome of the insurgent problem here, Aguinaldo has saved our troops a lot of desperately hard campaigning. The Spaniards are completely hemmed in [with] no hope for them but surrender."

Dewey, awash in contradictions, also praised the Filipinos, telling visitors that their military progress had been "wonderful," and that their treatment of Spanish captives was humane. He felt sure that Aguinaldo would await the arrival of the full U.S. ground force for a joint attack against Manila. Shortly before, he had disregarded Aguinaldo's declaration of independence, but now he informed General Anderson that Aguinaldo had proclaimed independence and "seems intent on establishing his own government." The situation could turn "awkward," he explained, should McKinley decide to annex the Philippines.

Dewey seldom left his flagship, but now he offered to conduct Anderson to Aguinaldo's headquarters. The meeting, Dewey advised, should be "as unofficial as possible—no sidearms, no ceremony [and] no indication to Aguinaldo that we take his government seriously."

The session was tense. Aguinaldo, sullen and remote, had by now come to distrust Dewey and addressed Anderson, again evoking the issue of U.S. support for his cause. Embarrassed, Anderson replied that he was a simple soldier, only there to set up and supply a military base. He added, however, that the Americans had come to free the Filipinos from "Spanish tyranny," and that they ought to "get along amicably together" against a "common enemy." But, he later recalled, the U.S. troop presence "bitterly disappointed" Aguinaldo, who wanted to capture Manila alone and thus gain credibility as the savior of the Philippines.

Anderson, a tall, weathered veteran with sharp eyes and a spade beard, was no great intellect. Like his colleagues, he viewed the Filipinos with condescension. Yet only he among the top American officers dealt with them directly, and he realistically appraised their traits. They were sincere and determined, he told Washington, warning that the creation of a U.S. military administration would "probably bring us into conflict" with them. "We have heretofore underrated the natives," who were "industrious" and "not ignorant, savage tribes, but have a civilization of their own, and though insignificant in appearance are fierce fighters." Aguinaldo also merited gratitude. At first suspicious, he had become "more friendly and . . . willing to cooperate" in the huge task of housing and feeding the U.S. troops who had landed, and in preparing the terrain for those on the way.

Aguinaldo had indeed shifted his headquarters to the town of Bacoor, ten miles from Cavite, to minimize friction betwen his men and the Americans. After some reluctance, he also furnished the U.S. force with supplies. Anderson's favorable estimate of him riled the War Department hawks, who buried his report in Washington's bureaucratic catacombs—where it remained until senators critical of U.S. policy in the Philippines made it public years later.

Anderson also argued in an article published after his retirement that Aguinaldo had every reason to expect U.S. support, since Dewey had brought him home aboard an American vessel. But Anderson had been just as duplicitous as Dewey and other American officials during his service in the Philippines. Once, when Aguinaldo asked if the United States meant to keep the islands, Anderson assuaged him with the same bromide that the Filipino had heard before: "In one hundred and twenty-two years we have established no colonies. I leave you to draw your own inference." Aguinaldo, eager to placate the Americans, nodded agreement. He had studied the U.S. Constitution "attentively," he claimed, and could not find any "authority for colonies." Thus he had "no fear."

Other kibbitzers meanwhile confused him. Howard Bray, writing from Singapore, urged him to deny landing rights to the Americans until they recognized his "duly constituted" government. Spencer Pratt, also in Singapore, exhorted him to seize Manila quickly, and requested a souvenir of the battle. Rounseville Wildman, in Hong Kong, admonished him for doubting America's altruism. The Americans had only gone to war, Wildman wrote, to emancipate Cuba from Spain and were "actuated by precisely the same feelings toward the Philippines." So, "whatever the final disposition of the conquered territory . . . you can trust the United States that justice and honor will control all its dealings with you."

Aguinaldo, perplexed, became testy. He boycotted a Fourth of July party organized by the Americans because the invitation addressed him as "general" instead of "president." He detained two U.S. officers who had strayed into his zone, releasing them only after Anderson's intercession, and he periodically spurned American requests for supplies. Heeding Bray's counsel, he warned

Anderson against new U.S. troop landings without his permission. When Anderson ignored the protest, he implored Pratt and Wildman, as if they carried any weight, to urge the American government to "define" its relations with him in a "formal convention."

The usually calm Dewey became peevish toward the Filipinos. On one occasion, he threatened to shell their positions if they moved closer to Manila; on another, he invited a group of them aboard his flagship to complain that their tiny "mosquito" boats, which buzzed his fleet, were a nuisance and should be curbed. When one of the natives muttered an oath, Dewey had him tossed overboard.

Aguinaldo grew more and more petulant as fresh U.S. detachments disembarked during July under the command of generals Greene and MacArthur. With Merritt's arrival in late July, the strained ties between the Americans and Filipinos began to fray rapidly.

Conditions, Dewey warned Washington, were now "most critical." If the Spanish surrendered Manila to the Americans, the Filipinos might react violently at having been deprived of a prize they regarded as theirs. Merritt's "most difficult problem," Dewey speculated, would be to control Aguinaldo, who had "become aggressive and even threatening toward our army." Merritt would have preferred to deal with the Filipinos as U.S. soldiers of his generation had handled the Indians: by wiping them out. But McKinley, still fearful of arousing anti-imperialist sentiment at home, had instructed him to avoid at all costs a "rupture" with the insurgents. Merritt therefore chose to shun them, presumably on the theory that they would evaporate if ignored.

Merritt later blamed Dewey for having "more or less encouraged" Aguinaldo by meeting with him. Merritt himself might receive Aguinaldo as a "subordinate" prepared to "offer his services" to the Americans, but otherwise intended to avoid all contacts with him until after the U.S. forces had captured Manila. At that point, the Filipino's "pretensions should not clash with my designs."

But Merritt faced a dilemma: He could not attack Manila without breaking through the Filipino encirclement of the city, which would have transgressed McKinley's order to him to maintain peace. On the other hand, he could not essay a diplomatic attempt to persuade them to pull out of their positions without violating his own rule against talking with Aguinaldo. He resorted to a ruse.

He delegated General Greene to approach Noriel, the Filipino commander nearest Manila, with an "unofficial" offer. Greene would give him several "fine pieces of artillery" in return for yielding the sector south of the city to the Americans. The proposal tempted Noriel, whose only cannon was an old muzzle-loading columbiad captured from the Spanish, but he needed approval. Pressed by Greene to decide immediately, he sent an aide through a blinding rainstorm to Aguinaldo's headquarters at Bacoor, twelve miles away. Aguinaldo, always striving to gain formal recognition from the Americans, would only comply if Merritt signed the request. Anticipating Merritt's rejection of the transaction, Greene pledged to forward Aguinaldo the desired document after the Filipinos withdrew. Aguinaldo naïvely conceded.

Greene delivered neither the document nor the artillery pieces. As U.S. troops moved into the vacated Filipino trenches, Noriel realized that he had been duped. Nearly in tears, he rushed to Aguinaldo, shouting: "Look what they are doing! If we're not careful, they will soon be replacing our flags with their own all over the country!"

Aguinaldo, humiliated, feared that his own officers might doubt his leadership. Certainly, he could no longer expect them to trust the United States. But, precisely because Greene's deceit had stung him, he felt compelled to justify the Americans—almost as a defense of his own gullibility. "You are being tragic!" he snapped back to Noriel. "They are our allies, always remember that!"

At night on July 31, to flex their muscles at the U.S. troops entering the area, the Spanish unleashed a series of senseless artillery and infantry attacks. Ten Americans died—the first to be killed in action in the Philippines.

Manila, now in its third month under siege, had become unbearable. The Intramuros, whose normal population numbered ten thousand, held seventy thousand people, many sleeping in the streets. Water was scarce, fruit and vegetables rare, and horseflesh a delicacy. Disease had spread, especially among women, children and the elderly, and the sick crammed churches already packed with wounded soldiers. It was only a matter of time before the city fell.

Spanish officials contemplated capitulation with dread. Terrified by the prospect of "savage" Filipinos investing Manila, they would only surrender to the Americans. But, under Spain's quaint code of honor, a court-martial awaited them unless they put up a fight. So a sham battle with the U.S. forces had to be contrived to save them from disgrace, much less punishment. Dewey had earlier shunned the idea when Governor Augustín suggested it through the British consul. He then lacked the men to block the natives, who would "wreak their vengeance upon the Spaniards and indulge in a carnival of loot," as he later explained. Now that the U.S. infantry had arrived, however, the rebels could be kept at bay. Dewey sent a message through the Belgian consul, Edouard André, to the new governor, General Fermín Jaudenes, named in July to replace Augustín, who had been dismissed for "defeatism." The Americans were ready for the charade.

The news of Spain's rout in Cuba demoralized the Spanish in Manila. They could no longer entertain the hope of a flotilla steaming in to rescue them—the illusion that had sustained them during the siege. Merritt was now eager to dash into the city. But Dewey stalled, quietly maneuvering to work out a bloodless scenario with Jaudenes.

Despite his orders to fight, Jaudenes had intimated to André that he might cede to the Americans—"to white people, never to niggers," as he put it. On August 4, Dewey and Merritt gave him forty-eight hours to lay down his arms, then extended the deadline for five days, setting the attack for the next morning. They confected the ultimatums in part to furnish Jaudenes with the face-saving evidence that he had buckled only under U.S. pressure. But they also meant the threats to be credible, should he actually resist. For the same reason, they kept the charade secret from their own senior officers and naturally excluded Aguinaldo from the deal. American troops were ordered to keep the Filipinos outside the city—if possible by persuasion.

Covert negotiations continued through André until the phony operation was scripted and scheduled for August 13. Dewey was to lob a few shells at both the Intramuros and Fort San Antonio Abad, a decrepit structure on the southern edge of Manila. His flagship would then fly the international code letters for surrender, the signal for the Spanish to raise a white flag. After officers from the two sides signed a truce, U.S. troops would stride into the city, unmolested. The exercise was to be over by afternoon "without loss of life," as Merritt noted. But it ran into snags.

Divulging the hoax to four of his ship captains, Dewey directed them to feign a bombardment that would spare Manila any serious damage. One of the skippers deliberately gave his gunners the wrong range for their targets. But, assuming that he had miscalculated, they corrected their sights and scored several direct hits. Dismayed, he sounded a cease-fire and withdrew his vessel from the line.

On land, the masquerade was even more difficult to manage. The Colorado volunteers, approaching Manila from the south, sloshed through mud as their band played the hardy perennial "There'll Be a Hot Time in the Old Town Tonight." The ease of it all gratified them: Fort San Antonio Abad, their initial objective, was empty, and a white flag fluttered over the Intramuros, their second goal. In another zone, the Filipinos exuberantly joined a U.S. column, thinking the attack was genuine. Spanish troops panicked at the sight, and started shooting back. Six Americans and forty-nine Spaniards died in the skirmish.

Dewey, lamenting the losses, later faulted Merritt for having "rushed in too soon." But the casualties were really the consequence of a communications gap. Had Dewey not severed the cable, Manila would have learned that Spain, beaten in Cuba, had signed an armistice with the United States the day before. As it was, news of the cease-fire reached the capital via Hong Kong three days after the sham battle. Spanish jurists contended during the later peace negotiations that, under international law, the prior truce had nullified the U.S. victory; the situation, therefore, should have returned to *status quo ante bellum.*

The phony fight for Manila further strained the already threadbare ties between the Americans and Filipinos. The nationalists, dismayed at having been left behind, pressed toward the city. Anderson urged Aguinaldo to restrain them "until we have received the full surrender" from the Spanish—at which stage, he pledged, "we will negotiate with you." Aguinaldo reluctantly complied. But four days afterward, McKinley ruled that the Americans alone would control the capital. "The insurgents and all others," he told Merritt, "must recognize the military occupation and authority of the United States." Angry at the apparent betrayal by the Americans, Apolinario Mabini forecast worse ahead: "The conflict is coming sooner or later, and we shall gain nothing by asking as favors of them what are really our rights."

He could have blamed Aguinaldo for gullibility, however. By trusting the Americans, and not attacking Manila before the U.S. forces landed, Aguinaldo was denied a role in the defeat of Spain, an outcome for which he had struggled for two years. Dewey and Merritt also barred him from the surrender ceremony. General Greene, presiding over the austere ritual, accorded the Spanish "all honors" and the status of war prisoners until the United States and Spain concluded a peace treaty.

Jaudenes later blamed the disaster on Spain's disregard for the Philippines.

Only his prudence, he pleaded before a court-martial in Madrid, had saved Manila from "pillage and devastation" by the Filipinos. The judges, torn between respect for his achievement and fidelity to military tradition, declined to reach a verdict. Jaudenes soon retired, his honor intact but his reputation stained.

Spain was not alone in defeat. Like vultures hovering over a carcass, European and Japanese warships had entered Manila Bay in May, after Dewey destroyed the Spanish fleet. Kaiser Wilhelm of Germany, then seeking dominions overseas, had sent in a flotilla of five cruisers under Vice Admiral Otto von Diederichs, his naval commander in the Far East. Wilhelm had received a preposterous report from an agent in Manila that the Filipinos were contemplating the creation of a monarchy and might welcome a German prince as king. He also hoped to acquire a Philippine base if the archipelago were carved up—or perhaps he could use Germany's presence there to bargain for territory elsewhere. Dewey, who hated Germans, was certain that they had come to help the Spanish.

He found confirmation for his suspicions in early July, when a German cruiser evacuated women and children from a provincial Spanish garrison besieged by the Filipinos. He accused Germany of breaking his blockade of the islands and authorized his men to board and search German vessels. When Diederichs protested, Dewey flew into a tantrum: "If Germany wants war, all right, we are ready!" Cables crackled between Washington and Berlin as alarmed diplomats in both capitals cooled tempers. Finally, at the beginning of August, the German fleet steamed away—Kaiser Wilhelm having concluded that his prospects in the Philippines were dim.

The flap with Germany, though trivial, nevertheless set ripples in motion. Reports of Dewey's prowess, exaggerated to lavish proportions by an adoring U.S. press, inflated his already legendary stature to towering heights. Like many another hero, he soon made the fatal mistake of believing his own publicity—and even began to imagine himself a presidential candidate. Meanwhile, grossly distorted by distance, the spectacle of Germany's bluster lent substance in Washington to the theory of "contingent necessity." It became axiomatic to American strategists that, unless the United States took over the Philippines, another of the foreign imperialist powers would grab the archipelago.

★ ★ ★

"Why is President McKinley's mind like a bed?" "Because it has to be made up for him before he can use it."

That popular joke of the period was all too true in late July, two or three weeks before the armistice. By now resigned to defeat, the Spanish hoped to win generous terms from the United States by proposing negotiations. They transmitted a peace overture through Jules Cambon, the French ambassador in Washington. The offer confronted McKinley with the ordeal of making decisions.

Congress had already voted in favor of independence for Cuba, so he was mercifully spared that issue, but McKinley had to define a policy for the Philippines. After a chat with him on the topic, Lodge cryptically remarked that he "means to go much farther than anyone I think guesses." But McKinley had no plan except to negotiate the future of the archipelago as part of a comprehensive settlement with Spain.

Seeking guidance on his reply to the Spanish proposal, he turned to his cabinet members. Summer enveloped Washington, and he invited them to escape the stifling heat by cruising the Potomac aboard a lighthouse tender. Puffing cigars and sipping cool drinks, they discussed the subject for four consecutive days, with McKinley acting more like a moderator than an arbiter. John Griggs, the shrewd attorney general, advocated holding the Philippines for its reputed commercial advantages—a view backed by Cornelius Bliss, the patrician secretary of the interior. James Wilson, the secretary of agriculture, a gray-bearded Scottish farmer from Iowa, was a devout Presbyterian who saw the archipelago as a field ripe for evangelical endeavor. Secretary of State Day found annexation unappealing. Lodge and Mahan tried to sway him with visions of America's strategic role in the Pacific. Day objected, saying that America was unsuited to rule "eight or nine millions of absolutely ignorant and many degraded" Filipinos. He also maintained, as a judge, that colonialism violated the constitutional precept of government by consent of the governed. At best, he allowed, the United States might keep only Manila as a naval base—a "hitching post," McKinley interjected.

In a note to himself, scribbled beforehand, McKinley had outlined a basis for talks with the Spanish, one that coincided with the cabinet consensus: Spain must yield Cuba and Puerto Rico unconditionally, but the status of the Philippines could be negotiated. As soon as the Spanish agreed to a truce, McKinley would appoint a delegation to pursue peace talks.

Day and his staff thereupon drafted a formal "protocol" to initiate the process. Cambon cabled the text to Spain, and it shuttled back and forth between Madrid and Washington for weeks, undergoing revisions. Cambon performed a dual role that proved him to be one of the most talented diplomats of the time. Representing the Spanish, he urged McKinley to soften his terms, pointing out that the United States could afford to be charitable. As their adviser, he persuaded the Spanish to acquiesce, candidly reminding them that defeat had limited their options. They finally agreed to give up Cuba and Puerto Rico and to concede to the American occupation of Manila until subsequent negotiations determined "the control, disposition and government" of the Philippines.

Bare electric bulbs flickered in the White House Cabinet Room on the afternoon of August 12, as a summer storm lashed its dim windows. Stiff and unsmiling, as if to emphasize the solemnity of the occasion, McKinley peered down on the table as Cambon and Day signed four copies of the armistice accord. Day had never been a true imperialist, but now his appetite for territory was whetted. Scanning a globe in the room, he said to an aide, "Let's see what we get by this."

Reflecting the expansionist mood creeping over the nation, the Senate had just voted after many delays to bring Hawaii into the U.S. fold. But Congress was still split, largely along party lines, over the wider issue of America's global role. McKinley, who detested discord, recoiled from exacerbating the dissonance—especially with legislative elections due in the fall. A peace treaty would also require Senate ratification, and he hoped for its endorsement with minimum debate. Thus, as the talks with the Spanish neared, he sought negotiators who would heed his wishes yet seem to be impartial—and, above all, deliver a settlement that aroused as little domestic opposition as possible.

He eventually formed a five-man delegation that was constitutionally dubious and politically tilted. Blurring the doctrine of separation of powers, he chose three senators who would later ratify a pact that they had negotiated. He also weighted the group with three avowed expansionists: senators Cushman K. Davis of Minnesota and William P. Frye of Maine, both Republicans, and Whitelaw Reid, publisher of the *New York Tribune*. The only strong anti-imperialist on the panel was Senator George Gray, a conservative Democrat from Delaware. William Day, who had been uncomfortable handling foreign policy as secretary of state, resigned to head the delegation. He anticipated a federal judgeship afterward, and McKinley expected him to be pliable. McKinley named John Hay, the urbane ambassador to London, to succeed Day, believing him more qualified to handle the intricacies of international affairs.

The delegation prepared to depart on September 18 for Paris, the site of the peace conference. The evening before, McKinley gave its members their instructions in the form of a long sermon at a farewell White House banquet. America had gone to war "only in obedience to the dictates of humanity and in the fulfillment of high public and moral obligations," with "no ambition of conquest," he said. For that reason, he had not acquired Cuba. But the Philippines was different. The capture of Manila had imposed on the United States "new duties and responsibilities, which we must meet and discharge as becomes a great nation." Foremost among these was "the commercial opportunity to which American statesmanship cannot be indifferent." Accordingly, he told his negotiators, he would accept nothing less from Spain than "the cession in full right and sovereignty" of Luzon.

"The march of events rules and overrules human action," McKinley intoned, the ponderous phrase again a reflection of his preference to follow rather than lead. Only ten months before, he had vigorously opposed a war for territory, saying that such a conflict would, "by our code of morality . . . be criminal aggression." But now he was sliding deeper into the imperialist camp and, within weeks, would demand total U.S. acquisition of the Philippines.

His conversion was a gradual process. He had at first been tempted to retain only Manila as a trading post and coaling station, as Secretary of State Day had recommended. But naval strategists advised him that the port was indefensible, and their counsel prompted them to order his peace negotiators to demand Luzon. He could have guaranteed the independence of the Philippines under a U.S. protectorate, an alternative favored by the Filipinos. He also rejected that solution, however, reasoning that America ought not assume the burden of responsibility without the benefits of authority. Thus he drifted toward complete annexation of the islands.

In one of the most singular explanations for the formulation of a foreign policy ever devised by an American president, McKinley divulged to members of a Methodist missionary society visiting him at the White House a year later that he had been inspired by divine guidance. He detained them as they rose to leave his office. "Not quite yet, gentlemen! Before you go, I would like to say just a word about the Philippine business." With that, he proceeded to tell the tale of his revelation.

In "truth," he said, he had not wanted the islands and had no idea what to do "when they came to us as a gift from the gods." He had paced the floor of the White House nightly, even kneeling to beg "Almighty God for light and guidance." Then, suddenly one night, a list of options appeared. It would be "cowardly and dishonorable" to restore them to Spain and "bad business and discreditable" to give them to France or Germany, "our commercial rivals in the Orient." Nor could they be abandoned to the natives, who "were unfit for self-government [and] would soon have anarchy and misrule." His only choice, therefore, was to take the archipelago and "to educate the Filipinos, and uplift and Christianize them, and by God's grace do the very best we could by them, as our fellow men for whom Christ died."

Devoutly religious, McKinley may indeed have been swayed by prayer, but he might have explored other courses of action. In particular, he did little to understand the aims of the Filipinos in his only encounter with one of their spokesmen, treating him instead with polite indifference.

Felipe Agoncillo, a rich Filipino lawyer and Aguinaldo's chief diplomat, arrived in Washington in September in quest of U.S. support. Granted an audience by McKinley at the White House on the afternoon of October 1, he appeared in a dark suit and bowler hat, the *ilustrado* uniform, and with typical Filipino gusto launched into a rhetorical exegesis. He recalled the iniquities of Spanish colonialism, expressed admiration for American democracy, described the Filipino nationalist program and evoked Dewey's purported pledge to back Philippine freedom. Cadenzas of elegant Castilian cascaded from his lips, his vibrato voice rising and falling in dramatic cadence as Alvey A. Adee, the State Department factotum, translated. McKinley had never heard anything like it. He listened fitfully, trying to remain awake as the afternoon light waned and Agoncillo, carried away by his own eloquence, swept on.

Finally, McKinley responded. He rejected Agoncillo's request for Filipino representation at the peace talks in Paris on the grounds that Spain would object. Nor could he authorize the U.S. delegation to hear the Filipino case, lamely explaining that Agoncillo's command of English was inadequate. But, unfailingly courteous, McKinley thanked his visitor, shook his hand warmly and saw him to the door with an invitation to submit a memorandum to the State Department. Adee later accepted the memorandum "in the most informal manner" and promptly interred it in a file. McKinley's rebuff notwithstanding, Agoncillo sailed for Paris. There too, the American negotiators brushed him off.

Had his bureaucracy operated efficiently, McKinley might also have gathered an insight into the Philippines from two young U.S. naval officers, Paymaster W. B. Wilcox and Cadet L. R. Sargent, whom Dewey had sent on a survey of Luzon. No Americans until then had undertaken so extensive a study. They toured the island for two months, interviewing hundreds of people. Aguinaldo, they learned, enjoyed wide support. The Filipinos overwhelmingly desired independence, preferably under U.S. protection, yet believed that whatever America "may have done for them, it has not gained the right to annex them." Dewey praised their report as the "most complete and reliable" available, but, for some inexplicable reason, he delayed for weeks before mailing it to Washington, where Navy Department officials relegated it to the archives.

General Greene, on the other hand, heavily influenced McKinley. He returned to Washington an instant expert after spending six weeks in a peanut field near Manila, having compiled a huge memorandum on the Philippines covering everything from its ethnic diversity to statistics on taxes and trade. Its sheer volume impressed McKinley. They had several conversations as well in which Greene, a champion of U.S. annexation of the islands, contended that Aguinaldo was a potential despot disliked by most Filipinos. Despite severe eyestrain, McKinley also read a recent article in the *Contemporary Review,* a London periodical, that was being widely quoted in the American press. Its author, John Foreman, a former British resident of Manila, claimed that Aguinaldo's movement was limited to Luzon. Consequently, he concluded, perhaps accurately, that bitter regional squabbles would rapidly rip an independent Philippines apart, making it prey to Japan, Germany or another imperialist power.

But nothing propelled McKinley more dynamically toward total annexation of the Philippines than his perception of U.S. opinion. He "seemed to fear," one of his aides noted, that anything less than full acquisition of the islands would incur the wrath of the nation.

Dewey had repaired the cable out of Manila, and American correspondents were filing glowing accounts of the glorious activities of U.S. soldiers in the Philippines. The stories gradually changed the national mood. A survey conducted in September showed eighty-four major newspapers in favor of keeping the archipelago, a sharp switch from only a few weeks before. Finley Peter Dunne described the shift in his column in the *Chicago Journal.* " 'I know what I'd do if I was Mack,' said Mr. Hennessy. 'I'd hist a flag over th' Ph'lippens, an' I'd take in th' whole lot iv thim.' 'An' yet,' said Mr. Dooley, ' 'tis not more thin two months since ye larned whether they were islands or canned goods.' "

Just as he had heeded God's word, so McKinley tuned into the voice of the American people. He toured the Middle West for ten vivid days in early autumn, stumping for Republicans in the forthcoming election and canvassing reactions to America's new global role. As usual, he spoke piously of justice, humanity and morality, but he felt—or thought that he felt—a surge of imperialist sentiment. Crowds cheered enthusiastically in Nebraska, Iowa, Illinois and Ohio as he talked of assuming "the trust that civilization puts upon us" and keeping "territory that sometimes comes to us when we go to war in a holy cause." At an exposition in Omaha, he rhetorically asked, "Shall we deny to ourselves what the rest of the world so freely and so justly accords to us?" "No!" the audience shouted, and he went on: "The war was not more invited by us than were the questions . . . laid at our door by its results. Now as then we will do our duty."

He exultantly returned to Washington, confirmed in his estimate of the public's expectations. On October 26, he sent new orders to his negotiators in Paris. He now wanted the Philippine islands in their entirety. "The cession must be of the whole archipelago or none. The latter is wholly inadmissible, and the former must therefore be required."

The peace talks had by then dragged on for nearly a month in a sumptuous salon of the French foreign ministry. The Spanish, after some bickering, had finally acquiesced to the loss of Cuba, Puerto Rico and Guam. But they refused to yield the Philippines, contending that the Americans had captured Manila after the signature of the armistice and that they did not hold much beyond the city in any case.

Splits within the U.S. delegation further snarled the negotiations. Former Secretary of State Day, a scrupulous jurist, echoed the Spanish view that the prior armistice agreement nullified the seizure of Manila. Senator Gray, an ardent isolationist, dissented even more adamantly. To take over the islands would reverse America's traditional "continental policy," risk "dangerous complications with foreign nations" and increase military expenditures and the "burdens of taxation." He also threw back at McKinley the president's own claim to have gone to war with "no ambition of conquest."

McKinley, decisive for the first time on this issue, would not budge. The Republican election triumphs in November had shown him the light. The "one plain path of duty," he replied, was full U.S. acquisition of the archipelago.

But even the imperialists on his peace delegation were now worried. The liberal Spanish prime minister, Práxedes Mateo Sagasta, was being harassed by his right-wing rivals. Unless a compromise were found he might be compelled to break off the talks and resume fighting. Senator Frye finally came up with the crassly practical idea of paying off Spain. His weary colleagues concurred, and so did McKinley. On November 21, Day suggested the figure of $20 million to Montero Ríos, the head Spanish negotiator. Ríos forwarded the proposal to Madrid and, chain-smoking nervously, read his government's florid reply two days later. Spain, for "lofty reasons of patriotism and humanity," ceded to "the law of the victor, however hard it may be," rather than return to "the horrors of war."

The peace treaty, signed by the two delegations in Paris on December 10, granted independence to Cuba and made Guam, Puerto Rico and the Philippines U.S. possessions. It only awaited ratification by the Senate to become legitimate. But to become a reality in the Philippines, it would have to be accepted by the Filipinos.

★ ★ ★

The American forces faced staggering problems after they entered Manila in August 1898. Crowded with refugees, the capital suffered from critical food and water shortages. Garbage that had accumulated during the siege littered the streets, many of them flooded for lack of drainage. Municipal bureaus and courts were closed, and former Spanish officials sullenly refused to cooperate in restoring services. Swindlers, gamblers, adventurers and other riffraff soon landed, lured by the chance to bilk the Americans. Prostitutes flocked in from San Francisco, Shanghai, Hong Kong and Tokyo. The Escolta, one of the city's main shopping thoroughfares, rapidly became a honky-tonk of noisy bars and saloons filled day and night with boisterous drunks.

Racial tensions inevitably mounted. Later generations of U.S. troops in Asia were to pin derisive labels on the natives, like "slopies" for Chinese and "gooks" for Koreans and Vietnamese. The early Americans to reach the Philippines at first referred to Filipinos as "niggers" and subsequently called them "gugus"—an epithet derived from the tree bark used as shampoo by the local women. Ugly incidents multiplied as the Americans clashed with native soldiers in the area around Manila. Private William Christner, a Pennsylvania volunteer, wrote to his father: "We killed a few to learn them a lesson, and you bet they learned it."

Characteristically, though, the Americans combined contempt for the natives with an evangelical impulse to improve their conditions. They swiftly brought law and order to Manila by creating a police force and military tribunals. They repaired roads and reopened schools. Concentrating on public health, they set up clinics, vaccinated children against smallpox and banned the local practice of dumping slops out of windows. One American team even devoted weeks to the repulsive task of removing the human excrement piled up under houses, whose toilets consisted of a hole in the floor. Soon Manila regained a semblance of normality. The U.S. Army band performed every afternoon at the Luneta, the city's central park, playing "There'll Be a Hot Time in the Old Town Tonight" so frequently that Filipinos reverently bared their heads, assuming it to be the American national anthem.

But the American and Filipino forces seemed destined to collide. Fatuous and arrogant, U.S. officers made no effort to appreciate Aguinaldo's aspirations. He, in turn, felt increasingly frustrated. Hoping that the Senate would repudiate the treaty with Spain and instead press McKinley to recognize Philippine independence, Aguinaldo pursued a dual policy. He deployed his troops throughout Luzon, reckoning that the control of territory would confirm his power and thus strengthen his bargaining position with the United States. Similarly, he bid for status by creating a formal government, complete with a constitution and an elected assembly. His military gains bolstered his claim to represent the only true nationalist force, but his political initiative faltered, with serious consequences for his movement.

He had moved late in the summer from Cavite to Malolos, a bustling market town twenty miles north of Manila. There he established his headquarters in a handsome old monastery and draped himself in the trappings of office. He furnished the building's chambers with loot stolen from Spanish homes, and posted uniformed halberdiers to guard its gates. On September 15, 1898, in an adjacent church, he convened a national assembly amid a fanfare of flags and martial music. The hundred delegates were hardly the primitive natives depicted in travelogues of the time. Wearing top hats and cutaway coats, most were lawyers, doctors, merchants, schoolteachers and writers, many of them educated in Europe. Aguinaldo, also dressed for the occasion, looked in swallowtails like a doll on a wedding cake. They indulged in such puerile French revolutionary rituals as addressing each other as "citizen," and reveled in an extravagant banquet, its dozen or more courses running the gastronomic gamut from *saumon hollandaise* through *coquilles de crabes vol-au-vent* and *dinde truffée* to *gelée de fraises*—all accompanied by fine wines and liqueurs. An American correspondent present remarked of the event, "They conducted themselves with great decorum, and showed a knowledge of debate and parliamentary law."

Dazzled by their wealth and prestige, Aguinaldo deferred to the *ilustrados,* who voted him president and appointed Mabini prime minister, titles they intended to be cosmetic. A rich attorney, Felipe Calderón, had drafted a constitution that vested authority in a legislature dominated by the upper classes—an "oligarchy of intelligence" better qualified to govern than "igno-rant" soldiers, as he put it. He discarded Mabini's egalitarian ideas, limited suffrage to the landed gentry and rebuffed proposals for agrarian reform.

Radicals protested against the conservative program, and the congress split into factions whose differences persisted, eventually debilitating the nationalist movement. Afterward, when war broke out between Filipinos and Americans, many conservatives chose to collaborate with the U.S. side, which promised to protect their economic and social privileges. The rivalries sapped Agui-naldo's struggle for independence and facilitated U.S. annexation of the Philip-pines. But the basic liberties guaranteed by the Malolos constitution were sufficient to justify Aguinaldo's later claim that it marked "the first crystalliza-tion of democracy" in Asia.

Despite his disappointments, Aguinaldo tried to prevent his men from clash-ing with U.S. units flanking Manila during the early fall. But his troops, hard to restrain under the best of conditions, were doubly difficult to discipline in the face of nearly constant American pressures.

Merritt had gone home in late August at his own request, annoyed by McKinley's refusal to allow him to conquer the entire archipelago. He had spent his three weeks in Manila aboard a ship anchored in the bay, learning nothing. Major General Elwell Stephen Otis stepped in.

At sixty-one, Otis was a portly figure with mutton-chop whiskers and a shrill voice. A Harvard Law School graduate, he had fought in the Civil War and against Indians and had founded the army's staff school at Leavenworth, Kansas. But despite his gilt-edged credentials, he was an inauspicious choice for a job that required tact and imagination. A head wound had left him an insomniac, and he sought solace at his desk from dawn until midnight— "counting the beans," as an aide described his obsession with trivia. Dewey called him "a pincushion of an old woman," and he reminded MacArthur of "a locomotive bottomside up on the track, with its wheels revolving at full speed." Though he never met Aguinaldo, he later charged him with "duplic-ity." Filipinos, he said, were "robbers" who aimed to "drive the Americans into the sea, and kill every white man in Manila."

McKinley, anxious to placate Spain, insisted that the native forces be barred from Manila by "whatever means" necessary. Otis confidently replied that with "delicate manipulation," he could handle them. He then proceeded to act like a bully.

American reinforcements were due to land soon, raising the U.S. force to twenty-two thousand men. Seeking to deploy them in a Manila suburb occu-pied by the Filipinos, Otis sent Aguinaldo an ultimatum. The peace talks with Spain had not yet started, but, his law degree notwithstanding, Otis argued that there was "no legal question as to the propriety of full American sover-eignty" over the sector. He wanted the native troops out in a week—or else, he warned Aguinaldo, he would take "forcible action" and "hold you responsi-ble for any unfortunate consequences that may ensue."

Otis was on dangerous terrain. The Filipino force, comprising about thirty thousand men, had lately received new weapons. A skirmish might flare into fighting and embarrass McKinley, who then hoped for a compromise with Spain. But Otis had stared down Sitting Bull in a confrontation at Yellowstone in 1876 and could cope with Filipinos. He told Washington, "I shall not yield to any of their requests, or make any concessions."

Aguinaldo, also awaiting the peace talks, hesitated to defy the Americans. He offered to comply if Otis softened his language. Otis consented. On September 14, two thousand Filipino soldiers marched out of two zones near Manila to the tempo of three bands. They saluted the Stars and Stripes as it replaced their flag over the trenches.

Otis sent Aguinaldo a note of thanks for his "friendly spirit." But Aguinaldo's moderation only convinced him that he could easily bend the Filipinos—and, again threatening force, he demanded that they yield other positions. Again retreating, Aguinaldo finally ordered his troops to recognize America's "military occupation and jurisdiction" over Manila and its suburbs.

Otis concluded by early December that the independence movement was crumbling, basing his view on talks with a few conservative Filipinos who had lost confidence in Aguinaldo. Trinidad Pardo de Tavera, a distinguished scholar and early nationalist, argued that "under no circumstances" should the United States leave the Philippines. He was seconded by Florentino Torres, a rich lawyer, who proposed the "frank and loyal acceptance" by the Filipinos of a permanent American presence—or else, he said, the islands would be taken over by another foreign power. Assuming these *ilustrados* to be representative, Otis cabled McKinley: INSURGENTS REPORTED FAVORABLE TO AMERICAN ANNEXATION.

A bizarre episode proved him wrong. On December 13, a message reached him from the port of Iloilo, located on the island of Panay three hundred miles south of Manila. The Spanish garrison there was still defending the town against Filipino nationalists, and local merchants sought American help to lift the siege, which was hurting trade. Otis, lusting for action, assigned Brigadier General Marcus Miller to lead a U.S. force to the scene. But Dewey refused to provide ships without Washington's approval. Unlike his eager army colleagues, he felt that control of Manila and another base or two suited America's aims. He also feared a war with the natives, who to him were "little more than children." McKinley, however, authorized the expedition "to preserve peace and protect life and property" in Iloilo. Miller departed with 2,500 men aboard four transports, with a cruiser as an escort.

McKinley was then in Georgia, striving to heal the wounds of the Civil War by evoking the U.S. defeat of Spain as a national achievement. He also hoped to rally public support for ratification of the treaty with Spain in the Senate, whose southern members suspected annexation of the Philippines on the grounds that brown people would enter America. Warm ovations convinced him of the wisdom of his overseas venture, but he persisted in sending muddled messages to his commanders in Manila after Miller's task force had steamed into the harbor of Iloilo.

The Spanish had withdrawn from the port on Christmas Day, and the Filipino commander denied Miller the right to land without "express orders" from Aguinaldo. Having come to terms with the nationalists, the merchants who had originally requested U.S. aid now advised Miller against disembarking troops. Miller, a crusty Civil War veteran, nevertheless favored an attack, but Otis checked him as he attempted to decipher McKinley's confusing directive, which ordered the American expedition to be firm yet conciliatory and to capture the town without risking a fight.

The U.S. troops at Iloilo were to remain aboard their ships for the next six weeks, stifling in the tropical heat. McKinley, later reversing himself, praised Otis's prudence: "Glad you did not permit Miller to bring on a conflict. Time given the insurgents cannot hurt us and must weaken and discourage them. . . . They will see our benevolent purpose."

But McKinley's virtuous intentions eluded the Filipino militants. The newspaper *La Independencia,* founded by the hotheaded General Antonio Luna, unleashed a tirade against the United States despite Otis's efforts to suppress its publication. The atmosphere became more feverish when Aguinaldo, in what Otis later termed "a virtual declaration of war," warned that he would "open hostilities" if Miller tried to seize Iloilo. "I denounce these acts before the world," Aguinaldo intoned, "so that the conscience of mankind may deliver its infallible verdict as to who are the true oppressors of nations and the tormenters of humanity. Upon their heads be all the blood that may be shed."

McKinley committed another blunder that aggravated the strained situation. Dewey, alarmed by the tension, had urged him to "allay the spirit of unrest" by issuing a proclamation defining U.S. policy toward the Philippines. With nobody on his staff competent to guide him, McKinley turned to Dean Worcester, a University of Michigan zoologist then visiting Washington. Worcester, later a key figure in the American colonial administration of the islands, was unqualified as a political adviser. He had studied wildlife in parts of the archipelago, but had never been to Luzon, the crucible of Filipino nationalism and knew nothing about its leaders or their objectives. McKinley nevertheless enlisted his help to draft a proclamation, which he cabled to Otis on December 26 with instructions to make it public immediately.

America's "earnest and paramount aim," said McKinley, was to "win the confidence, respect and affection" of the Filipinos by "proving to them that the mission of the United States is one of benevolent assimilation." They could hold office if they acknowledged American "supremacy." But "the strong arm of authority" would be "sedulously maintained" to "repress disturbance and to overcome all obstacles to the bestowal of the blessings of good and stable government." Meanwhile, the U.S. presence was to be "extended . . . to the whole of the ceded territory," since America had acquired "sovereignty" over the islands through the treaty with Spain.

Otis recoiled from publishing the document. McKinley, he realized, could not legally affirm U.S. control over the Philippines until the Senate had ratified the peace treaty. He also feared that radical Filipinos, spoiling for a fight, would react against McKinley's virtual decision to take over the archipelago. So, though a mere soldier, he rewrote the statement, replacing milder phrases for inflammatory terms like *supremacy* and *sovereignty.* He "did not think the president understood the situation," he recalled later, and "under the conditions then prevailing" felt "perfectly justified . . . to make such amendments."

Otis's revisions might have averted a crisis had not General Miller, sitting off Iloilo, inadvertently bungled. Washington had transmitted him a copy of McKinley's original text, which he naïvely handed to the local Filipino commander as evidence of America's benign intentions. The native officer forwarded the version to Aguinaldo, who immediately concluded that McKinley meant to seize the Philippines.

Aguinaldo prepared for war. Early in January 1899, he directed his provincial commanders to stockpile rice and other supplies. He also instructed the *sandatahan,* a fifth column of native commandos inside Manila, to plan an attack against the Americans in the capital. The Filipinos were sure to win, he told his generals, revealing to them that he had dreamed the night before of a triumphal march into Manila four hours after the fighting began. The prospect excited Colonel Juan Cailles, the Filipino commander of one zone near the city. When an American officer ordered him to withdraw his men fifty paces from the boundary line, Cailles sent him a challenging note: "Since Maquinley [*sic*] opposes our independence, I refuse to deal with any American. War, war is what we want!" Aguinaldo commended Cailles: "I approve and applaud what you have done."

Otis also braced for combat. Ignoring Aguinaldo's protests, he moved the Nebraska volunteers to Santa Mesa, on the western fringe of Manila, claiming that its climate was healthier than that of their former camp. In fact, the area was strategically situated at the juncture of the Pasig and San Juan rivers, the city's key waterways, and it also dominated a vital road. The Americans tightened their communications throughout the sector with a network of telegraph wires. Dewey deployed his ships within range of the Filipino positions, but he seemed to be troubled by the mounting tensions. "We may be fighting with the insurgents at any moment," he wrote to his son on January 23, adding that he preferred to abandon the archipelago "rather than have . . . a war with them."

The army did not share Dewey's reticence. Despite McKinley's earlier plea for peace at any price, the War Department publicly disclosed that Otis was now under orders to use force for the purpose of "defending himself and the interests confided to his charge." Otis, anticipating an outbreak, said: "The least spark may start a conflagration."

The two sides poised for war, but neither was ready to fire the first shot. Instead, they agreed to make a last stab at a reconciliation. The Americans issued safe-conduct passes to a delegation of Filipinos to come to Manila for a series of six meetings that dragged on through January.

The U.S. officers at the talks, proceeding without guidance from Washington, had no clear objective. They were vaguely aware of McKinley's desire for peace, but they also knew that he now favored annexation of the Philippines— a policy that would probably lead to war with the Filipinos. Nevertheless, they saw the sessions as a useful delaying tactic. As one of them later explained, they were "trying to gain time" until the arrival of four fresh U.S. battalions, "which we needed very much."

The Filipinos, for their part, still seemed to believe in the possibility of independence under a U.S. protectorate—a proposal that they repeated again and again in the course of the conferences. But they were also stalling in the hope that the Senate might disapprove the treaty with Spain and thus compel McKinley to consider a Philippine policy more attuned to their aspirations.

* * *

The real question, however, was far broader than the future American relationship with the Philippines: Would the United States shun this new obligation
abroad and cling to its traditional insularity, or would it advance toward larger
global responsibilities by becoming an imperial power? It was a question for
the nation to decide.

The Anti-Imperialist League, the most vocal lobby against expansion, held
its first meeting in Boston in November 1898. Patrician conservatives composed
its upper echelons. George Boutwell, the president, was a vintage Republican
who had been governor of Massachusetts and Grant's secretary of the treasury.
Grover Cleveland and Andrew Carnegie figured among its distinguished members, along with numbers of prominent lawyers, educators, editors and clergymen. But Theodore Roosevelt's cruel portrayal of them as "men of a bygone
age" was apt. Many, in their sixties or seventies, yearned to keep America
unfettered by foreign entanglements. Several, abolitionists before the Civil
War, equated the Filipino quest for independence with the Negro struggle for
freedom; some even compared Aguinaldo to John Brown.

By contrast, militant imperialists like Roosevelt, Lodge and Beveridge were
young, dynamic, progressive and, in their way, infused with idealism. Roosevelt had returned from his moment of glory as a horseless Rough Rider in
Cuba to run for governor of New York. In October 1898, as his campaign
gathered momentum, he pleaded in one of his more memorable speeches for
retaining the Philippines. "The guns of our warships have awakened us to new
duties. We are face to face with our destiny, and we must meet it with a high
and resolute courage. . . . Let us rather run the risk of wearing out than rusting
out."

As the test approached on Capitol Hill, the two senators from Massachusetts, both Republicans, represented opposite extremes of the spectrum. Henry
Cabot Lodge, managing the fight for approval of the treaty, warned that its
rejection would mean "humiliation of the whole country in the eyes of the
world" and show America to be "unfit as a nation to enter into the great
questions of foreign policy." George Hoar, meanwhile, had been arguing for
months that the seizure of territory abroad would transform America into "a
vulgar, commonplace empire founded upon physical force, controlling subject
races and vassal states, in which one class must forever rule, and other classes
must forever obey."

The Senate appeared to be split along party lines—with the notable exception of Hoar, a loyal Republican on nearly every other issue. An illustrious
New Englander, then seventy-two, his ancestors included a Harvard president
and a signer of the Declaration of Independence. A colleague called him the
"most cultivated man" in the Senate, and he did indeed collect rare books and
read poetry. He had been in Congress for thirty years, laboring for civil-service
reform and antitrust legislation. Round, bespectacled and white haired, he
resembled a jovial elf; the image, however, concealed a fickle crank. He had
voted to annex Hawaii and at first hailed the conflict with Spain as "the most
honorable single war in history," believing that McKinley would resist the
imperialists. Now he charged the president with plotting the "downfall" of the
republic. But McKinley continued to worship and respect him. One day, when

he asked Hoar how he felt, the senator replied, "Pretty pugnacious, I confess, Mr. President." McKinley grasped his hand warmly and, eyes moistening, said, "I shall always love you, whatever you do."

William Jennings Bryan, the Democratic standard-bearer, had zigzagged. Fearful of trailing public opinion, he had initially acclaimed the war with Spain, even recruiting a regiment of Nebraska volunteers with himself, commissioned a colonel, as its commander. But his men, bound for Cuba, got no further than a filthy camp in Florida, where they swatted mosquitoes and sand flies and fell ill in droves. Mustered out, he became a critic of imperialism; by December 1898 he had switched again. He now supported the treaty with Spain, reckoning that the Republicans would come to grief in the Philippines, and thus improve his chances for the presidency in 1900.

As he counted votes before the debate, McKinley realized that he lacked the two-thirds majority needed for approval. Of the ninety seats in the Senate, the Republicans occupied forty-six, some held by defectors like Hoar. He had to convert at least a dozen Democrats and others—no mean task.

The expansionists received a boost from Rudyard Kipling, the British apostle of imperialism, whose poem "The White Man's Burden" was then circulating in America prior to its publication in *McClure's* magazine. He had timed the verse to the Senate debate, subtitling it "The United States and the Philippine Islands." It warned of the frustrations of ruling "new-caught, sullen peoples, half devil and half child," who would "bring all your hope to nought." But Americans must "have done with childish days," and rise to maturity by assuming the responsibility of governing distant lands.

> Comes now, to search your manhood
> Through all the thankless years,
> Cold-edged with dear-bought wisdom.
> The judgment of your peers!

The debate opened on a lofty plane as skilled jurists among the senators wrangled over interpretations of the Constitution. The learned George Vest of Missouri, a strict constructionist, observed that federal statutes contained no provision for colonies. In any case, he argued, the United States could not annex territories abroad against the will of their people without violating its own principle of "government by consent of the governed." Orville Platt of Connecticut, an equally serious student of the law, contended to the contrary that America's acquisition of Louisiana, Alaska and parts of Mexico had never been hindered by such scruples. The level of debate declined. Arthur Gorman, a conservative Maryland Democrat, warned that retention of the Philippines would open America to Filipinos, and "downgrade" white supremacy. Benjamin "Pitchfork Ben" Tillman of South Carolina took up the same theme, objecting to "the injection into the body politic of the United States . . . that vitiated blood, that debased and ignorant people." The Senate also approved a resolution disclaiming any intention of making the archipelago "an integral part" of the United States—another racist ploy designed to deny eventual statehood to the islands or citizenship for their people. Lodge, pleading for ratification, pledged that McKinley had no plans to keep the Philippines permanently. McKinley, however, promptly punctured the promise by refusing to permit an amendment to that effect. Nor would he support an effort by several senators to pledge independence to the Philippines upon the establishment of a stable government there.

Thomas Brackett Reed, the elephantine speaker of the House of Representatives and a premier Washington wit, injected a note of levity from the sidelines to the solemn rhetoric in the Senate. Deflating the imperialists, who saw value in America's new Pacific dominions, he quipped: "If you travel westward you'll reach the Philippines by way of Hawaii, and if you travel eastward you'll reach Hawaii by way of the Philippines. The whole question is whether you prefer to take your plague before your leprosy, or take your leprosy before your plague." Later, commenting on the $20-million-dollar indemnity owed Spain for the Philippines, he predicted that the expenditure would not stop there. "We have about ten million Malays at two dollars a head unpicked, and nobody knows what it will cost to pick them."

The Senate, pressed by other business, agreed to vote on February 6, a Monday. But, as the deadline neared, McKinley was still shy of the required majority. Lodge and Mark Hanna cornered senators in the cloakrooms, bartering their votes in return for coveted committee slates and funds for projects back home. McKinley, himself playing patronage, promised a federal judgeship to a crony of Louisiana's Samuel McEnery and gave John McLaurin of South Carolina the right to name his state's postmasters. He also won over George Gray, the anti-imperialist Democrat from Delaware who had served on the peace delegation in Paris, with a seat on a circuit court.

The treaty passed narrowly. Eleven Democrats had changed sides, a few of them in deference to William Jennings Bryan. Only two Republicans, the intractable Hoar and Eugene Hale of Maine, remained opposed. It had been, Lodge observed, "the hardest, closest fight I have ever known, and probably we shall never see another like it in our time."

McKinley had expected victory since the Saturday night before the vote. He was dictating the text of a speech when, at about eleven-thirty, an aide interrupted with a dispatch from the *New York Sun* correspondent in Manila. The Americans and Filipinos had clashed, the U.S. soldiers sustaining casualties. McKinley read the report several times, laid it on his desk and, with a mixture of sadness and satisfaction, said to his secretary: "It is always the unexpected that happens, at least in my case. How foolish these people are. This means ratification of the treaty."

6. CIVILIZING WITH A KRAG

★ ★ ★

General Otis knew that he was courting trouble in the middle of January 1899, when he moved the Nebraska regiment to Santa Mesa, an eastern suburb of Manila. The area, located at the juncture of the Pasig and San Juan rivers, lay inside territory claimed by the Filipinos, and they protested against the intrusion. Tensions mounted as, night after night, soldiers on both sides exchanged invective. But Otis disregarded the danger. He clung like a limpet to his desk at the Malacañang palace, the former residence of the Spanish governor, firm in the belief that Spain's surrender legally entitled the United States to impose its presence anywhere in the Philippines. Despite President McKinley's directive to preserve the peace, he authorized his troops to resort to force if necessary to defend themselves. They were bored and restless after months of tedious drilling and sentry duty and welcomed the slightest pretext to go into action.

Private William Walter Grayson was typical. A lean youth of twenty-three from Beatrice, a small Nebraska market town on the Big Blue River, he had worked at a local inn until the lure of adventure inspired him to volunteer to fight against Spain. Service in the Philippines had so far been monotonous, and now he eagerly anticipated a bit of excitement to break the tedium.

He later expressed the view that it had been "damned bull-headedness" on Otis's part to deploy the Nebraskans in the disputed Santa Mesa suburb. But his was not to reason why on the evening of February 4, 1899, a Saturday, when he and a buddy, Orville Miller, started out on a routine patrol of their camp perimeter. The tropical twilight had faded fast, and soon they were treading nervously in the silent night through the scrub vegetation of the desolate zone, tormented by mosquitoes, the relentless humidity bathing their bodies in sweat. As they approached a rickety bridge spanning the sluggish San Juan River, low whistles, possibly signals, pierced the stillness, and a red lantern mysteriously flashed ahead from a ramshackle old Spanish blockhouse, now used by the Filipinos as a barracks. Suddenly, not more than twenty feet in front of them, they discerned the shadowy shapes of four natives, almost certainly drunk and probably unarmed.

"Halt!" shouted Grayson, raising his cocked Springfield.

"¡Alto!" echoed one of the figures mockingly.

Grayson repeated his challenge, and again the voice mimicked him. Grayson fired. The man crumpled, and two others sprang out of the dark. Miller shot one as Grayson, reloading quickly, dropped the other. The Americans then raced back to their camp, Grayson crying, "Line up, fellows, the niggers are in here all through these lines!"

Within minutes, the crackle of rifles and the roar of artillery resonated along the ten-mile front separating the U.S. and Filipino forces. "The thing is on," remarked General Robert Hughes with visible relief, and Major Wilder Metcalf of the Kansas detachment awoke his sleeping commander, Colonel Frederick Funston, ecstatically yelling: "Come on out here, colonel. The ball has begun."

The Americans subsequently termed the ensuing struggle the "Philippine insurrection"—the euphemism contrived to convey the impression that they were subduing a rebellion against their lawful authority. For the same reason, they later referred to their Filipino enemies as insurgents and rebels, and in some instances *ladrones,* or bandits. But, to the Filipino nationalists, America had embarked on a war of conquest against an independence movement that had formed a government no less legitimate than the young republic founded by the American revolutionaries a century earlier. The war afterward fueled controversy in the United States as many Americans grew more and more weary of an overseas venture that, like the Vietnam War two generations later, gradually lost its original luster. In contrast to the Vietnam experience, however, the United States prevailed in the Philippines—even though the fighting persisted in parts of the archipelago long after Theodore Roosevelt, then president, formally proclaimed victory in July 1902. An estimated two hundred thousand people died, the overwhelming majority of them Filipino civilians.

Elihu Root, appointed secretary of war by McKinley in August 1899, asserted in a retrospective version of the initial outbreak that natives "under the leadership of Aguinaldo, a Chinese half-breed, attacked in vastly superior numbers our little army." But senior U.S. officers in Manila later depicted the event differently. General Arthur MacArthur, conceding that the Americans had fired first, testified that "our soldiers were under great provocation, and it was getting hard to restrain them." Otis similarly explained that "our picket discharged his piece" when a Filipino violated "the line that had been mutually agreed upon"—adding as justification that Aguinaldo would have in any case begun fighting in "two or three more days." Nor did Willie Grayson ever deny his role. On the contrary, proud of having ignited the conflict, he afterward petitioned the War Department in Washington for a cash bonus—only to be told that "no pecuniary rewards are made by the government for extraordinary bravery in action."

Aguinaldo may have expected an eventual war but, Otis's allegation notwithstanding, he had no plans to launch an imminent assault. As incidents multiplied during the days prior to the first clash, he repeatedly pulled his

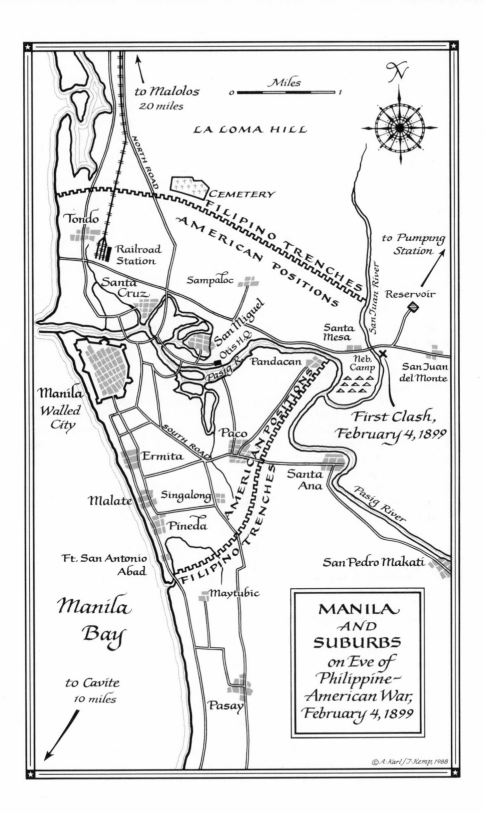

to Malolos
20 miles

Miles
0   1

LA LOMA HILL

N

CEMETERY

FILIPINO TRENCHES

AMERICAN POSITIONS

NORTH ROAD

Tondo

Railroad
Station

Santa
Cruz

Sampaloc

San Miguel
Otis H.Q.

Pasig R.

Pandacan

to Pumping
Station

Reservoir

San Juan River

Santa
Mesa

Neb.
Camp

San Juan
del Monte

First Clash,
February 4, 1899

Manila
Walled
City

SOUTH ROAD

Paco

Ermita

Singalong

Pineda

AMERICAN POSITIONS

FILIPINO TRENCHES

Santa
Ana

Pasig River

Malate

Ft. San Antonio
Abad

FILIPINO TRENCHES

San Pedro Makati

Maytubic

Manila
Bay

to Cavite
10 miles

Pasay

MANILA
AND
SUBURBS
on Eve of
Philippine-
American War,
February 4, 1899

© A. Karl / J. Kemp, 1988

troops out of contested territory rather than provoke the Americans. Moreover, nearly all his key officers had left their posts on that crucial weekend. General Antonio Luna, the chief Filipino commander, was visiting his family in the province of Pampanga, north of Manila, and Mariano Noriel, in charge of the sector south of the capital, had gone to Parañaque to prepare for his wedding. Other top Filipino soldiers were meanwhile attending a ball in Malolos, their capital, to celebrate the new Philippine constitution. Compared to the Americans, who were elated by the collision, Aguinaldo's melancholy reaction reflected his disappointment that war had not been averted: "No one can deplore more than I this rupture. . . . I have a clear conscience that I endeavored to avoid it at all costs, using all my utmost efforts to preserve friendship with the army of occupation, despite frequent humiliation and many sacrificed rights."

John F. Bass, the perceptive correspondent for *Harper's Weekly,* who was in the Philippines at the time, attributed the outbreak of hostilities to "race antipathy." The Americans and Filipinos differed from one another "so absolutely in mind, body and soul," he wrote, that they "could not live together under the then existing conditions." The Filipinos considered the U.S. troops to be "rough and tyrannical," while the Americans saw the natives as "tricky and dishonest," leaving the two "more or less undisciplined" forces poised "to jump at each other's throats."

Bass detested Filipinos—the most "unlovable people" he had ever met, as he put it. Nevertheless, he observed, the United States had aggravated the friction by failing to take into account their aspirations for independence. The "bone of contention," Bass wrote, was the question of sovereignty over the archipelago. Though the Filipinos may have lacked the skill to rule themselves, they could not have been worse than "many of our own communities at home," whose administrations were "wretched." Besides, the issue at stake was not whether their government pleased the United States, but whether it suited them. McKinley, rather than recognize that reality, had declared that "the islands were American property, that the army would proceed to take possession of them and that anyone resisting our authority would be repressed by force." As a consequence, the "hope of a peaceful settlement" had faded, and "we have fallen heir to the hatred that the natives felt for the Spanish." Bass concluded his dispatch on a note of regret: "Formerly we might have compromised with them. Now we must crush them."

But crushing the Filipinos was not to be easy. The U.S. forces, for all their superior military skill and firepower, were nagged by relentless heat, torrential rains, pervasive disease and the other afflictions of a tropical campaign as well as the challenge of pursuing an elusive foe fighting on familiar ground. They performed effectively despite these obstacles, but they owed their ultimate victory less to their own brilliance than to the errors committed by Aguinaldo and his followers.

★ ★ ★

Like the start of a race, Willie Grayson's first shot hurtled the Americans forward against the Filipino positions around Manila. The Kansans, commanded by the swashbuckling Colonel Funston, rushed up the coast, driving

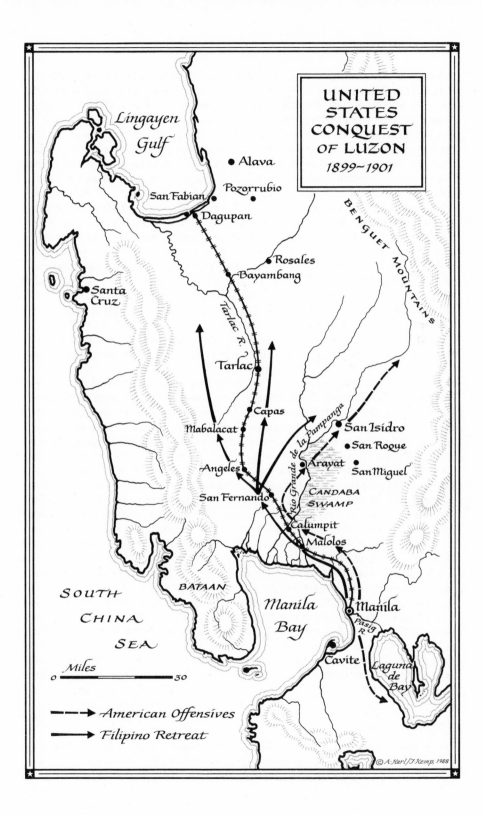

UNITED
STATES
CONQUEST
OF LUZON
1899~1901

Lingayen
Gulf

Alava

Pozorrubio

San Fabian

Dagupan

BENGUET MOUNTAINS

Rosales

Bayambang

Tarlac R.

Santa
Cruz

Tarlac

Capas

Mabalacat

Angeles

San Fernando

Rio Grande de la Pampanga

San Isidro

San Roque

San Miguel

Arayat

CANDABA
SWAMP

Calumpit

Malolos

SOUTH

CHINA

SEA

BATAAN

Manila
Bay

Manila

Pasig
R.

Cavite

Laguna
de
Bay

Miles
0   30

– – –▶ American Offensives
——▶ Filipino Retreat

© A. Karl / J. Kemp, 1988

the natives back under a hail of shells from Dewey's warships, which also raked other parts of the littoral. The California regiment quickly captured its objective, an enemy ammunition dump at Santa Ana, a village situated to the east, then sped ahead to San Pedro Macati, two miles beyond the city limits. The Nebraskans, backed by the Utah artillery, took the San Juan bridge, where Grayson had dropped a native interloper hours earlier, and went on to seize the reservoir that supplied the city with water. Volunteers from Idaho and Washington meanwhile secured both banks of the Pasig, remorselessly slaughtering hundreds of Filipinos trying to cross the river. North of the capital, however, the nationalists put up stiff resistance. Crouching behind the tombstones of a Chinese cemetery, they pinned down the Montana outfit until the Pennsylvanians arrived, howling as they charged up the hill.

As dawn came, the area around Manila was ablaze, the flames blending with the early light to silhouette the devastation in a burst of gaudy colors. Squads of U.S. troops careened through the streets, destroying nipa huts and stone buildings alike as they flushed out Filipino snipers. They shot some on the spot and leveled a local church in one district to blast out a group of partisans. Thousands of people fled in panic, some seeking security outside the capital, others pouring into the city in search of safety. Still others, more inquisitive than cautious, crowded onto rooftops to observe the spectacle through binoculars.

The Americans, fanning out from the city, charged forward wildly—often against the orders of their superiors, who feared that their lines were being perilously overextended. The U.S. soldiers, mostly volunteers with little training, had been bridled too long, and now they were having "more fun than a turkey shoot," as one wrote to his parents. By nightfall, twenty-four hours after the hostilities began, some three thousand Filipino corpses littered the network of trenches and barricades ringing the suburbs. A British resident of Manila, viewing the gruesome sight, objected to a U.S. officer that this was a "simple massacre and murderous butchery" rather than war. But Otis was more concerned with the fifty-nine American dead and nearly three hundred wounded. He cabled Washington that the U.S. casualties during the day had been "quite heavy"—adding reassuringly, however, that "everything" had been "favorable to our arms."

The intensity of the American assault stunned Aguinaldo. At his behest, two prominent Filipinos in Manila approached Otis with the offer of a truce and the creation of a neutral buffer between the two armies, to be followed by peace talks. Otis spurned them. "The fighting, having once begun, must go on to the grim end," he said. He then informed Washington that he had snubbed the overture, since Aguinaldo's influence in the area had been "destroyed."

Diplomacy thus discarded, Otis turned to the business of waging war. He ordered General Marcus Miller, who had been languishing off Iloilo since late December, to take the port as U.S. units seized the Visayan islands of Cebu and Negros. Shortly afterward, the Americans occupied the southernmost Sulu archipelago, a Muslim area, where a beleaguered Spanish garrison finally surrendered. But Aguinaldo's movement controlled Luzon, and there Otis concentrated his army in a two-pronged offensive. He ordered one division, under General Thomas Anderson, to head south from Manila while a second, commanded by Arthur MacArthur, went north.

America's total strength on the ground at that stage totaled only twenty-four thousand men, roughly one third of the Filipino force. Otis quickly realized that, while he could win battles, he could not hold territory. Soon he was tangled in contradictions of the kind that subsequently nagged U.S. commanders in Vietnam. Eager to publicize his effectiveness, he issued rosy reports of progress, but he contravened his optimistic estimates by requesting more and more troops. Late in February, at a time when he claimed to have already "dispersed" the enemy, he cabled Major General Henry W. Lawton, then on the way with a fresh regiment: SITUATION CRITICAL. YOUR EARLY ARRIVAL NECESSARY.

MacArthur drove toward Malolos, the seat of Aguinaldo's government, his troops marching north along the country's only railway line. Their first target was the coastal town of Caloocan, three miles from Manila, where the Filipinos awaited them in trenches threaded through a grove of trees. The Americans attacked in the early afternoon of February 10, their artillery and warships shelling the area to open the way for the Kansas and Montana regiments. John Bass of *Harper's Weekly* accompanied the Montana volunteers.

The two U.S. units went forward in waves. One rushed ahead along the edge of a forest as the other covered its advance from behind irrigation dikes bordering the rice fields. "At first the bullets were few and far between, but soon they began to zip past and kick up the dust about us in an unpleasant way," Bass wrote. "With each breath of powder and smoke our men seemed to gain new enthusiasm," the roar of their old Springfields drowning out the modern German-made Mausers wielded by the Filipinos. Forty natives held firm a half mile before the town, checking the drive until the Montana volunteers outflanked them. Then the white-clad figures fled one by one from their trenches into the woods. Flouting army regulations forbidding officers to expose themselves unnecessarily, a Major Jones flamboyantly wheeled his horse up and down the line, dodging enemy fire as he shouted: "Those fellows can't shoot. As long as they aim at us, we're all right."

He was mistaken. As the Americans crossed a plain near Caloocan, "the bullets came thicker and thicker." A soldier next to Bass fell—"not as we read in books, throwing up his arms and clutching at his coat, but sinking in a limp heap." A moment later, a lieutenant colonel slumped to the ground, shot through a lung. "Curiously enough, as the excitement grew the men seemed to notice the bullets less and less." They no longer sought cover. Instead, they scrambled ahead, yelling and firing as they ran, occasionally stopping to take surer aim at a fleeing Filipino.

Entering the town, Bass continued, they climbed over trenches heaped high with native bodies. "The smoke was thick and the din of battle deafening" as U.S. squads moved from house to house, clearing out the remaining enemy troops, while "in the road dead Filipinos lay here and there like great disfigured dolls thrown away by some petulant child." The first Kansans to arrive unfurled the Stars and Stripes atop the church steeple to the cheers of their comrades. Then, as the sun set, the Americans stretched out on the ground, exhausted. They had put Caloocan to the torch to dislodge snipers. "In the fading light of the day, the dry nipa huts, set afire, shot great gothic spires of flame into the sky. The main street of the town was roasting hot, and we rode through on a gallop. . . . Homeless dogs ran howling through the streets.

Motherless broods of chickens peeped helplessly. . . . Over the battlefield, doctors were still wandering about in the darkness, calling into the night to make sure that they had left no wounded." Bass made no mention in his dispatch of his own slight wound.

Anderson meanwhile entrusted the spearhead of the offensive south of Manila to Brigadier General Lloyd Wheaton, who with his black beard, swirling cape and strident voice resembled a bloodthirsty buccaneer—an image he carefully cultivated. Wheaton had enlisted as a sergeant during the Civil War and ultimately won promotion to brevet colonel, earning the Congressional Medal of Honor for leading a charge, sword in hand, against a Confederate gun embrasure. He remained a regular-army captain for the next twenty-five years, probably because he had the mentality of a corporal. He would stride among his men during battle, booming: "Don't you see them over there, running? Shoot! Don't stand there looking! Shoot!" Once, replying to a correspondent who had remarked that the Filipinos were brave, he pounded the table and bellowed: "Brave! Brave! Damn 'em, they won't stand up to be shot!" But his gruff exterior concealed a grain of compassion. On one occasion, he spared the life of a native spy about to be executed, ordering: "Shut the little runt up till the hike is over, and then let him go."

Official spokesmen in Washington proclaimed Wheaton's offensive as "the opening of a determined campaign" to be "carried on without cessation until the authority of the United States in the Philippines should be, as far as the native were concerned, undisputed." Launched in the middle of March, it was the first big American push of the war. But one correspondent observed shortly after it began that the operation had brought Otis "face to face with the fact that we did not have enough men to carry the war into the interior, and still protect Manila and its suburbs." Otis reluctantly agreed. Prodded by the War Department, he requested more troops. By the summer of 1899, straining the levels set by Congress, some sixty thousand Americans were serving in the Philippines, and a year later their number had grown to more than seventy-five thousand—three quarters of the entire U.S. Army. They included two Negro regiments known as "buffalo soldiers," a label pinned on them by the Indians, whom they had fought in the West. "What are you coons doing here?" a bystander shouted as they landed in Manila—to which one of the blacks replied, "We've come to take up the white man's burden."

Wheaton's so-called flying column, composed of regular and volunteer infantry and cavalry buttressed by gunboats, proceeded southeast from Manila along the Pasig River. Its aim was to capture the towns of Guadalupe, Pasig and Taguig, and eventually dominate Laguna de Bay, an immense lake, thus bringing one of the country's most fertile areas under U.S. control. Once again, John Bass accompanied the expedition.

Traveling on horseback, Bass galloped through the suburb of San Pedro Macati, then a flat landscape of paddy fields, and now Manila's bustling financial district, a canyon of skyscrapers. The fighting had started there and became heavier farther on. Wheaton's two gunboats, equipped with Gatling and Hotchkiss automatic weapons, steamed up and down the Pasig River, mercilessly raking the sleepy towns along its banks as his infantry and cavalry pressed forward day after day, routing the Filipinos from their trenches or blasting them out of churches and other buildings. Bass, by now inured to the spectacle of enemy dead, nevertheless paused to report one sight that haunted his memory. "A middle-aged, grizzly-headed native sat bolt-upright. A bullet or a piece of shell had passed through his neck, and completely shattered his jaw. He was perfectly conscious, but showed no evidence of suffering . . . and looked at us with expressionless face and ghastly, staring eyes."

By the end of the week, the Americans occupied the shattered remains of Taguig, on the northern shore of Laguna de Bay, and Wheaton called the operation a success. But his declaration was premature. Three companies of regulars, pursuing a group of Filipinos, ran into an ambush, losing five men. Wheaton announced that he "would hit back very hard" at belligerents and civilians alike whenever his men were lured into a trap. With that, he ordered his troops to burn every house and rice bin within a radius of five miles. "It was a very desolate picture as I rode between the charred ruins of former homes," wrote Bass. "Nearly all the people had fled. Occasionally a woman with her children or an old man sat disconsolately near a heap of smoldering ashes." He vented his anger against Americans as well as Filipinos—predicting that "our government, with its weak, vacillating policy and want of tact, and Aguinaldo and his followers, with their nagging trickiness and misrepresentation of our every act, would both be called to account for all this destruction when historians, in cold blood, should write the truth." He also warned that, with the rainy season only six weeks away, the U.S. forces would become bogged down, and "we hold only the province of Manila and the town of Cavite."

Otis, by contrast, continued to exude confidence—especially at the end of March, after Arthur MacArthur overran Malolos, the Filipino nationalist capital. The "insurgent" government, Otis said, was "in perilous condition, its army defeated, discouraged and scattered." His forecasts of forthcoming victory heartened members of the McKinley administration in Washington. Seeking to counter the spreading disillusionment with the war back home, they began to hint to the press that Aguinaldo's collapse was imminent.

But, apart from a few loyal officers on his staff, few Americans in the Philippines supported Otis. This was not a football game being played on a circumscribed field, observed one correspondent, pointing out that Aguinaldo had a movable headquarters and merely "took up the goal-posts and carried them back" whenever the U.S. forces approached. Even before Malolos fell, he had shifted the seat of his movement to the town of San Fernando, in Pampanga province. He later fled north as the Americans advanced, and eventually resorted to guerrilla tactics, thereby prolonging the struggle.

★　★　★

By early summer, Otis's rhapsodic appraisal of the situation had earned him the scorn of nearly all the American correspondents covering the war, igniting a dispute of the sort that subsequently recurred in Vietnam. As one of them put it, he capriciously managed the news to fit his own illusions, issued "wholly ridiculous estimates" of enemy killed or turned every battle into a "glorious American victory" even when the army had bungled. Otis, in response, branded them "troublemakers" whose spread of "baseless rumors" had a negative impact on opinion at home and indirectly played into the hands of the enemy.

But Otis had an advantage over his counterparts in Vietnam, where press operated without constraints. The War Department had permitted him to exercise censorship, which he imposed through his control of the only cable out of Manila. The outraged correspondents, headed by Robert M. Collins of the Associated Press, drafted a joint statement protesting that Otis was conspiring to feed the American public "an ultra-optimistic view that is not shared by the general officers in the field," rather than "a correct impression of the situation." Otis threatened to court-martial them for "conspiracy against the government." Undeterred, they transmitted the statement to their journals through Hong Kong to elude Otis's restrictions, and even proimperialist newspapers published it. McKinley naturally backed up his commander, contending that there was "nothing tangible" in the charges—though he instructed Elihu Root, the secretary of war, to urge Otis to adopt a more liberal policy. Otis haughtily disregarded Root's suggestion. He withheld cable privileges from the representative of the *Chicago Record,* who had reported among other things what nearly every senior American soldier in the Philippines believed: that the U.S. force was inadequate to cope with the challenge.

Most U.S. officers in the Philippines were contemptuous of Otis. He was too timid, as evidenced by his practice of mounting big U.S. expeditions, then withdrawing them from areas they had conquered and letting the fluid Filipino units retrieve lost ground. Worse still, he refused to delegate authority, as John Bass reported in June in a dispatch sent through Hong Kong to dodge censorship. Besides focusing on the "minutest details," including "every small bill or petition," Otis "forms every plan for every military movement and directs its execution, not day by day, but literally hour by hour." The commanders he interviewed, Bass wrote, bitterly complained "they cannot move hand or foot" without orders from Otis. "He sits in his office from early morning until late at night. . . . He has never been out on the lines, and I venture to say that he is the only American officer of the original army in the Philippines who has not seen a fight or a skirmish. . . . The fact that we have been floundering about in the wilderness for months without accomplishing anything is the result of the efforts of one man to manage the wholesale as well as retail department, without allowing any freedom of action to those officers who, from their positions on the line, have a better knowledge of the details of the campaign."

Some officers, blaming Otis for having provoked the war, argued that a compromise might have been reached with the Filipinos. Most, however, concurred with General Irving Hale, the head of a volunteer detachment, who faulted Otis for excessive caution and, in a personal confrontation, audaciously accused him of "cowardice." Ordinary soldiers similarly denounced Otis as a "foolish old woman" who lacked the aggressiveness to "smash the gugus." Otis's leading critic was Major General Henry Ware Lawton, who had landed in Manila in the middle of March to take over Anderson's first division. Lawton's motives may not have been entirely pure; he was bucking to succeed Otis, an aspiration that had been encouraged by several influential political figures, among them Theodore Roosevelt.

Lawton, then fifty-six, was a bold, romantic, sometimes reckless figure—the antithesis of Otis. Six feet four inches tall, he modeled himself on a British colonial officer, his iron-gray hair and matching mustache trimmed to perfection, and his pith helmet pipe-clayed to a glistening white. His men revered him as he rode erect astride his black horse or strode among them with cavalier disdain for danger during what he would term "a beautiful battle." He cultivated correspondents, whom he often took into his confidence, always providing them with "good copy." But there was, deep within him, some hidden tension that accounted for his heavy drinking and periodic tantrums. An inner volatility may have also propelled him into the foolhardy risk that cost him his life.

Orphaned as a child, Lawton was raised by an uncle in Indiana. He left college at the start of the Civil War to enlist in the Union forces as a private, displaying such courage that by the age of twenty-one he had soared to the rank of brevet colonel, with a regiment under his command. He won the Congressional Medal of Honor for a daring attack against a Confederate bastion at Atlanta. Like many another hero, he could not cope with civilian life after the war. He entered Harvard Law School, but soon dropped out to join the regular army as a second lieutenant in charge of a black infantry unit. A decade of monotonous garrison duty followed before he was again fighting, this time against Indians. He spent ten years combing the vast and rugged West, tracking different tribes and learning their distinctive customs. The education was to serve him well when, in 1886, he accepted a new assignment.

General Nelson Miles had just been ordered to subdue Geronimo, the elusive Apache chief and one of the last holdouts against white domination. Miles handed the mission to Lawton, whose light cavalry pursued the Indians for the next six months, riding some two thousand miles through the Arizona territory and into Mexico. Lawton employed a British invention, the heliograph, which reflected the sun to flash Morse coded messages signaling Geronimo's whereabouts. His men kept Geronimo on the run, but they themselves underwent a grueling ordeal. They scaled peaks and crossed deserts, often in heat so intolerable that their gun barrels burned their fingers and their horses and mules collapsed. Once they ran out of food for a week and survived on rats and lizards. On another occasion, short of water, some sucked their own blood to slake their thirst. Lawton finally trapped Geronimo in August 1886, and Miles appeared to preside over the surrender. He promised to resettle the Apaches in Florida. Instead they were shunted from one exile to another and forced into labor gangs, their ranks dwindling as they died from disease and mistreatment. They were ultimately banished to virtual imprisonment in Fort Sill, Oklahoma—near a town later named for Lawton.

Eventually promoted to the rank of major general, Lawton again distinguished himself in Cuba, where he was appointed military governor of Santiago following Spain's capitulation. But his addiction to alcohol hastened his transfer home on the pretext of poor health. Detailed to a presidential trip, he attracted the attention of McKinley, who had heard of his exploits and offered him the Philippine job. McKinley privately lectured him on temperance before his departure, and Lawton took the oath. Surprisingly, Lawton abstained after reaching Manila—even though Otis frustrated him to the point of desperation.

Lawton had sailed in January 1898, before the war with the Filipinos broke out. He assumed, despite McKinley's typical vagueness on the matter, that Otis would soon retire, and leave him at the helm. At the very least, he expected an independent field command that would enable him to display his skills. But Otis relegated him to diversions while entrusting MacArthur with the big campaigns. And even when Lawton turned minor operations into major victories, Otis would squelch his achievements.

Lawton had launched his first action early in April, three weeks after arriving. He drove south of Manila against the town of Santa Cruz, situated at the easternmost side of Laguna de Bay—a region razed by Wheaton a month before. He captured the town with only a few casualties in three days, and was preparing to set up a garrison there when Otis instructed him to withdraw. The Filipinos, who had prudently retreated in the face of the American push, thereupon reoccupied the area. A month later, while on an expedition to the north in support of MacArthur's larger offensive, Lawton seized the town of San Isidro, where Aguinaldo had fled following the fall of his other capitals. Certain of cornering Aguinaldo, he begged for permission to press on. Once again, Otis peremptorily ordered him to return to Manila.

Back in the capital, Lawton stormed into Otis's cluttered office at the Malacañang palace with a proposal. With two regiments, he promised, he would deliver Aguinaldo dead or alive within sixty days and win the war. He offered to stake his reputation on the pledge, and brought along a fellow officer as his witness. Otis listened placidly, then did something that he had never been seen to do: He laughed. It was an ironic, perverse, almost scornful guffaw—prompted perhaps by the sight of this charimastic soldier dramatically pleading his cause, possibly inspired by the vision of him thrashing through swamps in search of a little Filipino. But whatever the motive for Otis's unprecedented mirth, Lawton departed even more livid than when he had entered. Baring his heart to the journalists based in Manila, he criticized Otis's complacency by contending that a total of a hundred thousand American troops would be needed in the Philippines to attain victory. He urged the correspondents to circumvent Otis's censorship, and the rift between the two generals, duly published in the U.S. press, triggered a tempest back home. Several politicians and editorialists chided Lawton for indiscipline, while others demanded Otis's dismissal. Lawton, startled by the controversy he had sparked, dutifully disclaimed any animosity toward his boss. In the short time left to him, however, he neither forgot nor forgave Otis's ridicule.

Otis also quarreled with an official civilian commission recently arrived in Manila. Dewey had advised McKinley to create such a group as early as January, before the fighting between the Americans and Filipinos erupted. The panel, Dewey suggested, might "adjust differences" between the two sides, and conceivably avert a clash. McKinley concurred, reckoning as well that the group could furnish him with a fresh assessment of the situation in the Philippines, and help to clarify a future policy for the territory. After casting about for a respected figure to head the board, he finally selected Jacob Gould Schurman, the president of Cornell University and a noted professor of philosophy. Schurman demurred. At forty-five he had too bright an academic career ahead of him to embark in that *galère*. Besides, he candidly told McKinley, he opposed the acquisition of the archipelago. McKinley, in another admission of his inadequacies as a leader, confessed that he had succumbed to forces beyond his control. "I didn't want the Philippine islands, either," he explained to Schurman, and had deliberately "left myself free not to take them" in the cease-fire accord with Spain. "But in the end," McKinley sighed, "there was no alternative."

Schurman acquiesced, and McKinley appointed two other civilians to the group—Dean Worcester, the zoologist who had spent years in the Philippines, and Charles Denby, a conservative Democrat with long experience as the U.S. envoy to China. Otis and Dewey were to join the commission in Manila. The peace treaty with Spain, which then awaited Senate ratification, was not strictly lawful. Nevertheless, McKinley sent the panel off with orders to "facilitate the most humane, pacific and effective extension" of America's authority throughout the islands, and to secure "with the least possible delay the benefits of a wise and generous protection of life and property to the inhabitants."

Schurman and his team landed in Manila on March 4, 1899, exactly a month after the war with the Filipinos began, and immediately opened hearings. Dressed in wool suits and starched shirts, they sweated through the interrogations, held daily either at the *audiencia,* the former Spanish supreme court, or in informal sessions at their downtown headquarters. Their survey was flawed from the outset.

They proudly asserted later that they had listened to "all varieties of opinion" from "all classes" of the population. But they never once ventured outside the city. Most of the sixty witnesses they heard were American, British and other Western residents of Manila, who predictably argued that the "ignorant" natives lacked the competence to govern themselves. The few Filipinos they interviewed, moreover, were rich attorneys, bankers, physicians, landowners and other *ilustrados* who had abandoned the independence movement, contending that Aguinaldo had abdicated his leadership to dangerous radicals and terrorists. Trinidad Pardo de Tavera repeated, as he had earlier told Otis, that the United States should under no circumstances forfeit the islands. Felipe Calderón, the author of the nationalist constitution, claimed that the resistance to U.S. rule was being fomented by only a handful of selfish malcontents striving to advance their "individual interests" and did not reflect the real sentiments of either the elite or the masses, who merely wanted peace. Still, he stressed, the United States would not win the sympathy of the people until it demonstrated tangible evidence of its beneficence. "The important thing," he said, "is to show them actual deeds."

The commissioners had been given neither the time nor the authority to conceive a policy for the Philippines. Even so, Schurman hastily distilled the group's limited findings into a proclamation of so-called regulative principles. He published the document on April 4, precisely a month from the day that his group began its proceedings, and it essentially confirmed McKinley's concepts. The United States intended to grant the archipelago a modicum of political autonomy, an honest civil service, an equitable judicial system, public-works projects, economic development programs and other reforms, including universal education. But the velvet glove enclosed an iron fist. America's "supremacy" would be "enforced" throughout the islands, and "those who resist it can accomplish no end other than their own ruin."

Before departing Manila in September, the commission put out a comprehensive report underlining the necessity for "complete harmony between the aspirations and needs of the Filipinos, and the desire and capacity of the Americans to satisfy them." Americans and Filipinos, despite their different values, could cement a relationship based on their shared belief in "religious liberty, fundamental personal rights and the largest practicable measure of home rule." The panel thus recommended, among other proposals, a degree of self-government under U.S. supervision. Provinces and municipalities would be run by elected Filipino officials with the guidance of resident American advisers, and a national legislature would function with a civilian U.S. governor exercising a veto over its decisions. The study was then only an abstraction, yet it served to shape future American efforts to apply McKinley's virtuous if vague idea of "benevolent assimilation" to a strange and alien society.

Dewey, though a member of the commission, attended none of its meetings—nor, he later admitted, did he ever even read its reports. Having attained immortality, he preferred to remain in aloof grandeur aboard the *Olympia*, anchored in Manila Bay. He rose at dawn, strolled around the deck, performed a few fleet chores after breakfast, napped following lunch and then, as the afternoon cooled, went ashore for a carriage ride along the seaside boulevard that subsequently bore his name, sometimes stopping to call on acquaintances. At sixty-two, with a year in the tropics behind him, he was feeling his age, and he eagerly looked forward to going home.

Otis also belonged to Schurman's delegation, but he shunned its meetings for other motives. As a soldier, he resented the intrusion onto his turf of civilians promoting such notions as the elimination of military government. He had tried in vain to persuade the War Department to have them recalled, maintaining that their mission was invalid, since they had been appointed to avert the outbreak of hostilities. His annoyance approached apoplexy late in April, when Schurman favored exploring a peace bid from the Filipinos.

Aguinaldo's deputy, Apolinario Mabini, had derided the Schurman commission's proclamation. It was nothing less, he said, than an "ingenious scheme" by the Americans "to promise us the amplest autonomy and fullest political liberty, that afterward they may oppress us at will." The pledges were specious, since the United States "hates the colored race with a mortal hatred." So the Filipinos would carry on the struggle. "War is the last resource left to us for the salvation of our country and our national honor. Let us fight while a grain of strength is left us [and] generations to come, praying over our tombs, will shed for us tears of love and gratitude." Aguinaldo, however, agreed to seek an accommodation. Despite his tirade, Mabini not only switched, but drafted a conciliatory letter for a Filipino emissary, a Colonel Manuel Arguelles, to deliver to the Americans.

Arguelles, given safe conduct into Manila, handed the letter to Schurman. The nationalists had confidence in America's "friendship, justice and magnaminity," the message said, and it proposed a three-month truce to gauge the Philippine population's attitude toward an association with the United States. His comrades, Mabini vowed, would not take advantage of the armistice to redeploy or rearm, but merely sought to permit the people to "reflect on their sad situation" and to weigh the American offer of self-government. Straying from his script, Arguelles then revealed that he had been authorized to say that Aguinaldo had dropped his demand for independence and was fighting solely "for the honor of the army." Schurman, astonished by the disclosure, pressed the question. "You accept, then, the sovereignty of the United States?" Arguelles, repeating that he represented Aguinaldo, replied: "Yes, we do."

Hardly a disciplined diplomat, Arguelles may have been exaggerating Aguinaldo's views, or he could have simply been speaking for himself. But Aguinaldo was indeed receptive to a compromise at that stage. Though the Americans had not yet come even close to victory, they were pushing his troops out of the towns and he, a city boy, had no taste for retreating into the hills—*bundoks,* or "boondocks," as the Tagalogs called the mountain jungles. His ranks were also shrinking. Most of the *ilustrados* had deserted him, and his remaining followers were split over whether to negotiate terms with the United States. General Antonio Luna, his hotheaded army commander, adamantly opposed concessions.

Schurman, lacking credible sources of information, could only guess at Aguinaldo's dilemma. Nevertheless, he believed in the possibility of a settlement. He cabled the substance of his talk with Arguelles to Secretary of State John Hay, who urged him to explore the peace bid further. McKinley, said Hay, "earnestly desires the cessation of bloodshed."

Otis would have none of it. Mabini's assurances to the contrary, he was certain that the Filipinos only wanted a cease-fire to gain the time to strengthen themselves. To negotiate, he warned Washington, was a "fatal" course that would "cost soldiers' lives and prolong our difficulties." Worcester and Denby, the other civilians on Schurman's team, backed Otis. McKinley regretfully acceded to the hard-liners. The slow progress on the battlefield puzzled him, but his faith in the general remained unshaken, and the president's support bolstered Otis. He spurned other attempts by the Filipinos to arrange an armistice. Finally, Aguinaldo was left with only the slim hope that a Democratic triumph in the U.S. presidential elections of 1900 would reverse McKinley's policy toward the Philippines.

For all his intransigence, however, Otis realized that guns alone were not the answer. He encouraged civic action programs to win the sympathy of the natives—as long as his military establishment managed them. He steered the U.S. Army into such projects as sewer construction, food distribution, the hospitalizing of lepers and vaccination of villagers against smallpox. He focused on education, which rural families especially welcomed as an opportunity for their children. American troops, transformed into teachers, improvised classes in nipa huts or outdoors. They used ponchos as blackboards and lumps of starch as chalk and made do without textbooks. They introduced English, which eventually became the lingua franca of the Philippines—as it is today. The educational effort, later taken over by young American civilians, proved in time to be the single most important element in reconciling Filipinos to the U.S. presence. An enlisted man remembered his teaching stint as "the best six years of my life." Generations afterward, a distinguished Filipino lawyer recalled, "I'll never forget that big American soldier who first taught me how to read."

Otis sponsored other civic initiatives. A lawyer by training, he took a personal interest in the legal structure. He renovated the Spanish judicial system, putting native magistrates in charge of both civil and criminal cases, and founded a supreme court with Cayetano Arellano, an eminent *ilustrado* jurist, as chief justice. In July 1899, he also ordered the formation of local governments, to be directed by Filipinos under the aegis of U.S. military advisers. Town councils were to be elected, the vote restricted to literate adult males who owned or leased land. Lawton had already set up such an administration in Baliuag, a Luzon town that he had captured in May, declaring that pacification hinged on demonstrating "our good intentions" to the natives. Otis introduced the political experiment on a larger scale to the island of Negros, where Aguinaldo's influence was weak. But the Americans learned to their dismay that many Filipinos who participated in the process, and had even sworn allegiance to the United States, were in fact secret nationalist agents. And they discovered, as American soldiers in Vietnam did later, that nothing is more nerve-wracking in war than the difficulty of distinguishing friend from foe.

The pervasive fear of danger and doubt spurred the U.S. troops in the Philippines to increasing brutality, especially after the nationalists switched to guerrilla warfare, with its deception and duplicity. But even early in the struggle, many Americans approved any measures that halted the enemy. "No cruelty is too severe for these brainless monkeys, who can appreciate no sense of honor, kindness or justice," said one volunteer; another confessed, "I am in my glory when I can sight some dark skin and pull the trigger." Racist sentiment, still strong in the United States, stimulated much of the antagonism toward the natives among American soldiers, who commonly wrote home, as one did, that he wanted to "blow every nigger into nigger heaven." Fresh in the minds of these youths as well was the conquest of the West, which prompted the remark from a Kansan that the islands would not be pacified "until the niggers are killed off like the Indians."

But some U.S. troops recoiled from violating the rules of war. After the battle for Caloocan in February 1899, five Kansas volunteers accused their commander, Captain William Brenner, of having ordered them to "take no prisoners." He had, they alleged, insisted on their shooting four captured Filipinos, thundering: "Kill them, damn it, kill them!" Arraigned before a military court, Brenner denied the charge, and the judge dismissed the case, ruling that "considerations of public policy sufficiently grave to silence every other demand require that no further action be taken." Nearly seventy American soldiers were punished for crimes against the natives during the first year of the war. As in all wars, though, crimes were defined loosely. John Bass, who covered the fight for Caloocan, reported that the Americans had burned the town only to flush out snipers. But one of the Kansans wrote home that he had, "with my own hand, set fire to over fifty houses of Filipinos after the victory."

The Philippine war, like the Vietnam experience, gradually dehumanized the U.S. troops, who had volunteered out of a conviction that they were carrying America's values abroad. Captain Matthew Batson, to cite an example, at first deplored the sight of his comrades looting villages. "We come as a Christian people . . . and bear ourselves like barbarians," he observed in a letter to his family. After losing a friend in an ambush, however, he ordered the nearest town annihilated. "The time has come," he now concluded, "when it is necessary to conduct this warfare with utmost rigor." Many American soldiers similarly justified the torture of Filipinos—reports of which eventually scandalized the U.S. public. Over time, indeed, accounts of atrocities by their boys eroded support for the war among numbers of Americans who had originally believed in the benison of the mission. But their boys, equipped with modern Krag-Jorgensen rifles, were marching to a venomous song.

> Damn, damn, damn the Filipinos!
> Cut-throat khakiac *ladrones*!
> Underneath the starry flag,
> Civilize them with a Krag,
> And return us to our beloved home.

The Americans in the Philippines simultaneously hated the war and upheld its aims, as an enterprising reporter for the *Pittsburgh Post* divulged. After interviewing six hundred Pennsylvania volunteers as they returned to San Francisco during the summer of 1899, he wrote that sixty-two percent of the officers and ninety-three percent of the enlisted men denounced the conflict. They agreed unanimously, however, that the United States should not leave the archipelago until the Filipinos were "whipped first." A corporal typically asserted that "we should get out as soon as we can with honor"—but not before "we've beaten them into submission." To many, America could not walk away from its sacrifices. "If their comrades hadn't been killed," said Private John Kenney, "the men of the volunteers would have been ready to withdraw and let the Filipinos try their hand at governing themselves. Now they believe the job must be finished."

★ ★ ★

In June 1899, John Bass filed a long dispatch through Hong Kong. "The American outlook is blacker now than it has been since the beginning of the war," he concluded, providing the evidence to substantiate his grim assessment.

The U.S. forces, unable to hold territory, controlled a region that reached no farther than thirty miles north of Manila. The "whole population" supported Aguinaldo, and "only those natives whose immediate self-interest requires it are friendly to us." The "hostile attitude" of the Filipinos was visible in their refusal to cooperate with Americans as well as in such other signs as the curfew imposed in Manila by Otis out of fear of "an uprising." Bass then proceeded to enumerate the reasons for the U.S. failure.

In the first place, he stated bluntly, "the people of the Philippines do not wish to be governed by us." The U.S. Army, moreover, was "absurdly" equipped for the struggle. American soldiers, each laden down with two hundred rounds of ammunition, were being marched back and forth "in the broiling sun over a country without roads." As a result of this "positively criminal" strategy, the hospitals overflowed with five thousand men, sixteen percent of the total expedition. Finally, the United States lacked a coherent policy, but was instead waging "a harsh and philanthropic war at the same time." Official spokesmen professed America's aim to civilize the islands, while U.S. troops burned and looted everywhere. An American general, entering Malolos after its capture, instructed his men to protect private property for the sake of their "honor." Not far away, a U.S. regiment was razing the town of Guiguinto to the ground.

Bass echoed Lawton's plea for implanting garrisons throughout the archipelago, an approach that would require at least a hundred thousand men. As it was, "the American advance has about reached the end of its rope." So, unless the Filipinos collapsed "by natural disintegration," an unlikely prospect, they "will prosper for some time to come."

But Bass overlooked the factional disputes troubling Aguinaldo. In May, two of the few *ilustrados* still in his movement, Pedro Paterno and Felipe Buencamino, maneuvered to jettison Mabini, blaming him for botching the peace bid to the Americans. Though he regretted the loss of Mabini, who retired to a remote retreat, Aguinaldo did nothing to censure his advisers' rivals. Their move, however, angered the volatile General Antonio Luna.

Then thirty-one, Luna came from a wealthy *criollo* family of Ilocos Norte, in northern Luzon. A handsome man with a black mustache, he had studied chemistry in Madrid, where he wrote for *La Solidaridad,* the Filipino nationalist journal, and excelled as a fencer. His equally hotheaded brother, the painter Juan Luna, who lived in Paris, had killed his wife for allegedly committing adultery and was acquitted by an indulgent French court, which ruled the *crime passionnel* to have been excusable—especially for a semisavage.

Luna returned home with a shelf of books on military science. Aguinaldo, impressed, named him his senior commander, but Luna's instability marred his behavior. His rages terrified rather than inspired his men. He virtually handed the Americans the town of Malolos, the nationalist capital, by leaving the front to scold a subordinate—who, it should be added, deserved a reprimand for drifting off to a nearby fiesta. Implacably opposed to a compromise with the United States, he decried the *ilustrados* who favored such a deal and knocked down Buencamino during the debate on the topic. Aguinaldo, who was present, intervened to stop the scrap. Having appointed Buencamino, he took Luna's gesture to be a personal insult—and, though he remained distant from the incident that ensued, later gave it his discreet approval.

On June 5, Luna received a telegram signed by Aguinaldo, requesting his presence at the nationalist headquarters, a convent in the town of Cabanatuan. On guard were troops from Aguinaldo's native province of Cavite. They hated Luna both as a northerner and for trying to disarm them some months earlier for insubordination. Aguinaldo, suspiciously, was absent, and Luna found himself alone with Buencamino. They began to quarrel when Luna, hearing a shot, rushed out to investigate. One of Aguinaldo's officers, standing at the door, slashed his head with a *bolo* as other soldiers crowded in, their knives hacking. Luna fell, gasping: "Cowards! Traitors! Assassins!" Buencamino rifled his body, removing the telegram that might implicate Aguinaldo in the murder.

"The loss of Luna was, of course, a very heavy blow to our armed efforts," Aguinaldo later recalled. But he purged several of Luna's sympathizers, thus enfeebling the Filipino movement even further. Otis, learning of the dissension, could have shortened the war then by offering concessions to Aguinaldo. Instead he vowed to grind the Filipinos into submission.

The torrid climate ravaged the Americans, debilitating thirty percent or more of the force. His men, remarked one commander, were fighting under a "scorching sun almost as destructive and much harder to bear than the enemy's fire," the strain so severe that "they are now completely worn out and broken in health." The U.S. surgeon general reported that the "weakened hearts and quickened pulses" of the troops "indicate a condition akin to typhoid fever." A captain described an operation against the town of Las

Pinas, south of Manila. Of the seven hundred soldiers engaged, two thirds failed to reach the starting point for the attack.

Torrents of rain had fallen during the night, preventing the troops from sleeping. At dawn, after a breakfast of wet hardtack and coffee, they began a march that, the captain wrote, had "no equal in the annals of our army." By ten o'clock in the morning, a searing sun blistered them. "The heat was something horrible. Our canteens were dry, our heads splitting and throats parched." Desperately thirsty, they drank from pools filthy with slime and the excrement of water buffalo. Men collapsed "in twos or threes from sheer exhaustion" until only twenty-three remained from his company of ninety. Finally, at their bivouac area, they dropped to the ground from utter fatigue, only to be molested by ants, flies and mosquitoes. Another storm drenched them during the night, and next morning they resumed their advance across flooded rice fields "so gluey," one said, "I could hardly extricate my legs." They occupied the town without firing a shot as the natives, waving white flags, bowed and cried *"amigo."* A week later, the "same devils" counterattacked and, the captain added, "It came near being our first defeat."

In November, as the rains abated, Otis sought to break the deadlock on Luzon by launching a pincer movement against Aguinaldo. Two thousand American troops under Wheaton staged an amphibious landing at Lingayen Gulf after U.S. warships had shelled the region. They soon joined up with a column commanded by Arthur MacArthur, who had pushed north to capture the coastal town of Dagupan, the terminal of the island's only railway, which ran between there and Manila. The Filipinos scattered in all directions before the drive. With the U.S. cavalry on his heels, Aguinaldo and his family fled north from Tarlac to the town of Bayambang. There he assembled his tattered legions and defined a fresh strategy.

He ordered his men to switch from big battalions to small mobile units capable of launching lightning raids against the Americans. The shift partly reflected his realization that he could no longer confront a superior U.S. force without sustaining frightful losses. But his new tactics also mirrored a political perception. He still hoped for a change of American policy toward the Philippines—perhaps when the U.S. Congress again debated the issue in December or as the consequence of a Democratic victory in the presidential election the next year. A protracted war, he calculated, would gradually erode the patience of Americans at home, arouse their opposition to the conflict and intensify the pressure on Washington to concede to a settlement. He expected as well, by resorting to hit-and-run raids, to increase U.S. casualties on the battlefield— further stimulating the American public to clamor for peace.

MacArthur now foresaw a filthy guerrilla war of surprise and guile—a war in which every Filipino was a potential enemy. He urged Otis to adopt a stiff plan disguised as an amnesty. Natives who laid down their arms would be granted the lenient status of prisoners of war. But, after that, those caught killing Americans would be "regarded as murderers and treated accordingly." Obdurate though he was, Otis imagined the hazards of such a program. He rejected the proposal, observing that it would accelerate the cycle of violence as both U.S. and Filipino soldiers increasingly committed "barbarities."

The U.S. offensive had by now become a manhunt as Lawton, in the vanguard, pursued Aguinaldo across central Luzon—just as he had tracked

Geronimo through Arizona and Mexico. But Lawton's dazzling momentum worried Otis. Accustomed to classic troop movements, he ordered Lawton to stop until his detachments could take on additional equipment and supplies, most of them unnecessary. Aguinaldo, benefiting from Lawton's delay, escaped. Ahead of him, however, lay awesome hardships and personal losses.

Even before starting out, Aguinaldo suffered a tragedy when his infant daughter died of a fever at Bayambang. He trekked north, with his wife and sister in the advance column of two hundred and fifty men, also accompanied by their families. The U.S. troops soon dealt him another blow by capturing his mother and four-year-old son along with Felipe Buencamino, whose rear party had lagged behind. Pedro Paterno, his other senior deputy, deeming the resistance to be futile, had earlier defected to the Americans with ninety thousand pesos of the movement's funds.

One of Aguinaldo's aides, Colonel Simeon Villa, an ophthalmologist by profession, recorded their ordeal in his diary. They climbed from the coastal plain into highland forests, their only clothes soaked through from the humidity. As they scaled dizzy peaks, the "strong wind and cold air made our teeth chatter," and the precipices fell so sharply that they imagined themselves to be "on the edge of death." They traveled at night, the Americans close behind them, Villa noting that "our vision grows dim, our legs and knees are already weak and tremulous, our breathing laborious and our thirst intense." At one stage, they fought off a jungle ambush by aboriginal Igorots, who "awaited the opportunity to cut off our heads." With their plight worsening, Aguinaldo ordered the women to surrender to the U.S. forces. Finally, two months later, they reached Isabela province, on the eastern coast of Luzon. But Aguinaldo kept moving as the Americans followed him. He would have been caught earlier had it not been for the sacrifice of one of his generals, Gregorio del Pilar, who is canonized today in the Filipino pantheon of martyred heroes.

Del Pilar, then only twenty-four, was the son of a minor official from Bulacan province, in eastern Luzon. Joining the nationalist army as a teenage student in Manila, he soon acquired a legendary reputation in the fight against the Spanish, performing such feats as seizing an arms cache by masquerading as a woman. He charmed Aguinaldo, who took him into temporary exile in Hong Kong and back home afterward, promoted him to general. Filipino historians depict him as a combination of Byron and Casanova. He played the romantic role to the hilt in a starched uniform, polished boots and silver spurs, his fingers adorned with diamond rings and his billfold filled with perfumed letters from his mistresses. Superstitious, he wore an *anting anting,* a traditional amulet that supposedly shielded him from danger, and he constantly fretted over his dreams. But he was also bestial. After Luna's assassination, he presided over the torture of the late general's aides, one of whose daughters he had courted.

Now, bringing up Aguinaldo's rear echelon, del Pilar paused at Triad Pass, a narrow route located in the misty mountains of Abra province, nearly five thousand feet high. There he ordered sixty men to dig in to block the pursuing U.S. forces. "The Americans can never take this place," he said. "If they did, it would only be over my dead body."

On the morning of December 2, three U.S. companies led by Major Peyton March trudged up the dizzy trail, guided by an Ilocano with the improbable nom de guerre of January Galoot. Richard H. Little of the *Chicago Tribune,* covering the action, observed del Pilar in full view astride a white charger. As the Americans inched ahead under volleys of Filipino bullets, he exhorted his men—"scolding them, praising them, cursing, appealing one moment to their love of their native land and the next instant threatening to kill them if they did not stand firm." He himself sat motionless in his saddle, retreating slowly only after the U.S. troops, dashing forward or sniping from behind boulders, wiped out his first line of defense. The climax finally came at noon. "We who were below saw an American squirm his way out to the top of a high flat rock, and take deliberate aim. . . . We held our breath, not knowing whether to pray that the sharpshooter would shoot straight or miss. Then came the spiteful crack of the Krag rifle, and the man on horseback rolled to the ground. . . . The boy general of the Filipinos was dead."

The rest of the Filipinos routed, the U.S. soldiers flew out like buzzards to strip del Pilar's body of everything from his pants and collar button to a locket containing a curl of woman's hair and an American twenty-dollar gold piece he had carried in his pocket. The cadaver lay naked in the sun for days before a U.S. cavalry lieutenant, Dennis Quinlan, out of respect for his dead enemy, buried the corpse with honors. Quinlan inscribed on a headstone: *An Officer and a Gentleman.*

The Filipinos settled the score seventeen days later, when Lawton went to the town of San Mateo, eighteen miles northeast of Manila, a nationalist stronghold since the outbreak of the war. Accompanied by William Dinwiddie, a correspondent for *Harper's Weekly,* he rode overnight by horseback through a steady drizzle, dismounting at dawn on a bluff overlooking the site. A towering figure in his white pith helmet, a long yellow slicker hanging like a mandarin's gown to his feet, he made a conspicuous target as he peered through his binoculars and issued orders to his adjutants, warning them to disperse to avoid enemy fire. Soon an aide standing next to him whirled and fell, struck by a bullet. "I am afraid this isn't a good place for a general," Lawton remarked casually, and apologizing for leaving the line, strode across a nearby rice field, stopping from time to time to survey the scene. Suddenly, swatting his chest as if an insect had stung him, he spat a clot of blood and muttered: "God!" Two officers rushed to his side, asking where he had been hit. "In the lungs," he replied, then sank into their arms, dead. The Filipino marksman who shot him belonged to a unit commanded by a general whose name, by coincidence, was Licerio Geronimo.

The evening before, Lawton and his wife had entertained a few friends at their Manila home—a grand Spanish mansion decorated with embroidered draperies, its polished floors reflecting the soft light of crystal chandeliers. Lawton, chatting with the guests, could not rightly gauge whether the conflict was winding down or only beginning. He asserted, however, that the Filipinos could have been routed long ago "if we had gone after them." Contrary to Otis's rosy claims, he said, "They have not surrendered." Then, as he prepared to depart for San Mateo, he mused on his future plans. When the fighting in the Philippines ended, he hoped to observe the Boer War, which had recently erupted in South Africa. "No, you will not, dear," his wife objected. "You're going home with me to southern California to raise oranges."

Lawton's body was shipped back to an elaborate military funeral at Arlington Cemetery. McKinley used the occasion to evoke his glorious career, even though he had favored Otis.

★ ★ ★

On the afternoon of February 16, 1899, McKinley arrived in Boston. Flags throughout the country had been lowered to half-mast the previous day to mourn the first anniversary of the sinking of the *Maine,* the disaster that had catapulted America into an unprecedented overseas war. A shot fired outside Manila twelve days earlier now pitted America against a people fighting for freedom, and the gulf was widening in the United States between the champions and the opponents of ventures abroad. The past year had been one of the most tumultuous in the nation's history. That evening, McKinley was due to address an audience of nearly six thousand at a banquet of the Home Market Club in the cavernous Mechanics' Hall, in a city vivid with anti-expansionist sentiment.

The speech had been scheduled for months. McKinley and his staff polished the text as they traveled by train from Washington in the wake of a blizzard that had crippled the eastern seaboard. Now, standing on a dais bedecked with bunting, beneath large portraits of Washington, Lincoln and himself, McKinley spoke in gently persuasive tones as he reiterated his policy toward the Philippines.

The issue was divisive and the challenge daunting, and he possessed no prophetic "light or knowledge." Still, he maintained, God had entrusted the archipelago to the United States. Its inhabitants must therefore be made to understand that "their welfare is our welfare, but neither their aspirations nor ours can be realized until our authority is acknowledged and unquestioned." And looking beyond "the blood-stained trenches around Manila, where every red drop, whether from the veins of an American soldier or a misguided Filipino, is anguish to my heart," he saw a vision: The people of the Philippines, their children and children's children, "shall for ages bless the American republic because it emancipated and redeemed their fatherland, and set them in the pathway of the world's best civilization." In short, the United States intended to conquer the natives for their own good, whatever their views on the matter.

The applause was deafening. McKinley had disarmed his detractors—even *The Nation,* a consistent critic, conceding that he was "one of the rare public speakers who are able to talk humbug in such a way as to make their hearers think it excellent sense." As a seasoned politician, however, he knew that opinion was fickle, and that patriotic zeal could turn to antipathy toward the war—especially if it dragged on. To sustain a pitch of popular support for a protracted conflict was difficult. But he could at least appeal for patience, pleading that America's idealistic purpose would be rewarded. He seized on every opportunity to convey that message to the nation. He was afforded a unique moment in the fall, when Dewey returned home to the biggest ovation ever accorded an American until then.

Dewey, aboard the *Olympia,* sailed back in his own sweet time, taking nearly four months to savor the glory of his global reputation. He stopped at Hong Kong, Singapore, Suez and Trieste, and each port hailed him enthusiastically.

Finally, on September 27, he cruised into New York harbor to a frenetic welcome, with Theodore Roosevelt, then governor of the state, leading the hosts. As fireboats sprayed jets of water into the air, his flagship piloted the Atlantic fleet and a flotilla of smaller craft up the Hudson River amid a din of shrieking sirens and whistles. The next day, at the head of thirty-five thousand men, his crew in the vanguard, he paraded down Fifth Avenue to Twenty-third Street. There he unveiled the magnificent Dewey Arch, a wood and plaster replica of the monument to the Emperor Titus, which was to be sculpted in granite once a million dollars in donations had been collected. Following other festivities, including a glittering reception at the Waldorf-Astoria, he entrained for Washington to celebrate Dewey Day.

McKinley eagerly anticipated the rejoicing. Though he perceived the political advantages to be accrued from basking in the reflection of Dewey's acclaim, he also shared the patriotic mood of the public. He had contemplated a trip to New York to greet "the admiral," as everyone now called Dewey—as if he were the only naval officer of that rank. But Secretary of State John Hay dissuaded him with the acid reminder that it was below the dignity of his office to go out of his way to honor a sailor returning from a tour of duty, whatever his accomplishments. McKinley instead awaited Dewey in Washington, where the celebration was to surpass anything ever seen in the capital.

The fanfare marking the end of the Civil War thirty-four years before had been memorable. Now, on an evening in early October 1899, it seemed dim by comparison. Electricity made the difference. Lights bathed the city in radiance, from the Union Station to the Capitol and down Pennsylvania Avenue to the White House. They illuminated the new post office, its Florentine façade ablaze with Dewey's famous order to Captain Gridley, and shone on the colonnaded Treasury Building, where a reviewing stand had been constructed to represent the prow of his flagship. Floodlights brightened inscriptions strung across other government buildings, while searchlights played on the Stars and Stripes unfurled from their staffs. Lamps twinkled in side streets, in parks and in the windows of private homes. The incandescence not only glowed in homage to Dewey, but through him it symbolized the coronation of the United States as a global power.

The parade was formless. Dewey, seated in the reviewing stand alongside McKinley, watched as labor, church and various civic organizations filed past amid a din of firecrackers, each carrying placards extolling him. He slipped away, exhausted, after one group of marchers broke through the cordon around the reviewing stand to press toward him. Crowning the Washington events, however, was the award to him of the golden Tiffany sword on the steps of the Capitol. John D. Long, the secretary of the navy, delivered a long-winded address, replete with references to America's "imperial moral" and "manifest destiny." But McKinley, handing Dewey the sword, mentioned the U.S. commitment to the Philippines in a simple phrase. "There was no flaw in your victory. There will be no faltering in maintaining it."

McKinley had deliberately cited the Philippines briefly, assuming that the delirious turnout for Dewey reflected widespread approval of his policy. Hoping to benefit from Dewey's presumed wisdom and experience, however, he invited the admiral to the White House on the morning of October 3 for cigars and a quiet talk. Dewey knew virtually nothing about the Philippines, having

confined himself to his flagship in Manila Bay except for a daily visit ashore.
But he had spent a year there and was famous—qualifications that in McKinley's eyes made him an authority. Before the meeting, McKinley had jotted
down some questions, leaving spaces for Dewey's answers. The scribbled notes,
one of McKinley's few handwritten mementos to survive, suggest that he
found in the replies what he continually sought—confirmation of his own
righteousness:

> Self Govt—are they capable?
> No & will not be for several years.
> The US must control and supervise giving
> Philipinos [sic] participation as far as capable.
> What does AG represent? in population and sentiment.
> He has no more than 40,000 followers
> of all kinds out of 8 or 10 millions
> What is our duty?
> Keep the islands permanently
> Valuable in every sense
> How many troops needed?
> 50,000
> Have we ships enough?
> Ought to send more. Recommends
> that Brooklyn go & smaller vessels
> Should we give up the islands?
> Never—never
> The stories of church desecration & inhumanity. . . .

McKinley was delighted to have the accolades for Dewey rub off on him.
But he was mystified by Dewey. Several kingmakers pondered the prospect of
sponsoring the admiral for president; one, publisher Joseph Pulitzer, seriously
explored the possibility. Dewey baffled them as well. He evaded the subject,
creating the impression that he was biding his time before announcing his
candidacy. His silence also fueled speculation as to his party sympathies.
Nobody was willing to accept at face value his comment, made to a correspondent in Manila before his return home, that "a sailor has no politics." It
strained credulity to believe that a hero of his dimensions would forgo the
chance to parlay his prestige into high office.

Dewey in reality bore little resemblance to the deity fabricated by a fawning
press in quest of copy and exalted by a naïve public in search of heroes. Thrust
by events into prominence, he enjoyed the adulation, which inflated his vanity.
He held forth at Washington dinner parties, his anecdotes titillating the ladies
and his pompous pronouncements impressing the men. But he was merely a
competent naval officer of no special brilliance, who, save for an accident of
history, would have retired to comfortable obscurity.

Some months later, Dewey reconsidered the idea of the presidency. He
fatuously confided to a reporter for the *New York World* that he would respond
to a draft and could easily handle the job. But by then his popularity had
waned. He suffered from overexposure, the curse of instant celebrities. His
marriage to Mildred McLean Hazen, a rich and stylish widow thirteen years

his junior, also tarnished his image. She was reputedly cold and snooty. Besides, she had recently converted to Catholicism, an affront to America's solid Protestants. A disclosure that more than fifty thousand dollars had been raised through public subscription to purchase him a large mansion in Washington further cooled the nation's ardor toward him. There he was, effusively accepting a gift that his rich wife could have multiplied a dozen times over. Worse still, it leaked out that he had transferred the title of the house to her—in effect rejecting the country's gratitude. Donations to the Dewey Arch fell off, and the decaying wood-and-plaster model was soon relegated to the garbage dump. Dewey died early in 1917, at the age of eighty, as the United States entered the war with Germany that he had repeatedly forecast. He had become a memory.

Jacob Schurman, the head of the Philippine commission, was also back from Manila; like Dewey, he gratified McKinley. Having gone out opposed to the acquisition of the islands, he returned an enthusiast for annexation. He also felt that America was justified in imposing its sovereignty over the archipelago. But he urged McKinley to replace U.S. military rule with a civilian regime. Only liberal measures, including limited self-government, he contended, would win the allegiance of the Filipinos.

McKinley, as usual, meditated at length on the advice. To establish a civilian administration in the Philippines would entail legislation, but he was reluctant to revive debate in Congress, where passions on the subject ran high. Nor did he want to rekindle disputes over the issue as the 1900 presidential elections approached. In addition, he had qualms about ceding the extraordinary power that he exercised through the U.S. Army's management of the territory. So he argued that Aguinaldo's "insurgents" had to be crushed first. He suggested, though, that the political role of Filipinos loyal to the Americans could be gradually built up "from the bottom," first in the towns and later at the provincial level—under the control of the U.S. forces. The plan did not require legislative approval. Nevertheless, he would send it to Congress as a courtesy, expecting its easy endorsement by the Republican majority.

As a veteran politician, McKinley reveled in communion with the voters. He knew that the august presence of the president almost alone swayed public opinion, which in turn influenced Congress. But he sought reassurance from the acclaim of the people, even though he often chose to hear only the echo of his own views. The state elections scheduled for the fall of 1899 offered him an opportunity to reach out to the country. After fêting Dewey, he toured the Middle West as far as the Dakotas, campaigning for Republican candidates. He spoke as always of wages and prices, crops, jobs, industry, trade and sound currency. And, everywhere, he unabashedly waved the flag, now flying abroad over America's possession in the Pacific. The crowds—farmers, workers, merchants, businessmen and bankers—responded warmly to his warmth. He returned to Washington reinvigorated, his self-confidence reinforced. The nation was unified behind him; there was no need for controversy.

Thus, in January 1900, Albert Beveridge annoyed him. The pale, handsome, earnest young Republican senator, just elected from Indiana, had undeniable gifts. Then only thirty-seven, he was a skilled lawyer and mellifluous orator, and he exuded an air of authority. He was the only member of Congress to have actually been to the Philippines, where he saw action on Luzon and visited other islands. But he was a zealot who traveled merely to confirm his preconceptions. He was also a political amateur, unaware of the difference between arousing voters and dealing with his colleagues, nor had he learned to relate to the president. Now, in his maiden speech to the upper chamber, he revealed his flaws in a grandiloquent display of rhetoric.

Beveridge had drafted legislation asserting America's right to rule the Philippines in perpetuity. Referring to a small red notebook, a theatrical device contrived to enhance his credibility, he stressed the importance of the islands as the gateway to the vast China market—the guarantee of U.S. commercial preeminence. America had also been divinely ordained, as the crucible of the master race, to impose its supremacy on inferior peoples. To grant freedom to the Filipinos was folly, if not treason. "What alchemy," Beveridge intoned, "will change the oriental quality of their blood, and set the self-governing currents of the American pouring through their Malay veins?" The United States could not abandon "this combined garden and Gibraltar of the Pacific" to the stupid and indolent natives without abdicating both its obligations to itself and to its global role. Nor could the Senate in good conscience reject his bill while "our boys" were fighting and dying to fulfill America's providential mission to regenerate the world.

Though Beveridge had been purveying the same purple prose around the country for a year, the Senate galleries erupted in applause when his star-spangled oration ended two hours later. Correspondents dashed out to file their reports, which inspired banner headlines and pious editorials across the land. The cheers eclipsed Senator George Hoar of Massachusetts, the septuagenarian foe of imperialism, who replied frostily: "I have heard much calculated to excite the imagination of the youth seeking wealth, or the youth charmed by the dream of empire, but the words Right, Justice, Duty, Freedom, were absent my young friend must permit me to say from that eloquent speech."

After the fuss faded away, Beveridge's performance had also chafed his colleagues on both sides of the aisle. As a novice, he had transgressed Senate etiquette by arrogantly lecturing his fellow legislators on their responsibilities. Henry Cabot Lodge shared his expansionist outlook but tartly remarked that he had "a very imperfect idea of the rights of seniority." Moderate Republicans were especially irritated. They supported America's overseas ventures as an exercise in altruism and flinched at Beveridge's crass emphasis on trade and profit. Though they may have been racial bigots, his prejudices were too blatant. Veterans of the chamber were slighted as well by his crude lobbying for chairmanship of a committee on the Philippines. He had intimated that McKinley backed his candidacy, a patent untruth; in fact, McKinley feared that rashness might provoke the Senate into resisting his Philippine policy and privately criticized Beveridge's "unwise methods of securing recognition." Beveridge gained a seat on the Philippine committee; Lodge, however, was named chairman.

McKinley had no reason to worry. Faithful Republicans dominated the Senate. They also controlled the House of Representatives, which became more accommodating following the retirement of its speaker, the acerbic Thomas Reed, who hated McKinley. The Anti-Imperialist League's opposition no longer counted, largely because its leaders, as Theodore Roosevelt had noted, were figures of "a bygone age," out of tune with the nation's rambunctious mood. The movement virtually disappeared after McKinley's landslide reelection in November 1900, yet its demise testified to the validity of its cause. The U.S. public, more and more appalled by the war in the Philippines, had by now largely lost interest in acquiring new dominions overseas, thus obviating the need for protests against expansion. But the dream of foreign trade, particularly with Asia, lured Americans as much then as it does today, and it militated in favor of the strong U.S. presence in the Pacific that McKinley desired. Secretary of State John Hay worked to fulfill America's aspirations in Asia through the Open Door doctrine—an approach, clothed in piety, that essentially aimed to advance joint U.S. and British ambitions in China.

Hay, then sixty-one, was extraordinarily versatile. A man of striking appearance, with chiseled features and a spade beard, he had variously been an attorney, historian, novelist, journalist, poet, diplomat and cabinet member— never sacrificing his charm, sincerity or iconoclastic wit. He was born in Indiana, the son of a country doctor, and moved after college to Springfield, Illinois, to clerk in a law office next door to Abraham Lincoln. Elected president, Lincoln hired him as a private secretary and afterward made him a military aide with the rank of colonel—which prompted Hay to tease McKinley, who had held a lower grade in the Civil War, as "the major." He had also referred irreverently to Lincoln, whom he worshiped, as the "backwoods Jupiter."

Rewarded with diplomatic posts, Hay served in the U.S. legations in Paris, Vienna and Madrid. The sinecures left him the time to travel, write and enjoy the cultural and social life of Europe before boredom drove him home. He became an editorial writer for the *New York Tribune* and published poems and novels. He also collaborated with John Nicolay, a colleague on Lincoln's staff, on an immensely successful ten-volume history of the Lincoln presidency. He wisely wed the daughter of a rich Cleveland businessman, which gave him both financial security and the Ohio political connections that brought him into McKinley's inner circle of advisers. McKinley appointed him to the coveted post of U.S. envoy to London, where he gained a reputation as an Anglophile—an unhealthy image in the anti-British atmosphere of America at the time. Hay maintained, however, that a "friendly" relationship with Britain was the "one indispensable feature of our policy." He acted accordingly in formulating the Open Door doctrine.

Late in the nineteenth century, Britain faced the loss of its predominant commercial position in China to Germany, Russia and Japan as they carved up the moribund empire into spheres of influence. The British had suggested to Hay, then the ambassador in London, that the United States cooperate with them in curbing the other imperialist powers. McKinley ignored the proposal until he reached his decision to retain the entire Philippine archipelago. At that stage, to bulwark the new policy, he found it expedient to stress the benefits of wider markets for America in Asia. He authorized Hay, by now secretary of state, to pursue a common effort with Britain.

Short of Asia specialists, Hay recruited as an adviser William W. Rockhill, a former secretary at the U.S. legation at Peking and currently the minister to Greece. Rockhill in turn enlisted Alfred E. Hippisley, his brother-in-law and a British employee of the Chinese customs service. In September 1899, they sent notes to the European powers and Japan, informing them of America's wish for a formal declaration supporting free trade in their spheres of influence in China. With some reservations, each country agreed. Hay emerged as a bold and creative diplomat who had ended the sordid squabbling to slice up China. Later, after Russia had moved into Manchuria, the Open Door concept was amplified to recognize Chinese "territorial and administrative integrity." The doctrine rang hollow during the 1930s, when neither the United States nor the rest of the world intervened to block the Japanese invasion of China. But early in the century it symbolized America's assumption of responsibilities in Asia— a role that originated in the almost inadvertent takeover of the Philippines.

★ ★ ★

As he contemplated the future of U.S. tutelage in the Philippines, McKinley began to realize the inadequacies of his war powers.

Complicated political, economic, social, judicial and other problems would confront America when the conflict wound down. Congress, consequently, had to enact legislation to give the islands an administration capable of coping with the challenges. In contrast to the European imperialists, Americans lacked a colonial experience to serve as a precedent. Their dedication to the constitutional process, or at least in form, also spurred them to conceive legal solutions. Few men were better suited to devise a plan than John Spooner, the senior Republican senator from Wisconsin.

A respected jurist who with his disheveled hair and bulging eyes looked like an untidy owl, Spooner had not been an ardent expansionist. The acquisition of the Philippines had been, he said, "one of the bitter fruits of the war" with Spain. But, loyal to McKinley, he argued cogently in defense of America's right to annex dominions abroad. The possession of territories overseas, he claimed, was no different than the expansion of the United States within its continental limits. Indeed, he had studied the statute that enabled Jefferson to govern Louisiana. He finally introduced a bill to apply to the Philippines, at least provisionally.

It was designed to blunt Beveridge, who had called for permanent American control over the archipelago. Skirting the controversial issue of sovereignty, Spooner recommended that the direction of the islands be vested in the president pending further legislation. The audacious transfer of authority to the executive branch alarmed both Republicans and Democrats in Congress, and eventual passage of the proposal into law was to be laborious. But it represented a step toward the replacement of army by civilian rule in the Philippines.

McKinley cast around for an honest, able figure to supervise the transition. In the middle of January 1900, he sent a cryptic telegram to William Howard Taft, a federal circuit judge in Cincinnati: I WOULD LIKE TO SEE YOU IN WASHINGTON ON IMPORTANT BUSINESS WITHIN THE NEXT FEW DAYS.

7. LITTLE BROWN BROTHERS

★ ★ ★

A jovial giant, William Howard Taft seemed to personify turn-of-the-century America. He was ambitious, optimistic, diligent and, above all, big—from his bejowled face and elephantine torso to the boisterous laugh that erupted from beneath his extravagant blond mustache. Passionately devoted to his family, he exuded a warmth that also charmed his friends and colleagues, whose admiration of him frequently bordered on reverence. He had surprisingly few enemies for a public figure. Indeed, as a biographer later observed, he was "almost too perfect," and might have even been "obnoxious" had it not been for his good nature. But his cheerful manner was deceptive. Like many fat men who outwardly appear to be jolly, he had a simmering and sometimes uncontrollable temper. His emotions frequently made him erratic, and a streak of moral rectitude colored his perspective, rendering him stubbornly opinionated. Anxious for approval, he refused to read newspapers that criticized him, and he nursed grudges for years. Theodore Roosevelt, with whom he later clashed for subverting his political ambitions, called him "one of the best haters" he knew.

Taft's career, spanning a half-century, was impressive. Industrious rather than creative, he climbed steadily from assistant county prosecutor at the age of twenty-three to president of the United States at fifty-one and ultimately to chief justice of the Supreme Court—each advance the consequence of a previous accomplishment.

"No Taft, to my knowledge, has ever neglected a public duty for the sake of gratifying a private desire," remarked his mother, whose husband had inculcated their children with a spirit of earnest endeavor. Alphonso Taft, an austere Vermonter of Scottish descent, had immigrated to Cincinnati to practice law. President Grant rewarded his fidelity to the Republican party by naming him secretary of war and afterward attorney general before sending

him as U.S. envoy to Vienna and later to the Czar's court at St. Petersburg—
where his Yankee innocence amused the cosmopolitan nobles of both capitals.
Alphonso puritanically exhorted his five sons to high achievement through
"self-denial and enthusiastic hard work." One was to die insane, but the others
fulfilled his expectations. The eldest, Charles, became a multimillionaire businessman, publisher and philanthropist. Henry soared to prominence as a New
York lawyer, and Horace founded the prestigious Taft School in Connecticut.
Will, forty-two when McKinley's telegram summoned him to Washington in
January 1900, was then serving his eighth year on the federal circuit bench. His
wife, Helen, the "fascinating Nellie," the granddaughter and niece of congressmen, shared his ambition despite her aloof intellectual inclinations.

McKinley had met Taft for the first time three months earlier, during a
campaign swing through Ohio. Taft, a dedicated jurist uncomfortable with
compromises and contrived conviviality, had avoided politicians—even
though, as an inbred Republican, he could not entirely avoid politics. He rated
McKinley a mediocrity, and made no secret of his view. Thus the call to
Washington puzzled him. His sole dream was a Supreme Court seat, and he
could not conceive of McKinley appointing him. Besides, the bench was full.
Obeying the command, however, he took a night train to the capital and
hastened to the White House. The January day was gray and cold, and McKinley awaited him in his lighted office, flanked by Secretary of War Elihu Root
and Secretary of the Navy John Long. McKinley got straight to the point:
"Judge, I'd like to have you go to the Philippines."

He wanted Taft to head a commission to "establish a government there" to
exercise both executive and legislative authority in preparation for civilian
rule. The ensuing dialogue was a replay, nearly word for word, of McKinley's
bid to recruit Jacob Gould Schurman. Taft demurred. He had opposed the
acquisition of the archipelago, feeling that "we had quite enough to do at
home," and suggested that McKinley instead find someone "more in sympathy
with the situation." McKinley replied, much as he had to Schurman, that he
had not sought the islands either. "But," he told Taft, "we have got them, and
in dealing with them, I think I can trust the man who didn't want them better
than I can the man who did."

Taft was not an ardent anti-imperialist. The constitution, he felt, allowed the
possession of overseas dominions without necessarily according their inhabitants the rights of U.S. citizens or extending to them the benefits of free trade.
He was also in favor of giving the islands a sound administration aimed at
ultimate self-government. As he listened to McKinley's plans, however, he
recoiled from an assignment that might abort his judicial future.

Root finally intervened with an appeal to his sense of virtue and spirit of
adventure. "Your country needs you. You may go on holding the job you have
in a humdrum, mediocre way. But here is something that will test you, something in the way of struggle and effort, and the question is, will you take the
harder or easier task?" McKinley, aware of Taft's hopes for a Supreme Court
seat, followed up with a virtual pledge. The Philippine job would only be
temporary and, he promised, "If I last and the opportunity comes, I shall
appoint you." After consulting his family, Taft consented. He insisted, however, on total control in the Philippines so that only he would be "responsible
for success or failure." McKinley had weakened his resistance, he afterward

recalled: "I never came in contact with a more sweetly sympathetic nature, nor one more persuasive in his treatment of men."

Taft, later promoted to governor, was to remain in Manila for the next four years, declining repeated offers from Roosevelt, by then president, of a Supreme Court slot. Ironically, Roosevelt had himself longed to be the first civilian governor of the Philippines and had conceded to run for the vice presidency in 1900 only after Henry Cabot Lodge assured him that McKinley would eventually grant his wish.

Unlike Schurman's group, which had nominally included Otis and Dewey, the Taft commission was composed exclusively of civilians. McKinley reappointed Dean Worcester, the only holdover from the Schurman panel, along with three other distinguished figures. Luke E. Wright, a conservative Democrat from Tennessee, was a former Confederate general and state attorney general. Henry C. Ide, a Vermont lawyer, had been a U.S. magistrate in Samoa, and Bernard Moses was a professor of Latin American history at the University of California. Mark Sullivan, the celebrated chronicler of the epoch, reckoned their mean weight to be 227 pounds—Taft, at 325, substantially raising the average.

In February 1899, when fighting with the Filipinos broke out, responsibility for the Philippines was transferred from the State Department to the War Department. Seven months later, McKinley appointed Elihu Root his secretary of war to replace Russell Alger, who had been tarnished by scandal. McKinley reckoned that Root, a New Yorker, would lend regional balance to his cabinet. As a lawyer, Root also seemed to have the skills to cope with the legal problems involved in managing the islands and defining a policy for the archipelago.

Apart from moments of puckish humor, Root, with his slit eyes, willowy mustache and grave demeanor resembled the stereotype of an inscrutable Chinese mandarin. Then fifty-four, he came from upstate New York, where his father taught college. He had prospered as a clever and ruthless corporate lawyer, but social conscience propelled him into the progressive wing of the Republican party—a faction often derisively dubbed silk-stocking reformers, whose stalwarts included Theodore Roosevelt. His sacrifice of a lucrative legal practice to enter government earned him praise and also channeled him into a lifetime of public service. Roosevelt, as president, appointed him secretary of state. Later, as head of the Carnegie Endowment for International Peace, he won the Nobel Peace Prize for his valiant if futile efforts to avert war through arbitration. McKinley relied on Root's keen mind and sharp talents, though the two men never became close personally.

Root was an unalloyed expansionist. In his first speech as secretary of war, he asserted that the U.S. claim to the Philippines, legitimized by the Senate's ratification of the treaty with Spain, was "better than the title we had to Louisiana." He argued that the majority of Filipinos hated Aguinaldo's "band of brigands" and favored American rule. Regurgitating the biased reports of U.S. officials in Manila, he insisted that the "great mass" of the natives, "little advanced from pure savagery," could not possibly comprehend the concept of government by consent of the governed.

But he was too intelligent to cling to simplistic formulas as he sought to shape a U.S. colonial structure for the Philippines. He carefully studied the

British experience rule in India, finally discarding it as a model. America, itself a former colony, would be violating its basic tenets unless it upheld its own values in administering a foreign people, regardless of the legalities of the relationship. "Whether there be consent or not," he said, the "immutable laws of justice and humanity" demanded "that the weak shall be protected, that cruelty and lust shall be restrained."

So even though he could not foresee independence for the Filipinos in the near future, Root concluded that they deserved the same rights as Americans—except for trial by jury in criminal cases and the prerogative to bear arms. He thereupon drafted McKinley's orders to Taft. The directive was to guide the U.S. colonial endeavor until the Philippines attained autonomy thirty-six years later.

A lawyer's document, it was both rigid and flexible. It reaffirmed U.S. sovereignty over the islands, yet encouraged Taft and his team to adapt to local realities. They "should bear in mind that the government they are establishing is designed not for our satisfaction, or for the expression of our theoretical views, but for the happiness, peace and prosperity of the people of the Philippine islands, and the measures adopted should be made to conform to their customs, their habits and even their prejudices." Still, America considered "certain great principles of government" to be "essential to the rule of law and the maintenance of individual freedom," and the Filipinos must adhere to these precepts "for the sake of their liberty and happiness."

Thus the United States, imbued with evangelical zeal, would "civilize" the natives according to its standards. As usual, Finley Peter Dunne's Mr. Dooley summed it up: "Poor dissolute uncovered wretches, ye miserable, childish-minded apes, we propose f'r to larn ye th' uses of liberty. We can't give ye anny votes . . . but we'll threat ye th' way a father shud threat his childhern if we have to break ivry bone in ye'er bodies." The policy was enlightened compared to the repressive practices of the European powers in their colonies at the time. But the effort of the United States to transplant its values and institutions in the Philippines eventually became what the historian Glenn Anthony May has termed an "experiment in self-duplication," spurred by a belief still ingrained in Americans: that they can remold other lands in their own image. A noble dream, it proved in later years to be largely an exercise in self-deception.

★ ★ ★

On April 17, 1900, Taft sailed from San Francisco aboard a U.S. Army transport ship, accompanied by his wife and three children. He deposited them temporarily in Japan to spare them the hot season in the Philippines, then proceeded with his fellow commissioners to Hong Kong. There, like a modern tourist, he ordered a wardrobe of custom-made shoes, shirts and white cotton suits—none of which, his wife afterward complained, ever fit properly. In early June, bathing in sweat, he landed in Manila to an unpleasant welcome.

Otis, to everyone's relief, had gone home at his own request a month before, having typically worked at his desk until midnight before his departure. General Arthur MacArthur, his successor as military governor, refused from the outset to recognize Taft's mandate, and even snubbed the commissioners on their arrival. Instead of meeting their ship personally, he sent an aide to conduct them to his office—where, as Taft quipped, the frigid greeting dried his perspiration. As a further sign of disapproval, MacArthur assigned Taft and his associates to one small room in his headquarters. MacArthur also declined to give up his residence in the Malacañang palace, a symbol of his status, compelling Taft to rent a dilapidated house in the suburbs. A generation later, his son Douglas would be equally rude to presumed intruders.

Arthur MacArthur, at fifty-five, was a stocky man with pince-nez spectacles who, despite his fastidious uniforms, looked like a grocer. Vain and solemn, he constantly tried to gild his image by building minor skirmishes into major battles, with himself in a heroic role—a practice that his son emulated. Like Douglas, he had a grandiose idea of his intellect and would discourse pompously on global power balances and geopolitical strategies. He shared his colleagues' belief in innate white superiority. America's "wonderful" thrust into Asia, he told a Senate committee in 1902, was the preordained destiny of the "magnificent Aryan people," who were "thus initiating a stage of progressive social evolution that may be reasonably expected to result in . . . the unity of the race and the brotherhood of man."

Born in Massachusetts and raised in Wisconsin, where his father had served as governor, MacArthur spurned West Point to fight in the Civil War. He won the Congressional Medal of Honor for gallantry and, at the age of twenty, was promoted to brevet colonel. He spent the next quarter-century as an army captain in remote frontier outposts, chasing Indians. His elevation to U.S. commander in the Philippines coincided with Aguinaldo's shift to guerrilla warfare, a switch that altered the nature of the conflict. In 1899, the first year of combat, one American was killed for every four or five wounded; the ratio changed during the next year to one U.S. soldier killed for every two wounded—testimony to the growing effectiveness of the Filipinos.

The new circumstances exacerbated the dispute between MacArthur and Taft. Just as Otis had resented Schurman's commission, so MacArthur felt that civilians had no place in a war. Unlike Otis, who had exuded optimism to justify his claims of success, MacArthur projected gloom to dramatize his pleas for toughness. His analysis, if not his prescription, was realistic. A seasoned soldier, he had seen Filipino troops die in droves for their cause. He respected their courage and determination too much to accept the nebulous notion of duping them into surrender with offers of autonomy under U.S. supremacy. The idea of winning their "hearts and minds" he felt, was nonsense.

Prior to his departure, Otis had begun to organize town councils composed of Filipino elites elected through limited suffrage, with U.S. officers in charge. MacArthur dismissed the scheme as chimerical. Native officials, he observed, "acted openly in behalf of the Americans and secretly in behalf of the insurgents, and, paradoxical as it may seem, with considerable apparent solicitude for the interests of both." They helped the U.S. forces to build roads, bridges and schools, but covertly provided Aguinaldo with money, supplies, recruits and intelligence. It was wrong to suppose that the nationalists gained support solely though coercion: "Fear as the only motive is hardly sufficient to account for the united and apparently spontaneous action of millions of people." This "adhesive principle," MacArthur concluded in his ponderous style, "comes from ethnological homogeneity, which induces men to respond for a time to the appeals of consanguinous leadership, even when such action is opposed to their interests and convictions of expediency." In simple language, it was us against them—and, he believed, as his son later did, that there could be no substitute for a total U.S. victory.

Taft disagreed. MacArthur, he said, viewed all natives as implacably hostile to the United States and looked at his task as "one of conquering eight millions of recalcitrant, treacherous and sullen people." The charge was partly true. Soon after taking command, MacArthur proclaimed an amnesty for enemy troops who gave up their arms and swore allegiance to America. But the offer excluded those who had violated the "rules of civilized warfare"—which by definition meant guerrillas. It misfired badly. Fewer than five thousand Filipinos responded, most of them innocents only too happy to receive rewards for turning in their vintage rifles.

But MacArthur was neither as harsh nor as myopic as Taft portrayed him. He championed leniency for prisoners of war, partly out of fidelity to his soldier's code of honor, and also in the hope that Aguinaldo would treat American captives with equal compassion. He infuriated Taft by releasing many captured nationalists and allowing them to keep their property.

Though a jurist, Taft advocated a stern approach. Root may have stressed America's adherence to the immutable laws of justice and humanity, but Taft argued that the Filipino resistance was a "conspiracy of murder and assassination," proposing that enemy troops be executed or exiled "as they are captured." He was aghast in March 1901, when MacArthur invited Aguinaldo to the Malacañang palace after the Filipino leader's capture and publicly exonerated him in exchange for Aguinaldo's pledge of loyalty to the United States. Taft, then traveling outside Manila, warned that Aguinaldo would soon be agitating for independence through peaceful means and should have been deported to Guam, where the Americans banished obstreperous natives.

Coping with MacArthur baffled Taft. Neither McKinley nor Root had promised to back him in a quarrel, and he could not appeal to them for support. But Taft had been given control over appropriations for the Philippines, and management of the money reassured him that, in a showdown, he could bring MacArthur to heel. In contrast to MacArthur, he believed that "the back of the rebellion" had been broken and, in time, America would prevail. He urged his commission to exercise patience "in this climate," quoting from Kipling's novel *The Naulakha,* a warning to Westerners who sought to impose their pace on Asia:

> And the end of the fight is a tombstone white
> with the name of the late deceased,
> And the epitaph drear: "A Fool lies here
> who tried to hustle the East."

In fact, Taft drove his team at top speed. Assigned to different fields, the commissioners spent the summer amassing information. They labored ten or twelve hours a day in the torrid heat, interviewing Filipinos, Americans and other witnesses. Dean Worcester covered agriculture, mining and health. Luke Wright, an attorney, focused on the militia, the police and criminal codes while Henry Ide, the former Samoa judge, studied the courts, banking and currency, and Bernard Moses, the historian, surveyed education. Taft reserved for himself the touchiest topics: the civil service, the disposition of public lands and the status of the remaining Spanish friars. Late in August, at a cost of $40,000, he cabled their findings to Root.

The "ignorant, superstitious and credulous" natives had been gulled by "unscrupulous leaders" into defying America, he said. But now, MacArthur's gloomy appraisal to the contrary, the war had been reduced to sporadic guerrilla actions. Most people wanted peace under U.S. sovereignty, and a victory by McKinley in the presidential election in November would confirm his policy to retain the Philippines. The remnant Filipino nationalists, their hope for independence gone, thus had no alternative except surrender. So the United States sought to sponsor, under civilian auspices, a local constabulary, a new tax structure, public works, judicial reform and universal education in English.

On September 1, 1900, as scheduled, the Taft commission assumed the functions of a legislative body—with authority to raise taxes, appropriate funds, fix tariffs and set up law courts. In helping Root to draft his instructions, however, Taft had failed to carve out for himself the post of chief executive, which MacArthur held and naturally refused to relinquish. But Taft and his associates could now enact laws. In addition, they controlled $2.5 million, accumulated by the U.S. Army from customs duties and other sources. MacArthur's power had been "cut down to almost nothing," Taft cheerfully noted in a letter to a friend. Still, he directed a stream of grievances against MacArthur in messages to Root until, ten months later, he was appointed governor.

Officials usually embark on missions with preconceived attitudes, and Taft fit the pattern. He had already decided before reaching Manila, as he told a friend, that Aguinaldo and his disciples were "desperate men" fighting to convince the U.S. public that the "task of settling that country is hopeless." Unless they were eliminated, they would "overawe the more peaceably inclined inhabitants and the better educated class" in the Philippines. Nothing he heard during his first few months in Manila changed his mind.

He conferred with the same upper-class lawyers, doctors and landowners who had testified before the Schurman panel. They held their own people in low esteem, validating Taft's estimate of most Filipinos as abysmally backward. Shortly after his arrival, he privately ventilated his views in letters home. He described the "vast mass" of the natives as "superstitious and ignorant" and unqualified for either universal suffrage or autonomy. "They need the training of fifty or a hundred years before they shall even realize what Anglo-Saxon liberty is." He even decried the *ilustrados,* whose opinions he valued. "There are not in these islands more than six or seven thousand men who have any education that deserves the name"—most of them "intriguing politicians, without the slightest moral stamina" and motivated only by "personal interests." Few Filipinos could be entrusted with responsibility, since a "certain tendency to venality characterizes them in every position in which there is the slightest opportunity to 'squeeze' the public." He similarly denounced the natives in an informal message to Root as "generally lacking in moral character . . . prone to yield to any pecuniary consideration and difficult persons out of whom to make an honest government." They were "born politicians, as ambitious as Satan and as jealous as possible of each others' preferment."

But Taft felt bound by duty "to do the best we can." Though the Filipinos would never attain more than a small measure of autonomy under "careful" U.S. tutelage, they could be taught, through "political education" and "widespread" schooling, the "possibility of the honest administration of government." He would be their missionary, steering them into the pastures of righteousness. He condescendingly referred to them as "little brown brothers"—a memorable epithet that inspired an anonymous American soldier to compose an equally memorable ditty.

> They say I've got brown brothers here,
> But still I draw the line.
> He may be a brother of Big Bill Taft,
> But he ain't no brother of mine.

Taft's fellow commissioners were no less biased. Moses, the California historian, foresaw "the beginning of a rapid return to barbarism" if the United States withdrew from the Philippines, and Dean Worcester remarked to a reporter that "honesty among Filipinos is a theme for a humorist." But they shared Taft's conviction that, under America's guidance, the natives could be improved. Moses maintained that it was America's duty to turn the "barbarian" into an "ally of civilized society." Worcester, who regarded the Filipinos to be "naturally unfit" for self-government, also believed in their future. Often patronizing and truculent, he devoted much of his life to bearing the "white man's burden" as a senior official in the U.S. colonial administration.

The United States had acquired in the Philippines a possession that, in one key respect, differed from Europe's overseas territories: The British in India or the French in Vietnam had taken over lands whose native rulers, whatever the sophistication of their own culture, had been unfamiliar with the West. In the Philippines, by contrast, America inherited a cosmopolitan upper class, composed mostly of Spanish or Chinese *mestizos* who were the intellectual equals or even superiors of their U.S. masters.

Taft might voice contempt for these *ilustrados,* but he perceived that they could be useful, if only as an expedient. He had read the testimony of Felipe Calderón, the prominent local lawyer who had earlier warned the Schurman panel that while defeating the Filipinos by force would be difficult, they could more easily be dominated by "leading them on by attraction." Almost intuitively, Taft evolved what he labeled a "policy of attraction," designed to induce the elites to cooperate with the Americans. A credible native opposition would deflate Aguinaldo's movement. Over the long run, too, the participation of able Filipinos in the colonial administration would spare the United States the stigma of outright imperialism. The policy was to leave a deep imprint on the Philippines. From start to finish of America's rule, the Filipinos essentially governed themselves under increasingly light U.S. supervision.

Many contemporary Filipino historians, belatedly imbued with nationalism, have branded the pro-American collaborators as traitors, to some degree a valid charge. Several wealthy professionals and landowners were indeed selfish and aloof. "The people do not know what is good for them," said Benito

Legarda, a rich lawyer and planter, who feared that Aguinaldo's radical followers would threaten his privileges. He shifted his allegiance to the United States, as did another *ilustrado,* Trinidad Pardo de Tavera, and Taft soon helped them to found a political party.

But these men, and others like them, were not solely concerned with their narrow interests. Some sincerely saw American sovereignty as a boon to the Philippines. In their eyes, they were the true heirs to José Rizal, the martyred patriot who had rebuffed the revolutionary *Katipunan*'s call to arms against Spain and appealed instead for the same rights granted Spaniards. "All we demand," Rizal had said, "is more care, better instruction, better officials, one or two representatives and more security for ourselves and our property." These rights were precisely what America offered when McKinley originally promised the Filipinos "benevolent assimilation."

Trinidad Hermenegildo Pardo de Tavera, the archetypal *ilustrado,* was a lean figure with a spade beard and rimless spectacles perched on his aquiline nose. His father, a distinguished Spanish lawyer, had been the son of a nobleman assigned to the Philippines as an army officer. The Spanish readily crossed racial lines to enrich themselves, and the family united with affluent *mestizo* dynasties. Pardo de Tavera's mother came from a wealthy merchant clan of Spanish, Filipino and Chinese origins, and he himself married a cousin of Felipe Calderón, whose ancestry was mixed. His sister wed Juan Luna, the painter, also of a prominent background—who had shamed his kin by murdering her for suspected adultery.

Pardo de Tavera went from college in Manila to medical school in Paris, doubling in the study of Oriental languages. He published several esoteric works, among them a treatise on Tagolog words borrowed from Sanskrit and a survey of curative Philippine herbs, and was honored with election to the Royal Academy of Sciences in Madrid. Like his fellow *ilustrados,* he was a classic nineteenth-century liberal. He championed capitalism, separation of church and state, civil liberty and universal education, all encapsulated in that magic term of the time: *progress.* But he believed that, without a modern society and mature political institutions, self-government in the Philippines would be fatal. After all, Rizal had warned: "Of what good would be independence if the slaves of today become the tyrants of tomorrow."

As Aguinaldo's foreign-affairs adviser, Pardo de Tavera had implored him to beg McKinley "under no circumstances" to forsake the Philippines. He quit the nationalist movement when Aguinaldo spurned his suggestion. Pardo de Tavera himself wrote to McKinley: "Providence led the United States to these distant islands for the fulfillment of a noble mission, to take charge of the task of teaching us the principles that . . . have made your people the wonder of the world and the pride of humanity." In a letter to MacArthur, he pledged that "all our efforts will be directed to Americanizing ourselves" in the hope that "the American spirit may take possession of us," infusing the country with "its principles, its political customs and its peculiar civilization," so that "our redemption may be complete." He was one of the rare Filipinos to testify before the Schurman panel. Along with Legarda, he had gone to the dock to welcome Taft to Manila. Pardo de Tavera was, to Taft, the prototypical "little brown brother."

Despite his private disdain for all natives, Taft respected Pardo de Tavera's "common sense"—his euphemism for moderation. Here was a solid, educated, refined Filipino, who shared his own conservatism, not one of Aguinaldo's murderers. Indeed, by some stretch of the imagination, Pardo de Tavera might even pass for a Republican back home in Ohio. Accordingly, Taft put his considerable weight behind the *Partido Federal*, popularly called the *Federalistas*, which Pardo de Tavera, Legarda and other *ilustrados* founded late in 1900. They were assisted by a U.S. colonial official, Frank Bourns, who subsequently created a spy network to collect scandalous tidbits about Filipino politicians. He helped draft the party's program, which outlined the evolution of the islands under American tutelage. As the country was pacified, local administrations would be set up and education encouraged. A "constitutional period" would then follow, with elections to a national legislature and accreditation for a resident Filipino delegation to represent the Philippines in Washington. A year later, the party added a visionary plank to its platform: statehood in the Union.

The *Federalistas* formally inaugurated their party on February 22, 1901, George Washington's birthday. Crowds jammed Manila's central park, the Luneta, as brass bands played and children carrying papier-mâché eagles paraded past a reviewing stand flying the Stars and Stripes—the flag of Aguinaldo's republic having long before been banned. Pardo de Tavera, as party president, delivered the keynote address, unabashedly evoking his dream of Americanization. "I see the day near at hand . . . when it shall transpire that George Washington will not simply be the glory of the American continent but also our glory, because he will be the father of the American world, in which we shall feel ourselves completely united and assimilated."

Taft counted on the *Federalistas* to concentrate the "conservative forces in the islands." He gave $6,000 to Pardo de Tavera's ailing newspaper, *La Democracia*. Under a new sedition act, he also banned opposition movements—claiming that one, which recognized U.S. sovereignty but advocated eventual independence, would crystallize "all the lawless, restless, lazy and evil members of society." He further granted the *Federalistas* a monopoly on official jobs reserved for Filipinos. They rapidly attracted more than two hundred thousand recruits, who calculated that the party, as a creature of the powerful Americans, would provide schools, roads, health services, employment and other plums. The United States thus introduced its own system of patronage to the Philippines, and the Filipinos were to make the pork barrel a pillar of their political practice in later years. Taft rewarded Pardo de Tavera and Legarda, along with a rich sugar planter named José Luzuriaga, with places on his commission. Their appointments were only cosmetic; he privately noted that "the majority will be American at any rate."

The *Federalistas*, with more tangible benefits to offer Filipinos than could Aguinaldo, helped erode his support. They also played a role in the transition from U.S. military to civilian rule by serving the American regime. Taft's embrace, however, eventually proved to be their kiss of death. Despite the relative benison of U.S. tutelage, Filipinos were gradually acquiring a veneer of nationalism, and no movement could appear for long to be subservient to the Americans. Root, then Roosevelt's secretary of state, also shattered the *Federalistas'* dream of integration into the Union in 1904, when a delegation of the party leaders visited him in Washington. "Gentlemen," he said with disarming candor, "I don't want to suggest an invidious comparison, but statehood for Filipinos would add another serious problem to the one we have already. The Negroes are a cancer in our body politic, a source of constant difficulty, and we wish to avoid developing another such problem."

Two years later, Pardo de Tavera and his associates scuttled their statehood plank and, taking advantage of relaxed U.S. political curbs, instead called for "ultimate independence." But their party had crumbled by then. Taft had gone home in February 1904, depriving them of their patron. They succumbed to internecine rivalries. And they could not match shrewder Filipino leaders, like Sergio Osmeña and Manuel Quezon, who contrived to present themselves as dynamic nationalists—even though they were also American protégés and thus, in their fashion, "little brown bothers" as well.

Taft's promotion of the *ilustrados* reinforced a pattern that endures in the Philippines to this day. By cultivating the upper crust, he strengthened the wealthy families that had originally emerged during the Spanish colonial era, and many still hold sway. Ferdinand Marcos was to smash the old oligarchs seventy years later, but he supplanted them with his greedier cronies. The dispossessed dynasties, determined to regain their privileges, were instrumental in ousting him in favor of Corazon Aquino. She, however, also belonged to the landed gentry and showed no signs of drastically renovating the society. So while Filipinos echoed the rhetoric of U.S. democracy, often to soothe American ears, the Philippines remained, as Ninoy Aquino wrote in 1968, "an entrenched plutocracy."

Taft was not entirely responsible for this system, however. Subsequent American governors, for the sake of expedience, perpetuated the Filipino oligarchy, which continued after independence to ignore the need for economic and social reforms—a major cause of the country's recurrent rebellions. But, at the start, Aguinaldo did not promise a progressive alternative. On the contrary, he failed because he offered the population even less than did the Americans.

★ ★ ★

In May 1900, before leaving Manila, Major General Elwell Otis announced that "the war in the Philippines is already over" except for "little skirmishes that amount to nothing." His rosy view was to be contradicted by two more years of tough fighting, followed by mopping-up operations. Aguinaldo, at the time a fugitive in northern Luzon, was losing momentum. He had shifted to a protracted guerrilla conflict in the hope that the likely Democratic candidate for president, William Jennings Bryan, would defeat McKinley in November and fulfill his goal of independence. But the strategy only prolonged and intensified the struggle without improving his prospects.

Aguinaldo had changed his approach at the end of 1899, after Otis's rejection of his recent peace bid convinced him that negotiations were fruitless. He also recognized the futility of a conventional resistance when the Americans overran his last capital, Bayambang. As he fled north to presumed safety, he ordered the mobilization of "guerrillas and flying columns," and issued voluminous directives that read like Mao Zedong's later manuals on "people's war." He told his men to ambush American units, harass their supply lines and cut their communications. He recruited spies to monitor U.S. movements and inform on Filipino collaborators, and warned his troops against abusing villagers, lest they lose popular support. To make his army flexible, he placed it under autonomous commanders—one of whom wrote that "the war should now be waged more through craft than by force of arms." The struggle became uglier, for both sides.

The Filipinos, formerly visible in big battalions, began to blend into the landscape. One U.S. officer claimed to have observed a native shed his weapon, grab a farm tool, slip into a nearby field and shout *"amigo"* to a passing American soldier. Another recalled a village where "the people all greet you with kindly expressions while the same men slip into the bushes, get their rifles and waylay you further down the road." Like their descendants in Vietnam, the American troops in the Philippines became more and more frustrated by the elusive enemy. "Everything possible is being done to locate the insurgent bands in this vicinity," reported a U.S. commander in the eastern Luzon province of Nueva Ecija, "but so far without success. . . . They will no doubt concentrate somewhere again soon."

Aguinaldo's forces meanwhile turned increasingly to terrorism—even though, fearful of alarming U.S. public opinion, he had urged them to avoid atrocities. They invented lethal contraptions of the kind later made notorious by the Vietcong, such as pits concealing sharpened bamboo stakes, or spears and arrows triggered by hidden trip wires. Sergeant Herbert O. Kohr recalled an incident one Sunday in the Luzon town of Nueva Caceres, when a farmer peddling eggs approached an American sentry playing solitaire. Before the sentry could look up, the peasant severed his head from his body with a *bolo* and escaped. Scouts arrested several natives, but Kohr reported, "They were never certain if they had got the proper one." The Filipinos sometimes castrated American captives and stuffed their genitals into their mouths. In June 1900, a U.S. infantry patrol in Leyte reported finding the remains of an American prisoner who had been buried alive up to the neck: "His mouth had been propped open with a stick, a trail of sugar laid to it through the forest. . . . Millions of ants had done the rest."

Such horror stories, exaggerated in the retelling, rippled through the U.S. ranks. Indignant American troops retaliated in kind despite official communiqués praising their benign pacification effort. "No more prisoners," one wrote home; the guerrillas "take none . . . we will kill wounded and all of them." A volunteer remarked: "With an enemy like this, it is not surprising that the boys should soon adopt 'no quarter' as a motto and fill the blacks full of lead before finding out whether they are friends or enemies." By the end of the war, fifteen Filipino soldiers had been killed for every one wounded—the lopsided ratio suggesting that the Americans either left the wounded to die or shot prisoners.

Civilians fared no better. Colonel Robert Bullard noted in his diary in August 1900 that "ultimately we shall be driven to the Spanish method of dreadful general punishments on a whole community for the acts of its outlaws." But many U.S. officers had long demanded stiffer penalties for Filipino suspects. One argued, for example, that pacification would falter if the Americans attempted "to meet a half-civilized foe" with the same measures conceived for "people of our own race, country and blood." The rambunctious

General Lloyd Wheaton similarly advocated "swift methods of destruction." He sneered at the tactic of "going with a sword in one hand, a pacifist pamphlet in the other hand and trailing the model of a schoolhouse after," adding that "you can't put down a rebellion by throwing confetti and sprinkling perfumery." General S.B.M. Young recommended a plan for dealing with "Asiatics," who had "no idea of gratitude, honor or the sanctity of an oath." To deny the guerrillas support, he proposed the concentration of the rural population into controlled zones—a practice ironically denounced by Americans when the Spanish had imposed it in Cuba. He also favored the summary execution of natives who resumed fighting after swearing allegiance to the United States, and the arrest of anyone "deemed prejudicial" to the Americans.

A Civil War statute, later adopted as an international convention to safeguard human rights during war, forbade the indiscriminate killing of civilians. But it prescribed draconian measures for those caught aiding guerrillas, and MacArthur stressed that aspect when he declared martial law in December 1900. Natives implicated in activities judged to be "inimical" to American "interests" would be considered "war rebels" or "traitors" and punished accordingly. Captives unaffiliated with a "regularly organized force" were not to be classified as soldiers and would be denied the rights of prisoners of war. Loosely interpreted, as it was by most U.S. troops, the decree heralded open season on Filipinos, whatever their status. Taft subsequently claimed that while "war of course provokes some cruelty in everyone," he knew of no conflict, "whether against inferior races or not, in which there were more compassion and more restraint and more generosity."

American soldiers remembered the war differently. After some U.S. troops were "hacked to pieces" near the town of Malabon, "we got orders to spare no one," recalled Anthony Michea, an artilleryman. "We went in and killed every native we met, men, women and children. It was a dreadful sight, the killing of the poor creatures." Usually unable to tell friend from foe, the American forces frequently burned any town or village believed to be an enemy sanctuary—even though, as Colonel Arthur Lockwood later conceded, innocent civilians suffered in the process. Lockwood cited the Bible as justification. "The Almighty destroyed Sodom," he said, "notwithstanding the fact that there were a few just people in that community." Similarly, U.S. soldiers in quest of intelligence often tortured local officials and other civilians. Former Sergeant Charles S. Riley of Northampton, Massachusetts, was one of several veterans to describe the so-called "water cure" at a Senate hearing early in 1902.

Speaking in a New England monotone, Riley recounted the interrogation of the *presidente,* or mayor, of a town on the island of Panay two years before. His company, pursuing partisans reported to be near the town, presumed the mayor to be a source of information. When he refused to speak, Riley's commander ordered the torture. A couple of American soldiers pinned him down under the faucet of an iron tank, while another held open his mouth. as water poured into the man's throat, a native interpreter translated the officer's questions. Every few minutes, a soldier would stomp on the victim's stomach to make him vomit, and the ordeal would resume. Finally, after salt water had been squirted up his nose through a syringe, the mayor talked. Riley's grim tale ended on a fatuous note when Senator Julius Caesar Burrows, a Republican from Michigan and former Civil War captain, asked if the man had suffered. "Yessir," the sergeant nodded, but "of course he could not holler or make any noise." "Why not?" Burrows pressed—to which Riley replied dryly: "On account of the water being in his mouth."

The Filipinos usually remained silent. Nationalist partisans pervaded the countryside, retaliating against informers with impunity. Most vulnerable were local officials functioning under U.S. supervision—unless they doubled as covert nationalist agents, as many did. In February 1900, one of Aguinaldo's generals, Pantaleón García, directed his officers to "apply the proper punishment" to pro-American sympathizers, citing as a precedent some two hundred men on the island of Negros who were executed "for having accepted U.S. sovereignty." Another Filipino general, Arcadio Maxilom, threatened to level any town that acknowledged American authority, and even minor infractions like paying taxes in areas under U.S control invited retribution. Offenses ranged from disobedience to treason, and the penalties from fines to decapitation or burial alive. Guerrilla death squads often liquidated suspects capriciously despite Aguinaldo's pleas to his followers to conduct trials. Taking advantage of the fluid situation, rival village factions frequently went on killing sprees to settle old vendettas.

Juan Cailles, a Filipino general of part-French origin, commanded a freewheeling collection of guerrilla bands in Laguna province, a flat area of rice fields, marshes and scrub vegetation southeast of Manila. The region had been combed and presumably cleaned out by the Americans several times over. But, though outnumbered, Cailles's men constantly staged hit-and-run raids against the U.S. forces. They killed some fifty Americans in twelve separate attacks during a two-week period in September 1900. "This record," remarked a U.S. officer, "shows how hard the insurrection is dying."

The key to their success, as in all guerrilla struggles, was control of the population, through either intimidation or sympathy. Cailles and his men, moving swiftly to escape capture, collected food and taxes, and drafted recruits by compelling families to contribute their unmarried sons to the cause. They treated American collaborators brutally. They shot the mayor and destroyed the town of San Pablo after its residents had presented an American officer with a homemade U.S. flag as a mark of their esteem. Cailles decreed death for *Federalistas,* the pro-American party, and he killed for reasons unrelated to the war. On the pretext that they had committed treason, for example, he executed a married couple involved in a lawsuit against one of his friends. But, in Filipino style, he tempered rough justice with religious reverence. Directing an aide to wipe out two men, he declared that their murder conformed to "the law of God, because it is dictated by sound reason." Afterward, as a gesture of respect for the victims, he sent a message to his troops: "Let us offer up a prayer for their eternal rest." Betrayed by a disgruntled follower, he was finally captured in June 1901. He promptly took an oath of allegiance to the United States and, with equal zeal, joined the Americans in flushing out his former comrades.

★　★　★

At the end of June 1900, the Republicans gathered in Philadelphia to acclaim McKinley for a second term. A dispute arose over moves to name Theodore

Roosevelt, the governor of New York, as his running mate. McKinley, at home in Ohio, mysteriously remained neutral as his former campaign manager, Mark Hanna, fought to block Roosevelt—warning with uncanny prescience that "there's only one life between that madman and the presidency." Nor did Roosevelt want the empty honor. He preferred the governorship of the Philippines, and asked Henry Cabot Lodge to lobby on his behalf with McKinley. By then, however, McKinley had already decided on Taft. Tom Platt, the New York Republican boss, who could not abide Roosevelt, finally maneuvered to secure his nomination as a way of banishing him from the state. Roosevelt acquiesced after Lodge pledged him Taft's job later as compensation for his sacrifice. To record his displeasure, Roosevelt cast the sole vote against himself. Lodge, the convention chairman, then went on to assure the delegates sweltering in the early summer heat of the party's plan to fulfill its Asia policy. America would stay in the Philippines, guide its people "to entire freedom and to self-government under our flag" and thus gain the "inestimable advantages" of Manila as a base for trade with China—the "greatest of all markets."

The Democrats met three weeks later in Kansas City to renominate William Jennings Bryan, their candidate in 1896. As number two on the ticket, they picked a prominent Illinois politician, Adlai Ewing Stevenson, vice president under Cleveland and grandfather of a subsequent presidential aspirant. Bryan had supported both war with Spain and the treaty to retain the Philippines. But now, his mellifluous voice ringing out as he stood beside his own bust on the podium, he criticized McKinley's acquisition of the islands. The Democratic platform awkwardly combined two themes in an attempt to bridge northern liberals and southern conservatives. Affirming that "the constitution follows the flag," it argued that America could not lawfully rule another land: "No nation can long endure half republic and half empire." And to placate the racists, it denounced the annexation of territories whose people, like Filipinos, were not "fit to become American citizens."

The issue of the Philippines loomed large in the campaign, and the candidates reiterated familiar platitudes as they toured the country. Aguinaldo, fleeing from one refuge to another in northern Luzon, tried to keep track of the contest. At that distance, he could only rely on information from his far-flung agents, whose conclusions were invariably clouded by wishful thinking. One asserted that the anti-imperialists in America were "growing more and more confident of victory," while another observed that "the probabilities of Bryan's success improve day by day." Buoyed by the optimistic reports, Aguinaldo called the election "a ray of hope." He urged his men to carry on their fight by emulating George Washington and, oddly enough, William Tell. When the results came in, however, McKinley scored the biggest Republican triumph since 1872, beating Bryan by a margin of 155 electoral votes and a popular plurality of nearly 1 million.

Aguinaldo's prospects also dimmed as his best officers either surrendered or were captured and swore fidelity to the United States. Even Apolinario Mabini, confined to a Manila jail following his arrest months earlier, was no longer implacably hostile to the Americans. An amiable intellectual, he enjoyed occasional chats with senior U.S. officers and, at their behest, wrote to Aguinaldo in November 1900, offering to arrange a new round of peace talks. The letter, carried by courier over rugged mountain trails, took four months to reach Aguinaldo, who by now had retreated to Palanan, a remote village on the Pacific coast of Luzon. There, for the sake of security, he referred to himself as "Captain Emilio." He promptly drafted a reply, favoring fresh negotiations—on condition that the United States recognize the "legitimate rights and inherent liberties" of the Filipinos. One of the most dramatic episodes of the war intervened to render his response pointless.

Brigadier General Frederick Funston was, like Aguinaldo, a bantamweight. Five feet four inches tall, he looked with his ruddy face and red beard like an adolescent masquerading as a man, but at thirty-six he was already a legend. The son of a Kansas farmer turned politician, he had quit college to work on the railroad, then became a newspaper reporter before embarking as a botanist on government expeditions to Death Valley and Alaska—his exploits including a daring solo journey down the Yukon. One spring evening in 1896, while strolling in Manhattan, he casually dropped in on a rally promoting Cuban freedom from Spain. The appeal of the cause, coupled with the lure of adventure, converted him. He volunteered to serve as an artillery officer with the Cuban rebels, even though he had never heard a cannon fired in anger. He proved his mettle in battle. Twice wounded, he was finally captured by the Spanish and narrowly escaped execution by pretending to have deserted the Cuban forces. He returned home, preceded by press accounts of his prowess, to cash in on the lecture circuit. When the war between the United States and Spain began, he persuaded the governor of Kansas to commission him a colonel in command of a state regiment of volunteers. Soon he reached the Philippines.

As a former newspaperman, Funston knew that reporters cherished quotable comments, and he accommodated them. The average Filipino, he declared, was a lazy lout who "is born tired, stays tired and dies tired." He called Aguinaldo a "cold-blooded murderer" whose followers were a "drunken uncontrollable mob," and he bragged about summarily executing natives to avenge American deaths. In some ways he shared Theodore Roosevelt's boyish brashness. They started a correspondence that lasted until Roosevelt, elected president, prudently disassociated himself from Funston's outrageous opinions.

But Funston was a brave soldier, as he demonstrated soon after the war with the Filipinos broke out. He personally led a squad across a river under heavy fire to silence an enemy machine-gun nest, sustaining a wound in the assault. The exploit won him promotion to brigadier general and the Congressional Medal of Honor. Then, in February 1901, a stroke of luck brought him the chance for real glory.

He was commanding a brigade in central Luzon, when sentries hustled a frightened Filipino into his headquarters. The native turned out to be a courier who had been captured carrying, among other papers, a coded letter from Aguinaldo to a subordinate in the province of Cavite, south of Manila. Funston and his staff, fortified by whiskey and black coffee, spent a night deciphering the message: "I have not sufficient people. Send me about four hundred men at the first opportunity." Under questioning, the captive revealed the location of Aguinaldo's sanctuary at Palanan. Funston concocted an audacious scheme.

He would form a unit of bogus reinforcements, composed of natives loyal to the Americans. They would have five U.S. officers in tow, pretending to be prisoners they had captured. Once at Aguinaldo's headquarters, they would surprise and seize him. MacArthur approved the concept, and Funston worked out the details.

He hired eighty Macabebes, members of an ethnic group in Pampanga province, to pose as the sham reinforcements. The clan, traditional foes of the Tagalogs, had served the Spanish as mercenaries and had been mobilized by the U.S. forces as scouts. He also enlisted Lázaro Segovia, a former Spanish officer who had deserted to the Filipinos and then secretly defected to the Americans. To avoid a hard trek across the mountains, he persuaded the U.S. Navy to take his men by sea to a spot within range of Aguinaldo's lair. In addition, he sent fake messages to Aguinaldo to assure him that help was arriving. On March 6, 1901, two days after McKinley's inauguration in Washington, the team left Manila aboard the gunboat *Vicksburg*. MacArthur, the evening before, had melodramatically bid him farewell: "Funston, this is a desperate undertaking. I fear I shall never see you again."

In the early hours of March 24, the commandos landed on the coast at Casiguran Sound, on the east side of Luzon. The Americans were dressed as enlisted men, in khaki breeches and blue shirts without insignia, and the Macabebes wore tattered guerrilla garb. Drenched by the surf and a steady drizzle, they huddled under palm fronds, afraid to light fires lest they be detected. Their objective lay a hundred miles ahead.

The inhabitants of the first village they entered greeted them with music and flowers, believing the Macabebes to be real partisans and the Americans genuine prisoners. But the operation soon became arduous. Rain fell constantly as they slogged across muddy beaches, waded streams and scaled cliffs. After running out of food, they subsisted on snails and limpets. Funston later recalled that they had "stumbled along in a half-dazed condition . . . some of them so weak that they reeled as they walked" while he himself doubted that "the madcap enterprise could succeed"—the prospect of failure filling him with "regrets that I had led all these men to such a finish." Their morale sagged when they learned—wrongly as it turned out—that Aguinaldo had just been strengthened by the arrival of four hundred fresh troops. They also heard, to their alarm, that March 22 had been Aguinaldo's thirty-second birthday and that Palanan was crowded with his supporters. Nevertheless, they plodded on—their hopes bolstered ten miles from his redoubt by a welcome note from Aguinaldo's chief of staff, who had been informed of their whereabouts. The ruse was working.

A complication arose: Aguinaldo intended to release the American captives, and denied them entry to his camp, fearing that they might identify it later. He ordered them to be held instead at a nearby village, but Segovia gambled, trusting that his defection had not been betrayed. Forging a directive from Aguinaldo to authorize their passage, he told the Americans to follow with an escort as he, leading the rest of the column, went on to Palanan. There his men lined up in the square, facing Aguinaldo's troops. Filipino officers ushered him and an aide up to a second-floor room of a modest house on stilts. Aguinaldo soon appeared, in a starched khaki uniform and polished black boots. They talked pleasantly, Aguinaldo thanking him for the help. Finally, Segovia signaled to a comrade outside, who shouted: "Now is the time, Macabebes! Give it to them!" At that, they began shooting at Aguinaldo's astonished men.

Aguinaldo, thinking his troops were firing salutes, cried from the window: "Stop that foolishness. Don't waste ammunition!" Then, seeing men dropping, he wheeled around, perplexed. Segovia, his gun drawn, barked at him and his officers: "You are our prisoners! We are not insurgents, we are Americans! Surrender or be killed!" Two of Aguinaldo's officers moved abruptly, and Segovia shot them. A third pulled a white handkerchief from his pocket. "We surrender," he said softly. "This is a flag of peace."

Funston arrived shortly afterward, introduced himself to Aguinaldo and pompously proclaimed him to be "a prisoner of war of the army of the United States of America," adding: "You will be treated with due consideration." Aguinaldo, stunned, muttered, "Is this not some joke?"

News of Funston's feat flashed across the Pacific, making him famous overnight. KANSAS WILD WITH JOY, *The New York Times* headlined, reporting moves to run him for governor. "You have added your name to the honor roll of American worthies," wrote Roosevelt. Thomas Edison turned the exploit into a pioneer movie at his New Jersey studio. Enraged anti-imperialists charged Funston with "treachery" against Aguinaldo, a "brave patriot and lover of liberty." They were ignored.

Back home ten months afterward, Funston exultantly continued in lectures, interviews and magazine articles to disparage both the Filipinos and their American sympathizers. But the public was wearying of the war. Theodore Roosevelt, by now president, sensed the mood, and told Funston to cease his "very unfortunate" rhetoric. Funston went on to direct an effective relief effort in San Francisco after the earthquake of 1906. Eight years later, when American forces seized Veracruz during the Mexican revolution, he acted as the city's military governor. He died in 1917, at fifty-one, another forgotten hero.

Despite his disdain for Filipinos, Funston had admired Aguinaldo's "dignified" style. After his capture, he had taken the rebel leader to Manila aboard the *Vicksburg,* and they had chatted amiably during the voyage. To Taft's dismay, MacArthur graciously invited the vanquished foe to the Malacañang palace. Three weeks later, under pressure from his wife and children, Aguinaldo issued an eloquent proclamation. "Enough of blood, enough of tears and desolation. . . . By acknowledging and accepting the sovereignty of the United States throughout the entire archipelago, as I now do without any reservation whatsoever, I believe that I am serving thee, my beloved country. My happiness be thine!"

Aguinaldo then retired to his family mansion in Kawit, and he wore a black bow tie forever after, in mourning for his lost republic. Apart from a fruitless foray into politics, he remained a largely private figure. He naïvely broadcast pro-Japanese propaganda during World War II, a blunder for which he was pardoned. Surviving all his contemporaries, he died on February 6, 1964, just before his ninety-fifth birthday—and nearly sixty-five years to the day from the outbreak of his war against the Americans. Six years before, as a gesture of reconciliation, Charles Bohlen, then the U.S. ambassador in Manila, had returned to him his Spanish sword. Tarnished, it hangs on a wall of his gingerbread house, now a dusty museum cluttered with mementos, among them the autographed photographs of American presidents and generals. In the garden, shaded by tamarind trees, stands his white marble tomb, its simplicity a symbol of his innocence. Sympathizers still lobby for his enshrinement as the national hero, but he lived too long for martrydom—the prerequisite for idolatry in the Philippines.

Some historians have drawn parallels between Aguinaldo's resistance and the Vietnamese Communist struggle against the Americans nearly seventy years afterward. Both, fueled by fierce nationalist sentiment, relied heavily on guerrilla tactics, and both spurred dissent in the United States. But their differences overshadowed their similarities.

The Filipinos, in contrast to the Vietnamese, had an edge over the Americans. At its peak in Vietnam in the late 1960s, the joint force of more than 500,000 American and approximately 1 million South Vietnamese troops outnumbered the enemy by a proportion of roughly six to one. There were never more than 70,000 Americans in the Philippines, compared to almost 100,000 Filipino regulars and tens of thousands of militiamen—a ratio of two to one in Aguinaldo's favor. The Americans in Vietnam had a formidable arsenal of artillery, aircraft and other advanced weapons, while the Krag-Jorgensen and Springfield rifles of their forefathers in the Philippines were no better than the Remingtons and Mausers wielded by the Filipinos. Late in the Vietnam War, their guerrillas virtually annihilated, the Communists fought in big battalions that were devastated by overwhelming U.S. firepower. The Filipinos, however, became increasingly elusive after switching to guerrilla tactics. Thus, by military measure, America should have prevailed in Vietnam and, at least, been held to a deadlock by Aguinaldo. Why did the two wars end differently?

Aguinaldo and his staff were egregiously inept. General Vo Nguyen Giap, the chief Vietnamese strategist, brilliantly waged a protracted war of attrition, coupling Mao Zedong's doctrine of "people's war" with lessons learned from fighting France. He slowly escalated from guerrilla to conventional tactics, accepting huge casualties while building a broad base of support in the expectation that, over time, he would erode America's will to fight. Aguinaldo, to his detriment, took a diametrically opposite course. Inexperienced as a soldier, he at first relied on Antonio Luna, his main field commander, whose smattering of knowledge came from classic military texts. He consequently sustained immense losses in set-piece battles from the outset. And he belatedly switched to guerrilla warfare only as a desperate last resort. Had he begun by pursuing an unconventional strategy, he might have prolonged the struggle, and ultimately exhausted the patience of the U.S. public—whose ardor increasingly waned as the war dragged on. The Vietnamese, on the other hand, figured that the resolve of Americans at home would weaken if they could only endure on the battlefield in Vietnam. Their calculation proved to be correct.

The Vietnamese had another advantage over the Filipinos. Their troops could escape to safety in nearby North Vietnam, Cambodia and Laos while Aguinaldo's security, as Funston demonstrated, was not inviolable even in a remote village. The Vietnamese also benefited from a strong and pervasive sense of national cohesion. Ho Chi Minh, their leader, could rally them, first against France and later against America, by invoking the memory of centuries of resistance to foreign invaders. The Filipinos lacked a recorded history and common identity. Their chain of islands had been a geographical accident rather than a society before the arrival of the Spanish, who had deliberately perpetuated the disunity of the archipelago to maintain their rule. Ethnic and regional rivalries chronically nagged Aguinaldo's crusade as factions in areas outside central Luzon resented the intrusion of his predominantly Tagalog commanders.

But one ingredient absent from Aguinaldo's program may, above all others, have contributed to his collapse: He failed to offer genuine change to the Filipino masses. The Vietnamese gained support and strength, especially during their war against the French, by simultaneously challenging colonialism and promoting a revolution that pledged to improve the plight of dispossessed peasants. They fulfilled the vow in areas under their control by liquidating landlords and distributing property to the poor. Their campaigns appealed to both the nationalistic sentiments and the tangible demands of the population, a highly charged combination. Aguinaldo, however, focused exclusively on winning independence, showing little concern for even modest economic or social reforms.

Himself a member of the rural gentry, he courted rich provincial families to boost his own prestige. He upheld their power and privileges, and gave them official positions, even though many had collaborated with the Spanish. Like feudal nobles, they often reciprocated by joining his ranks with private armies composed of dragooned villagers, but they were opportunists who later shifted their allegiance to America when it suited their interests. So the majority of sharecroppers, tenant farmers and other poor folk did not give Aguinaldo their full sympathy. Numbers saw him as the champion of the oppressive oligarchy rather than as a Robin Hood. Their expectations for radical change disappointed, they remained indifferent to his movement or accommodated to both sides. Without their consistent support, he could not maintain his momentum.

The regional elections conducted by his regime late in 1898 merely confirmed the authority of local notables. The *ilustrados* who drafted the constitution had limited suffrage to the affluent upper classes, who naturally buttressed their own power. The Luzon town of Ilagan, capital of Isabela province, exemplified the process. There, out of a population of nearly fourteen thousand, only seventy-three citizens were qualified to vote. They chose as province chief a wealthy tobacco merchant, Dimas Guzman, a skilled survivor who had been rewarded by the Spanish for meritorious service, and was later elected to the Philippine legislature organized by the Americans. Like hereditary dynasties, the same clans were to control their native regions for decades, and many present-day Filipino politicians trace their present influence back to the prominence of their forebears.

Aguinaldo made dubious deals with vested interests. He once broke a strike by railway employees to placate the railway company, which in return gave his regime ten percent of its income, allowed his aides to travel free and provided him with a special train. Though not numerous, the workers he alienated could nevertheless have helped his cause. He maintained the heavy taxes formerly imposed by the Spanish on rural communities, and he shut his eyes to the fact that several local mayors and their cronies were pocketing the money.

Worse still, he ignored the country's appalling agrarian problems. Deaf to the tenants clamoring for a reduction of the exorbitant rents that they paid plantation owners, he also disregarded farmers who demanded restitution of land seized from their families by the Spanish. Nor did he deal equitably with property confiscated from the Spanish monastic orders. In Laguna, for instance, his officials kept the estates for themselves and their friends on the pretext that they were now government custodians. They refused to renew the leases of tenants—one of whom claimed that, under Aguinaldo, his fate was "a thousand times more miserable" than it had been during the Spanish era. Many frustrated peasants joined messianic sects to oppose Aguinaldo. They continued to fight the Americans, who instead of introducing reforms, branded them "bandits." Areas of the Philippines, as bleak today as then, are the crucible of the Communist insurgency that feeds on injustices dating back decades.

Late in February 1899, shortly after the war between the Filipinos and Americans broke out, Mabini issued a warning that could be the epitaph of Aguinaldo's cause. "We cannot conquer today, but we can hope to achieve victory tomorrow if the people are with us. If not, we will be defeated."

★ ★ ★

Americans at home, elated by Aguinaldo's capture in March 1902, could finally discern the light at the end of the tunnel. But brutal episodes yet to unfold in the waning war were to horrify many of them. The U.S. mission in the Philippines no longer seemed to be an exercise in benevolence.

The cast of characters involved in the venture had largely changed as 1901 drew to a close. On September 14, McKinley died, eight days after being shot by Leon Czolgosz, a presumed anarchist, during a visit to Buffalo. Roosevelt, not yet forty-three, had become the youngest president in U.S. history. Taft, still in Manila, was the first civilian governor of the Philippines. MacArthur had returned home, but Taft continued to bear a grudge against him. Years afterward, as secretary of war and subsequently president, Taft denied MacArthur promotion, including appointment to Army Chief of Staff. Taft also clashed with MacArthur's successor, Major General Adna Romanza Chaffee, who landed in Manila in July 1902.

Chaffee was a dour Ohioan of sixty, with narrow eyes, a lantern jaw and the bowlegged gait of a cavalryman. Another boy wonder of the Civil War, he had joined the Union army at nineteen as a private, earning a field commission before being wounded and captured at Gettysburg. He remained with the same regiment for the next twenty-five years, mostly fighting Indians, winning notoriety for ordering during one skirmish, "Forward! If any man is killed, I'll make him a corporal!" The war with Spain elevated him to the rank of brigadier general in command of a detachment in Cuba, where he gained Roosevelt's admiration. He went on to head the U.S. units sent to China in 1900 as part of the international force assembled to crush the Boxers, a fanatic cult that had besieged the foreign legations in Beijing. There he was remarkably humane compared to his European colleagues, who had few compunctions about slaughtering innocent Chinese.

Chaffee showed no such sensitivity in the Philippines—which he called a "volcano" on the verge of eruption. Tough and sinewy despite his age, he derided Taft's corpulence as symptomatic of a flabby attitude toward the Filipinos. They could be checked only by force, as he sought to illustrate in Batangas province, south of Manila.

Following Aguinaldo's capture, General Miguel Malvar, a middle-aged veteran with a satanic beard, proclaimed himself supreme commander of the remnant Filipino forces and vowed to pursue the "difficult and arduous" struggle. He deployed his guerrillas in Batangas, his native province, hoping as Aguinaldo had that the U.S. public, tiring of the war, would swing to his side. "Perseverance, perseverance and always perseverance, without fear of sacrifice," he told his men. "Let us continue, as the will of the people has always been more powerful than the most powerful armies."

Chaffee had singled out Batangas as his first target and coaxed Taft into putting the province under military control. The enemy operated there, he said, "through the connivance and knowledge of practically all the inhabitants," who had to be taught "a lesson." He handed the job to Brigadier General J. Franklin Bell, a burly Kentuckian who had arrived in the Philippines as a major and won a promotion for gallantry. Bell, invoking the Civil War code that authorized severe punishment for anyone suspected of helping partisans, issued a rigorous order to his men: "Neutrality should not be tolerated." Only those who provided the American forces with intelligence, guided operations against the guerrillas or identified them and their sympathizers would be judged guiltless. Prisoners would be executed by lot in retaliation for the murder of U.S. soldiers or Filipino loyalists, and all civilians were to be herded into zones where they could be monitored. The inhabitants of the region would thus be filled with such "anxiety and apprehension" as to deter them from cooperating with the nationalists. "Even though they call me a brute, as I know they do," Bell said, "I shall follow out the course I have planned."

Driving into Batangas early in January 1902 with four thousand men, he was merciless. A congressman who later visited the area reported that "there isn't anybody there to rebel," since U.S. troops had raked the region "in a most resolute manner." They "took no prisoners [and] kept no records," but "simply swept the country, and wherever or however they could get hold of a Filipino they killed him." A correspondent covering the push called it "relentless." The American soldiers killed "men, women, children, prisoners and captives, active insurgents and suspected people, from lads of ten and up, an idea prevailing that the Filipino . . . was little better than a dog" who belonged on "the rubbish heap." They rounded up natives, stood them on a bridge and, "without a shred of evidence" against them, shot them "one by one, to drop into the water below and float down as an example to those who found their bullet-riddled corpses." It was "not civilized warfare," the correspondent admitted—yet he wrote approvingly: "We are not dealing with a civilized people. The only thing they know is force, violence and brutality, and we give it to them."

Bell's strategy, whatever its ethics, worked. Alone and unarmed, Malvar surrendered in April. He explained that he had been deserted by his closest aides, and chased from one place to another until, "without a single gun" left, he could no longer hold out. In any case, his men would have starved eventually, since Bell's scorched-earth tactic had prevented the local farmers from planting next season's rice crop.

The ferocity of the U.S. troops in Batangas was a reaction to the earlier massacre of their comrades on the island of Samar, in the Visayas. That episode, in turn, provoked an incident that was to shock and sober American public opinion.

Samar, the first land sighted by Magellan as he neared the Philippines in the sixteenth century, is the third largest island in the chain, and among the wildest even to this day. Its interior, still largely unmapped, is a rugged terrain of jungle-clad hills, with no roads and few trails. General Vicente Lukban, a rotund man in his fifties, had gone there late in 1898 with a hundred armed followers, announcing himself Aguinaldo's governor. The scion of a rich Chinese *mestizo* family from Luzon, he cemented an alliance with the leaders of the *Dios-Dios,* a religious sect. He won their confidence by executing the local Spanish friars, who had branded the movement heretical. The cult, which dressed in red, had been founded years before by a self-styled messiah, who inspired his disciples with the promise of eternity in a golden heaven. They were fearless fighters, convinced that their *anting antings,* or amulets, rendered them invincible. Twirling huge knives, they would charge in suicidal waves— like "breakers dashing against the rocks," recalled one U.S. soldier who had faced one of their assaults. Lukban employed them as spies, and encouraged their cruelties against real or imagined traitors. One of their punishments for a native suspected of pro-American sentiments was to turban his head in a U.S. flag soaked in kerosene, set it aflame and mutilate his corpse. As a warning, they staged the spectacle before the victim's fellow villagers.

American troops first landed on Samar in early 1901, setting up coastal outposts as Lukban prudently retreated inland. In August, a company of seventy-four U.S. officers and men arrived at Balangiga, a town on the south side of the island. The men carried Krag-Jorgensens and the officers Colt forty-fives, a powerful revolver of Indian war vintage recently reissued as the only weapon capable of stopping a fanatic in close combat. One soldier, noting the two hundred nipa huts clustered around a flaking church and a mildewed town hall, remarked: "Boys, we're in guguland for sure now."

The company was there to establish a garrison at the request of the mayor, Pedro Abayan, whose plea for protection against "pirates" had been greeted by the U.S. authorities in Manila as a sign that the Filipinos were joining the American side. But the Americans were unaware that Abayan had earlier advised Lukban of his "deceptive" plan to lure the U.S. troops to the town and, at a "favorable opportunity," launch an uprising against them. Shortly before, an American patrol had captured Abayan's incriminating letter in a raid on Lukban's hideout. Judged unimportant, it was buried in the army files.

Captain Thomas W. Connell, the company commander, was a West Pointer in his late twenties and something of a prig. A devout Catholic, he believed that the Filipinos esteemed him because of their common faith. But they actually regarded him with a mixture of indifference and contempt. They could not fathom his disdain for cockfights, their main diversion, nor did they appreciate his prudish attempt to make their girls exchange their seductive sarongs for more seemly dress. Abayan, however, feigned submission. He obeyed Connell's order to clean up the piles of garbage, excrement and dead animals that littered the town. Connell naïvely accepted Abayan's offer to bring laborers in from the nearby countryside to do the job. They were, of course, guerrillas in disguise.

On September 26, a boat brought the Americans mail from home along with their first news of McKinley's assassination. Connell ordered a mass for the president to be held at the church on Sunday, two days hence. He was puzzled by the numbers of native women from nearby areas entering the church bearing coffins that, they claimed, contained the bodies of children who had perished in a cholera epidemic. Had his sentries investigated, they would have found the coffins to be filled with *bolos*—and the mourning women to be men. Connell was baffled as well by the odd absence of the town priest, whom he had hoped would celebrate the mass for McKinley. Had his intelligence been even routine, he would have learned that the priest was in league with Lukban.

Most of the Americans awoke before reveille on that sultry Sunday morning to reread their mail. At six o'clock, as the bugler sounded mess call, they straggled across the town square to the tents where the company cooks were serving breakfast. Twenty minutes later, it happened.

Only three American sentries were on duty. The local police chief, stopping to chat with one of them, suddenly seized his rifle and fired a signal shot. The church bells then pealed crazily, and natives appeared from everywhere, brandishing *bolos,* picks and shovels. Rushing into the mess tent, they decapitated a sergeant—leaving him, as one of his buddies recollected, "leaning forward with a spoon clutched in his hand . . . his head lying on the table." They pitched another soldier into a barrel of boiling water as he washed his utensils. Screaming and slashing, they stormed the huts that lodged some of the U.S. troops. A survivor later recalled the sight of one man "bleeding from a gaping wound in his forehead, sitting bolt upright on a ladder in front of our shack, dying," as another crawled "on his hands and feet like a stabbed pig, his brains falling out" from a head wound. Guided by Abayan, a group of natives invaded the convent adjacent to the church, which also had served as a barracks. After killing two officers in their beds, they crashed into Connell's room, where he had been reading his breviary. He leaped from the window and ran, only to be chopped to ribbons by a howling gang. A corporal who shot Abayan remembered that he "died in a very pretty way," rising "in the air like a toe dancer."

The unarmed Americans fought back desperately with everything from baseball bats to rocks, and a cook fended off his assailants by hurling cans of beans at them. The unit's three officers dead, Sergeant Frank Betron took command. He considered holding the town while sending for help, but with only thirty-six soldiers left, most of them wounded, he decided to escape by sea. He led them to five native dugouts that lay on the shore. They were embarking when Private Claude Wingo saw the Stars and Stripes still flying over the town at half-mast, in tribute to McKinley. Though injured himself, Wingo took three volunteers back to rescue the colors. Only two returned, the flag in their possession.

Harassed by snipers, swamped by rough water and pursued by sharks, the men drifted throughout the day, suffering from exposure and thirst. Only three boats finally reached safety at Leyte and the U.S. garrison at Basey, thirty miles up the coast. Seven more men died during the voyage, Wingo among them, and another eight succumbed from wounds at the Basey infirmary. Only twenty of the company's original seventy-four members survived. "In my dreams," one wrote years afterward, "I often live over again that dreadful morning of slaughter, and wake up screaming." Lukban called the massacre a manifestation of God's "justice."

A fresh American detachment of fifty-three volunteers promptly steamed to

Balangiga, their ship's machine gun and cannon scattering a mob of natives defiantly shouting from the shore. The soldiers, bayonets fixed, charged through the surf to behold a ghastly sight. Their dead comrades had been mutilated beyond belief—as if an arcane rite had driven the townsfolk into a barbaric frenzy. Disemboweled bodies had been stuffed with molasses or jam to attract ants. The sergeant killed while washing his mess kit was still upended in the water barrel, his feet chopped off. A bag of flour had been poured into the slit stomach of an unidentified corpse. Even the company dog had been slain, its eyes gouged out and replaced with stones. Captain Connell's head was found in a fire, far from his torso, his West Point ring missing along with the finger.

Captain Edwin V. Bookmiller, commander of the column, buried the dead Americans. Despite the pleas of two old women, who begged that the two hundred and fifty natives slain in the melee be given a Christian burial, he had them cremated. His men, scouring the vicinity, gunned down twenty Filipinos hiding in the nearby jungle.

News of the Balangiga massacre jolted the U.S. public. The press rated it with the Alamo and Custer's defeat as one of the worst tragedies in American military annals. Chaffee, his pessimism confirmed, remarked that Taft's "silly talk of benevolence and civilian rule [and] the soft mollycoddling of treacherous natives" was no substitute for "shot, shells and bayonets." He thereupon directed Brigadier General Jacob W. Smith to end the resistance on Samar once and for all.

At sixty-two, Smith was another leathery veteran of the Civil War and the Indian campaigns. His formal education had consisted of a year at a Connecticut commercial school, where he learned copperplate penmanship, a system of writing based on engraved models and an enviable skill before the advent of the typewriter. A cranky little man with a ragged mustache whose wrinkled white tropical uniform looked like he slept in it, he was known for his bellowing voice as "Hell-Roaring Jake."

To command the mission, Smith selected a swaggering marine major of forty-five improbably named Littleton Waller Tazewell Waller, who had fought in Egypt, Cuba and against the Boxers in China. Smith, giving him four companies, said: "I want no prisoners. I wish you to kill and burn, the more you kill and burn the better you will please me. I want all persons killed who are capable of bearing arms in actual hostilities against the United States." Waller, a scrupulous professional, asked Smith to define an age limit. "Ten years," replied Smith. Waller pressed for clarification. "Persons of ten years and older are those designated as being capable of bearing arms?" "Yes," responded Smith.

Smith repeated similar orders in different forms as Waller launched the offensive. "Short severe wars are the most humane in the end," one stated, adding that every native should be "treated as an enemy until he has conclusively shown that he is a friend." In another, unsigned, he wrote in his exquisite copperplate that Samar "must be made a howling wilderness." The message, later made public, earned him a new nickname, "Howling Wilderness" Smith.

Waller, appalled by Smith's directives, confided to an aide that "we are not making war on women and children." Nevertheless, he ordered his men to shoot all native suspects as he led an expedition against Lukban's redoubt, located in the mountains of the interior. They captured the Filipino commander and then, obeying Smith's instructions to make Samar a "howling wilderness," Waller and his troops marched across the island, destroying every village along the way. Not only did food shortages, torrential rains and leeches afflict them as they hacked through the jungle, but some narrowly escaped an attack by mutinous native porters, whom they arrested. When he returned to his base, Waller was informed of a plot by local Filipinos to murder marines who had remained behind in the town. One of his subordinates convened a court-martial and sentenced the mutineers and the conspirators to death. Waller, feverish following his trek, approved their execution. He sent a laconic message to Smith's headquarters on Leyte: "It became necessary to expend eleven prisoners."

Domestic politics now began to weigh heavily on policy abroad. The American public, horrified by the slaughter on Samar, was more than ever frustrated by the seemingly endless struggle. Senator George Hoar, the senior Republican from Massachusetts and a foe of the war from the start, perceived the trend. On his insistence, the Senate committee on the Philippines, headed by Lodge, opened hearings on the conflict in January 1902. Lodge summoned a collection of friendly figures, among them Dewey, Otis and MacArthur in addition to Taft, who was then home for medical care. But the panel included a a minority of vocal critics, notably Thomas Patterson of Colorado and Edward Carmack of Tennessee, both Democrats, and Eugene Hale of Maine—the only Republican to have joined Hoar in opposition to the treaty annexing the Philippines. They grilled the administration witnesses, even getting as shrewd a jurist as Taft to acknowledge that natives had been tortured "on some occasions." Officers and men appeared to recall atrocities, and newspapers played up their accounts corroborated by other tales of brutality culled from letters by soldiers to their families.

The testimony confirmed the view of the anti-expansionists, who had warned that America would violate its tenets in imperialist wars. One of the most eloquent, Mark Twain, was then at the pinnacle of his fame. The year before, he had published an essay, "To the Person Sitting in Darkness." Cast in the form of a letter to McKinley, it recommended that Old Glory be redesigned—"the white stripes painted black and the stars replaced by the skull and cross bones." Finley Peter Dunne's Mr. Dooley swelled the criticism. The Supreme Court, bowing to McKinley and the Republicans in Congress, had ruled in a tortuous decision that the Constitution did not necessarily follow the flag, and that people in U.S. colonial possessions could be denied the rights of Americans. Mr. Dooley remarked with his usual acuity: "No matter whether th' constitution follows th' flag or not, th' supreme coort follows th' illiction returns." In his poem "On a Soldier Fallen in the Philippines" young William Vaughn Moody deplored America's loss of its idealism:

> The proud republic hath not stooped to cheat
> And scramble in the market place of war. . . .
> Ah no!
> We have not fallen so.

Roosevelt now feared that the ferment over the war would damage his election chances two years hence, when he ran for president on his own. Root, sharing his concern, made a stab at rectitude. To prove that malefactors were punished, he published the cases of thirty-nine U.S. soldiers convicted of cruelty. His move misfired. Most, it turned out, had merely been fined or reprimanded for torturing or shooting captives, and the document was widely berated as a farce.

Chaffee, sniffing the mood at home from the distance of Manila, smelled trouble. Apprised of Waller's execution of the Filipinos at Basey, he sailed to Smith's headquarters on Leyte to investigate the incident himself. "Smith," he asked as he landed, "have you been having any promiscuous killing on Samar for fun?" Smith denied any knowledge of the affair. Chaffee concluded, however, that a scapegoat would deflect possible accusations against his own command. He decided to prosecute Waller for murder—even though Waller had been no worse than many other American officers. Root concurred, as did the army chiefs in Washington, who were only too willing to sacrifice a marine to protect their branch of the service.

Waller's trial opened in Manila on March 17, 1902. He confessed to having approved the execution of the Filipinos, but based his defense on the Civil War order that decreed stiff penalties for civilian suspects. As the proceedings dragged on, opposition newspapers at home dubbed him a "butcher," and exhorted the Republican party to cleanse its "sins." Roosevelt impatiently demanded action, and Root cabled Chaffee to press the case "forcefully." Chaffee, with no alternative, reluctantly conceded to put his old friend Smith on the stand. "It looks as if Jake Smith is going to be in the soup too," he told his wife.

Waller had honorably refrained from revealing Smith's harsh directives to absolve himself. Smith, showing no such nobility, implicitly blamed Waller for the Filipino deaths. He claimed that he had told his officers to respect "the laws of war," and refer prisoners to an army commission. Waller, his career if not his life at stake, finally divulged Smith's instructions, from the order to kill children to the "howling wilderness" message. Witnesses bore him out. The court quickly acquitted him, but the episode stunted his career. Though he subsequently became a major general, he was passed over for promotion to the position of marine corps commandant by Taft, then president—for whom he personified the anguish and embarrassment of that period.

Waller's revelation logically led to Smith's indictment on the ambiguous charge of conduct prejudicial to "military discipline." Smith denied his guilt, but his prospects for acquittal were slim. A scapegoat was still needed, and he fit the role. He stubbornly spurned Chaffee's advice to plead that he had not intended his directives to be taken literally and insisted instead that he had meant what he said. Even the imperialists abandoned him. His behavior had been "revolting," Lodge averred. Roosevelt, having urged the American forces to act tough, now disclosed that he had told Chaffee that "nothing can justify the use of torture or inhuman conduct" by U.S. troops. Smith could not escape conviction. Nevertheless, Root urged a lenient sentence, citing the hardships of waging war against "cruel and barbarous savages." Roosevelt agreed, and Smith was merely "admonished." He retired, disgraced in the eyes of the U.S. public. Soldiers, though, held him up as a hero. They cheered his return to San

Francisco in August 1902—one of his aides remarking: "If people know what a thieving, treacherous, worthless bunch of scoundrels those Filipinos are, they would think differently. . . . I do not believe that there are half a dozen men in the U.S. Army that don't think that Smith is all right." Smith, added Chaffee, had made Samar "more peaceful than many parts of the United States."

But the American conquest of the Philippines was not to be completed for a decade. The *Dios-Dios* sect on Samar went on harassing isolated U.S. garrisons. On Luzon, aboriginal tribes also defied submission, periodically staging head-hunting campaigns against Americans and their Filipino auxiliaries. The most obdurate resistance meanwhile came from the Muslims of Mindanao and the other southern islands. The Spanish had named them Moros because of their resemblance to the Moors of North Africa, even though they represented a dozen or so different ethnic groups—each led by a local sultan or self-styled prophet. Dressed in gaudy turbans and embroidered vests, they launched massive attacks, waving spears and knives, and shouting bloodcurdling cries. Two senior U.S. soldiers gained distinction in the fight against them. Brigadier General Leonard Wood, a Harvard Medical School graduate, had been Roosevelt's superior as commander of the Rough Riders in Cuba and later became governor of the Philippines. John J. Pershing had been promoted by Roosevelt from captain to brigadier general over nearly nine hundred officers after his first battles against the Moros. He returned to administer the region, crushing a large Moro movement in a bloody fight waged in 1913 on the slopes of a volcano—and subsequently commanded the American Expeditionary Force in Europe during World War I. Moro dissidents continued to struggle against the infidels for years, and their heirs are striving to this day to establish an autonomous state.

The war ended officially on July 4, 1902. On that day, Roosevelt formally declared its conclusion in a proclamation commending the American army for its "courage and fortitude . . . indomitable spirit and loyal devotion" in defeating the "great insurrection" against "the lawful sovereignty and just authority of the United States."

By standards of the time, the conflict had not been inexpensive for America. The U.S. toll was 4,234 dead and 2,818 wounded—and thousands later succumbed at home to diseases contracted in the islands. It had cost the United States some $600 million—or roughly $4 billion in today's currency—and additional millions have gone to families of its veterans, many of whom continue to this day to receive pensions.

The Filipinos paid heavily. The U.S. forces, by their own count, killed some twenty thousand native soldiers. As many as two hundred thousand civilians may also have died from famine and various other causes, including atrocities committed by both sides. The devastation of the country was reflected in a single statistic: The number of *carabao,* or water buffalo, without which the rural population could not plant or harvest rice, the staple food, shrank by ninety percent during the war.

The U.S. victory aroused none of the jubilation that had marked America's first overseas foray four years before. On the contrary, the public reacted to

Roosevelt's announcement with muted relief, and the nation's press mostly gave the news perfunctory treatment.

It now remained for the United States to chart a new course for the Philippines. A fresh debate began to develop, in Washington as well as in Manila, over a timetable for the dominion's independence.

8. AMERICA EXPORTS ITSELF

★ ★ ★

Under a slate sky on a sultry August morning in 1901, a converted cattle ship, the *Thomas,* steamed into Manila Bay. Crowding its decks were five hundred young Americans, most of them recent college graduates, the men wearing straw boaters and blazers, the women in long skirts and large flowery hats. Like vacationers, they carried baseball bats, tennis rackets, musical instruments, cameras and binoculars. Few had ever been abroad, and they scanned the exotic landscape with a mixture of fascination and anticipation. Precursors of the Peace Corps volunteers of a later generation, they were arriving as teachers. They quickly fanned out across the archipelago to set up schools and soon became known as "Thomasites," after the vessel that had brought them. The label, pinned on all American teachers of the time, had the ring of a religious movement. But their vocation, though secular, did have an evangelical design. Education would Americanize the Filipinos and cement their loyalty to the United States. "We are not merely teachers," Philinda Rand later wrote to her family in Massachusetts from the island of Negros. "We are social assets and emissaries of good will."

Not all Americans who landed in the Philippines during those early years were so dedicated. There were swindlers, hucksters and dubious adventurers among them. Many who began with noble motives became lonely and discouraged and vented their bitterness in racial slurs against the Filipinos. But many—doctors, engineers, agronomists, surveyors, sanitation specialists and teachers like Philinda Rand—were driven by an unflagging faith in the virtue of their commitment.

The U.S. conquest of the Philippines had been as cruel as any conflict in the annals of imperialism, but hardly had it ended before Americans began to atone for its brutality. Inspired by a sense of moral obligation, they believed it to be their responsibility to bestow the spiritual and material blessings of their exceptional society on the new possession—as though providence had anointed them to be its savior. So, during its half-century in the archipelago, the United States refused to be labeled a colonial power and even expunged the word *colonial* from its official vocabulary. Instead of establishing a colonial office, as the British did to govern their overseas territories, President McKinley consigned the Philippines to the Bureau of Insular Affairs, an agency of the War Department. Nor did Americans sent out to supervise the islands call themselves colonial civil servants, a term that evoked an image of white despots in topees, brandishing swagger sticks at cringing brown natives. In their own eyes, they were missionaries, not masters.

The venture had originally been infused with apostolic fervor when McKinley divulged his divine directive to "uplift and civilize" the Filipinos—a goal he had earlier advertised as "benevolent assimilation." Elihu Root, his secretary of war, codified the doctrine in his instructions to William Howard Taft to promote the "happiness, peace and prosperity" of the natives in conformity with "their customs, their habits and even their prejudices." Seconding that sentiment soon after becoming governor, Taft intoned: "We hold the Philippines for the benefit of the Filipinos, and we are not entitled to pass a single act or to approve a single measure that has not that as its chief purpose."

Compared to European colonialism, the United States was indeed a model of enlightenment. Americans were banned by law from acquiring large tracts of land in the Philippines—a sharp contrast to Britain's mobilization of coolies on Malayan rubber plantations or France's forced recruitment of native labor to cultivate huge rice fields in Vietnam. The Americans avoided such egregious schemes as the opium monopolies, maintained by the British, French and Dutch in their Asian dominions to raise revenues. Nothing they did to preserve order even remotely matched the repression of the French in Vietnam, who in 1930 executed nearly seven hundred native dissidents without trial. Even the supposedly benign British summarily imprisoned a hundred thousand Indians for civil disobedience during the same period. On the other hand, the Filipinos renounced violent opposition to U.S. supremacy after Aguinaldo's defeat—precisely because they finally concluded that American rule would not be harsh.

Aware from the start that the Filipinos would judge them by actual deeds, the Americans launched practical programs to demonstrate their benevolence. They bought and redistributed the rural estates held by the Catholic friars, whose excesses had provoked Filipinos to rebel against Spain. To improve the economy, they constructed dams and irrigation facilities, expanded markets, developed mines and timber concessions, built roads, railways and ports. Their legal reforms gave the archipelago, for the first time in its history, an honest judiciary under native magistrates. They introduced a tax system to make the country self-sustaining, and renovated the financial structure, which had been a chaos of currencies. Unlike the Europeans elsewhere in Asia, who plundered their colonies for their own profit, they displayed deep concern for the welfare of the natives. Their expenditures on health helped to double the population from 1900 to 1920, and schools spurred a climb in the literacy rate from twenty percent to fifty percent within a generation. Fearful of mutinies, the Europeans forbade native troops from outnumbering their own soldiers and maintained their forces at the expense of the colonies. By the 1920s, more Filipinos than Americans were serving as army regulars and police in the Philippines.

The United States also accorded the Filipinos unusual latitude to govern themselves, even though its motives were less than idealistic. Taft encouraged the ambitions of the upper classes to subvert diehard native nationalists, and the Republicans back home endorsed liberal moves to deflect their Democratic critics. But whatever the reasons, Filipinos were running for local office even before the Americans had fully conquered the archipelago. They conducted elections for a national legislature as early as 1907.

But the U.S. performance in the Philippines was flawed. The Americans coddled the elite while disregarding the appalling plight of the peasants, thus perpetuating a feudal oligarchy that widened the gap between rich and poor. They imposed trade patterns that retarded the economic growth of the islands, condemning them to reliance on the United States long after independence. The American monopoly on imports into the Philippines also dampened the development of a native industry. At the same time, the unlimited entry of Philippine exports to the United States bound the archipelago inextricably to the American market. Economically at least, the Filipinos were doomed to remain "little brown brothers" for years—though many, despite their nationalist rhetoric, found security in the role.

Above all, the U.S. effort to inculcate Filipinos with American ethics proved to be elusive. Filipinos readily accepted American styles and institutions. They learned to behave, dress and eat like Americans, sing American songs and speak Americanized English. Their lawyers familiarized themselves with American jurisprudence, and their politicians absorbed American democratic procedures, displaying unique skills in American parliamentary practices. But they never became the Americans that Americans sought to make them. To this day, they are trying to define their national identity.

Taft oversaw U.S. rule of the Philippines for thirteen years, first as governor in Manila and later from Washington as secretary of war and president. He undertook the gigantic task of implanting in the archipelago the foundations of a modern state. Rather than steer them toward independence, he sought to convince the Filipinos that their own interests would best be served by a close and permanent bond with the beneficent United States. But he underestimated the dynamics of nationalism, which drove Filipinos to push for sovereignty despite their recognition of America's generosity. Nor did he anticipate the shifting pressures that came from changing attitudes in Congress and the White House. Thus, while he left an indelible imprint on the islands, U.S. policies in the archipelago lacked consistency.

★   ★   ★

Pioneer U.S. officials were not blind to the magnitude of the task as they set out to modernize the Philippines. As Daniel Williams, an aide to Taft, observed in a letter home, they had inherited a Spanish regime "so antiquated and disorganized as not to admit of patching or repair." Worse yet, America had never governed a foreign land, and now it faced staggering problems "with few, if any, precedents to guide." But they were energetic, optimistic Americans, confident that they could cope with any challenge. A year later, in a rhapsodic report, Williams wrote: "I doubt if in the world's history anything similar has been done. . . . The whole fabric is being made over [and] scarcely anything is left as it was. Having started to mend the machinery, we have found that all the parts must be replaced in order to make the thing move."

The ossified Catholic establishment in the Philippines was a priority target. If American-type secular institutions were to be created, Taft believed, the Spanish friars must be expelled from their rural fiefdoms. Their ouster would also make America popular with the Filipinos, who, despite their fidelity to the Catholic Church, equated the friars with Spanish tyranny. Taft's prudish sensibilities were shocked as well by lurid tales of their greed and depravity, including their purported sexual escapades. They had "ceased to be religious ministers," he wrote to a friend in Ohio, and were nothing more than "political bosses" preoccupied solely with "money and power." Only two hundred Spanish priests were then left in the islands—most having fled, or been slain or jailed by the Filipino nationalists. Nevertheless, the monastic orders still owned some four hundred thousand acres of farm land, which they leased to sixty thousand tenants. Confiscate the estates, Taft concluded, and their power would be crushed.

But America had pledged to respect all property rights in the Philippines, those of the church included. The friar lands would have to be acquired legally.

In a cable from Manila late in 1901, Taft urged Theodore Roosevelt, by now president, to appoint an American envoy to negotiate a deal with the Vatican. Soon afterward, when Taft returned home for surgery on an abscess, Roosevelt summoned him to the White House and gave him the job.

It was no routine business deal. Catapulted into the White House by McKinley's assassination, Roosevelt needed all the support he could muster to win on his own in the election two years hence. But there were potential political perils even in talking with the Vatican. A dispute might antagonize Catholic voters, a potent force in America's big cities. An accord might anger anti-Catholics, then strong in rural America. Secretary of War Elihu Root, aware of the hazards, cautioned Taft against conveying the impression that the overture was "in any sense or degree diplomatic." Eager to enhance its international prestige through U.S. recognition, the Vatican had meanwhile spread rumors that Taft was acting in an official capacity.

He arrived in Rome in June 1902 with, among others, his seventy-four-year-old mother, a vigorous lady who joined the party to shield her boy from the evil papists. But Leo XIII, the famous liberal pope then in his nineties, was so amiable during the splendid audience that, Taft wrote to a friend, he had found the "old boy . . . quite bubbling with humor." The papal effervescence, however, failed to stir the cardinals assigned to the case. Though willing to sell the monastic land, they rejected Taft's demand that the friars be removed from the islands. Taft, back in Manila, spent the next seventeen months in long-distance haggling. The United States finally paid $7 million for the estates. Never officially withdrawn, the friars gradually died off—taking with them a last vestige of Spain's presence in the Philippines.

Taft had no clear vision for the country as he began his term as governor. He doubted that the Filipinos, whom he privately disdained despite his warm displays of paternalism, would ever qualify for independence—though perhaps, under U.S. auspices, they might be trained to manage their internal affairs. Perhaps, over time, they could also be persuaded that the prosperity and protection assured by American rule was preferable to parlous sovereignty. For the moment, then, he would only continue to try to improve them. "If a policy is to be declared at all," he advised a Senate committee in 1902, it should be "to hold the islands indefinitely, until the people shall show themselves fit for self-government."

When would the Filipinos be ready to govern themselves? Who would judge their competence? What system would suit them? Often asked those questions, Taft replied vaguely. There were "many discouraging defects" in the "character" of the natives that could "only be cured by careful tutelage," he wrote to Henry Cabot Lodge. It would take "at least a generation," maybe longer, to prepare them for "a large participation" in government.

But he would "do the very best" he could for them, as McKinley had pledged after his fitful night of prayer. He would bless them with the three ingredients that had made America great: mass education, economic development and democratic government. Free public schools accounted for America's enlightenment, economic growth for its prosperity and citizen involvement at the lowest levels of government to its devotion to republican precepts. The United States thus embarked on a unique experiment: to duplicate itself in a drastically different terrain. Taft and the other Americans committed to the effort were talented men who would surely have thrived had they stayed at home. Their willingness to work among unfamiliar people in a cruel climate dramatized a singular dedication to their cause. Yet an innocent, naïve and frequently overweening faith in their own virtue often propelled them into fantasies that, to their disappointment, were later punctured by reality.

★ ★ ★

The spread of schools has been applauded as America's single greatest achievement in the Philippines. Guided by American teachers, the Filipinos rapidly attained the highest literacy rate in Southeast Asia and, after Christianity, the English language became the centripetal force that brought at least a semblance of unity to the far-flung archipelago. But the U.S. educational effort failed in many ways to satisfy its American promoters—partly because their expectations were illusory and partly because they could not agree on a consistent policy.

American propaganda notwithstanding, Spain had not condemned the Filipinos to abysmal ignorance. On the contrary, during the latter half of the nineteenth century, they were the most Westernized, sophisticated, modern elite in Asia. Rich families sent their sons to private Manila secondary schools and European universities and, by the 1890s, some two hundred thousand pupils were in primary schools throughout the islands. But the system was stymied by a lack of money and teachers as well as by the friars, who resented intrusion onto their turf. Even so, the Filipinos had tasted education and wanted more, and the U.S. Army saw on its arrival that their appetite could be turned against Aguinaldo's forces. American troops were ordered to conduct classes, largely to pacify the natives by demonstrating the benison of the U.S. mission—a strategy that, in later wars, was to be called "winning hearts and minds." Education, an American official noted, would make the Filipinos "less liable to be led by political leaders into insurrectionary schemes."

Following the U.S. conquest, many Americans maintained that education would deter native agitation for independence. Taft's aide, Daniel Williams, reckoned that "the Filipino, with a wider range of knowledge, would better appreciate his natural limitations and hesitate before demanding that he be cut adrift." McKinley had earlier judged that schools would deepen the allegiance of the natives to the United States and thus induce them to accept America's permanent presence in the Philippines. In April 1900, he transferred control of education from the army to the Taft commission, then poised to depart for Manila to create a civilian administration. He directed Taft to set up a system of free primary instruction to "fit the people for the duties of citizenship and for the ordinary activities of a civilized community."

The typically amorphous order left Taft to contrive a practical plan. On the recommendation of Charles W. Eliot, the president of Harvard, he hired Fred Atkinson, a high school principal of thirty-five from Massachusetts. Six feet four inches tall, Atkinson was a Harvard graduate with an advanced degree from Germany who knew nothing about primary instruction. But Taft named him director of education for the Philippines, explaining indulgently that the Americans were only experimenting. "Experience in the United States can hardly seem to furnish much of a guide for what must be done here. It will be largely original work."

Atkinson, once in Manila, swiftly confected a centralized school system, with himself at its head and Americans supervising local districts. Costs would be shared by the U.S. administration in Manila and municipal councils throughout the islands, but scarce funds precluded compulsory education for all children. Devout Filipinos, inflamed by Atkinson's plan to bar religion from the schools, threatened a boycott unless the curriculum included Catholic instruction. As a compromise, Taft agreed to allow priests to teach the faith after hours—a concession that annoyed some Americans. Still, Philippine education was to be free of church control for the first time in three centuries.

The Americans violated a cardinal rule of imperialism. The Europeans, to insulate their colonial subjects from supposedly subversive Western concepts like liberty and equality, confined them almost entirely to education in the local language—if they educated them at all. Spain had similarly limited instruction in Spanish to only a handful of the Filipino elite. But Atkinson concluded that to teach the Filipinos in their vast assortment of languages and dialects would entail "a large corps of translators [and] books of every sort." Thus, for strictly practical reasons, English was to become the lingua franca of the Philippines. Yet the decision, perhaps subliminally, also reflected a basic purpose of the Americans: They intended to Americanize the Filipinos, not Filipinize themselves. As usual, Finley Peter Dunne's perceptive Mr. Dooley detected the distinction. "We'll larn ye our language," he remarked, "because 'tis easier to larn ye ours thin to larn oursilves ye'ers."

Most Americans hailed the move as idealistic, and it also drew praise from some Filipinos. Trinidad Pardo de Tavera, whose *Federalista* party favored statehood for the Philippines, warmly welcomed the initiative. English, he declaimed, would instill the "American spirit" in Filipinos, inspire them to "adopt its principles, its political customs and its peculiar civilization" and thus further "our complete and radical . . . redemption." But to other Filipino intellectuals, English was a threat to tradition. Teodoro Kalaw, a popular polemicist, deplored its potential impact on Filipino women, the symbol of continuity. He could already see their degradation, he wrote in a florid essay in 1904. There they were, reading books in English and "chattering in a strange language," having become "unconscious victims of modernity," bereft of their "native simplicity," insisting on being known as "girls" instead of *dalagas,* or maidens. Corrupted by "Anglo-Saxon influence," these emancipated females would soon be "walking out alone" without *duennas,* "a handbag under the arm, just like bold little American misses." Eventually, too, they would even be taking "nonchalant trips" abroad—and all this after "only six years of American occupation."

For better or worse, however, English quickly caught on. By 1910, U.S. officials estimated that more Filipinos could read, write and speak English than any other single language. Critics of America's educational program ridiculed the claim, contending that most spoke a brand of English that was barely comprehensible. But whatever they learned was due to the pioneer American teachers in the Philippines.

More than a thousand young Americans volunteered to teach Filipino children and to train native instructors. Recruited from nearly every part of the United States, most were college graduates with some classroom experience. Eight thousand had applied, either out of altruism or for adventure. Money was also an attraction: As an inducement, they were offered as much as $125 a month, substantially more than teachers earned at home. Two groups reached Manila during the early summer of 1901, before the *Thomas* landed on August 21 with the largest contingent. Many kept journals or wrote often to their families, and their accounts frequently reveal an innocent exuberance. But the solitude, strangeness and hardships of a faraway land also made many melancholy, depressed and disgruntled.

Philinda Rand, a tall, slender Radcliffe graduate of twenty-three, had been teaching grade school for two years in Bethel, Massachusetts. She responded eagerly to the call, telling her diary with romantic expectation that this was "a grand opportunity to see life on the frontier of civilization." Arriving in Manila, she and her companions plunged into its exotic bustle. They clambered down from their ship into small boats that zigzagged up and down the Pasig, the city's main waterway, a noisy jumble of steamers, lighters, barges, junks and *cascos,* straw-covered sampans that lodged the river folk. Once ashore, they were encircled by natives, some jostling to help, others merely curious. They struggled with their bags, books and cameras into *carromatas,* flimsy two-wheeled carriages whose tiny ponies dashed off through the city's narrow streets, careering "between houses covered with moss and hanging vines and plants growing from cracks in their red-tiled roofs . . . as black heads stuck out and black eyes looked with amazement at these new school ma'ams." For the next week, Philinda crammed her journal with vignettes.

She observed coolies nimbly balancing huge crates on bamboo shoulder poles as they trotted beside lines of water buffalo lazily tugging carts piled high with sacks of sugar or bags of rice. A horse-drawn tram jammed with native men passed her, its horn squawking as it rumbled across a plaza, and she caught a glimpse of an elaborate funeral procession preceded by eight solemn priests in black robes and white wigs. Venturing out at night, she wandered through an open market, its stalls lighted by flickering lamps burning sweet coconut oil. And, of course, she was mesmerized by the spectacular sunset over Manila Bay.

From Manila she sailed south in a "wallowing little tub" to the island of Negros—then as now a landscape of sugar plantations set against a horizon of jungle-clad mountains. She had heard that the natives there were "quite friendly to Americans," and her information proved to be correct. After landing at the only port, she traveled by oxcart through a pouring rain to the town of Silay, her destination, where *el presidente* welcomed her with an attempt at a ceremony. She could speak neither Spanish nor Ilongo, the local language, and a group of women who had come to greet her "shrieked with laughter" whenever she opened her mouth. But the mayor was "a dear," and did "everything he could to make it pleasant." He provided her with a nipa hut with oyster-shell windowpanes and a five-gallon kerosene can for a bath. Her domestic staff comprised three servants, among them a cook who gambled the food allowance on cockfights, so that she had "a poor dinner if he loses." She took to the costume of the "better class": gowns with long trains made from silk or *pina,* a gossamer muslin woven from pineapple plants. At five feet ten, tall even for an American girl of the period, she must have looked gawky in a dress designed for small native women, and she also towered over the men. Yet she never felt uneasy—at least socially. Traditionally hospitable, the Filipinos treated her graciously, and she had a sense of humor.

Her job was less amusing. The school consisted of "a dirty, dismal room" furnished with "a few rough desks and a long table," and her undisciplined pupils would "walk around, spit on the floor and talk aloud." Her two native aides, both young women, were little help. They were supposed to interpret for her until the class acquired some skill in English, but their knowledge of English was scant. As an alternative, Philinda began to tutor pupils individually by repeating the word in English for specific objects. One day, when she showed a knife to a little girl, the child ran off screaming that "the big American was going to kill her."

At first disappointed by the low attendance, Philinda hoped to nurture it "naturally" by convincing local families of the advantages of education. But the American district supervisor demanded long rosters to improve his image with the U.S. authorities in Manila, who in turn wanted "fine reports" to impress Washington. "So," Philinda noted, "our obliging *presidente* sends out policemen every morning to round up children, and I arrive to find eighty or a hundred cowering youngsters. The next morning they hide, and the policemen get a new lot."

She was equally dismayed by her Filipino aides, slated to become teachers themselves. Frequently tardy or absent, they would casually explain that they had been diverted by family chores, or had simply overslept. They were also often unprepared and unmotivated, and Philinda confided her chagrin to her diary. "They have never been farther in arithmetic than fractions, and do not know east from west on a map. I am just beginning to appreciate fully the fact that education means much more than learning. Both are considered educated—that is, they have been to what they call colleges and one has been to Manila. Neither can reason in the least. . . . They have no power of concentration [and] their minds are so untrained as to take days to grasp what a grammar school American child would know in an hour." Bewildered at times by America's "overwhelming" undertaking, she wrote in her journal: "I wonder what will become of it all."

Other American teachers were frustrated by the clash of cultures in a society whose values differed almost diametrically from their own. They had brought a puritanical devotion to diligence and hard work, virtues they intended to ingrain in their pupils—only to find them ambling to an insouciant drumbeat. Students chronically cut classes to attend weddings, baptisms and fiestas, regular features of Philippine towns, or they simply went fishing. As apostles of democracy, the Americans were stymied as well by a stiff social structure that blocked their efforts to imbue the children with egalitarian principles. To promote the dignity of labor, for example, many encouraged gardening as a school activity—whereupon the sons and daughters of rich families showed up with servants to till their plots. Wealthy parents often protested, too, against the presence of poor youngsters in the same classroom as their children.

Compounding their problems, the Americans lacked books, paper, pencils, blackboards and chalk. Their schools, often barns or sheds, leaked during rainy weather or broiled in the hot season. Within the first three years, twenty teachers died of dysentery, cholera or smallpox, six were murdered by bandits and one blew his brains out. Isolation in a tiny town could be sheer tedium. Benjamin Neal, stationed in Pangasinan province, nostalgically awaited mail that brought him and a fellow teacher football scores, fraternity gossip and other news from Syracuse University, their alma mater. "After supper each night," he wrote in his diary, "we sit in the front window and whistle the good old college tunes while the tropical sun sets gradually, fades and twilight deepens. Memory helps us to bridge over many an hour that otherwise would be lonesome." Roy Matthews, in Tayabas province, confessed to a quaint moral quandary in a letter to a friend. Despite his "rigid observance of Methodist principles," he was tempted to accept the gift from the town council of a live-in "*signorita* [*sic*]." How he resolved the dilemma remains a mystery.

Several American teachers exulted in the notion that they were the progenitors of a mighty transformation. His hope, Paul Gilbert lyrically wrote, was to "stir the Filipino from his dream of the dark ages, and point the way to modern progress." Others were content to discern fainter signs of Americanization in the natives. They were delighted when their students serenaded them with such popular American classics as "Good Night, Ladies" and "There'll Be a Hot Time in the Old Town Tonight," and they took special pride in their school bands, which gustily played Sousa marches—as school bands in even the smallest Philippine towns do to this day. Nothing impassioned them more, however, than the promotion of baseball, the obvious antidote to the native addiction to cockfighting. Baseball, wrote a Chicago *Daily News* correspondent, was vital to America's "civilizing" effort.

Many teachers sank roots. Philinda Rand married a fellow American, gave birth to a daughter and remained in the Philippines for seven years. Maud Jarman, who went to Manila to teach in 1901, died there a half-century afterward. Some spawned families that made the islands their home. Frederic Marquardt, the son of a Thomasite who founded a school in an obscure town on Leyte, served as a magazine editor in Manila until the start of World War II. Early in 1987, he returned to the town to unveil a bust of his father erected by local citizens—who, eighty-five years later, still remembered an early American benefactor. But the legend of the selfless American teacher in the Philippines, like the subsequent legend of the "ugly American" elsewhere in Asia, was also largely mythical.

Harry Cole lost heart in November 1901, after only three months on Leyte. "I find this work very monotonous, trying to teach these monkeys to talk," he wrote home. "Most of these people are lazy and indolent, and I do not think they can stick to it to get an education. . . . And oh! they are so dirty. Of course they have not been taught any better, and so they can hardly be blamed, and yet I do not believe they would care to exert themselves to clean up. . . . Their habits are frightful." Four months later, he was ready to quit. "The more I see of this lazy, dirty, indolent people, the more I come to despise them. I came here to help them, to enter their homes and to try to uplift them. But it seems to me a useless task. I am becoming more and more convinced that for years and years to come, the only business Americans ought to have over here is to rule them with severity."

Cole's wife, Mary, shared his disenchantment. "Everything mildews" while "pigs run about the streets and around the house," she lamented in a letter to her folks. There was "no butter, no flour, no milk except condensed [and] you never know when the cook is going to wash his feet in the dish pan or wipe them on the tea towel." The heat sapped her morale, as did her pupils. "Sometimes I get disgusted with the whole race and think it useless to try to teach them anything. . . . Only eight months and three weeks more of this detestable work, and we shall leave. Oh, how happy I shall be." But she did not despair that America might one day convert the Filipinos. "I suppose with patience and perseverance they will progress little by little until within two or three hundred years they may be quite Americanistic."

Some teachers were less charitable. Blaine Free Moore, a vintage Thomasite, hated "being shut up with a lot of little brown kids," as he wrote home. They were "wriggling, squirming, talking barbarians," and the United States had adopted a "pernicious" policy by "teaching these people that they are as good as anybody, that this country is for them and the Americans are only here for their benefit." His formula was simple. "If these people don't improve, it will show the absolute uselessness of this 'benevolent' business, and prove that the only way to manage these people is the way they understand . . . to which they will respond much quicker, viz., a show of force." Paradoxically, he later became a top U.S. educational official in the Philippines.

Taft soon realized that Atkinson had been a bad choice. Atkinson deluged teachers with memos on their decorum, dress and haircuts, and paid their wages erratically. He had also imported a curriculum better suited to Massachusetts than to the Philippines. History included George Washington's cherry tree and Paul Revere's midnight ride as "patriotic" lessons. He introduced the *Baldwin Reader,* a popular American primer that taught "A is for apple," a fruit alien to Filipinos, and pictured John and Mary in the snow, an equally odd substance.

A racial bias also skewed his concepts. He had visited Tuskegee Institute, the Negro school in Alabama run by the celebrated Booker T. Washington, who believed that American blacks should strive to attain equality through the "dignity of common labor" rather than through political agitation. Somehow seeing a parallel, Atkinson decided that Filipinos, like Negroes, were unfit for academic studies and ought to acquire such "practical" skills as pig breeding, carpentry and handicrafts. Taft received similar advice from his brother Horace, headmaster of an exclusive Connecticut prep school, who maintained that vocational training ideally suited the "deficient races." Rich Filipinos, who regarded manual labor as demeaning, backed the idea for the lower classes. But it was rejected by the lower classes, who saw formal education as an opportunity for their children to climb the social ladder.

Taft dropped Atkinson late in 1902 and brought in David Barrows, who ran the program until Frank White succeeded him six years later. The turnover was normal enough. But each man approached the job differently, and educational policy seemed to lurch from one extreme to another.

Barrows, an anthropologist from California, had worked in the archipelago since 1900 as an expert on aborigines. Intelligent, dynamic and ambitious, he hoped to parlay the assignment into a political career at home. He diagnosed the fundamental flaw of the Philippines to be its static social structure, which condemned the ignorant and submissive masses "without protest to the blind leadership of the aristocracy." As long as that structure remained, the Filipinos could never attain real self-government, America's goal for them. He prescribed a Jeffersonian answer: the creation of a literate peasantry through "universal primary instruction for . . . all classes and every community." He opened more schools and hired additional native teachers. His curriculum accented reading, writing and arithmetic, and he prepared textbooks especially for Filipino children. The primers now showed Juan and María walking through rice fields instead of John and Mary in the snow, and avocados and coconuts replaced apples and pears. Barrows also ordered teachers to deliver civic homilies. Mayors "are elected by the people" and should not "act like little kings," one went. Advised another, "If you want to be a farmer, you ought to own your own farm. You will be richer and happier."

Barrows also inaugurated a program for young Filipinos to study in America. Called *pensionados,* the first hundred sailed for the United States in October 1903. They included Francisco Benítez, later a prominent educator, who jokingly compared them to the barbarian children sent as hostages to imperial Rome to be converted into loyal Roman citizens.

Benítez spent five years at a cow college in Illinois, where he joined a fraternity, went to football games, dated American girls—and returned home "totally brainwashed," as his daughter Virginia Licuanan recollected. He insisted on speaking English to his family, which became "as American as any Filipinos could be." His children grew up on American food, and adopted American nicknames. They learned to quote Patrick Henry and Benjamin Franklin, sing "The Star-Spangled Banner" and eagerly awaited Santa Claus at Christmas—even though their house of course lacked a chimney.

Back home, however, Benítez and his fellow *pensionados* were snubbed by both Filipinos and Americans. The Filipinos, ridiculing their American dress, manners and speech, dubbed them "Amboys." Having been treated as equals in the United States, they had expected on their return to receive the same treatment from Americans in Manila. But they were ostracized as inferiors by the city's American community, which excluded them from clubs reserved for whites, even as guests. Most nevertheless retained a lifelong devotion to the

United States. Benítez, later a passionate partisan of Philippine independence, attributed his nationalism to his American tutelage. The United States, he said, had blessed Filipinos with the "inspiration and vision of American ideals [and] we would be unworthy if we did not seek for our people what American ideals have given to America itself."

During the 1930s, following in her father's footsteps, Virginia Licuanan enrolled in a small college in Missouri, where she too became a football fan. She also dated an American boy—alarming her mother, who shuddered at the prospect of an American son-in-law despite the family's admiration for the United States. Her mother had no cause to worry. Among upper-class Filipinos in those days, Licuanan recalled, "nobody married Americans." But her U.S. education did leave a deep imprint. Though she married a Filipino, she confessed that "I never learned to make love in Tagalog."

Barrows left some four thousand elementary schools in the Philippines when he quit in 1909—a threefold increase during his seven-year tenure. He had doubled the number of pupils to more than four hundred thousand, and tripled the size of the native teacher corps to some eight thousand. But behind the impressive statistics, the system lacked quality. Most of the Filipino teachers had not gone past the sixth grade and merely served as monitors. Truancy was endemic, especially among farm children who had to help their parents in the fields during the planting and harvesting seasons. Of all the pupils who enrolled in school, only one sixth reached the fourth grade. The rest dropped out to work.

Senior U.S. officials finally decided that Barrows had been misguided. The Jeffersonian concept of an educated yeomanry could not be replanted in foreign soil simply by teaching students a few lofty notions for a few hours a day over a few years. The United States returned to Atkinson's aborted idea of vocational training in hopes of preparing the natives for productive labor. Barrows left to teach at the University of California, and never went into politics.

Frank White, who took over in 1909, had already worked at various jobs in the Philippine educational system. At thirty-four, he was a picture-book American: the tall, handsome, clean-cut young man in the Arrow collar ad. His ideas coincided with those of Cameron Forbes, then the U.S. governor, for whom economic development was primordial. Until his death from tuberculosis in 1913, White concentrated on such "useful occupations" as basketry, weaving, embroidery, pottery and raising poultry at the expense of "impractical" subjects like reading, writing and arithmetic. He reduced the number of primary schools, and instead stressed secondary instruction for fewer students—a measure that reassured the Filipino oligarchy, which had been uncomfortable with the political and social implications of mass education.

By the 1920s, however, U.S. experts had concluded that the educational effort was faltering. A group led by Paul Monroe of Columbia University's Teachers' College, which visited Manila in 1925, found after testing thirty-two thousand pupils that very few who had finished four years of school were equal to American second-graders. Teaching was "so deficient," Monroe reported, that young Filipinos had not learned enough English for "a functional control over the language in adult life." He criticized the vocational courses as well for training students either in unwanted skills or to manufacture unwanted products. The verdict was harsh and probably unjust, since it assessed the Filipinos by American standards. But the Americans had no other yardstick than their own. Besides, America's objective was to Americanize the Filipinos.

To give high marks to the U.S. school system, as most Americans and Filipinos do in retrospect, is a fair judgment—as far as it goes. But education in itself was not a miraculous remedy for all the country's ills. The instrument could only be as effective as those who used it.

English, still the most widely spoken language of the Philippines, brought a degree of cohesion to the sprawling archipelago, which the Spanish had deliberately kept divided as a device to perpetuate their control. But its popularity deterred the development of a national Philippine language. Education also transformed political behavior. As Filipinos became more and more literate, they increasingly compelled their leaders to respond to their demands. The traditional *ilustrados,* no longer able to wield power arbitrarily, now staged elections that, with their campaign hoopla, resembled U.S. elections. The similarity was deceptive. The oligarchy continued to exercise authority through money, patronage and a web of dynastic alliances—as it does to this day. Yet Americans, to justify the U.S. tutelary role, proclaimed the Philippines a "showcase of democracy"—when Filipinos, with their talent for imitation, had merely learned enough from their American mentors to make the charade seem real.

Not that Filipinos have been insincere in their fondness for the United States. A sense of obligation toward those who render them service was deeply imbedded in their society, and their expressions of gratitude, couched in flowery Latin style, could be sentimental, even mawkish. A distinguished jurist, Benvenido Tan, effusively recalled some years ago that "next to God and my parents, I owe all that is good in me to my former American teachers." Older Filipinos still retain fond if misty memories of "Mr. Parker," from whom they learned to read, or "Miss Johnson," who taught them algebra.

The U.S. system created an almost compulsive appetite among Filipinos for education—or at least the appearance of being educated. Since the beginning of the century, primary-school enrollment has vaulted from two hundred thousand to ten million, a climb of forty-five times compared to a sevenfold growth in population. By the 1980s, more than a million students were attending universities and colleges. But, once again, the figures fail to convey the distortions in the Filipino obsession with education.

Young Filipinos shunned floundering American vocational programs, preferring instead academic courses that promised the nebulous respectability of white-collar jobs. They even spurned skills like engineering and agronomy, sorely needed by the society, and flocked to diploma mills that ground out graduates in law, advertising and public relations. Thus, along with other developing countries, the Philippines has suffered from a scarcity of qualified labor in its rural areas and a surplus of nominally educated urban youths either unemployed or working as shop clerks and taxicab drivers. Ambitious students meanwhile struggle for gilt-edged degrees from a few elite institutions, like the University of the Philippines or the Ateneo de Manila, a Jesuit school. But nothing surpasses the prestige of an Ivy League laureate as Filipinos persistently seek an American imprimatur despite their search for a distinctive national character.

The Filipinos became Americanized without becoming Americans. But whatever the alchemy that finally shapes their national identity, a process that could take generations, the ultimate amalgam is bound to bear traces of their U.S. education.

★ ★ ★

The Europeans claimed to need raw materials for their home industries, markets for their manufactured products and targets of investment for their capital, and they bled their colonies, at times flagrantly, for the exclusive profit of the mother country. To many Americans, overseas possessions were equally crucial. The fiery Senator Albert Beveridge pleaded for retaining the Philippines as a fulcrum for trade with China, "our natural customer." But other Americans, big businessmen among them, maintained that the United States, with its expanding population and seemingly limitless natural wealth, was the central arena. Instinctively isolationist, they also saw peril in commitments abroad. Senator Alexander Clay of Georgia articulated their view: "Wars, entangling alliances, domestic insurrection are not the proper means to induce foreign consumers to buy our goods and wares."

The dispute reached back to the acrimonious debate over McKinley's decision to annex the Philippines, and it continued into the 1930s to cloud the question of how to govern the islands. Efforts to formulate a coherent American economic policy for the archipelago thus bogged down in chronic controversy.

Congress was largely responsible for the lack of coherence. The war powers granted to McKinley had enabled Taft to deal directly with such matters as education and the disposal of church land in the archipelago. But Congress, sensitive to vested interests at home, balked at giving him and later governors the freedom to manage the Philippine economy. Economic programs would therefore require legislation, which was tilted by influential lobbies and often tangential political squabbles. As a result, a zigzag of improvised expedients rather than a consistent policy dictated America's development of the islands.

Nevertheless, America's colossal weight deeply and durably dented the Philippine economic, social and political fabric. The Americans shackled the country's economy to the United States in a quintessentially colonial relationship that continued, in modified form, long after the islands had gained independence.

The Philippines was in dismal condition during the early years of the century. Many peasants, deprived of their land in the shift to export commodities like sugar, tobacco, hemp and coconuts, slid into poverty as tenants and laborers. The reduction of acreage devoted to rice and corn caused famine in several regions. Worse yet, wide areas lay in waste after years of war, and aggravating the devastation were floods, droughts, insect plagues and a cholera epidemic that claimed more than a hundred thousand lives. Congress dawdled for two years before voting $3 million in relief funds as crime and other symptoms of unrest surged alarmingly. The crisis convinced Taft that the country required nothing less than a complete overhaul.

He and his commission had begun to contemplate possible long-range economic plans even before they sailed for Manila in the spring of 1900. They were not economists, nor did they have professional economic advisers—a rare species in those days. But they had been witness to America's titanic growth during their own lifetime, and they reasoned that the same strategies that had transformed the United States would work in the Philippines—and for the good of the Filipinos. "Nothing will civilize them so much," Taft declared, "as the introduction of American enterprise and investment."

His prescription combined three ingredients: He would construct and improve roads, railways and ports to modernize the country's archaic transportation system; agriculture, mining and logging would be revived through heavy doses of U.S. capital; and special tariffs, aimed at spurring trade between the United States and the Philippines, would further stimulate the development of the islands. But at each step of the way, Taft and his successors clashed with Congress, which had its own agenda.

No economic plan could begin before order was imposed on the chaos of Philippine currencies. Spanish gold coins were still in circulation, but Filipinos preferred large Mexican silver dollars, a vestige of the galleon trade with Acapulco. Then came the U.S. dollar to exacerbate the turmoil. Speculators gambled on fluctuations in the value of gold and silver, sparking wild swings in import and export prices. Bankers could not keep pace with the pendulum of exchange rates, and merchants were confounded by the confusion. Taft hired two experts to deal with the situation—Charles A. Conant, a New York financier, and Jeremiah W. Jenks, an economist familiar with Asia. They eventually proposed a dual currency of both gold and silver pesos, each worth fifty U.S. cents. The idea fueled a fierce fight in Congress as backers of the gold standard tangled with spokesmen from the silver-producing states. The reform finally passed after a year of bickering, and the islands got a sound currency for the first time in memory. The episode served to remind Taft, however, that he would face as many obstacles in Washington as he would in the Philippines.

Manila, meanwhile, was a mess. The city had scarcely changed since the seventeenth century, when the Spanish had transformed it from a stockade into the seat of their Asian empire. Still a walled medieval town of ancient buildings clustered around a cathedral, it was surrounded by swamps that bred cholera and malaria—scourges that recurrently killed thousands of natives jammed into bamboo huts on its outskirts. Not until 1882 did the Spanish install a fresh water supply, which provided only four hundred spigots for a population of three hundred thousand. Nor did they enforce even basic health precautions. The first U.S. soldiers to enter Manila in August 1898 nearly suffocated from the stench of rotting garbage and excrement littering the streets.

So did Taft. Indeed, the filth claimed him as a victim. He contracted amoebic dysentery soon after arriving, probably from food fertilized with human feces, and the agony was unbearable for a man of his obesity. But at least he could appreciate the plight of the natives, and he acted promptly.

He brought in American medical and hygiene specialists to help the U.S. Army's sanitation programs. Their progress was slow but remarkable. They built the city's first sewage system and a new reservoir as well as a modern hospital whose free clinic was soon handling eighty thousand outpatients a year. Fresh from the Caribbean, where they had learned to treat tropical diseases, American doctors virtually wiped out cholera by teaching the Filipinos to boil water. They reduced malaria through mosquito control and eliminated smallpox by compulsory vaccination. By 1914, the year after Taft left the presidency, Manila's death rate had dropped to twenty-three per thousand population—nearly half of what it had been when he first landed in the city.

The renovation of Manila eventually became one of Taft's pet projects. A vogue for urban renewal, dubbed the City Beautiful movement, was then sweeping America, promoted by reformers who believed that grimy industrial areas could be redeemed through an esthetic revival. Captivated by the idea, Taft decided to apply it to Manila as part of his Philippine economic plan. He gave the commission to Daniel Burnham, the celebrated architect whose achievements included Manhattan's daring Flatiron building and the splendid Washington mall stretching from the Potomac River to Capitol Hill. Taking advantage of Manila's unique natural location, Burnham laid out wide plazas, broad boulevards and spacious parks in a majestic arc facing the magnificent bay. A young aide, William E. Parsons, designed landmarks that still stand, among them the Manila Hotel, the Army and Navy Club and an array of pseudo-Grecian government buildings of the kind that grace Washington. Just as the Spanish had made Manila the symbol of their imperial power in Asia, so the United States turned the city into the emblem of its Pacific presence.

The "Pearl of the Orient" was the luminous label pinned on Manila by tourist promoters. For Americans who could tolerate the heat, it was a pleasant town around the turn of the century. The New York Medical Journal even judged its climate to be healthier than that of Chicago and Philadelphia. Most of its five thousand American residents were civilian and military officials, representatives of U.S. corporations or private entrepreneurs. As anywhere, status and money counted. Bureau chiefs, top army and navy officers, company managers and successful businessmen occupied lavish villas set amid luxuriant gardens, with legions of servants at their constant beck and call. Even junior employees reveled in colonial privilege—as one confessed to an American writer. "If I were working back in the States, we couldn't live like this—a big house, two barefooted Filipinos in white waiting on us, a yard boy, a chauffeur, a Chinese amah for the baby. . . . I clap my hands loudly for service or yell 'Boy!' or 'Psst!' and the Filipinos jump to wait on us. Back home I could never afford all this."

Manila's rhythm, as befits the tropics, was leisurely. Americans rose early, spent the morning at their offices, took a siesta after lunch, returned briefly to their desks and quit at four or five in the afternoon. They might then listen to the daily band concert at the Luneta, go horseback riding along the beach, or play golf, tennis or polo before drinks at their clubs as the sun set in a splash of effulgent colors. Evenings offered dinners and bridge parties, the opera or a touring vaudeville show, or perhaps that new form of entertainment, the cinematograph. For a livelier night, there was the Santa Ana Cabaret in suburban Pasig, owned by a New Yorker of Italian descent named John Canson, who owes his admirable epitaph to the historian Lewis E. Gleeck, Jr.: "He never watered his liquor and his girls never rolled a customer." A reception at Malacañang, the U.S. governor's residence, superseded all other social engagements.

"Manila is the most thoroughly typical American city I have ever visited outside the United States," declared Edwin W. Stephens, a Missouri editor, in an interview in the *Manila Times* in February 1908. Other Americans would have agreed. Manila was home away from home.

The *Manila Times,* one of four newspapers edited by and for Americans, first appeared in early 1900 and is still published in English under Filipino direction. A vintage advertisement introduced a Dr. Stevens, a "painless dentist" with the "only laughing gas" in town. Adolpho Roensch and company announced the arrival of "American shoes, crushed caps and crush hats, styles Fedora, such as are worn in New York and Washington during the summer." The latest Caruso records were on sale at Erlinger and Galinger, authorized distributors for Victor gramophones, while Heacock's plugged Elgin watches. Ike Beck's American Bazaar, true to its name, stocked Kellogg's Corn Flakes, Ivory Soap and Borden's canned milk among its U.S. imports. Before the Manila Hotel opened in 1912, the Waldorf claimed to have the best accommodations—at a dollar and a half a day for room and board. On steamy mornings, American officials and businessmen would drift over to Clarke's ice cream parlor to sip coffee and trade gossip under the purr of ceiling fans, as though they were back in New England or the Middle West. Years later, an American woman who spent her adolescence there recollected that, yes, there was a difference between the American high school in Manila and her children's high school outside Boston: "It was too hot for us to have a football team."

But its American veneer only transparently veiled large areas of Manila that were—and are still—an urban jungle without electricity, plumbing and other modern facilities. And behind the monumental façade, Americans regarded the Filipinos, rich or poor, as racial inferiors.

The prejudice was frequently subtle. W. Cameron Forbes, one of Taft's successors as governor, was widely admired for his decency. But once, advising a colleague to hire a male Filipino secretary, he added that the native "need not live in the house." Many esteemed Americans, by contrast, derided Filipinos openly. The Episcopalian bishop Charles H. Brent remarked that despite their "awakening" by the United States they had yet to learn "how to dress themselves." Frederick O'Brien, the editor of *Cablenews,* one of the city's American newspapers, called them a people "without initiative" mired in a "slough of ignorance and sloth. Though the Americans acclaimed elections as a step toward democracy, the *Manila Times* lamented when Filipinos took over the municipal council in 1908 that the capital would henceforth be governed "by men with whom we decline even to brush elbows in the street."

The racial bias went beyond words. Taft, denouncing the "blind folly and weak viciousness" of bigotry, regularly invited upper-crust Filipinos to formal functions at the Malacañang palace. But neither he nor other Americans in Manila at the time would invite the same Filipino notables to their clubs, the center of their social life, much less have them as members.

A classic colonial institution, in the Philippines as well as in European possessions, clubs generated complicated psychological contradictions in the relationship between the rulers and the ruled. They evolved from the natural impulse of Westerners in an alien land to create a familiar enclave in which they could share their own culture, speak their own language, even eat their own food. But clubs soon became racial bastions behind whose barricades whites could defend their sense of supremacy. And that, paradoxically, was their magnet for the native elite, for whom access to the sanctum of their imperial masters meant validation as equals. George Orwell depicted the phenomenon brilliantly in *Burmese Days*. For Dr. Veraswami, the Indian physician, election to the club would signify his acceptance as the equivalent of the figure he most admired—the English gentleman.

Older Filipinos may have mellowed over time, or perhaps pride prevents their admitting that prejudice troubled them. Whatever the reason, many later looked back on discrimination with an unusual lack of rancor. Maria Kalaw Katigbak, whose father was a noted writer, denied to me in an interview in 1987 that her upper-class family had ever felt any resentment toward Americans. "We had nothing in common with them anyway," she recalled. Nor did the issue seem to annoy the contemporary Filipino press, which tended to treat it more ironically than abrasively. In 1912, for instance, the Spanish-language newspaper *La Vanguardia* caricatured the American as a "man of a superior race [and] of almost supernatural character . . . white, rich, powerful, armed, wise and feared." The essay added sarcastically, "Fortunately for the natives, he is so paternal and good-hearted."

Filipinos were barred from the Elks, and except as servants denied entry to the Army and Navy Club, whose lovely garden of bougainvillea, palms and flame trees faced Manila Bay. They could not play golf at the Manila Club or belong to the University Club, created by Taft for leading American civilians. Nor were they welcome at the Columbia Club, which Bishop Brent had founded as an American social center. Not until 1936, a year after his election as president of the autonomous Philippine commonwealth, was Manuel Quezon granted honorary membership to the Polo Club.

The Polo Club had been founded in 1909 by Forbes, a keen sportsman. The toniest spot in town, it was the venue for such smart occasions as the later visit of the Prince of Wales to Manila. Finally, after twenty-two years of white exclusivity, its barriers fell in 1936 after the membership committee rebuffed two *mestizos* proposed by the four Elizalde brothers—world-class polo players of Spanish origin and scions of one of the wealthiest families in the Philippines. The Elizaldes were outraged, perhaps less out of liberal indignation than because their honor had been slurred. In any case, they promptly organized a desegregated club, the Tamaraw, which was just as snooty socially as the Polo Club had been racially. The Polo Club thereupon erased its color line, and thus snobbishness triumphed over prejudice.

American women in Manila largely set standards. Like the British *memsahibs* of India, they were determined to preserve their code of conduct in a foreign land—which did not include social ties with the natives, regardless of rank. Frances Parkinson Keyes, the wife of a U.S. senator, was shocked to discover during a trip in 1927 that longtime American women residents of Manila had "never entered a Filipino home" and so shut themselves off from people "of culture, refinement and intellect." Florence Horn, a writer, found American wives in the city remarkably similar to "the station-wagon set in Westchester county" as they whirled through hectic schedules of bridge parties, receptions and dinners—with other Americans. The only Filipinos they knew were their servants, whose foibles they discussed constantly in a tone of "contempt . . . that almost reaches fear."

Like Americans in America during those years, Americans in Manila were repelled by racial intermarriage. And they were equally hypocritical on the subject. Just as Americans at home discreetly accepted illicit liaisons between white men and black women, especially in the south, so Americans in Manila tolerated compatriots who kept a native *querida,* or mistress—a practice common among Filipinos. Indeed, it was no secret years later that General Douglas MacArthur had an exquisite *mestizo* girlfriend. But matrimony was taboo—and in that respect the Americans were less progressive than their European colonial contemporaries. A Frenchman married to a Vietnamese elevated her to his social level, and a Javanese woman gained status from her Dutch husband. Americans wed to Filipino women, by contrast, were ostracized by the U.S. community. They were "squaw men," a pejorative tag tacked on whites who married Indians back home.

Ironically, to many Americans, intermarriage seemed more sinful than did cohabitation. A spirited exchange on the topic enlivened the letters column of the *Manila Times* in 1907, after a Mrs. Lingo Lyon denounced intermarriage as "evil." One American sardonically responded that his Filipino wife "knows what a toothbrush is, and wears shoes and stockings," and another invited Mrs. Lyon to visit his "native señorita" and their "half-caste pickaninnies." But a Filipino woman clinched the debate. "I am married to an American," she wrote, "and think that every woman should be proud of her husband, whatever his color."

Mrs. Lyon's reference to "evil" typified the piety of many American do-gooders. A Judge W. A. Kincaid, founder of the Moral Progress League, battled prostitution and other depravities until his campaign fizzled amid disclosures of his intemperate drinking. The Manila Women's Club and the Young Men's Christian Association, among other American groups, also fought against sexual laxity. The crusades were futile. The Filipinos, like Latin Catholics, observed a double moral standard, and pursued their vices behind various masks that eluded prudish Americans. In 1926, for example, the Filipino majority on the Manila municipal council voted to license dancing schools as an antidote to brothels. But the schools were actually disguised bordellos, as evidenced by a realistic regulation requiring the woman teachers to be examined periodically for venereal disease. A recent reform mayor died in the saddle in a Chinese whorehouse where, he would quip, he regularly repaired for "afternoon tea."

But if Manila never acquired more than the cosmetic look of a U.S. city, the Americans did give the Philippines a carbon copy of a town back home. Baguio, nestled in the mountains nearly two hundred miles north of Manila, was another of Taft's innovations—and it remains to this day a charming remnant of the U.S. presence in the archipelago.

Taft was tormented by the torrid Manila weather from the moment of his arrival in June 1900. Hardly had he landed, in fact, than he concluded that the city's American community needed a cool retreat like Simla or Darjeeling, the British hill stations in India. He asked Dean Worcester, a member of his commission, to find a spot. Worcester dug out an old Spanish medical report that claimed that the climate of mountainous Benguet province "benefited and in many instances cured . . . anemia, malaria, inflammation of the kidney, digestive diseases, asthma, neuralgia caused by malaria, chronic catarrhs of the bladder and urinary tracts" as well as "nostalgia and hypochondria." Without further research, he formed a party to explore the area.

There, atop a plateau of green meadows and pine groves, he discovered a village known as Baguio, its population a clan of Igorots and a bizarre German scientist named Otto Scheerer, who had gone native after a broken marriage. After the climb from the steamy tropics below, Worcester wrote, the "delightful cold breeze" that swept the landscape "literally dumbfounded" him. And he noted, with the judicious eye of a realtor, the "scores of places where, in order to have a beautiful house lot, one need only construct driveways and go to work with a lawn mower."

Taft, elated, commissioned Daniel Burnham to turn Baguio into a summer capital. Burnham took the job without a fee—"for the sake of the poetic thing itself," as he said. Taft also ordered a road built to the site, a span of twenty-eight miles from the main route, entrusting its completion to Cameron Forbes, then a young U.S. official in Manila. Baguio appropriately means "storm" in the local dialect. Bedeviled by typhoons, the road ultimately cost $3 million, a vast sum for the time, as four thousand coolies worked for a decade to hack through the dense mountain jungles. At one stage, though sick with dysentery, Taft inspected the road, finally reaching Baguio, whose bracing air reminded him of the Adirondacks. Enthusiastic, he dictated a cable to Root in Washington: STOOD TRIP WELL. RODE HORSEBACK TWENTY-FIVE MILES TO FIVE THOUSAND FEET ALTITUDE. Root, visualizing Taft's girth, replied, HOW IS HORSE?

Baguio was too far from Manila to serve as a summer capital, but it became truly American. Indeed, except for the odd Igorot wandering through its streets, it might have been a resort in the Berkshires or upstate New York. As Worcester had foreseen, rich Americans constructed large gabled houses set behind deep lawns. Bishop Brent opened a boarding school along New England lines, denying admission to native and even *mestizo* boys with the specious argument that he was preparing American students for U.S. universities. In 1910, a group of prominent Americans also founded an American country club. Forbes wrote the prospectus, promising a golf course "equal to the finest in Scotland," with "great fireplaces in which pine logs will crackle merrily night and day." The club lived up to his blurb. American women in silk gowns graced its Saturday-night dances and, along with their husbands or fiancés, appeared in sensible tweeds at Sunday tiffin. In contrast to Manila practice, the Americans invited a token number of wealthy Filipinos to join the club, and several built vacation homes in the area.

An American flavor still pervades Baguio. Streets commemorate American governors, among them Francis Burton Harrison and Leonard Wood, and a park honors Burnham. A Philippine army camp, still bearing the name of McKinley's secretary of state, John Hay, once ignited a marathon legal battle. The Americans had seized the site from an Igorot chief, Mateo Carino, who sued the U.S. government. Five years later, in February 1909, the Supreme Court ruled in his favor—Justice Oliver Wendell Holmes stating that America's "first object" in the Philippines was to "do justice to the natives, not to exploit the country for private gain." In addition to receiving a $5,000 award, Carino proved that U.S. law had a long arm.

William Cameron Forbes was more than a Baguio booster. During his nine years in the Philippines, four of them as governor, he made the transportation system a priority—prompting the Filipinos to call him *el caminero,* "the road builder." He also concentrated on the economy as a whole.

Forbes is remembered in Manila today only by an exclusive residential district named for him. Even more than Taft, however, he adopted the Philippines as his personal responsibility. One of his "most important functions in this world," he later wrote, was to care for the Filipinos "in the manner that I felt best for them, regardless of whether they liked it or not." Unlike his colleagues, who shunned the label, he considered himself a career colonial civil servant, almost in the British mold. His models included British imperial giants like Lord Cromer, the viceroy of Egypt, and he admired Kipling. But he personified an American of the industrial age. Iron, steel and coal, speed, efficiency, modernization and economic growth, he maintained, were the engine that drove human progress.

A confirmed bachelor, prematurely bald, Forbes was a small, taut man with obsessive energy. He worked tirelessly and expected the same of his staff, unwinding in intense physical activities like polo and hiking. His journals flexed with muscular phrases of the kind that rippled off Teddy Roosevelt's robust pen. He was constantly "slashing away" at problems and "crashing through" to solutions, and a tribute that he once addressed to American officials in the Philippines might have been autobiographical. They labored to the "limit of their capacity" with "loyalty, enthusiasm, diligence and the spirit that wins," yet received "little appreciation" from the Filipinos, and only "half-hearted support" from an "ungrateful government at home." But his personality was precarious. Peter W. Stanley, a historian of the Philippines, has suggested that Forbes may have been driven less by his mission than by "a compulsion to measure up . . . to the dynamic pattern set by his ancestors."

His patrician forebears fused the two predominant strains in Boston brahminism: intellect and commerce. Ralph Waldo Emerson, his maternal grandfather, represented the former, but Forbes leaned toward his father's lineage. His paternal grandfather, John Murray Forbes, was a shrewd banker who had earned a fortune in the China trade, and his father had been a founder of the Bell Telephone Company. Forbes was a frail youth who, like the young Roosevelt, strengthened his body through strenuous swimming and riding. A superb football player at Harvard, he remained in Cambridge after graduation as a varsity coach, then joined an accounting firm and, in his early thirties, inherited the family bank. At that stage, a multimillionaire, he underwent a conversion common to flush businessmen. He decided to join the government. Taft, now secretary of war, offered to put him in charge of commerce and police for the Philippines under Luke Wright, the new governor. Roosevelt, a Harvard man who liked Harvard men around him, exhorted Forbes to enlist. "It is doing some of the world's work," he said. "It is more important work than you can get otherwise."

Though keen to go, Forbes canvassed his Boston friends and associates for their opinions. Most, though averse to overseas ventures in that crucible of anti-imperialism, urged him to accept. William James, the philosopher, had doubts: "Nurse no extravagant ideals or hopes," he wrote. "Be contented with small gains, respect the Filipino soul whatever it prove to be, and try to educe and play upon its possibilities for advance rather than stamp too sudden an Americanism on it. They are abysses of crudity in some of our popular notions in that direction that must make the Almighty shudder."

Forbes ignored the advice. No sooner did he arrive in Manila in August 1904 than he had already formed a judgment about Filipinos who favored an end to American rule: "They want independence," he confided to his diary, "very much as a baby wants a candle, because it is held out to him." As for those who championed autonomy under U.S. protection, they cynically sought "the honor, the patronage and the salaries," while leaving to America the "expense of keeping an army here to suppress the wild tribes, the Moros and insurrection [and] to keep off the Japanese and Germans."

Too civil to show his personal feelings, Forbes treated the Filipinos politely, and they appreciated his courteous style. But he never changed his preconception of them as credulous, crafty and opportunistic. Still, having committed himself to their welfare, he indefatigably pursued that goal—his own "white man's burden."

Philippine nationhood, he insisted, depended on a sound economy. And, spurning abstract theories, he told Filipinos to focus on "practical questions" rather than on self-government or independence. He would set the example, he pledged, by helping people "to better their conditions, to increase the products, of rubber, hemp, sugar, tobacco, lumber and other things, by which money can be made." In a flight of fancy, he foresaw a day when the natives would "crowd around me" to suggest ways to "live better, have better houses, better food and better clothes." He appealed for "fifty or a hundred first-rate American businessmen with ample capital" to invest in the country, and thereby "do more toward real civilization than I can express." The *Manila Times,* the voice of U.S. interests, seconded him with a string of alliteratives. "We have always been for more rice than reasons, more meat than manifestoes, more hemp than harangues, more potatoes than politics."

★ ★ ★

Improved transportation ranked high in Taft's plan for the Philippine economy. Like other Americans of his time, he believed that the United States owed much of its phenomenal growth to its rail network, which expanded twentyfold during the nineteenth century to cover almost two hundred thousand miles. It reached into nearly every corner of the nation, stimulating agriculture, industry, trade and, above all, national unity. The sole railway in the Philippines, by contrast, was a quaint kind of Toonerville Trolley owned by a British syndicate, which ran for only a hundred miles north from Manila to Lingayen Gulf. American investment in new rail lines, Taft wrote in the sonorous tones of a tourist brochure, would "revolutionize life and business in these wonderfully rich, beautiful and healthy islands." He also proposed modern port facilities for Manila, Cebu and Iloilo, where ships unloaded their cargoes onto lighters at sea for lack of docks, cranes and breakwaters—a risky operation in rough weather. Many foreign shipping firms either boycotted the Philippines or charged exorbitant freight rates, with damaging consequences for the economy.

Another legacy of Spain's neglect was the desperate need for roads. At the time of the American arrival, the entire archipelago had only about three hundred miles of what were generously termed "first-class" rural roads. The rest were dirt tracks that turned into impassable bogs during the wet season. Sir John Bowring, a British traveler of the 1850s, eloquently described the countryside under the torrential tropical rains: "I have seen beasts of burden struggling in vain to extricate themselves, with their loads, from the gulf into which they had fallen, and in which they were finally abandoned by their conductors. I have been carried to populous places in palanquins whose bearers, sometimes sixteen in number, were up to their thighs amidst mire, slough, tangled roots, loose stones and fixed boulders." John Foreman, a British resident of Manila, reckoned forty years later that rain regularly closed sixty percent of the roads to vehicles. Emphasizing the obvious, Taft declared that without roads "people are necessarily savages, because society is impossible and . . . real progress is retarded."

Forbes began to translate Taft's lofty statements into action. To stimulate interisland trade, he commissioned American and Filipino contractors to build breakwaters, warehouses and wharves in Manila, Iloilo and Cebu to enable even big ships to enter the harbors instead of unloading their cargoes at sea. But his "magnum opus," as he noted in his journal, was to be a modern road system that opened up new farming areas, gave peasants access to markets, and would spur them to switch from subsistence agriculture to cash crops. He approached the problem scientifically, calibrating such complicated details as the ratio of traffic to maintenance costs. Then, as if he were launching a project in the United States, he plunged forward zealously.

Movement in the Philippines was slow, however. Local Filipino officials rejected his plan to draft workers—a measure reminiscent of the labor gangs mobilized by the Spanish—and years slipped by before he could raise money for roads through higher taxes. He should have remembered Kipling's epitaph to the "fool who tried to hustle the East," but the delays strained his patience. Eventually, though, he achieved results. By 1913, when he retired as governor, he had quadrupled the number of first-class roads to a total of thirteen hundred miles and completed or improved three thousand miles of minor roads.

Constructing railways would be even harder. As early as 1901, the Taft commission had contemplated a rail web covering a thousand miles of Luzon and five hundred miles on Mindanao—to be constructed by private American companies with U.S. government guarantees on their investment. Sir William Van Horne, the American-born founder of Canadian Pacific, soon conceived a more ambitious scheme for an integrated rail and shipping grid linking the major islands. The proposal mildly attracted such railway magnates as E. H. Harriman of Union Pacific and J. P. Morgan, whose holdings included New York Central. Typical of the "robber barons" of the period, they preferred the certain profits to be made at home to the perils of committing capital abroad, and were reluctant to subscribe until Congress actually approved the underwriting.

The issue split Congress. The House of Representatives, deferential to railway lobbyists, granted the companies assurances of financial security and complete freedom from supervision in the Philippines. But the bill was blocked in the Senate by Democrats and Republican reformers, who opposed privileges for private business in general, and particularly detested the powerful railway trusts that had marauded the western states. As the debate dragged on, Harriman, Morgan and even Van Horne backed out. Two syndicates finally won franchises, one for Luzon and the other in the Visayas, and they were to flounder for lack of funds. They did expand the Philippine rail system from a hundred to more than six hundred miles during the next decade—far short of the grandiose plan to span the archipelago.

Taft had also expected liberal incentives to induce U.S. companies to put capital and technical skill into Philippine mining, logging and agriculture. Everyone would presumably benefit—the American firms from the return on their investments, the Filipinos from the "trickle down" effect of American profits. Again, the experience would duplicate the successes at home, where Americans derived their prosperity from bold entrepreneurship. All hinged on granting American investors in the Philippines generous concessions to justify, among other things, their "expenditure of large amounts for expensive machinery and equipment." Early in 1902, during his Washington visit, Taft laid his plans before Congress—which proceeded to nibble them to shreds.

Fired by his own enthusiasm, Taft imagined dynamic U.S. companies tapping the "magnificent mineral possibilities" of the archipelago: gold, copper, iron and coal deposits long neglected by the Spanish. But Congress regarded the giant U.S. mining corporations to be as rapacious as the railway trusts and refused them privileges. Among other restraints, they would be limited to one claim on the same lode. Thus discouraged, American prospectors filed only eight thousand claims during the first decade of U.S. rule, most of them small.

As in every gold-rush story ever told, the luckiest American failed to cash in on his strike. Nils Peterson, a Dane by birth, had tried mining in California before joining the U.S. Army at the outbreak of the war with Spain. Sent to the Philippines, he heard tales of abandoned Spanish lodes awaiting rediscovery, and the yarns rekindled his dream of hitting it rich. He stayed on after the war, trekking the islands for four years in quest of gold. Finally, in the jungles of Benguet province, Igorot tribesmen led him to a spot where they panned the streams for nuggets from which they carved amulets. The site seemed to be promising, and he persuaded Met Clarke, the proprietor of Manila's popular ice cream parlor, to grubstake him in return for a majority share. By 1911, he had a mine and a simple amalgamation mill working. He also cut out a road to nearby Baguio, and other Americans pledged investments. A series of typhoons then swept the area. The mine crumbled and the mill washed away, along with the offers of money. To top it all, Clarke went broke. His creditors, including a bank owned by the Catholic archdiocese of Manila, liquidated his assets to collect their debts—except for the jinxed mine that nobody wanted. Clarke died poor soon afterward. Peterson, equally penniless, went home in 1917 to rejoin the army as America entered World War I. But instead he succumbed to pneumonia, leaving his widow, Mary, destitute—at least for a time.

Clarke's creditors had meanwhile turned to "Judge" John W. Haussermann, a Manila lawyer, to save the cursed mine. He agreed—and became the Midas of the Philippines as well as its richest and probably most influential American.

At the peak of his wealth in the 1930s, Haussermann was a portly man with pudgy fingers, silver hair and a white mustache—a patriarchal appearance deliberately cultivated to lend credibility to his lofty pronouncements. The contemporary press canonized him as a Horatio Alger hero who had succeeded through hard work, perseverance and thrift, and even before the Xerox age he always had stacks of fuzzy Photostats of the adulatory articles to hand out to visitors. But he lived modestly despite his immense fortune, professing that he was merely God's "trustee for the worldly goods that He has given me." An ardent Republican, he regularly led the party's Manila delegation to the presidential conventions to lobby against Philippine independence. The natives, he argued, could never recover from "the end of Anglo-Saxon influence" if America withdrew from the archipelago. The Filipinos nevertheless admired his affluence and authority, which had after all contributed significantly to the economy. In 1954, not long before his death at the age of ninety-five, the Philippine government decorated him.

The son of a Cincinnati meat dealer, Haussermann was a young attorney in Kansas when America declared war on Spain. He enlisted, went to Manila as an army lawyer and arrogated for himself the bogus title of "judge." Electing to remain there in private practice, he had drafted the legal documents for Peterson and Clarke, and accepted shares in their mine in lieu of a fee. So it was logical for their creditors to ask him, as the only solvent stockholder, to salvage the defunct enterprise. He raised fresh capital, resurrected the mine, imported modern equipment, increased production, opened new mines elsewhere in the country and expanded into logging. With much fanfare contrived to gild his benign image, he gave his workers free rice, houses, schools and clinics. Ironically for a Republican, he owed his breakthrough to a Democratic president, Franklin Roosevelt, who in 1933 hiked the price of gold to $35 an ounce. Philippine gold production surged, and so did Haussermann's profits. By the end of the decade, his company had produced $150 million worth of gold and paid $35 million in dividends—fabulous sums in those lean Depression years.

Haussermann himself piled up millions, and even the heirs of an investor who had fluttered a few hundred dollars at the start would now be millionaires. The corporation, currently Benguet Consolidated, has long been listed on the New York Stock Exchange. Haussermann would be astonished by its present directors—Filipinos in three-button suits and button-down shirts who absorbed their "Anglo-Saxon influence" at Ivy League business schools.

Peterson's widow, affectionately known to Manila high society as "Aunt Mary," recouped smartly. She married Jan Marsman, a stout Dutchman who had come to the Philippines in 1920 to sell sugar machinery. Parlaying some of her late husband's claims into a gold-mining firm that became second only to Benguet, they went into trucking, trading and real estate, and reached out to Hong Kong and Indonesia, then the Netherlands East Indies. Unlike Haussermann, who shunned showiness, Mary draped herself in diamonds at Manila parties. But she was equally at home in dungarees at mining camps, barking orders in the vernacular of a veteran prospector.

★　★　★

A potent blend of U.S. capital and enterprise, Taft also maintained, would modernize Philippine agriculture. And he felt that, with four fifths of the land in the archipelago in the public domain, Americans should be allowed to purchase or buy tracts of twenty-five thousand acres or more, especially in the sugar regions. It was elementary business. Only large holdings promised the profits that would induce U.S. companies to make large investments. Once again, he ran into snags in Washington.

By early 1902, Congress had begun to discuss so-called organic legislation to regulate U.S. rule of the islands. Henry Cabot Lodge, chairman of the Senate Committee on the Philippines, included Taft's land concept in the bill. Taft personally testified before the committee, explaining that his plan would attract American capital "without bringing about an abuse." The appeal fell flat.

Democrats like Edward Carmack of Tennessee, a strident anti-imperialist, predictably denounced the proposal as an invitation to "carpetbaggers" to pillage. Republicans whose states had been plundered by predatory real estate syndicates attacked the plan with equal fervor. The idea also aroused the wrath of senators from California, Colorado, Michigan, Nebraska and other beet-sugar-producing areas, which feared Philippine competition. Congress finally limited public land acquisitions by Americans in the islands to thirty-five acres for individuals and about twenty-five hundred acres for a company. Lodge, initially a champion of unchecked American investment in the Philippines, went along—explaining later that, after all, excluding speculators from the archipelago would preserve its "ultimate peace, prosperity and good government." A vindictive man beneath his jovial exterior, Taft never forgave him for the shift. Lodge, he wrote privately, had resorted to a "subterfuge" to protect his position on Capitol Hill.

So Congress, more out of self-interest than rectitude, saved the Philippines from U.S. agricultural exploitation. During the decade prior to 1913, Americans bought or leased a total of only some forty thousand acres of public land in the archipelago, and their later attempts to amend the curbs were blunted. Harvey Firestone, the tire mogul, had an exemplary experience. He visited Manila in 1926 in an effort to lease a half-million acres on Mindanao, whose location outside the seasonal typhoon corridor made it ideal for growing rubber. General Leonard Wood, at the time U.S. governor, pleaded his case with the Filipinos, who by then had become increasingly nationalistic and would only grant him the statutory twenty-five hundred acres. Similarly, the Goodyear tire company could never get more than a tract of that size on Mindanao, which it used as an experimental station.

But some Americans, operating within the restrictions, earned handsome if unspectacular incomes off the land. One, a Dr. J. W. Strong, was the unofficial potentate of Basilan, a remote island in the Sulu Sea south of Zamboanga. A traveler who visited him during the 1930s found a "serene, amazingly young-looking man" of sixty-five ensconced in a gracious white house framed by palms, tamarinds and flame trees, its lush garden radiant with bougainvillea, hibiscus and a dozen varieties of orchids. Married to a cheerful Filipino woman who had given him a sprawl of children, he warmly welcomed guests with the hospitality of a lonesome expatriate, serving them sundowners on his broad veranda—whose furniture included, along with the usual rattan armchairs and divans, a large refrigerator, which in those days symbolized affluence.

Strong had landed in the Philippines thirty years before as a U.S. Army dentist. Pressed into fighting cholera and typhoid in Zamboanga, he sailed over to nearby Basilan, where he bought two thousand acres for next to nothing and planted rubber. He employed local Muslims known as Yakans, who wore baggy pantaloons and bright turbans. Besides paying their wages, he provided them with food and medical care—but, despite his métier, did nothing to improve their teeth, which they filed down to stubs and painted black. He settled their disputes, and they revered him as their rajah. Though he was the largest single rubber producer in the archipelago, his yield rarely exceeded a million pounds a year—a driblet compared to the millions of tons then exported annually by, say, the French-owned Michelin plantation in Vietnam. He prospered, however, by selling his rubber either in America or in the Philippines under a trade umbrella that protected him against competition.

A few U.S. companies circumvented the restrictive land law, and disclosures of their maneuvers periodically ired Congress. The protests usually came from special-interest groups, but they reflected the extent to which at least some factions in Washington kept a sharp if partisan eye on the islands. Unlike the powerful viceroys who governed Europe's colonies, U.S. officials in Manila were constantly being held accountable to the authorities back home.

One case involved the former monastic estates purchased by Taft in 1903. Earmarked for sale to their tenants on the installment plan, the tracts had become a drain on the U.S. treasury in Manila, which was paying for their maintenance. Forbes flippantly suggested at one point that it would be cheaper just to give the farms away, but their status was vague under the land legislation. Late in 1909, however, agents for the American Sugar Refining Company secretly bid for fifty-five thousand acres that had previously belonged to the Catholic Church on the Visayan island of Mindoro. The *Washington Evening Star* broke the story, and a juicy scandal appeared to be brewing amid the familiar Washington swirl of disclosures and denials. Among other possible improprieties, Taft's brother Henry was a lawyer for the company.

The potential transaction seemed to be stuck in a legal snarl until Taft himself intervened. Though now president, he still regarded the Philippines as his personal preserve, and a major U.S. investment fit his original economic plan for the islands. He approved the sale of the plantation to the American Sugar Refining Company for some $300,000, roughly $40,000 more than he had paid for it. Many Americans saw the deal as a precedent, and rumors spread of other large estates on the market elsewhere in the archipelago. In Congress, however, representatives of the sugar-beet interests demanded an investigation, and they were backed by an assortment of other groups with causes to plead. But there was not enough former church property to make a fight worthwhile. For that reason, too, many U.S. firms were reluctant to become engaged in the dispute. The controversy soon faded away—at least in Washington.

In Manila, though, young Filipino leaders assailed the transaction. What riled them was less the deal itself than the fact that they had not been consulted. They were not so naïve as to deny the need for U.S. investment in the economy. But they contended that, unless they exercised control, big American corporations would carve up the country for their own benefit—and, in the process, block eventual Philippine independence. A rising Filipino politician, Sergio Osmeña, made the point in September 1910 in a lengthy memorandum to Taft's secretary of war, Jacob M. Dickinson, who was then visiting Manila. Osmeña agreed that "capital from without" was vital to develop the islands. However, "the invasion of that capital" would, "once invested here . . . be opposed to any change of sovereignty, because it will not consider itself to be sufficiently safe and protected, except under its own."

Osmeña, and other Filipino politicians then and later, were nationalists rather than agrarian reformers. They were not troubled by large estates as long as the land remained in Filipino hands. Indeed, many were in the pockets of the big property owners. Similarly, Congress did not apply its land curbs to private holdings, nor did U.S. governors in Manila tamper with the rural gentry, the pillars of stability. Thus wealthy Filipino clans, usually of mixed Spanish or Chinese origin, amassed fortunes that their heirs later multiplied.

Some of the biggest Filipino fortunes dated back to the sugar boom of the nineteenth century. During the 1860s, for instance, Eugenio Lopez acquired nine thousand acres of sugarcane fields on the island of Negros, and his descendants today control utilities, newspapers and television stations. The powerful Locsin, Lacson and Ossorio dynasties also grew out of Negros sugar. The Elizaldes, who claimed to be pure Spaniards, were the largest single exporters of Philippine sugar to the United States during the 1930s, and their assets extended into gold mines, insurance firms, timber companies, paint, wax and rope factories, a fleet of interisland ships and a cattle ranch. Corazon Aquino derives her wealth from her great-grandfather, José Cojuangco, a poor Chinese immigrant who by the 1890s had vast sugarcane fields among his fifteen thousand acres in Tarlac province, north of Manila.

The United States thus blocked Americans from plundering the archipelago, but did nothing to prohibit its exploitation by Filipinos. The old dynasties prevail to this day despite years of harassment by Marcos, who created his own oligarchy. They comprise roughly sixty families, which preserve a system that is still largely feudal. "The gap between the entitled few and the masses," historian David Joel Steinberg has observed, "is comparable to that of eighteenth-century France."

Taft was correct to argue that U.S. capital would spur Philippine agriculture. Hawaii's big sugarcane plantations, fueled by American money, became the most efficient in the world. Irrigated and mechanized, they produced record yields and also operated year-round, providing full-time jobs. Philippine sugar estates, by contrast, languished for lack of investment. Reliant on seasonal rains, they could function for only four months a year, leaving their labor idle for long stretches. The tractor symbolized the Hawaiian industry, while a barefoot little boy astride a lazy *carabao* personified the Philippines— and still does.

If Philippine sugar and other commodities thrived at all, however, it was only because of artificial U.S. trade policies. The sham stimulant superficially appeared to be inspired by American benevolence. But, over the years, it cemented the economy of the archipelago to the United States.

The Republicans, defenders of big business, had erected high tariff walls to shield U.S. enterprise against foreign competition. But Taft, bucking the party line, advocated an exception for Philippine products like sugar, hemp, tobacco and coconut oil. Grant those goods easy access to the United States, he reasoned, and the money to be earned from their cultivation would attract American investors to the islands. There were also political gains to be derived from the trade, he candidly told the Harvard Alumni Association in 1904. If the Filipinos could be made to understand that the American market offered them profits, he explained, they would surely prefer "some sort of bond" with the United States rather than "become independent and lose the valuable business that our guardianship . . . has brought to them."

Taft also conceived a formula to grant benefits to U.S. business in exchange. If Philippine agricultural goods were to be given an unlimited market in America, then American manufactured goods deserved an unrestricted market in the Philippines. But the arrangement, subsequently entitled "reciprocal free trade," transgressed every tenet of free trade. For, by imposing duties on the products of other nations entering the archipelago, it hiked their price and assured U.S. exporters a virtual monopoly in the islands. And all this, ironically, as the United States was piously proclaiming the Open Door policy in an effort to persuade the European powers to respect free trade with China.

The tariff issue was a legal labyrinth. In 1898, as an incentive to Spain to cede the archipelago, the United States had agreed to allow Spanish goods into the Philippines for a ten-year period at the same duties paid by Americans. To cut those duties would mean a serious loss of revenues. So U.S. business would have to wait for its exclusive market in the islands. At the same time, the problem of American tariffs on Philippine imports raised a basic constitutional question: What was the precise relationship between the United States and its new dominion? If the Philippines was a foreign land, its products would face the prevailing duties. But, as an integral part of the United States, its commodities would be exempt. In May 1901, the Supreme Court delivered—or rather evaded—a decision. For tariff purposes, the Philippines was neither "foreign" to nor "incorporated" in the United States. Thus it was the responsibility of Congress to pass special tariff legislation for the archipelago.

The ruling freighted the issue with politics, as Taft rediscovered in Washington in 1902, when he urged Congress to lower the duties on Philippine imports. Again he was caught in the crossfire of a partisan battle. The Democrats, though supporters of tariff curbs, refused to endorse his proposal, coming as it did from a Republican. The Republicans, though sympathetic to his appeal, refused to retreat from their high tariff doctrine. Both parties felt pressure from lobbyists for the beet sugar, tobacco and other interests, some of whom sounded hysterical in defense of their cause. In the end, Congress would go no further than to approve only a token twenty-five-percent cut in the tariff on imports from the Philippines.

Filipino producers, still suffering from the ravages of the war and natural calamities, continued to clamor for lower duties. The sugar planters of Negros, for example, warned that only reduced levies could save Philippine agriculture "from the ruin to which it is doomed." But Congress, deaf to the cries for help, repeatedly rejected tariff revision in the years ahead—for an obvious motive. The Filipinos were half a world away while agents for groups like the American Beet Sugar Association coursed the corridors of the Capitol, cautioning against competition from "cheap oriental labor," as one put it. As usual, the lobbyists were duplicitous. A spokesman for New England's tobacco industry publicly decried the dangers of lower duties yet privately confided to Senator Orville Platt of Connecticut that Americans would probably never acquire a taste for harsh Philippine cigars. After a few puffs, Platt coughed and concurred. Responsive to his constituents, however, he went on voting for high tariffs.

Spain's equal right to the Philippine market ended in 1909. American manufacturers, eager to corner the market, now pressed for the elimination of the Philippine tariff. However, Taft still insisted that the duties on Philippine goods entering the United States be slashed in return. To calm the fears of American beet-sugar and tobacco growers, he cited studies showing that their Filipino rivals could not produce enough to threaten them. Just elected president, he expected the influence of the office to work. But even a Republican majority in Congress was no guarantee of success.

The Philippine problem was only a footnote to the tariff debate of 1909—one of the major disputes in U.S. economic history. The pivotal question was whether America ought to maintain its prohibitive duties or adopt free trade. But a larger issue was at stake: Did the United States intend to play a broader world role or remain isolated behind its formidable tariff barriers?

The Republicans had vowed to shave the tariff during the last year's presidential campaign, partly at Taft's behest. He ran on that platform, arguing for competition, efficiency and ingenuity rather than protectionism. But the party was still split as Congress pondered new tariff legislation. The key figures on Capitol Hill were Nelson Aldrich, chairman of the Senate Finance Committee, and Sereno Payne, head of the House Ways and Means Committee. Another power, cranky "Uncle Joe" Cannon, was then in his fourth term as speaker of the House. Taft had little reason to trust them. Aldrich, a surrogate of the U.S. sugar refiners, had long favored high duties, and Cannon had stacked the House panel against the bill despite his promise to help Taft. Lobbyists of every stripe had joined the struggle as it dragged into the summer. Taft sweated in the heat of Washington as he had in Manila. Sometimes he would repair to his White House bedroom to wrap his huge torso in a silk kimono that, as he wrote to his brother Horace, made him look like a "Chinese idol."

The legislation, which finally passed in August, barely furthered Taft's cause. Of the two thousand items up for tariff revision, more than half remained unchanged, and the levies on some two hundred were actually raised. The United States was not ready for free trade. Taft signed the bill, but it left a schism in the Republican party that was to contribute to its defeat two years hence.

To Taft's delight, however, the law granted Philippine products duty-free access to the United States. American manufacturers had exerted pressure for the change, realizing as they did that only an unchecked U.S. market for Philippine goods would open the Philippines to limitless quantities of their goods. Forbes ecstatically wrote to Taft from Manila soon afterward that the economy was experiencing a "magical awakening" as peasants returned to formerly idle fields and commodity prices began to rise sharply. "From all over the islands comes the same story," he added in his journal, "better crops, more cultivation, better feeling and more prosperity." The statistics bore out his elation. Exports, most of them to the United States, increased forty percent during the next four years. By the 1920s, as expected, America was buying nearly every ounce of Philippine sugar and coconut oil shipped abroad in addition to most of the tobacco and hemp.

It was lopsided growth. The sugar kings of Negros and the coconut barons of Zamboanga flourished while the rice farmers of Luzon lagged in poverty. The Philippine economy, largely reshaped to supply the United States, was also headed for a roller coaster of boom and bust as it trailed the ups, downs, twists and turns of the American economy.

During World War I, for example, demand skyrocketed for coconut oil, which contains glycerin used in the manufacture of explosives. Forty new coconut-oil factories multiplied across the islands, amassing fat profits from the limitless demand. All collapsed after the war, but some resurfaced during the U.S. economic revival of the roaring twenties. Within a decade, however, the depression again spelled doom as the devastated American dairy industry protested that coconut oil, an ingredient in margarine, menaced butter. The cycle was to persist even after independence, when America for its own purposes imposed tight trade ties on the Philippines.

The American trade affected millions of Filipinos, many of whom probably had no inkling of their reliance on the U.S. market. They cut fibers to be woven into hats, collected tobacco to be rolled into nickel cigars and, on remote island beaches, gathered shells to be molded into buttons—all for American consumers. Cotton dresses, nightgowns and baby clothes, made in U.S. factories, were shipped to Manila to be embroidered by native women in slum shacks, then shipped back to be sold in U.S. department stores. The list could go on almost interminably of sugarcane laborers, coconut workers, rope weavers, gold miners, stevedores, insurance agents, bank clerks and the boy astride the water buffalo, every one of them dependent on the vagaries of the U.S. economy.

Equally perilous for the Philippine economy was the U.S. corner on imports into the archipelago. A stroll along the arcaded Escolta, the main shopping street of Manila, was like a stroll along Main Street in any American city. Its stores carried all the familiar American brands, and American agents elsewhere in the city sold such American durables as cars and refrigerators. Apart from dampening the development of even light Philippine industry, the U.S. import monopoly obliquely instilled a taste for expensive American articles in affluent Filipinos who might have otherwise been induced to practice a somewhat greater degree of austerity.

Taft, rejoicing in the apparent success of his laborious struggle to forge close trade links between the United States and the Philippines, confidently wrote to his wife that the new arrangement would "greatly clear up the difficulties of Philippine politics." He was wrong. Many Filipino politicians saw "reciprocal free trade" for what it was: a device to preclude Philippine independence by locking the archipelago into the American economic orbit. But the same Filipino politicians were equivocal about sovereignty, and the inconsistency of U.S. policy fueled their ambivalence. Passionate rhetoric poured forth from both sides of the Pacific during the years to come, yet the sound and the fury often signified uncertainty.

9. STUMBLING TOWARD SELF-RULE

★ ★ ★

Paralleling their educational and economic programs, the Americans pursued an ambitious effort to train the Filipinos to govern themselves. Once again, they were propelled by missionary zeal, hoping to convert their new protégés to their own exceptional system. But the political evolution of the Philippines under U.S. tutelage was to be a series of spasms, as priorities and personalities changed both in Washington and in Manila. The Americans soon discovered to their disappointment that, for all their benign intentions, they were never able to transplant their ideals in a society with totally dissimilar values.

A high moral purpose had inspired Elihu Root as early as the summer of 1899, when as McKinley's secretary of war he inherited the responsibility for shaping a policy for the new U.S. possession. It was the first time in history that America had acquired an overseas territory, and he studied Europe's colonies as possible models. None fit. So, he concluded, the United States would have to be guided by its own principles. Trusting reports from American army officers that the Filipinos were "little advanced from pure savagery," he considered it absurd to grant them the U.S. constitutional guarantee of "government by consent of the governed"—much less the right of self-determination. But America could not dismiss the "immutable laws of justice and humanity," whether at home or abroad. Thus he directed William Howard Taft to promote "the happiness, peace and prosperity" of the Filipinos in accord with "their customs, their habits and even their prejudices."

The same impulse motivated President Theodore Roosevelt, who echoed the martyred McKinley with his pious affirmation that "the justification for our stay in the Philippines must ultimately rest chiefly upon the good we are able to do." Taft similarly declared that it was America's duty to be "a blessing to the people of these islands," and Cameron Forbes injected a familiar evangelical note into the rhetoric of redemption when he wrote to a friend in Boston, "We are doing God's work here."

Taft assumed from the outset that the Filipinos, given internal autonomy and economic prosperity, would prefer a permanent connection with the United States to the perils of independence. He reduced the idea to a formula: Create a "well-ordered government" under U.S. tutelage, the islands would thrive and, logically, the Filipinos would not "want to sever the bonds between us and them." The problem, however, was to teach them to manage their own affairs.

Just as he had set up American schools to educate native pupils as Americans and persuaded American business to bring American enterprise to the archipelago, so Taft imagined a version of America's political structure for the Philippines. In January 1901, after seven months in Manila, he floated the notion to his commission. Quoting Alexis de Tocqueville's classic *Democracy in America,* he stressed the French writer's observation that America owed its sound government to a basic political unit, the town, and pointed to the "self-sustaining and self-administering" New England township as a paradigm: "The town government is the practical way of building up a general government. Make the town government autonomous so that the seeds of popular government might be sown there."

Taft's dream mirrored his belief that the elements that had gone into the making of the U.S. political system would yield the same results in the Philippines. But authority in America reposed on impersonal institutions, while power in the Philippines revolved around the complex kinship networks of the *compradrazgo* system.

In later years, borrowing American hoopla, Philippine political practices acquired a modern gloss. But little had fundamentally changed since Taft's cloudy dream of bringing New England democracy to the islands.

A typical Philippine town at the start of the century was managed by a few local landowners, merchants, lawyers, doctors and priests collectively known as the *principalía,* whose authority usually dated back to the Spanish era. One of them served as *presidente,* and the *principalía* supervised everything from tax collecting to law enforcement. As the sole voters, they perpetuated their power over the area's farmers, tenants, laborers, fishermen and artisans. James LeRoy, an early U.S. official, sketched a scene that scarcely resembled Tocqueville's America: "Imagine a rural community where only two, four or twelve families out of a population of ten thousand or more live in stone houses with wood floors, and the rest in cane shacks, dependent on those above them for employment or a piece of land to till, or the money advances inevitably needed each year to till it."

As in small towns everywhere, the leading local families had been squabbling forever. The introduction of elections by the Americans, however, simply formalized the quarrels as the competing clans created political parties as vehicles for their disputes. So old feuds masqueraded as modern politics. Like Philippine parties today, the factions were identical ideologically. They fought partly for prestige—but, more often, for the power to sequester land, steal tax receipts, demand kickbacks for licenses or hand out profitable and frequently fake public-works contracts to their relatives. Officials grew rich in subsequent years by pocketing funds allocated by the Manila government to develop municipalities.

Early in the century, when only literate landowners and taxpayers exercised the franchise, they chose officials through compromise and consensus. But, as the electorate broadened, politicians were compelled to campaign. Nevertheless, class prevailed as prominent families mustered their *compadres* and invoked *utang na loob,* the debts incurred for past favors. To win, a candidate had to persuade voters to shift loyalties—a tough task in a social structure where all the townsfolk were linked by kinship bonds to one faction or another. He would obviously not try to sway his rival's relatives. Nor, if he were running for mayor, would he attempt to convert the town treasurer, policeman or dogcatcher, who owed their posts to the incumbent—unless he had learned that they now bore a grudge against him. However, he would strive to influence the less committed by fair means or foul, from promising them jobs to buying their votes—both strong inducements to poor peasants and workers. He might form teams of "flying voters" to cast ballots in different precincts, or to register names off tombstones. His thugs might even threaten recalcitrant citizens with violence, or actually murder some as an example to others. "Gold, goons and guns" have long determined the outcome of Philippine elections.

Yet a code of honor ruled the game. During the 1950s, for instance, a landlord in one region of Luzon dispossessed a tenant who was campaigning for a rival party. The penalty not only abused the man's civil rights, but denied him his livelihood. Even so, the landlord felt that he had treated the tenant generously, and was justifiably owed fidelity. The tenant had violated the concept of *utang na loob,* and even the landlord's enemies agreed.

Such customs have been fading in Manila and other big cities, where the pressures of urbanization have naturally loosened loyalties. But tight kinship alliances are still alive in rural areas like Mindoro, an island in the Visayas, whose political hierarchy has not changed in a century. Its power elite, the Abelada clan, reaches back to an ancestor who arrived from Luzon in 1825. His descendants intermarried with other immigrants, so that one third of the present population of two hundred thousand are related. Strollers along the dusty main street of Mamburao, the capital, greet each other as *kang,* the local patois for brother, uncle, cousin or nephew. Family members have owned the island's rice fields and sugar plantations for as long as anyone can remember. They are also entrenched in public office, a key to their wealth. The dynasty supported Marcos until his ouster in early 1986, then nimbly accommodated to the Aquino camp. During legislative elections held later, the family split behind three rival candidates—two of them relatives and the third a clan surrogate. They realistically united behind the winner, however, thus assuring the dynasty's sway. Mindoro, an official frankly confided to a visitor, was still medieval: "Feudalism, that's what we have here. We have feudal families, feudal landlords and feudal politicians."

★ ★ ★

As early as the summer of 1899, Major General Elwell Otis, the crotchety U.S. military commander during the war against the Filipino nationalists, had prescribed municipal elections on the theory that the Filipinos, shown America's good will, would cooperate with his pacification campaign. Most could not have cared less, knowing as they did that the same elite would retain power. After establishing his civilian administration, Taft launched a larger program of political tutelage in response to Root's instructions to grant the Filipinos the "opportunity to manage their own local affairs to the fullest extent of which they are capable . . . consistent with the maintenance of law, order and loyalty." But basic contradictions, in himself as well as in the situation, were to bedevil the enterprise.

Tilted by racial prejudice, Taft privately lamented the "oriental duplicity" of the Filipinos, deploring their lack of "Anglo-Saxon" ethics. But he and his associates, who shared his views, were no more bigoted than most conservative Americans of the time—few of whom, for example, favored political equality for Negroes at home. Despite their disdain for the Filipinos, however, they accepted the premise that the archipelago could, under U.S. guidance, be steered toward self-rule. Taft named three *ilustrados* to his commission as window dressing—or, as he put it, "to show our desire to consult Filipino sentiment."

As an American convinced of America's superiority, Taft fervently hoped to ingrain Filipinos with American values. But he was nagged by doubts. Most Filipinos, he wrote to a friend, were unfit "by nature, education and moral stability" to serve on juries. Nor, he told Root, was it "wise to give too much power in the administration of provincial affairs to the native, until he is educated up to a greater care in the expenditure of money and greater probity in the letting of contracts." Despite his talk of bringing U.S. democracy to the Filipinos, therefore, he could not imagine them actually practicing politics in the American way—at least for years to come. "The masses are ignorant, credulous and childlike," he declared in late 1900. So "the electoral franchise must be much limited, because the large majority will not, for a long time, be capable of intelligently exercising it." Thus, though he scheduled new municipal elections, he limited suffrage to a handful of landowners and taxpayers. Other elections were to be held during the decade ahead, yet in none would more than three percent of the population vote.

Having been anointed by the Americans, the old families assumed that they could run their fiefdoms arbitrarily, and many flagrantly misused their authority, as they had under the Spanish. They squeezed bribes out of merchants, demanded tribute from peasants, embezzled tax revenues and pocketed funds earmarked for schools, roads and other public purposes. Native judges handed out stiff sentences to innocent rivals and exonerated guilty cronies.

By way of comparison, Taft would remind critics that Tammany Hall and other big city machines in the United States were hardly a "shining success." Still, he felt betrayed, baffled and embarrassed by the widespread abuses of Filipino officials, who had presumably been learning America's ideals, not its evils. His staff probed reports of misconduct, but enforcing the law was not easy. The Filipinos, enmeshed in coils of mutual loyalties, declined to testify against each other. Local magistrates were reluctant to try influential figures, and provincial governors refused to defy regional structures to whom they owed their power. The Americans, citing Root's instruction to Taft to respect "the customs, the habits and even the prejudices" of the natives, treated suspects leniently. James F. Smith, the U.S. governor in 1908, admitted his reticence to "remove officials who have been named by the people." Out of some twenty-five hundred Filipinos investigated for misbehavior during the first decade of the century, very few were convicted.

Taft, chagrined that the political experiment had fallen short of his aspirations, deplored the pervasive "tyranny" of Filipino officials who never understood that "office is not solely for private emolument." In 1913, as his presidency ended, he concluded in retrospect that he had gone "a little too rapidly in extending the political power of the native Filipino." But it eluded him that he may have been at fault in backing a selfish indigenous oligarchy primarily concerned with preserving its own privileges. Instead, he singled out the shortcomings of the system to caution against Philippine independence. Only the United States, with its "power and resources . . . to punish disturbances and maintain order," stood between stability and anarchy. For the Americans to abandon the archipelago to the Filipinos, he warned, would spark "a chaos of ever-recurring revolt and insurrection."

Taft's collaborators, the *Federalistas,* whom he had chosen to serve as America's surrogates, proved to be a disappointment. He had used the party to build support for the United States by funneling patronage into the provinces through its leaders, Trinidad Pardo de Tavera and Benito Legarda. Earnestly pro-American, they had championed statehood for the Philippines until Elihu Root deflated their dream during a conversation in Washington in 1904, when he crudely told them that "the Negroes are a cancer in our body politic" and to naturalize the Filipinos would "add another serious race problem to the one we have already." Now, for several reasons, their movement began to crumble.

They had antagonized Taft's successor as governor, Luke Wright, an amiable if tactless former Confederate officer and corporation lawyer. Pardo de Tavera derived much of his vast wealth from tobacco and Legarda's assets included distilleries, and they protested against Wright's decision to tax cigars and alcohol in an effort to make the archipelago financially self-sufficient. Wright accused them of seeking to feather their own nests, and they assailed his "profound contempt" for Filipinos. They were even more aggrieved when, dismayed by their party's internal rifts, he had ceased to employ them as a conduit for American patronage. Without U.S. money to disburse, they swiftly lost their popularity.

Alarmed that the political edifice he had left behind was collapsing, Taft sailed for Manila in 1905 to adjudicate the quarrel. He tried to placate his Filipino protégés by replacing Wright with James F. Smith, a devout Catholic who had first landed in the Philippines as a U.S. Army officer. But he had been away too long to grasp the changes that had occurred since his departure. The Americans had lifted an earlier ban against public agitation for independence, and educated Filipinos were becoming increasingly nationalistic. The *Federalistas,* having scuttled their statehood platform, joined in the clamor to salvage their political reputation. Renaming themselves the *Partido Nacional Progresista,* the label denoting their nationalism, they came out for eventual Philippine sovereignty—thereby shattering Taft's hope that they would be his spokesmen for an indefinite U.S. presence in the islands. However, they were no match for a younger Filipino political breed then emerging.

Two men represented the new species: Sergio Osmeña and Manuel Luis

Quezon y Molina. Born within a month of each other in 1878, they might have been taken for brothers. Both were slim and sinewy, with sharp, handsome features. And, like siblings, they were alternately friends and rivals. Quezon ultimately upstaged Osmeña, however, and has even effaced him from memory. Little was written about Osmeña, while Quezon has been exhaustively described, eulogized and vilified by colleagues, journalists and scholars in articles and books, including his self-serving memoir and a reverent biography that borders on hagiography. Except in his native Cebu, not a town or street throughout the islands now commemorates Osmeña. By contrast, Quezon's home province of Tayabas was renamed in his honor, and Quezon Boulevard reaches northwest from Manila into adjacent Quezon City, the formal capital of the Philippines. But together they dominated the political scene for almost the entire period of America's rule of the archipelago—despite diametrically different personalities.

Osmeña, part-Chinese, was as poised and unperturbable as a picture book. Yet his remote manner shrouded an inner warmth that sometimes hovered on sentimentality. Deeply loyal to his associates, he defended them at the peril of his own position. Nor could he bring himself to clash with his often emotional adversaries, whose pomposity he would puncture with subtle barbs rather than with frontal assaults. "I want you to know," an irate foe once warned him as he warmed up to an attack, "that when I get angry, I send everybody to hell—my wife, my children, everybody." Smiling gently, Osmeña responded, "That is terrible, but I never intervene in family affairs." His skill at compromise earned him the respect of U.S. officials. With monastic discipline, he would study an issue in detail before acting—a trait, observed one American, that made him "the master of every important problem." His plodding style, though, paled in the glare of Quezon's brilliance.

A Spanish *mestizo,* Quezon had the impulsive, mercurial, flamboyant temperament of a prototypical Latin. From one hour to the next he could be solemn, frivolous, petulant, gloomy, optimistic, generous, conceited—and yet he was, as one of his aides remarked, "sincere each time." Misquoting Emerson, he decried Osmeña's consistency as "the hobgoblin of a little mind," vaunting his own unpredictability as a virtue. "You can't find consistency in my speeches over a period of six months," he boasted to an American friend. "I run the risk of making myself look ridiculous, but I've discovered that the people rather like it when I come out and say in so many words, 'I've made a mistake.' " Politics to him was artifice, caprice, comedy. "The trouble with you," he lectured Osmeña, "is that you take this game of politics too seriously. You look too far behind you and too far ahead of you. Our people do not understand that. They do not want it. All they want is to have the present problem solved, and solved with the least pain. That is all."

If Osmeña impressed the Americans with his diligence, Quezon dazzled them with his virtuosity. Cameron Forbes, who was familiar with them both, wrote of Quezon that he had "the most brilliant mind of any Filipino that I know." Quezon understood, Forbes added, "that the United States is doing the right thing out here . . . and wants to help." Quezon's wiles exasperated Forbes and other U.S. officials—yet they begrudgingly respected his talents. "He is probably the most unscrupulous little person in the world [and] will knife you in the back," Forbes later noted. "But he can be extremely useful because he can get things done. The danger of using him is that each time you do so, you add to his power, which is a great power for evil as well as for good."

Florence Horn, an American writer of the 1930s, argued that most Filipinos favored politicians of Chinese origin, seeing them as fellow Asians, but suspected Spanish *mestizos* of preferring their white antecedents. Thus, she suggested, Osmeña's sense of psychological security accounted for his simplicity, while Quezon constantly sought to prove himself. Whatever the validity of the theory, Osmeña was in fact the epitome of sobriety and Quezon almost a paragon of ostentation. Osmeña dressed modestly. Inspired by the wardrobe of his friend Roy Howard, the American publisher, Quezon indulged in expensive silk shirts, bizarre hats and tight jodhpurs that flattered his lithe figure. Osmeña was abstemious. Quezon adored fine food and good liquor, balls, cabarets and all-night poker sessions with cronies in smoke-filled rooms. Osmeña shunned publicity. A natural actor, Quezon postured in the tradition of *palabas,* a Tagalog word meaning "showiness," often applied to the garish melodramas popular at village fiestas. Quezon would erupt in tantrums, melt into tears, then explode again—all for theatrical effect. The pattern has persisted. Marcos, a consummate performer, contrived elaborate legalisms to camouflage his chicanery, and his wife, Imelda, joined in with her vulgar extravagance and sleazy show-biz connections. Nor was *palabas* entirely absent from Corazon Aquino's role as Joan of Arc, campaigning with the sainted spirit of her dead husband against the satanic Marcos.

Osmeña, devoutly Catholic, was a model husband; Quezon, by comparison, was an obsessive libertine—to the anguish of his wife, who found solace in prayer and the Philippine law against divorce. His flirtations were frequently juvenile diversions devised to project his rakish image. Even in his twilight years, he liked to be seen in nightclubs with lovely damsels, swaying sensually to "La Comparsita," his favorite tango. But he was also a serious philanderer who "had always been fascinated by beautiful women of all ages and climes," as his biographer approvingly put it. Dean Worcester, who maintained a stable of spies, circulated a report of his "intimate relations" during an ocean voyage with a Chicago widow named Lillian Lynche. Such accounts only gilded his romantic image, however, and scores of women succumbed to his charms. The stunning British film actress Madeleine Carroll, whom he first met in Hollywood in 1937, pursued him to Washington and New York, bold behavior for those rather prudish days. As a souvenir of the affair she gave him a photograph of herself inscribed: *To Manuel, the prince of his people, from his make-believe princess.* Their glamorous romance contrasted sharply with the tawdry fling in the 1970s of Ferdinand Marcos and an obscure Hollywood starlet, Dovie Beams, who perversely taped and broadcast their acrobatics in bed, complete with kinky dialogue and heavy breathing.

There was an undeniable alchemy in Quezon's magnetism. An American woman who often danced with him recalled that "he had a way of holding you in the lower back and, with a touch of the spine, making you do just what he wanted." He also worked magic on men, manipulating even adamant enemies with abject apologies for his errors and poignant pleas for help "in this most crucial period of our history." Above all, he captivated crowds. Nattily garbed in khakis and pith helmet, he would enter a town adorned with triumphal palm and bamboo arches, mount a platform festooned with flags and deliver a marathon oration, his eyes moist with emotion, his voice modulating from soft tones of persuasion to peaks of passion. He often spoke in English, barely comprehensible to most of the people. But, oblivious to the time and the sun, they would listen for hours as his ardor kindled their sympathy. Osmeña's sincerity could not compete with such charisma.

Osmeña was born illegitimate. But the sins of fathers are not laid on children in forgiving Filipino families, and he was never stigmatized by his Chinese *mestizo* clan, one of the wealthiest in Cebu. Raised by his mother, he was put into the care of local Catholic priests, who recognized his potential. They enrolled him in a seminary and later sent him to Santo Tomás, the Catholic university in Manila, where he met Quezon, a classmate. After the war between the United States and Spain interrupted his studies, he returned to Cebu to try his hand as a free-lance journalist. Early in 1899, when fighting between the Americans and Filipinos broke out, he started a newspaper, *El Nuevo Día,* to represent the nationalist cause. Like most of the defeated nationalists, however, he shifted his fidelity to the United States—later writing with the fervor of a convert: "The Filipinos will never forget the inspiring spectacle of American soldiers leaving their guns and, as emissaries of peace and good will, with book in hand, repairing to the public schools to teach Filipino children the principles of free citizenship."

Turning to the law, Osmeña found patrons among the rich Chinese merchants of Cebu, who were always looking for talent to defend their interests. He was also hired as an aide by the local political boss, Juan Climaco, a former nationalist general who had been elected governor after defecting to the Americans. Tireless and dedicated, Osmeña could be trusted. When Climaco visited the United States in 1904, he appointed Osmeña acting governor during his absence and later named him regional prosecutor. Osmeña won plaudits for renovating Cebu City following a devastating fire—a job that entailed the negotiation of delicate property disputes caused by the disaster. American officials commended him to Forbes, who hailed Osmeña's "fine example of unselfish, constructive statesmanship." Bolstered by Climaco's support, the accolade propelled Osmeña into the provincial governorship. Soon he gained national status as head of a countrywide league of governors. By 1907, his political future was assured.

Quezon's more adventurous youth had all the ingredients of a picaresque novel—or so he embellished it in his own accounts. His father, a former soldier in the Spanish army, had migrated to Baler, a remote town in Tayabas, a province on the east coast of Luzon. He taught at the local school, wed the town's woman teacher and bought a small rice field to augment their slim income. Both Spanish *mestizos,* fluent in Spanish, they were treated as equals by the Spanish officers in the garrison and by the Spanish parish priest— thereby acquiring a social status higher than that of richer Filipino families. They sent Manuel to Manila at the age of nine, and there he remained for ten years, first at a Dominican school, and afterward at Santo Tomás, where he studied law. He witnessed Dewey's defeat of the Spanish fleet in Manila Bay on May 1, 1898, and watched American troops stage their sham battle for the city three months later. Like his parents, he supported the Spanish. Indeed, his father and a younger brother were slain by Filipino partisans while on a mission to procure supplies for the Spanish troops in Baler. Subsequently, as provincial prosecutor, Quezon avenged their deaths by having the killers imprisoned as "bandits."

It was a label that could have been pinned on him. Early in 1899, when the Filipinos and Americans went to war, he joined the nationalists as a guerrilla. The first shots stirred in him "an irresistible impulse to run away," he recalled, but a "sense of shame and humiliation, stronger even than the fear of death, brought me instantly back to myself." He fought for the next two years, mostly in the hills of the Bataan peninsula, rising to the rank of major. In one clash, he and his men ambushed a company of fifty U.S. troops, killing two whose bodies he himself buried. Combat was less of an ordeal than dysentery, malaria and hunger in the damp, mosquito-infested jungles—though the agony did not dim his lust for women. He wed a coffee-colored peasant beauty in a "revolutionary" ritual later annulled as illegal. When his commander ordered him to Manila to confirm the report that Emilio Aguinaldo, the nationalist generalissimo, had been captured, Quezon went to a nearby U.S. Army post, disclosed his mission and was sent under escort to Manila. Conducted to Malacañang palace, he was received by General Arthur MacArthur, who silently waved him toward a room where Aguinaldo sat in forlorn isolation. Quezon evoked the moment with typical pathos in his autobiography. "As I write these lines, forty-two years later, my heart throbs as fast as it did then. . . . My whole world had crumbled, all my hopes and dreams for my country were gone forever!"

Jailed for six months by the U.S. authorities in Manila on charges of murdering American prisoners, Quezon was finally released for lack of evidence. His health broken, he resumed his law studies and, in 1903, began to practice. Soon he returned to his native Tayabas province to recover his family farm, claiming that it had been stolen by one of his father's rivals. His political career was now about to be launched under the auspices of the area's U.S. officials.

Tayabas, later a lucrative producer of coconuts, was then a pristine backwater of 150,000 people. Bandits and dissident religious sects roamed its rugged mountains, which overlooked a fertile coastal plain of towns and estates dominated by a few rich families. Anxious to protect their interests, the powerful clans bent to the prevailing wind with astonishing flexibility. After serving the Spanish, they rallied behind the Filipino nationalists, then bowed to U.S. superiority. In March 1901, when Taft visited Lucena, the provincial capital, the town dignitaries greeted him with American flags, a huge portrait of President McKinley and an enthusiastic rendition of "The Star-Spangled Banner." As a further mark of fidelity, they urged Taft to name as provincial governor a singular U.S. Army colonel, Cornelius Gardner, whose comrades had ostracized him for criticizing their atrocities against the natives. Gardner bequeathed a legacy of paternalism to his successor, Major Harry H. Bandholtz, who along with Paul W. Linebarger, the U.S. district judge, and Colonel James G. Harbord, another American officer, were to be among Quezon's early mentors.

Bandholtz, a strapping, dynamic, self-confident West Pointer, was the local potentate. He had arrived in the Philippines in 1900 as an infantry captain of thirty-five after serving in Cuba. Assigned to Tayabas, he set up town councils composed of natives presumed loyal to the United States. He and his American wife might have been born to the tradition of colonial paternalism. Learning Spanish and some Tagalog, they befriended what they called the "better class" of Filipinos: the region's landowners, merchants, lawyers, doctors, priests. They invited them into their home, and regularly attended local baptisms, weddings, funerals and other rituals, developing unique insights into the complex kinship web that underlay the community's power structure.

A senior U.S. official in Manila dismissed Bandholtz as "first, last and all the time a politician." But the elite of Tayabas, out of genuine admiration, elected him governor of the province—the only American ever so honored in the Philippines. His carrot-and-stick technique of patronizing protégés and penalizing opponents earned him respect. He resigned in 1903 to take over all of southeastern Luzon as commander of the constabulary, the force comprised of Filipino troops and American officers. Yet he continued to exert immense influence in Tayabas, both by maintaining his headquarters in its capital and through a Filipino surrogate whom he had arranged to succeed him as governor.

Linebarger had originally landed in Manila as a soldier in the Wisconsin regiment after practicing law in Europe, and his experience naturally suited him for the judicial system being set up by the Americans as the war with the Filipinos wound down. Trading his uniform for a robe, he accepted a judgeship whose far-flung jurisdiction stretched from Tayabas south to the island of Mindoro. He had tried Quezon's suit for recovery of his father's farm. Impressed by Quezon's court performance, he not only ruled in his favor but offered him a job as prosecutor for the Mindoro district. He also introduced him to Bandholtz, who was always eager to meet bright young Filipinos. After all his troubles with the Americans, it now dawned on Quezon, as he confessed later, that they "were not as bad as I thought them to be." He realized as well that it was only through cooperation with them that he could fulfill his budding political ambitions.

His Mindoro sojourn was tumultuous. Within six months, he had been indicted for nine felonies, including the rape of a local girl, armed assault and suppressing evidence in a pending criminal case. He claimed to have been framed by the regional American army commander, who allegedly resented the presence of a Filipino prosecutor. Whatever the truth, he escaped punishment. Bandholtz and Linebarger, reckoning that his skills outweighed his faults, managed to save his skin by procuring him the post of provincial prosecutor for Tayabas.

There was a measure of condescension in their protection—as if they felt that Filipinos should not be held up to the same ethical scrutiny that applied to Americans. Even the puritanical Forbes disregarded Quezon's "extremely loose" morals as irrelevant. To their U.S. patrons, moreover, even Filipinos as gifted as Quezon required supervision, like children. Recommending him to a fellow officer, Bandoltz called Quezon "intelligent and influential," but cautioned that he needed "proper handling," since he was "young and liable to commit mistakes at any time [and] it is well to keep a paternal eye upon him to keep him from going astray."

Quezon also needed the right connections—the key to advancement in the boondocks. His father, a Spanish protégé, had not belonged to a regional clan, and he himself was an outsider. The Americans became his foster family. Bandholtz adopted him, taught him English and, as Quezon later wrote, "made me feel at home in his company." He also backed Quezon in a major legal fight.

The case involved the American publisher of a Manila newspaper, Francis J. Berry, whom Quezon prosecuted and convicted for illicit land deals in Tayabas. Berry, himself a lawyer, had hired a battery of American defense attorneys, and the trial loomed as the test of a Filipino's authority to pursue a powerful American. Quezon might have failed had not Bandholtz dredged up dirt damaging to Berry's reputation; Linebarger's role as judge also helped. The first Filipino to defeat an American in court, Quezon resigned to go into private practice as a prelude to politics.

Savoring his new prestige, he aimed for the governorship of Tayabas, due to be contested in an election scheduled for early 1906. He won after tricky maneuvers by his American patrons, who played Filipino politics instead of bringing New England town-hall democracy to the Philippines.

Governors were then chosen indirectly by an electoral college of town officials who gathered in their provincial capital. The conclave usually degenerated into a litigious roil as rival factions challenged each other's credentials. The verdict depended on a panel controlled by U.S. officials, but their decision required care. They could not afford to alienate the region's dynasties by endorsing an unpopular candidate. Nor were they themselves always unified.

Bandholtz, who had been reassigned to Manila late in 1905, ordered his successor, Colonel James G. Harbord, to promote Quezon. A shrewd soldier of forty, later to become chairman of the board of the Radio Corporation of America, Harbord plunged into the local political swirl. Quezon belonged to none of the leading clans and was opposed by the region's American teachers, who resented his association with U.S. military officers. Undaunted, Harbord sponsored his campaign and publicized a letter from Bandholtz, who had enormous prestige in the area, designating Quezon as his man. When the time came to convene town officials for the vote, Harbord mobilized U.S. Army trucks to carry his supporters to the provincial capital. Quezon, winning by a narrow margin, now set his sights higher as the United States prepared to raise the Philippine political stage to national dimensions.

★   ★   ★

Taft had envisioned a national Philippine assembly whose legislation would be subject to an American veto. It was to be, in his vision, a political academy in which the Filipinos would learn parliamentary procedures. Congress had approved the idea, President Roosevelt set an election date for 1907 and two main Filipino parties braced for the contest.

Despite his disappointment with them, Taft was rooting for the *Federalistas,* now the *Partido Nacional Progresista.* To James F. Smith, then the American governor, the party comprised the "most conservative, best educated and talented Filipinos in the islands," and he had no doubts about their influence. "When this body of men gets to work," he wrote to Taft, "it usually makes itself felt." But Forbes, Bandholtz and other U.S. officials discounted them as a spent force.

Their leaders, Pardo de Tavera and Legarda, were Manila figures. But America's new encouragement of local authority had shifted the center of power to the provinces, where fresh factions now represented influential regional clans. Mostly headed by younger men, they were supported by U.S. officials who encouraged the trend. Osmeña and Quezon personified the change. In March 1907, five months before the legislative elections, they fused a collection of bickering cliques into the *Partido Nacionalista*. Known as the *Nacionalistas*, they were to dominate Philippine politics for decades to come. They captured fifty-eight of the eighty seats in the infant assembly. The first parliament ever freely elected in Asia, it was a tribute to the liberalism of U.S. colonial rule.

American democracy it was not. With suffrage limited to landowners, taxpayers and the literate, only three percent of the population had voted. But at least the new legislature could claim continuity. Its members were the same *ilustrados* who had served the Spanish and U.S. administrations.

Traveling with his wife, Taft arrived in Manila in October 1907 to bless the assembly, which had gathered in the Ayuntamiento, an ancient Spanish building nestled inside the walled city. The spacious hall, draped with American flags, might have been located anywhere in the United States. Taft, perspiring profusely in a rumpled white suit, dwarfed the Filipino delegates, lean brown men also in white. Though his *Progresistas* had only won sixteen seats, he accommodated to the *Nacionalista* victory. He joined the ovation for Osmeña, whose unanimous election as speaker made him the undisputed Filipino political leader. And, at the glittering inaugural ball held at the Malacañang palace that night, he further inclined to the *Nacionalistas* with grace. Instead of dancing the opening rigadoon with his appointed partner, the wife of Pardo de Tavera, he upset decorum by taking the arm of a startled Mrs. Osmeña.

His speech to the assembly was less tactful. Alarmed by the *Nacionalista* campaign platform of "complete, absolute and immediate independence," he warned that an end to America's presence in the Philippines would end "mutually beneficial trade relations" with the United States. It was a stale and tiresome lecture that showed him to be badly out of date.

Had he been in touch, Taft would have known that most Filipino politicians were ambivalent toward independence. Convinced that nationalism had potent popular appeal, they never missed a public opportunity to clamor for sovereignty. They were also to use the issue in their continual bargaining with the Americans for greater autonomy, increased economic aid, improved education and other advantages. In private, though, they realized that to cut themselves off from the United States would be disastrous. Apart from sacrificing a market in America for their commodities, they might also lose U.S. protection from Japan, then flexing its muscles in Asia. Quezon encapsulated the contradictions with his consistent inconsistency. He put on a show of demanding sovereignty while maneuvering behind the scenes to delay a break with the United States. Years later, for example, he publicly denounced a Filipino politician who warned that independence would bring "economic ruin and desolation." But in fact he had secretly approved and even edited the politician's speech in advance.

American officials in Manila could distinguish between rhetoric and reality. Governor James Smith, in an analysis as valid then as today, shrewdly perceived "the only genuine political parties" in the Philippines to be the "Outs" and the "Ins." As he wrote to Taft: "The Ins are generally conservatives, the

Outs are always radical—until they get in." He therefore reckoned that the *Nacionalistas,* after stridently demanding independence during their campaign for election, would relax once in power. Forbes, now the deputy governor, agreed. Osmeña and Quezon had been recommended to him by provincial U.S. officials. He had met both men during his tours of the islands and regarded them to be trustworthy moderates. Even before the election, he noted in his diary, they had confided to him that their pleas for sovereignty were "really a catchway of getting votes." What mattered to them most, he observed, "was office, not independence." He recalled that Osmeña himself had explained: "The Filipinos wanted independence only when it seemed to be getting farther off, and the minute it began to get near they would begin to get very much frightened."

Forbes tested his thesis as the new assembly opened in October 1907. Taft, taking their campaign talk literally, expected the *Nacionalistas* to demand immediate independence. To block the move, Forbes drafted a resolution pledging the body to obey U.S. law, which would implicitly commit it to recognize American supremacy. Quezon, the majority leader, compliantly promised to make it the assembly's first act. But Forbes suddenly began to fear the motion might drive the radical Filipinos into a showdown with the Americans, thus weakening Osmeña and Quezon. Anticipating the worst, Forbes rushed to the assembly and raced up the stairs to Osmeña's office. Osmeña, placid as usual, informed him that the resolution had passed unanimously.

Over the next two years, Osmeña skillfully sidetracked several radical bills calling for immediate independence. But his moderation exposed him to rivals who attacked his subservience to the Americans. His fiercest critics, ironically, now included the formerly pro-American *Progresistas,* who had become ultra-nationalistic in a blatant bid for popularity. American officials in Manila did little to help him. They repeatedly vetoed attempts by the assembly to increase the number and authority of Filipinos in the administration, or raise their salaries to American levels. Forbes, appointed governor in 1909, rebuffed one measure with the remark that the legislature "can send up more fool bills in less time than it takes to say it." To many Filipino politicians, such condescending comments meant that the Americans considered the parliament to be a debating society rather than a source of power. Their perception was largely true. Forbes's predecessor, James F. Smith, had earlier described the assembly as little more than a school for "educating the people as to their responsibilities and benefits of modern government."

The trade issue, which surfaced with the passage of new tariff legislation by Congress in 1909, upset the Filipinos as well. Though they welcomed the elimination of duties on their exports to the United States, they recoiled from the reciprocal arrangement that gave American products unchecked access to the Philippines. Also worrisome to them were fresh drives by U.S. business for land, railway, mining and other concessions in the archipelago—efforts spurred by Forbes, who proudly declared his devotion to "material progress." The Filipino political leaders were too sophisticated to oppose U.S. investment. As Quezon said: "We are not living in the fifteenth century. . . . We want to see our country prosper and develop." But they were chilled by the prospect of American companies dominating their economy, then lobbying against eventual independence on the pretext that it would menace U.S. interests. Even pro-American Filipinos would have probably agreed with *El Renacimiento,* the radical Manila newspaper: "We fear absorption, monopoly, special privileges in perpetuity, the very death of our nationality."

In today's era of instant global communications, Filipinos devour the American press for clues to U.S. policy. But at the turn of the century, when news traveled slowly, many had read Lincoln Steffens and Ida Tarbell, the celebrated muckrakers of the period, who had skewered America's giant trusts. Quezon echoed their heady language. If Americans "have not yet succeeded in throwing off the yoke of great corporate capital," he intoned on one occasion, "what, then, can the Filipinos hope for in the undoubtedly forthcoming struggle between them and these powerful corporations in the Philippines?" His apprehensions found confirmation, however, in statements by U.S. businessmen in Manila, whose claims to exploit the Philippines sounded as rapacious as anything a muckraker could have invented.

Osmeña also sought to display his nationalism by defying the Americans during the summer of 1910. Now president, Taft sent his secretary of war, Jacob M. Dickinson, on a trip to Manila, and Osmeña seized the moment. He decried the U.S. program of political tutelage for its "lack of confidence in the capacity of the natives," arguing that it prevented them "from developing themselves by their own methods." But he refrained from demanding immediate sovereignty. He merely called for a formal American pledge of eventual independence, coupled with a larger role for Filipinos in the bureaucracy. Plainly, he was implying, greater autonomy would strengthen moderates like himself and block the rise of extremists.

Forbes ridiculed the idea. Speaking at a banquet for Dickinson, he warned the Filipinos that they could "talk just as much as you want about politics" as long as "you do not let it reach a point that will disturb the public order and interfere with the business of the country." Dickinson, a seasoned Tennessee politician, was more flexible. At one point during his visit, he stunned a petitioner for independence by snapping: "Well you won't get it, that's all." But, recognizing the importance of assuaging the Filipinos, he recouped with the kind of cant they loved to hear. While he hoped that they would stay within the U.S. fold, he said, his purpose was not to "further any plan that contemplated the denial of ultimate Philippine independence"—which, he added, was "a consummation devoutly to be prayed for." The Filipinos were appeased. Dickinson, wrote a local newspaper, had shown a "noble desire to impel us upward"—in contrast to Forbes's "insulting phrases."

But Dickinson went home, while Forbes remained to face fresh challenges. Stirred by "turbulent spirits," he noted shortly afterward, the assembly was "getting a little out of hand" as Osmeña put himself "in the forefront of the popular movement in order to hold his power." Soon another battle brewed over Filipino representation in Washington. Could the Filipinos, supposedly headed toward self-rule, pick their own men? Or were they required to submit to American candidates?

Congress in its original law regulating U.S. rule of the archipelago had authorized two Filipino members of the House of Representatives, where they could speak but not vote. One was to be chosen by the U.S. governor in Manila, the other by the Philippine assembly. At Taft's behest, one of the posts had gone to Benito Legarda, his *Progresista* protégé. Quezon, figuring that both his

William Howard Taft, the first U.S. civilian governor of the Philippines, weighed 325 pounds. He strongly influenced American colonial policy.

This school for Filipino children, founded by Americans, used an American curriculum. Education was one of America's main achievements in the Philippines.

Americans at the mountain resort of Baguio, built for Americans by Daniel Burnam, the celebrated city planner.

American women stroll through a Philippine town. Numbers of American women served as teachers.

An American picnic in the mountains. Very few Americans mixed socially with Filipinos during the U.S. colonial period.

Governor Francis Burton
Harrison flanked by
Manuel Quezon *(right)*
and Sergio Osmeña.
Burton, a liberal
Democrat, opened the
colonial administration to
Filipinos.

President Franklin D. Roosevelt signs act in 1935 pledging Philippine independence in ten
years; Quezon behind him *(to right)*.

The National Archives

General Douglas MacArthur was military adviser to Quezon, with Major Dwight Eisenhower *(in white suit)* as his aide. MacArthur and Eisenhower detested each other.

Lyndon Baines Johnson Library, Drew Pearson Papers

Isabel Rosario Cooper—"Dimples"—was MacArthur's Filipino mistress.

Japanese bombing of Clark Field on December 8, 1941, as the Japanese saw it.

Sam Grashio, a U.S. fighter pilot in the Philippines at the outbreak of World War II.

General Jonathan Wainwright surrenders to Japanese General Masaharu Homma, a Japanese view.

American and Filipino prisoners following the fall of Corregidor, May 1942.

Americans on the Death March from Bataan, sketched by an American survivor.

José Laurel, president of the puppet Philippine republic founded by the Japanese. He was later exonerated.

General Tomoyuki
Yamashita, commander of
the Japanese forces in the
Philippines.

The U.S. invasion force
heading toward Leyte in
October 1944.

General MacArthur splashes ashore at Leyte with Sergio Osmeña
(in pith helmet), president of Philippine commonwealth.

Americans freed from Japanese internment in Manila following the liberation of the city in 1945.

Manila, after Warsaw, was the most destroyed Allied city of World War II. Thousands of Filipinos died in the battle for the city.

country's future and his own destiny lay in Washington, had persuaded the legislature to give him the other slot in 1909. Two years afterward, however, the assembly rejected Legarda's reappointment, arguing that he was an American "creature." Taft, in a fury, told Forbes to "leave nothing undone" to promote Legarda. Congress finally broke the deadlock by extending the terms of the two Filipino incumbents. The compromise left Quezon in Washington, where he was to flourish until his ultimate departure late in 1916.

★　★　★

Apart from its cold winter, Washington enchanted Quezon, and he in turn captivated the capital. He adored strolling the corridors of Congress, stopping here or there to banter with politicians, who liked his easy style. Journalists found him to be good copy, and aware of their influence, he assiduously courted them. Naturally gregarious, he thrived on long lunches and dinner parties, lingering at the table to soak up the small talk and gossip and inside tips, or holding forth himself with stories, often in a ragout of Spanish and fractured English. His libido ever active, he flirted with the ladies, melting many with his exotic charm. He also toured the country, his top hat and tails a disappointment to locals who expected a tribal chief in loincloth and plumes. At a Tammany Hall gathering in New York, one of the sachems jokingly introduced him as the descendant of an Irishman who had fled to Spain, where his name had been hispanicized from Casey to Quezon. Henceforth, most of his American friends and a few Filipino cronies called him "Casey."

Quezon's maiden speech to the House of Representatives, delivered on May 14, 1910, was untypically muted. He expressed gratitude to America for giving the Filipinos "more personal and political liberty than they ever had under the Spanish crown." But, in a mild plea for independence, he said: "Ask the bird, sir, who is enclosed in a golden cage if he would prefer his cage . . . to the freedom of the skies and the allure of the forest." Rebuked by his colleagues for his diffidence, he replied that riling Congress would accomplish nothing. He had become, he wrote, "the enemy of demagogy."

Opportunity knocked after the U.S. legislative elections of November 1910, which for the first time in fourteen years put the Democrats in control of the House of Representatives. The committee in charge of the Philippines now came under the gavel of William Atkinson Jones of Virginia, whom Quezon had cultivated. Together they altered American policy toward the islands, but it was a tortuous process.

Jones, a gray figure of sixty, was Virginia gentry. As a cadet at the Virginia Military Institute during the Civil War, he had fought to defend Richmond in the last gasp of the Confederacy. He had spent twenty undistinguished years in Congress when Quezon met him. Forgotten in America, he was to attain immortality in the Philippines, where nearly every town has a street or park bearing his name. The Philippine government even built an incongruously ornate shrine to him in the Episcopal church of Warsaw, Virginia, his birthplace. His anticolonialism, he claimed, stemmed from his family's opposition to the British during the American Revolution. But Forbes called him a raw opportunist: "He wanted to get his name on a bill without caring too much what the bill was. It was a pity that a man of such little judgment happened by the rule of seniority in the House to get into a place where he could do so much mischief."

The bill, which Quezon actually drafted in early 1912, pledged Philippine sovereignty in eight years, with American forces to remain for twenty years to deter foreign threats. An upper chamber of the Philippine assembly would be elected, thus granting the Filipinos full legislative power except for the U.S. governor's veto. The measure in effect prescribed home rule for the islands—an unprecedented step at a time when the Europeans were denying even cosmetic concessions to their colonial subjects. Equally unique, it acknowledged the principle of Philippine sovereignty.

Despite his role in writing the bill, Quezon privately agreed with Forbes that Jones was galloping toward Philippine independence for partisan political motives. But Quezon could not publicly deprecate an apparent friend of the Filipinos without jeopardizing his own nationalist image. So he kept up with Jones—and even tried to outpace him. The motion went nowhere, however, with Taft still in the White House and the Republicans dominating the Senate.

The prospects for Philippine independence suddenly brightened in November 1912, when Woodrow Wilson was elected president, sweeping the Democrats to complete victory in Congress. In Manila, anticipating a new deal, ten thousand Filipinos celebrated by parading through a torrential rain as the nationalist newspaper *La Vanguardia* portrayed Wilson as Moses reincarnate: "He will preside over our triumphal entrance into the Promised Land after redeeming us from the long captivity to which the imperial Pharaohs reduced us."

The elation in Manila was premature. The Democrats had championed Philippine independence in every election since 1900, but Wilson, the dour former Princeton professor of political science, had not clearly committed himself during his campaign. An early advocate of America's acquisition of the islands, he later theorized that the Filipinos should be denied self-rule until "a long apprenticeship of obedience" had taught them maturity. Though he had hinted more recently that he might endorse the Jones bill, his intentions were uncertain. Quezon, unperturbed by Wilson's vagueness, again intimated to a Washington confidant that his present goal for the Philippines was merely legislative autonomy.

Taft could not abide the prospect of the islands, his personal domain for a dozen years, even loosening its ties to the United States. Late in 1912, now a lame duck, he launched a campaign to prevent any change of the status quo. Forbes, back on leave, joined him, and he hired Martin Egan, the former editor of the *Manila Times,* who had returned home after selling his share of the newspaper. They founded the Philippine Society, organizing U.S. businessmen, bankers and others with interests in the archipelago to lobby for their cause. Ironically, considering that Taft had divested the Vatican of its Philippine estates, they warned American Catholics that the Filipinos, once sovereign, would seize church property amid "civic unrest and disturbances." Taft also cautioned Protestants that their missionaries would be menaced if America left the islands. The "mere advocacy" of Philippine independence, he wrote in the *New York Tribune,* "inspires false hopes, checks present progress, provokes dissension and makes for dissatisfaction" among the natives. Jones, he said, was a "bad man" for defaming "everyone who has been out there working and sweating for the good of the Filipinos and the good name of the United States." Several congressmen from Catholic constituencies rallied to the campaign, and a protracted battle over Philippine independence seemed imminent.

Paradoxically, Taft had triggered the trend that he was now attempting to arrest. He had encouraged autonomy for the Filipinos in the hope that they would choose to remain within the U.S. orbit. By promoting their liberties, however, he had indirectly whetted their appetite for complete sovereignty. So, having raised aspirations that now had to be satisfied, he bequeathed the dilemma to Wilson. America could not plausibly return to force to rule the Philippines, but the Filipinos would cooperate with the United States only if their wish for a pledge of eventual sovereignty were fulfilled.

Wilson's cabinet was split, its views ranging from the pious isolationism of William Jennings Bryan, his secretary of state, to the fervent imperialism of William C. Redfield, his secretary of commerce. Seeking unbiased guidance, Wilson did what presidents often do: He sent a personal friend to the Philippines to evaluate the situation for him.

Henry Jones Ford, another Princeton professor of political science, toured the islands for two months during the spring of 1912, tirelessly gathering details on everything from education to aboriginal tribes. The "magnificent" work of U.S. health and welfare officials impressed him, but he found it "deplorable" that the Filipinos "seem unappreciative of our efforts and resentful of our domination" and foresaw a revolt unless they were given political autonomy. He urged Wilson to pledge them ultimate independence and to enlarge their authority in the interim.

In Washington, meanwhile, Wilson's new secretary of war, Lindley M. Garrison, sought advice from the Bureau of Insular Affairs, the agency under him that managed the archipelago. He particularly heeded General Frank McIntyre, its chief, and his young legal aide, Felix Frankfurter. An erudite career army officer with an encyclopedic knowledge of the islands, McIntyre had a gentle, considerate manner that Filipinos of every political stripe respected. Frankfurter, not long out of Harvard Law School, was already displaying the skill that would later make him a distinguished American jurist. Both were far more prudent than Ford.

Frankfurter argued that the "small, masterful, highly educated, wealthy" Filipino elite had "little community of interest and little sympathy" with the mass of people, and only the Americans could broaden the country's political base. So he opposed any disruption of the "continuity and stability" of the U.S. administration in the islands—pleading, in effect, against change. Thus he was being conservative for liberal motives, as he would later be as one of the preeminent Supreme Court justices of the century.

Garrison was also uncomfortable with a definite date for Philippine independence, but he counseled Wilson to give the Filipinos more authority while clarifying America's aims for the islands. Wilson assented, also agreeing to Garrison's proposal that a new U.S. governor be appointed to regain the trust of the Filipinos. The prize position was the American equivalent of a Roman proconsul, and Wilson would not decide without consulting Quezon. They had discarded more than a dozen possibilities when, one day in August 1913, a New York congressman named Francis Burton Harrison approached Quezon on behalf of a friend, Oscar T. Crosby, a company executive whose firm owned railways in the Philippines. Rejecting Crosby on those grounds, Quezon turned to Harrison: "Why in the world shouldn't you yourself be the candidate?"

Harrison, at first amused, agreed. With that, Quezon orchestrated the appointment in four days—his swift success testimony to his talent as a Washington operator. After obtaining Secretary of State Bryan's endorsement, he won over Garrison and rallied key members of Congress. Wilson promptly sent Harrison's nomination to the Senate committee on Philippine affairs, which confirmed him in fewer than six hours.

Quezon's choice was not entirely fortuitous. He knew Harrison, a veteran of ten years in Congress, as a reformer who had promoted lower tariffs and a federal antinarcotics law that bore his name. Harrison, a faithful Democrat, had toed the party line by criticizing imperialism, but he had been slow to champion Philippine independence. Only shortly before being tapped for governor, he confided to a friend, had he "become more earnestly impressed with the necessity of severing our bonds with the Philippines," since America had "no justification for holding those people in bondage." He also shared Theodore Roosevelt's concern that the islands would prove to be " 'our heel of Achilles' in time of war."

At forty, Harrison was tall, trim and handsome, with grayish hair and clipped mustache. A pedigreed blueblood, he traced his forebears back to Lord Fairfax, a supporter of Cromwell against Charles I during the English Civil War of the seventeenth century. The family had grown rich from its vast estates in the Virginia colony, siring several prominent figures, among them Thomas Jefferson. Harrison's father, a lawyer, had been secretary to Jefferson Davis, the president of the Confederacy, and his mother was a noted novelist. His parents moved to New York after the Civil War, and Harrison seemed destined for stardom from youth. Skull and Bones at Yale, he studied law and joined the U.S. Cavalry at the start of America's war with Spain, but never saw action. Politics soon lured him. Like nearly every white southerner of the period, he was a Democrat, which in Manhattan meant Tammany Hall. The machine steered him into Congress—though, to advertise his social conscience, he would point out that he represented an Italian working-class district. Women were one of his frailties; though a convert to Catholicism, he was married five times—a habit that raised eyebrows among Filipinos, who frowned on divorce despite their tolerance for extramarital male philandering.

Harrison was to adopt the Philippines, just as Taft and Forbes had. Unlike his predecessors, however, he was adopted by the Filipinos—and became, with the exception of Douglas MacArthur, their favorite American. Fifteen years after his tenure as governor, he returned as an adviser to Quezon, who made him the first American to be named an honorary Philippine citizen, and he was eventually reburied in Manila following his death in New Jersey in 1957. But while he espoused the Filipino cause, Harrison lacked interest in the Filipinos themselves. He seemed to be a pastiche of the patrician liberal: devoted to mankind yet uneasy with people. Though he reveled in the company of Osmeña, Quezon and other luminaries, he recoiled from natives below their rank. He seldom ventured into the countryside—and then only with trepidation. Once, on a visit to a tribe of Igorot aborigines, he was seen washing himself with carbolic soap after shaking their hands.

Landing in Manila on October 6, 1913, he drove to the Luneta, where thousands erupted in jubilation at his message from Wilson—which, for the first time, pledged America to Philippine sovereignty: "Every step we take will be taken with a view to the ultimate independence of the islands." Then, speaking for himself, Harrison struck an apostolic note of the sort that impassions Filipinos: "We place within your reach the instruments of your redemption. . . . Under divine providence the event is in your own hands."

The Philippine assembly excitedly voted a resolution stating that "colonial exploitation has passed into history." But its leaders were more prudent. Soon after his arrival, Harrison invited Osmeña to supplant the entire American administration with Filipinos, saying: "Take every bureau chief." Staggered, Osmeña remonstrated that "we want not only a Filipino government, we want a good government" and urged him to "go more slowly." Quezon, tracking events in Manila from Washington, was equally incredulous at Harrison's haste. "He thinks he can turn us loose in about four years," he nervously told a senior U.S. official.

But Harrison rushed ahead with his so-called program of Filipinization, drastically purging the U.S. establishment. He restructured the executive commission, which the Americans had controlled, to give Filipinos five of its nine seats. Then he replaced Americans with natives throughout the bureaucracy.

Actually, the number of Filipino officials had doubled to some six thousand in the decade before 1913, but most held minor jobs in contrast to Americans—who, for example, directed all except one of the twenty-four departments in the administration. During his eight years as governor, Harrison tipped the scales dramatically, shrinking the American corps from roughly three thousand to about six hundred, and raising Filipino representation to more than thirteen thousand.

Harrison's housecleaning methods did not always match his righteous rhetoric. Many of the U.S. officials he dismissed were involved in shady business—even though, in those permissive times, their activities were unethical rather than illegal. He sacrificed several able Americans by cutting salaries under the guise of economizing and fired Republicans while hiring Democrats. His promiscuous streamlining elevated numbers of inept Filipinos.

Many Americans in Manila, predictably outraged, recalled Reconstruction after the Civil War, when carpetbaggers put uneducated former Negro slaves into responsible posts. "The business community is suffering acutely . . . from unwholesome fear," wrote the *Manila Times* as the voice of the business community. Had there been an award for hyperbole, it might have gone to Representative Clarence B. Miller, a Minnesota Republican, who told the *New York Sun* after a trip to Manila: "Not Attila of the Huns nor Theodoric of the Goths ever laid such destructive hands upon human institutions."

Harrison, versed in Tammany Hall techniques, struck back at his American business critics with threats to audit their finances, but many Americans adapted. Big corporations in particular abhor uncertainty, and their executives preferred the clarity of Philippine independence, to which they could adjust, to Taft's vagueness. Harrison also tried to reassure U.S. firms and in one instance used public funds to rescue a bankrupt American company. He was lucky during World War I, when the huge global demand for raw materials enriched the islands. Unluckily, postwar prices plummeted, shattering the economy and leaving him the target of recrimination.

Whatever Americans thought of him, Filipinos revered Harrison, whose rare trips outside Manila caused a commotion. Paz Marquez, then a teacher and later an author of considerable wit, reported the fuss as her hometown in Tayabas province awaited him in the fall of 1913. Writing in English to her fiancé, she described a meeting of a women's committee formed for the event. "You should have seen that noisy assembly. Someone proposed a typically Filipino lunch. But no! the idea is ridiculous. We wish to convince the Americans that we are civilized enough to be independent, and we shall be refused if we eat off banana leaves. Yet is it very uncivilized to eat from banana leaves? When Italians eat macaroni they turn their faces heavenward with their mouths generously open, and they have their independence and their king. . . . Thus the discussions went on, all high pitch and fortissimo—none of those soft and gentle voices, a good thing in women according to old-fashioned Mr. Shakespeare."

A week later, the preparations were still incomplete, nor had the flurry subsided. "Everybody is in a ferment over the Harrison reception and politics in general," continued Paz. An American resident of the town groused that he would not "pay ten pesos to hear speechifying about independence." The local students, by contrast, were planning to applaud Harrison for his statements in favor of freedom, and "the faculty has been praying with all its might for rain" to dampen their spirits. A triumphal arch had been designed, the mayor and municipal council had drafted orations and a girls' choir was rehearsing a song of greeting, its opening lyric: "We welcome thee, O Burt-on Har-ri-son."

★ ★ ★

Harrison's arrival speech in Manila notwithstanding, America's promise of Philippine sovereignty had yet to be legitimized. The Jones bill was gathering dust, and Quezon had done little to promote its passage.

On the contrary, Quezon had been lobbying in Washington against an early American withdrawal from the islands, having heard that Japan might try to fill the vacuum. He conceived a plan to delay independence for at least twenty-five years, during which time the Filipinos would be autonomous. After Wilson approved the idea, however, Quezon dropped it in reaction to criticism that he was betraying Philippine nationalism and went back to renovating the first Jones bill—but Jones, now in poor health, waffled over revisions. Finally, in June 1914, Quezon handed Jones a new draft.

The measure prescribed the vote for all literate adult Filipino males and the election of a senate, thus vesting virtually full internal authority in a bicameral Philippine legislature. Rather than risk controversy, Quezon avoided a timetable for sovereignty, and instead confected an amorphous preamble pledging the United States to recognize Philippine independence "as soon as" the Filipinos could establish a "stable government." Like many another expedient, the phrase was to provoke chronic disputes during the decades ahead as Americans, Filipinos, Democrats and Republicans wrangled over the definition of "stable government."

The House of Representatives easily passed the revised Jones act in October 1914—yet it was to wait sixteen months to become law. Taft again mustered U.S. business and church leaders, and Republican senators managed to hobble the bill in committee. Taft's fervid struggle against the motion mirrored his desperation. Theodore Roosevelt, whose Bull Moose dissidents had split the Republicans and thwarted his bid for a second presidential term in 1912, now dealt him another blow by supporting Philippine independence out of fear that the United States could not defend the islands against Japan. Quezon also subverted Taft's appeals by cautioning American corporations that alternatives to the measure might be worse.

The jockeying went on into January 1916, when the success of the bill seemed sure. Then came a last-minute hitch: Senator James P. Clarke, an Arkansas Democrat, proposed an amendment to approve Philippine independence within four years.

Clarke, prodded by Republican taunts that the Jones act was a subterfuge, sent its sponsors into a frenzy as their neatly crafted consensus seemed about to collapse. They further panicked when Wilson, who had not long before opposed Philippine sovereignty, backed Clarke's innovation. Secretary of War Garrison objected strenuously—eliciting from Wilson the foggy reply that while he too had doubts about the Clarke amendment, they should defer to Congress. Garrison resigned. The Taft lobby, suddenly in remission, mobilized a bloc of Democratic senators, most of them Irish Catholics, to rebuff the amendment, and it passed only by the casting vote of Vice President Thomas Marshall. Quezon, torn between his nationalist credo and his desire to slow down the movement toward independence, slumped into bed in exhaustion. Osmeña, back in Manila, faced a cacophony of noisy Filipino legislators, some insisting on immediate sovereignty, others protesting against independence without U.S. protection.

The House of Representatives axed the Clarke amendment in early May as thirty Catholic Democrats swung the vote in response to secret instructions from Cardinal James Gibbon of Baltimore, whom Taft had recruited. But Taft could not stop passage of the Jones bill, which the Senate approved and Wilson signed into law in August 1916. However flawed, it was a landmark gesture. No other Western power at that stage had conceded autonomy to a colony, much less promised it independence. Osmeña indirectly made that point in a congratulatory cable to Quezon: YOUR SINCERE AND STEADFAST EFFORTS HAVE SAVED YOUR COUNTRY CENTURIES OF SUFFERING THAT OTHER PEOPLES HAVE TO GO THROUGH ON THEIR WAY TO FINAL EMANCIPATION.

Emotional celebrations followed. Quezon, addressing the House of Representatives, predicted that Jones's name would be engraved "in letters of gold" in Philippine history—and it would, indeed, be pinned on one of Manila's main bridges. With characteristic immodesty, Quezon also threw a huge party for himself at the old Willard Hotel, performing as his own toastmaster as a hundred Washington dignitaries sang his praises. In Manila, meanwhile, forty thousand people marched through the streets, and the city sent Wilson a silver tablet inscribed with words of gratitude.

His keen political antennae now told Quezon to seek his destiny at home. He sailed back, precariously disembarking in a typhoon to a wet but raucous ovation of parades, brass bands and speeches. Girls in pink showered him with flowers, and a poet composed a sonnet in his honor. At a gaudy banquet, he hinted at his future course. Thanking those who had helped to pass the Jones bill, he conspicuously omitted mention of Osmeña. He ran for the Philippine senate in the elections held soon afterward, and a *Nacionalista* landslide vaulted him into the presidency of the new body. The seat, with its authority to ratify official appointments, gave him immense power—which he was to manipulate during the years ahead to displace Osmeña to become the country's unchallenged leader.

Harrison now pressed Wilson to set a date for Philippine independence, contending that the country had a "stable government" as stipulated in the preamble to the Jones law. But a scandal partly of his own making punctured his plea.

In 1916, eager to give the new political authority of the Filipinos an economic base, Harrison founded a national bank with the help of H. Parker Willis, a scholarly veteran of the Federal Reserve Bank in the United States. Willis soon learned that the Filipinos on the board of directors regarded the institution as an instrument for dispensing patronage. He quit, leaving its direction to one Venancio Concepción, an absurd choice for the position.

A Spanish *mestizo,* Concepción was a former Spanish army officer who had defected to the Filipino nationalist forces, in which he rose to the rank of general before surrendering to the Americans. Osmeña, who owed him a favor, appointed him to the bank despite his lack of financial experience. A temperamental figure given to fustian outbursts, Concepción rejected technical advice and instead operated in Filipino tradition through an arcane skein of personal contacts. The result, a U.S. official subsequently concluded, was "nearly unbelievable mismanagement, graft and the violation of every rule that good banking dictates."

At first the bank flourished, as World War I spurred the global lust for Philippine commodities. In just three years, for example, exports of coconut oil, used to make explosives, soared in value by some twelvefold. But Harrison's brother Archibald, one of the bank's two American directors, charged Concepción with grave abuses—alleging that he had granted fat loans to his friends without collateral and written off their debts or allowed them to relend the bank's money at exorbitant interest rates. Because the bank lacked a central accounting system, its reserves were $11 million less than claimed. Concepción, backed by Osmeña and Quezon, refuted the accusations. Refusing to believe that his Filipino friends could be corrupt, Harrison also spurned his brother, who promptly returned home, furious and humiliated.

The restraints on him gone, Concepción plunged ahead despite signs that the World War I boom was about to bust. Rather than retrench when hemp prices crumbled in the summer of 1918, he expanded credit to producers, crippling the bank with massive defaults. He exceeded the bank's statutory loan limits to underwrite new sugar mills, ignoring evidence that the world sugar market was collapsing, and again disaster followed. Nor did he curb his employees from wild currency speculation, another costly venture. The total losses may have run as high as $30 million, a huge amount for those days. Jittery international financiers convened in Shanghai to explore ways to save their investments should the Philippine economy sink, and their discussions resembled the talks held during the 1980s, when foreign bankers met in New

York, London and Tokyo in an effort to reschedule the vast debt incurred by the profligate Marcos regime.

In November 1920, an American banker arrived in Manila to relieve Concepción, who was to be convicted and jailed for fraud—a penalty, some older Filipinos ruefully recall today, that could have been imposed only under the U.S. judicial system. Harrison, always ready to defend his Filipino protégés, later observed that they were "only partially responsible" for the debacle, yet "received all the blame." He was correct. The bank's ruinous currency gambles were the fault of an American agent, and many American hemp and coconut-oil processors had been the beneficiaries of its unsecured loans. But Harrison absolved himself of any guilt, lamely explaining that he had been abroad when Concepción committed his worst misdeeds. In any event, after winning the 1920 U.S. elections, the Republicans inflated the scandal in an effort to suggest that the Filipinos had not established a "stable government"—and thus were not ready for sovereignty.

★ ★ ★

The new president, Warren Gamaliel Harding, fatuously announced a return to "normalcy," which in the case of the Philippines meant forgetting promises of independence. As a senator from Ohio, he had opposed any plan to relinquish the islands, calling it a "national disgrace" to condemn the Filipinos "to walk alone when they had not been taught fully to creep." Now, on the eve of his inauguration, he leaked his view of the Philippine situation to the pro-Republican *New York Sun,* which ran the story on page one under the headline

PHILIPPINES IN CHAOS
BIG HARDING TASK

GOVERNOR HARRISON
BLAMED FOR MISRULE

Harrison's record, the inspired account read, was "not considered creditable either to himself or to the [Wilson] administration." During his term, "American sovereignty in the islands had been undermined, Filipino demagogues and adventurers who urge independence for their own selfish purposes have come to the front, American authority has been sadly impaired, the fiscal affairs of the islands have been thrown into chaotic shape and things have gone backward instead of forward." Harding, the newspaper added, would send Forbes or General Leonard Wood to the Philippines to counsel him on how to deal "justly" with the Filipinos and define a policy that Americans could "sanction and support."

Before departing for Manila in May 1921, Forbes advised Harding to maintain the political concessions already made to the Filipinos but recommended tighter U.S. controls to avoid another catastrophe like the bank scandal. He and Wood then toured the islands for four months, producing a report that confirmed their preconceptions. Beginning in the tone of a travel guide, they praised the Filipinos for their "many fine and attractive qualities—dignity and self-respect, personal neatness and cleanliness, courtesy. . . ." Predictably, however, they concluded that "it would be a betrayal of the Philippine people, a misfortune to the American people, a distinct step backward in the path of progress and a discreditable neglect of our national duty were we to withdraw from the islands . . . without giving the Filipinos the best chance possible to have an orderly and permanently stable government."

Just as predictably, the Filipino leaders flayed the report in public to preserve their nationalist image, while conceding in private that it was fair. But the Republican comeback augured renewed tensions with the Americans that, Quezon reckoned, could be turned to his political advantage.

Though Quezon had dominated the Philippine senate since 1916, he resented Osmeña's preeminence as speaker of the lower chamber. By 1923 he had maneuvered to supplant Osmeña with Manuel Roxas y Acuña, a young protégé from the island of Panay, and soon his power was uncontested. Osmeña was to survive thirty-nine more years, half that span as Quezon's subordinate, accepting his eclipse as humbly as a Buddhist monk for whom all life is transient.

Quezon was now prepared to risk a clash with Leonard Wood, whom Harding named U.S. governor in 1921. Win or lose, he calculated, a quarrel with the American viceroy could only enhance his reputation as a Filipino nationalist.

Wood, then sixty-one, had sterling credentials. The son of a Cape Cod physician, he joined the army as a doctor after graduating from Harvard Medical School but went into combat. He participated in the Indian wars and earned the Congressional Medal of Honor for his role in Geronimo's capture. Theodore Roosevelt, impressed by his performance, recommended him as commander of the Rough Riders, and afterward, as president, named him U.S. governor of Cuba. He later went to the Philippines to lead the American troops fighting the Moros, stayed there to head the U.S. military establishment and returned home to become Army Chief of Staff. Annoyed by his arrogant manner, Wilson denied him command of the American forces during World War I. Wood also alienated key members of Congress, and his bid for the Republican presidential nomination in 1920 worried Harding, who offered him the Philippine governorship to keep him at bay. Though Wood could hardly refuse after his mission to the islands with Forbes, he was an unpropitious choice.

Distressed by Harding's turnaround after the indulgent Harrison years, the Filipinos needed a sympathetic American governor to foster their experiment in self-rule. Above all, they yearned to be trusted by the Americans, whose tutelage they respected despite their nationalistic posturing—much as a rebellious adolescent seeks a parent's approval. This psychological nuance eluded Wood. Stern and aloof, he gave Filipinos the impression that he viewed them with suspicion. His rigidity particularly dismayed Quezon, who by contrast was elastic and nimble—but, in his way, equally stubborn.

Quezon's combustible ego would erupt at what he regarded as condescension by Wood's "cavalry cabinet"—which included young Lieutenant George S. Patton. Wood piqued Quezon as well by vetoing his Filipino appointees and protecting American officials. In March 1923, a complicated episode catapulted them into a squabble that raised the issue of where the locus of political power lay in the Philippines.

The case involved a raffish American detective on the Manila vice squad, whom the Filipino mayor had suspended on charges of corruption. Spurning the mayor's claim to handle the case administratively, Wood ordered a trial. The court acquitted the cop for lack of proof but cast doubts on his probity, and Wood retired him with full benefits. Angry at Wood for usurping his turf, Quezon staged a theatrical showdown.

Late on a hot night in July 1923, he strode into the Malacañang palace, the governor's residence, flanked by six top Filipino politicians in formal garb. Wood awaited them in a white dress uniform ablaze with medals. Quezon accused him of breaking America's "sacred pledge" to extend to the Filipinos "the greatest possible measure of self-government" and announced the resignation of the council of state, a cosmetic panel of native advisers. Wood denounced the "preconcerted attack" against U.S. supremacy, and Manila soon rippled with rumors of an impending American military putsch against the Filipino legislature.

Quezon, asserting that his target was Wood, not America, sent a mission to Washington to explain the Filipino side to Harding. But Harding, hit by pneumonia on a visit to Alaska, had suddenly died in San Francisco on August 3, 1923. The Filipinos now faced Calvin Coolidge, who bluntly warned them that their protests would only delay their independence. For them to antagonize "as good an administration" as that of Wood, he declared, would be "rather a testimony of unpreparedness for the full obligations of citizenship than an evidence of patriotic eagerness to advance their country." The futile encounter convinced Quezon that his dealings with the United States would remain deadlocked until "someone" was "taken out of the way." Indeed, nothing was to budge before 1927, when Wood died in Boston during surgery for a brain tumor.

Quezon went to Washington soon afterward to lobby for a more congenial governor. His candidate was Henry L. Stimson, who had visited Manila years earlier as Taft's secretary of war. Coolidge, bored by the subject, acquiesced.

Stimson, at sixty, belonged to America's peerage. The son of a rich New York banker who had forsaken finance for medicine, he was Skull and Bones at Yale and a Harvard Law School graduate and subsequently joined Elihu Root's Manhattan law firm. Theodore Roosevelt's influence made him a Republican reformer, a political path into Taft's cabinet. During World War I, though already fifty, he served briefly in France as a field artillery colonel and proudly bore the rank for the rest of his life. His family fortune further cushioned by the Wall Street boom of the 1920s, he replied to a plea from Coolidge to mediate a rebellion in Nicaragua. He had just finished that task when the Philippine assignment beckoned as a "last short adventure" before old age, as he later put it. He held the job for less than a year before becoming Herbert Hoover's secretary of state, but he was to profoundly determine the fate of the Philippines.

Little in Stimson's attitude should have commended him to the Filipino leaders. He candidly told Quezon and Osmeña that he opposed independence because their "Malay tendency to backslide" would wreck the archipelago. Only the Americans could promote "free institutions" and check the country's "undemocratic oligarchy," which had no interest in the "great farming masses." And, he added, a U.S. presence was vital to defend the islands against

Japan. He would accept the assignment only on condition that they cooperated with him while recognizing his "final authority." Quezon agreed.

He admired Stimson's rectitude. Stimson was in fact a moralist who later vetoed the creation of a U.S. espionage agency because "gentlemen don't open each other's mail" and truly believed such homilies as "the best way to make a man trustworthy is to trust him." Full sovereignty as a goal was also receding in Quezon's mind as he considered a tie with America like Canada's autonomous status within the British empire. Stimson was thinking along similar lines, and Quezon confided in him, "Give us certainty, and we will take dominion status." But, fearful of ceding the independence issue to his rivals, Quezon warned, "If you quote me on this, I will say you lie."

★ ★ ★

By the late 1920s, a growing number of groups in the United States pondered the future of the Philippine connection, and the Filipinos swiftly lost control of their own destiny as the debate intensified.

Predictably defending the status quo were a few big U.S. companies with investments in the Philippines, the American community of Manila, the U.S. importers of duty-free products from the islands and exporters with a virtual monopoly there for their goods. The American partisans of change comprised a crazy quilt of bedfellows, most of them also concerned with their special interests. With world sugar prices sliding, U.S. beet sugar producers decried Philippine competition—even though their real rival was Cuban sugar. American dairy lobbies denounced Philippine coconut oil as an ingredient in margarine, when in fact most of it went into soap. Though the U.S. textile business reaped fat profits from its market in the islands, Senator Thomas J. Helfin of Alabama called them a "millstone about the necks of the cotton producers." He was, he asserted, "in favor of freeing the Philippine people and hereafter, when their cheap and inferior stuff comes in to swamp our American farmers, we can put a tariff on it, protect our interests and preserve the home market for our American home people."

In October 1929, as the Wall Street crash spread to Main Street, sugar, dairy and other lobbyists stepped up their demands on Congress to block Philippine imports while labor unions clamored for curbs on the flow of Filipinos into the country. Some sixty thousand had arrived by 1931, unaffected by the exclusion law against Asians. Welcomed at first as cheap farm and domestic workers, mostly on the Pacific coast, they rapidly became pariahs as unemployment among Americans proliferated. The American Federation of Labor joined the American Legion and other self-styled patriotic movements to insist that they either be denied entry to the United States or that America's links with the Philippines be severed. In early 1930, a Filipino died in a California race riot against Asian workers.

And more than economics stirred the ferment. Japan's invasion of Manchuria in 1931 foreshadowed its aggressive aims in Asia, splitting Washington over the issue of U.S. strategy toward the Philippines. Hoover and Stimson, now secretary of state, championed an American presence in the archipelago to deter the Japanese. They had an eloquent supporter in the new Army Chief of Staff, General Douglas MacArthur, recently back from a tour of duty as

U.S. military commander in the islands. Worried by the fate of their colonies in Asia, the British and Dutch not only advocated a stiff U.S. stance, but hinted that they might take over the Philippines should America withdraw. His rhetoric apart, however, Hoover balked at the expense of bulwarking the U.S. forces in the Pacific. Nor did Congress or the American public welcome a firm commitment to the area. Pacifist sentiment, in reaction to the horrors of World War I, combined with the isolationist feelings that recurrently envelop U.S. opinion. Many Americans scorned the Japanese threat as inflated, while others, acknowledging its reality, preferred a U.S. retreat to Hawaii to a faraway Philippine involvement.

Several bills proposing sovereignty for the islands had been defeated by Congress until Senator Harry B. Hawes, a Missouri Democrat, embraced the issue early in 1930. Hawes, a stout figure with white hair and heavy jowls, resembled a statesman. In fact, he was a prototype politician who had climbed through the ranks back home to serve three terms in the House of Representatives before winning a Senate seat in 1926. He owed his career to various vested interests, including the American cordage industry, which resented competition from Philippine hemp and favored scuttling the archipelago. But Hawes convinced Filipino nationalists of his devotion to their cause. During their frequent trips to Washington, he put them in touch with legislators, lobbyists and journalists, explaining, "I should like to feel that I have contributed something toward the happiness of a large section of mankind."

Quezon, suffering from a bout of tuberculosis, was unable to go to Washington himself. Instead, he sent Osmeña and Manuel Roxas with ambivalent instructions. The Japanese menace disturbed him, and he also feared that sovereignty would cost the Philippines its U.S. market at a time when, like the rest of the world, its economy was in tatters. But, as usual, he had to maintain his nationalist image. So he told Osmeña and Roxas to deny that "we are not in favor of immediate independence," while directing them to float the idea of Philippine sovereignty "after a period of preparation of, say, ten, fifteen or twenty years." With the U.S. public increasingly cool to keeping the islands, though, they could not plausibly plead for time. Thus they answered Hawes in the affirmative when he asked them, "Do you and your people honestly and truly want independence?"

In June 1930, Hawes and Senator Bronson M. Cutting of New Mexico drafted legislation to grant independence to the Philippines in five years. But the bill was to languish in committee for twenty months even though the Democrats had meanwhile regained control of the House of Representatives. Finally, in April 1932, the measure easily passed the House—promoted by Butler Hare, a Republican from a North Carolina tobacco area. The farm bloc would have scuttled the islands overnight had not the motion been rammed through at top speed by Speaker John Nance Garner of Texas, soon to become Franklin D. Roosevelt's vice president. The few nays came mainly from the industrial states, alarmed by the potential loss of their captive Philippine export market. "What a travesty, what a tragedy!" lamented a Massachusetts congressman. "Forty minutes to found a nation!"

His panic was premature. Senator Arthur Vandenberg, a wily Michigan Republican, maneuvered to shelve the bill until late 1932, by which time Hoover had been buried by the Roosevelt landslide. Vandenberg still hoped to retain the Philippines despite clear evidence that Congress, appalled by the Depression, was determined to relieve America of its overseas commitment.

Congress now differed only on a timetable for Philippine independence and such details as future trade and strategic ties. Even so, the debate was rich in hyperbole. Vandenberg urged a slow transition to avert the "absolute collapse" of the archipelago, and Senator Roscoe G. Patterson of Missouri foresaw "possible revolution" following a U.S. withdrawal. By contrast, Senator Huey Long of Louisiana denounced the "Wall Street imperialists" and "gods of greed" who clung to the islands while Americans starved; some, he claimed in one preposterous speech, were even reduced to practicing cannibalism. Just as Kipling had exhorted Americans early in the century to take up the "white man's burden," so Winston Churchill gratuitously intervened to warn that the "national duty, dignity and honor" of the United States were at stake.

By January 1933, however, the two chambers of Congress had compromised on a bill that crushed the advocates of a long-term U.S. hold over the Philippines. The Filipinos were to be accorded independence in ten years, during which time they would govern themselves as a commonwealth. American business was to be favored during the interim, and Philippine goods could enter the United States under generous quotas. The U.S. Army and Navy bases were to remain intact.

Hoover flung the bill back at Congress with a stinging rebuke. It violated "the idealism with which this task in human liberation was undertaken," he said, and confronted Americans and Filipinos with "new and enlarged dangers to liberty and freedom." However, he made no dent on the House, which in only two hours overrode the veto by a huge majority. Four days later, on January 17, 1933, as the Senate followed with equal ferocity, Hoover conceded, "It's a rout." William Randolph Hearst, whose strident newspapers had screamed for war with Spain a generation before, had personally telephoned a score of influential senators in a desperate attempt to help Hoover. But the old jingoist magic was gone—and, with it, thirty years of Republican policy for the Philippines.

There was a denouement to the episode, however. Quezon had sent Osmeña and Roxas back to Washington to lobby for the measure while he remained in Manila. Once the bill passed, he suddenly perceived his political blunder. His rival Osmeña, he realized, would now be hailed as the hero who had achieved Philippine independence. He foresaw Osmeña returning to win the forthcoming election as president of the new commonwealth while he disappeared into obscurity. With more than his usual petulance, he accused Osmeña and Roxas of capitulating to unfavorable trade terms and violating the country's future sovereignty by permitting U.S. military and naval bases to remain on Philippine soil. He then resorted to a device to regain the limelight.

The U.S. measure required the approval of the Philippine assembly, and Quezon set out to prevent its endorsement. He assured the radical nationalists that he could persuade the Americans to hasten independence, and promised the sugar barons that he could guarantee their U.S. market by delaying independence. The legislature thereupon rejected the American bill, having isolated Osmeña, Roxas and other moderates who had pleaded for its ratification. In November 1933, Quezon departed for Washington, promising to secure a better deal. If nothing more, his performance was testimony to America's extraordinary benevolence. At a time when other Asian nationalists could not extract the slightest concessions from the European imperial powers, here was a Filipino spurning a pledge of sovereignty from his colonial masters for the sake of promoting his personal ambitions.

Franklin D. Roosevelt had just named as governor Frank Murphy, the former mayor of Detroit, who years later was to become governor of Michigan and a Supreme Court justice. The Filipinos admired him as a devout Catholic and, like many of them, an unabashed philanderer. To many his liberalism was naïve, yet Quezon trusted him enough to enlist his support before going to Washington. His goal, Quezon explained, was to shrink the schedule for independence while prolonging the period under which the islands would enjoy trade benefits.

At first Quezon found Washington unreceptive. Roosevelt had neglected the Philippines during his campaign, expecting the Hoover administration to have settled its status, and now in office he was too busy with more pressing problems. Over an amiable lunch, however, he asked Quezon to draft a set of concrete proposals—which Roosevelt, of course, never read. Quezon turned to Millard Tydings of Maryland, who chaired the Senate committee responsible for the islands. Tydings, knowing that Quezon mainly hoped to advance himself politically, was cool. But Hawes had recently left the Senate and Quezon, flush with sugar money, enlisted him as a paid lobbyist. Together they convinced Tydings that only Quezon had the influence to line up the Philippine legislature behind an independence bill. He and Representative John McDuffie of Alabama essentially repackaged Hawes's motion of the previous year, and Roosevelt's blessing steered it to an even bigger majority in Congress in March 1934. For Quezon, success had justified duplicity. "When the historian passes on what we have all said and done at this momentous period," he wrote at the time, "how petty and how small must our dissensions and disputes seem to him."

Quezon returned to Manila in triumph. The legislature, which had supinely obeyed his orders to reject the earlier independence measure, at his behest now ratified its carbon copy unanimously. He easily won the commonwealth presidency in the elections held in September 1935, far outdistancing Emilio Aguinaldo, the vintage nationalist generalissimo, still spry at sixty-six. A constitution promulgated months before had even been tailored to his measure. Though superficially patterned on the U.S. model, it gave the Philippine executive almost limitless powers—including the prerogative to decree martial law that Marcos was to use thirty-five years later. Americans who yearned to believe that the United States had instilled a love for democracy in the Filipinos misunderstood their traditional respect for authority. In an analysis of the constitution, Quezon stressed its crucial difference from the American concept of government: "The good of the state, not the good of the individual, must prevail."

He might have also borrowed Louis XIV's imperious words "l'état, c'est moi." By now, he was so transfixed by a sense of his own importance that he insisted on being ranked above Governor Murphy at the inauguration of the commonwealth on November 15, 1935. He threatened to boycott the ceremony unless he received a salute of twenty-one guns, the protocol reserved for a foreign head of state. Only after a personal plea from Roosevelt did he acquiesce to a nineteen-gun salvo, but he sulked throughout the event.

It was a momentous occasion. A bright blue sky bathed Manila as a half-million Filipinos packed the area around the Philippine legislative building, its Greek style redolent of Washington. The official American delegation was headed by Vice President Garner and Secretary of War George Dern, with forty-three members of the U.S. Congress and their wives filling its ranks. Among the visiting journalists were Quezon's crony Roy Howard, boss of the Scripps-Howard chain, and William Allen White, the legendary editor of the *Emporia Gazette,* who ironically had been a vocal imperialist. The ritual was largely American despite its celebration of Philippine home rule. The band played "The Star-Spangled Banner" to the unfurling of Old Glory, and "Hail to the Chief" in honor of Quezon. The speeches were mercifully brief. Dern read a message from Roosevelt voicing the hope that Filipinos would look with gratitude on America's role as having been a "benediction." Quezon appealed to God "to give me light, strength and courage."

The Philippines would need all that and more during the decade ahead. Few of the dignitaries at the ceremony sensed the coming crisis more acutely than did a tall, erect figure with the chiseled profile of a matinee idol. General Douglas MacArthur had just returned to Manila. No American was to earn greater reverence from the country—which, he once said, "fastened me with a grip that never relaxed."

10. MacARTHUR'S MANDATE

★ ★ ★

Douglas MacArthur was a protean figure—a kaleidoscope of diverse and divergent notions and emotions, actions and reactions, shapes, shades and sizes whose paradoxes and contradictions challenge easy portrayal. Vain, flamboyant and sanctimonious, he was also considerate, sensitive and charming. He could be generous and petty, inspirational and ignoble, sublime and absurd, wise and shallow. His rhetoric extolled duty, honesty and patriotism, all of which he truly believed even as he contrived shabby schemes to advance his overweening ambitions. A die-hard conservative, his political opinions reassured right-wing ideologues, yet he appreciated the need for economic reform, social justice and racial harmony. He blurred his self-image of bravura by weeping in public, and his proud masculinity clashed oddly with an almost pathological submission to a pushy mother. Though his courage earned him a record array of decorations, some of his own men accused him of cowardice. Whatever attitudes he aroused, indifference was not among them. Views of him ranged from blind admiration to fierce animosity. He relished the acclaim and resented the criticism, reveling in the controversy as proof of his towering stature.

To the Filipinos, he was nothing less than superhuman. In July 1961, as Asia correspondent for *Time* magazine, I covered his valedictory visit to the Philippines—his first since the end of World War II. The reception for him approximated religious idolatry. Aware of his reputation as a consummate actor, I had anticipated an artful performance, but he exceeded my expectations. He seemed to have practiced every step, planned every gesture, rehearsed every statement. Frail but erect at eighty-one, his noble profile as firm as ever, he descended from a U.S. Air Force jet at the Manila airport, dressed in familiar khakis and crushed cap. He saluted the dignitaries assembled to welcome him and, his baritone still resonant, expressed pleasure at his return to "the land that I have loved so well, among people who I have loved so well." Then, as a tinny band mournfully blared "Old Soldiers Never Die," he and his wife Jean boarded a limousine for the ten-mile drive into the city. I soon sensed that, despite its mawkish flavor, this was the celebration of a personality cult.

MacArthur called the trip "a sentimental journey," and it ignited an electrifying charge of adulation among the millions of Filipinos who turned out to mark the occasion, officially declared a national holiday. As his procession snaked through Manila, the metropolis exploded in pandemonium. Banners proclaimed him OUR SAVIOR and OUR LIBERATOR. People dangled from windows, perched atop lampposts and packed the streets, slowing the parade to a crawl as they pressed toward his car for a closer glimpse of him. Children chanted songs in his praise, and girls tossed flowers in his path. Filipino veterans of World War II, many in bemedaled uniforms, jostled to grasp his hand—or, still better, to be photographed with him. Later, as he drove into the Luzon countryside, the scene of his battles, triumphal arches draped with American and Philippine flags adorned the road, throngs surging forward at every town to greet him with garlands and cheers. Mothers held up their babies, as if his glance might endow them with glory, and small boys raced for miles alongside the motorcade, hoping to be rewarded for their exploit with a nod or a wave. Afterward, at the Luneta, the central park of Manila, his eyes narrowed against the harsh glare of the tropical sun as he peered into the crowd and beyond to the azure bay he had seen a thousand times, and his peroration struck a melancholy chord. "Even as I hail you, I must say farewell. . . . So, dear friends, I close with a fervent prayer that a merciful God will protect each and every one of you, and bring this land peace and tranquillity always."

A Manila newspaper columnist, eager to create a stir, derogated the "ballyhoo" as "utterly nauseating." But such blasphemy was rare. Carl Mydans, the *Life* photojournalist, whose experience in the Philippines went back years, savored a remark that accurately caught the mood. After a luncheon at the Manila Hotel, the guests spontaneously broke into "Let Me Call You Sweetheart" as MacArthur bussed his wife. At that, Mydans related, a Filipino beside him beamed: "General MacArthur kisses his wife only in the presence of his family, and we are his family." So MacArthur was, to the Filipinos, their *compadre*—intimately linked to them through mutual sacrifice, loyalty and obligation. With the tendency of Filipinos to translate institutional ties into personal bonds, he more than any other American blazed in their eyes as the power, prestige and patronage of the United States.

Above all other Americans, too, MacArthur understood and accepted this responsibility—but with a strong strain of condescension. The U.S. commitment to the Philippines was his own liability, his proprietary mission, his own "white man's burden." Motivated by a quaint spirit of noblesse oblige, he was the country's custodian, dedicated to the welfare of its common people. Unlike most Americans in Manila, he shunned racial bigotry, numbering many Filipinos among his friends—including Manuel Quezon, his son's godfather and thus his ritual kin. Yet, while he disregarded color, he respected class. He confined his social circle of Filipinos to rich landlords, entrepreneurs and their political cronies, who gave him as biased a perspective of the Philippines as he derived of America from his big-business acquaintances back home. The

Tarlac sugarcane cutter was as alien to him as the Georgia sharecropper. Nor was he any more familiar with the Manila intellectual communities than with their counterparts in Boston and New York.

His father's memory haunted MacArthur. General Arthur MacArthur, military governor of the islands early in the century, had viewed himself as a kind of U.S. viceroy for Asia, and Douglas inherited that conceit. Fortune had cast him as the star of an unprecedented drama, the birth of the Philippine nation as the only Christian democracy in the Far East, and fate had also chosen him to guide America's destiny in the Pacific. The Philippines fit into the vision, and its salvation was to be his obsession, his illusion, his tragedy and, ultimately, his finest hour.

★ ★ ★

The lone eagle image that MacArthur sought to project of himself was deceptive. In fact, he relied inordinately on his parents—a phenomenon, one of his biographers has theorized, that revealed his anxieties. He acquiesced to his mother, a southern belle nicknamed "Pinky," who regulated his life. She meddled in his first marriage and subverted his only known love affair, lobbied for his promotions and accompanied him almost everywhere except the battlefield. At sixty-five, he still craved the approval of his austere father, then dead for thirty years. "Whenever I perform a mission and think I have done it well," he confessed, "I feel that I can stand up squarely to my dad and say, 'Governor, how about it?' "

The youngest of three sons, MacArthur was born in January 1880 in Little Rock, Arkansas, then a remote frontier town. His father, a captain despite two decades in the army, was transferred six months later to the New Mexico territory to pursue Apaches, and the family went along. There Douglas spent his early childhood in the romantically rugged region. In the style of the time, his mother kept him in skirts and curly long hair until he was five, just as across the country, at a mansion in Hyde Park, New York, an equally determined mother, Sara Roosevelt, dressed her boy Franklin as a girl.

Arthur MacArthur rocketed through the ranks in 1898, when the war with Spain put a premium on seasoned officers. Made a brevet brigadier general, he was sent to the Philippines and later became military governor. Douglas, meanwhile, had earned an appointment to West Point. He traveled there with his mother, who stayed for the full four years, lodging at a hotel near the academy grounds. During their strolls every evening, she would exhort him to excel, and he fulfilled her ambitions. He topped the class of 1903, the most brilliant cadet since Robert E. Lee seventy-four years earlier. Soon he embarked for the Philippines, then one of the few spots overseas where a young American officer could serve.

Despite his father's position, Douglas was just another shavetail, and his superiors treated him accordingly. They assigned him to an engineer unit improving harbors and other facilities in the Visayan Islands and, while exploring the region, he experienced his baptism of fire. He was walking alone through the jungle near the town of Iloilo when two native guerrillas or bandits ambushed him, a bullet piercing his campaign hat. Instantly drawing his pistol in cowboy style, he killed them both. "Participated in no battles, engagements or actions," he modestly recorded in his annual report. He had not yet learned to inflate his exploits to gild his reputation—as he did in later years.

After six months in the field, he was shifted to desk duty in Manila, a move that would have annoyed most eager young officers, but MacArthur enjoyed the city's placid colonial ambience. He roomed at the Army and Navy Club, with its superb view of the bay, and spent his evenings at the opera or theater, or playing poker. Far from his mother, he also carried on a mild flirtation with an American girl. He was too energetic and inquisitive, though, to restrict himself to the U.S. community. Roaming Manila on foot, a rare practice for an American, he soaked up its sights, sounds and smells. Even more untypically, he met Filipinos socially. Colonel James G. Harbord, chief of the Philippine constabulary, who made a profession of cultivating promising young Filipinos, introduced him at dinner to a couple of recent law school graduates, Manuel Quezon and Sergio Osmeña. Like MacArthur, they were in their twenties, and their political chitchat captivated him. Both later presidents of the Philippines, they were to recall proudly that their friendship began that evening.

MacArthur would have remained in the Philippines for three or four years had he not contracted malaria while on a survey of the Bataan peninsula. Repatriated to California, he had hardly recovered before he landed a dream assignment. His father, then U.S. military attaché in Tokyo, enlisted him as his aide on an extensive Asian tour; Pinky naturally joined them. They traveled for eight months by rail, river boat and ocean liner, visiting nearly every country on the continent and seeing everyone of note. From Singapore they crisscrossed Java and went to Burma, where they sailed up the Irrawaddy to Mandalay. In India they trekked through the Himalayas and over to the fabled Khyber Pass, then descended to Calcutta for an audience with Lord Kitchener, the crusty commander of the British forces. Given a lavish banquet in Bangkok by King Chulalongkorn of Siam, whose father was to be immortalized on Broadway by Yul Brynner in *The King and I,* they became court celebrities when Douglas repaired a blown fuse. They reviewed the French garrison in Saigon, voyaged north along the China coast and finally returned to Japan. The splendid trip, Douglas afterward wrote, was "the most important . . . in my entire life." From it he concluded that "the future and, indeed, the very existence of America, were irrevocably entwined with Asia and its island outposts."

Sixteen years were to elapse before MacArthur went back to Asia. By then he had emerged from World War I as one of America's most glamorous soldiers.

The British and French were near collapse late in 1917 as Germany shifted troops to the Western front after Russia's withdrawal from the conflict. Only the United States, which had entered the war in the spring, could reverse the trend. MacArthur, now a colonel, arrived in France in October as Chief of Staff of the Rainbow division—so called because its men came from a spectrum of states. General John J. Pershing, commander of the American expeditionary force, had served under his father in the Philippines.

MacArthur promptly set his own sartorial style, boasting to a comrade that "it's the orders you disobey that make you famous." Instead of a steel helmet, he sported a crushed cap, the rakish headgear later adopted by hotshot pilots.

He also traded the regulation tunic, baggy pants and puttees for a turtleneck sweater, riding breeches, cavalry boots and long muffler knitted by his mother, wielding a swagger stick as his only weapon. The doughboys derided him as "Beau Brummel" or "d'Artagnan" until his valor—and frequent foolhardiness—changed their sneers to admiration.

One night, unarmed and bizarrely attired, he joined a French unit on a raid into the German lines. Accompanied by a junior officer, he crawled across no-man's-land, cutting barbed wire and ducking into shell holes as bursts of flares lighted the sky. Then the French attacked, and machine guns rattled and artillery roared in the "savage and merciless" fight, as he later described it. Fading into the darkness, he and his companion were feared lost. But they appeared at dawn with a French party and a bag of prisoners—one of them a German colonel being prodded by MacArthur's swagger stick. Awarded the *Croix de guerre* by the French commander on the spot, he was the first American soldier in France to win that decoration. By the end of the war, his chest glittered with ribbons—only the Congressional Medal of Honor conspicuously missing.

His division commander, Major General Charles Menoher, hailed him as "one of the ablest . . . most popular" officers in the U.S. Army. But Menoher expected him to be killed sooner or later, since "there's no risk of battle that any soldier is called on to take that he is not liable to look up and see MacArthur at his side." Neglecting paperwork to be with his troops in combat, MacArthur quipped that nothing would raise their morale more than to see a senior officer being "bumped off." To his growing circle of critics, however, he was a blatant exhibitionist—an assessment shared by Pershing, a strict disciplinarian. Still, Pershing promoted MacArthur to brigadier general under pressure from President Woodrow Wilson's secretary of war, Newton D. Baker.

MacArthur's mother had ardently lobbied for him, perhaps behind his back. In a "heart-to-heart" letter to Pershing, she recalled "my late husband's great admiration for you," listed her son's qualities and divulged her dream to "live long enough" to see him raised to general. She later thanked Pershing in another effusive letter, pledging, "You will *not* find our Boy wanting!" But MacArthur owed his first star less to her exertions than to Baker's influence following an incident that illustrated the advantages of propinquity. An Ohio politician who valued good publicity, Baker eagerly hoped to visit the trenches during a trip to France in March 1918, and MacArthur obligingly escorted him up to the front in defiance of Pershing's orders. A German shell exploded harmlessly nearby, enabling Baker to brag to the folks back home that he had been "under fire." From then on, Baker was a solid MacArthur fan, and Pershing despite his misgivings could not buck his civilian boss. He reluctantly elevated MacArthur—who, Baker proceeded to tell reporters, was "the greatest fighting front-line general" in the U.S. Army.

So persuaded was MacArthur of his own superiority that he may have been blind to Pershing's reservations about him. Evidence to the contrary, he later claimed that Pershing had called him "the greatest leader of troops we have." He also wooed journalists long before the invention of modern public relations, having intuitively learned that nothing captivates the press more than colorful copy. Just after World War I, while on occupation duty in Germany, he dazzled William Allen White, the celebrated editor, over lunch at a Rhine castle that he had appropriated as his headquarters.

"I had never before met so vivid, so captivating, so magnetic a man," White subsequently wrote—adding, in what must rate as one of the howling misjudgments of all time, that MacArthur "seemed to be entirely without vanity." Yet, even then, MacArthur was showing paranoiac symptoms. The faintest criticism would convince him that he was the target of plots, and his surly reaction provoked fresh slights that in turn confirmed his sense of persecution. In France, he had seen himself to be the victim of a "clique" around Pershing that included officers like George C. Marshall, who was to become the Army Chief of Staff during World War II. Two decades afterward, while fighting in Asia, he still felt that foes from Pershing's old entourage were conspiring to hobble his campaign. By then, too, he had acquired new rivals, among them a former aide, Dwight D. Eisenhower, whom he loathed. During World War II and again in Korea, he was to use press censorship not only for legitimate security purposes but also to promote his personal image.

But even paranoiacs have enemies, and MacArthur did in fact alienate U.S. Army reactionaries who, besides their disdain for his extravagant style, resented his broad-gauge approach to soldiering. Military progressives, on the other hand, esteemed him perhaps more than he realized. In 1919, they maneuvered to put him in charge of West Point, with orders to "revitalize and revamp" its musty curriculum. He agreed that officers ought to be familiar with national and foreign affairs as well as other modern subjects, including human behavior. Predictably accompanied by his mother, he arrived with plans for courses in history, government, economics, even psychology. The entrenched faculty and conservative alumni combined to resist, however, and only years later did his reform become the core of the contemporary academy.

In 1922, his tenure at West Point abbreviated, MacArthur was sent back to the Philippines. Now, instead of his mother, his companion on the voyage was a wife.

Louise Cromwell Brooks was a tony socialite straight out of the Sunday rotogravure. Her late father had been a rich Manhattan attorney, her stepfather a multimillionaire Philadelphia banker and her brother one of the myriad husbands of Doris Duke, the tobacco heiress. She had wed a rich Baltimore contractor, by whom she had two children. They moved to Paris, where they remained during World War I as members of the madcap "international set," wantonly dining and dancing despite the death and destruction at the front only a few miles away. Eroded by her infidelities, her marriage crumbled. She went to Washington to join a new coterie that included Pershing, whom she had known in Paris. Now U.S. Army Chief of Staff, Pershing was a widower, and she often acted as his official hostess. Gossip of a liaison between them spread. But Louise then fell for MacArthur at a weekend party, and they immediately announced their nuptials. "If he hadn't proposed the first time we met," she confided to reporters, "I would have done it myself."

MacArthur's mother, shattered by the prospect of a divorcée daughter-in-law, brushed off the relationship as "purely physical." She may have been correct. MacArthur, then forty-two, was tall and lean and, with his sculpted profile, as handsome as any silent-movie idol of the day. Louise had reached the shady side of thirty-five, but she could still pass for a seductive jazz age flapper in her short skirt and shingled hair. Her stepfather presided over their elaborate wedding celebration at his Palm Beach estate, inspiring one newspaper to headline MARRIAGE OF MARS AND MILLIONS. None of MacArthur's friends attended. Nor did his mother.

Louise spread the story that Pershing, infuriated by her jilt, was "exiling" MacArthur to the Philippines in reprisal. "Poppycock," retorted Pershing, and MacArthur echoed the denial. She may have wholesaled the rumor out of fear for the future. Jittery as she faced an experience drastically different from her giddy life until then, she must have also felt that the unfamiliar, distant destination would test her marriage—as, indeed, it did.

The newlyweds, accompanied by Louise's children, landed in Manila late in 1922. They were given a splendid old house atop a rampart of the inner city, which Louise delighted in decorating with Spanish colonial furniture and Chinese rugs. But the exotic excitement of discovery soon faded. To keep busy, she turned to pious if futile endeavors, like scolding native coachmen who beat their ponies. Amusement consisted of bridge and drinks with other Americans at their incestuous clubs or formal dinners with U.S. and Filipino officials. She soon found it all "extremely dull," she wrote to friends. She begged MacArthur to resign and go into business, offering her stepfather's assistance to open doors. When he declined, she attempted in vain to have him transferred to a U.S. post. His mother, back home, meanwhile aggravated their tensions by alarming them with her real or imagined ailments—a reminder to MacArthur that he could not escape her clutches.

MacArthur, by contrast, was thrilled to be back in the Philippines. The U.S. governor was now General Leonard Wood, one of his father's former subordinates, whose cold manner chilled Manuel Quezon and other local leaders. MacArthur, as an officer, owed his loyalty to Wood, but he hoped to remain on good terms with the Filipinos, whose friendship he valued. Treading a fine line, he avoided politics and only saw the Filipinos socially. Even so, he later recalled, he incurred the "resentment and even antagonism" of many Americans in Manila. His racial tolerance may have also taxed his relations with Louise, who shared the prejudices of her clubby circle.

MacArthur was chiefly absorbed by his command of a U.S. infantry brigade. The Philippine garrison was merely a token force, numbering only about eleven thousand American regulars and six thousand Filipino auxiliaries. It had just been cut to placate the Japanese, who had recently agreed to curb their navy in concert with the major powers on condition that the United States and Britain reduce their bastions in Asia. Congress, reflecting America's isolationist mood in the wake of World War I, had also slashed military outlays. Strategists in Washington were reviewing a subject that they and their predecessors had studied several times during the past decade: the defense of the Philippines.

The probable enemy was no secret. Since 1905, American experts had postulated that Japan, after defeating Russia that year, would eventually challenge the United States for control of the Pacific. They concurred on the necessity for American naval bases to span the ocean. Pearl Harbor was the logical spot in Hawaii, but the Philippines posed problems. The army rejected Subic Bay, the navy's favored site, as too vulnerable to land attack, while the navy replied that the fleet would be strangled were it confined to Manila Bay, the army's preferred location. The sort of debate that keeps strategists employed, it had dragged on for years. Building installations at all in the Philippines, however, hinged on the question of whether the archipelago was defensible.

Contingency plans had been drafted in Washington for war with various hypothetical enemies, each designated by a code color. The Orange Plan, designed for hostilities with Japan, foresaw a conflict being waged mainly at sea, and contained few provisions for protecting the Philippines. President Theodore Roosevelt dissented with his usual bluster. To expect the archipelago to be spared in the event of war, he argued, was preposterous—Congress must either provide funds or vote to withdraw from the possession. In August 1907, writing from his summer home at Oyster Bay, he aired his views in a rambling letter to William Howard Taft, his secretary of war. To retain the islands "without adequately fortifying them" against the Japanese, he warned, "would be disastrous in the extreme." As it was, they "form our heel of Achilles." So, to "remove a temptation from Japan's way," the Philippines ought to be given independence "with perhaps some kind of international guarantee." But largely out of inertia, the bold proposal was to hang in limbo, with nobody willing to turn the islands loose or to make the investment to protect them.

The power balance tilted further against America after World War I. The Japanese, awarded Germany's former Pacific islands for joining the Allies, currently straddled the U.S. sea lanes to the Philippines. Now they could throw three hundred thousand men into the archipelago within weeks, and easily crush its token American garrison. Governor Wood, in Manila, foresaw with remarkable prescience the "abandonment of American posts, American soldiers, an American fleet, American citizens in the Far East." But he cautioned that to tell the truth would have a "disintegrating and demoralizing effect" on U.S. opinion. Perhaps, by continuing to pore over the problem, American strategists could somehow "work it out."

The strategists could not work it out. Nor would they admit openly that war with Japan would doom the Philippines. Instead, in 1924, they revised the Orange Plan, ordering the U.S. garrison to secure Manila Bay until the American fleet arrived to defeat the Japanese and rescue the archipelago. They knew the formula to be unrealistic—but, like military men throughout history, they clung to the thesis because any plan was preferable to none.

During the years ahead, U.S. officers were to revise and refine the scenario more than a hundred times in board games and chart maneuvers, always concluding that the Philippines could not be defended, even temporarily. Therefore, as one planner put it, reliance on the Orange Plan "would literally be an act of madness." Some proposed that the United States pull back to its "natural strategic peacetime frontier in the Pacific": a perimeter stretching from Panama through Hawaii to Alaska. But that option violated the doctrine, especially espoused by the navy, that war must be "waged offensively"; worse yet, it reeked of "defeatism." So, even though its members doubted its plausibility, the conservative U.S. military establishment stood by the Orange dogma.

Such lofty issues were then outside MacArthur's purview, but the plan to defend Manila Bay saddled him with the job of surveying the Bataan peninsula, which flanked its entrance. He had contracted malaria there two decades before, and it was still an unhealthy area. Leading a party of engineers, he mapped forty square miles of the tough terrain—scaling steep mountains, hacking through jungles, wading across flooded paddy fields. The achievement, impressive for a man in his forties, enthused him. Nearly twenty years later, when Bataan and Corregidor had become his Calvary, the inadequacies of the Orange Plan would be gruesomely apparent.

Late in 1924, as Pershing prepared to retire as Chief of Staff, MacArthur's mother unabashedly importuned him again. "Dear Old Jack," she begged in another of her smarmy letters, be "real good and sweet [and] give my Boy his well earned promotion before you leave the army." Whether or not her appeal made a difference, Pershing did elevate MacArthur, and he returned home from the Philippines as America's youngest major general. But his life for the next three years was to be sad and lonely.

Hardly had he taken command of the Washington military region, his new job, than he received what he later termed "one of the most distasteful orders" of his career: to sit on the court-martial of Brigadier General William Mitchell. A rambunctious advocate of air power, Mitchell had alienated the army hierarchy, which charged him with misconduct and indiscipline. Convicted and suspended from duty, he would ultimately be enshrined as a martyred prophet. MacArthur claimed to have voted for acquittal, but he was notably silent during the trial, presumably to placate his superiors. He also depicted himself subsequently as having acclaimed the airplane, yet nothing in his record showed his support for Mitchell's crusade. In fact, he had shared the bias of the brass and braid, who had woefully disparaged aircraft until after the outbreak of World War II. He was to pay dearly for his neglect of the new technology.

His return home should have saved MacArthur's marriage. He and Louise moved into her mansion nestled in the rolling hills outside Baltimore, and she resumed her familiar social pace, but the relationship soon soured. Though MacArthur tried to mingle with her stylish friends, their talk of fox hunting and charity balls bored him. Louise, for her part, could not fathom his fidelity to the army when fortunes could be made overnight from stock and real estate deals. One of MacArthur's biographers, Carol Morris Petillo, has also attributed their tensions to sexual problems. Petillo has speculated that MacArthur had little experience with women and may have even been a virgin when he met Louise, a liberated flapper with several affairs under her sash. Louise hinted as much to her brother, cruelly remarking that MacArthur, despite his rank, was just "a buck private in the boudoir." His failings, if real, could have driven him back to his mother, who resided in nearby Washington. Pinky's intrusions, Louise later claimed, "eventually succeeded in disrupting our married life."

Finally divorced in 1929, the MacArthurs blamed the break on "incompatibility." In a sense, the routine alibi was true. They personified two diametrically opposite currents then polarizing the United States. Rootless and restive, Louise was the paradigm of an F. Scott Fitzgerald heroine, roaring through America's topsy-turvy twenties like Daisy Buchanan in *The Great Gatsby*, discarding husbands in her quest for a "gold-hatted, high-bouncing lover." Aloof and austere, MacArthur flinched at frivolity and indulgence, blights that threatened to sap America of the strength to pursue its world mission, and he sought a wife who shared his total devotion to flag and duty. Louise and

MacArthur did not understand each other's America or each other. But MacArthur too could be described by Fitzgerald: "Show me a hero and I will write you a tragedy."

★ ★ ★

"No assignment could have pleased me more," remarked MacArthur late in 1928, when orders reached him to return to the Philippines as U.S. commander for the entire archipelago. Besides offering escape from his private woes, the job stood high in the American military hierarchy—a tribute to an officer of only forty-eight. But his ambitions had begun to stretch beyond soldiering. The new position, he mused, might propel him into loftier realms.

Recently elected president, Herbert Hoover named as his secretary of state Henry L. Stimson, the U.S. governor in Manila. MacArthur, seeing a chance to flatter a potentially useful contact, sent Stimson a syrupy note of felicitations, voicing the hope that the position would be "a stepping stone to that last and highest call of America, the presidency." He then bid for the vacant governorship, enlisting Manuel Quezon, at the time head of the Philippine senate, to propose him in a letter to Hoover. Fearing that Quezon might not be extravagant enough in his praise, he even drafted the letter himself. MacArthur, it read, was the "unanimous" choice of all Filipinos, and to select him "would be a master stroke of statesmanship and diplomacy." Quezon never sent the message. Despite his admiration for MacArthur, he balked at backing a soldier for the job after his troubles with Leonard Wood.

MacArthur continued to yearn for bigger things. In April 1929, *The New York Times* reported from Manila that he had "his eyes on the White House for eight or twelve years hence" and that he hoped to get there first by serving as governor of the Philippines and then holding a cabinet position. The unsigned story, attributed to his "close friends," may have been based on local gossip, but MacArthur, who unabashedly ventilated his ambitions, could have been the source. He had not forgotten that William Howard Taft had pursued precisely that path to the presidency a generation before.

In any case, Hoover gave the governorship to Dwight F. Davis, a former secretary of war and wealthy sportsman known mainly as the donor of the tennis trophy that bears his name. But MacArthur eclipsed Davis as the favorite American of the upper-class Filipinos, and he reciprocated their affections.

MacArthur and Quezon deepened their old friendship during those years. They frequently dined together at Quezon's home, MacArthur listening attentively as Quezon spun his dream of eventual independence—an aspiration that most Americans in Manila would have treated as treasonable. The rising shadow of Japan worried them as well, and they often discussed the security of the Philippines. MacArthur knew by now that the Orange Plan was a sham. Nor could he count on Congress to furnish adequate funds for the U.S. garrison, especially after the Wall Street crash of October 1929 sent America's economy into a tailspin. One of his colleagues had bluntly advised him, "There isn't any plan, and you won't get any money, so go to it and do the best you can." Still, MacArthur was buoyed by his training programs and field maneuvers, which seemed to be working. He had also raised the pay and benefits for the Filipino auxiliaries serving with the American forces, and their morale had apparently improved. But, most of all, he desperately wanted to believe in his own success whatever the realities—a trait that would prove disastrous a dozen years later.

In July 1929, Hoover offered him command of the U.S. Army engineers, who were then building massive flood controls for the Mississippi valley. MacArthur, however, longed to be Army Chief of Staff, the honor denied his father. In an effort to ingratiate himself with Hoover's secretary of war, Patrick J. Hurley, a boisterous Oklahoma oil mogul, he sent him an unctuous letter lauding one of his banal speeches as "the most statesmanlike utterance that has emanated from the American government in decades." Hurley, disturbed by MacArthur's divorce, refused to endorse "a man who couldn't hold his women." Nevertheless, Hoover promoted MacArthur to Chief of Staff as a model of the "younger blood" needed by the army.

Quezon and other local luminaries toasted MacArthur at a grand farewell banquet at the Manila Hotel in September 1930. MacArthur, in reply, emphasized the "inescapable necessity" for Americans and Filipinos to share a "sympathetic understanding of each other's desires, hopes and aspirations." His plea for racial harmony again reminded the Filipinos that he was unique among the senior American officials in Manila.

On one occasion, praising the Philippines in typically florid rhetoric, MacArthur digressed into raptures over the "moonbeam delicacy" of its women. The phrase was more than rhetoric. Five months before leaving Manila, he succumbed to such a woman in a liaison that was to end years later as a costly embarrassment to him—and a tragedy for her.

Isabel Rosario Cooper, when MacArthur first met her, was an exquisite creature in her early twenties, with pearly skin and long ebony hair. The daughter of a Scottish businessman and his Chinese *mestizo* wife, she was a popular Manila movie actress and vaudeville star known as "Dimples." MacArthur was soon seeing her regularly, disregarding the gossip that rippled through town. His Filipino friends, after all, kept *queridas,* and Americans attached no opprobrium to native mistresses as long as the line was drawn at intermarriage. Most important, his mother was too far away to inhibit him. But before sailing for Washington, he took a bold step. He arranged for Dimples to join him there.

Just as boldly, he deluged her during his long voyage home with letters and cablegrams and wrote to her frequently during his later travels. To this day, fortunately for his literary reputation, the MacArthur estate prohibits direct quotation from the correspondence. It bears the imprint of an impassioned schoolboy—or worse yet, the infatuation of a man of middle years for a beauty half his age. Blushing with references to hearts and flowers, kisses and undying love, the passages read like greeting cards.

Back home, MacArthur lodged his infirm mother in his official mansion at Fort Myer, across the Potomac from the capital, and installed an elevator for her convenience. He meanwhile ensconced Dimples in a comfortable apartment near his office adjoining the White House and, presuming that she would rarely go outdoors, provided her with more kimonos and lingerie than street clothes. Soon, with the dexterity of a trapeze artist, he was vaulting from one place to the other.

His hope of locking Dimples into a love nest forever was romantic fantasy, however. A vivacious young woman who had been a celebrity in Manila, she resisted confinement. He soothed her with a limousine and chauffeur to tour the city and, after she had seen all the sights, sent her on a cruise to Havana. Again bored on her return, she enrolled in law school, where she had a fling with a fellow student while MacArthur paid the bills. By early 1934, his passion cooled and his pocketbook depleted, he offered to pay her way back to the Philippines. When she refused, he forwarded her a newspaper classified section advertising menial jobs, along with a crude note: "Apply to your father or brother for any future help." She moved to a sleazy rooming house and began to hunt for work. By then, the affair had remained secret for four years, an amazing phenomenon for leaky Washington. Soon it would rattle MacArthur.

Professionally, too, those were dim years for him. As Chief of Staff, he was at the peak of his career, but his army comprised only 130,000 troops, ranking it sixteenth in the world—below the Portuguese and Greek forces. His men lacked modern rifles, artillery and other equipment, and their wages had not been raised in a decade. Small wonder, then, that the service was a dump for poor, uneducated and often illiterate outcasts. The officers were also largely an uninspired lot for whom duty represented membership in a "gentleman's club" in which they played polo in the afternoon and bridge in the evening, often drank to excess and awaited glacially slow advancement. MacArthur's rapid rise had been unique. The Chief of Staff during World War II and later one of America's great secretaries of state, George C. Marshall, did not become a brigadier general until 1936, at the age of fifty-six.

The army partly owed its problems to the economic slump, which had caused Congress to slash appropriations. But the atrocities of World War I had also turned Americans against military solutions. They showed their feelings in the spread of peace and disarmament groups as well as in their acclaim for novelists like Ernest Hemingway and John Dos Passos, who vividly depicted the horrors of war. To MacArthur, however, any sentiment short of total loyalty to country was evil, as he argued in 1931. A majority of clergymen, surveyed by a religious journal, had objected to any U.S. role in a future war. Asked for his comment, MacArthur replied: "I can think of no principles more high and holy than those for which our national sacrifices have been made in the past. . . . Religion and patriotism have always gone hand in hand, while atheism has invariably been accompanied by radicalism, communism, bolshevism and other enemies of free government."

During the summer of 1932, obsessed by alleged leftist trends, he committed a blunder that was to blemish his image for years to come. Some twenty thousand veterans of World War I, mainly jobless victims of the Depression, had marched on Washington to urge Congress to vote for a deferred bonus. Many came with their families. Camped in empty government offices or in flimsy huts outside the city, most were orderly men who merited compassion. But, to MacArthur, they were subversives, and he assumed personal charge when Hoover ordered them dispersed. One of his aides, an overaged major named Dwight D. Eisenhower, later recalled telling "that dumb son-of-a-bitch" to keep away from the fracas. MacArthur ignored him. Donning his uniform and ribbons, he referred to himself in the third person as he declared:

"MacArthur has decided to go into active command in the field. There is incipient revolution in the air."

Mobilizing eight hundred troops, he first evicted the veterans from the public buildings. Then, disregarding a directive from Hoover to halt, he pursued them with bayonets and tear gas across the Anacostia River southeast of the capital. There, as women and children fled in terror, his men burned their encampment of shacks and tents. Shocked by the spectacle of "ragged, ill-fed" former soldiers being "badly abused," Eisenhower afterward remarked of MacArthur, "I just can't understand how such a damn fool could have gotten to be a general." But MacArthur proudly declaimed that he had routed a "bad-looking mob" bent on "insurgency and insurrection." To protect his own reputation, however, he cleverly shifted responsibility for the operation to the feckless Hoover. The president's "force and vigor," he told reporters, had averted "a very grave situation" that would have "severely threatened" the government.

Conservatives cheered, but MacArthur worried Governor Franklin D. Roosevelt of New York, who had just been nominated Democratic candidate for president. Chatting with friends at his Albany office, Roosevelt cited Senator Huey Long, the Louisiana demagogue, as "one of the two most dangerous men in the country"; the other, he said, was MacArthur. However, Roosevelt added, he would "tame" right-wing officers like MacArthur and "make them useful to us."

MacArthur's posturing made him an easy target for columnists like Drew Pearson and Robert S. Allen, who reveled in puncturing pomposity. They assailed him in a cascade of adjectives as "dictatorial, insubordinate, disloyal, mutinous and disrespectful of his superiors," calling his rout of the veterans "unwarranted, unnecessary, arbitrary, harsh and brutal." He promptly sued them for $1.75 million in damages and, facing disaster, they desperately began to build a defense.

A Mississippi congressman helped. A friend of his lived in the same apartment house as a lovely Eurasian woman whom MacArthur visited frequently. She was Dimples, of course, and Pearson discovered to his delight that she had saved MacArthur's love letters. His lawyer casually informed MacArthur's counsel at a pretrial hearing that a Miss Isabel Cooper would appear as a defense witness.

The rest resembled a bedroom farce. Pearson, alleging that MacArthur had ordered army agents to abduct her, concealed Dimples in a Baltimore hideout with a colleague, whom she reportedly seduced—or vice versa. Amid these escapades, MacArthur abruptly abandoned the case. He gave Dimples $15,000 for the letters and paid an equal sum to defray Pearson's legal fees. The episode cost him the equivalent of his salary and allowances for three years. He never mentioned the affair. But a friend, Admiral William Leahy, later observed that he could have defeated Pearson in court had he not feared that his mother would learn about Dimples. "He was a bachelor," Leahy remarked. "All he had to do was look everybody in the face and say: 'So what? Cunt can make you look awfully silly at times!'"

The farce ended in tragedy. Dimples eventually drifted out to Hollywood, where she played a few bit movie roles and tried in vain to tell the tale of her romance. In 1960, despondent, she committed suicide by swallowing an overdose of barbiturates.

MacArthur, meanwhile, felt increasingly alienated from Roosevelt's circle. He was uneasy with New Dealers, whose liberal ideas transgressed his traditional views. They in turn resented his Republican sympathies and imperious manner and denounced him as a "bellicose swashbuckler" or "polished popinjay." Above all, MacArthur battled Roosevelt's efforts to put domestic priorities ahead of defense spending; both stubborn men, they clashed bitterly. Following one shouting match, in which Roosevelt rejected his resignation, MacArthur retched on the White House steps. He clearly could not continue as Chief of Staff. The Philippines, once again, offered an escape.

★　★　★

Late in 1934, Quezon visited Washington. Expecting to preside over the Philippine commonwealth recently created by Congress, he sought advice on managing the new government. He had one question for his old friend MacArthur: Could the islands be defended after independence? Refuting the opinion of nearly every U.S. strategist, MacArthur replied: "I don't *think* so. I *know* they can defend themselves." He thereupon proposed a Swiss formula—a reserve of citizen conscripts, trained and commanded by a core of regulars, to be mobilized in the event of war. Reassured, Quezon invited him to become military adviser to the autonomous regime.

Roosevelt, by now eager to banish MacArthur, approved. The offer also tempted MacArthur, who faced either a corps command at home or retirement at the age of fifty-five, but he imposed stiff terms on Quezon. He demanded $33,000 a year, the same salary and allowances paid the U.S. governor of the Philippines, in addition to a fully air-conditioned penthouse atop the Manila Hotel, almost equal in size to the governor's quarters in the Malacañang palace. Quezon agreed, and MacArthur accepted, pledging to "devote the remainder of my life if necessary" to defending the archipelago. Soon, however, he was jockeying to be made high commissioner, as the senior American official would be entitled under the commonwealth. Roosevelt seriously considered him until he overplayed his hand by reviling the incumbent governor, Frank Murphy, whose liberal opinions he detested. To MacArthur's distress, Roosevelt later chose Paul V. McNutt, the former governor of Indiana. McNutt hoped to be the Democratic presidential candidate and Roosevelt, already eyeing a third term, wanted him out of the way.

MacArthur landed in Manila late in 1935, accompanied by his octogenarian mother and a token staff that included Major Eisenhower, whom he had dragooned into serving as his chief aide. He was stunned when his mother died six weeks later, but her death emancipated him. Aboard ship, he had met Jean Marie Faircloth, who was traveling to China to visit friends. A small, sparkling spinster of thirty-six from Tennessee, she may have reminded him of the southern belle his mother had been. She was proud of her Confederate forebears, one of whom had fought against MacArthur's father during the Civil War. Captivated by soldiers, she could not resist MacArthur, a prototype of the breed. After his mother's death, Jean returned to Manila to console him, and they were married the next year during a furlough in New York. A year later, she bore his son, whom he named Arthur, for his father.

Exalted by his new job, MacArthur arrogated for himself the rank of field marshal, the only U.S. Army officer in history to hold that grade. He also concocted a comic-opera uniform of black trousers and a white tunic filigreed with intricate designs. The ludicrous costume not only reflected his vanity but also caught the flavor of the Philippines, which then appeared to be devolving into a coconut republic.

Quezon, now president of the commonwealth, articulated the language of American democracy, but he was, in practice, an autocrat primarily preoccupied with preserving his power. Recalling his mythical peasant past, he would rattle on about "social justice" as he wielded nearly absolute authority to control wages, prices and profits as well as to ban strikes and other "unwholesome agitation." Such was his ego that he peremptorily canceled an experiment with daylight savings time after stubbing his toe in the early-morning darkness. Exercising his prerogative as head of government, he moved into the Malacañang palace, whose lovely gardens he used for large parties devised to depict himself as successor to the Spanish and American colonial masters. He also entertained lavishly on his sleek white yacht, and spent huge sums on clothes, nightclubs and other luxuries during his trips abroad, staffing his private railway coaches with native cooks to prepare his favorite fare. One of his delights on his visits to New York was to take over the Roseland ballroom for the night, paying the taxi girls to dance with him and his friends. Filipino and American businessmen underwrote him, often with blank checks, and he usually repaid them with patronage. Once, in need of funds to finance a journey to the United States, he cleaned out the bank account of a big Manila footwear manufacturer. Finding the industrialist in trouble on his return months later, he breezily told him, "Oh well, you can have the contract to supply the entire Philippine army with shoes."

Nothing sustained Quezon's sense of self-importance more than being treated as a chief of state on visits to China and Japan, whose leaders courted him as part of their own policy of encouraging Asian nationalism. He genuinely rejoiced in the banquets, salutes, decorations and other gestures, which appealed to his opulent tastes. But he would repeatedly be reminded of his semisovereign status, as he was in 1936, when Roosevelt denied him permission to attend the coronation of King George VI of Britain as an independent ruler.

Despite his pretenses, though, Quezon realized that the Philippines was an American dependent. "Every Filipino," he would intone, "owes allegiance to the United States . . . without mental reservation." But he identified America with MacArthur, his *compadre.* Quezon's wife, Aurora, along with her husband a godparent of MacArthur's son, once explained it to Murphy, who envied their intimate relationship: "Frank, you don't seem to understand. Douglas is our brother."

Quezon, by entrusting MacArthur with the security of the Philippines, felt that the United States was consecrated to his country's protection. But MacArthur's concept for defending the archipelago was at best clouded, and, as Quezon discovered when the chips fell, the American commitment was murky.

Guided by the Swiss example, MacArthur envisioned a core of eleven thousand Filipino regulars who would train four hundred thousand native troops to be mobilized at the outbreak of war. Buttressed by a fleet of fifty patrol boats and two hundred aircraft, they would fight in small mobile squads from their assorted home areas to defend the beaches against attack—and then, as MacArthur put it, continue to resist "to the furthermost retreat left available." He saw the force as primarily a deterrent that would, as he pledged in his sententious rhetoric, confront an enemy with "such difficult problems as to give pause even to the most ruthless and powerful." To conquer the islands, he calculated, would require "a half million men, ten billion dollars, tremendous casualties and three years' time"—far more than any rational adversary would want to expend. His program, on the other hand, would cost a comparatively modest $8 million a year over the span of a decade.

Elihu Root, who as secretary of state had pioneered the U.S. presence in the Philippines, turned MacArthur's equation upside down with uncanny foresight. In 1937, just before his death at the age of ninety-two, he reckoned that the Japanese could take the archipelago within a week, compelling America to commit "five years and twenty-five billion dollars to beat them." Official U.S. strategists were equally gloomy. With the patience and fortitude of Talmudic scholars, they had been analyzing and modifying the Orange Plan for years, and still it was little more than a formula for withdrawal. Nor did MacArthur's Swiss model infuse them with much confidence. Unlike Switzerland, a survey by War Department experts noted, the Philippines was not a "compact land unit" that could be protected by flexible troop units, but a sprawl of islands vulnerable to various enemy assaults. The Japanese navy, they also warned, could easily blockade the archipelago, thus cutting its lines of supply. They suggested that the infant Filipino force concentrate instead on "internal disorders," such as banditry and peasant dissidence. The United States, however, no longer governed the Philippines completely. The commonwealth regime now legislated its own defense policies, and Quezon had placed his faith in MacArthur.

Domestic instability was indeed worrisome. As it is today, the Philippines was then a social volcano, constantly rumbling with discontent, erupting periodically in local revolts. The U.S. administration in Manila, after a few abortive attempts at liberal measures, had delegated the agrarian issue to Filipino officials, most of them servile to an entrenched gentry implacably opposed to reforms. The worldwide economic slump had also shriveled the foreign market for exports like sugar and coconut oil, and a surging birth rate exacerbated the problem. Conditions in the countryside had steadily deteriorated, driving the average income below subsistence levels. One statistic in a census conducted during the 1930s illustrated the gravity of the situation: Out of a population of sixteen million, about three and a half million were classified as "agricultural day laborers"—in short, a dispossessed fourth of the nation.

Farms had become unproductive as swelling families split up their acreage into increasingly smaller plots, and tenancy spread as creditors foreclosed on insolvent peasants. Hunger and poverty paralyzed what had been America's two most notable programs: education and public health. Parents pulled their children out of school to help make ends meet, while malnutrition, dysentery and tuberculosis grew to epidemic proportions. An American researcher dubbed the *barrios* a "rural slum," saved from starvation only by the fecundity of the tropics. Early in 1931, a U.S. official in central Luzon saw a crisis ahead. "Take a man's land away from him and he is desperate," he declared, warning that the area was "ready for an uprising."

The same could have been said of almost any spot in the Philippines at almost any time. The provinces swirled with a profusion of mystical cabals, secret societies, clandestine brotherhoods, seditious associations and other such groups. Many, rooted in religious factions and messianic movements that dated back centuries, were animated by assorted patriotic zealots and political dissenters. Understandably, they attracted the alienated and aggrieved, who had little to lose from hopeless ventures.

During the recession after World War I, for example, a fishmonger named Flor de Entrecherado organized the indigent tenants and sugar workers of the Visayas, and soon became a potent figure in the area. He proclaimed himself "Emperor of the Philippines" under the title of Florencio I, converting his villa into a "royal palace" in which, seated on a rattan throne on the veranda, he held court in a purple robe and bejeweled crown, scepter in hand. In 1925, he announced a crusade to "liberate" the archipelago, alerting his faithful to await the order for "the poor . . . to kill all the rich." He issued the order two years later, and the comedy turned ugly. Wielding axes, knives and homemade guns, his disciples raided police stations and constabulary garrisons in several towns—fortunately causing more furor than casualties. The American governor, Leonard Wood, checked the violence by going to Iloilo, where he induced Florencio to surrender by plying him with a gourmet dinner. Psychiatrists diagnosed the emperor as mentally unstable and confined him to a Manila asylum, where he spent his final years writing voluminous memoirs while puffing perfumed cigars. His chief lieutenants, deemed sane, went to jail.

The Florencio episode may have been a squall, but more severe social storms hit Luzon with typhoon intensity. Early in 1931, scores of dejected farm laborers occupied Tayug, a town in coastal Pangasinan province. They seized municipal offices and burned hated land records before troops arrived, losing five of their own and killing six rebels in a fight that raged for twelve hours. One of the slain insurgents was a young woman, shot by soldiers as she strode barefoot across the town square in the afternoon sunshine, apparently in a trance, waving the Philippine flag above her head in cadence to her steps. Several alarmed Americans in Manila called for reform. The *Free Press*, a liberal weekly, asserted that "no nation can be founded on a downtrodden peasantry," and urged that "facts" be "looked in the face." However, neither senior American nor Filipino officials would confront facts.

A bigger upheaval was to rock Luzon four years later. Its leader, Benigno Ramos, was a prolific Tagalog-language journalist and poet who had moved to Manila from nearby Bulacan province. His writing attracted Quezon, who gave him a staff job in the Philippine senate. In 1930, lusting after elected office, Ramos bid for nationalist support by protesting against an American high school teacher accused of maligning Filipinos as "monkeys." Quezon, then striving to soothe the United States, disowned him. At that, Ramos founded a weekly, *Sakdal*, meaning "accuse" or "strike" in Tagalog, and flayed Quezon for helping the Americans to exploit the "masses." Filipinos thrive on abusive polemics, and Ramos's vitriolic genius made him an instant celebrity. He formed a political party, also called *Sakdal*, capturing three seats in the national legislature and several municipal posts in central Luzon. Frank Murphy guardedly advised Washington that while the movement "may become dangerous," a populist antidote to the reactionary oligarchy "might be a welcome development."

To maintain his nationalist momentum, Ramos decried the commonwealth status then scheduled for the Philippines and demanded immediate independence. He went to Japan in quest of support and, during his absence, local Filipino officials harassed his followers—denying them, among other things, the right to speak publicly. Japanese sympathizers financed Ramos's propaganda, which he smuggled back to the islands. It was puerile stuff that, for instance, labeled Frank Murphy a "Frankenstein" and Quezon his "Super-Servant." But the restive farm laborers and tenants of central Luzon needed no prodding. By 1935, they were ripe to explode in revolt, and *Sakdalista* agitators touched off the fuse.

Early in May, a month of dense heat and humidity, some six thousand peasants flared up in the area around Manila—as if ignited by a single spark. Spilling through the region in hundreds of bands, they brandished knives, sickles, clubs and primitive guns. They converged on municipal offices, constabulary barracks and police stations, naïvely expecting to be supported by seditious soldiers and friendly townsfolk. Instead, to their astonishment, they met withering fire everywhere. The bloodiest battle occurred in Laguna province southeast of Manila. The governor there was Juan Cailles, a part-French *mestizo*, who as a swashbuckling young nationalist guerrilla at the turn of the century had been one of the last holdouts against the American conquest of the Philippines. Though now middle-aged, he had lost none of his verve. Pistol in hand, he rushed forth at the head of his troops against three hundred insurgents crouched behind an ancient Spanish stone wall in the town of Cabuyao, killing fifty of them in the assault. Another ten or twenty rebels died elsewhere in the area as the survivors fled in panic, dazed and disillusioned that the rural population had failed to rally to their cause. By the end of the day, the odor of cordite hung in the air as corpses began to rot under the scorching sun. Benigno Ramos, safe in Tokyo, later served the Japanese during their occupation of the Philippines in World War II—as did many of the rich Filipinos he detested.

In different guises, under different leaders and spurred by different ideologies, larger uprisings were to disrupt the Philippines during the decades ahead—nearly all of them rooted in social dissatisfaction. But the *Sakdal* rebellion had been the biggest within memory, and it stimulated a few prescient Americans in Manila to clamor again for reforms.

One of the more liberal, A.V.H. Hartendorp, editor of *Philippines Magazine,* cautioned that despite their "vague, foolish and uncoordinated" principles, the *Sakdalistas* had nevertheless manifested "a groping for remedies that have not been brought to them by the politicians." Murphy, ever the New Dealer, shared that opinion and released almost all the convicted rebels as his last official act as governor in late 1935. Many Filipinos also began to appeal for progressive measures, but, like the Bourbons, the wealthy landowners neither forgot nor learned. In parts of central Luzon, they formed vigilante groups to crush the dissidents and instructed their surrogates in the Philippine legislature to reject proposals aimed at easing the plight of the peasantry.

Presumably an expert on the archipelago, MacArthur must have been aware of the ferment. But he seemed to be blind to its revolutionary potential. He was a conventional officer assigned to create a conventional army capable of waging a conventional war against a conventional enemy.

Eisenhower, detailed by MacArthur to create the Filipino force, doubted from the start that an army could be cobbled together, and his frustrations rose as he grappled with the task. Local draft boards were casual about enlisting youths, who dodged service by vanishing into the jungles or simply staying at home. Those conscripted defied molding into even passable soldiers. They lacked modern weapons and adequate rations, and their pay amounted to "little more than cigarette money," Eisenhower lamented. As he toured the country, he found training camps to be ramshackle affairs in which the rookies, most of them uneducated farm boys, hated discipline, disobeyed orders and even mutinied. But he was particularly dismayed by the native officers, supposedly the spine of the makeshift army, who impressed him as indolent, corrupt and quarrelsome. He soon came to expect of them, as he confided to his diary, "a minimum of performance from a maximum of promise."

MacArthur made matters worse. In 1936, in his initial report on the embryonic Filipino army, he said that "progress . . . has exceeded original anticipation." The absurd estimate, partly contrived to quiet skeptics, also reflected his belief in his own infallibility, since any project he undertook would by definition succeed. But an ulterior motive prompted his enthusiasm as well. His Filipino troops relied on surplus U.S. weapons and other equipment, which he feared might be denied them unless he convinced Washington that they were making strides. Eisenhower dismissed his report as "far too optimistic," commenting that there was no native force "to speak of"—and he continued to puncture MacArthur's roseate rhetoric. To evade reality, he contended, would only build up illusions that could prove to be dangerous in the future.

The two men waged acrimonious disputes. MacArthur would fly into tantrums at Eisenhower, denouncing his doubts as defeatist and threatening to wreck his career. His temper equally volatile, Eisenhower dared MacArthur to fire him, sputtering, "Godammit, you do things I don't agree with, and you know damn well I don't." Both obstinate, they were to vilify one another for the rest of their lives. Years later, jealous of Eisenhower's fame, MacArthur deprecated him as "the best clerk I ever had." Eisenhower, afterward asked if he had ever met MacArthur, snorted, "I studied dramatics under him for seven years." The rancor between them was to grow especially acute immediately after the United States entered World War II, when Eisenhower as a key planner in Washington plotted policies that clashed with MacArthur's priorities.

MacArthur nevertheless retained Eisenhower, whose skill as an organizer he needed. Eisenhower was also vital as a liaison with Quezon—who, wary of MacArthur's flights of fancy, respected Eisenhower's integrity. He gave Eisenhower an office in the Malacañang palace and counted on him for the unvarnished truth. Dismissing MacArthur's cheerful forecasts, Eisenhower warned that the Philippines would be swiftly conquered unless the Japanese were stopped at the coast. To boost Quezon's morale, however, he added a more encouraging note that presaged his own invasion of Normandy in 1944: "Successful penetration of a defended beach is the most difficult operation in warfare." Late in 1939, as Eisenhower prepared to return home, Quezon praised his candor at a farewell banquet: "Whenever I asked Ike for an opinion, I got an answer. It may not have been what I wanted to hear, it may have displeased me, but it was always a straightforward and honest answer."

In part, Eisenhower was departing out of exasperation. His effort to forge a Filipino army had faltered and, as he put it, "I can't afford to go on teaching schoolboys any longer." By then, the native reserve consisted of only about a hundred thousand men, one fourth the number called for in MacArthur's plan. MacArthur continued to exude optimism, but Quezon had gradually become morose.

"If I did not believe that the Philippines could defend itself," Quezon had told an American editor in 1937, "I would commit suicide." Vowing to stand by the United States, he affirmed that "the cause for which America would fight is our cause." He also pondered delaying Philippine independence to guarantee U.S. protection of the islands. His attitude evolved over the next two years as he watched Japan tighten its grip on China and saw Germany march into Austria and Czechoslovakia. Small nations, he concluded, could not rely on the democracies to defend them. He began to contemplate a deal between the Philippines and its probable foe, Japan.

He took a shadowy trip to Tokyo in June 1938, claiming that it was a vacation. In fact, he hoped to induce the Japanese to give him a formal pledge to respect Philippine neutrality following independence—which he would now seek to achieve sooner than scheduled. He conferred at length with senior Japanese officials, and the emperor tendered a lunch in his honor, an arcane sign that his mission was being blessed with celestial favor, but the Japanese made no commitments. They knew, as did everyone else, that the erratic Quezon could zig as quickly as he zagged.

Back home, Quezon moved to placate Japan. To declare neutrality, he requested Philippine independence in 1940, six years ahead of schedule. He created a Defense Department, curbing MacArthur's authority to procure supplies, construct facilities or enroll recruits without his approval. Hitler's invasion of Poland in September 1939 further convinced him "of the futility of spending money to carry on our program of defending the Philippines from foreign aggression." He cut his military budget, closed training camps and reduced arms purchases. The archipelago, he told a crowd packed into a Manila stadium, "could not be defended even if every last Filipino were armed with modern weapons."

Despite their kinship ties, Quezon visibly repudiated MacArthur—proposing in late 1939 to Francis B. Sayre, who had replaced Paul McNutt as high commissioner, that Roosevelt recall him. He dropped the idea after Sayre prudently asked for it in writing. But he henceforth required MacArthur to go through his private secretary, Jorge Vargas. The snub hurt MacArthur, but he was accustomed to Quezon's whims. He also reckoned that, with war approaching, Quezon would sooner or later need his services. Once, when Quezon denied him access, he predicted to Vargas: "Jorge, some day your boss is going to want to see me more than I want to see him."

The publisher Roy Howard wrote to Quezon in late 1939 that "the American public is badly balled up as to just what your ideas are." But Quezon's caprices truly reflected his quandary. The Roosevelt administration, by rejecting early independence, had thwarted his plan to proclaim neutrality. Congress would not furnish the U.S. forces with the funds necessary to protect the islands. And MacArthur's native army, which had been intended as a cheap alternative, was a failure. Quezon was gambling on the slim prospect that Japan might concede to an accommodation. For years, however, the Japanese had been crafting a strategy whose objectives included the takeover of the archipelago.

★ ★ ★

All Japanese aspired to make Japan preeminent in Asia, but their island nation lacked the resources vital for modern industry to generate its power. The attainment of their dream depended on the acquisition of raw materials to be found overseas—rubber, tin, bauxite and especially oil. One largely civilian group of leaders championed such peaceful means as trade and diplomacy. Another, primarily military, favored conquest. The line between them was fuzzy, however. There were pugnacious politicians and prudent soldiers, and Japan's policies vacillated as their influence rose or fell. The Japanese high command nevertheless played a crucial role in steering Japan toward war with the United States.

The Japanese officer corps traced its singular status back to the ancient *shizoku,* the warrior nobility. Besides enjoying the patronage of the emperor, whose mandate from heaven endowed him with absolute authority, senior generals and admirals headed the ministries responsible for their respective services, which permitted them to act without interference. As cabinet members, they also exercised immense political leverage and could topple governments that foiled their aims, but they were not a monolith. Their ranks were riddled with competing factions that chronically squabbled among themselves, and even murdered their rivals.

In 1894, army zealots concocted a war with the decrepit Chinese empire that led to Japan's annexation of Taiwan; a decade later, the navy engineered a conflict with Russia, whose defeat put Korea under Japanese control. The global slump that began in the late 1920s hit Japan hard, bringing famine to many of its rural areas. Claiming that expansion was the only path to recovery, an army clique fabricated an "incident" in 1931 as a pretext to gobble up Manchuria in northeastern China and founded a puppet regime there called Manchukuo. The League of Nations, meeting in Geneva, could only censure Japan, thereby convincing its hard-liners that they could push ahead with impunity. In July 1937, they plunged Japan into a full-scale war against China.

The senior Japanese commanders had by then reached a broad compromise following a debate of the kind common to military bureaucracies everywhere. The army, spearheading the costly offensive in China, demanded fresh appropriations to continue its drive. Vying for funds, the navy designed a two-front strategy to assure itself a role. While the ground forces waged a "continental" campaign in China, the fleet would launch a "blue-water" offensive into Southeast Asia against French Indochina, the Dutch East Indies and the British colony of Malaya, with its presumably impregnable bastion at Singapore. The advance held out the promise of the region's natural resources. The Philippines would figure among the targets—which inevitably augured a collision with the

United States. At that stage, however, the plan was a broad set of intentions rather than a clear course of action.

Japan's ultranationalists, humiliated by discrimination against Japanese immigrants in America, had been clamoring for reprisals against the United States since the start of the century. Some even floated the idea of a future war, a notion that struck a chord among extremist naval officers, who started planning for that contingency as early as 1907. Ironically, they were inspired by Captain Alfred Mahan, the American naval theorist, whose works had been translated into Japanese years before. In typical Japanese fashion, however, they adapted his tenets to their needs. They embraced his belief that success hinged on climactic sea battles. Indeed, they credited his influence for their dramatic victory over the Russians, whom they smashed in two stunning naval engagements. But Japan lacked the industrial might to achieve quantitative superiority, one of Mahan's fundamental doctrines, and they blended his teachings with traditional Chinese and Japanese military concepts of maneuver, attrition and deception.

Their plan was to attack the Philippines and Guam at the outbreak of a hypothetical war, thus luring an American fleet across the Pacific to defend the U.S. possessions. Then, benefiting from the proximity of its home bases, the Japanese navy would intercept and destroy the American ships, their crews exhausted by the long voyage, in a decisive encounter. Fierce domestic debates were to roil Japan, however, before the strategy could be accepted as national policy.

During the decade after World War I, the United States and Britain had persuaded Japan to agree to curb the size of its navy. Several Japanese civilian leaders, champions of cooperation with the Western democracies, backed the pacts. A number of admirals concurred, maintaining that a rash arms race with the Americans at that point would cripple Japan. By no means pacifists, they believed, as one senior officer wrote, that the navy should be strengthened "calmly and with circumspection." In 1930, after the Japanese legislature ratified one of the treaties, the expansionists went berserk. A fanatic assassinated the prime minister, Osachi Hamaguchi, a partisan of disarmament, and a clique in the navy ministry ousted the moderates. Japan now hurtled headlong into the ranks of the major sea powers.

To Americans in those days, "made in Japan" signified dime-store gimcrackery, but Japanese engineers and artisans, as skilled then as they are now, were investing their talents in the war machine. Transgressing the treaty curbs, they perfected the world's deadliest torpedoes, along with a fleet of fast boats to carry the weapons, and developed the most modern cruisers and destroyers then afloat. In 1937, they secretly began construction of the *Yamato* and the *Musahi,* the most powerful battleships to be built anywhere until then. To equal the *Yamato,* which displaced sixty-four thousand tons, the United States would have had to design a vessel too large to pass through the Panama Canal.

Nothing in the Japanese arsenal, however, surpassed the redoubtable Zero fighter, which for speed and flexibility outclassed any airplane in the U.S. Army or Navy when it first entered action in 1940. Its chief flaw was its light weight, the key to its maneuverability, a weakness that American pilots later learned to detect. Lieutenant General Claire L. Chennault, whose corps of volunteers, the Flying Tigers, flew missions against the Japanese in China before the United States entered World War II, had cautioned against the Zero's lethal performance. But the American military establishment, complacently refusing to acknowledge Japan's technological capabilities, ignored his warning—with fatal consequences for U.S. airmen during the early stages of the war.

Nor could Americans conceive of the Japanese, little people who ate rice and raw fish, as formidable fighters, but many of Japan's top officers had studied in the United States, Britain or Germany. Nearly all kept up with the the latest military theories, which were regularly translated into Japanese. Like their aircraft, Japanese pilots were precision instruments. Numbers of them had years of combat experience in China, and even novices could not join their units before clocking three hundred hours aloft. Japanese sailors, trained under rigorous conditions in the frigid climate off the coast of northern Japan, sardonically joked that their relentless schedule consisted only of weekdays. Above all, a martial spirit of almost religious intensity charged Japanese servicemen, inspiring them to sacrifice themselves in battle out of a conviction that their death would purify the "soul" of Japan.

Crucial to Japan's strategy were some thirty thousand Japanese citizens then living in the Philippines. Most were concentrated on the southern island of Mindanao, a pristine frontier region, where they ran hemp plantations, lumber companies, sawmills, fishing fleets, canneries and other enterprises, often with silent Filipino partners to comply with the curbs on alien proprietorship. Their engineers built roads, and their agronomists introduced new farming methods. They worked hard, obeyed the law, paid taxes and were widely esteemed. The area's major city, Davao, was a Japanese town—with Japanese schools, Japanese shops, Japanese cafés serving Japanese beer and Japanese commercial firms handling its imports, eighty percent of which arrived from Japan aboard Japanese freighters. A contemporary U.S. official, awed by their dynamism, wrote after a trip to Davao that they had created "a well-nigh perfect organization for the economic penetration and development of a new country." They were also potentially a "fifth column" of subversives.

Japan's pivotal operative in the Philippines then was Kiyoshi Uchiyama, the consul in Manila. Conceiving a scheme to win support for Japan, he urged Tokyo to authorize him to undertake such "behind-the-scene measures" as financing a "pro-Japanese newspaper" to arouse "anti-American sentiment." He received approval in 1936, along with advice that Japan's plan to advance southward was no "empty dream." Ordered to muster sympathy for Japan among influential Filipinos, he was fortified with the funds to dispense largesse. He made little headway. A few Manila journalists pocketed his money, and he squandered $30,000 on a candidate who failed to win election to the Philippine legislature. He did bankroll one illustrious Filipino—José Laurel, a Yale Law School graduate and Supreme Court justice, who later presided over the puppet republic set up by the Japanese during their World War II occupation of the islands. Some of his critics accused Quezon of taking Japanese subsidies, but the charges were never proved. In any case, as historian Theodore Friend has written, Quezon received gifts in the spirit of the Aga Khan, who was paid his weight in diamonds, without feeling obligated to give anything in return. Uchiyama, finally frustrated by his slipperiness, described his attitude toward Japan as "thoroughly ambiguous."

Like Laurel, many elite Filipinos collaborated with the Japanese during World War II, out of necessity but also out of admiration for their skill, discipline and authoritarian ethic. The Japanese also attracted Filipino radicals enthralled by the spell of Asian nationalism. They largely benefited as well from their compatriots residing in the Philippines, who had long awaited the chance to serve their motherland. Carlos Romulo, the eminent Filipino diplomat, recalled his surprise at learning after the war that "my gardener had been a Japanese major and my masseur a Japanese colonel."

★ ★ ★

A telephone call jarred President Roosevelt at three o'clock in the morning of September 1, 1939. William C. Bullitt, his ambassador in Paris, was on the faint line, his voice trembling with the news that the Germans had invaded Poland. The war in Europe had begun. After a moment's silence, Roosevelt replied: "Well, Bill, it has come at last. God help us all."

In a startling pact four weeks later, Germany and the Soviet Union divided Poland between themselves, and a lull followed—dubbed by cynics the "phony war." Then, in May 1940, Hitler suddenly launched a new offensive. Within a month, his panzer divisions swept across Holland and Belgium, driving the British forces off the Continent and capturing Paris within a month. The French cabinet fled, and Marshal Henri Philippe Pétain, a World War I hero then near senility, set up a pro-German regime in Vichy, a fashionable spa in central France. Americans, to whom Europe had once seemed remote, now realized that only Britain, precariously battling a German bombing blitz, separated them from the Nazis.

In Tokyo, half a world away, the Japanese welcomed the German victories as a boon to their ambitions. France and Holland, in shambles, could no longer protect their colonies in Southeast Asia, and Britain's territories in the area were nearly as vulnerable. In July 1940, a Japanese army faction installed as the new prime minister Prince Fumimaro Konoe, a sensitive but pliable aristocrat. The power in the cabinet, however, belonged to Lieutenant General Hideki Tojo, the war minister. A strict, dedicated, incorruptible soldier known as "The Razor," he resembled the prototypical Japanese villain, with his thin lips, narrow eyes and bullet head—an image tailor-made for American propagandists during World War II. He had bucked Japan's civilian leaders as one of the officers involved in the unlicensed military takeover of Manchuria in 1931. Again promoting the army's aims, he now intimidated the French authorities in Indochina, whose masters in Vichy were hostage to Germany, into allowing the Japanese forces to use its northern zone to stage forays into southern China.

Japan and the Soviet Union had meanwhile opened talks that were to conclude soon afterward in a nonaggression pact of vast value to them both. With Japanese pressure on them reduced, the Russians could transfer troops from Siberia to their European borders should they go to war with Germany. And, with the Soviet threat to them lessened, the Japanese could focus on their blue-water strategy.

But they knew that a thrust south threatened war with the the United States.

Once more, they reviewed their strategy, debating whether to fight or negotiate. They decided, for the present at least, to pursue both tracks.

Until 1940, hoping to avoid a clash in Asia that might divert him from Europe's fate, Roosevelt had ordered Cordell Hull, his secretary of state, to be "firm but conciliatory" toward the Japanese. A flinty Tennessee mountain boy, Hull had climbed through Congress into the improbable role of America's chief diplomat. He believed in the virtues of persuasion and would lecture visiting Japanese officials on the "principles of good behavior" and their government's lapses therefrom as they nodded politely. The approach left the U.S. public ambivalent. Deeply sympathetic to the Chinese, traditionally the object of their missionary zeal, Americans were appalled by Japan's hideous atrocities in China, the daily fare of their newspapers and newsreels. Yet, still strongly isolationist, they recoiled from foreign entanglements. As he observed the increasing truculence of the Japanese, however, Roosevelt gradually stiffened his stance toward them, and their posture hardened in response.

Alarmed by the army's key role in the Konoe cabinet, Roosevelt took a first tough step by banning U.S. sales of aviation fuel and scrap metal to Japan. In retaliation, the Japanese signed an alliance with Germany and its partner, Italy. By late 1940, in preparation for action in Southeast Asia, they were training troops to fight in the tropics. Their planes began to fly photo reconnaissance missions over Malaya and the Philippines, and their War Ministry started to print military currency for the conquered lands. At that point, too, Japanese planners began to contemplate an almost incredible operation: a carrier-based air attack against the huge U.S. naval complex at Pearl Harbor. The officer behind the project was Admiral Isoroku Yamamato, a stocky little man who had studied at Harvard and subsequently served as a naval attaché in Washington.

American strategists now faced a daunting dilemma as they realized that the United States, menaced by both Japan and Germany, lacked the means to wage war simultaneously on opposite sides of the globe with equal vigor. After long debates, they gave priority to Europe at the expense of Asia. They might have derived some comfort from the knowledge that their Japanese counterparts were also wrangling over their next moves. American cryptanalysts could by then intercept secret Japanese messages under a program code-named "Magic." Roosevelt, after reading the traffic, described the internal Japanese dispute with his typical flair for drama as "a real drag-down and knock-out fight . . . to decide which way they were going to jump—attack Russia, attack the South Seas [or] sit on the fence and be more friendly with us."

The Japanese had indeed been thrown into disarray by the German invasion of the Soviet Union in June 1941. They had not been informed in advance by Hitler of his offensive, which placed them in an awkward predicament. The Russians could now tear up the treaty they had signed two months before and attack them as German allies, thereby derailing their plans to push south. The emperor hastily convened his commanders, and they haggled over various options, including a proposal to join the Germans in the war against the Soviet Union. In the end, they voted to stick with their original strategy. They would embark on their venture in Southeast Asia in the hope of acquiring the raw materials to sustain their costly campaign in China, the real prize, but they were not averse to a deal with the Americans that might serve their goals. They had been exploring that possibility since early 1941, when they sent as their ambassador to Washington an amiable, one-eyed retired admiral, Kichisaburo Nomura.

He was preceded by several free-lance intermediaries, including a pair of gullible American Catholic priests who visualized Japan, under U.S. auspices, as an anticommunist bastion. Hull was to meet with Nomura several times during the months ahead, without success. There could be no settlement, Hull repeated in his Tennessee drawl, until Japan conceded to withdraw from China. The protracted war in China was then bleeding their economy, but the Japanese leaders could not conceivably comply with a demand that, to them, signified surrender. Instead, they stepped up their preparations for the drive into Southeast Asia. On July 21, 1941, they occupied all of French Indochina, deploying fifty thousand troops throughout the country, shifting their planes to its southern airfields and stationing their warships at the Cam Ranh Bay naval base. Now they were poised to strike at Malaya, the Dutch East Indies and the Philippines.

Roosevelt, worried about Europe's fortunes, feared that a tough reaction to Japan's bold move might precipitate a premature conflict in Asia, but, unable to disregard the challenge, he contrived a complicated maneuver. He issued a directive freezing all Japanese bank deposits, without which Japan could not pay for U.S. exports. To avoid a showdown, he licensed limited Japanese purchases of oil. Either he failed to explain the gesture to his aides or they deliberately ignored his subtle ploy. Whatever the truth, during one of his absences from Washington, they completely banned the sale of U.S. commodities to Japan. Roosevelt could not plausibly retract the decision on his return without seeming weak. Thus American fuel shipments to the Japanese totally stopped, and deprived of a product indispensable to their military effort, they again reassessed their alternatives.

One group in Tokyo implored the emperor to approve a compromise with the Americans, at least as a stall, warning that the navy's oil reserves were adequate for only eighteen months of hostilities—too short a time to score a "sweeping victory." By contrast, the expansionists demanded a quick war to acquire the raw materials of Southeast Asia. Pleading the case, one of their spokesmen reported that the army in China was "so horribly strained that we cannot endure it much longer." Thus, he asserted in a jumble of metaphors, Japan must immediately "break asunder this ever-strengthening chain of encirclement being woven under the guidance of . . . the United States, acting like cunning dragon seemingly asleep." Admiral Harold C. Stark, the U.S. chief of naval operations, grew increasingly worried by the feverish tone of the Japanese messages intercepted through Magic. Unsure how to respond to a potential attack, he sent a classic gobbledygook order to his officers in Asia, instructing them to take "appropriate precautionary measures against possible eventualities."

At the same time that he froze Japan's assets, Roosevelt redeemed MacArthur by appointing him commander of "U.S. Army Forces, Far East," a wholly new organization incorporating his ragtag Filipino units into the American garrison in the Philippines. Roosevelt's secretary of war, Henry L. Stimson, promptly gave MacArthur priority status, pledging him modern antiaircraft guns, rifles and other up-to-date weapons along with more than three hundred B-17 bombers, the redoubtable Flying Fortresses, capable of long-range strikes against an invading armada. Shortly afterward, MacArthur persuaded his bosses in Washington to change his mission drastically. No longer would he be shackled to the old Orange Plan, which had envisioned only the defense of Manila Bay. Nor was he to be strapped by a later strategy, Rainbow Five, recently drafted by the United States and Britain to designate Europe as the principal theater of operations. Henceforth the Philippines would be a main arena and, authorized to protect the entire archipelago, he was mandated to repulse the Japanese on its beaches. Quezon, now convinced of America's commitment to shield his country, abruptly scrapped his notions of a deal with Japan and again embraced MacArthur, telling him, "All that we have, all that we are, is yours."

MacArthur, elated by his fresh lease on life at the age of sixty-one, ecstatically told his staff, "I feel like a new dog in an old uniform." A few months earlier, he had assured John Hersey, then a *Time* correspondent, that there would be no war, since a "bristling united front" composed of the British, Dutch and Americans was deterring Japan from pushing into Southeast Asia. Nor would the Japanese test the Americans, having agreed to help Germany by bottling up the U.S. fleet at Pearl Harbor. Even if war broke out, Japan did not stand a chance against the Allied forces in Asia. Infected by MacArthur's optimism, Hersey wrote, "You go out feeling a little brisker yourself, a little more cheery and more confident about things."

Others were equally buoyant. Clark Lee, an Associated Press correspondent in Manila, saw the U.S. warships at anchor in the bay as vivid proof that the Philippines was secure. "When the Japs come down here," he reported, "they'll be playing in the big leagues for the first time in their lives." A young pilot, Lieutenant Samuel C. Grashio of Spokane, perceived the same mood among the American officers aboard his transport headed for Manila in November 1941. "To a man," he recalled years later, "they were convinced that there would be no war because the Japanese would not be so stupid as to start a war they would be certain to lose within a few weeks." MacArthur's promotion, coupled with the fresh U.S. investment in the Philippines, also spurred a belief in Washington that the islands could be shielded.

But MacArthur's glow was soon to dim—partly through no fault of his own. Delays plagued the pledged B-17 bombers, and only thirty-five were to land by early December—without adequate fighter escorts. Other equipment moved at an excruciatingly slow pace, taking weeks to cross the American continent to California ports, then weeks more to reach Manila by sea. Much of it was obsolete and worthless. Defective old Enfield rifles arrived instead of modern Garands, and ammunition was scarce. There were no hand grenades. The artillery lacked sights, and many machine guns were unserviceable. Most of the mortar shells would prove to be duds, and the mortars themselves were antiques. Promises of the latest technology notwithstanding, MacArthur received only two radar sets, so that his warning system against enemy planes was to consist of spotters armed with primitive telephones or radios.

MacArthur rightly blamed his superiors later for giving him "too little too late." But he had deluded himself and others by blurring fact and fancy in an attempt to publicize his success—a symptom, again, of his infallibility complex. After assuming his new command, he had informed Washington that his strength totaled more than a hundred thousand American and Filipino troops.

In fact, three quarters of the force consisted of a paper roster of Filipinos available for service. He also declaimed as his defense program began that it was "progressing by leaps and bounds" as the Filipinos soared from "a feeling of defeatism to the highest state of morale I have ever seen." An American officer in the field painted a different scene. His recruits lacked everything from steel helmets to clothes, and they wore sneakers "so deteriorated from age and use that most of the men were barefooted within a few days." Their units were undermanned, and "practically no Filipino officers above the grade of captain were capable of functioning properly." MacArthur's decision to defend the whole archipelago, moreover, would prove to be a colossal blunder. For, in their desperate last gasp, his beleaguered forces were denied the food, medicines and other supplies that he had dispersed around the country.

Central to MacArthur's planning was his calculation that if the Japanese attacked at all, it would not be before April 1942. By then, he anticipated, his defenses would be ready. But he had no evidence of the enemy's timetable. So, locked into his own convictions, he spurned any advice or even solid information that violated his preconceptions.

Nor were Japan's commanders paragons of rationality. In September 1941, after weighing various specific plans, they chose to strike the Philippines and Malaya concurrently, then invade the Dutch East Indies. The strategy was the trickiest they could have picked, raising as it would perilous problems of coordination and timing. But it was the only one to win the support of both the army and navy—and the Japanese function by consensus. Like MacArthur, they overflowed with optimism. They expected to seize the Philippines in seven weeks, take Malaya in a hundred days and control the Dutch East Indies within five months. The U.S. Navy, to be destroyed at Pearl Harbor, would not intervene. Handed the plan, the emperor skeptically noted that, four years before, the same officers had promised to conquer China swiftly, and now they were venturing into Southeast Asia and the Pacific—a region, he observed, "more immense" than the vast Chinese hinterland. Still, he ratified the project, including the strike against Hawaii, then retired to compose a poem in praise of peace. War clearly loomed by the middle of October, when General Tojo supplanted Prince Konoe as prime minister.

Peace might have won a brief reprieve, however. Admiral Nomura, continuing his desultory talks with Cordell Hull in Washington, had essayed a partial accord under which Japan would eventually evacuate Indochina and arrest its move into Southeast Asia in exchange for a resumption of U.S. trade. With Roosevelt's assent, Hull pondered the offer as a chance to buy time for MacArthur to reinforce the Philippines. But the Chinese government would not acquiesce, and Hull replied with a plan for an overall settlement in Asia—its key point again the demand that Japan quit China, including Manchuria. By November 27, the Japanese had not answered, and Hull lost hope. Diplomacy had failed and, he told colleagues, "I have washed my hands of it." That morning, unbeknownst to him, a Japanese fleet of aircraft carriers and other ships steamed forth from the bleak, fog-shrouded Kurile islands of northern Japan, headed eastward across the Pacific toward Hawaii. The day before, a group of senior Japanese admirals and generals had assembled aboard a cruiser off the Taiwan coast to put the finishing touches to a plan to invade the Philippines.

★ ★ ★

Some of Roosevelt's critics later accused him of having provoked the war with Japan; others claimed that he was aware of the imminent conflict, yet neglected to warn his top officers. It is true that U.S. experts analyzed masses of secret Japanese messages, but they could not determine at the time which ones accurately revealed Japan's intentions. So, with remarkable hindsight, many historians have fostered the impression that Roosevelt and his staff must have known of Japan's exact deployments beforehand—when, in reality, they were uncertain and confused. Still, clues abounded of the impending collision with Japan.

As early as November 7, reflecting his sources, Hull urged the cabinet to be "on the lookout for a military attack by the Japanese . . . at any time." Stimson learned two weeks later that a Japanese force had left Shanghai for Southeast Asia, and U.S. experts intercepted a message from Tokyo to the Japanese ambassador in Berlin, directing him to advise the German leaders that "war may come quicker than anyone dreams." Amid all this, the War Department ordered MacArthur to prepare for "hostile action" by Japan "at any moment." The Washington brass, to avoid charges of provocation, insisted that the Japanese be permitted to "commit the first act"—a detail, American troops afterward complained, that gave the enemy the benefit of surprise. MacArthur dismissed the "alarmists" at a meeting in Manila with Francis Sayre and Admiral Thomas C. Hart, the American navy commander in Asia. Puffing a black cigar as he strode around Sayre's office, he declared with oracular certitude that he could tell from the "existing alignment and movement" of the Japanese forces that "there would be no attack before the spring."

Even today, with instant communications reflecting the intimacy of global relationships, U.S. commanders abroad are often denied the details of sensitive Washington decisions. So it may have been routine for MacArthur's superiors at home to insulate him from developments in the capital. He was not informed when, on December 5, Japan's diplomats began packing to leave—a sign that their endeavor had aborted. Nor was he apprised, two days afterward, of Roosevelt's final futile appeal to the emperor for peace. Neither was he told that a marathon Japanese note, decoded that night by U.S. experts, spelled war. But then, nobody bothered to notify the Army Chief of Staff, General George C. Marshall, who went riding next morning, a Sunday, in a Virginia meadow later to be the site of the Pentagon. At that moment, in choppy waters off the Hawaiian island of Oahu, six Japanese carriers turned east to the wind as their Zero fighter pilots warmed their engines. Twelve hours separate Washington from the Philippines, and it was Monday in Manila.

It was also the feast of the Immaculate Conception, a major Catholic holiday, offering Filipinos and Americans alike a leisurely long weekend. The weather, typical for the season, was pleasantly warm and dry. Many Filipinos had left the city on Friday afternoon to visit relatives in the nearby countryside, or had departed by car, bus or train for Malolos or Malabon, towns noted for their garish annual celebrations honoring the Virgin Mary. Some Americans drove up to Baguio, the mountain resort, while others went to the beach or remained in town to play golf or tennis at Wack Wack or the Army and Navy Club. Officers from the U.S. naval base at Cavite, in off-duty white-linen civvies, rode the ferry to the capital, perhaps to eat at an air-conditioned restaurant, take in a movie or dally with a girl at one of the bars tucked inside the walls of the Intramuros. Men of a U.S. Air Corps unit avidly awaited a Sunday-night stag party at the Manila Hotel, its raunchy entertainment touted as the liveliest "this side of Minsky's."

The noise from the raucous affair scarcely disturbed MacArthur, whose spacious penthouse spanned the west wing of the hotel. His schedule rarely varied. He returned there punctually from his office to play with his son, now a frisky three-year-old. Then he would dine with his wife and read for an hour or two. Before going to bed, he customarily stepped onto the balcony for a breath of fresh air, inhaling the sweet, almost cloying scent of bougainvillea, frangipani and hibiscus from the lush tropical garden five floors below. Gazing at the bay, he could discern in the distant darkness the few flickering lights of Bataan and Corregidor—names, at the time, barely known outside the Philippines.

He was sleeping soundly when the radio message crackled into Manila at three o'clock on Monday morning—eight A.M. on Sunday in Hawaii. Another forty minutes passed before an aide awoke him to one of the ghastliest days of his career.

11. WAR AND REDEMPTION

★ ★ ★

At ten minutes before eight o'clock on a bright Sunday morning, December 7, 1941, the first formation of Japanese fighter, bomber and torpedo aircraft roared over Oahu, and successive squadrons followed. Their main target was the massive U.S. naval base at Pearl Harbor, its anchorage crowded with nearly a hundred vessels. Three hours later, amid the wreckage of sunken ships and destroyed planes and the ruins of docks, oil tanks, hangars and barracks, some four thousand Americans were dead or wounded. The sudden raid surprised and shocked the United States unlike any disaster in its history. The nation, its Pacific fleet in shambles, was crippled—at least temporarily.

President Franklin D. Roosevelt, his voice vibrating with emotion, denounced the "infamy" of the attack at noon the next day in a short speech to Congress, which promptly declared war on Japan. General Hideko Tojo, the Japanese prime minister, proclaimed the hostilities as Tokyo radio broadcast a martial hymn, its morbid lyrics a prescient dirge for the thousands of lives to be lost in the struggle over the next four years.

> Across the sea, corpses in the water.
> Across the mountain, corpses in the field.

Whatever their short-term gains from the strike, the Japanese had blundered. They kindled America's wrath, thus ordaining their ultimate doom. They might have pushed with impunity into Southeast Asia at a time when the U.S. public was in no mood to fight a war to protect the vestiges of European imperialism. They could have also bypassed the Philippines, which possessed none of the raw materials crucial to their forces and avoided a clash with America there as well. But, by then, their military machine was being propelled by its own momentum, and they attacked the archipelago with a speed that caught its U.S. garrison off guard in a debacle that matched the fiasco at Hawaii.

AIR RAID AT PEARL HARBOR—THIS IS NO DRILL read the message that reached Manila at three o'clock in the morning of December 8, its brevity denoting a crisis. Sent via U.S. Navy channels from Hawaii, it was addressed only to Rear Admiral Thomas C. Hart, the fleet commander, who detested MacArthur and neglected to notify him. Instead, MacArthur was awakened forty minutes later by a telephone call from Major General Richard K. Sutherland, his chief of staff, who had heard the news from a commercial radio report. He was dressing hastily when Brigadier General Leonard T. Gerow, head of army planning in Washington, telephoned. Gerow had given him the "impression," MacArthur was to recall, that Japan had "suffered a setback." In fact, the record showed, Gerow said that the Japanese had inflicted "considerable damage" at Pearl Harbor. He also warned MacArthur to brace for a strike against the Philippines "in the near future."

Japanese aircraft had flown over the Manila area within minutes of the attack on Pearl Harbor, striking the U.S. naval station at Cavite. But MacArthur did virtually nothing for nine hours after receiving the report of the Hawaii debacle. The Japanese hit their major Philippine targets with an ease that astonished nobody more than themselves.

They had assigned some two hundred Zero fighters and Mitsubishi bombers to the initial phase of the operation, and their pilots expected the worst as they waited to leave for Luzon from bases on Taiwan and carriers near the island. Due to take off at dawn, they were delayed by dense fog. They assumed that the Americans knew about Pearl Harbor and would either stage a preemptive strike before they got aloft or intercept them along the five-hundred-mile route south. But they were relieved at about a quarter past noon, as they approached their primary objective, Clark Field, northwest of Manila. The sky was crystal clear, and they could plainly see the scene twenty-five thousand feet below. There lay America's largest array of planes in the archipelago, its biggest air armada anywhere overseas. Lined up, their wings tip to tip, sat thirty-six P-40 fighters and seventeen B-17 bombers, the famous Flying Fortresses. Forty miles to the west of Clark, at Iba Field, another Japanese group sighted an American squadron of sixteen P-40s on the ground.

Filipino spotters, tracking the Japanese, had urgently signaled a U.S. warning center in Manila by radio, telephone and teletype. Garbled or imprecise, the reports nevertheless cited Clark as the prime enemy goal. An officer in Manila shouted the information over the telephone to a lieutenant at the field, who presumably forgot to tell his commander. The lone radar technician at Iba, detecting blips on his screen, also attempted to contact Clark. Still trying, he was blown to bits as more than a hundred Japanese planes swooped down to annihilate the base. At Clark the radio operator had gone to lunch along with most of the pilots and ground crew.

Ignorant of Iba's fate, they were ambling out of the mess hall, smoking and chatting before resuming work. An officer was chuckling at a radio newscast that Clark was under attack. His comrades joined the laughter, one of them remarking that some "eager beaver" had invented the rumor to keep them alert. But soon they heard "a low moaning sound," as Lieutenant Dupont

Strong later described it, as a "whole crowd of airplanes" darkened the horizon.

Waves of Mitsubishi bombers arrived above the range of the old U.S. antiaircraft weapons, setting oil dumps ablaze, obliterating buildings and gutting the runway. Pilots and mechanics dashed out in a futile effort to get their planes into the air. An eerie lull suddenly followed, and dazed survivors rose slowly from slit trenches, stumbling past corpses, too shaken to attend to the wounded. Then came the Zeros and, unopposed, they machine-gunned the base for more than an hour. They destroyed all except three Flying Fortresses and every P-40 apart from four that had somehow scrambled.

Lieutenant Samuel Grashio was lucky. We met by chance in Manila in May 1987, when he was revisiting the Philippine battlefields, and one hot afternoon we drove out to the vast U.S. military cemetery in the suburbs. Strolling through the rows of crosses, we observed the ironic sight of Japanese tourist groups spilling from buses to photograph the site. But Grashio displayed no trace of rancor at their presence as he recollected that day forty-five years before, only three weeks after landing in Manila as a young pilot just out of training school. Attached to a squadron of P-40s based at Nichols Field, southwest of the city, he flew up to Clark at noon on December 8, amid confused reports of an imminent attack. He arrived minutes after the enemy raid. "It was astounding. Where the airfield should have been was an area boiling with smoke, dust and flames. Though I didn't know it then, some of my classmates and friends had been killed while struggling to get their planes off the ground." Returning later, he found chaos. "Command, leadership, discipline, even simple order, had vanished utterly. Officers, enlisted men and civilians had scattered headlong in all directions."

Their first strike cost the Japanese only seven pursuit planes, and during the next two days they repeatedly attacked other U.S. installations throughout Luzon, including the Cavite naval base and Nichols Field in the vicinity of Manila. About eighty Americans had perished in the raids against Clark and Iba, moderate casualties compared to the number killed in Hawaii. MacArthur had lost his air power, and the blow was to be calamitous both for the Philippines in the weeks ahead and for America's long-term position in the Pacific.

Following investigations, Admiral Husband E. Kimmel and General Walter C. Short, the commanders at Pearl Harbor, were cashiered for negligence. But MacArthur was considered too valuable during the war to be dragged through an official inquiry, and he had become too popular a hero afterward to face potentially embarrassing questions. So his handling of the Japanese attack has never been fully clarified, and the subject is still snarled by controversy.

The debate has largely centered on his failure to send his planes aloft early on December 8. At the news of the Pearl Harbor debacle, his air commander, Major General Lewis H. Brereton, rushed to his office for approval to bomb both Japan's bases on Taiwan and its convoys headed for the Philippines. MacArthur's zealously protective chief of staff, General Sutherland, denied him access to the boss but told him to await further orders. About seven hours later, Brereton was authorized to fly a reconnaissance mission to identify enemy targets prior to a strike, presumably to be launched afterward. By then it was too late.

His Flying Fortresses were still being fueled and armed at Clark Field when the Japanese destroyed them. General Henry H. Arnold, the U.S. Army Air Corps chief, called him from Washington, demanding to know "how in hell" his planes had been trapped on the ground. Brereton was the only top U.S. officer to be officially reprimanded. MacArthur was never formally admonished—or, at the time, even criticized.

He was not solely at fault, however. Brereton, whom he had earlier ordered to move his B-17s south to the island of Mindanao, beyond range of the Japanese, had delayed so his men could attend the Sunday night party at the Manila Hotel. Imperious and arrogant, Sutherland also erred by insulating MacArthur from Brereton and other commanders, whom he should have seen on that hectic morning. Nor was the brass in Washington guiltless. The Flying Fortresses lacked adequate fighter escorts, radar equipment and other protection, and there were shortages of everything from nuts and bolts to spare parts. Most U.S. pilots were woefully inexperienced. Lieutenant Grashio's only target practice during his brief training in California had been to fire "a few bursts at silver slicks on the sea." But MacArthur consistently denied any fault for the disaster.

"We took a hell of a beating," said General Joseph W. Stilwell after his rout in Burma, and other senior officers have been equally candid in defeat. Not MacArthur. Indeed, throughout the Pacific war, he was to attribute every victory to himself and rebuke others for setbacks—effacing skilled generals like Walter Krueger and Robert L. Eichelberger and humiliating Jonathan Wainwright for the loss of Bataan and Corregidor. In Europe, by contrast, Eisenhower consistently gave credit to such subordinates as George Patton and Omar Bradley, thereby making them household names.

MacArthur later explained his inaction at the outbreak of hostilities in the Philippines by citing Washington's order to allow the Japanese to strike first. Two hours after the events in Hawaii, however, he was officially advised that a state of war existed with Japan and told to execute the prearranged plan to defend the archipelago. He implied that Manuel Quezon, the commonwealth president, had insisted that the islands could remain neutral and thus be spared by the enemy. In reality, he was out of touch with Quezon, who had gone to the mountain resort of Baguio, suffering from a bout of tuberculosis. Far from championing neutrality, moreover, Quezon vowed that every Filipino would "stand by" the United States in a radio broadcast that MacArthur's aides must have heard. MacArthur also denied any knowledge of Brereton's proposal to attack the Japanese, saying that in any event he would have "unequivocally disapproved . . . such a suggestion." Yet, in a message at the time to General George C. Marshall, the Army Chief of Staff, he mentioned a forthcoming raid against the enemy bases. He had previously pledged to conduct "strong offensive air operations" at the outbreak of war. But he later claimed to have shown restraint because his "token force" was "hopelessly outnumbered and never had a chance of winning." Perhaps he was correct, though, when he said subsequently, "Nothing could have saved the day."

MacArthur's reputation never entirely recovered from his odd conduct during those terrible hours. Secluded in his office, he issued no orders and saw nobody except Sutherland, who later explained lamely that he was studying intelligence reports. Nor have his other aides been enlightening. So only conjecture remains. Nevertheless, as D. Clayton James concludes in his judicious biography: "When all the evidence is sifted, however contradictory and incomplete it may be, MacArthur still emerges as the officer who was in overall command in the Philippines that fateful day, and he must therefore bear a large measure of the blame."

That day, though, only prefaced the long, devastating, mortifying ordeal that was to confront MacArthur during the months ahead as he grappled with the biggest crisis of his career in a land to which he had devoted so much of his life.

★　★　★

Two days after eliminating America's air fleet in the Philippines, the Japanese scored another great victory off Malaya as their bombers sank the British battleships *Repulse* and *Prince of Wales,* the two largest Allied vessels in the western Pacific. Germany and Italy declared war against the United States a day later. Over the next week, Japanese troops crossed from China into Hong Kong, landed in Malaya and seized the tiny U.S. garrison on Guam. Japanese infantry units hit parts of Luzon and Mindanao, but their main force had yet to attack the archipelago. Even after the debacle at Clark, however, American officers derided the Japanese army as an "untrained mass of young boys," as one assured Clark Lee of the Associated Press. "When our tanks and planes go into action," he added, "we'll chase them back to the sea."

Exuding the same confidence after snapping out of his catatonic state, MacArthur deluged Washington with requests for men and supplies—demanding that America's total global war effort be redirected from Europe to Asia, where the Philippines was "the locus of victory or defeat." But the only convoy sent to aid him was diverted to Australia after U.S. Navy commanders refused to run Japan's blockade of the archipelago. With the navy yard at Cavite a ruin following Japanese raids, the American fleet, apart from some patrol boats, left for the Dutch East Indies. His air power gone, MacArthur had now also lost his sea power.

Hoping that good news would win him support at home, he ordered his press chief, Major LeGrande A. Diller, to report only success. To verify one rosy communiqué, Carl Mydans of *Life* drove a hundred miles to Lingayen Gulf, on the west coast of Luzon north of Manila, where Filipino troops had purportedly repulsed a huge Japanese assault. The shore was supposed to be strewn with enemy bodies, but Mydans found only Filipino soldiers lolling on an empty beach. Returning to Manila, he informed Diller that there had been no battle, much less a Japanese defeat. Diller, unperturbed, pointed to his handout: "It says so here." The United Press, however, described a clash in which 150 enemy ships had been sunk, and *The New York Times* headlined JAPANESE FORCES WIPED OUT IN WESTERN LUZON.

MacArthur's cosmetic glow quickly faded in the harsh light of dawn on December 22, when some forty-three thousand Japanese troops tumbled ashore at Lingayen Gulf, the roaring breakers swamping their boats. Their commander, Lieutenant General Masaharu Homma, an amateur dramatist who had served with the British army during World War I, admired the West and had publicly deplored Japan's expansionist policies. But now, as a professional soldier, he intended to capture Luzon within fifty days to fulfill the Japanese schedule to conquer the whole archipelago in seven weeks.

Major General Jonathan Mayhew Wainwright IV, his U.S. counterpart, was a boozy cavalryman of fifty-eight called "Skinny" because of his skeletal frame. With four divisions and a cavalry regiment, Filipino reservists stiffened by American regulars, he had twice as many men as Homma. But MacArthur's illusory native army was untrained and poorly equipped. Some units resisted valiantly. Reduced to fewer than five hundred survivors, the cavalry regiment held off enemy tanks for two hours at the Agno River, thus enabling Wainwright to fix a first defense line on the road to Manila. Thousands, however, flung away their weapons and fled into the jungles before the Japanese juggernaut—though numbers later fought as guerrillas. On Christmas Eve, another ten thousand Japanese disembarked at Lamon Bay in southeastern Luzon and advanced toward Manila.

MacArthur, still determined to stop the enemy at the coast, continued to appeal for help from Washington. There his former aide, Colonel Eisenhower, now head of the Asia desk at the War Department, pleaded for him despite his feeling that MacArthur "might have made a better showing at the beaches and passes," as he privately noted. But the U.S. high command was concerned with Europe, and MacArthur finally ceded. Reluctantly, he reverted to the old Orange Plan, the defense of Bataan and Corregidor, which he had once vilified as "defeatist." He declared Manila an "open city," as Paris had been, to spare its population. Then he prepared for the most difficult of all military maneuvers: retreat.

The daunting task entailed moving two different armies totaling eighty thousand men, separated by a distance of more than 150 miles between northern and southern Luzon, into the Bataan peninsula—funneling them, in effect, into a narrow corridor.

He knew Bataan's rugged terrain from his days as a young engineer. Its five hundred square miles, dangling like an earlobe from Luzon, are dominated by a spine of jungle-clad mountains craggily jutting out to sea on the west and sloping gently down to farmland on the east. Few regions in the Philippines were better suited for defensive warfare—on condition that its defenders had adequate supplies.

The operation, which MacArthur planned to complete in two weeks, required exquisite coordination to converge the two forces, lest they be cut off from one another and chewed up by the enemy. To give the force south of Manila time to swing north toward Bataan, he ordered Wainwright to pull back slowly through central Luzon, delaying the Japanese at a series of five defense lines. One slip might have imperiled the entire project. Bridges had to be dynamited at precisely the right moment, roads secured, scattered units regrouped and supplies shipped swiftly to the new redoubt. Above all, inexperienced and frightened Filipino conscripts had to be inspired to hold their positions by American officers who were frequently just as inexperienced and frightened.

MacArthur managed the maneuver from Corregidor, the island citadel at the mouth of Manila Bay, where he had gone on Christmas Eve. The turning point came early in January, after Wainwright's destruction of a key bridge at the town of Calumpit slowed down the Japanese at the torrential Pampanga

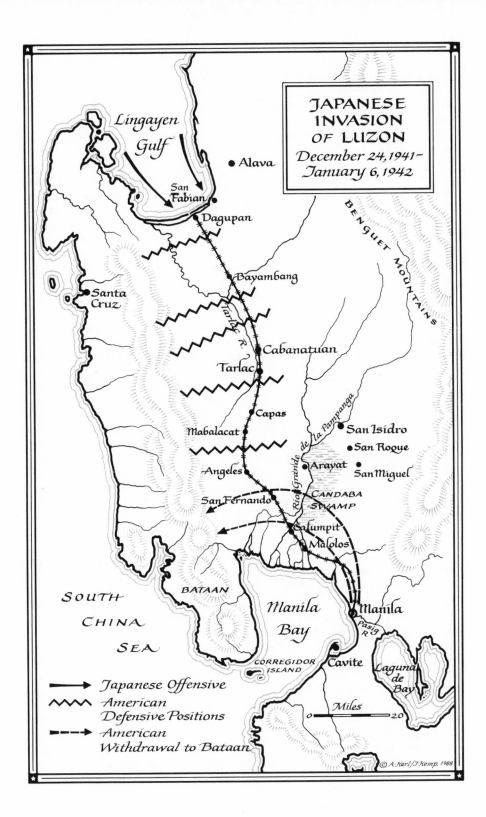

JAPANESE
INVASION
OF LUZON
December 24, 1941–
January 6, 1942

Lingayen
Gulf

• Alava

San
Fabian

Dagupan

BENGUET MOUNTAINS

Bayambang

Tarlac R.

Santa
Cruz

Cabanatuan

Tarlac

Capas

San Isidro

Mabalacat

• San Roque

Rio Grande de la Pampanga

Arayat

• San Miguel

Angeles

San Fernando

CANDABA
SWAMP

Calumpit

Malolos

BATAAN

Manila
Bay

Manila

SOUTH

Pasig
R.

CHINA

CORREGIDOR
ISLAND

Cavite

Laguna
de
Bay

SEA

→ Japanese Offensive

Miles

〰 American
Defensive Positions

0   20

⇢ American
Withdrawal to Bataan

© A. Karl / J. Kemp, 1988

River. The retreat was to rank among MacArthur's glories. General John J. Pershing, neither a MacArthur fan nor inclined toward superlatives, spoke up from retirement at the age of eighty-two to call it "one of the greatest moves in all military history."

Homma's errors contributed to the triumph. Wainwright's route had been congested for miles with refugees on foot or bicycle, in gaudily decorated buses, old jalopies, ramshackle trucks and peasant carts piled high with belongings. But despite his mastery of the air, Homma inexplicably refrained from strafing or bombing the horde—a tactic that would have caused chaos. A prudent officer, he also halted periodically to await supplies rather than maintain his momentum. Wrongly expecting MacArthur to defend Manila, he failed to press rapidly to block the roads to Bataan. By the middle of January, the Americans and Filipinos were inside the Bataan perimeter. His schedule to conquer Luzon in fifty days was severely set back—along with his reputation in Tokyo.

MacArthur also miscalculated badly. After persuading Washington to supplant the Orange Plan with Rainbow Five, his grand scheme to resist from the beaches to the boondocks, he stocked depots throughout the provinces with food, medicine and military equipment. But now the reversion to the Orange Plan required the swift transfer of the supplies to Bataan and Corregidor—an exercise that was to abort dramatically.

The logistical disaster began even before the enemy had landed. Alarmed by rumors of war, railway crews deserted, thus paralyzing the single line from central Luzon to Manila. Jittery troops prematurely evacuated Fort Stotsenburg, near Clark Field, without carrying away or at least destroying its stores of food, weapons and ammunition. Quezon, sensitive to the needs of the population, had induced MacArthur to ban American officers from confiscating food and clothing from warehouses—including those owned by Japanese. MacArthur also enforced a law prohibiting the movement of rice across province borders. So, for example, his quartermasters could not buy rice from a stock of fifty million bushels located at the town of Cabanatuan—a fifth of which, specialists later estimated, would have fed the Bataan garrison for a year.

"If we had something in our bellies," Wainwright said afterward of the Bataan experience, "things would have been a little more endurable." His eighty thousand men started their ordeal on two thousand calories a day, and the ration shrank during the months ahead—along with their morale. Hunger drove them to steal or hoard the tiniest scraps, and officers faked rosters to feed their troops. Sam Grashio, there with the remains of his squadron, quickly felt his energy sapped by famine. He foraged for bananas, coconuts and edible roots in the jungle and joined his comrades in killing any animal in sight: chickens, pigs, deer, dogs, cats, iguanas, snakes and water buffaloes, the ubiquitous beast of burden, whose leathery meat was indigestible. Mosquitoes, leeches, lice and flies plagued them—and "hanging over everything," he later recalled, "were enormous clouds of choking dust and a horrendous stench rising from filth of every variety." They suffered from malaria, dysentery, scurvy and beriberi. Hit by dengue fever, with its spasms of chills and sweat, Grashio tried to treat himself. "The grimmest places were the field hospitals," packed with patients who "moaned or screamed in pain from wounds or disease or both, that the medical staff could do little about from lack of drugs and equipment."

By contrast, MacArthur's presence had assured Corregidor of supplies to sustain ten thousand men for six months. The island, roughly the size of Manhattan, bristled with coastal artillery and smaller guns, its Malinta tunnel an impregnable cave of storerooms, offices, barracks and medical facilities. It had once been touted as America's answer to Singapore—a comparison that proved to be unfortunate for both places.

MacArthur had sailed there aboard an interisland steamer on Christmas Eve, along with his wife Jean, their son, Arthur, and the child's Chinese amah, Ah Cheu. The party included Francis Sayre, the U.S. high commissioner, his wife and her fifteen-year-old stepson. Quezon, after first objecting that he had to "take care of the civilian population," finally went with Sergio Osmeña, his vice president. Knowing him to be close to the Japanese, he had persuaded José Laurel, then his secretary of justice, to stay behind in hopes of curbing their excesses. He also asked his private secretary, Jorge Vargas, a skilled administrator, to remain as mayor of Manila for the same purpose. Flushed with emotion as he bid them farewell, Quezon said, "Keep your faith in America, whatever happens." MacArthur warned Laurel not to swear allegiance to Japan—or else, "when we come back, we'll shoot you."

He saw "no reason for immediate worry," MacArthur told Quezon after two weeks on the island, predicting that they could resist for "several months." As Japanese pressure mounted, he told his troops that "help is on the way," and exhorted them to "hold until these reinforcements arrive." But his promises, though intended to boost morale, were either fatuous or deceitful, since he knew the chances of relief to be remote despite the predictable messages of encouragement from Washington. Frustrated by rebuffs, he accused Roosevelt, George Marshall and Henry L. Stimson, the secretary of war, of indifference. His special nemesis was Eisenhower, one of those "faceless staff officers" ranged against him, as he described the War Department bureaucracy. Worse than their misguided pro-Europe strategy, he believed, was their conspiracy to subvert his career.

Eisenhower, rankled by his virtual paranoia, did indeed reproach him—though only privately. MacArthur, he confided to his diary, was "as big a baby as ever" and appeared to be "losing his nerve"—his demands for immediate aid "a refusal . . . to look facts in the face, an old trait of his." But Eisenhower worked around the clock on his behalf, noting that "we've just got to keep him fighting." His labors were in vain. Offers of $10 million notwithstanding, few private shippers were willing to run the Japanese blockade of the Philippines. War Department planners figured that to aid MacArthur effectively would take at least seven battleships, five carriers, fifty destroyers, sixty submarines and fifteen hundred aircraft—an effort, even if feasible, that would mean an "entirely unjustifiable diversion of forces from the principal theater, the Atlantic." Even Patrick J. Hurley, the never-say-die former secretary of war, saw no hope. Sent by Roosevelt to Australia to speed supplies to MacArthur, he admitted, "We were out-shipped, out-planed, out-manned and out-gunned by the Japanese from the beginning."

Quezon was meanwhile in another of his zigzags—perhaps due to his tuberculosis, which had worsened in the humidity of Corregidor. Like MacArthur, he was becoming increasingly embittered by the delays in American assistance.

He had won a second term as president of the Philippine commonwealth just before going to Corregidor, and MacArthur improvised an inaugural for him there. Standing on a crude wooden platform, his voice cracked by coughing, he extolled MacArthur for "your devotion to our cause, the defense of our country and the safety of our population." He also broadcast a message to the Filipino soldiers on Bataan, pledging that "America will not abandon us." But, as the weeks dragged by without help, his trust in the United States waned. After learning that Roosevelt was sending aircraft to Britain, he decried those in Washington who favored Europe, branding them *sinvergüenzas*—"shameless ones." "How typically American," he railed, "to writhe in anguish at the fate of a distant cousin while a daughter is being raped in a back room!"

Hideko Tojo, the Japanese prime minister, had recently offered to respect Philippine sovereignty under a separate peace—a transparent device to drive a wedge between the Filipinos and the Americans. Tempted by the idea, which he had explored before the war, Quezon bounced it off a member of his staff on Corregidor. "Do you expect me to continue this sacrifice? The fight between the United States and Japan is not our fight. . . . We are not getting protection from those who promised us protection. . . . We must try to save ourselves, and the hell with America."

Increasingly despondent, he bombarded Roosevelt with a series of gloomy radiograms. It was senseless, he said in one, for "all these men to be killed when . . . the shedding of their blood may be wholly unnecessary." Finally he urged Roosevelt to grant the Philippines immediate independence so he could declare neutrality and "save my country from further devastation as the battleground of two great powers."

MacArthur later claimed that he had "bluntly" warned Quezon against the illusory notion. In any case, he wrote in his memoirs, Quezon knew it was impractical, and had only intended to "shock" Roosevelt into recognizing his dilemma. As usual, MacArthur revised history. Mercurial but never flippant, Quezon did indeed hope for a deal with the enemy. MacArthur, moreover, had himself endorsed the proposal in a parallel message to Washington, terming it "the sound course to follow." He could not vouch for the continued loyalty of the Filipinos, whose "temper . . . is one of violent resentment against the United States." His own men also faced "complete destruction," and a cease-fire "might offer the best solution of what is about to be a disastrous debacle."

Given his heroic view of himself, MacArthur's approval of Quezon's willingness to capitulate remains yet another MacArthur mystery. Maybe, as historian Theodore Friend has speculated, he saw it as the only way to save his army, his family and his reputation. He might have conceivably argued that, as a soldier, he had no authority to interfere with Quezon, who as president of the Philippine commonwealth had every right to surrender. Or, endowed as he was with a fertile imagination, MacArthur could have manufactured all kinds of other alibis to justify his conduct.

The messages stunned Stimson as "most disappointing" and "wholly unreal." He could understand Quezon's frustrations—but, he noted in his diary, MacArthur was remiss for going "more than half way" to endorse virtual surrender at this "ghastly" juncture. Marshall shared his annoyance, and they promptly conferred with Roosevelt, who listened attentively as Stimson outlined their views like the seasoned lawyer he was, "standing as if before the court." Roosevelt approved a firm stance and, with Eisenhower's help, drafted two responses—one to MacArthur and the other to Quezon, both to bear the president's signature.

They sent MacArthur an exhortation to stand and fight, better suited to "noble Romans" than to "ordinary" Americans, as Stimson later reflected with regret. The men on Bataan should resist as effectively "as circumstances will permit and as long as humanly possible" to delay Japan's advances throughout the Pacific. MacArthur recanted. He had never meant to allow Quezon to quit, he replied. As for himself, he intended to hold his "present battle position in Bataan to destruction" and then struggle to the finish on Corregidor, where his family would "share the fate of the garrison."

The message to Quezon was gentler. The present plight of the Filipinos, it warned, was "infinitely less than the sufferings" that awaited them if he struck a deal with Japan. The United States would defend them "to the death" or return to "drive the last remnant of the invaders from your soil" should Bataan fall. Quezon, shifting again, vowed to "stand by America regardless of the circumstances." As he put it later, he could not "in decency" have been less generous or less determined than Roosevelt, who had promised to save the Philippines through "the sacrifice and heroism of his own people." So, melted by U.S. influence, he discarded his idea of an accommodation with Japan. Late in February, planning to form a government-in-exile in America, he left Corregidor with his wife and the Sayres. Before boarding the submarine, Quezon slipped his signet ring onto MacArthur's finger. "When they find your body," he said morbidly, "I want them to know that you fought for my country."

On the eve of his departure, he also gave MacArthur half a million dollars and paid smaller legacies to three of his aides as "recompense" for their "magnificent defense" of the archipelago. The sums were transferred to their banks at home from Philippine government funds in the United States. Quezon evidently believed that he owed MacArthur a debt of gratitude in the tradition of *utang na loob,* which imposes mutual obligations on *compadres.* But MacArthur's motive for accepting the gift was puzzling, since he must have known that U.S. Army regulations prohibited officers from taking "emoluments." He may have been reluctant to offend Quezon, or perhaps felt that the honorarium was due him as a field marshal in the Philippine army—a job he hoped to resume after the war. Or he could have been greedy. Eisenhower, interestingly, declined a similar offer. Underlining the words in an elegant report for the record, he wrote that he told Quezon that it was "inadvisable and even impossible" for him to "accept a material reward for the services performed." Any "misapprehension or misunderstanding," he said, might spur gossip, hurt his reputation and damage the war effort. Instead he would welcome a medal, which "would be of great and more lasting value to me . . . than any amount of money."

Many of MacArthur's own men were meanwhile losing faith in his leadership. They resented his self-promotion—as reflected by the fact that two thirds of his hundred and fifty communiqués during the first three months of the war, most of which he personally edited, cited only one soldier, Douglas MacArthur. His aloofness also alienated them. "They were filthy, and they were lousy, and they stank. And I loved them," he subsequently wrote of the Bataan defenders. He later dubbed his personal plane the *Bataan,* and after the war he reveled in reunions of the "Bataan gang." Yet, during his seventy-seven days on Corregidor, he visited Bataan only once, in an apparent effort to bolster sagging morale. He was no coward. On the contrary, as reckless as he had been in World War I, he would stand unflinchingly during air raids as shrapnel flew around him—joking that "the Japs haven't yet fabricated the bomb with my name on it." Even so, his troops were unmoved. An anonymous GI set a taunting ballad to the tune of "The Battle Hymn of the Republic":

> Dugout Doug's not timid, he's just cautious, not afraid.
> He's carefully protecting the stars that Franklin made.
> Four-star generals are as rare as good food on Bataan,
> And his troops go starving on.

But Roosevelt, always seeking to buoy up support for the war at home, persuaded Congress to award him the Medal of Honor, and overnight he became the "Lion of Luzon," a living legend. Newspapers ran extravagant reports of his exploits, confected of course under his own supervision, and even the Olympian columnist Walter Lippmann vaunted his "vast and profound conceptions." Babies, streets, schools and dams were named for him along with the "MacArthur narcissus," a flower, and the "MacArthur glide," a dance. An Indian tribe made him an honorary chief, and the University of Wisconsin gave him an honorary doctorate. He was exalted by Democrats despite his conservative views, while Republicans began to consider him presidential. A missionary in Panama discovered that natives there had carved wooden idols of him to ward off evil spirits. The acclaim recalled the enthusiasm generated forty-four years before for Admiral George Dewey, after he defeated the Spanish fleet. The occasions, obviously, were different.

Once again, Eisenhower dissented privately: "The public has built itself a hero out of its own imagination." But he saw the value of the myth. MacArthur, he wrote in his diary, should be left on Corregidor, where he was "doing a good job" in a situation freighted with "all the essentials of drama." If he were withdrawn, "public opinion will force him into a position where his love of the limelight may ruin him."

But Roosevelt had decided by the middle of February to pull him out—not merely for his safety. The Japanese had by then invested Singapore, taken Borneo, landed in Sumatra and were poised to attack Java, the main island of the Dutch East Indies. Ahead lay Australia, whose best troops were loyally fighting for Britain against the Germans in North Africa. Prime Minister John Curtin threatened to bring them home to protect their country unless America bore the burden. Roosevelt accepted. He assumed responsibility for Australia's defense, named MacArthur supreme army chief for the Pacific and created a separate navy command with Admiral Chester W. Nimitz in charge. It was a momentous decision. The Australians stayed in North Africa, playing a vital role in the German defeat at El Alamein, a victory that saved the Suez Canal for the Allies. And Australia was to dilute its relations with Britain to become intimately associated with the U.S. presence in the Pacific—as it is to this day.

Roosevelt's order to quit Corregidor posed a dilemma for MacArthur. He had pledged to go down fighting and now, as writer Robert Sherwood observed, he was like a captain abandoning the sinking ship first. But he finally obeyed Roosevelt, asking only that he choose the "psychological" moment to depart. On March 11, 1942, after waffling for more than two weeks, he boarded a patrol boat with his wife, son, the child's amah and a few aides. They had a harrowing journey, risking capture by Japanese ships to reach Mindanao, whence they flew to Australia. Before leaving, MacArthur entrusted his command to Wainwright, telling him to "hold."

A week later, while traveling by train across Australia, he stopped at one town and proclaimed to reporters waiting for a statement, "I have come through and I shall return."

MacArthur's critics denounced the personal pronoun as yet another symptom of his megalomania, while his supporters marveled at his ability to improvise memorable phrases. His massive ego notwithstanding, MacArthur usually selected his words for a purpose, and his public remarks were seldom extemporaneous. In this case, his pledge had been carefully crafted weeks before by Carlos Romulo, the chief Filipino propagandist on Corregidor. Having anticipated MacArthur's departure, he had conceived a promise directed at Filipinos. They had long ceased to expect salvation from America, yet their faith in MacArthur was still firm. So, as Romulo put it, "if *he* says that *he* is coming back, he will be believed." MacArthur, after all, was their *compadre*—and both he and they knew it. Their liberation was to become his primary goal, his obsession, his atonement for having forsaken them.

★　★　★

By the middle of February 1942, Bataan was in deadlock. Homma, far behind schedule, was distraught. Weeks earlier, reassured by his successes, the high command in Tokyo had moved his best men to Malaya, instead sending him overage veterans trained for occupation jobs. "Absolutely unfit for combat duty," as one of his staff described them, they were no better prepared for the jungle than the Americans. Their ranks also dwindled from hunger and disease—and, Homma revealed, the U.S. force could have "walked" through them "without encountering much resistance." He clamored for help, his pleas to Tokyo an echo of MacArthur's appeals to Washington. Unlike MacArthur, he eventually received relief, but his supplications had signified a confession of failure, a humiliating "loss of face" for a proud Japanese soldier, and he was to be retired prematurely.

He had exaggerated his problem, however. The Americans and Filipinos, despite their numerical edge, were too feeble physically to counterattack. Even if they could have fought their way back to Manila, they would have faced the hopeless task of defending the city without reinforcements. So their plight had been ordained beforehand, when MacArthur dispersed supplies across Luzon. With ample food, medicine and equipment, the Bataan garrison could have resisted for a year—rather than being starved into submission.

Like all protracted struggles, the battle for Bataan was a seesaw series of attacks interrupted by lulls as both sides collapsed from exhaustion. They engaged in artillery duels, but the worst of the fight was personal. Drenched in sweat, gasping for breath in the suffocating heat and humidity, they grappled in flooded rice fields, amid dense jungles, on dizzy mountain cliffs, snipers and booby traps a continual menace. The Americans and Filipinos often shot prisoners summarily, claiming to be retaliating for atrocities. The Japanese did indeed torture, disembowel, decapitate or castrate prisoners, sometimes flinging the mutilated corpses into the bay. In an attempt to demoralize the Americans and Filipinos, their sound trucks broadcast nostalgic music or shrieks, groans and other weird noises throughout the night. They circulated primitive propaganda tracts—one, for example, showing a half-naked woman beside the caption *Don't wait to die. While there is still a time and place, feel soft against me and rest . . . rest your warm hand against my breast.*

Enemy infiltrators were everywhere, slipping stealthily through the lines at night to murder and steal. Captain Paul Ashton, a U.S. Army doctor, was dozing in his foxhole, a razor-sharp bayonet within reach, when a scraping noise awoke him. "Very slowly and quietly," he later wrote, "I brought my arm out in the complete darkness and touched the end of a rifle, then brought my hand beneath it, past a helmet and felt a nose and face. In one motion I grabbed the rifle with my left hand and thrust the long knife along the collar bone, driving it deep into the neck." The Japanese "screamed in surprise, fear and pain," trying to roll away as Ashton held him long enough "to plunge the weapon again and again deep into his neck." The enemy soldier's body went limp, but Ashton remained awake, having heard that even dying Japanese often pulled the ring of their grenades to "take killer and killed to hell together." Examining the corpse at dawn, he concluded with the coolness of a coroner that his victim had bled to death from a severed windpipe and carotid artery. He counted himself lucky, thinking of the terror that struck, night after night, up and down the line.

Late in March, with Japan's offensive in Southeast Asia advancing, Homma finally received new troops as well as air and artillery units for a decisive push against Bataan. Its defenders were now down to a thousand calories a day, and Wainwright reported that their rations would run out within two weeks. Nearly all had malaria, and seventy-five percent dysentery. "Under no conditions" should they yield, radioed MacArthur from Australia. He ordered them to counterattack, seize a Japanese supply dump at Subic Bay and drive into northern Luzon, fighting as guerrillas if necessary. Despite his misgivings, Wainwright passed the directive to Major General Edward P. King, the stocky, courteous, cerebral artilleryman who had succeeded him as commander on Bataan.

Homma, now reinforced, delivered his coup de grâce on April 3, Good Friday. The assault hit "like a hurricane," as Sam Grashio recalled. Japanese aircraft and artillery unleashed a fierce barrage, the bombs and shells setting the sector ablaze. Into this inferno of strangling smoke and dust "poured wave after wave of enemy troops," shattering the defense lines and destroying leadership, discipline, order. "Sick, starved, dazed, terrified men abandoned arms and equipment, and milled about aimlessly, many so tired that they fell asleep as soon as they sat down. Communications broke down, and nobody knew what anyone else was doing. Some Filipino detachments had to be driven to their positions at gunpoint. Roads were jammed with men and vehicles headed in every direction. The Japanese strafed jungle trails crowded with stragglers pouring from the battlefield to escape captivity. It was confusion beyond my wildest imagination."

After five days, King decided to submit regardless of MacArthur's directive—not telling Wainwright in order to absolve him of responsibility. On the morning of April 9, his face taut with weariness, he drove with two aides to the enemy lines to talk terms with Homma's chief of operations, who demanded unconditional surrender. "Will my troops be well treated?" asked King. Offended, the Japanese replied, "We are not barbarians." King laid his pistol on the table. Never in history had so large a U.S. military force capitulated.

MacArthur, though enraged, could not decently derogate the martyrs of Bataan. Instead, he delivered one of his more ponderous epiphanies: "No army has done so much with so little. . . . To the weeping mothers of its dead, I can only say that the sacrifice and halo of Jesus of Nazareth has descended upon their sons, and that God will take them unto Himself." Taken captive, Brigadier General William Brougher wrote in a squalid Japanese prison camp soon afterward: "A foul trick of deception has been played on a large group of Americans by a commander in chief and small staff who are now eating steak and eggs in Australia. God damn them!"

The Japanese now faced Corregidor, three miles across a channel, its coastal guns the final obstacle to their control of Manila Bay. Packed into the Malinta tunnel, ten thousand troops, casualties and refugees sweltered in the heat and humidity. Water was scarce, and the power plant exposed to assault. Soon the enemy artillery was pounding away from the heights of Bataan. Homma, pressed by Tokyo to capture the island swiftly, attacked on the night of May 5.

It was almost suicidal. Their boats capsized in the surf or were blown to bits as they came within point-blank range of the U.S. guns, but swarms of Japanese had landed by morning. Wainwright, in despair, sent a poignant valedictory to Roosevelt. "With broken heart and head bowed in sadness but not in shame," he was surrendering "to end this useless effusion of blood and human sacrifice."

MacArthur vindictively vetoed a proposal to award the Medal of Honor to Wainwright, who was given it only after his release from Japanese internment following the war. For public consumption, however, MacArthur delivered another of his proclamations. Corregidor had "scrolled its own epitaph on enemy tablets," and "through the bloody haze of its last reverberating shot, I shall always seem to see a vision of grim, gaunt, ghastly men, still unafraid." Eisenhower again writhed privately. "Poor Wainwright! He did the fighting in the Philippine islands. Another got such glory as the public could find in the operation. . . . MacArthur's tirades to which . . . I so often listened in Manila would now sound as silly to the public as they did to us. But he's a hero! Yah."

MacArthur was to assert after the war that the defense of Bataan and Corregidor delayed Japan's offensive in the Far East and thus contributed to America's ultimate victory. But his claim, though understandably designed to lend meaning to the tragic defeat, lacked substance.

With the exception of the Philippines, the Japanese conquered Southeast Asia on schedule. They lagged behind in the archipelago only because it was a lesser priority to them than acquiring the resources of Malaya, Sumatra and Java, which their military machine needed to capture the real prize: China. For that reason, they deprived Homma of his best men at a moment when he could have easily crushed the Bataan garrison and taken over all of Luzon.

To America early in the war, the Philippines was also an area that "did not in 1942 possess great strategic significance" from a global perspective, as the official U.S. Army history later put it. So the Roosevelt administration neglected MacArthur—and the "battling bastards" of Bataan, as they called themselves, were expendable from the start. But the epic illustrated the unique political and psychological quality in the relationship between Americans and Filipinos.

Japan destroyed European rule in Southeast Asia at the outbreak of the war, and the British, French and Dutch soon forgot their empires as they resisted German aggression at home. Asian nationalists emerged, many rallying behind the Japanese against their colonial masters. But the fight for Bataan, as a symbol of America's broader struggle for the Philippines, had different consequences. Like Pearl Harbor, it ranged the U.S. public behind the war effort in a quest for vengeance and victory. Since then, it has become another Valley Forge or Alamo, a piece of folklore that inspires the national spirit. The spectacle of Americans dying alongside their troops also touched Filipinos deeply, and thousands joined guerrilla movements to resist the Japanese. To this day, they evoke the memory of Bataan to symbolize their special bond with the United States. The disaster did not end at the gate to Manila Bay, however. An abominable sequel awaited the American and Filipino prisoners of the battle, and the agony they shared was to be a crucible in which their two countries forged even closer links.

Soldiers usually treat prisoners of war leniently, if only to avoid reprisals against captured comrades. But the savagery vented by the Japanese on the vanquished Americans and Filipinos was unparalleled, at least in modern military annals. During the notorious Bataan Death March, as many as ten thousand men died from disease, malnutrition and wanton brutality. The exact figure is unknown even today.

Giving him the benefit of the doubt, historian John Toland has written that Homma expected twenty-five thousand prisoners and planned to treat them as he did his own men, but suddenly found himself burdened with three times that number. He may have been too busy as well to prevent racial fanatics among his officers from torturing and killing white captives. Cruelty was also common to Japanese troops, whose superiors regularly slapped them for the slightest misconduct, and so they considered brutality routine. Taught to equate surrender with disgrace, they further believed that prisoners deserved to be punished as severely as they themselves would for submitting. And, too, a bizarre brand of romantic sadism pervaded the Japanese army. Enemy diaries discovered after the war, for example, revealed vivid accounts of beheadings, the poetic passages exalting the skill of the executioner, the beauty of his blade and the courage of his victim.

Assembled in central Bataan, the captives were destined for Camp O'Donnell, a Philippine army installation eighty miles to the north. Their guards began by stealing their jewelry, watches, pens and other valuables, kicking, beating or even bayoneting anyone found with a Japanese item on the presumption that he had looted a Japanese body. There were coincidental cases of kindness, however. A Japanese officer returned a stolen ring to Mario

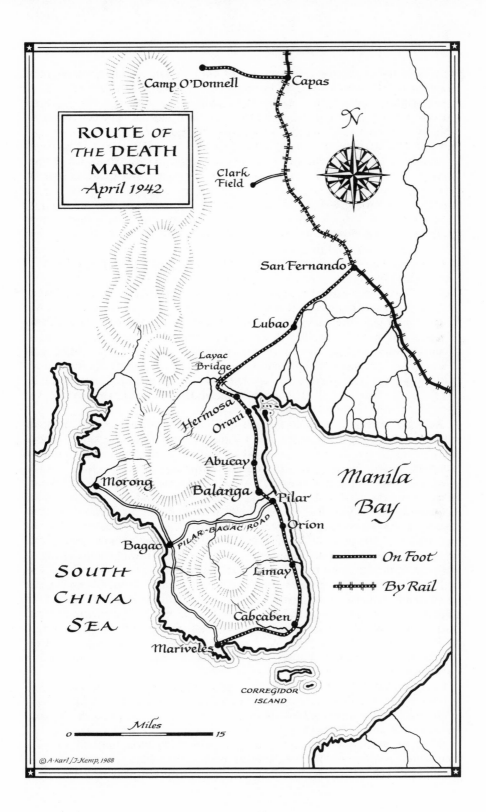

ROUTE OF
THE DEATH
MARCH
April 1942

Camp O'Donnell
Capas

Clark
Field

N

San Fernando

Lubao

Layac
Bridge

Hermosa
Orani

Abucay

Balanga
Pilar

Morong

Orion

Manila
Bay

Bagac
PILAR-BAGAC ROAD

On Foot
By Rail

Limay

SOUTH
CHINA
SEA

Cabcaben

Mariveles

CORREGIDOR
ISLAND

Miles

0   15

© A. Karl / J. Kemp, 1988

Tonelli, a former Notre Dame fullback. As a student at the University of Southern California in 1935, he explained, he had seen Tonelli play in Los Angeles. But Sam Grashio's description of the ordeal was truer: "A macabre litany of heat, dust, starvation, thirst, flies, filth, stench, murder, torture, corpses and wholesale brutality that numbs the memory."

Four decades later, though, Grashio's memory was still keen, and he wept at moments as he related his experience to me. "As we started out, the Japanese took away whatever food we had, and refused to give us any in return. They wouldn't let us near the springs and streams along the route, but only allowed us the muddy, scummy water from buffalo wallows. And even when men almost crazy from thirst rushed to the filthy ponds, the guards often clubbed them back into formation or shot them. One day a case of milk fell off a passing truck, and the prisoners swarmed over it like ants. The Japanese leaped in, swinging their fists, kicking and flailing with rifle butts, pounding them back into line."

Blair Robinette, a former army engineer, said as we sat in the living room of his house near Baltimore: "It's been forty-five years, and I'm still mad." As the march began, a Japanese guard grabbed his canteen, took a swig and threw it to the ground. "He watched my reaction. Trying not to act angry, I bent to pick up my canteen. Next thing I knew, he hit me with his rifle butt, and I was flat on the road, blood running down my face. I got to my knees and looked up, and he's pointing his bayonet at me. He was just a little guy, but his gun made him ten feet tall, and you realized that you would've been a damn fool to argue with him."

Robinette saw a U.S. lieutenant lashed to a telephone pole and decapitated with a single swish of the sword by a Japanese executioner, who left the body dangling in the sun. He lost count of other headless corpses sprawled in ditches along the road, the gaping necks covered with flies. Grashio dodged as a Japanese tank deliberately swerved to crush an American too weak to get out of its path. He witnessed a guard, bayonet drawn, prod an American into burying another American alive. Rank was irrelevant. Japanese soldiers threatened to shoot Brigadier General Clifford Bluemel, one of the Bataan commanders, for aiding a crippled comrade. Nor were Filipinos spared. "I don't know what he did," Robinette recalled, "but I saw the Japs string a Filipino from the limb of a tree and beat him to death."

Filipino villagers along the road surreptitiously handed water, rice and sugar to the famished men, or even waved to them, and many suffered. At one point, Japanese soldiers caught an old peasant and his wife passing out rice, burned them alive and displayed their charred bodies on the stake to discourage similar acts of generosity. If any Americans had harbored racist feelings before the death march, the risks taken by the Filipinos converted them into paragons of tolerance.

The first Americans to straggle into Camp O'Donnell, the internment center, were addressed by its Japanese commandant, resplendent in black boots, white shirt and starched shorts. His arms folded across his chest, he barked at them: "You are captives, not prisoners of war, and will be so treated."

Sixty thousand men jammed the camp, a sprawl of bamboo huts built to hold one sixth that number. Their daily food ration consisted of a handful of rice gruel, but even worse was the lack of water. Only two spigots served ten thousand Americans, who would wait for hours under the fierce tropical sun to fill their canteens, standing on paths slimy with excrement from their dysentery. When General King, who had made the trek on foot with his troops, begged the commandant to alleviate their suffering, the Japanese slapped him in the face and shouted: "You are my enemies! I will shoot anyone who disobeys me!" Nearly two thousand Americans and some twenty-five thousand Filipinos died within three months.

Similar horrors awaited thousands of Americans later transported to Japan as slave labor. Men crazed by thirst in an airless hold of one Japanese ship slashed the wrists and throats of their comrades in a savage attempt to suck their blood. American submarines or aircraft, unaware of their cargo, sank several such vessels. In one case, as a ship went down, Japanese guards machine-gunned the prisoners even as they themselves struggled to keep afloat.

★ ★ ★

On Christmas Eve of 1941, when Francis Sayre fled with MacArthur to Corregidor, he left behind his executive aide, Claude Buss, to assist the eight thousand American civilians about to come under Japanese rule. Buss had been visiting a friend in the hospital on January 2, when he saw the enemy troops invest the city. "They were in jeeps, and they knew exactly where they were going," he recalled to me forty-five years later. "Some drove to this street or to that avenue, and in nothing flat, they had everything in hand."

Unlike their comrades on the death march, many Japanese officers assigned to manage Manila were silky smooth. Buss dealt with one who jokingly referred to himself a "chocolate soldier," explaining that he was really a civilian employee of the army. Educated in Britain, he spoke fluent English. "Everything's going to be fine," he assured Buss. Not long afterward, three Americans had just been beaten to death with coils of barbed wire for attempting to escape from the suburban University of Santo Tomás campus, which the Japanese had transformed into a civilian internment camp.

To prevent overcrowding, Buss had advised the officer to lodge the Americans in schools, clubs and office buildings throughout Manila. The Japanese, realizing that their dispersal would pose control problems, ordered the Americans confined to Santo Tomás—where, though civilians, they were to be treated as prisoners of war.

Journalists were no exception. Carl Mydans of *Life* and his wife, Shelley, were loaded onto a truck along with other Americans bound for Santo Tomás. The university, a Spanish vestige from the seventeenth century, was an array of mildewed buildings set in a weedy campus. Mydans promptly realized that the Japanese "had no program whatsoever" to provide the prisoners with rations, medicines or other basics. Filipinos helped, as they did during the death march. Assembling outside the enclosure, they tossed food and bedding over the wall and went on supplying the inmates despite Japanese threats. Again, even the most biased Americans lost their last shreds of racial prejudice.

Abundantly equipped with time and skills, the Americans swiftly made the prison habitable—repairing the lighting, building toilets, creating schools, improvising a clinic and organizing a police force to cope with thievery and other offenses committed by their companions, lest the Japanese impose their brutal code. They also elected a committee to deal with the Japanese—whose main concerns, as Mydans put it, were "to keep us there and to keep us quiet." After the Japanese killed the three escaping Americans, nobody else tried. Prisoners would sometimes be taken away, presumably to a Japanese army center elsewhere in Manila. Many never came back. Three years later, when the city was freed, a few were found, wasted and bleached, in ancient Spanish dungeons. But, Mydans recalled, the most terrifying were those who returned to the camp. One reappeared, his body bruised, his wrists and legs ulcerated under the marks of ropes. Still traumatized, he replied nervously when Mydans asked him to relate his ordeal: "Don't talk. Don't ever talk in here."

After eight months, not knowing what to expect, Mydans and his wife traded Santo Tomás for a Japanese internment camp in Shanghai and luckily won repatriation in a prisoner exchange. Mydans was to cover the American army's liberation of Santo Tomás early in 1945. By then, nearly half of the first batch of inmates had died of hunger and disease. The survivors resembled skeletons.

Though thousands of Filipinos helped prisoners or joined guerrilla groups, many cooperated with the Japanese, at least at the start of the occupation. Nationalist zealots embraced them as fellow Asians, and local officials submitted to their rule for the sake of survival. Above all, they were widely supported by the old political, landed and entrepreneurial dynasties that had traditionally accommodated to the imperial power to preserve their own prestige and privilege. Scions of the *ilustrados* who had earlier served both Spain and the United States, they were to retain their position after the war by closing ranks—and because MacArthur, despite his pledge to purge pro-Japanese collaborators, exonerated them to keep the conservative governing class intact.

Jorge Vargas, whom Quezon had left behind to deal with the Japanese, felt harassed and helpless as their troops reached the outskirts of Manila at dawn on January 2, 1942. With Quezon in Corregidor, he naturally turned to an American for advice. He telephoned Claude Buss, asking: "Can we hinder their progress, make things tough for them?" Buss, knowing that resistance was hopeless, replied, "Use your head and do nothing to bring retribution to the people." After days of agonizing, Vargas gave way to the Japanese, and delivered a radio broadcast on their behalf.

He promised that they would be "benign and liberal," and urged Filipinos to "resume their normal life to the end that law and order may be restored"— in particular, to "refrain from committing acts . . . inimical to the interests" of the new masters. The Japanese, confident that he could be managed, appointed him head of their surrogate administration.

Just as the United States had governed through the upper classes, so the Japanese recruited them on the theory that the mass of Filipinos, traditionally subservient to the entrenched oligarchy, would pliantly follow. Besides Vargas, they enlisted such *ilustrados* as José Laurel, Benigno Aquino—father of the later martyred Ninoy—and Manuel Roxas. But these men, the best known of the collaborators, rapidly lost respect as Japanese occupation troops alienated the population by their cruelty. Nor could they maintain their credibility as it became clear over time that America would win the war.

Vargas later contended that he had served the Japanese only to comply with

Quezon's instructions. If so, he was carried away by the masquerade. "The prestige of all Asian nations has been vindicated" by Japan's "sweeping victories," he declared on one occasion and, on another, extolled the Japanese for emancipating the Philippines from the "hopeless bondage" of U.S. rule. He even praised the Japanese commandant of a notorious prison camp for his "considerate treatment" of the captives. But despite his ingratiating rhetoric, the Japanese sought a more plausible figure to act as president when, in 1943, they contemplated the creation of a puppet republic.

They planned to set up the sham regime out of fear that President Roosevelt might grant independence to Quezon's government-in-exile in the United States and thereby usurp their claim to have freed the archipelago. Their candidate for president was Manuel Roxas y Acuña, a slim, brilliant, moody man in his late forties, who had held several top public positions, including speakership of the legislature. Quezon, his patron, would have preferred him to Osmeña as his vice president, and MacArthur, also an admirer, had made him a colonel in the U.S. Army. He had joined them on Corregidor and escaped before its fall. Captured by enemy troops, he would have been executed had not a senior Japanese officer, seeing him as an ideal puppet president, interceded to save his life. Roxas declined the job, pleading poor health, and later played a double game: handling food distribution for the pro-Japanese administration while secretly providing the Americans with intelligence. He was cleared of collaboration charges after the war by MacArthur, who helped to elect him as first president of the truly independent Philippines.

The Japanese finally chose José Laurel, who had earned a law degree in Tokyo and lobbied for their business interests in the Philippines before the war. They also read an incident as an auspicious omen of his fidelity. In June 1943, while playing golf, he was gravely wounded by an assassin's bullet—surely proof of his pro-Japanese sympathies.

Like Vargas, he later claimed to have been following Quezon's orders. But Laurel was a complex man, prompted by complicated impulses, who conceded to becoming a puppet in hopes of pulling his own strings. The Japanese, however, were to manipulate him for their purposes.

Indicted as a youth for murdering a rival in a love triangle, he studied law and won acquittal as well as a reputation for brilliance. He returned home after a stint at Yale, gaining cabinet rank in the local government by his early thirties. A spat with U.S. officials stunted his career and embittered him toward America, and an eventual supreme court seat did not alleviate his frustrations. Increasingly nationalistic, he accused the Americans of stifling Filipino aspirations. More and more, he saw Japanese values as an antidote to the corruption, waste and indolence of his own society. "Life is nothing, duty everything," he declaimed, stressing that honor, hard work, racial pride and similar virtues within an autocratic system had made Japan great—and could renovate the Philippines as well. Inaugurated president in October 1943, he yielded to Japanese pressure to declare war on the United States the next year. The regime, President Roosevelt said in a radio broadcast beamed to the Philippines, had been conceived "in fraud and deceit . . . to confuse and mislead the Filipino people."

Laurel's pretensions to sovereignty were an illusion. Every Filipino knew that Japanese "consultants" managed the bureaucracy, and that Japanese soldiers enforced martial law. The Japanese also invented a legislature composed of a single party known as the *Kalibapi,* an acronym derived from the *Kapisanan Sa Paglilingkod Bagong Pilipinas,* the Association for Service to the New Philippines. They selected as its leader Benigno Aquino.

A sturdy, gregarious man then in his late forties, Aquino belonged to the landed gentry of Tarlac province, north of Manila. His father, who had fought the Americans as a general in the Filipino army early in the century, quaintly continued to balk at the U.S. presence in the Philippines by refusing to learn English. As a young politician during the 1920s, Aquino decried the U.S. school system as an "instrument for the Americanization of our customs [and] mannerisms" and regularly denounced "American imperialism" before that term became trite. His vision blurred by intense chauvinism, he believed the Japanese to be the wave of the future. Soon he was one of their foremost apologists. "We belong to the East," he declared, calling the Philippine link to the United States "artificial, unnatural, illogical and untenable." Once, visiting a prison camp, he even had the temerity to tell the sick and starving Filipino veterans of Bataan and Corregidor, most of them volunteers, that America had sacrificed them as "a symbol of resistance." He aspired to the presidency of the puppet republic, but his leadership of the *Kalibapi* put him in an equally key role as boss of its regional apparatus. Charged with treason after the war, he died shortly before his trial, and the case against him was posthumously dismissed. His son Ninoy, inspired by filial respect, claimed that he had acted under duress—though radical Filipino nationalists to this day glorify him for his defiance of the United States.

The ambitious design of the Japanese was to incorporate the Philippines, along with the other lands under their flag, into a coherent system grandly entitled the Greater East Asia Co-Prosperity Sphere. But neither they nor their surrogates could make their policies work.

They were deluded from the outset by their dream of converting easygoing Filipinos to such Japanese virtues as diligence, discipline and frugality. Blind to the pervasive imprint left on the archipelago by American teachers, doctors and engineers, they mistakenly derogated the "oppression and tyranny" of U.S. colonialism. Their accent on common Asian ties also misjudged the appeal of Western influence to the people. "As the leopard cannot change its spots, you cannot alter the fact that you are orientals," was a favorite line of General Homma, the senior Japanese commander. But that kind of racism, echoed by his aides, convinced few Filipinos. For whatever their doubts about themselves, they were not about to permit Japan to define their national identity under the pressures of war. In forty years of peace, after all, the Americans had only superficially reshaped their culture.

Filipinos rapidly learned as well that "co-prosperity" meant servitude to Japan's economic requirements. Amply supplied from their Taiwan colony, for example, the Japanese had no use for Philippine sugar, but they desperately needed cotton, which they had imported before the war from India and the United States. They thereupon launched a program to grow cotton instead of sugar, with ruinous results. Lacking the seeds, pesticides and technological skills for the new crop, they reduced hundreds of thousands of acres of cane fields to stubble and impoverished the ten percent of the population involved in the sugar industry. Jobless farm workers glutted the cities, swelling the ranks of the urban unemployed, whose enterprises had been crippled by the slump. Severe shortages of salt, soap and other basics developed as Japanese troops cornered those items for themselves, and famine spread as they seized vast stocks of local food. As scarcities sent prices soaring, Japanese officials aggravated the inflation through financial maneuvers. They sent what remained of the country's gold and dollar reserves to Tokyo to enrich Japan, thus depriving the Philippine currency of support. As a substitute, they printed billions of worthless pesos that Filipinos, familiar with Hollywood lingo, derisively dubbed "Mickey Mouse" money.

Confronted by chaos, they decreed the death penalty for economic offenses, but the society spun out of control. The prime culprits were Japanese officers themselves, who, despite their propaganda pleas for austerity, took over luxury villas and hotel suites, spent lavishly in restaurants and nightclubs, cruised around in commandeered limousines and plundered private homes for art objects and other valuables. Filipinos quickly discarded their scruples. "Buy and sell" became their byword and black marketeering their principal vocation as they dealt in everything from cigarettes and matches to jewelry and cars. Judges and lawyers forged documents, and the police routinely accepted bribes. The Japanese army paid whopping sums in fake pesos to Filipino middlemen for spare parts, sheet metal and other items that, they knew, were stolen from Japanese warehouses by Filipino gangs. Prostitution flourished as movie stars, respectable matrons and ordinary housewives exchanged their bodies for cash. To relax the strain on marriages, the Laurel regime legalized divorce—which, under pressure from the Catholic Church, was again banned after the war.

Thirty years later, the Filipino writer Carmen Nakpil Guerrero recalled the "suspicion and apprehension and abused faith" that had etched "our souls like acid and marked them forever." Only survival mattered. "It sharpened the mind, distorted appetites and dulled the moral sense. The old values and ideas of order, decorum and limits eroded. . . . Pious old ladies lived on what their cooks looted from the neighborhood grocer. Brothers hid little bags of sugar or lard from each other. Fathers ate their ill-gotten slice of pork while their children languished from a vegetable diet." Once secure, Filipinos now resorted to "savage and ardent cunning . . . plain deceit, pimping, hoarding and furnishing the enemy with war matériel," becoming "callous and miserly . . . a race of spies, thieves, saboteurs, informers." The endemic venality and corruption that nags the Philippines today is largely a legacy of the ethical degradation of that period.

Nothing damaged the reputation of the Japanese, however, as much as their promiscuous cruelty. Their propagandists publicized Japan's "fraternal affection" for the Filipinos, and some of their enlightened officers did indeed befriend and protect them. But compassion was rare. The *Kempeitai,* the Japanese version of the Gestapo, tortured and summarily shot suspects, imposing death even for listening to American radio broadcasts. Japanese commanders tyrannized villagers, and equally arrogant enlisted men beat anyone who failed to bow to them. Frustrated in their efforts to rule an elusive population, they increasingly beheaded innocent victims and displayed their bodies as an example. They turned to similar ruthlessness as the guerrilla resistance spread, executing ten Filipinos at random in retaliation for every Japanese soldier ambushed or assassinated. Several Japanese civilian officials cautioned that brutality would only alienate the people. They were overruled by their military colleagues, who insisted that force be met by force.

The guerrillas multiplied, however, until their various movements numbered some two hundred thousand men. They never seriously dented the enemy's superior military machine. But they harassed isolated Japanese garrisons, transmitted useful intelligence to the approaching U.S. forces—and, above all, boosted the morale of Filipinos who yearned to believe that they were participating in the struggle against Japan.

Like the anti-Nazi partisans in Europe, their motives were lofty, base or a mixture of both. Some were American and Filipino fugitives from the Bataan Death March or from Japanese prison camps. Russell Volckmann, a U.S. colonel, eluded captivity to form a guerrilla movement in Luzon and another American officer, Wendell Fertig, mobilized Muslim and Christian Filipinos in Mindanao. Two Filipino colonels, Marcario Peralta and Ruperto Kangleon, founded similar groups in the Visayas. By early 1943, MacArthur was supplying these organizations by submarine with weapons, radios—and, of course, cigarette packages and matchboxes bearing his vow I SHALL RETURN. He also sent in agents to distinguish the authentic from bogus partisans—no easy task. Thousands of jobless youths, unable to make ends meet in the cities, fled into the hills to call themselves guerrillas. Adventurers and bandits of every stripe posed as partisans, and local factionalism riddled the various movements as well, as rival families and clans settled old feuds, duplicitously fighting or helping the enemy to suit their aims. Late in 1944, when the U.S. landings in Leyte presaged the liberation of the archipelago, self-styled guerrillas surfaced everywhere in a final frenzy of plunder.

The strongest force was the People's Anti-Japanese Army, in Tagalog the *Hukbong Bayan Laban sa Hapon—Hukbalahap* for short, run by a coalition of communists and socialists. Its leaders, though mainly urban intellectuals, astutely realized that central Luzon, long a caldron of rural unrest, was ripe for their efforts. Within months after the war erupted, they commanded twenty-five thousand guerrillas and thousands more supporters throughout the area of sugar and rice fields, jungles and mountains stretched in an arc north of Manila.

Their guerrillas, popularly called Huks, were mostly poor sharecroppers and farm workers looking for any chance to improve their abysmal lot—just as their forebears had often rallied behind religious mystics promising change. Now they saw new hope in the dislocations caused by the Japanese. The hated landlords, who represented local authority, had fled to Manila for safety, abandoning their plantations and leaving the Japanese in charge. So, to the Huks, the fight against the enemy was an opportunity to seize the vacated estates, fill the power vacuum—and, in effect, stage a revolution.

The *Hukbalahap* military commander, Luis Taruc, then in his thirties, was one of the few senior leaders of peasant origin. When I first met him twenty-five years later, he was still a sinewy figure with taut skin, chocolate eyes and a prodigious memory. He had organized small mobile squads, training them with the help of an imported Chinese Communist instructor who taught Mao Zedong's principles of guerrilla warfare and used Edgar Snow's *Red Star Over China* as a text. Among their officers, he recalled suggestively, was a lovely young woman with the nom de guerre of *Liwayway,* or "Beautiful Morning," who had enlisted to avenge her father's murder by the Japanese—and led an ambush against a column of their troops. Their ability to blend into the local population assured their protection, but they suffered badly when, out of overconfidence, they challenged superior Japanese forces. Eventually they adopted defensive tactics, such as tightening their grip over harvests to deny food to the enemy. They also prepared to seize future political power by setting up provisional administrations in the areas under their control.

The Huks would have welcomed U.S. aid without submitting to American orders, and attempts to strike a deal foundered. Nevertheless, they later helped the U.S. drive to liberate Luzon, acting as guides in the push toward Manila and freeing Americans from Japanese prison camps. MacArthur's attitude toward them was blurred. He denied them formal recognition, having been warned by his intelligence staff that they aimed to set up "a communistic government in the Philippines after the war, on the early Russian model." But he grasped their desire for change and, vetoing a proposal to send a force against them, said: "If I worked in those sugar fields, I'd be a Huk myself." In several areas, however, U.S. soldiers disarmed them, leaving many to be beaten and even killed by returning landlords and their surrogates, rival guerrilla groups, former enemy collaborators and other foes. American military police also arrested Taruc and two of his comrades. Though subsequently released, their mistreatment shocked and humiliated their followers, and the United States and its Filipino protégés were to be confronted by a tougher phase of the *Hukbalahap* rebellion a few years hence.

No guerrilla, true or false, exalted his exploits more loudly than did Ferdinand Marcos, who never ceased to laud the *Ang Mga Maharlika,* or Noblemen, the partisan movement that he claimed to have commanded in northern Luzon. In early 1986, his claim was revealed as fraudulent by an American scholar, who based his conclusions on documents in the National Archives in Washington. But Marcos was not the only Filipino to invent stories of his guerrilla exploits. Thousands of others did the same, partly to petition for U.S. Army pensions after the war. Many were actuated as well by genuine feelings of fidelity to America, and that sense of allegiance intensified as it became increasingly clear that MacArthur would fulfill his personal pledge to return.

★ ★ ★

Events began to favor America as early as May 1942, when the U.S. Navy routed a Japanese fleet near Midway, an island astride a key Pacific supply route. Their logistical problem thus eased, MacArthur's men were soon leapfrogging northward, ousting the Japanese from remote atolls like Saipan, Tinian and Truk, names once known only to geographers, now the stuff of headlines. By early 1944, as U.S. strategists pondered the next major target, the navy called for circumventing the Philippines and instead striking at Taiwan, three hundred miles closer to Japan, the bull's-eye. MacArthur, appalled, warned that to bypass the archipelago would not only incur the "open hostility" of the Filipinos and damage America's image throughout Asia, but "cause extremely adverse reactions" at home. "We have a great national obligation to discharge," he said—implying, of course, his own obligation.

President Roosevelt traveled to Hawaii in July 1944 to confer with MacArthur and his navy equal, Admiral Nimitz, ostensibly to resolve the issue. In fact, his journey was political. Just nominated by the Democratic party for an unprecedented fourth term, he was eager for visibility as the nation's commander in chief and spent most of his time being photographed with his senior officers. MacArthur privately fumed at having been summoned for a "picture-taking junket," but he won over Roosevelt during their discussions with his emphasis on America's "moral" duty to the Philippines as well as his economical casualty record. In two years of fighting in the Pacific, he had lost twenty-eight thousand men—fewer than the deaths in the recent Normandy invasion and one third the number of GIs killed on the beaches of Anzio.

But Roosevelt, once home, deferred to the joint chiefs. They finally approved MacArthur's plan to land in Leyte and later endorsed his proposed assault on Luzon, dropping the Taiwan option. He had promised them quick, dramatic results—and, as usual, his optimism was contagious.

Set for late October, the Leyte attack would demonstrate the might of American industry, now running at full throttle. Some seven hundred craft were to be engaged, from warships to transports for two hundred thousand troops. Supplies for the first month, to total two million tons, included weapons, ammunition, rations and the candy and cigarettes vital to GIs, with three hundred thousand tons to land every month thereafter—all coming from nine separate Pacific bases in a logistical operation of monumental proportions.

Blamed for Japan's reverses until then, Prime Minister Tojo had recently been purged, paving the way for his rival, Lieutenant General Tomoyuki Yamashita, to be named Japanese commander in the Philippines. Yamashita, six feet tall and weighing two hundred pounds, was renowned as the "Tiger of Malaya" for his capture of Singapore. Tojo had banished him to minor jobs in China. Now he hoped to stage a comeback, but he would face long odds when MacArthur struck at Leyte.

Yamashita, having learned from the Pacific campaign that clinging to the beaches under withering U.S. naval fire was costly, planned to fight from the Philippine interior rather than along its shores. With two hundred thousand troops to defend the entire archipelago, he concentrated on Luzon at the expense of the other islands. He assigned only twenty thousand men to Leyte and ordered them to harass potential U.S. invaders from the mountains instead of trying to hold the coast. But he had cause for worry. Japan was no longer master of the air as raw recruits replaced the expert pilots killed over the past years. Worse yet, the high command in Tokyo, gulled by its own propaganda, still believed in Japan's invincibility—an illusion soon to prove disastrous. Yamashita was also dismayed by the ignorance of many of his field officers. As the first American troops reached Leyte, he informed a newly arrived aide in Manila of their landing. "Very interesting," the officer replied. "Where is Leyte?"

The U.S. invasion force steaming toward Leyte stretched for a hundred miles across the sea, the vast array of ships looking from a distance like black spots on a silver sheet. MacArthur's entourage aboard the cruiser *Nashville* included Osmeña, now president of the Philippine commonwealth since Quezon's death in upstate New York in August. At midnight on October 19, 1944, the vessel slid into the waters off Leyte—not far from the site where, in 1521,

Magellan had erected a cross for Spain and Christendom. As a novice second lieutenant, MacArthur had served in the region four decades earlier. Years later, writing in his memoirs, he vividly evoked the moment before the Leyte battle: "Men lined the rails or paced the decks, peering into darkness and wondering what stood out there beyond the night. . . . There is a universal sameness in the emotions of men, whether they be admiral or sailor, general or private, at such a time as this."

The American fleet opened fire at dawn, and four U.S. divisions landed soon afterward to little resistance. Four hours later, MacArthur inadvertently strode into the most famous scene of his career when a harried navy beachmaster, too busy unloading supplies to provide his party with a boat, barked, "Let 'em walk." Cameras caught him wading ashore, his scowl a look of determination. Sensing its theatrical value, he reenacted the performance on Luzon.

He also dramatized his arrival in rhetoric of redemption contrived to electrify the emotions of pious Filipinos—even though it rankled many Americans at home. Oblivious to enemy snipers not far from the beach, he proclaimed through a radio transmitter: "People of the Philippines, I have returned. . . . Rally to me! . . . The guidance of divine God points the way. Follow in His name to the Holy Grail of righteous victory!"

Alarmed by MacArthur's landing, the Japanese went for a showdown. Had they succeeded, MacArthur's Leyte venture would have been doomed—and the whole U.S. offensive in the Pacific stymied. But the battle of Leyte Gulf, the greatest naval engagement of all time, was to shatter their fleet. Thus the Americans were able to advance in the Philippines and edge closer to Japan. The critical U.S. victory at sea, however, hinged as much on luck as it did on skill and courage.

Japan's naval chief for the area, Admiral Soemu Toyoda, had drafted a plan as complex as a *Go* game. His aim was to destroy the U.S. logistical armada off Leyte, and so deprive MacArthur of supplies, but first he had to lure away Admiral William Halsey's protective fleet. To bait Halsey, he sent a decoy of empty carriers north of Luzon, while ordering three other groups to Leyte to annihilate the nearly naked American support flotilla. Coming from Singapore, Borneo and Japan, they were scheduled to converge on their target on October 25—a feat that required perfect coordination.

Halsey, diverted, steamed off. But the rest of Toyoda's maneuver went awry—partly because the remaining U.S. forces resisted bravely. A group under Rear Admiral Jesse Oldendorf virtually wiped out one Japanese fleet in Surigao Strait, at the entrance to Leyte Gulf, and drove another from the same spot. American navy pilots also scored decisively—one of them, Commander David McCampbell, downing nine enemy planes on a single flight. The Japanese, however, largely suffered from their own blunders.

The commander of their most powerful task force, Vice Admiral Takeo Kurita, had fought in almost every major action until then. Aware of the perils ahead, he expected to lose half his flotilla—yet, he exhorted his men as they departed their base on Borneo for Leyte, it would be a "shame for the fleet to remain intact while our nation perishes." He was prescient. Soon afterward, his flagship was ripped apart by torpedoes from two American submarines, which also crippled one of his heavy cruisers. The next day, U.S. Navy planes spotted his force knifing through the Visayan Islands. For twelve hours they strafed, bombed and torpedoed the *Musahi,* the world's most formidable battleship, finally sinking it with a thousand of its crew. Kurita, the bulk of his force still afloat, nevertheless drove to within eighty miles of the Leyte coast. There, at sunrise on October 25, a group of small U.S. escort carriers valiantly tried to block him. He was about to crush them when, suddenly, he reversed course and retreated—in effect snatching defeat out of the jaws of victory. Had he continued, he could have pushed into Leyte Gulf and devastated MacArthur's supply vessels and beachhead positions. But, exhausted and confused from lack of sleep, he had deduced from radio intercepts that Halsey was bearing down on him. In fact, Halsey was far away. Toyoda's decoy plan, though successful, had ironically been futile.

Japan had unveiled a fearsome weapon during the fight, *kamikaze* pilots. They sank one of the six U.S. ships lost in the engagement and would sink or damage several more in the months ahead. To employ suicide fliers, however, was an act of desperation. The debacle off Leyte cost the Japanese half of their naval tonnage—including three battleships, four carriers and ten cruisers. Their fleet was no longer an offensive force but, as a Japanese admiral said, the defeat had been "tantamount to the loss of the Philippines."

But the Japanese ground forces were far from finished as MacArthur's men pushed inland to conquer Leyte. Yamashita, reluctantly forgoing his plan to focus on Luzon, began to reinforce the island within days of the U.S. landing. American planes were to sink eighty percent of his convoys—yet, by December, he had tripled his Leyte force to sixty-five thousand men.

Leyte, a grim tropical battlefield, presaged Vietnam. Monsoon rains and a fierce typhoon delayed construction of runways for American pursuit planes, and Japanese fighters repeatedly raided the U.S. beachhead, impeding the unloading of supplies. They bombed and strafed the coastal town of Tacloban, where MacArthur had taken over a large house, once almost hitting him as he was shaving. His troops, meanwhile, were enduring agonies as they penetrated the island. Laden with equipment, they hacked through steamy jungles, the heat and humidity soaking their clothes. They waded waist deep across swamps alive with leeches that sucked their blood, and they clawed up craggy cliffs whose sharp rocks slashed their boots and feet. Ambushes menaced them constantly, and they faced recurrent fire from tenacious Japanese concealed in trees, mountain caves, and holes in the ground. The going grew slower, tougher and deadlier as enemy reinforcements poured in.

The bloodiest battle of the campaign occurred near the town of Cariaga, on the northern littoral, from which MacArthur planned to drive across the island to the port of Ormoc, on the west coast—thereby dividing the enemy force. Blocking the way was a mass of hills that a U.S. patrol, mauled during a probe of the area, dubbed Breakneck Ridge. The Japanese had carved its ridges, slopes and crevices into a fortress of trenches, bunkers and hidden gun emplacements. They hurled back the first Americans to storm the redoubt on November 5, and the combat dragged on for ten days—men often fighting hand to hand in the stifling heat for inches of ground. As the enemy dug deeper, GIs brought in flamethrowers, one of them shouting as five burning Japanese rushed out of a cave, "Fry, you bastards, fry!" Superior U.S. artillery prevailed, however, and the Americans finally won control. But, after killing two thousand Japanese, they had advanced only a mile.

Sheer U.S. firepower ultimately beat the Japanese on Leyte—at a cost of nearly four thousand Americans dead and fifteen thousand wounded. MacArthur, eager to stick to his schedule, had declared on December 26 that the campaign was over "except for minor mopping up." In reality, the "mopping up" was to take another four months of "bitter, exhausting, rugged fighting—physically the most terrible we were ever to know," as a U.S. Army history put it. MacArthur stated as well that the Japanese had sustained the "greatest defeat" in their "military annals," but there was a sour taste to his triumph. The struggle for Leyte had been longer and harder than he expected, hardly a boon to his image. Leyte, he also learned, was unsuitable as an air base to attack Luzon. He would have to invade the island of Mindoro to edge closer to the target, relying for air support on the U.S. Navy, which he hated almost as much as he did the Japanese.

He might have derived some consolation from the plight of Yamashita. Despite his initial opposition to the venture, Yamashita had by Christmas squandered sixty thousand troops, nearly his total force on Leyte. He now elected to abandon the island, knowing that the bloodbath had already sapped his strength to defend Luzon, his main priority. Signaling his decision to Lieutenant General Sosaku Suzuki, his chief field commander on Leyte, he added that he was shedding "tears of remorse" for those being left behind. Suzuki later fled with a few aides in a small boat. Adrift at sea for weeks, they were strafed one day by a U.S. plane. Suzuki, killed in the attack, had earlier composed a portentous poem for a friend.

> Be thankful that you can die at the front,
> Rather than an inglorious death at home.

Fugitive Japanese troops continued to roam the island, a scene of appalling carnage. A veteran, Shohei Ooka, recalled his own ordeal in a novel, *Fires on the Plain.* Fleeing into the hills from U.S. artillery barrages, he entered a deserted village amid a sickly smell of rotting Japanese corpses. The men, marauders, had probably been surprised and slain by the villagers themselves. Dogs and crows picked at the cadavers, their ragged uniforms the only clue to their identity. "From some of the bodies, intestines as large as thumbs protruded where the stomachs should have been. . . . The heads too were bloated and looked as if they had been stung by thousands of hornets, the hair tightly glued to the skin by a liquid that had oozed out in the process of decomposition." Elsewhere, American shellings had littered the landscape with dead whose "vivid guts and blood shone in the sun's rain-washed beams," the severed limbs resembling "so many broken dolls." Ooka, also coming upon carcasses with buttocks stripped of flesh, slowly surmised to his horror that they had been cannibalized by starving comrades. Though starving himself, he resisted the temptation, and instead survived on plants and insects. He was later captured by Filipino guerrillas, who turned him over to the U.S. Army. Committed to a mental institution in Japan, he wrote his novel as a catharsis to overcome a "sense of desolation and a profound knowledge of betrayal."

MacArthur's drive through Luzon was to be his major campaign, second in size only to the U.S. push across central Europe. With nearly three hundred thousand American troops and Filipino guerrillas under his command, he confronted an almost equal force of Japanese. The contrast in casualties would be staggering. Some two hundred thousand Japanese died in battle—compared to eight thousand Americans. The final fight to liberate Manila killed at least a hundred thousand civilians in a holocaust of savage Japanese atrocities and furious U.S. artillery bombardments. After Warsaw, no other Allied city suffered such destruction during World War II.

MacArthur could find no better spot for landings than Lingayen Gulf, where Homma's force had attacked late in 1941. Its spacious beaches, ideal for an amphibious venture, also offered him direct access to the road and railway to Manila, a hundred miles to the southeast. The site debouched as well into the island's broad central plain, just the terrain for his large mechanized units. Following a frenzy of airfield construction on Mindoro to guarantee his men air support, he scheduled the assault for January 9, 1945.

Yamashita had no intention of gambling on a showdown at the shore. To lose such a clash, he feared, would propel the Americans toward their ultimate goal: an invasion of Japan. He planned instead to delay their advance by tying up their troops, ships and aircraft in Luzon, thereby buying time for his compatriots at home to prepare for the protection of the sacred homeland. His options were slim in any case. The U.S. fleet dominated the surrounding sea since the Japanese naval debacle at Leyte Gulf, and he could not expect fresh weapons and ammunition for his dwindling arsenal. Nor could he rely on reinforcements to replenish his ranks, which had been gravely depleted by the Leyte bloodbath.

He envisioned a protracted defense of Luzon designed to inflict heavy casualties on the Americans and so impede their progress. Dividing his army into three groups, he deployed one in the highlands above Clark Field to deny the base to U.S. aircraft, and another in hills east of Manila to control the city's source of water. His own force, 150,000 men, withdrew to the Cagayan Valley east of Lingayen Gulf, a fertile mountain region rich in rice. He himself moved from Manila to Baguio, where he took over a comfortable American villa as his headquarters. Recalling the U.S. ordeal of three years before, he avoided Bataan—though he did stiffen his garrison on Corregidor.

MacArthur's staff, distrusting intelligence reports to the contrary coming from guerrillas on Luzon, assumed that Yamashita would resist on the Lingayen beaches. Thus a U.S. flotilla, ordered to pound the coast beforehand, anticipated a classic response from big coastal guns and was inadequately equipped to handle enemy aircraft. The results were devastating. As the American ships entered Lingayen Gulf, waves of *kamikaze* fighters attacked from every direction. One crashed through the deck of the *Ommaney Bay,* sinking the escort carrier with a hundred of its crew. Another, slamming into the bridge of the battleship *New Mexico,* claimed among its victims a *Time* correspondent and a British general on a liaison mission. With the fanatical pilots shattering his other vessels, the fleet commander, Rear Admiral Jesse Oldendorf, considered a retreat to spare the approaching troop transports a similar fate. But, after a week, the Japanese ran short of planes—having destroyed twenty-four U.S. ships and damaged seventy others. Their suicide attacks continued on a smaller scale until, finally, they were virtually bereft of air power in the Philippines. MacArthur's ground forces would henceforth have little to dread from the sky.

They began to land at about ten o'clock on the morning of January 9, almost strolling ashore to no opposition except scattered shots from a few enemy snipers. MacArthur followed four hours later, this time deliberately wading through the surf for the cameras. He could not wait to race to Manila. Knowing the record of Japanese cruelty, he was concerned for the interned Americans. "We must move fast . . . to save as many of those prisoners as we can," he had confided to Carl Mydans aboard his flagship the night before. He also dreamed of a grand victory parade in the liberated capital on January 26, his sixty-fifth birthday, à la General Charles de Gaulle's procession down the Champs-Élysées the previous August. But his zeal was more than a quest for ego gratification. He was profoundly committed to the crusade to free a country that he regarded as his own, whose salvation he considered to be his personal responsibility. Years later, he evoked the emotions that had gripped him as he scanned the hazy Luzon horizon on the eve of the invasion: "At the sight of those . . . scenes of my family's past, I felt an indescribable sense of loss, of sorrow, of loneliness and of solemn consecration."

His return to Luzon exhilarated MacArthur and, as usual, he recklessly disregarded danger. He would inspect the front almost daily in his jeep, its pennant defiantly bearing his new rank of five-star general. Once, coming upon a platoon pinned down by the enemy, he refused to heed a young captain who frantically waved him away, saying: "I'm not under fire. They're not shooting at me." Another time, striding beyond his own lines on foot, he nearly stumbled into a Japanese machine-gun nest, saw his mistake and coolly backed off.

A supreme commander, he always said, should avoid "back seat driving" by delegating tactical decisions to his senior field officers. But now, obsessed with speed, he impatiently prodded his top subordinates—in particular General Walter Krueger, his ground-force chief. Krueger, at sixty-four, was a muscular figure of phenomenal stamina. A soldier's soldier, he once remarked that he preferred a regiment to an army so that he could "think a lot, scold a little, pat a man on the back now and then—and try to keep a perspective." He knew Luzon as intimately as did MacArthur, having surveyed its terrain as a young army engineer thirty-five years before. In contrast to MacArthur, however, he was extremely prudent. Expecting stubborn resistance from the Japanese even though they had ceded Lingayen Gulf, he was reluctant to dash toward Manila until he had mobilized his full strength. MacArthur, in a gesture of scorn for his procrastination, leapfrogged ahead of him, moving his own headquarters thirty-five miles nearer the enemy lines to Hacienda Luisita, later the Tarlac estate of the Cojuangcos, the family of Corazon Aquino.

Krueger was correct to be cautious. Under orders from MacArthur, he rushed his troops south to capture Clark Field without adequate protection against possible enemy attacks from the nearby hills. They ran into stiff opposition as the Japanese, fighting inch by inch, delayed the advance for a week. The Americans finally broke through, yet progress was still too slow for MacArthur. After one of his jeep tours of the sector, again defying snipers and exploding shells, he sharply rebuked Krueger for his "noticeable lack of drive and aggressive initiative" in following up the push. He also hounded Major General Verne Mudge, whose armored unit, the 1st Cavalry Division, had recently arrived in Luzon from the southwest Pacific. "Go to Manila, go around the Nips, bounce off the Nips—but go to Manila."

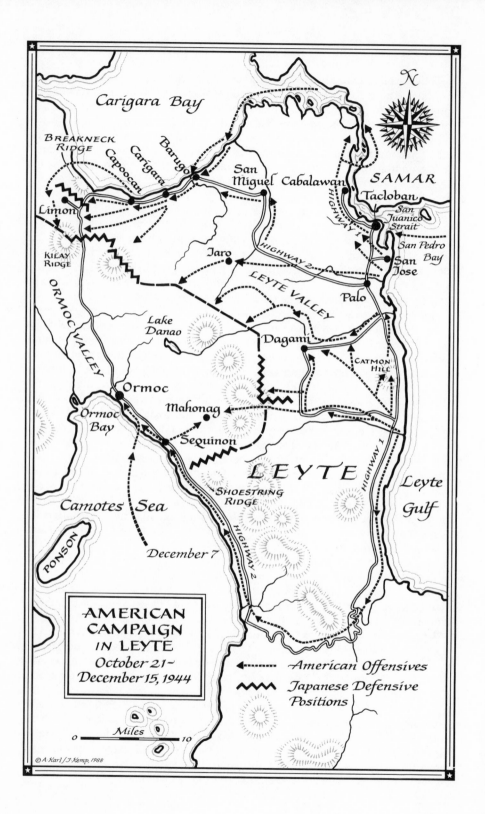

Carigara Bay

N

BREAKNECK
RIDGE
Capoocan
Carigara
Barugo
San
Miguel
Cabalawan

SAMAR

Tacloban

San
Juanico
Strait

San Pedro
Bay

HIGHWAY 1

Limon

KILAY
RIDGE

Jaro

HIGHWAY 2

LEYTE VALLEY

San
Jose

ORMOC VALLEY

Lake
Danao

Dagami

Palo

CATMON
HILL

Ormoc

Ormoc
Bay

Mahonag

Sequinon

LEYTE

HIGHWAY 1

Camotes Sea

SHOESTRING
RIDGE

Leyte
Gulf

PONSON

HIGHWAY 2

December 7

AMERICAN
CAMPAIGN
IN LEYTE
October 21~
December 15, 1944

American Offensives

Japanese Defensive
Positions

0   Miles   10

© A. Karl / J. Kemp, 1988

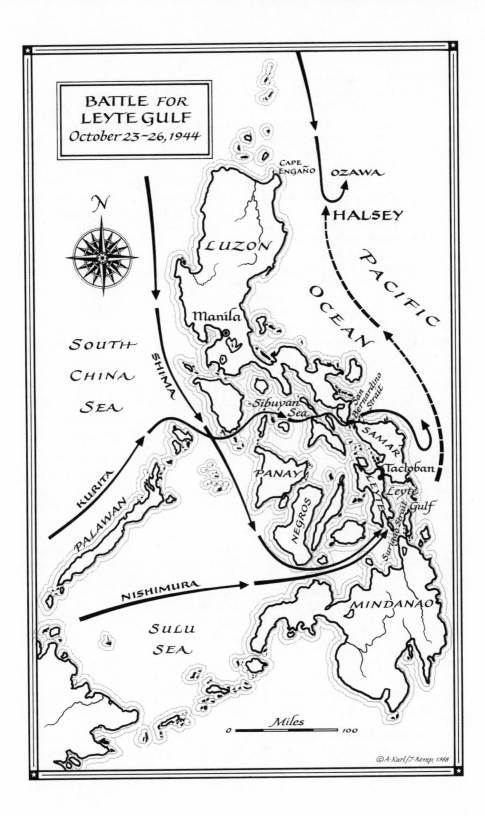

BATTLE FOR
LEYTE GULF
October 23~26, 1944

N

SOUTH CHINA SEA

SHIMA

KURITA

PALAWAN

NISHIMURA

SULU SEA

LUZON

Manila

Sibuyan Sea

PANAY

NEGROS

CAPE ENGAÑO

OZAWA

HALSEY

PACIFIC OCEAN

San Bernardino Strait

SAMAR

Tacloban

LEYTE

Leyte Gulf

Surigao Strait

MINDANAO

Miles
0   100

©A·Karl/J·Kemp, 1988

Three U.S. divisions competed for the honor of reaching the capital first, but the "First Cav" won the race. Its two "flying columns" of Sherman tanks, spearheading truckloads of soldiers, had forded rivers and demolished road-blocks with lightning speed, finally entering the city's northern limits at dusk on February 3. Filipinos spilled into the streets to cheer as guerrillas guided the U.S. force to Santo Tomás, where some four thousand American men, women and children awaited deliverance. They had been alerted the day before, when a U.S. plane dropped a message: ROLL OUT THE BARREL. SANTA CLAUSE [sic] IS COMING MONDAY OR TUESDAY! Now the American tanks smashed the gate, and GIs poured through to flush out enemy guards still holed up in buildings around the campus. They soon freed the prisoners, most of whom had been there since 1942. Many, looking like scarecrows from hunger and disease, welcomed Carl Mydans, formerly a fellow inmate, who had accompanied an armored column. "As I passed from thin hand to thin hand," he later recollected, "each voice had a strangely familiar sound and each unlocked a flurry of memory fragments from long ago."

Other U.S. soldiers seized Malacañang palace, and still others stormed Bilibid jail, releasing more than a thousand American civilian and military prisoners. On February 7, at his headquarters in Tarlac province, MacArthur announced that his men had "surrounded" the Japanese and were "rapidly clearing" them from the city, adding that "their complete destruction is immi-nent." He was showered with messages of congratulations from President Roosevelt, Winston Churchill, Chiang Kai-shek and other Allied leaders. But his compulsion for public relations had once again carried him away. The struggle for Manila was only unfolding, and it would be one of the most horrendous episodes of World War II.

Yamashita, later hanged for war crimes, was convicted in part for his alleged role in the city's martyrdom. In fact, he bore no responsibility for the cata-clysm—having ruled from the start against defending the capital. He realized as a professional soldier that the sprawling metropolis, a mass of eight hundred thousand people mostly jammed into flammable bamboo huts, would be a nightmarish battlefield. Also moved by a streak of humanity, he hoped to spare its "law-abiding citizens . . . the ravages of war," as he put it. So, in effect declaring Manila an "open city," he ordered the withdrawal of all Japanese troops to the nearby hills.

But Rear Admiral Sanji Iwabuchi, commander of the naval defense force, ignored the decree. His duty, he felt, was to prevent the Americans from taking the Manila harbor intact—an advance that would spur their eventual push toward Japan. Though untrained for ground combat, his twenty thousand sailors bristled with automatic weapons, mortars and heavy cannons salvaged from damaged ships. Iwabuchi deployed them south of the Pasig, the river traversing the city, placing a strong group inside the Intramuros, whose stout walls and narrow alleys made it a redoubtable bastion against an infantry assault. Above all, he was relying on their fanatical determination to fight to the end.

As the Americans entered Manila from the north, Iwabuchi unleashed an urban variation of the scorched-earth policy, burning docks, warehouses and other port installations. The flames, fanned by the wind, quickly whipped across the city to the slums, igniting jumbles of flimsy shacks and panicking thousands. Trapped in the chaos, the Japanese embarked on an orgy of atrocities matched only by the pillage of Nanking in 1937. They impaled babies on bayonets, raped women, beheaded men and mutilated the corpses. Setting houses ablaze, they shot the fleeing inhabitants, and started fires in hospitals after strapping patients to their beds. They focused on the upper classes, as if by design. A prominent Filipino, then a youth, recalled to me years later how he had returned home to discover the bodies of his parents, brothers and sisters—machine-gunned in the garden behind the family's home in a rich residential district.

But the majority of the slain civilians were casualties of awesome American and Japanese artillery exchanges. Vicky Quirino, a child at the time, had been caught with her family in the fierce cross fire, and the experience still haunted her forty years later. "We were in a kind of no-man's-land, with the shells and bombs coming from the two sides. A shell fell right in our bathroom, killing my grandmother instantly. My aunt, I don't know what hit her, but it cut her body in two, one half dangling from the other. And the cook. I'd gone to her, on the back stairs. Suddenly I heard a noise, like a loud shot. I looked up and saw her head blown off, one eye hanging out and brains splattered all over. By now our house was burning, and we climbed over the wall to the next house, and to the next when it started burning. There were dead bodies everywhere. We ran blindly from one place to another, with nothing to eat, drinking water from wells even though they were filled with corpses. My father and I got separated, then luckily we found each other. After two, three days we reached the American lines. They gave us some rice."

By the middle of February, as they started to tighten the noose around Manila, the American forces confronted the ghastly job of dislodging the deeply entrenched Japanese. MacArthur's senior field commanders, aware of the enormous challenge ahead, recommended dive bombing and napalm strikes before the final assault. But, just as leery of air power as ever, he spurned them on the grounds that the "inaccuracy" of such attacks would "beyond question" cause "the death of thousands of innocent civilians." It was a specious point, considering his approval of equally indiscriminate and often deadlier artillery bombardments. In any case, his decision condemned the GIs to cruel, remorseless, treacherous city combat—the kind of warfare detested by even the most seasoned soldiers. Their task was doubly difficult in the face of an enemy prepared for self-immolation.

The struggle raged for weeks as the two armies grappled street by street, house by house, room by room and frequently hand to hand. American troops, coming from the south, inched up palm-studded Dewey Boulevard beside the bay, battling the enemy dug into landmarks like the Army and Navy Club and the Manila Hotel. The Japanese had fortified the Philippine General Hospital in violation of international conventions, and GIs finally killed them all after fighting from floor to floor. Joining another U.S. group moving in from the north, the Americans converged on the Intramuros, the site of the fiercest Japanese opposition. Squads of GIs, equipped with flamethrowers and explosives, scaled its buildings, dropping down from rooftops to corner the enemy below. An American veteran of the operation described one room after his team had blasted it with a flamethrower. "The heat had glued the Japs to the wall, literally. They looked like wallpaper."

The Japanese resistance in Manila was finally subdued in early March, leaving the city a rubble pervaded by the sickly stench of unburied corpses. But signs of life began to stir. Merchants slowly reopened their shops. People who had fled to the countryside returned to poke through their shattered homes, while others traveled to villages to see relatives for the first time in years. A Filipino band performed for the U.S. soldiers amid the ruins, gustily playing Sousa marches and climaxing with "God Bless America." A few weeks earlier, MacArthur had visited his old apartment at the Manila Hotel to find his books and antiques destroyed, and he came back soon afterward for a ceremony at the Malacañang palace. The Japanese had taken Laurel, Aquino and their other puppets to Tokyo, while MacArthur revalidated Sergio Osmeña as president of the Philippine commonwealth. Reiterating a familiar theme, he extolled America's "redemption of your soil," adding: "My country has kept the faith!"

To symbolize his return, he had ordered the recapture of Corregidor. The Japanese on the island, caught off guard, lost more than a thousand men in wild attempts to repulse the first U.S. attack. Then, in a monstrous gesture of defeat, they sacrificed two thousand more in a mass suicide by detonating an underground arsenal—the explosion accidentally killing scores of Americans. But the fight for the Philippines was far from over. MacArthur, seeing himself as the savior of the whole archipelago, waged costly campaigns for southern islands of no strategic value. The diversions depleted his forces, hobbling their offensive in northern Luzon.

There, in the highlands, Yamashita initially conducted skillful defensive actions—his design, as always, to delay the ultimate American assault against Japan. Soon, though, even his sturdy soldiers stumbled. They were devastated by U.S. bombers in the biggest napalm raid of the Pacific war. Torrential rains drenched them. They suffered from hunger and disease as their supplies shrank, and their plight worsened as they withdrew deeper into the mountains. "We were like a band of bandits or beggars," wrote Tetsuro Ogawa, who survived. "Our clothes were glossy with dried filth and mud, our faces unshaven, our boots broken. . . . All of us now had glinty eyes and gaunt faces." Two of his comrades shot themselves. Others were slain by deserters desperate to rob food or to practice cannibalism. Still Yamashita refused to contemplate capitulation. He planned to resort to guerrilla warfare—and, if that failed, to commit *hara-kiri.* Then, on a sunny August morning, a biplane flew overhead, scattering tracts. Neatly written in Japanese, they read: THE EMPEROR OF JAPAN HAS ORDERED PEACE TO BE NEGOTIATED WITH THE ALLIED NATIONS. Ogawa rejoiced at the end of his agony—without knowing that, over the past ten days, American aircraft had dropped atomic bombs on Hiroshima and Nagasaki.

MacArthur presided over the formal surrender ritual on September 2, 1945, aboard the U.S. battleship *Missouri* at anchor in Tokyo Bay. Officials from all the Allied powers were in attendance. But the only representative of the Philippines was an honorary Filipino—Douglas MacArthur.

12. DEPENDENT INDEPENDENCE

★ ★ ★

Nationalists emerged across Asia after World War II to liberate their lands from the remnants of European colonial authority. Indonesians defied Dutch rule; resistance to the British intensified in India, Burma and Malaya; and Vietnam erupted as the French prepared to reassert their power. Only in Manila did the transition occur peacefully as America transferred sovereignty to a Philippine government. Ironically, the gesture earned the applause of Ho Chi Minh, the Vietnamese Communist leader who later became America's prime enemy in Southeast Asia. Late in 1945, as he braced to fight France, he remarked to Major Archimedes Patti, a U.S. liaison officer in Hanoi, "If the Americans had been our masters, they would now be giving us our freedom."

The ceremony that unfolded in Manila on the morning of July 4, 1946, was indeed unprecedented. For the first time in history, an imperial nation was voluntarily relinquishing a possession as the United States kept its pledge to emancipate the Philippines—a half-century after its original conquest.

The twisted concrete and shattered columns of the city's buildings recalled the battle that a year earlier had cost a hundred thousand lives. Braving torrential rains, crowds of jubilant Filipinos packed the Luneta before a makeshift stand in front of the monument to Rizal, the national martyr. At a few minutes after nine, President Manuel Roxas hoisted the Philippine flag on the same white cord that Paul McNutt, former U.S. high commissioner and now ambassador to the new republic, had lowered the Stars and Stripes. Bands played "The Star-Spangled Banner" and the "Marcha Nacional," the Philippine anthem. A warship fired a twenty-one-gun salute, church bells pealed, sirens screamed and speakers tried to outshout the din. General Douglas MacArthur, who had flown in from Tokyo, commanded the most attention. The occasion, he thundered, foretold "the end of mastery over peoples by force alone—the end of empire as the political chain that binds the unwilling weak to the unyielding strong."

Exulting in the celebration, which resounded to his own glory, he said to a friend: "America buried imperialism here today." But the Philippines was to remain almost as reliant on the United States as ever—and, his noble sentiments to the contrary, MacArthur himself played a crucial role from the start in perpetuating the dependent connection.

★ ★ ★

Many Americans and Filipinos, appalled by the ruins of the war, doubted if the Philippines could grapple with the colossal challenges of independence. Some talked of turning the clock back, but it was too late to reverse policy.

McNutt had been cool to Philippine sovereignty as early as 1938, during his first tour as high commissioner. With his silver hair and plastic smile, he looked every inch a president—and had indeed aspired to the Democratic bid in 1940, when Franklin D. Roosevelt, sensitive to competition, had shunted him off to Manila. There he bluntly declared that Philippine independence would deny America its pivotal place in Asia and condemn the Filipinos to "economic disaster" by depriving them of their privileged U.S. market. He advocated a "reexamination" of U.S. policy, proposing a "dominion" under which the Filipinos would enjoy "every ounce of domestic autonomy" while America managed their finances, defense and foreign affairs. Manuel Quezon, then president of the commonwealth, spurned the idea—though, he conceded, its economic logic was "unassailable." But McNutt clung to the concept even after World War II, when President Harry Truman reappointed him high commissioner for lack of another candidate. "It is an open secret," McNutt tactlessly said at a news conference late in 1945, "that most Filipinos do not particularly want independence."

Quezon's successor, Sergio Osmeña, would have agreed—in private. He had returned with MacArthur, and a glance at the ravaged country convinced him that reconstruction was too big a job for the Filipinos. But to defer independence would prompt his rivals to denounce him as unpatriotic—even though the perils of freedom also alarmed them. "If we don't take it now, we'll never get it," Osmeña said dubiously.

Despite their differences, virtually every Filipino political figure subscribed to the view of Quezon, who nearly a year before his death in August 1944 had written his last "testament" in the form of a letter to Roosevelt: "One would be very blind indeed not to see that the postwar relationship between the Philippines and the United States should be as close, if not closer, than our relationship before the war." Since then, Americans and Filipinos have pondered the issue of how close the relationship should be—amid confusion and tensions inherent in a lopsided alliance.

Despite its pious pledges, America has pursued a spastic policy toward the Philippines. The archipelago ranked low on the global U.S. agenda at the outbreak of World War II, then rated high during America's postwar crusade against communism in Asia. So a fever chart would resemble a zigzag of ups and downs, ranging from long periods of benign neglect to moments of intense concern—leaving the Filipinos uncertain of their importance to Washington.

The Filipinos have been equally inconsistent. Like the poor relatives of a rich *compadre*, they have assumed U.S. support to be their due. Yet, out of national pride, they have resented American interference in their affairs. Thus they have charged the United States with showing them either too little or too much attention. But Quezon's statement remained their article of faith for years after the war, when they welcomed America's reimposition of its power over them as the renewal of the U.S. commitment.

Addressing a group of Filipino dignitaries assembled at the Malacañang palace in February 1945, MacArthur announced: "Your country is again at liberty to pursue its destiny." But, he told an aide, he alone would be "in control" during that formative interlude before independence. He, MacArthur, intended to guide his adopted land toward its destiny.

As U.S. commander in occupied Japan following the war, MacArthur encouraged civilian American specialists to promote a spectrum of liberal programs from dismantling monopolies to land reform—measures that revolutionized Japanese society. But he aborted change in the Philippines by reinstalling the traditional dynasties, whose primary aim was to protect their vested interests. By revamping Japan totally, he felt, he would exorcise its lust for aggression. The upper-class Filipinos, however, were his friends.

Early in 1944, long before his return, he contemplated a future system for the Philippines. Haunted by the specter of civilian American officials invading his turf, he forecast a revolt by the Filipinos "if we send a big staff of outsiders in there . . . to run their affairs." He treated an aide to one of his slanted history lessons. His father's military regime at the turn of the century had been "getting on smoothly with the Filipinos when that selfish man Taft came in" and "made enemies of [those] who were being converted into friends." The result, he recalled, was the "insurrection"—the war between America and the Filipino nationalists. Now, as their redeemer, he would delegate authority to the Filipinos, and restore their "sacred right of government by constitutional process." By barring rival Americans from the archipelago and vesting power in Filipinos beholden to him, he would of course enhance his own stature. After his decades of service there, who was better fit to shape the country for the years ahead?

He valued the advice of two aides—both unalloyed reactionaries, who equated reform with revolution. One was Colonel Andrés Soriano, a wealthy Spaniard whose holdings included gold mines, real estate and the lucrative San Miguel conglomerate. He had skirted U.S. law before the war by failing to register as the Manila agent for Generalissimo Francisco Franco, the dictator of Spain. The other was MacArthur's chief of intelligence, Brigadier General Courtney Whitney, a prewar Manila lawyer closely linked to the local oligarchy. Together they not only shielded MacArthur from progressive ideas, but reinforced his paranoiac belief that enemies were conspiring to usurp his prerogatives.

They were not entirely wrong. Various proposals for administering the Philippines were then being considered by a Washington committee heavily influenced by Harold Ickes, the churlish secretary of the interior, whom MacArthur detested. Both monumental egotists, they had been squabbling since the dawn of the Roosevelt era. Ickes, a sectarian New Dealer, regarded MacArthur as a right-wing fanatic; MacArthur, a die-hard Republican, dismissed Ickes as a wicked liberal. Their feud had reached into the Philippines, which MacArthur coveted as his personal domain even though it came under the Bureau of Territories, formerly Insular Affairs, an agency of Ickes's department.

Ickes predictably suggested that MacArthur share power with a senior U.S. civilian. MacArthur angrily replied that Ickes "seemed to think of the islands as one of his national parks" and would resist any "meddling" in his activities. Should Washington assign a high commissioner to Manila, he would "put him on a boat and send him home." Nor would he abide a "cloud of carpetbaggers," as he derogated civilian experts. Just before the Leyte invasion in October 1944, Roosevelt conceded to his demands. Only after MacArthur had moved to his occupation job in Japan was Paul McNutt allowed to assume his duties in Manila. By then, MacArthur had largely designed the postwar pattern for the Philippines.

Ickes had earlier advised Osmeña against accompanying MacArthur to the archipelago, saying, "The country will be entirely under military command, and you as a civilian leader will be powerless." Demurring, Osmeña replied: "My place is in the invasion. Otherwise the Filipinos will say, 'Where is our government? Where is our president?' They might even think I was afraid." Ickes pressed Osmeña to request a U.S. high commissioner as a counterweight to MacArthur. Osmeña again balked, and this time Secretary of War Henry L. Stimson interceded, cautioning Ickes "not to gum up the game by his hostility to MacArthur." Ickes, finally acquiescing, told Osmeña: "Very well, but don't blame me later."

Despite his bias, Ickes was correct. "I can't work with Osmeña," MacArthur confided to a visitor, explaining that the Filipino leader, then in his sixties, lacked the energy to cope with that parlous period. MacArthur, eager to spotlight himself as the country's sole savior, also eclipsed Osmeña following their return to the Philippines. He delayed the distribution of food, clothing and other supplies to the destitute population, which blamed Osmeña for the slowdown, or administered relief in his own name, thereby denying Osmeña political credit for the program. Further blistering his image, he made Osmeña tell Philippine army veterans that America would grant them only eight pesos a month in back pay rather than the fifty pesos they expected.

Frustrated, Osmeña journeyed to Washington in search of help in the spring of 1945, only to find himself in a fog. Roosevelt, whom he finally saw in Warm Springs after weeks of waiting, sounded compassionate—but he died soon afterward. Truman listened to him sympathetically, but he had just been vaulted into the White House, and his mind was elsewhere. Osmeña forlornly returned to Manila to face a fresh challenge from MacArthur's favorite, Manuel Roxas.

Then in his forties, Roxas was MacArthur's kind of man. Unlike the frail, plodding Osmeña, he was a tense workaholic whose cigarette habit would soon kill him. He had impeccable family credentials. Born on the Visayan island of Panay, he traced his forebears back to an eighteenth-century Spanish merchant and landowner who also sired the Ayala, Zobel and Soriano clans—to this day the cream of Philippine society. Excelling as a law student, he entered politics and, at the age of thirty, became speaker of the lower chamber of the legislature. He married into a rich Luzon dynasty, acquiring three Manila publications among his other enterprises. Long Quezon's protégé, he was presumably his heir, and he had also been anointed by MacArthur with a U.S. Army colonelcy. His record was blemished by doubts about his role during the Japanese occupation, but MacArthur shortly put that right.

MacArthur had promised to "run to earth every disloyal Filipino" after his return. The traitors, Roosevelt also decreed, "must be removed from authority," and Ickes demanded prosecution of the "timid, craven, opportunistic helots who basely collaborated with the enemy." Ickes crudely warned Osmeña as well that the United States would withhold relief aid from the Philippines unless he "diligently and firmly" punished the pro-Japanese elements. This posed a dilemma for Osmeña. Not only had his two sons been quislings, but so had much of the nation's elite. To eliminate the entrepreneurial, land-owning and political class would estrange him from his colleagues and *compadres,* associates linked to him through intricate kinship ties, men whose values he shared. Such a purge would leave a power vacuum as well. The Philippines was not Europe, where the underground resistance against the Nazis included moderate and even conservative figures capable of forming stable governments. Here, Osmeña judged, the only alternative to the old oligarchy was chaos. He was prepared to let bygones be bygones and shelve the issue.

MacArthur also cherished the *ilustrados* as friends and, besides, they represented continuity. But, after his wartime pledge, he could not ignore the question. He contrived an expedient; instead of trying Filipinos, he would prosecute Japan's senior officers in the Philippines as war criminals.

In September 1945, shortly after his arrival in Tokyo, he indicted General Tomoyuki Yamashita, the former Japanese commander, who had been captured in Baguio. Yamashita, the charge read, had violated "the laws of war" by permitting his soldiers "to commit brutal atrocities and other crimes." The court-martial, conducted by five American generals without legal training, opened a month later in a reception hall of the U.S. high commissioner's residence in Manila. It was the distraction that MacArthur had sought. Crowds of indignant Filipinos, taunting Yamashita as guards escorted him to and from the premises, seemed to forget that many of their own leaders had cooperated with the enemy. The inexperienced judges admitted questionable evidence, and MacArthur denied a plea for a delay from the five U.S. Army lawyers appointed to defend Yamashita, who tried in vain to explain that the rape of Manila had been committed against his orders. Yamashita was sentenced to death by hanging, a humiliating punishment for a Japanese. The decision aroused controversy then and for years thereafter.

Petitioned by Yamashita's defense team, the U.S. Supreme Court confirmed the verdict, with justices Frank Murphy and Wiley Rutledge dissenting. The "uncurbed spirit of revenge," Murphy said, had been "masked in formal legal procedure." On February 23, 1946, Yamashita was executed in Los Banos, a town south of Manila. Lieutenant General Masaharu Homma, also convicted, was more honorably sentenced to death by a firing squad shortly afterward.

In April 1945 MacArthur had summarily exonerated Roxas of assisting the Japanese. Learning that Roxas had reached the American lines near Baguio, he flew him to Manila, publicly hugged him and promoted him to brigadier general in the U.S. Army. Roxas, he later declared, had been "one of the prime factors in the guerrilla movement," and a source of "vital intelligence." Though he had "tried to find Roxas's connection with the underground," an official U.S. investigator reported afterward, "no one knew anything about it." MacArthur had spoken, however, and that was that.

MacArthur now took another step to restore the oligarchy—and to exculpate Roxas. He directed Osmeña, as commonwealth president, to convene the Philippine legislature during the transition to independence. Elected in 1941, the body had never met, and most of its surviving members had collaborated with José Laurel's pro-Japanese regime. Osmeña summoned them to Manila in June 1945, spelling his own doom in the process.

As MacArthur had hoped, Roxas was chosen president of the upper chamber and chairman of the powerful appointments committee. Roxas maneuvered to dismiss two members of Osmeña's cabinet who had criticized his war record. With both houses under his control, he also obstructed Osmeña's legislative proposals. But he displayed his gratitude to MacArthur by making him an honorary Philippine citizen, ordering his name to figure "in perpetuity" on Philippine army rosters. When MacArthur appeared at the legislature to accept the tribute, Roxas called him "one of the greatest soldiers of all time."

MacArthur replied with an avuncular lecture on the need for national unity. "Petty jealousy, selfish ambition and unnecessary misunderstanding," he counseled, "must not be permitted to impede progress and rend your country." He then proceeded to aggravate their dissension with his meddling.

In August 1945, he freed five thousand collaborators, among them many officials. Paul Steindorf, the U.S. consul in Manila, reported to Washington that Filipinos who fought the enemy were "very bitter" at the release of these "rich and powerful" traitors. MacArthur's own counterintelligence chief, Brigadier General Elliot Thorpe, sardonically noted that Roxas and his cronies had "developed a well-organized propaganda campaign to persuade the world that all those who collaborated with the Japanese had done so only from the finest motives of patriotism, and that the nation should really be grateful to them." David Bernstein, an American adviser to Quezon and Osmeña, later wrote that MacArthur's absolution of Roxas brought back "the puppet politicos and the buy-and-sell parasites," making U.S. policy toward the Philippines look "stupid, irrational and cynical."

McNutt shared the same concern after landing in Manila in September 1945 as high commissioner. He warned Washington that "enemy collaborators" dominated the legislature, and favored postponing independence pending an investigation. Truman, for once attentive to the Philippines, consulted his attorney general, Tom Clark, who ordered a deputy, Walter Hutchinson, to study the situation. Hutchinson concluded after his survey that the snarl was "one of our own making."

Nearly all the collaborators were known to U.S. intelligence officers, he wrote, and America ought to have dealt directly with the "basic and gigantic problem" rather than buck it to the Filipinos, numbers of whom had themselves been traitors. The United States had a duty to "the thousands who died in a sacred democratic cause," he went on, proposing war-crimes trials presided over by Filipino judges supported by American aid. Otherwise, it was "almost a certainty" that Roxas would declare an amnesty after his probable election as president of the independent Philippine republic and free "many if not all the leading collaborators." The report was soon buried in a Washington archive as interest in pursuing World War II enemies receded before America's new focus on "containing" communism. But Hutchinson was uncannily prescient.

The momentum for Roxas had been accelerating for months. Beginning in July 1945, his newspapers went from emphasizing MacArthur's exoneration of him to asserting that MacArthur had "recognized" him as a "leader" of anti-Japanese resistance. Roxas's cronies were soon touting him for president, even though an election had not been scheduled. Joaquín Elizalde, one of the country's richest men, spent four hundred thousand pesos on his behalf and MacArthur's former assistant Colonel Soriano put up even more. They mostly bought the support of politicians, but a fat sum went to a Manila journalist for a syrupy biography entitled *And Now Comes Roxas.* Their hopes were buoyed when MacArthur, before departing for Japan, set the presidential election for April 23, 1946. The date was a blow to Osmeña, who had dreamed of being in office for the independence ceremony on July 4.

McNutt had remarked to MacArthur during a visit to Tokyo that a fair election was impossible in a country as venal as the Philippines. "Paul, you're absolutely right," MacArthur replied, "but the Filipinos will hold as honest an election as you ever had in the state of Indiana."

Roxas had organized a new party, the Liberals, whose activists waged a dirty campaign against Osmeña. Maligning him as "old, decrepit and impotent," they circulated sinister references to his Chinese origin, as if he were an alien. They also decried him as a communist for accepting support from the former *Hukbalahap* guerrillas. Yet these tactics paled beside the perception that MacArthur—thus the United States—had sanctified Roxas.

In fact, MacArthur had not endorsed Roxas publicly, but to Filipinos, with their keen political antennae, the proof was plain. MacArthur had judged Roxas innocent of aiding the Japanese and was responsible for his legislative power. And it was no secret that MacArthur disliked Osmeña. If all this was not enough, Roy Howard, the voluble proprietor of the Scripps-Howard newspaper chain, put America's imprimatur on Roxas in an interview with the *Manila Times:* "If he's good enough for General MacArthur, he's good enough for the United States." With MacArthur's approval, the U.S. Army gave Roxas access to its radio network in the Philippines, and voters assumed that American soldiers patrolling the precincts were helping Roxas. Paul McNutt clumsily intervened by seconding Roxas's charge that Osmeña's followers were engaged in "terroristic practices."

But Osmeña blundered. Reckoning it beneath his dignity to campaign, he forfeited the hustings to Roxas. He also misjudged the impact of Roxas's money, figuring that local political bosses still considered him, as president, to be the fountain of patronage. By refusing to disavow Huk support, he failed to realize that he was alienating the United States, which now distrusted any group with even faint leftist tendencies.

Roxas and his running mate, Elpidio Quirino, scored an unspectacular victory, winning fifty-four percent of the nearly three million votes cast. His Liberals also took over the legislature. Osmeña's *Nacionalista* party, which he and Quezon had founded forty years before, had suffered its first defeat. Despite its excesses, however, the contest had been relatively peaceful, and both Americans and Filipinos publicized the Philippines emerged as the "showcase of democracy" in Asia. But its ossified oligarchy still wielded power, and the years ahead were to be nagged by mismanagement, corruption, social injustice and peasant revolt.

★ ★ ★

If MacArthur sculpted the political shape of the postwar Philippines, other Americans pressed the archipelago into the U.S. military and economic fold. So, behind the thin façade of independence, the former colony remained "neocolonized." But aside from a few ultranationalists, Filipinos generally welcomed the so-called special relationship as proof of America's concern for their welfare.

The relationship was periodically roiled during the postwar years by controversies—prime among them the status of Clark airfield and the Subic navy yard, America's largest overseas bases. The issue remains a lively one. Many Filipinos have maintained that the bases violate their sovereignty as well as imperil their security by making them a potential target in case of war between the superpowers. To many the installations have served as a reminder that the Philippines, though independent, has remained hostage to U.S. interests. Their grievances have often been legitimate.

After World War II, American negotiators did indeed force Filipino leaders to accept onerous conditions in the bases agreement as the price for freedom. But the majority of Filipinos, then yearning to be part of America's global strategy, would have been disappointed had the United States rejected them. So they submitted voluntarily to their own exploitation. Their dream, as historian Theodore Friend has put it, was to be "a favored and exemplary party within a Pax Americana, a kind of inverse Cinderella, most beloved adoptee of a benign and powerful stepmother."

Ironically, the bases issue had divided the American military establishment long before it troubled the Filipinos. As far back as 1900, Admiral George Dewey had begged for "an impregnable naval base" at Subic Bay. Congress waffled for four years before funding the project, which then floundered in disputes. The army, objecting that Subic was exposed to a land attack, proposed Manila Bay, which the navy rebuffed as vulnerable. As a compromise, a small naval station was built at Subic, and the army got Fort Stotsenburg, the location of Clark Field. But even passionate partisans of holding the Philippines flinched at more than token defense expenditures. Senator Henry Cabot Lodge, a vintage imperialist, adamantly opposed a big investment in the islands. "We shall never fortify them," he said in 1922. "It would cost hundreds of millions of dollars [and] we are not going to do it." A decade later, plagued by the Depression, Franklin Roosevelt was equally cool to a costly involvement in the archipelago. He saw an economical alternative in 1933, as Congress debated eventual sovereignty for the Philippines. Quezon had come to Washington to lobby for legislation that would squelch his nationalist rivals at home. Calling the bases a violation of "true independence," he urged their elimination. Roosevelt eagerly complied. At his behest, the final law prescribed the transfer of U.S. Army property to the Filipinos after independence, with the disposition of the navy bases to be settled through negotiations. Quezon, having demonstrated his patriotism, returned to a hero's welcome in Manila, and America was to be relieved of its Philippine burden.

But the experience of World War II altered American and Filipino attitudes. Once isolationist, Americans were now willing to bear the burden of global power. Filipinos, after the trauma of Japanese rule, feared the loss of America's protection. For different motives, the Philippine bases were thus seen as indispensable on both sides of the Pacific.

In September 1943, as he peered into the postwar period, Quezon reaffirmed his allegiance to the United States. Then living in exile in the Shoreham Hotel in Washington, he was about to go to Lake Placid, New York, where tuberculosis would take his life a year later. Despite his country's geographical location, he wrote to Roosevelt, "we are with the West." Permanent U.S. bases in the Philippines, he proposed, would safeguard both nations and guarantee "the future peace of the Pacific."

The idea at first enthused official Washington. Echoing turn-of-the-century imperialists, experts rediscovered the Philippines as the gateway to the "great" China market, the "rich resources" of the East Indies and the "possibilities for investment and development" throughout Asia. Strategists imagined the islands as "springboards" from which American ships, aircraft and troops could be vaulted into other parts of the region. Paul McNutt envisioned Manila as pivotal to "our diplomacy in the Orient."

In May 1945, Truman and Osmeña, successors to Roosevelt and Quezon, signed a "preliminary statement" calling for the "fullest and closest military cooperation" between the two countries. The U.S. Joint Chiefs of Staff, whose specialists had already drafted plans, requested twenty-three navy and thirteen army sites besides Subic Bay and Clark Field. They could have had anything. So anxious was Osmeña to keep the Americans in the Philippines that he placed no curbs on the size of their force or its deployments. Nor did he extract in exchange more than an amorphous U.S. pledge to defend the archipelago. The Philippine legislature approved the accord without dissent. But the bargaining over a final agreement turned out to be a tangle.

The negotiations opened on a sweltering Manila day in June 1946, a month before Philippine independence. McNutt headed the small American diplomatic team and Roxas, just elected president, directed the Philippine delegation through Elpidio Quirino, his vice president, who doubled as secretary of foreign affairs. McNutt had recently steered Roxas around Washington, figuring that exposure to America's bigwigs would make him more pliable. They could have avoided the trip. As MacArthur's protégé, Roxas was as loyal to the United States as any Filipino could be expected to be. Indeed, he assured McNutt as the negotiations began that "you can have what you want." But, realizing that he had to protect his nationalist flank at home, he quickly rejected a demand that the United States exercise jurisdiction over American soldiers, sailors and civilian employees, on or off duty, on or off the bases. The issue was more than abstract. The war ended, U.S. troops with little to do as they awaited repatriation were clashing with Filipinos in traffic accidents and brawling over women in bars. To authorize American military courts to try those cases, Roxas protested, would tarnish Philippine sovereignty—and his own reputation.

The United States and the Philippines are both litigious societies, and the complex issue elated American and Filipino lawyers alike. Rival U.S. agencies complicated the quarrel. To insist on extraterritorial privileges, American diplomats warned, would poison U.S. relations with the Philippines and discourage other nations from allowing bases on their soil. American army and navy officials disagreed, arguing that U.S. military personnel involved in disputes with Filipinos could never be fairly tried by a Philippine court.

As the debate dragged on into late 1946, however, U.S. world strategy had begun to evolve. Rising tensions with the Soviet Union turned America toward Europe. Pentagon planners preoccupied with Asia and the Pacific began to focus on such places as Japan, Okinawa, Korea and Guam as sites for air and naval stations and ground force deployments. But Congress was reluctant to finance a spending spree. The U.S. military establishment reviewed its options and gave the Philippines a low priority. The navy favored Okinawa and Guam because, as small islands, they were easier to defend. Eisenhower, then Army Chief of Staff, averred that he would rather remove America's troops from the archipelago than confront chronic friction with the Filipinos. In December 1946, McNutt was ordered by Washington to inform Roxas that the U.S. force in the Philippines would soon be reduced. Soon afterward, base construction was temporarily halted.

Fearing a U.S. withdrawal, Roxas ceded. In the formal agreement, signed in March 1947, he granted the United States ninety-nine-year leases on twenty-two sites, including Clark Field and Subic Bay. And, besides giving the United States the right to try Americans, he acquiesced to its juridiction over Filipinos working on the bases. Angeles and Olongapo, the towns adjacent to Clark and Subic, predictably became a tenderloin of bars, brothels and massage parlors, prostitutes and pimps managed by gangs protected by corrupt politicians. The bases not only brought unprecedented prosperity to the areas, but they became vital to the Philippine economy as a whole.

The bases issue nevertheless often rankled even the most pro-American Filipinos. They were slighted by the fact that the United States imposed tougher terms on the Philippines, its former colony and current ally, than it did on the Japanese, the former enemy, to acquire bases in Japan. Many were also appalled by American arrogance. In 1956, at a meeting to revise the original base agreement, the chief U.S. negotiator shoved a paper across the table to his Filipino counterpart, Emmanuel Pelaez, saying, "Here is your position." Pelaez, then a senator and later Philippine vice president, stalked out, stalling the talks for two years.

Many Filipinos had also sensed earlier that the United States assessed the strategic importance of the Philippines solely as an adjunct to its own security. The military value of the islands had dimmed in 1947, after the completion of the bases pact. But, two years later, China went communist and then the Korean War broke out. Meanwhile, the *Hukbalahap* rebellion had been spreading across central Luzon. Truman extended his "containment" concept to Asia. The Philippines regained status on Washington's agenda—and its fate again became inextricably intertwined with U.S. foreign policy.

★   ★   ★

Just as they had pressed Roxas into a favorable bases agreement, so the Americans exerted leverage on the Filipinos to obtain economic preferences. Americans paradoxically acquired greater privileges in the Philippines during the postcolonial years than they had during the colonial period.

The Filipinos, ravaged by the war, were too feeble to resist. The devastation amounted to nearly $1 billion—roughly $5 billion in today's terms. Manila and other cities lay in ruins, and the rural areas of Leyte and Luzon, where the fighting had been heavy, were a wasteland. Hundreds of thousands of people lacked clothing and shelter, and many subsisted on U.S. Army soup kitchens. Rice fields, vegetable gardens, coconut groves and sugar estates had been gutted. Peasants had lost their livestock and chickens, and the thousands of water buffalo that had been killed left them bereft of their essential beasts of burden, without which they could not till their farms. Wrecked roads and bridges prevented the available food from reaching markets. Hospitals, clinics and sanitation projects had been destroyed, and schools were closed. Prices, spurred upward by the shortages, had soared eightfold from prewar levels.

Worse yet, the moral fiber of Filipinos had unraveled during the Japanese occupation, when they had cheated and robbed to survive. Banditry and murder thrived, and graft and corruption pervaded high places. An official inquiry in 1947 disclosed that, over the previous two years, $300 million in U.S. military surplus vehicles, machinery, garments and other items given to the Philippine government had been stolen. One of the few culprits indicted was the senate speaker, José Avelino, who had amassed the equivalent of $300,000 from selling the loot to Chinese fences. In another case, millions of pesos in crop loans to tenant farmers disappeared—presumably into the pockets of officials and big landowners. An investigation, *The New York Times* reported, found "no tenants and no crops, and the money could not be recovered."

In May 1945, three months before war ended, Senator Millard Tydings of Maryland went to the Philippines to study conditions with a view to recommending relief programs. He had planned to tour the islands for a month but MacArthur, who distrusted snoopy politicians, confined him to Manila. Still, he learned enough in six days in the city to propose a rehabilitation bill to Congress. He envisioned a grant of $100 million to the Philippines to cover war damages, coupled with a trade act to resurrect its economy. As a sponsor of the legislation a decade before that pledged independence to the Filipinos, he sympathized with their plight. To sell his plan to penny-pinchers on Capitol Hill, he recollected that the Philippines had been America's sixth largest customer before the war, and its economic revival augured orders and jobs for U.S. industry. "Think of the Philippines as a great staging area for trade," he said.

Representative C. Jasper Bell, a conservative Missouri Democrat, thought differently. Head of the House Committee on Insular Affairs, which oversaw American policy toward the Philippines, he sought to ease U.S. taxpayers of the burden of rebuilding the archipelago. American companies would join in the task, he believed, if given concessions and guarantees of security. In September 1945, he introduced a companion to Tydings's motion, to assure them that "they can safely invest private capital" in the Philippines, and expect "a reasonable profit" in return. McNutt, supporting the bill, revealed its true intent when he said that its passage was "imperative for U.S. business to dominate in the Pacific."

Tydings advocated close bonds between the United States and the Philippines. But, as an old-fashioned champion of self-determination, he argued that America had to guide its former colony through the tough transition to independence. Bell's backers "fundamentally opposed" sovereignty for the Philippines, he alleged: Their "whole philosophy" was to control the islands "economically even though we lost them politically." The Bell bill, later passed as the Philippine Trade Act of 1946, did indeed rewind the clock.

The measure offered American businessmen an opportunity. By pegging the Philippine peso to the U.S. dollar, it protected them against currency fluctuations and permitted them free convertibility whatever the financial needs of the Philippines. Returning to the prewar system, American exporters would be granted a monopoly in the archipelago while Filipinos received unrestricted access to the U.S. market—until the reciprocal arrangement was replaced eventually by quotas and tariffs. Until then, however, Filipinos were prohibited from selling any products that might "come into substantial competition" with articles made in the United States—meaning no manufactured goods. So the archipelago, its industrial potential stunted, was to be preserved as an agricultural land dependent on America.

Tougher still was a so-called parity provision that entitled Americans to equal rights with Filipinos to own mines, forests and other resources—without granting Filipinos the same privileges in the United States. The clause violated the Philippine constitution, conceived a decade earlier under American auspices, which reserved the majority share of such holdings for Filipinos. The stipulation, aimed at preventing American exploitation, could be amended only by a nationwide referendum after ratification by the Philippine legislature. Resorting to coercion, a House committee linked the Tydings relief program to Bell's bill and limited war damages for Filipinos to $500 until the amendment passed.

The Bell bill went through seven months of debate and five versions before becoming law in April 1946. Its most vocal foes included State Department officials, then urging Britain to open its colonies to American trade. To favor U.S. business, they testified, contradicted their campaign. William Clayton, an assistant secretary for economic affairs, decried the measure as "clearly inconsistent with the basic foreign economic policy of this country" and a betrayal of "our promise to grant the Philippines genuine independence." Critics in Congress mainly represented the sugar and dairy states, always fearful of foreign competition.

The protests failed. Representative Harold Knutson of Minnesota, sensitive to the dairy industry, backed the bill after a stiff quota was imposed on Philippine coconut oil. "We have interests to look after, too," he explained— and, though he liked Filipinos, "we can't let our hearts run away with us altogether." Others approved concessions to American companies. "There is no other way out," said John Dingell, a Democrat from Michigan. "Capital will not go back into a devastated country without some assurances." Nor was the musty idea of imperial America dead. William Howard Taft's rhetoric resonated through his son Robert, a Republican senator from Ohio. With U.S.

bases and business implanted there, he declared, the islands should be "an American outpost in the Pacific." He ended with a patronizing anachronism worthy of his father: "The fact that they have a completely independent, autonomous government is, I think, a good thing. But certainly we shall always be a big brother, if you please, to the Philippines."

The law, finally passed, drew mixed reviews from U.S. business. Americans long established in the Philippines were dismayed by the parity clause, which they feared would annoy Filipinos. "In the interests of honesty and fair-dealing," one of them warned, "the United States should voluntarily abrogate the invidious provision at the earliest moment." By contrast, some big American corporations saw the legislation as a chance for trade with Asia. McNutt had claimed to have "no financial interest in the future of the Philippines." But he went from ambassador to chairman of the Philippine-American Trade Council, formed by U.S. firms to promote business in Asia, and also became a director of several Manila companies. He had earned the cushy jobs, having fought hard for the Bell act in Washington. "We used every contact, every stratagem, every trading point we could through those long weeks of negotiations, deliberations, committee hearings. . . . We buttonholed senators and congressmen in their offices, at their homes, at social gatherings [in] the most active and persistent lobby any bill has ever attracted."

But its passage by the U.S. Congress was only half the battle. The act also needed the approval of the Philippine legislature, where it faced juridical hurdles. Truman and his legal aides preferred ratification after Philippine independence, scheduled for July 4, 1946, to veil it as an accord between sovereign nations rather than an imperialist decree forced on a colony. That timetable was risky. Its Filipino foes could delay the agreement by arguing that it was actually an international treaty requiring confirmation by two thirds of the Philippine upper chamber. Doubtful of mustering that margin, Roxas feared that failure would damage Philippine relations with the United States along with his own image as America's surrogate. If a vote were held before independence, though, he could maintain that only a plurality was needed. He won U.S. assent for an early test following frantic telephone conversations with American officials in Washington. Then he drove his legislature into an all-night marathon of hearings and debate.

"I find no dream of empire in America," he had earlier said, and again he appealed for faith in the United States. Critics forecast "economic slavery," and some even called the Americans as cruel as the Japanese. But the measure passed on July 2, along with a concurrent resolution lamenting its "imperfections and inequalities." Most of the members reluctantly supported the motion as the "lesser evil." As one of them explained, he voted in favor "because we are flat broke, hungry, homeless and destitute."

Another storm, however, later broke over the provision to grant equal rights to Americans. Opponents and champions hammered each other with strident rhetoric typical of debates in the Philippines. Its enemies denounced the infringement of sovereignty, one of them forecasting that the Americans would seize the country and compel Filipinos to "live like Indians on reservations." Roxas predicted that rejection of the clause would strain relations between the United States and the Philippines, and lead to "national disaster and chaos." He pushed the amendment through the legislature by a tricky maneuver. But it was not an issue that gripped the population. The referendum in March 1947 drew only forty percent of the voters, many submitting to government pressures. Officials threatened foes of the amendment with reprisals, and polling booths were shifted out of hostile areas. Still, the motion scored massively even in places where sentiment ran strongly against Roxas—maybe because Filipinos felt that Americans, as their saviors, deserved to share their resources. Jasper Bell envisioned "a rich and ever-growing flood of commerce . . . based on private enterprise thriving in a free democracy."

But the Philippines swiftly became known instead as the "poor little rich country" of Asia as its outward prosperity concealed a precarious economy. Though trade boomed, it was wildly distorted. Flush with relief dollars, the Philippines imported huge quantities of American clothing, canned food and other manufactured goods, spending twice as much as it earned from selling commodities to the United States. Only a small fraction of the export earnings went into the equipment indispensable for economic development. So, while American and Filipino entrepreneurs and landowners piled up profits, little was done to improve the country's basic conditions.

Roxas's maneuver to grant parity rights to Americans had meanwhile sown the seeds of future trouble. Unlike the trade act, the motion clearly required a three fourths majority to pass the Philippine legislature. Roxas, realizing that he lacked the votes, resorted to the device of denying seats to eleven opposition members, accusing them of having been elected through "fraud and terror." The charge, if true, was absurd. Chicanery and violence were—and still are—a feature of Philippine elections. Roxas further weakened his allegation by seating his own supporters, though many were then under indictment for treason as Japanese collaborators. The Philippine supreme court upheld him notwithstanding, and the measure squeezed through. The short-term victory turned out to be a long-range blunder. Six of those deprived of seats belonged to the Democratic Alliance, a party recently formed by former Huk guerrillas. Frustrated by their exclusion from the legal political process, they returned to the boondocks to plan an uprising.

★　★　★

In March 1947, proclaiming the doctrine that bears his name, Truman pledged America's support for "free peoples who are resisting attempted subjugation by armed minorities or by outside pressures." His initial purpose was to aid the Greek regime fighting Communist rebels backed by the Soviet Union. But it soon became axiomatic in Washington that the Russians managed Communists everywhere, and that America's duty was to stop them. The dogma gained credibility in 1950, after Mao Zedong conquered China and the Korean War broke out. John Foster Dulles, then a State Department adviser and later President Eisenhower's secretary of state, warned Secretary of State Dean Acheson that Moscow and Beijing had designed a "comprehensive program . . . to eliminate all Western influence" from Asia, including the Philippines. American intelligence analysts agreed, concluding that the Huks "seek to further the objectives of world Communism."

In fact, the Huk ranks overwhelmingly consisted of poor peasants fighting for reform rather than revolution. Most opposed the abuses, not the concept,

MacArthur exculpated Manuel Roxas of helping the Japanese and engineered his election as president of the independent Philippine republic.

General Edward Lansdale *(left)* was a key adviser to Ramón Magsaysay, defense secretary and later president, during the Huk rebellion.

3/26/60

To my dear friend, Joe Smith, to whom we are grateful for his services to our people.

Gabriel Kaplan, a CIA man during the early 1950s, meets with a local Filipino official.

Philippine President Diosdado Macapagal with Joseph Burkholder Smith, his CIA benefactor.

Huk insurgents at a training camp in central Luzon. Most were dispossessed peasants.

Luis Taruc, the Huk leader *(right)*, surrendered to Benigno Aquino, Jr., in 1954. Aquino was then a young newspaperman.

President Lyndon Johnson with President Ferdinand Marcos and his wife, Imelda, in Washington in 1966.

President Richard Nixon and his wife, Pat, with the Marcoses in Manila in 1969.

Ronald Reagan, then governor of California, dances with Imelda as Nancy dances with Marcos in Manila in 1969.

Benigno Aquino in San Francisco, prior to his return to Manila in August 1983.

Nemesio Demafelis, alias Commander Iko, a Communist guerrilla on Negros.

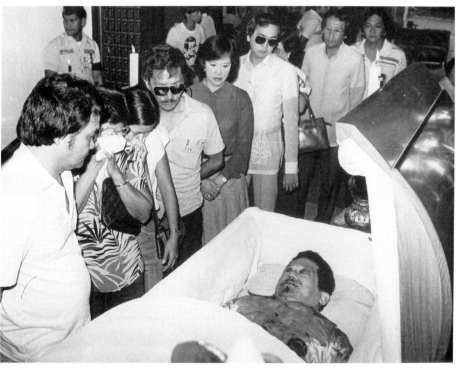

Aquino's body on display in Manila after his murder in August 1983. His mother insisted that nothing be done to clean the corpse.

Corazon Aquino campaigning for the presidency early in 1986. Until then a quiet housewife, she proved to be a vigorous campaigner.

Cory meeting with Cardinal Jaime Sin, archbishop of Manila, during her election campaign. Sin played a key role in promoting her candidacy.

General Fidel Ramos *(left)* and Defense Minister Juan Ponce Enrile staged a revolt against Marcos in February 1986.

President Reagan listens to special envoy Philip Habib *(far right)* as cabinet meets to determine Philippine policy in February 1986. Reagan acquiesced to removing Marcos from office.

Reagan and Cory Aquino following White House lunch in September 1986. Reagan was never entirely reconciled to Marcos's ouster.

Secretary of State George Shultz, wearing Cory doll, at State Department banquet for Aquino. Shultz had been one of her early supporters.

Cory applauded by joint houses of Congress on September 18, 1986. House Speaker Thomas "Tip" O'Neill (*left*) called her speech the best he had ever heard.

of feudalism. They were willing to serve as tenants as long as landowners gave them easy credit, a fair share of the crop and protection against repression by the local authorities. Few were hostile to the United States. Those who had known Americans before the war usually remembered them as benign school-teachers, and later they esteemed the United States for defeating the detested Japanese. By contrast, the upper echelon of the Philippine Communist party, the *Partido Komunistang Pilipinas,* was principally composed of Manila labor leaders and bourgeois intellectuals either unfamiliar or unconcerned with rural conditions. They clung to the classic Marxist belief in the primacy of the urban proletariat—an inane idea in a country without industry. In any case, their movement had never been a top item on Moscow's list of priorities.

The early Bolsheviks theorized that revolutions in Asia would deny markets and raw materials to Western capitalist nations and hasten their collapse. They had designated the Philippines as "an important strategic point in the Pacific," but their first agent only reached Manila in 1924. Reasoning that a U.S. colony was American turf, they had assigned the task to William Janequette, a shadowy American Communist who operated under the alias of Harrison George.

Janequette claimed to be a labor specialist, and Filipino officials, unaware of his real identity, were cordial. But his plan to form a Philippine Communist party advanced slowly. With the United States already committed to independence for the archipelago, he could not plausibly tout communism as the answer to American imperialism. Nor could he denounce U.S. oppression, since Manila was a swirl of political factions, their liberties guaranteed under American rule. Finally he spotted a possible Communist leader in Crisanto Evangelista, the head of a small printers' union, a slim man with ebony eyes and a tubercular cough who had picked up a smattering of Marxism from American radicals during a trip to the United States. Earl Browder, then an American Communist agent and later the party's general secretary, arranged for Evangelista and a few other Filipino comrades to visit Moscow in 1928. They founded a local Communist party two years afterward amid an anarchy of ideological disputes. Philippine government policy soon stiffened and, convicted of sedition, they were banished to the provinces. They made little impact on poor Filipinos, who logically ought to have been attracted by the appeal of revolution. Over those years, too, they remained outside the mainstream of international communism—except for rare contacts with their American "big brothers."

In August 1936, a young American couple, Sol and Isabelle Auerbach, landed in Manila. They were both Communist agents. A veteran organizer of Filipino merchant seamen in Brooklyn, she had been secretly sent to the Philippines the year before to enlist students for training in Russia. His real name was James Allen. He carried press credentials as a writer for *The Nation,* and this was his first trip to Manila. The heat stifled him, he had few contacts, limited funds and a delicate task ahead. They could have been any Americans arriving in an alien land. As Allen later recalled: "We wondered how we could live, let alone work, here."

Moscow had recently ordered Communists everywhere to join with liberal movements to resist the growing threat from Germany, Italy and Japan. Allen's assignment was to merge the Philippine Communist and Socialist parties in a "united front." He performed with uncommon skill.

His first step was to secure the release of Evangelista and the other banished Communists. Then president of the commonwealth, Quezon was easily accessible—as are Filipino leaders today. He invited Allen to the Malacañang palace for breakfast, and they chatted through lunch into dusk, rambling from the local economy to the state of the world. Allen was impressed by Quezon's "mental agility and virile personality"—though, he later wrote, he saw in his autocratic style "the qualities of a dictator." Quezon, at the moment apprehensive about Japan's aims, agreed that the Communists might play a positive role. He would free them on condition that they back him publicly. Complying, they praised his patriotism, and he eventually pardoned them.

Allen had also been urging the Socialist leader, Pedro Abad Santos, to unite with the Communists. Then sixty, Abad Santos was a gaunt, frail, gentle man—and, unique in the Philippines, a wealthy landowner with a social conscience. He had been captured while fighting as a guerrilla against the U.S. Army at the turn of the century, condemned to death and later amnestied. Entering politics, he won a seat in the Philippine assembly, and underwent a conversion when, as he recalled to a Manila journalist: "I saw the rich ride by in carriages, splashing mud on the street cleaners in the rain, and I asked myself why these things were so." Retiring to a modest adobe house outside San Fernando, the capital of his native Pampanga province in central Luzon, he took a vow of celibacy, donned peasant garb and devoted his life to helping the poor. He provided free legal advice to farm tenants and laborers, to whom he would slip peso notes from a steel safe, and organized young activists to plead their cases in court.

Though encyclopedic in his knowledge of Marxism, he admired moderates like Norman Thomas, the perennial American Socialist, and Leon Blum, the French Socialist leader, but his real hero was Gandhi, whose asceticism he imitated. He spurned the Soviet model, saying that he would be "satisfied . . . if our workers could approximate the living conditions, status and rights . . . that American workers have obtained under modern capitalism." Some of his followers, fearing Communist domination, urged him to rebuff Allen's plea for a merger. He disagreed, asserting that the Japanese threat required unity. The coalition was formed in October 1938 under the name of the Communist party, with Evangelista as chairman and Abad Santos as deputy.

Three and a half years later, following their seizure of Manila, the Japanese executed Evangelista and mercifully sent Abad Santos back to Pampanga province, where he died in 1945. The covert Communist party was taken over by Vicente Lava, a brilliant chemist with a degree from Columbia University. The "united front" shortly afterward became the guerrilla movement *Hukbong Bayan Laban sa Hapon,* the Huks. Its military commander, Luis Taruc, then twenty-eight, was a former deputy to Abad Santos and one of the few authentic peasants among the radical Filipino leaders.

I first interviewed Taruc in December 1965 in a Manila military prison, where he was serving a life sentence for sedition. For a man in his fifties who had spent a decade behind bars, he was still as sinewy as he must have been as a guerrilla—the result, he told me, of a lean diet and daily exercise. I could not picture him as the incarnation of "the Red menace," as he had once been portrayed in American and Filipino propaganda. Repudiating his past, he had returned to the Catholic fold, as dramatized by the icons of Christ and Pope

Paul VI on the walls of his cramped cell. His bookshelves—a pile of political treatises, trashy novels and, appropriately, *The Birdman of Alcatraz*—testified to his solitude. But his caramel eyes flashed and his voice vibrated with emotion as he spoke. Despite his conversion, it seemed to me, he had not forsaken his concern for the plight of the peasants.

He was later released by President Ferdinand Marcos, who with much fanfare publicized him as "the Communist redeemed." During our subsequent encounters, Taruc continued to maintain that the peasants still suffered from the injustices that had spurred them to support the Huk uprising. He also blamed the United States for failing to bring true democracy to the Philippines, and I realized that he was opposed less to the principles of colonialism than to its inadequacies.

Taruc was born in a *barrio* of Pampanga province, the son of a sharecropper. Typical of Filipino peasants, for whom education is an escape from poverty, his father sacrificed to put him through high school. The schools then operated under U.S. supervision, and Luis learned English and baseball. But above all, he loved American history. More than once, as we talked, he would digress into an emotional excursion on the subject. "My eyes watered when I read about Washington, Jefferson, Thomas Paine, Patrick Henry, Lincoln. I cherish Jefferson and Abraham Lincoln, especially Lincoln." To prove the point, he would recite the Gettysburg Address.

In a quantum leap for a peasant youth, he went on to college in Manila, where he worked part-time as a ditch digger to earn his keep. One day, out of curiosity, he attended a political rally at which he accidentally met an American army master sergeant whose name, Tom Farrell, he still remembered thirty years later. They fell into conversation, and Farrell disclosed his leftist sympathies. The next day, he brought Taruc some Soviet pamphlets and introduced him to Marxism. Taruc had exchanged a few words with his American school supervisor, but this was his first long talk with an American—and one critical of U.S. policy in the Philippines at that. "It was a revelation," he recalled. "Suddenly I knew that there were answers to our problems."

Too poor to complete college, he returned to central Luzon to work as a tailor—a craft his older brother had taught him. He buried an old clan vendetta by marrying the daughter of a local official who had once humiliated his father. They named their only son Romeo because, Taruc said, "our marriage had ended a family feud."

The worldwide economic slump of the 1930s was devastating the Philippines, causing commodity prices to plummet. Tenants and farm laborers, who lived near the margin even in the best of times, began to stage protest strikes. In 1935, caught up in the excitement, Taruc left his tailor shop to his wife and volunteered to work for Abad Santos in an attempt to direct the disorganized peasants. Abad Santos, shy and bookish, soon named Taruc his spokesman and later the Socialist party's general secretary—a grand title for a movement that numbered only two or three hundred members. But Taruc revealed his organizational skill in the 1940 elections, when he ran Socialist candidates throughout central Luzon. Though they lost the race for representation in the national legislature, they displayed their political potential by winning majorities in several towns. Despite his lack of military experience, Taruc's knowledge of the area made him a natural to command when the Socialists and Communists formed the Huk coalition to fight the Japanese.

When the war broke out, Taruc pledged in a radio message to MacArthur to struggle for "the defense of democracy and the territorial rights of both the Philippines and the United States" and begged for American "guidance and support." MacArthur disregarded him, but the Huks nevertheless helped the U.S. forces to liberate Luzon. Taruc later claimed that his men killed a total of twenty thousand Japanese soldiers and Filipino collaborators during the war. American officers praised their performance. They freed several towns from the Japanese and set up local governments, some expecting the Americans to reward them with medals or money. Instead, they were disarmed and even arrested by U.S. counterintelligence units, which often handed local authority to former Filipino collaborators who represented landowners and other powerful figures. In February 1945, with the consent of American officers, a rival guerrilla chief named Adonais Maclang and his followers rounded up a hundred Huks near the town of Malolos, forced them to dig a mass grave and shot them. The Americans subsequently appointed him mayor of Malolos. Taruc and a deputy were jailed on charges of preventing the region "from returning to a normal way of life."

The anti-Japanese resistance was a mosaic of factions, many fearful of the Huk threat to their postwar aspirations. Aware that the Americans favored conservative movements, they denounced the Huks as dangerous Communists, and the tactic worked. Evidently swayed by his Filipino informants, Major Robert Lapham, a U.S. guerrilla commander in central Luzon, described the Huks in a report as a "subversive . . . radical organization" committed to "carnage, revenge, banditry and hijacking . . . never equalled in any page of the history of the Philippines." MacArthur had rebuffed a proposal to send a U.S. force directly against the Huks, but determined to preserve the old power elite, he authorized, or at least acquiesced to, their piecemeal repression.

Despite the crackdown, the Huk leaders chose to enter the political process. In July 1945, a month before the war ended, Communists, Socialists, peasant unions and various other groups stitched together the Democratic Alliance. Their platform was hardly revolutionary. As Taruc recalled, they did not advocate "even the mildest socialization or change in the society" but aimed to develop "a healthy industrialized capitalist country out of the feudal agricultural condition" through "the ballot and the peaceful petition." But the big landowners, to whom any change was revolutionary, spurred local officials and police to harass their candidates during the 1946 election campaign. In the name of "law and order," mayors banned their public meetings and, on election eve, thugs ransacked their headquarters in the Pampanga province capital of San Fernando. "We weren't angels," a former Huk guerrilla recalled, admitting that his comrades fought back in many places. They were no match for the goons. Even so, six Democratic Alliance candidates won seats in the national legislature. Taruc beat his rival by a margin of twenty-nine thousand votes without delivering a single speech.

Roxas's maneuver to deny the party its seats was seen by the local authorities as a signal to subdue the Huks. Police, soldiers and private gunmen rounded up and often assassinated numbers of suspected radicals in what a U.S. Army historian called a "near pogrom." During the early summer of 1946, alarmed by the prospect of a bigger conflict, Taruc and his colleagues persuaded Roxas to agree to a truce: The peasant unions would disarm and the vigilante groups would disband. But the distrust was too strong on both sides to preserve the peace for long. On August 24, a veteran leftist leader, Juan Feleo, was driving with his wife to Manila from central Luzon to join Taruc at a conference with Roxas. He had been on a mission to monitor the armistice and was being protected by police. They did nothing to stop a squad of uniformed men from abducting him. A headless body, identified as his, was found a month later in a nearby river. The murderers were never apprehended.

Taruc, in a letter to Roxas, accused him of ceding to the "enemies of democracy and progress." He would be "of more service to our country and to our people . . . if I stay with the peasants," Taruc said, and he returned to the countryside. Implicitly, he had proclaimed the Huk uprising.

Vowing to wield a "mailed fist," Roxas pledged to vanquish the rebels in sixty days. He misjudged badly. His feckless troops alienated rural folk or drove them into the Huks' ranks by promiscuously bombing and terrorizing their villages, and the fighting intensified. He offered to resume peace talks, hinting at reforms, but Taruc and his comrades refused until he issued a blanket amnesty and gave them their legislative seats. Copying Mao Zedong's guerrilla force, they adopted a revolutionary new name, the *Hukbong Mapagplayang Bayan,* the People's Liberation Army.

In March 1948, Roxas virtually declared war by outlawing the movement as "subversive" and demanding its unconditional surrender. If he expected any Huks to submit, he negated the possibility by pardoning their worst enemies: all Filipinos who had collaborated with the Japanese. A few weeks later, on a visit to Clark Field, he died of a heart attack.

Elpidio Quirino, his successor, was a limp, indecisive figure, but like many other Manila politicians, he feared that a protracted fight against the Huks would be a costly venture at a time when the country was in financial straits. He proposed "accommodation instead of confrontation." Taruc, agreeing to talk, flew to Manila—and into a frenzy of radical chic. Business and academic groups invited him to speak. He became a celebrity guest on radio talk shows, and a movie producer paid him five thousand pesos for his life story. The legislature restored his seat, along with two years in back salary, part of which he gave to the Huk treasury. He and Quirino then opened two months of negotiations that were doomed from the start.

Quirino, hoping to defang the Huks, offered them amnesty on condition that they disarm. Detecting a trap, they conceded to register, not yield, their weapons. Local police tried to confiscate their guns, the guerrillas resisted, and clashes again erupted. At the same time, Taruc derailed the talks in Manila by demanding immediate agrarian reforms, the dismissal of officials deemed hostile to the Huks and the repeal of parity rights for Americans—none of which Quirino could, or would, grant. The talks collapsed in August 1948, and Taruc fled to the hills, claiming that Quirino had set thugs on him.

Ironically, considering the American portrayal of the Huks as Moscow's protégés, the Communists in the movement had at first been more moderate than Taruc. The party "does not believe in the use of force," its leaders stated, prescribing "legal and parliamentary struggle" until the urban proletariat could rise up according to Marx. Toeing the Moscow line, they rejected peasant revolution as heretical until early 1948, when they realized that they were fouling their claim to be the "vanguard of the masses." Suddenly reversing gears, they endorsed the insurrection. But no evidence indicates that the Russians were tracking, much less managing, their activities. During that period, as historian Charles B. McLane has written, the Soviet press "remained unaccountably silent on events in the Philippines."

Taruc built his original hard core into a larger, more efficient organization after his talks with Quirino aborted—doubling its size over the next two years to some seventeen armed partisans and fifty thousand reservists. He set up a jungle headquarters on the jungle-covered slopes of Mount Arayat, an extinct volcano overlooking the central Luzon plain. From there his regional commanders, mostly anti-Japanese veterans, directed mobile guerrilla squads able to melt into the countryside. New weapons could be acquired by robbing American arsenals, ambushing government troops—or merely purchasing them on the open market. To provide food, lodging, intelligence and communications for his men, Taruc developed a support network of two million peasants. But peasants did not simply sustain the guerrillas; they were the guerrillas.

In the spring of 1987, I drove about two hours north of Manila to Nueva Ecija province, the heart of "Huklandia," as the insurgent zone had been dubbed. A hazy horizon of hills frames a table of rice fields dotted with coconut groves, and villages sheltered by palms stretch along dusty roads alive with chickens, pigs, goats and naked children. I headed for San Ricardo, a *barrio* profiled by Benedict Kerkvliet of the University of Hawaii, who had pointed me toward the peasants he had interviewed for his massive study of the Huk uprising. They are no longer indentured to large landowners, as their ancestors had been. The government has furnished them with schools and clinics, and occasionally I spotted a television antenna. It occurred to me, however, that their plight a generation ago must have been appalling if conditions have improved since. Those I saw were jammed with their families into flimsy nipa huts without electricity or running water. As tenants, their fathers at least shared the crop. These men, though, were hired laborers who work seasonally—or, as many do, illegally grab land to grow food. Simeon San Pedro, a wiry old peasant with narrow eyes and a leathery face, had been a guerrilla. Seated in front of his shack, he was still indignant as he chain-smoked my cigarettes and looked back on the Huk uprising. "Nobody would give us our rights or hear our demands. They said we were Communists. I didn't even know what Communism was, and I still don't. But they called you a Communist, that was that. It made no sense to deny it, because they wouldn't believe you."

Many peasants tried to remain neutral. "We were caught in the middle," one explained. "I sympathized with the Huks, but the police were always passing through the village and questioning us. I couldn't afford to take risks. I gave rice to the guerrillas and answered the cops truthfully." Others were alienated by the excesses of the Huks. Though usually disciplined, the partisans did abuse women, steal cattle from farmers, murder innocent officials designated as "class enemies" and, calling it "taxation," bilked merchants. In April 1949, an insurgent band waylaid a motorcade carrying Manuel Quezon's widow, daughter and ten others, shooting them at point-blank range. Denying

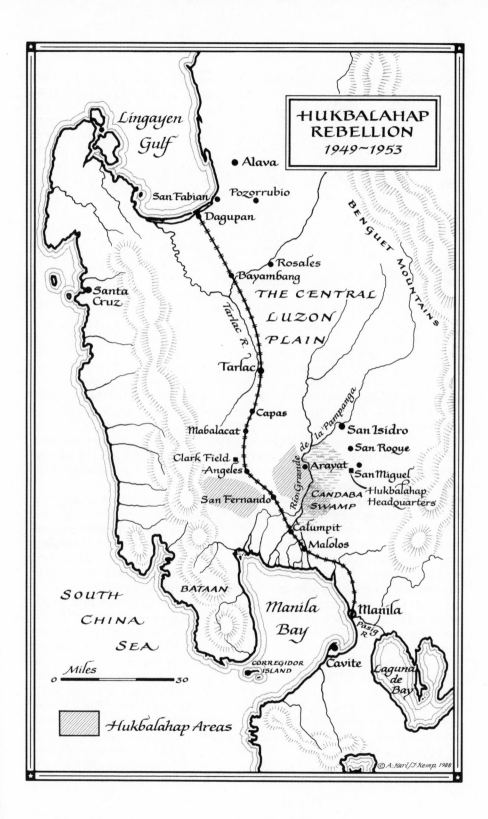

HUKBALAHAP
REBELLION
1949~1953

Lingayen
Gulf

● Alava

● San Fabian   ● Pozorrubio
● Dagupan

BENGUET MOUNTAINS

● Rosales
Bayambang

THE CENTRAL

Santa
Cruz

LUZON

Tarlac R.

PLAIN

● Tarlac

● Capas

Mabalacat   ● San Isidro
● San Roque
Clark Field
Angeles   ● Arayat
San Miguel
San Fernando   Hukbalahap
CANDABA   Headquarters
SWAMP

Río Grande de la Pampanga

Calumpit
Malolos

SOUTH   BATAAN

CHINA   Manila
Bay   ● Manila

SEA   Pasig R.

Miles
0   30   CORREGIDOR   Cavite   Laguna
ISLAND   de
Bay

Hukbalahap Areas

© A. Karl / J. Kemp, 1988

responsibility, Taruc blamed the crime on bandits and decried the government for "creating national hysteria" by implicating his followers. In fact, a rogue rebel group had staged the ambush, and the movement suffered a crippling blow to its reputation as a result. Nor could Taruc always trust his political cadres. Early in 1950, he instructed a comrade to go to China in hopes of persuading the Chinese Communists to send him advisers. "I gave this fellow ten thousand pesos, quite a tidy sum in those days," Taruc later told me. "I waited and waited until, finally, I learned that he had acquired a new wife and opened a grocery store in some remote province." American and Philippine government charges notwithstanding, there is no proof that the Huks ever received Chinese Communist aid.

But despite their failings, the Huks developed into a formidable force. On March 20, 1950, they marked the eighth anniversary of their founding by overrunning two towns and fifteen villages in central Luzon—and even littered the Manila city hall with propaganda leaflets. Six months later, in their most spectacular operation, they threw a battalion of two hundred men against a government garrison in Tarlac province. They slaughtered twenty-six army troops, massacred the patients in the camp clinic, raped and killed the nurses and freed the inmates from the local jail. Overall, however, Taruc pursued a strategy of attrition aimed at grinding down the government army. Swift and flexible, his guerrilla teams would strike, retreat, strike again, then evaporate. They ambushed army convoys, attacked military outposts, assaulted police stations and assassinated civilian officials. Large landowners fled as they ravaged estates, destroying homes, barns and draft animals. Desperate to escape the cross fire, refugees poured into the cities and towns, only to discover the government indifferent to their predicament. Numbers, disappointed and frustrated, returned to their *barrios* to embrace the Huk cause. Probably nothing accounted for the Huk successes, however, as much as the cowardice, corruption and incompetence of the Quirino administration.

Vaulted into the presidency by Roxas's death, Quirino spared no effort to gain his own mandate as the Liberal party candidate in the 1949 election. The opposition *Nacionalistas* had nominated José Laurel, who had served as puppet president under the Japanese. The race was the filthiest in Philippine history to date. "Every device known to fraudulent elections was used," observed a *Reader's Digest* writer. The two sides deployed goons to threaten citizens, stuff ballot boxes and abduct and often murder rival campaign workers. They lifted the names of voters from tombstones or just invented them. In some places, Filipinos sadly joked, "even the birds and bees voted." His incumbency enabled Quirino to bribe local political bosses, several of whom repaid him with exceptional zeal. In two provinces, his vote outnumbered the voters, and in many districts it exceeded the population. He won by a slim margin. Later, an official study estimated, one fifth of the ballots had been phony.

The Huks publicly boycotted the election, but many secretly worked as thugs for Quirino, reckoning that he would plunge the country into chaos and confusion and so turn the people toward them for salvation. The tactic proved to be correct. Quirino's triumph unveiled venality of prodigious proportions. Government contracts, import licenses, public jobs, immigration permits—all were on sale either to the highest bidder or to those with connections in high places. Civil servants sank into lethargy, functioning only to fill their own pockets. The image of the Philippines as the "showcase of democracy" had dimmed.

Nor was Quirino fit to cope with the Huk uprising, whose causes he had never understood. He fortified the Malacañang palace and moored a motor launch nearby to evacuate him and his family should the rebels enter Manila. His only response as the insurgency spread was to exhort his troops to fight harder, which they did by devastating villages, thereby driving peasants into the arms of the Huks. As Taruc subsequently remarked to me, "We couldn't have had a better recruiter."

America was now confronted by a dilemma it later faced in Vietnam, Iran, Panama—and the Philippines itself during the final phase of the Marcos regime: How to deal with a client government that has squandered its credibility? The problem tormented U.S. officials then as it has since.

In 1949, when Quirino visited Washington to plead for help, Truman bluntly replied that the aid "would be largely wasted" unless he put his house "in order." Quirino stalled after returning home and Myron Cowen, the U.S. ambassador in Manila, favored cutting him off—or else he would feel "that the situation is not truly urgent." Still Quirino waffled. His regime verged on bankruptcy, the Huk threat grew and the issue roiled State Department officials. Charlton Ogburn, an Asia analyst, urged toughness. To rescue every self-styled "anti-Communist" would make America a "refuge for weaklings and incompetents." Tell the Filipinos to reform—or else: "Darn it, *they* are the ones who are threatened with a fate worse than death—not we." To John Melby, the Philippine desk officer, the only choice "in the present impossible situation" was to give Quirino a long "breathing period." Melby prevailed, Quirino got a loan and America lost its leverage. Quirino now knew, concluded a State Department report, that the United States would bail him out "no matter what he does." And, indeed, he did nothing—with U.S. aid.

Dean Acheson, addressing the National Press Club early in 1950, fretted aloud over the $2 billion in U.S. assistance given to the Philippines since the end of World War II. "Much of that money has not been used as wisely as we wish it had," he said, warning that future funds might be stopped "if help continues to be misused." Soon afterward, Truman sent an economic mission to Manila headed by Daniel Bell, a private banker and former undersecretary of the treasury. Bell's report observed the obvious: "The profits of businessmen and the incomes of large landowners have risen very considerably [but] the standard of living of most people is lower than before the war." The team recommended tighter American supervision and, of course, drastic reforms.

The proposal was pointless. Quirino and his associates were well aware of the need for reforms, but they resisted progressive change because, as part of the oligarchy, their authority reposed on the status quo. So it was futile to hector them into behaving like "mature statesmen," as Cowen did early in 1950.

In a burst of cables to Washington, he derided Filipino politicians as "self-seeking and unscrupulous men." The most "evil" of them was Quirino, who demonstrated a "distressing disregard for his country's interests" by dismissing the Huks as a "less immediate danger" than his Manila rivals. Acheson similarly told Truman that Quirino was the "primary obstacle" to a solution:

"He would prefer to see his country ruined rather than compromise with his own insatiable ego." Acheson recalled the recent debacle in China, where America's blind support for the egregious Chiang Kai-shek regime led to the Communist takeover. The lesson of that disaster was clear: "If we are confronted with an inadequate vehicle, it should be discarded." In short: Dump Quirino.

Cowen came up with a daring proposal: the replacement of Quirino by Fernando Lopez, his vice president, the scion of a rich sugar family with powerful political allies. The gambit, he said, needed a "remorseless mind" like that of Fernando's "brainier brother Eugenio," a newspaper publisher and "cold-blooded strategist" whose "half-enlightened and half-feudal" clan had displayed a "capacity for ruthless operations." Though Cowen did not go into details, the plan would require the deployment of secret U.S. agents, who were then building an "infrastructure," as covert operatives term their clandestine allies inside foreign regimes. The scheme, however, reflected the American illusion that the answer to the Huk insurrection was simply fresh faces at the top—or, as Cowen phrased it, "a reshuffling of the cards." But a dynamic new figure did appear, as if by miracle, and he came from the bottom of the deck. His name was Ramón Magsaysay, and he ultimately became a legend.

★　★　★

American rather than divine intervention led to Magsaysay's emergence. As a member of the Philippine legislature, he had gone to Washington early in 1950 to seek benefits for Filipino war veterans. By chance he met Edward Lansdale, a U.S. Air Force lieutenant colonel on loan to the Office of Policy Coordination, a supersecret organization responsible for covert action, afterward absorbed into the Central Intelligence Agency as the "department of plans"—or "dirty tricks." Lansdale, who knew the Philippines, was alarmed by the Huk threat. He concluded after an evening with him that Magsaysay understood the problem as "very few Filipinos or Americans did"—and that "he should be the guy" to lead the fight against the insurgents. Magsaysay also impressed Lansdale's boss, Frank Wisner, who offered him undercover support for his political career if he would act as America's surrogate. Magsaysay agreed. Wisner sent Livingston Merchant, an assistant secretary of state, to Manila with a proposal for Quirino: Appoint Magsaysay defense secretary and U.S. military assistance would be increased.

Cowen, unaware of the deal, had meanwhile been recruited by Magsaysay to lobby Quirino on his behalf. By now Quirino knew that U.S. aid hinged on his appointment of Magsaysay. In August 1950, his defense secretary, Ruperto Kangelon, fortuitously resigned over a bureaucratic dispute, and he gave Magsaysay the job. The U.S. connection had again been crucial.

Filipinos henceforth identified Magsaysay as America's proxy. He reveled in the image, reassuring U.S. officials concerned for his nationalist credibility: "What do you know about Filipinos? They like Americans. They like to see me with Americans." To him, too, America's patronage not only promised the redemption of the Philippines but the salvation of all Asia. With U.S. "guidance and assistance," he said in a later speech, "this country can become the head of a family of democratic nations in this part of the globe."

Magsaysay's niche in the Philippine pantheon is secure—even though his premature death in an airplane crash was not exactly the martyrdom of a true Filipino hero. Like Corazon Aquino a generation afterward, he owed much of his celebrity to the U.S. press, whose hagiographies, reprinted in Manila, dazzled Filipinos. But his myth, like all myths, is clouded by reality. In contrast to his romantic portrait as a "man of the people," he came from a solid middle-class family with valuable clan affiliations. The defeat of the Huks, his most vaunted achievement, was also due less to his skill than to their blunders. Nor did America, through its experience with him, learn to cope with insurgencies, as events in Vietnam later proved. Nevertheless, Magsaysay appreciated more than any Filipino leader before or since the economic and social injustices that spur rebellion, and he earnestly introduced reforms. Above all, his relentless energy, uncommon honesty and personal charisma restored the faith of the population in government—at least for a brief shining moment.

A burly figure nearly six feet tall, Magsaysay towered above Filipinos. He did not smoke, drink or gamble—though, in the macho manner of Filipino men, he had an eye for women. Uneasy among Manila's opulent rich, he preferred to trade jokes and gossip at familiar hangouts with old cronies, who called him by his nickname, Monching. His spotty schooling had given him a sense of intellectual inferiority, and he often swallowed the cant of self-styled experts. He was particularly deferential toward his American advisers, but his impetuosity sometimes drove them to exasperation. Mostly he enjoyed what he did best, touring the country in a vintage C-47, the *Pagasa,* or "hope" in Tagalog. His sports shirt and khaki pants soaked by sweat in the tropical heat, he would stride into villages, spouting populist platitudes that he unabashedly believed. "I love to shake hands dirty with the mud of poor farmers. I love to shake the hands of greasy mechanics. I would rather shake their hands than those hands in Manila—perfumed hands washed ten times a day with the best kind of soap."

Magsaysay's paternal lineage reached back to a Chinese merchant who had settled with his Filipino wife in Zambales, a coastal province northwest of Manila. His father was a well-to-do shopkeeper and landowner, and his mother claimed descent from a Spanish noble. Born in 1907, the second of four children, he preferred to help his father's tenants in the fields than attend school. Like an American boy his age, he read *National Geographic* and *Popular Mechanics.* Also like a young American, he sported a second-hand Model-T Ford in high school. College in Manila bored him; besides, he hated city life. Dropping out, he returned home to find work in time-honored Filipino fashion: His father's uncle's wife's cousin was related to the proprietor of a local bus company, who hired him as a mechanic. He excelled at the grimy job, and his boss promoted him to manager. Late in 1941, when Japan invaded the Philippines, he left his wife and three children to join a guerrilla unit operating under American auspices in his native province.

He had lent his firm's vehicles to the U.S. forces at the start of the war, and several American officers knew him. One, who had formed the resistance group, made him a captain under the nom de guerre of Chow. He handled transportation—a routine task. But the experience altered his life. The U.S. Army, rewarding his integrity and enterprise, named him provincial military governor after the war, and his political career began. The job gave him the distinction of being in America's trust, and his control over U.S. food, clothing and other relief supplies gave him extraordinary authority. Running in the 1946 election for the national legislature, he easily won a seat in the lower chamber. He steered himself into the chair of the Defense Committee, where he observed the incompetence and corruption of the Philippine army. His trip to Washington in 1950 had benefited Filipino veterans, and he irked ultranationalists by extolling U.S. generosity. They were then assailing Ambassador Cowen for interfering in the country's domestic affairs, and Magsaysay lashed back, terming an "attack against a benefactor the bitterest dreg of ingratitude." He was, of course, repaying America for having promoted him as the next defense secretary.

Once appointed, he fled Manila's meddlesome politicians by shifting the Defense Department from the city to suburban Camp Murphy, named for an obscure U.S. officer. He moved his family into a modest cottage inside the compound and set up an office in a mildewed villa. His top priority was the Huk threat, now critical. Edward Lansdale soon arrived as his mentor and, like Magsaysay, he eventually became a legend.

Lansdale, who died in 1987, was a perennial topic of controversy. William Lederer and Eugene Burdick exalted him in *The Ugly American* as Colonel Hillendale, whose harmonica captured "hearts and minds" for the U.S. crusade against Communism. In *The Quiet American,* by contrast, Graham Greene caricatured him as Pyle, the naïve U.S. official who held that peasants taught the tenets of democracy would resist the Communist menace. I later knew Lansdale in Vietnam—and, genius or fraud, he was pie-à-la-mode American. Proud of his inability to speak a foreign tongue, he zealously advanced American values—as if the world awaited his Americanizing mission. As he wrote, "I took my American beliefs into these Asian struggles."

The clue to Lansdale was his youth in the advertising trade. Beneath his homey, gee-whiz veneer, he was a devious self-promoter who invented achievements that redounded to his credit. He also exuded an artless goodwill that ignored the economic and social roots of revolution. To him, radical insurrections could be checked by "psychological warfare" techniques borrowed from advertising gimmicks. During the 1960s, when the CIA was pondering ways to oust Fidel Castro, Lansdale proposed sparking a revolt in Havana by firing eerie flares over the city on a Catholic holiday, while broadcasting warnings of impending doom. An agency wag dubbed the scheme "elimination by illumination" before it was mercifully shelved. He made counterinsurgency sound simple, like the directions on a cake-mix box: "Communist guerrillas hide among the people," he would say. "If you win the people to your side, the Communist guerrillas have no place to hide. With no place to hide, you can find them. Then . . . finish them!" Unlike most career officers at the time, he realized that conventional tactics could not defeat peasant rebels. He taught Magsaysay to innovate and persuaded the conservative U.S. military establishment to support him.

The son of a peripatetic car-parts dealer, Edward Geary Lansdale was born in Los Angeles. He quit college to join a San Francisco advertising firm and entered the U.S. Army when World War II broke out. Assigned to the Office of Strategic Services, the precursor of the CIA, he expected a covert job overseas. Instead he spent the war at home, gathering maps and other data on combat areas. Only afterward was he sent to the Philippines as a military intelligence officer, and he loved the country. He explored the boondocks, but mostly he remained in Manila among its hothouse elite. His view of the Huk threat typified cold-war logic. Having observed the abysmal poverty of rural areas, he admitted that the peasants had legitimate grievances. However, he concluded, the fault lay less in the system than in "fallible" Filipino officials who had failed to make enlightened laws "work as perfectly as intended." The Huks, as "true disciples of Karl Marx," were "exploiting" the discontent as a consequence.

The CIA, created in 1947, was initially prohibited from cloak-and-dagger actions like toppling undesirable foreign leaders. But, the argument in Washington went, America needed a subversive organization to subvert Soviet subversion. So, the next year, the Office of Policy Coordination was founded under Frank Wisner, a high-strung wartime spy who committed suicide in 1965. Lansdale became his man in Manila.

Hired by Wisner in 1949, he was assigned to Manila a year later to manage Magsaysay. His job, like his outfit, was so hush-hush that the U.S. ambassador and the CIA had orders to assist but not question him. He signed his messages to Washington with the code name "Geoffrey Villiers," which he had taken out of a telephone directory. Quirino had been pressed into accepting him as an intelligence adviser without being told his true mission. Lansdale was under instructions to build Magsaysay's political base for the future while helping him annihilate the Huks.

One of his few CIA associates was Gabriel Kaplan, an astute operative who had been a liberal New York Republican lawyer and politician. Kaplan had been brought into the agency by Desmond FitzGerald, a senior dirty-tricks executive and onetime political friend. His camouflage testified to the CIA's sterling connections. First he went to Manila in 1951 for the Committee for Free Asia, later renamed the Asia Foundation, then headed by Alan Vallentine, president of the University of Rochester. Back the next year under another CIA guise, the Catherwood Foundation, he began a community development project whose patrons included prominent U.S. corporate executives. A handsome, gregarious man in his early fifties, he stayed for six years, spreading America's gospel to the Filipinos with homilies like: "A democracy is a light bulb—and the people are the electric current." He formed the National Committee for Free Elections to propel Magsaysay forward, and it was resurrected in 1986, presumably without U.S. money, to serve Corazon Aquino.

On the political side, Lansdale also relied on David Sternberg, whom I later saw frequently on my visits to Manila—though I had no idea that he was on the CIA payroll. He had arrived in the Philippines with his brother and sister in 1939 and suffered Japanese internment during the war. A paraplegic, confined to a wheelchair in his sprawling suburban home, he would chain-smoke as Filipino politicians, bureaucrats, journalists and businessmen filed through to seek his counsel—his infirmity having apparently endowed him in their eyes with the wisdom of a guru. Thus he collected information and dispensed advice. He disguised his CIA role as a contributor to *The Christian Science Monitor* and, besides his value as a source of intelligence, he wrote speeches for Magsaysay. Rumor had it that Lansdale once kayoed Magsaysay for refusing to deliver one of Sternberg's speeches. As Lansdale subsequently told the story, he had indeed knocked out Magsaysay—but it was Lansdale who had written the speech.

Lansdale's main American military sidekick was Charles Bohannan, a lanky army major who had fought as a guerrilla in the Philippines. His chief Filipino associate was Colonel Napoleon Valeriano, who commanded swashbuckling units called "skull squadrons" for their practice of beheading suspected Huks. But mostly he communed with Magsaysay, and they became *compadres.* Their talks rambled into the wee hours, the two of them often sharing a bedroom in Lansdale's villa. Lansdale usually ventilated ideas in his patient, sometimes didactic style, and Magsaysay listened reverently. It was "subliminal," speculated a contemporary observer. Lansdale went on day and night, weeks and months, so that "by the time Magsaysay stood up somewhere to speak, he knew what to say." A Filipino nationalist once charged Lansdale with keeping Magsaysay "in custody." Lansdale privately remarked years later that, having concluded that "Asia needed its own heroes," he had in effect invented Magsaysay.

They frequently toured the country together, arriving unannounced at army posts, and their discoveries appalled them. In many places supplies had disappeared into the black market, leaving soldiers without guns and even boots. They found cannibalized vehicles and crippled tanks whose spark plugs had been stolen. One morning, they surprised officers asleep after an all-night poker session. They realized the urgency of a massive overhaul and, under Lansdale's tutelage, Magsaysay energetically started the job.

To tighten his control, he shrank the constabulary, a scattered parallel force, and made the army the spearhead of the campaign against the Huks. He nearly doubled its size to fifty-six thousand men by 1952, reducing overweight units to mobile battalions. Half a billion dollars in U.S. economic and military aid between 1951 and 1955 blessed the venture with modern weapons and other equipment, including aircraft to bomb and strafe rebel targets—and often villages. Magsaysay, aware that guns and organizational changes were not enough, also boosted morale. He purged incompetents, broke up entrenched officer cliques and rewarded achievers. As the army gradually awoke from its torpor, he proclaimed "all-out force and all-surrender," a carrot-and-stick policy that signified surrender—or else.

His men, inspired by regular pay and rations, showed fresh vigor. He made them sleep in the fields rather than in barracks. They carefully guarded roads and bridges, and combed villages without molesting the inhabitants. Their officers, armed with cash, purchased intelligence. The Huks, forced into the mountains, faced attacks from army combat teams, often backed by air raids. Denied peasant support, they sought to survive in the jungle, some dying from eating poisonous plants, others fighting among themselves over rats, snails, insects. William J. Pomeroy, an American Communist who had joined the Huks, described the ordeal in his journal. "There was a time when the forest was wholly ours, and we lived in it as within a fortress, issuing forth at will to spread panic among our foes. . . . Now the forest is like a breached wall, through which government troops can pour at their will. . . . There is the sensation, now, of being in a vise." They foraged for food in nearby *barrios,* only to be rebuffed as pariahs. Fearing detection, they dared not build huts and huddled together at night under torrential rains. Pomeroy, both his feet "a mass of scored and bleeding flesh, bright red, with the look of rot," evoked revolutions to keep going: "I clamber over mammoth roots and . . . this is India and its people overcoming the obstacles to independence. I come up a long difficult slope and . . . this is China . . . and the fight against the running dogs of imperialism." Finally captured in 1952, he was deported home after ten years in prison.

Lansdale devised "psywar" gimmicks that, he later wrote, were "remarkably effective." He contrived to broadcast Huk "voices" from tombs, a sign to the superstitious of their malevolence, and conceived of making them victims of the *asuang,* a mythical vampire, supposedly to spread panic among the insurgents. One of his wilder schemes was to surface a U.S. submarine disguised as a Soviet vessel to "prove" that Moscow was helping the Huks. It was vetoed in Washington.

While no expert on revolution, Lansdale at least knew Mao Zedong's dictum that "Fish swim in water," and he spurred Magsaysay to promote projects to win the peasants away from the insurgents. Magsaysay created credit banks, clinics and agrarian courts in which army lawyers represented aggrieved tenants and laborers against landowners. His most publicized offer, however, was to give farms to rebels who surrendered. "They're fighting for a house and land," he would say with ebullient simplicity. "Okay, they can stop fighting, because I'll give it to them." But the pledges faded, as pledges do in the Philippines. The agrarian courts never curbed the power of the landowners, and the land grant benefited fewer than a thousand families, only a fourth of them Huks. In 1952, Robert Hardie, a U.S. land-tenure expert in Manila, expressed doubts about the reforms, and advised instead that the government buy big holdings and resell small plots to tenants on the installment plan. Denounced as a Communist by Filipino politicians, he was recalled home.

Magsaysay's ballyhoo made an impact, however. A Huk cadre derogated the promised reforms as "showcase"—but, he ruefully remarked, peasants "believed" them. I heard the same view thirty-five years later in central Luzon, where one old laborer recalled that Magsaysay "fought for our rights." When I noted that he still lacked his own land, he blamed the politicians who subsequently undid Magsaysay's "good deeds."

With American help, Magsaysay gained further glory in the 1951 legislative elections. Gabriel Kaplan's committee for free elections, nominally run by Filipinos on the CIA payroll, enlisted civic leaders, teachers and students to act as poll watchers. Lansdale also induced Magsaysay to assign troops to prevent violence and to assure secret balloting and a fair count. Fearing for his corrupt Liberal party, Quirino objected to the operation, but Magsaysay defied him, and the contest was relatively honest. More dramatically, a record four million voters ignored pleas by the Huks for a boycott designed, as one of their internal directives phrased it, to "make the masses realize the necessity . . . of revolution." A Huk analysis shortly afterward lamented the "illusion" of peasants who yearned for "peace and order even though they suffer poor living conditions."

By 1951, Magsaysay was predicting victory over the Huks—and his forecast soon came true. Official American studies later credited his success to his "aggressive" operations and the impact of U.S. aid. But despite the undeniable power of that amalgam, other elements combined to defeat the Huks.

Unlike the New People's Army, which spread its uprising thirty years later across the islands, the Huks concentrated on central Luzon. They lacked the flexibility to regroup in other regions as the pressure on them grew and could only retreat to the mountain jungles—a grim haven. In contrast to leftist rebels in other parts of the world, they received neither Soviet nor Chinese help, and their supply problems became severe as improved Philippine army discipline made stealing or buying weapons difficult.

But their worst setbacks were self-inflicted. They had foolishly planted a major apparatus in Manila, a city without secrets. Tipped off by an informer, government forces swept into twenty-two houses and apartments on October 28, 1950, capturing reams of Huk documents along with six senior leaders—among them José Lava, a noted jurist who had succeeded his brother Vicente as Communist party chief. On hearing the news, William Pomeroy recalled, insurgents in the boondocks felt like "men in mines when the tunnel behind them caves in." Many, their morale shattered, surrendered—and several betrayed comrades.

A bid by the Communists to control the movement further hastened its doom. José Lava, who fancied himself a Marxist theologian, had concluded from the scriptures that the United States was headed into an economic slump that would devastate the Philippines. He saw this inevitable event in America's reluctance to aid Quirino. So, he argued, the time had come to turn the peasant rebellion into a full-scale revolution aimed at establishing a Communist regime. The momentous move would require the reorganization of the guerrillas into a regular army under Communist command. Lava also championed big battalions to confront Magsaysay's forces in big battles.

Luis Taruc conceded that the "untrained and uneducated" guerrillas needed "firm leadership." But to escalate the rebellion into a conventional war, much less a revolution, struck him as madness. The Huks were militarily inferior to the government army. As for the peasants, Taruc explained to me, "they wanted land, not to die fighting if they could get reforms." In 1951, after criticizing his concern for the people as "excessive humanism," the Communists divested him of his command. Shortly afterward, fearing reprisals, he sent a secret signal to Magsaysay.

Lansdale, now with the CIA, had meanwhile been grooming Magsaysay for the presidency in 1953. Quirino's plan to run foreclosed Magsaysay's hopes of winning the nomination of his own Liberal party. He could defect to the *Nacionalistas*, but their old bosses, José Laurel and Claro Recto, had ambitions. Recto, a pudgy man with bedroom eyes, was especially mulish. Born into a humble family, he was an eminent legal scholar who had learned to speak fluent Castilian—and, affecting the manner of a Spanish aristocrat, liked to be called "Don" Claro. He decried America's "merciless materialism" and had collaborated with the Japanese out of intense nationalism. Nevertheless, under Lansdale's gentle suasion, he and Laurel deferred to Magsaysay—at least for then.

Ever the advertising man, Lansdale credited Magsaysay's image to his own "symbol manipulation." In 1952, escorting Magsaysay to America, he arranged for him to meet Truman, be awarded a U.S. Army medal and win an honorary doctorate from Fordham University. He introduced him to the press, which earned Magsaysay such plaudits as *Time*'s "Eisenhower of the Pacific." In Lansdale's best aw-shucks manner, Magsaysay repeated that he was "too busy knocking down Communism" to run for president. His "self-effacement," wrote a Manila newspaper, denoted "a truly great man."

Lansdale orchestrated the campaign back in Manila by feeding the Magsaysay myth to American correspondents, then having their roseate dispatches replayed in the city's major newspapers, three of which belonged to Americans. The U.S. Information Service furnished pro-Magsaysay pieces to the impecunious provincial press through the Philippine News Service, a CIA front, while the Voice of America transmitted pro-Magsaysay broadcasts to the forty-one radio stations it owned across the archipelago. Lansdale disingenuously said years later that he received no official U.S. funds, "secret or otherwise." In fact, the agency not only underwrote him, but Gabriel Kaplan's watchdog committee also served as a CIA funnel, and American companies in Manila pitched in as well. "As a practical matter," Joseph Alsop observed, "Magsaysay is the American candidate." His column, written for the *New York Herald-Tribune,* was replanted by Lansdale in the *Manila Bulletin,* an American property. To be so described elsewhere in Asia would ruin a politician. In the Philippines at the time, to be called an "Amboy"—"America's boy"—was a halo.

Magsaysay could have played in Peoria. Campaigning in English under the slogan "Magsaysay Is My Guy," he was soon known everywhere as "the Guy." He had a catchy theme song, the "Magsaysay Mambo," composed by Raul Manglapus—a jazz buff who was himself a subsequent CIA protégé and later became Corazon Aquino's secretary for foreign affairs. Reveling in the hoopla, Magsaysay would push into crowds, cuddling babies, bussing old women, shaking hands, smiling, always protesting his rectitude: "I will send my own father to jail if he breaks the law." Stomach ulcers had grounded Quirino in the Malacañang palace, confirming Magsaysay's picture of him as a sick old man. He decried Magsaysay as an American puppet—which only added to Magsaysay's popularity.

On election day, U.S. military advisers dispersed around the country—ostensibly to watch Filipino troops protecting the polls but actually to make America's presence felt. For the same purpose, American warships cruised into Manila Bay. Magsaysay was aboard a U.S. vessel when the results flashed. He won nearly seventy percent of the vote, beating Quezon's record in the race for commonwealth president in 1935. It was also a triumph for America and for Lansdale—whom the Indian ambassador to Manila nicknamed "Colonel Landslide."

Magsaysay kept up his populist image at his inaugural in January by wearing a cotton *barong Tagalog,* a native shirt. His speech resounded with platitudes, but the crowd went wild with enthusiasm. He was lifted into the air by elated fans, who tore his clothes as he tried to reach his car. He had invited fifty guests to a formal luncheon at the Malacañang palace. Five thousand came, and thousands more poured in during the days ahead. Kids raced around the halls, mothers nursed their babies on satin sofas, families picnicked on the lawn outside. The Age of Jackson had come to Manila.

As his first act, Magsaysay urged citizens to wire their gripes to an aide,

Manuel Manahan, at a special rate of one peso a telegram. Manahan was soon deluged by nearly thirty thousand complaints from peasants—proof, he later told me, that they now trusted Magsaysay more than they did the Huks. He also received a secret message from Luis Taruc, suggesting a talk. With Magsaysay's approval, Manahan was preparing to reply to Taruc by courier when a *Manila Times* reporter named Benigno Aquino, Jr., sauntered into his office. Aquino, then twenty-one, was ambitious, alert and brash. He was trying on his own to interview Taruc. Learning of this contact, he challenged Manahan: "You're cooking up something. I've got to get the story." Manahan, fearing a leak, co-opted him.

The two men, eluding an army cordon of the area, first saw Taruc secretly in a village north of Manila in January 1954. Never short of words, Taruc rambled on about poverty, injustice and the need for reform, and requested a complete pardon. Magsaysay, informed of the discussions, insisted on Taruc's absolute submission. Aquino pursued the talks alone, Taruc insisting on amnesty and Magsaysay refusing. Taruc's stamina eroded as Magsaysay's forces attacked the region, and he heard that the Communists planned to murder him. Finally, in early May, he summoned Aquino back. Aquino repeated the episode for the rest of his life, embroidering each account. The version he gave me later was probably as accurate as any.

Taruc had set the early-morning rendezvous at a *barrio* called Santa Maria, in his native Pampanga province. Now the army was involved. Aquino was to enter at six-thirty and, as he recalled, the troops would "blow the place to smithereens" if he failed to return by nine. "Taruc was surrounded by the villagers, and he looked like them, in a gray peasant shirt, brown pants and straw hat. After shaking hands, I asked him: 'Do you accept the president's terms?' He said: 'I accept.'"

Aquino got his exclusive story, and the boost that propelled him into a meteoric, tragic career. Given three life sentences, Taruc spent fourteen and a half years in jail. Lansdale left the Philippines for Saigon, where his effort to turn South Vietnam's austere President Ngo Dinh Diem into another Magsaysay faltered badly. Magsaysay's presidency was a disappointment.

The task of administering the country was an anticlimax after fighting rebels. Bored with routine, he dealt with problems spastically—wavering and vacillating, issuing and countermanding orders until his subordinates were dazed and confused. His dreams of reform foundered as he refused to learn the political and bureaucratic machinery. A Manila editor, sympathetic to him, commented at the time: "Everybody wishes him well, but it's about time he gave the people more than honesty, integrity and the common touch. The government must be capable, efficient and effective." Precisely the same criticism was directed more than thirty years later at Cory Aquino, who also had trouble descending from the dizzy peaks of glory to the daily grind of detail.

Nor could Magsaysay cope with the vintage politicians who had lent him support and were now calling in their IOUs. "Those old guys want to put me in their pocket," he confided to a friend. His particular nemesis was Claro Recto, the ultranationalist, who from his seat in the upper chamber of the legislature regularly assailed his obedience to America. John Osborne, a *Time* correspondent who then espoused America's cold war policies, saw the struggle starkly: "whether the Philippines remains a firm U.S. ally in Asia, as will be the case if Magsaysay wins . . . or becomes an uneasy neutralist" if the Recto camp prevailed. Sharing that apocalyptic view, the CIA's dirty tricksters attempted to smear Recto by labeling him a Chinese Communist stooge—and once, in a childish gesture, distributed defective condoms bearing his name.

Magsaysay backed every American enterprise in Asia to reciprocate for U.S. support. He endorsed the Taiwan Straits resolution, an American warning to Communist China, and he played host at the signing of the Southeast Asia defense treaty, a regional security pact that later fell into decay. The U.S. bases in the Philippines were never in doubt during his presidency. He allowed Lansdale to recruit Filipinos for a CIA front in Vietnam at first called the Freedom Company, then renamed the Eastern Construction Company to make it seem less political. Its agents trained South Vietnam's police, and one drafted the constitution. A subsidiary, Operation Brotherhood, helped to move thousands of anti-Communist refugees from North Vietnam to the south after partition—a pet Lansdale project.

On March 16, 1957, Magsaysay flew in a refurbished C-47 to the city of Cebu to mend his crumbling political fences in the Visayas. He planned to return to Manila that evening and, as usual in the Philippines, the schedule lagged. There were meetings with the local bosses, an honorary degree at the university, a kowtow to the archbishop and, capping the day, a banquet. The plane left at about one in the morning and crashed into a mountain fifteen minutes later, killing all twenty-six aboard except a newspaperman by the name of Nestor Mata. An investigation blamed pilot error. Gossips claimed that the aircraft was overweight with passengers and baskets of ripe mangoes, and some said that the pilot had been drinking. A year afterward, a new CIA man assigned to Manila was told by his boss: "Find another Magsaysay."

13. CONJUGAL AUTOCRACY

★ ★ ★

It was nearly midnight on September 22, 1972, when the telephone awoke Henry Byroade, the American ambassador. He recognized the soft voice of Richard Usher, the Philippine desk officer at the State Department, calling from Washington.

"Hank, what's happening?" Usher asked.

"What do you mean?" replied Byroade as he switched on his bedside light and fumbled for a cigarette.

"The press is reporting that Marcos has just announced martial law." Usher then began to read news dispatches describing tanks and truckloads of troops rolling through downtown Manila—miles from Byroade's spacious villa in Forbes Park, one of the city's fancy residential enclaves.

Byroade was dismayed. Over the past week, aware that President Ferdinand Marcos was planning to impose martial law, he had repeatedly advised him against the move on the grounds that it might antagonize the U.S. Congress and ignite an upheaval in the Philippines. They had again discussed the topic earlier that day at Malacañang, the presidential palace, and Byroade left convinced that he had dissuaded Marcos from acting rashly—at least for the moment. Byroade was so confident that he drove to his chancery office overlooking the shimmering expanse of Manila Bay and composed a confidential message for Washington: "For the time being, possibly for the next six weeks, the likelihood of martial law declaration has lessened." Now, deceived by Marcos, he awaited the worst.

Actually, he had known for at least a year that Marcos was jockeying to cling to power after his term expired in 1973. The president of the Philippines was limited by law to two terms; Marcos, always concerned with the façade of legitimacy, had been maneuvering to promulgate a new constitution that would enable him to run again. Meanwhile, he was hyping up a Communist threat as a pretext to retain authority. He had disclosed his objective to Byroade: Marcos alone, the World War II guerrilla hero, could cope with the Communist situation. Though he had publicly warned that he might impose martial law, he had deliberately avoided the phrase in their talks, fearful of evoking unsavory images of a military dictatorship. Instead, speaking in generalities, he confided to Byroade his intention to resort to "unusual measures" to put a stop to the killings, bombings and other violence, which he attributed to the Communists and their surrogates. Only on September 19, three days before the declaration, did Byroade obtain the text of the martial law decree from a CIA mole inside the Marcos entourage.

By then Byroade had served in Manila for more than three years—longer than any U.S. ambassador since the Philippines attained independence. Like his predecessors, he assumed from his arrival that America's colonial legacy entitled him to an intimacy with Filipinos denied to other foreign envoys. But he earned his close relationship with Marcos, who saw him as a reflection of the romantic figure that he fancied himself to be. Byroade, no striped pants diplomat, was tall and ruggedly handsome, with a cigarette habit that betrayed his inner tension. A West Pointer, he had been the youngest brigadier general in the U.S. Army during World War II—a record that matched Marcos's claim to have been a precocious guerrilla commander. His previous tours of duty in Egypt and South Africa had given him solid professional credentials, and his involvement in the clandestine CIA operation in 1953 that had secured the throne for Shah Mohammad Reza Pahlavi of Iran appealed to Marcos's taste for adventure. He had a weakness for women, another trait Marcos shared. Above all, Marcos figured that Byroade had a direct link to President Richard Nixon, whom he believed would back his anti-Communist cause.

Byroade had been informed by his CIA station chief, who had impeccable sources, that many of the alleged Communist incidents had in fact been concocted by Marcos as an excuse to crack down on his political rivals—most notably Ninoy Aquino, the probable candidate for the presidency in 1973. But Byroade was not a liberal concerned with human rights; his motives were purely practical. As an admirer of Marcos, he feared that the suspension of civil liberties, whatever the justification, would backfire. Years later, as we sat amid the exotic souvenirs of his career in his home in an affluent Washington suburb, he recollected his apprehensions: "I could imagine protests against Marcos sweeping through Manila and back here, on Capitol Hill, demands that we cut off his aid for raping democracy."

Over breakfast, after dinners, on the golf course and at other meetings, Byroade repeated his misgivings to Marcos. Finally, in August 1972, as his deadline approached, Marcos challenged Byroade: "I know what you think, but I want to know what your government thinks." In short, he wanted the word from Nixon, not just an ambassador's opinion.

Marcos's wife, Imelda, who had arrogated for herself the role of his global emissary, had earlier sought the same word. On October 22, 1971, during one of her extravagant worldwide journeys, she obtained an audience with Nixon at the White House. He was busy with weightier matters, among them his forthcoming trips to Beijing and Moscow, and in any case he could not abide her cloying manner. Trapped, he tried to fob her off on his wife, Pat, but she was also appalled by Imelda and fled in panic. Imelda presented him with a chestful of Philippine seashells, then sank into a sofa and talked for the next twenty minutes. She and her husband were "determined" to stay in office until the Communists were "licked," she said, adding that she would replace Marcos as president should he retire. Nixon's eyes glazed over as she babbled away, and finally he eased her out. Nevertheless, he communicated her warning of the Communist menace to a State Department expert, who muttered after a glance at the report, "Oh, crap."

Imelda, who invariably tailored her conclusions to fit her preconceptions, very likely assumed that Nixon's silence signified approval for Marcos to remain in power—and she carried that message back to Manila. Marcos, meanwhile, was receiving what he regarded as encouraging signals from other American sources. Years before, he had come to trust Francis Tatu, a political officer in the U.S. Embassy in Manila, whom he credited with helping his election as president in 1965. Tatu, now a middle-level State Department official, had since shifted to dealing with other countries, but he continued to monitor events in the Philippines. One day in the spring of 1972, chatting with the Philippine ambassador to Washington, Tatu casually suggested that Marcos ought to declare martial law to halt the violence in Manila. The ambassador was Imelda's brother, Benjamin Romualdez. "My guess," Tatu told me, "is that he reported to Marcos that I was speaking for the American government, since that's what he wanted to believe."

In August 1972, when Byroade journeyed to Washington at Marcos's behest, he was completely ignored by both Nixon and Henry Kissinger, the president's national security adviser. Nixon's schedule, jammed with Vietnam, the recent Watergate burglary and his campaign for reelection against George McGovern, could not accommodate the Philippines. Kissinger, equally absorbed in the last stages of the Vietnam cease-fire negotiations, dismissed the Philippines as trivial. Their snubs posed an embarrassing dilemma for Byroade. He estimated that Marcos, who had agents and friends in Washington, would know that Nixon had spurned him, and he could not plausibly manufacture a White House meeting that never occurred. But, if only for the sake of his own prestige, he could not return to Manila without the official U.S. position that Marcos had requested. So he himself drafted a message to Marcos that, as best he could recall it to me fifteen years later, pledged American "support for the president of the Philippines in the event of a genuine Communist danger." The language, he felt, was firm enough to placate Marcos, yet too vague to commit the United States to his martial law plan. He floated it past his State Department colleagues, who concurred, and flew back to Manila with a "policy."

Marcos interpreted the statement to mean that he had only to dramatize the Communist danger to win Nixon's endorsement for whatever measures he initiated. During the first half of September 1972, bombs blasted public buildings, private offices and department stores across downtown Manila. Marcos blamed the violence on the Communists, but much of it was his doing. The CIA learned from a reliable informer, for instance, that his henchmen were behind an explosion that wrecked the sewage system in suburban Quezon City. Taking advantage of the unrest, criminals and racketeers surfaced everywhere, murdering, pillaging and settling old scores, and crooked policemen joined in to bilk shopkeepers and motorists. Marcos, announcing that the Communists were moving toward "open war," affirmed that only he stood between anarchy and stability. The weather helped: A typhoon struck central Luzon, devastating hundreds of villages, laying waste to the rice crop and adding credibility to Marcos's contention that a state of emergency was necessary.

To execute his design, Marcos enlisted a dozen loyalists later dubbed the "Rolex Twelve" because he supposedly rewarded them with gold watches—though one of them afterward told me that his had merely been an Omega. The twelve included ten army officers, a business crony and the defense minister, Juan Ponce Enrile. Despite Marcos's attempt at secrecy, Manila leaked like a sieve, and Ninoy Aquino, then a senator, revealed the details of the plan to the U.S. Embassy as early as September 12. Byroade, who distrusted Aquino, did not believe his story until a week later, when he received the text of the martial law proclamation from the high-level Filipino on the CIA payroll. Armed with the decree, he again attempted to change Marcos's mind.

By now Manila churned with rumors of Marcos's imminent move. Students decried his "evil and oppressive" plan, and a caucus of local mayors vowed to accept martial law "only over our dead bodies"—one declaring that "we are all trembling with rage." Afraid of a bloodbath that might ruin his image, Marcos waffled. Enrile urged him to act quickly, explaining that delays would give the opposition time to mobilize. Still Marcos delayed—and Enrile proceeded to trigger the coup.

Late on the afternoon of September 22, Enrile headed home from his Manila office in his blue Ford sedan, trailed as usual by a security escort. The convoy was approaching Harvard Street, behind the Wack Wack golf course, when assailants shooting from another automobile riddled his Ford. As Enrile related the attack at the time: "My driver slammed on the brakes and jumped out, firing at the car, which sped away." He owed his providential escape, he revealed, to a last-minute decision to ride with his guards. Years later, after he had turned against Marcos, he admitted to me that the ambush had been a sham. He was nowhere near the scene but had simply ordered his own gunmen to shoot up his empty Ford.

Marcos signed the martial law decree at nine o'clock that night—backdating the document to September 21 to make it evenly divisible by seven, his lucky number. He intended to use his power, he said in a radio broadcast, to "eliminate the threat of violent overthrow of the government"—adding in pompous military jargon, "we have fallen back on our last line of defense." Just after midnight, as troops fanned out across Manila, a constabulary colonel rapped on the door of a room at the Hilton hotel, where Ninoy Aquino was attending a political meeting. Ninoy recognized the officer as a personal friend who probably would have allowed him to slip away. Instead he apologized to his colleagues that he could not address them, boasting with boyish bravado, "I'm being arrested." During the coming weeks, Marcos closed down newspapers and radio and television stations, imposed censorship on those that remained in operation, seized the airlines and public utilities, and rounded up some six thousand political rivals, journalists, professors and student activists, branding them Communist sympathizers or outright Communists. He eventually released most of them—but Ninoy, who misgauged Marcos's capacity for vengeance, was to languish in prison for seven and a half years.

Speculation to the contrary, nothing in the White House logs of the period indicates that Nixon gave Marcos the green light by telephone. Marcos also told me years afterward that he had not spoken directly with Nixon at the time—though, he seemed to recall, he had taken Byroade's ambiguous pledge of support to be approval for martial law. But if he had not acted with Nixon's complicity, he was reassured by America's acquiescence. For months to come, State Department spokesmen replied to every question on the subject, "No comment." The Pentagon was similarly mute, one officer warning against any remarks that might "rock the boat" and jeopardize America's bases in the Philippines—then vital to the Vietnam War.

A senior State Department official finally broke the silence in March 1973, when Marshall Green, the assistant secretary for east Asia, testified before a congressional subcommittee. As chargé d'affaires in South Korea in 1961, he had boldly attempted to prevent the army from abrogating the constitution. Now, ironically, he defended Marcos's action, saying that there had been a "deplorable breakdown in the whole social fabric of the country, and something had to be done and done very drastically." So it was "understandable" for Marcos to have imposed martial law. To a congressman who asked if Marcos could be pressured into restoring democracy, Green replied, "We shouldn't pressure him, but remind him." More than a decade later, the United States was still trying in vain to "remind" Marcos that he should abandon absolute rule and return to truly representative government.

Soon after seizing total power, Marcos told Lee Lescaze, a *Washington Post* correspondent, that the Philippines was a "sick society" desperately in need of reforms. By February 1986, when Cory Aquino ousted the Marcoses, it was economically ruined, financially bankrupt, socially divided and besieged by two insurgencies. But whatever his original motives for declaring martial law, Marcos's dismal diagnosis of the Philippines at the time was not exaggerated. "Raw democracy," as many observers indulgently labeled the rough-and-tumble Filipino style, was plainly in disarray. Ninoy Aquino, who paradoxically agreed with Marcos that the system had collapsed, confided to me before his arrest that he would introduce some sort of authoritarian regime if he ever became president. Despite his practice of quoting Jefferson and Lincoln, his models were Syngman Rhee and Park Chung Hee, the autocratic leaders of South Korea—and, during one late-night bull session, Aquino even professed admiration for the "positive achievements" of Hitler and Mussolini. He tended to ramble in sophomoric style, and I dismissed his talk as trivial. Still, my frequent trips to the Philippines during those years left me doubting whether American institutions, implanted there at the turn of the century, could really take root in its soil.

★ ★ ★

I began covering the Philippines in the summer of 1959 as chief Asia correspondent for *Time* magazine, and it differed dramatically from the other countries on my far-flung beat. Gathering news in Thailand, Indonesia, Vietnam or Burma was as difficult as divining oracle bones. Leaders were subtle, elusive and, as the stereotype goes, inscrutable. Manila, by contrast, was a reporter's paradise. From the president to the lowliest official, everyone was easily accessible and often exhaustingly garrulous. Conversation seemed to be the main industry as politicians, businessmen and journalists lingered for hours over breakfast or after dinner, trading gossip and weaving theories. Juicy scandals, allegations and denials, charges and countercharges filled the press, flanked by fiery editorials and endless commentaries by prodigiously prolific columnists. At first it all appeared to me to be a mirror image of America, but soon I learned that the mirrors reflected distorted images, like those at a carnival sideshow. If this was not Asia, neither was it America.

The president, Carlos García, was then being attacked for a tax bill amid a barrage of invective. His opponents were calling him "ignorant, inept and venal," adjectives one of his supporters qualified as "the most scurrilous, malicious, reckless and irresponsible" he had ever heard. The fever could become convulsive, as I fortuitously noted one morning during a visit to the Philippine legislature—its entrance bearing the sign NO FIREARM IS ALLOWED INSIDE THE SESSION HALL. The governor of the central bank, a frail man named Miguel Cuaderno, had just arrived to plead for García's tax plan when he was spotted by Alfredo Montelibano, a spokesman for the sugar bloc, which opposed the measure. "You are mentally dishonest," shouted Montelibano, to which Cuaderno riposted, "And you are a coward who deserves to be shot." At that they dipped into their briefcases, and the assembly scrambled for safety. Tepid heads prevailed, however, and the hearings went on. My Filipino colleagues laughed off the rhubarb as routine; indeed, it rated only a paragraph in the newspapers next day.

But the sound and fury was not insignificant. García's controversial tax, ostensibly a levy on foreign currency transactions, was in fact a device to line his pocket. And, I quickly discovered, money more than anything else ruled the country. Or as an old provincial boss put it, "Politics in the Philippines is addition."

Getting elected, the first step in the political process, was expensive. Aside from newspaper, billboard, television and radio advertising, candidates had to pay campaign workers and bribe voters. Legislative aspirants spent $50,000 or $60,000, and a presidential race could cost $30 million or $40 million. Holding office was expensive. Legislators then earned the equivalent of $3,000 a year— obviously not enough to keep a home in Manila and another in their district, besides maintaining aides, bodyguards, servants and sympathetic newspapermen, providing for hordes of real and ritual kin, supporting a mistress and running for reelection. Hence they peddled their influence, procuring import grants, foreign currency licenses and taking commissions on the deals. Rich provincial families chose and financed local candidates in the expectation of favors or kickbacks from their profits. There were vast personal fortunes to be made in politics, and the bigger the politician the greater the opportunity. To cite a case, the official capital of the Philippines was shifted from Manila to Quezon City, an inconvenient suburb, only because the powerful boss of the area manipulated the government into purchasing his real estate there. García, a small-bore crook compared with the Marcoses, was breaking all records for corruption during the late 1950s.

Graft pervaded his government, from customs officials who connived with smugglers to a rural development agency controlled by landowners. At the time, Japan had pledged to pay the Philippines nearly $300 million as war damages in the form of ships and industrial machinery; García had promised the equipment to his cronies even before the agreement was signed. His most lucrative racket was the allocation of import licenses, which his wife and private secretary distributed in exchange for kickbacks. In 1958, the transactions grossed García some $700 million—much of which he used to underwrite his party's candidates. The enterprise created financial havoc. Instead of importing goods, the recipients sold the licenses, or used them to procure U.S. dollars, which they traded on the black market at twice the legal exchange rate. By obtaining new licenses, they could repeat the operation and reap fortunes simply through currency dealing.

The Philippines had by then been independent for more than a decade, and in theory its internal affairs should have been none of America's concern. But U.S. officials in Manila and Washington still felt responsible for the former colony, both for pragmatic and idealistic reasons. García's misrule threatened to ruin the country, revive the Communist rebellion and jeopardize America's interests—especially the U.S. bases. The "showcase of democracy" was in danger of being shattered. So it was urgent to restore sound government—if necessary through covert action. The CIA was the natural vehicle for operation, and Al Ulmer, head of its Asia division, assigned the job to Joseph Burkholder Smith, who had previously served in Indonesia and Singapore. Ulmer recalled a similar crisis in 1950, when Colonel Edward Lansdale had secretly groomed Ramón Magsaysay to replace the egregious President Elpidio Quirino. Ulmer wanted "another Magsaysay."

A Harvard graduate, then in his late thirties, Smith arrived in Manila in March 1958, posing as a civilian air force employee. He was a clandestine Diogenes in search of honest Filipino politicians who could be recruited to topple García. Looking back thirty years later, he recalled his mission with pride: "It was the American century, and we Americans had been chosen to do good in the world. We had a unique relationship with the Filipinos, special obligations toward them. The CIA was on the side of the angels, there's no doubt about it. We hoped to bring a political, economic and social revolution to the Philippines, break up the old oligarchy and promote genuine democracy."

Philippine law barred foreign involvement in elections, but it was common knowledge in Manila political circles that Lansdale and other CIA operatives had propelled Magsaysay into the presidency in 1953. Their "infrastructure," as the agency terms its local surrogates, cover groups, financial contacts and safe houses, was still intact when Smith landed. A key Filipino figure, Jaime Ferrer, a former Magsaysay aide, had been on the CIA payroll for years. He introduced Smith to several politicians with long-standing agency connections, all of whom were avid to supplant the García regime. Each lusted for office, however, and Smith's task was to unify them. When they asked him how much support they could expect, he prudently replied, "Substantial." They promptly nicknamed him "Mr. Substantial Support."

In fact, Smith's budget of $250,000 was paltry compared with García's millions. Smith stretched his funds by buying pesos at the free exchange rate in Hong Kong and smuggling them back to Manila—an illegal maneuver that doubled his assets. The CIA, which had a cooperative bank in Hong Kong, did the same throughout Southeast Asia, where currencies were soft and local officials pliable.

The Philippine political scene in 1959 was an almost incomprehensible tangle of party splits, personal vendettas and rivalries within rivalries. The CIA itself was divided. García, a *Nacionalista,* was opposed by his vice president, Diosdado Macapagal, a Liberal and longtime clandestine agency informer. Macapagal was in turn hated by the old Magsaysay coterie, which also disdained García. The CIA station chief favored Macapagal, who had presidential aspirations for 1961. But Smith, mesmerized by the Magsaysay myth, preferred the "Magsaysay boys," as they were called in Manila. He set his plan in motion during the summer of 1959.

Eight of the Philippine senate's twenty-four seats were due to be contested in the legislative elections scheduled for November, and the winners would gain national prominence as presidential material, possibly eclipsing Macapagal. Working feverishly, Smith cobbled together a slate of six candidates labeled the Grand Alliance, which he endowed with $200,000. The group included Manuel Manahan, a former Magsaysay assistant, and Raul Manglapus, who had been a junior member of Magsaysay's cabinet. Smith's favorite was Emmanuel Pelaez, a rich young attorney and also a Magsaysay disciple. The ticket was badly beaten. Smith insists to this day that, with more money, the CIA could have given the Philippines an honest and efficient government—and averted the subsequent catastrophe of the Marcos regime.

Marcos, then a member of the lower legislative chamber, also ran for the senate as a Liberal—with stunning success. Even though he was present at its creation, he had cagily avoided involvement in Smith's coalition. He had never been one of Magsaysay's insiders, and felt uncomfortable among them. Nor, with ample funds from his native province, did he need CIA money. Through his marriage to Imelda, he had also forged links with her powerful political family.

At the time, according to Smith, his Filipino protégés had welcomed his financing. But in 1987, when I canvased them, all except one denied the former CIA affiliation—some heatedly. Manahan ducked the issue, and Raul Manglapus, then Cory Aquino's foreign secretary, had become a strident critic of the United States. Emmanuel Pelaez, by contrast, admitted to the covert connection in general terms. He had served as vice president during the early 1960s, later practiced law and eventually became Cory's ambassador to Washington. "Freedom is a universal value," he said. "If one country helps to promote democracy in another, I have no inhibitions about it."

The CIA had paid Macapagal $50,000 during his term as García's vice president. In 1961, when he ran for president, the agency partly underwrote his campaign and gave him advice. But hardly had he been elected than his American mentors regretted their choice.

Then in his early fifties, Macapagal came from a poor peasant family—a rarity for a Filipino politician. His father had scraped to send him to high school and college, but he interrupted his studies to become an actor. A wealthy benefactor financed his return to law school, where he excelled. He was invited to join an American law firm as a practicing attorney, an honor for a Filipino prior to World War II. Out of gratitude to his American patrons, he named a son Arturo, after General Arthur MacArthur.

After serving as a diplomat abroad, Macapagal returned home in 1949 to run for the legislature from Pampanga, his native province. His grandiloquence

earned him a handsome majority, and once elected, he favored farm credit
programs and rural health projects. The Manila press praised him, and his
Liberal party nominated him for vice president in 1957, hoping that his apparent virtue would offset its presidential candidate, a sugar baron. Splitting the
ticket, the voters elected Macapagal as García's vice president. García treated
him as a pariah, banishing him to a dingy office and giving him a battered car
that chronically broke down. Macapagal capitalized on his humiliation, advertising himself as sober, frugal and puritanical, an antidote to García's corruption. He dressed for the role in a rumpled sports shirt and parted his patent-
leather hair in the middle, looking like a scrubbed yokel. His slogan in the 1961
presidential elections was pure corn syrup: "Honest Mac, the Poor Man's Best
Friend."

The Liberal party's business and landowning backers, whom García had
ostracized, had arranged Macapagal's nomination in hopes of manipulating
him after his election. García was too ill to campaign, and his supporters had
become sick of him. Macapagal won, declared a "new era of the common man"
modeled on Franklin D. Roosevelt's New Deal and even harked back to 1933
with his theme song, "Happy Days Are Here Again." Then, announcing a vast
house cleaning, he banned his family from engaging in business, put the
presidential yacht up for sale and introduced a hodgepodge of plans, including
land reforms. Nothing changed. After famished years on the outside, his
supporters hungrily demanded privileges. He could not control the venal
politicians and bureaucrats, and his government soon slid into corruption and
inefficiency. But, he would rosily assure me during my trips to Manila, the
problems were merely "the growing pains of democracy."

The disarray was visible, widespread and, after a while, monotonous. The
port of Manila was a hive of graft, with gangs protected by politicians working
with customs officials to smuggle in everything from automobiles and air
conditioners to textiles and cigarettes. Rackets abounded in fake import licenses and fraudulent invoices, requiring businessmen to keep two or three sets
of ledgers. Thieves showed extraordinary ingenuity, as I learned on a visit to
Clark Field, where a group of Filipinos disguised as firemen had recently
walked briskly onto the base and driven away with the hook and ladder—the
U.S. Military Police smartly saluting them through the gate. Presumably they
dismantled the vehicle and sold the spare parts. Violence had reached epidemic
proportions: In 1964, Manila recorded eight hundred homicides, compared
with fewer than six hundred in New York City—whose population was eight
times larger. Calling on a Filipino acquaintance one afternoon, I found him
in his garden, target-practicing with a revolver as his small son picked up the
brass. He proudly showed me his arsenal, which included a dozen rifles,
shotguns and his prize, an automatic weapon. Ninoy Aquino, whom I first met
then, cruised around town in a bulletproof limousine, its upholstery fitted with
slots for machine guns.

Macapagal concocted nationalist issues as a distraction. Resorting to an old
tactic, he expelled numbers of Chinese, many of them naturalized citizens. He
deported an American businessman, Harry Stonehill, who had amassed an
estimated $50 million from real estate, tobacco and other enterprises, allegedly
with help from Filipino politicians, including members of Macapagal's cabinet.
To everyone's relief, Stonehill took his secrets with him. Macapagal won

nationalist applause by shifting the national holiday, July 4, the anniversary of independence from the United States in 1946, to June 12, the day in 1898 that Emilio Aguinaldo declared Philippine sovereignty. Years afterward, he told me the real reason for the change: "When I was in the diplomatic corps, I noticed that nobody came to our receptions on the Fourth of July, but went to the American Embassy instead. So, to compete, I decided that we needed a different holiday."

By 1965, as he prepared to run again, Macapagal was in distress. His agrarian reform proposals had infuriated the landed gentry, and his failure to enforce them disappointed the peasants. Prices and unemployment had risen, and he had not curbed corruption. Worse yet, he was abandoned by key Liberals—notably Ferdinand Marcos, who defected to the rival *Nacionalistas,* assailing Macapagal for reneging on a pledge to bequeath him the presidency. Marcos then gained the *Nacionalista* nomination for president—again illustrating the emptiness of party affiliations in the Philippines.

The 1965 campaign was the costliest on record. Together the two men spent more than $100 million on advertising and festivals, paying off local bosses, fixers, goons—and voters. Marcos bulged with cash. Through Imelda he had inveigled Fernando Lopez into running with him for vice president, bringing in the Lopez family's incalculable wealth. He was financed by rich Chinese, who recalled Macapagal's persecution of their compatriots, and donations arrived from Filipinos in California and Hawaii, many of them immigrants from Marcos's native province of Ilocos Norte. Marcos copied John F. Kennedy, picturing himself as young and dynamic, while Imelda tried to imitate Jackie. The U.S. Embassy in Manila remained neutral, but Francis Tatu advised them informally—suggesting among other show biz ideas that Imelda sing a revised version of "Hello, Dolly" entitled "Hello, Marcos."

Macapagal's publicists smeared the couple by spreading rumors that Imelda had played in porno films and, recalling that Marcos had once been charged with murder, labeled him a "deliberate killer." It was a moral struggle, Macapagal said, forecasting that his victory would represent "the triumph of good over evil." But he was no match for Marcos's eloquence and Imelda's beauty. Marcos beat him by more than six hundred thousand votes. About five percent of the eight million ballots were rigged, and roughly fifty people died in clashes—a quiet election by Philippine standards. On the morning of December 30, 1965, Marcos was inaugurated under a searing sun at the Luneta, the ebullient Vice President Hubert Humphrey among the dignitaries. He had been given a "mandate for greatness," Marcos intoned, vowing to end "every form of waste or conspicuous consumption and extravagance" and to uphold "the supremacy of the law."

★ ★ ★

Apart from watching him in action, I interviewed Marcos often before and during his years in power and following his fall. I talked with his friends and foes and read much of the literature about him, including his own accounts. He lied or distorted events beyond credulity, while his sympathizers and enemies, grinding their own axes, were frequently just as untrustworthy. Out of it all emerges the portrait of a complex, brilliant, cunning yet essentially cautious man. "When Marcos makes a sudden move," a Filipino commentator once remarked, "he has probably planned it years in advance."

Isolated in his airless palace, Marcos ultimately lost touch with reality. His corrupt administration was totally discredited by late 1985, yet his blind belief in his own invincibility prompted him to schedule the election against Cory Aquino that spelled his doom. The next year, broken and bitter, he confided to me amid the splendid solitude of his Honolulu exile, "It was the biggest mistake I ever made." Still, he had governed the Philippines for two decades, nearly half its span as a sovereign nation. He ruled absolutely for two thirds of that period, the extraordinary length of his tenure ranking him among the world's most durable leaders.

With the army buttressing him, Marcos wielded complete authority, imposing his will through decree. But he was not a classic dictator who arbitrarily jailed or repressed masses of opponents. On the contrary, he weaved and bobbed like the boxer he had been in his youth, jabbing, feinting, punching, retreating. He would crack down, loosen up, tighten his grip, relax—continually confecting earnest legalisms to cloak his skulduggery, constantly promising that his autocracy was only temporary. In brief, he was a grand master of manipulation. He persuaded many respectable Filipinos that he alone could restore order and prosperity, as indeed he did at the start of martial law. Similarly, he convinced successive American presidents that only he could crush the Communists and guarantee stability, thereby assuring the continuity of the U.S. bases.

Revolutionary rhetoric notwithstanding, Marcos was not overthrown in the end because Filipinos clamored for the return of democracy. He crumbled under the sheer weight of his flagrant mismanagement and venality, which bankrupted the country, alienating the Manila business community and the Catholic hierarchy, his most enthusiastic supporters at the beginning. They crystallized around Cory Aquino, who represented the old oligarchy that Marcos had dispossessed. Had Marcos been an honest despot who deprived his people of political freedom but offered them economic growth in exchange, as Singapore's Prime Minister Lee Kuan Yew and the South Korean generals have done, he probably could have lasted forever. However, in retrospect both he and his population were victims of his illusions.

Late in 1964, before he first ran for president, he hired an American writer named Hartzell Spence to produce his biography. The book, entitled *For Every Tear a Victory,* was unabashed hagiography that Marcos undoubtedly dictated—its dedication asserting that he "would today be counted one of America's greatest heroes" had he been born "white-skinned" in the United States rather than "brown-skinned" in the Philippines. He went on to embellish his life story over the years ahead until he seemed to be afflicted by an incurable case of mythomania. Even his private diaries were filled with falsehoods—lies about himself to himself. But he fabricated his image for a purpose.

He hoped to depict himself as the personification of the Philippines, just as the ancient divine emperors of Asia had embodied the soul of the nation. Emulating the legendary Khmer rulers, whose sculpted heads peer down from the temples of Angkor, he had his bust carved into a hillside of central Luzon. He contrived a cavalcade of noble, warrior, peasant, artistic, colonial and nationalist ancestors, as if their collective spirit resided in him. Imelda, who shared his delusions of grandeur, contemplated the commissioning of a panoramic mural of the country's history in which every face would bear a Marcos family resemblance. Consonant with all this, Marcos dreamed of founding a royal dynasty. His feckless son, Ferdinand junior, known as Bong Bong, whom he named governor of his native province of Ilocos Norte, would be his heir. He had Imelda, the potential queen mother, elected governor of Manila and gave her a seat in his cabinet as well as myriad other public positions. And, like a feudal monarch, he filled his court with faithful relatives and cronies, among them General Fabian Ver, the armed forces Chief of Staff, a cousin.

Imelda made no effort to conceal their ambitions either. She ordered a garish painting of them and their three children, their chests ablaze with regal sashes and decorations. The painting adorned the audience chamber of the Malacañang palace, where Marcos would preside over formal functions from a gilded throne. As befit his imperial presidency, he received visitors to his private study from behind a desk perched on a dais, majestically peering down on the guest as video cameras taped the session. Craning my neck one morning in July 1985, I listened for three hours as he delivered an often incoherent and incongruous monologue on his life.

He was born Ferdinand Edralin Marcos on September 11, 1917, in Ilocos Norte, the northernmost province of Luzon, a rugged region of hardy folk often compared to the Scots. As he told it, his forebears were Malay chiefs who dominated the area before the Spanish arrived and later intermarried with Chinese settlers. They served the Spanish as local officials, becoming rich landowners. Subsequently they rallied to the nationalists to fight for independence from Spain, afterward resisted the U.S. conquest and finally pledged allegiance to America. In the process, they renounced Catholicism to follow Gregorio Aglipay, a nationalist priest who defied the Vatican to found a revolutionary church. He escaped unscathed from World War II, Marcos said, because Aglipay had given him an *anting anting,* an amulet made of magic wood that rendered its holder invisible. On other occasions, he recalled that he had been badly wounded during the war, once by a Japanese mortar shell that ripped open his abdomen.

In the populist version, Marcos pictured himself as a regular boy whose parents "discouraged elitism" and urged him to befriend the peasants. He would contradict that account, however, by recalling that his mother, Josefa, a teacher, and his father, Mariano, a school supervisor who entered politics, exhorted him to excell—which he did. An obsessive achiever, he was an energetic and disciplined student whose phenomenal memory lifted him to the head of his class at the University of the Philippines Law School, where he swept the top prizes for debating, oratory and military science. He scored so high on the bar examinations that he was suspected of cheating—until, to refute the allegation, he recited legal texts by heart. The fear of failure tormented him. He yearned for an Ivy League diploma with such intensity that once he surprised an interviewer by referring to "my Harvard classmates." Asked to explain, he lamely replied that he was planning to go to Harvard when World War II intervened. Afterward, he went on, Harvard "threatened" to award him an honorary doctorate, but by then he was too busy and responded, "We'll do it some other time." In fact, he had desperately lobbied for an honorary Harvard degree prior to a trip to the United States in 1966;

despite promises to help, State Department officials did nothing. As an ultimate irony, Harvard in 1980 gave a fellowship to Ninoy Aquino, his archenemy.

Marcos claimed to have been an Olympic athlete—yet another fib. But in college he had been a varsity swimmer, wrestler and boxer as well as captain of the pistol and rifle teams. Taut and wiry at five and a half feet, he kept in superb shape into his fifties by playing golf and exercising daily and, until medical treatments made him puffy in his twilight years, maintained his weight at a hundred and thirty pounds. He neither drank nor smoked, and ate sparingly at Imelda's sumptuous banquets, which featured mounds of caviar and gallons of champagne. To eat with him alone, as I once did, was monastic. Seated in a luxurious chamber of the presidential palace, he picked away at a leathery cutlet and sipped a glass of water.

In December 1938, when he was twenty-one, he hit the limelight in a dramatic episode. Arrested shortly before his graduation from law school, he was charged with murdering the candidate who had humiliated and defeated his father in an election in their native province three years earlier. In the Philippines, where violence chronically mars politics, such incidents usually spin into endless clan feuds rather than court cases. Marcos later contended that Manuel Quezon, then president of the Philippine commonwealth, had personally ordered his prosecution in reprisal for his role as a student agitator. Marcos's accusation against Quezon was evidently designed to boost his own importance. Whatever the truth, he was convicted and sentenced to seventeen years in prison. He delivered an emotional plea to be released on bail so that he could finish law school and prepare an appeal to the Supreme Court. The judge, reduced to tears, consented.

By now Marcos had become a celebrity to the Filipinos, who cherish a juicy melodrama. Most probably believed that he had fired the fatal shot; years afterward, his intimates swore, he boasted of it. But even if he was guilty, he had vindicated his father's honor, as filial piety required. In a reciprocal gesture of family solidarity, his mother sold her property to cover his legal fees. His fellow students acclaimed him for challenging the authorities, and the press, which published the full text of his plea for bail, vaunted him as the valiant underdog struggling for justice against a mindless government machine. Several distinguished attorneys had filed petitions on his behalf prior to his appearance before the Supreme Court in October 1940.

Marcos wore a white sharkskin suit and white shoes to symbolize his purity and introduced a three-volume brief studded with quotations from Shakespeare, Melville and Henry James. Arguing in his own defense, he did not protest his innocence but pleaded that the verdict was technically flawed. He impressed José Laurel, the justice assigned to the case, who upheld Marcos after concluding that the country needed bright young men like him. Loyal to the Filipino custom of *utang na loob,* Marcos remembered his debt of gratitude to Laurel during the war. Despite his purported guerrilla resistance against the Japanese, he covertly cooperated with Laurel, who served as Japan's puppet president. He also left the Laurel family's property intact after his proclamation of martial law, while he confiscated the holdings of other old dynasties. Nor did he oppress Laurel's son Salvador, who belatedly turned against him in 1980 and subsequently ran as Cory Aquino's vice presidential candidate.

Marcos never forgave Quezon, however. As Marcos later told the story through Spence's biography, Quezon apologized after his acquittal and offered to appoint him chief public prosecutor. Marcos refused; he would not work for a regime that disregarded "the way justice should flourish in a nation of free men." The exchange probably never occurred, but it was daring for Marcos to have related it in 1964. Then dead for twenty years, Quezon was the immortal founder of the Philippine republic, and for Marcos to decry him at that early stage in his own career was as risky as an American politician disparaging George Washington. But Marcos was already driven by the overweening sense of moral superiority that he was to exhibit in power. Equally important, he was consumed by his clan obligations. Quezon had endorsed the opponent who had insulted his father, and so Marcos was fulfilling a family duty. Quezon's children, similarly moved by filial respect, sued Marcos for libeling their father in Spence's book. The suit, largely a gesture, went unresolved.

One of Marcos's most cherished conceits was his command of the Ang Mga Maharlika, the World War II group of eight thousand guerrillas who had roamed Luzon, harassing the Japanese and radioing intelligence to the U.S. forces. He claimed to have earned at least thirty awards, among them the Congressional Medal of Honor—a score that ranked him above Audie Murphy, the most-decorated American soldier of the war. Marcos's purported heroism was his rise to manhood, his profile in courage, his passport to political prominence, the symbol of his shared loyalty to America and the Philippines, his epiphany. "My forebears were great warriors," he would say, paying homage to his family. He adopted Maharlika as his badge of honor. As president he baptized one of the country's main arteries the Maharlika Highway, unveiled a Maharlika Hall at Malacañang and even contemplated Maharlika as a new name for the Philippines.

Marcos did serve as a lieutenant during the defense of Bataan, winning a medal for valor. Captured, he was later released from enemy internment. His story after that is a blur of exaggeration and invention. American and Filipino historians studied thousands of files without finding a trace of his name or unit, but he continued, undaunted, to relate his ventures. In January 1986, an American scholar named Alfred McCoy unearthed U.S. Army records in the National Archives in Washington that fully documented the fraud. American officers during the war had rejected Marcos's requests for funds and supplies on the grounds that his movement was phony. His postwar claims for benefits were also rebuffed—one U.S. investigator flatly declaring that he "did not exercise any control over a guerrilla organization" and another concluding that his men had been "hoodlums" engaged in trafficking with the enemy. John Sharkey of *The Washington Post* had meanwhile discovered that Marcos's medals were mostly fake. And on top of all this came new proof that his father, Mariano, whom he had portrayed as a patriot executed by the Japanese, had been hacked to pieces by Filipino guerrillas as an enemy agent.

The disclosures devastated Marcos just as he was reeling under the impact of the massive protests against his misrule inspired by Cory Aquino; like a punch drunk boxer, he flailed back, alleging plots to smear his reputation. His plaintive, almost pathetic reaction suggested that he had carried on the charade for so long that he actually believed it. But, for a long time, so did nearly everyone else.

Sifting fact from fiction in the Philippines after the war was virtually impossible. Many guerrillas emerged from the jungles without records to prove their exploits. Most Filipinos, after lying and conniving to survive the enemy occupation, were accustomed to deception. Nor did General Douglas MacArthur, their savior, do much to restore morality. By exculpating the Japanese collaborators, he erased the line between loyalty and treason, and now everyone could recount spurious stories of heroism—including Marcos.

Marcos also had a powerful patron in President Manuel Roxas, who owed his election in 1946 to MacArthur's blessing. Marcos was practicing law in Manila when Roxas, seeking young talent for the new Liberal party, persuaded him to enter politics. In 1949, at the age of thirty-two, Marcos ran for the lower house of the legislature. He attracted support from the old dynasties of Ilocos Norte by appealing to their provincial pride. "Elect me now," he repeated at rallies, "and I promise you an Ilocano president in twenty years." He won easily in the dirtiest race in Philippine history to date, becoming the youngest member of the legislature.

As chairman of the committee supervising import controls, he earned payoffs for expediting licenses. The tobacco lords of Ilocos Norte feathered his nest in return for favors, and he took sums from Harry Stonehill, the freewheeling American entrepreneur. But ethics were elastic in Manila, as they are today, and his career advanced. He mastered the rhetoric of reform, inveighed against corruption and espoused such popular causes as benefits for war veterans, while maintaining close ties to the oligarchy and coddling the press. After three terms in the lower house, he won a landslide victory in the senate election of 1959. He wisely spurned support from the CIA, whose slate was routed.

Filipinos may be pious Catholics, but in Latin fashion, they are not prudish, and Marcos suffered no opprobrium from his liaison with Carmen Ortega, a former beauty pageant winner by whom he had four children. As he calculated his future, however, he saw the advantages of marriage into a powerful political clan. He discarded Carmen and, in 1954, wed Imelda Romualdez after a whirlwind romance. Her family, rooted in Leyte, included an early Supreme Court justice, governors and senior legislators. Marcos knew that, though they were rival *Nacionalistas,* the Romualdezes would be bound by kinship obligations to back him despite his Liberal affiliation. He also factored the regional balance into the equation. "Imelda was from the south and I'm a northerner," he explained to me years later, "and together we covered the country."

I first met Imelda at an informal dinner with a group of their friends at the end of 1965, just after Marcos had been elected president. It was a relaxed party in typical Filipino style. The table groaned under a vast assortment of native dishes, and the beer flowed as freely as the talk, most of it *tsismis,* Tagalog for gossip, the common currency of Manila conversation. Then thirty-six and the mother of three, Imelda was imposingly beautiful. She was tall for a Filipino woman, a trait she spicily traced to Spanish priests in her lineage, and she accentuated her height by coiffing her black hair in a pile. Her round face and soft features betrayed her Malay origins, and there was a hint of Chinese ancestry in her sloe eyes. Nothing about her portended the grotesque egocentric of subsequent years. She seemed to be the ideal political wife, dutifully dedicated to her husband's career. Subdued, almost shy, she smiled and remained silent except to encourage the chattering men to eat. I remembered two decades later that Cory Aquino, whom I first met at that time, also served cake and coffee quietly as Ninoy talked a streak.

Imelda announced through a spokesman in 1965 that she planned to be more than "merely a decorative figure." At the beginning, however, she was all charm. In September 1966, she made her international debut on an official trip with Marcos to the United States. She entranced Lyndon Johnson, a pushover for pretty women, by singing at a White House evening that whirled on past one in the morning. The press gushed, a *Washington Star* columnist calling her "a blessing not only to her own country, but to the world." Then, moving to New York, she mingled with the Whitneys, Rockefellers and Fords at a Metropolitan Opera premiere. Still a schoolgirl at heart, she erupted enviously to a Manila magazine, "Wow! In America, when they're rich they're *really* rich."

But she would outdo them. The next month, when Johnson visited Manila, she gave him a reception that might have been staged by Cecil B. DeMille. Like Marie Antoinette playing peasant in the park of Versailles, she dubbed it a *"barrio* fiesta." She illuminated the expansive palace gardens with eight thousand paper lanterns and treated the three thousand guests, myself among them, to enough food to sustain a real *barrio* for a year. Lovely starlets and strolling musicians threaded through the crowd, troupes performed native dances and Imelda crowned the evening by singing for Johnson, who gazed at her in rapture. Lady Bird, a veteran of big Texas parties, said: "I have rarely seen a night to equal it."

Imelda intuitively understood Oscar Wilde's aphorism that nothing succeeds like excess, and from then on she tried to snare every visiting American president, congressman, company executive and journalist in her opulent web—both to bulwark Marcos and to enhance her own prestige. The strategy worked. Guests would return from Manila dazzled by her hospitality as she and Marcos drove the country into hock to defer the bills.

"Committed to the finer things in life," as her press releases declared, Imelda increasingly posed as a patron of the arts. Dame Margot Fonteyn, the dancer, and pianist Van Cliburn flew to Manila at her expense. She spent a fortune on a cultural center, a luxury the crippled economy could scarcely afford, and launched a film festival featuring porno movies. In June 1983, in a show biz extravaganza, she married her elder daughter Irene to Gregorio Araneta, the scion of a distinguished Spanish *mestizo* family. The event, held in Ilocos Norte, cost $10 million, more than $1 million of which went toward restoring the old church in Marcos's hometown of Sarrat, the site of the religious ceremony. Marcos constructed a jet airstrip in the remote area and chartered planes flew in five hundred guests, who were housed in a sprawling hotel built for the occasion—which later fell into disrepair. Imelda filched some of the money from a typhoon relief fund, and Marcos's rich cronies contributed. The groom's father had a heart attack after discovering that Imelda had painted his collection of antique altar candles white for the wedding, thus destroying their natural patina.

In January 1984, returning to Manila after an absence of several years, I was amazed by Imelda's transformation. By now stout and a bit blowzy, she suffered from insomnia, which she proudly termed her "surplus of energy." She would sit up until three or four in the morning, in effect talking to herself in an often incomprehensible stream of consciousness, as her courtiers, too faithful to leave, fidgeted or dozed fitfully. One of her pet topics was the need for a "cosmic vision of development" based on "a human order with a moral concept," gibberish that could keep her going for hours. Desperate for fresh company, she somehow located me one evening at an obscure café and sent a car to fetch me to a private club, where she was relating an interminable anecdote to a group of exhausted cronies—one of them actually asleep at the table. It was nearly dawn when she announced, "Oh, it must be midnight, and I'm keeping everyone awake."

By then Ninoy Aquino had been dead for six months, and the protests against the Marcoses were mounting, but Imelda behaved as if her reign would never end. On another evening, we zipped through Manila in her stretch limousine, a squadron of motorcycle police escorting us across the usually clogged city. Noticing that the traffic was blocked at every intersection, I remarked that the motorists must have been waiting for hours in the stifling heat. Tossing her head, she replied, "This is what power is all about."

With Marcos's approval, she appointed herself a roving envoy, relentlessly roaming the world to meet with Leonid Brezhnev and Fidel Castro, Emperor Hirohito, Pope John Paul II and the American presidents—basking in the reflection of their importance. Her private salon at the Malacañang was cluttered with their signed photographs, including a portrait of Nancy Reagan inscribed "With Love," and she reveled in her recollections of them. Mao Zedong, she boasted to me, had kissed her hand and called her "Meldy." She claimed to know that Muammar el-Qaddafi was having a homosexual affair with his foreign minister and expressed shock at Idi Amin's habit of urinating in public. Vaunting her big-business connections, she once apologized for keeping me waiting outside her study; she had been on an overseas call with Armand Hammer, chairman of Occidental Petroleum, discussing a deal to import coal from China. "I can give you a piece of the action," she joked in a display of entrepreneurial jargon. It was all *palabas,* Tagalog for "showiness," designed to radiate her image. During a trip to New York in 1984, when the Philippines was hemorrhaging from its multibillion-dollar debt to the global banking community, she had her picture taken with a leading financier. It soon appeared in Marcos-controlled Manila press above the caption FIRST LADY NEGOTIATES FOREIGN DEBT.

She even collected dead celebrities, once recalling to me how MacArthur had adopted her after his landing on Leyte in October 1944, when she was fifteen. As she told it, he would conceal her in his car as he reviewed his troops. He had heard her sing, she went on, and introduced her to Irving Berlin, who was there to entertain the U.S. soldiers, and he in turn invited her to join his act. She also intimated that MacArthur had a love affair with her aunt and even described in clinical detail their coupling on the beach. Astounded, I checked the story with one of her assistants, who irreverently whispered in my ear, "Bullshit." The tale mirrored Imelda's vision of herself. MacArthur had been a deity to Filipinos of her generation, and she was sharing his glory. Similarly, Marcos claimed that MacArthur had personally decorated him.

A prodigious social climber, Imelda pursued Rockefellers and Fords, and even dreamed of betrothing her daughter Imee to Prince Charles of Britain—a brainstorm that hit her in 1971 during a trip to Iran, where the shah's imperial splendor filled her with jealousy. Imee defiantly wed a divorced Filipino basketball coach, driving her mother to despair. Imelda's coterie included actor George Hamilton, Christina Ford, the former wife of Henry Ford II, and Van Cliburn, who would serenade her by telephone from Texas if he could not jet to Manila. After her disgrace, when having been linked to the Marcoses was tantamount to leprosy, the upper crust disowned her. "She was such an awful woman," said John Fairchild, publisher of *Women's Wear Daily,* whose pages she once graced. During her heyday, however, her fancy friends had accepted her costly gifts and flocked to her lavish parties, which she videotaped for her vast film archive; that she had amused them testified to their own tawdriness. Striving to sound liberated, she would gossip about the sex life of her chums, even circulating the rumor that she was a lesbian. She clumsily contrived to appear cosmopolitan. "I adore New York because it's so Jewish," she once exclaimed to me over dinner—then, to prove the point, she ordered the restaurant orchestra to play from *Fiddler on the Roof.* My wife, Annette, sized up Imelda in an instant. At their first meeting in 1985, Imelda scrutinized her from her toenails to her hairdo and blurted, "Stanley, you've got it all." Annette muttered under her breath, "Tacky."

Imelda was deeply upset by reports of the three thousand pairs of shoes found after her escape from Manila in February 1986. Though they were mostly French and Italian, she later insisted to me in Honolulu that she had accumulated them to promote the Philippine shoe industry "on my trips abroad." But her footwear fetish was merely neurotic compared with the madness of her global spending sprees. She traveled with film crews, hairdressers, bodyguards and other retainers, including her "blue ladies," wealthy matrons in aquamarine dresses whose husbands relied on Marcos for favors and usually financed the junkets—if anyone did. After the director of Philippine Airlines repeatedly dunned Imelda to pay for the chartered jumbo jets, Marcos nationalized the company.

Arriving in Tokyo, Rome or Paris, she would buy racks of clothes and trays of diamonds along with often unauthenticated antiques and paintings. She squandered $12 million on jewelry in a single day in Geneva. In Manhattan, where she stayed in MacArthur's former suite at the Waldorf-Astoria, she tipped the bellhops with $100 bills and once gave a Cartier watch to an amazed doorman. Bloomingdale's opened especially for her on Sunday, sending her courtiers into a frenzy. Igor Kropotkin, then president of Scribner's bookshop, recalled their assault: "They landed like locusts, taking every third copy off the shelves, sometimes every second copy—art books, poetry, classics, travel, history, biography." When he urged Imelda to examine his rare volumes, she pleaded lack of time and delegated him to pick whatever he liked for her—adding, "Make them pretty." Cory Aquino later exhibited the abandoned loot as a moral lesson in avarice. Piles of crates were still sealed, like those in the cellar of Citizen Kane's castle. I wondered whether Imelda too had her secret "Rosebud" among the airport souvenirs and other kitsch that, I noticed, filled the Marcos's house of exile in Honolulu.

"I have surpassed Cinderella," Imelda once said, but she was Cinderella with a twist. Instead of marrying the handsome prince and living happily ever after, she overcompensated for her miserable childhood by seeking revenge against the upper classes while claiming to be one of them. She invented a confused fairy tale of her early life that made Marcos's exaggerated reminiscences seem pale by comparison.

Her family, Imelda bragged, was "one of the mightiest political clans of the country," depicting her father as a lawyer, scholar, artist and composer—"a Renaissance man." Her story was partly true. Descended from Malays, Chinese and Spaniards, including a couple of friars, the Romauldez dynasty was indeed prominent on Leyte and in Manila, where its scions became judges, politicians and officials. But Imelda's father, Vicente Orestes, was a misfit who flitted from job to job. After his first wife died, burdening him with five children, he remarried and sired six more. Imelda Remedios Visitación, the eldest of the second brood, was born on July 2, 1929, in Tolosa, a lovely little Leyte port. Later she built a grandiose "ancestral home" there to dramatize the fiction of her nobility.

Troubles marred her youth. Her parents were constantly quarreling, separating and reconciling. Unable to make ends meet, they moved to Manila to mooch off relatives, who lodged the children in a squalid garage. When Imelda was eight, her mother died—a loss that perhaps she subconsciously resented thereafter. She effaced her mother's memory and mythologized her floundering father. A failure in Manila, he returned to Leyte on the eve of World War II, finding work as a minor administrator in a law school. He subsequently scrounged enough military surplus from the invading American forces to slap together a house so shabby that Imelda was too ashamed to invite her friends over. She sailed through high school on her popularity, which won her election as student body president in college. A classmate's autograph album reveals a typical American teenager. Her favorite dishes, Imelda wrote, were fried chicken and ice cream, her favorite musical composition George Gershwin's *Rhapsody in Blue,* her favorite expression the GI chant "Hubba-hubba!" With or without MacArthur or Irving Berlin, she visited the U.S. Army camps and sang for the troops. Years afterward, she flew a group of American veterans back to Leyte and entertained them throughout the night with wartime songs.

In 1952, at the age of twenty-three, Imelda arrived in Manila with five pesos in her purse, seeking her fortune. Every Filipino house, however humble, is open to poor kinfolk, and she moved in with a politically powerful cousin— sharing a room with a maid. He found her work in a government bank after her father objected to her singing in a music store. Through the cousin she also met politicians and journalists, occasionally dating Ninoy Aquino, then a young reporter. Her first break came in 1953, when a magazine editor featured her face on his cover. With that she entered a beauty contest and won the title of Miss Manila—as much from nerve as from good looks. The jury had crowned another woman, but Imelda tearfully appealed to the mayor, who vetoed the verdict and awarded her the prize. A formidable philanderer, he expired a few years later from overexertion in a Chinese brothel. His reputation spawned rumors that Imelda had swayed him with more than tears.

"I'm getting married," Marcos confided to a colleague on seeing Imelda's magazine picture. He arranged an introduction and, after an eleven-day courtship, won her hand. According to one account, she consented after he showed her his cache of illicit dollars. Until then a member of the independent

Aglipayan church, he quickly had himself baptized a Catholic. A thousand guests—mostly politicians, officials and their families—attended the wedding at a Manila cathedral on May 1, 1954. President Ramón Magsaysay, one of their sponsors, lent the couple the Malacañang gardens for the reception.

Imelda should have been overjoyed, but the adjustment to Marcos's career was difficult. Still a provincial, she was snubbed by Manila's socialites. Marcos worked hard and often left her alone with his mother, who by Filipino custom shared their house. A sexual acrobat, he was soon consorting with courtesans, including a beauty who specialized in servicing prominent politicians. In 1960, Imelda buckled under the pressure and flew to New York to consult a psychiatrist—who prescribed tranquilizers and advised: Either quit Marcos or adapt to his life-style. She adapted. Returning home, she learned to hobnob with his political cronies and appeared at fancy functions in expensive dresses and jewels. But she was never fully stable. Her subsequent shopping binges and insomniac soliloquies plainly reflected manic tendencies.

By 1964, Imelda was completely on the team. She helped Marcos to secure the *Nacionalista* presidential nomination by lobbying delegates at the party convention. Bursting into sobs, she persuaded Fernando Lopez to run as vice president—then crisply made him sign a pledge to finance the campaign out of his fabulously rich family fortune. The next year she played a vital role in the campaign, speaking and singing at rallies, organizing women and traveling to remote spots to win over the local bosses who decided the count. After his victory, Marcos said: "She was worth a million votes."

★ ★ ★

Certain that the United States engineered every event in the country, Filipinos concluded that Marcos was America's choice. The conviction improved Marcos's image; now, it was assumed, he would be able to obtain increased U.S. aid. The Marcoses also believed that the Americans, in some mysterious way, were responsible for their success. Shortly after the election, Imelda's brother Benjamin Romauldez, a deceptively oafish-looking character nicknamed "Kokoy," made a proposal to Francis Tatu, who had monitored Marcos's campaign and offered a few helpful hints. "Frank," he said, "we know that you placed America behind us, so write your own ticket. What if we got the State Department to name you our foreign affairs adviser?" Tatu demurred. Whatever his own sympathies, he explained, U.S. policy had been "hands off." In any case, he was not about to scrap his diplomatic career to serve Marcos. Kokoy dangled a fatter plum. Marcos, he mused, might nationalize Benguet, the big gold-mining and timber company. "Frank," Kokoy persisted, "we could appoint you director."

Tatu had told the truth: America had been neutral in the election. But, along with other U.S. Embassy officials, he was impressed by Marcos. "We had great faith in him," Tatu recalled years later. "Marcos was a tremendous guy, solid and dedicated. We believed his promises to renovate the society, to introduce land reform, social justice, real democracy." President Johnson's aide Jack Valenti, who attended Marcos's inauguration, was equally dazzled. Marcos, he wrote to Johnson, was "enormously intelligent" as well as "tough," and "one of the most magnetic speakers" he had ever heard. Persuaded by Valenti and others, Johnson invited the Marcoses to Washington in September 1966 as the American press lionized the couple. Imelda was extolled in *Life* as having a combination of Jackie Kennedy's "grace" and Eleanor Roosevelt's "energy," and *Time* praised Marcos's "dynamic, selfless leadership." A note of caution crept into a message to the State Department from William McCormick Blair, Jr., the U.S. ambassador to Manila. Despite his admiration for Marcos, he warned against expecting "extravagant" results from him. At that stage, Blair could not envision the future Marcos autocracy. Nevertheless, he foresaw "profound" problems if Marcos became so convinced of his own importance to the United States that he attempted to manipulate American policy and practice for his own purposes.

Blair was prescient. Beginning in late 1965, Marcos did in fact proceed to influence U.S. policy to suit himself. He started with the accurate perception that Lyndon Johnson was haunted by the nightmare of the Vietnam War. Johnson, then pouring American troops into the conflict, desperately hoped to show the American public that the nations of the region, the "dominoes" that would supposedly topple should the Communists prevail, shared his worries and were eager to participate in the struggle. In reality, the countries of the area were primarily preoccupied with their internal problems, but they would accommodate Johnson if he footed the bill. Thus, at America's expense, Australia, New Zealand, Thailand and South Korea sent in substantial forces relative to the size of their populations. Marcos, on the other hand, set out to extract a maximum profit from a minimal investment and, through shrewd bargaining, he succeeded. So, at the outset of his term, he learned to exert leverage over the United States. The lesson served him well for the next twenty years.

By the end of 1965, I had become Asia correspondent for *The Washington Post,* and Marcos was aware that Johnson, a newspaper junkie, would read my dispatches over breakfast. He granted me an interview in Manila in November to say that he would commit an engineer battalion of two thousand men to Vietnam following his inauguration a month later. Earlier, he explained, he had opposed Philippine involvement out of fear of an American withdrawal— but now that Johnson was displaying a "resolute will to slug it out, we have been reassured." Hinting that he would need more than the $6 million he already expected from Johnson to sustain the unit, he added that there was "real goodwill toward the United States in the Philippines [and] no problem between us cannot be solved easily." The interview was an opening bid in his bargaining. Soon he raised the ante.

On one pretext or another, he delayed the deployment of the Philippine battalion until Johnson fulfilled his request for an official invitation to the United States. Finally, in September 1966, the contingent embarked for Vietnam, landing on the same day that Marcos and Imelda arrived in Washington for their state visit. While Imelda hypnotized Johnson with her singing at the White House banquet, Marcos haggled with State and Defense Department officials at a series of sessions later described by one of them as "messy."

Of all the countries in the area, Johnson believed, the Philippines, with its historic attachment to the United States, should have been the first to volunteer soldiers for Vietnam. He wanted Marcos to commit more men, combat troops rather than merely engineers. But Marcos, sensing that Johnson was vulnerable, insisted on a heavy price. He would mobilize ten battalions at America's expense on condition that he be allowed to keep some of them at home for his own purposes. Anxious to have the Philippine flag among his Asian banners, Johnson ceded. In the end, Marcos sent only a token force to Vietnam, retaining nearly all the units to build roads and other pork barrel projects in the Philippines just before his next presidential campaign. A subsequent investigation by the U.S. Congress failed to determine precisely how he spent the funds, and Marcos muddled the matter further by claiming years later that he had received "no fee or payments of any kind" for his largely phantom contribution to Vietnam. Besides the military subsidy, Johnson had also given him $80 million in economic aid and other grants, including $3 million for Imelda's cultural center. Johnson, who usually referred to his allies in possessive terms, had called Marcos "my right arm in Asia." Afterward, realizing that Marcos had outwitted him, he barked to an aide: "If you ever bring that man near me again, I'll have your head."

Johnson also handed Marcos another lever with which to manipulate the United States. Following the Washington visit, he sent a top secret message to William Blair, the American ambassador in Manila, instructing him to disclose to Marcos that nuclear weapons were being stored at the U.S. bases in the Philippines. Marcos might have guessed as much, but until then no Philippine president had been officially given that information, which had never been made public—and which, to this day, is confidential. Johnson's motives for the gesture are still unclear. He may have believed that, by taking him into his confidence, Marcos would be more cooperative. Instead, Marcos realized that he was in a stronger bargaining position than he had previously imagined, and he held the bases as his trump card in negotiations with future American presidents. As a former Johnson aide later phrased it: "The instrument of our policy became the object of our policy. We had to submit to Marcos for the sake of the bases."

Richard Nixon placated Marcos for the same reason. Nixon had scheduled a brief stop in Manila in July 1969, during his first trip abroad as president. Marcos, who was running for reelection later in the year, invited Nixon to spend the night at the Malacañang palace in hopes of creating the impression that the United States endorsed his candidacy. Precisely to avoid that trap, Nixon planned to stay at a hotel. But Marcos pressed, and Nixon finally complied. Imelda hastily renovated the palace and put on one of her opulent dinners, followed by hours of entertainment. Despite their exhaustion, Nixon and his wife, Pat, endured the ordeal. Two months afterward, Imelda repeated the performance for Ronald Reagan, then governor of California, and his wife, Nancy. Nixon had sent the Reagans to Manila to represent him at the opening of Imelda's cultural center, and she fêted them at banquets and receptions that by comparison made Hollywood parties seem like church picnics. The Marcoses showed shrewd foresight. Reagan never forgot their hospitality, which he misinterpreted as a personal mark of friendship and, as president, he remained faithful to them long after their behavior had become scandalous.

Marcos was just as clever at manipulating his own people. Shortly after entering office in 1965, he promoted himself as modern and sophisticated by recruiting a staff of so-called technocrats, many of them educated in the United States, and announced agrarian reforms and other ambitious plans. Thanks to the engineer units underwritten by Lyndon Johnson, he did build roads and bridges, and he fortuitously benefited from a major scientific breakthrough. Largely financed by the Ford and Rockefeller foundations, agricultural experts at a center near Manila had recently developed new breeds of high-yielding rice that were now producing record harvests. The Philippines became a food exporter for the first time in nearly a century, and the achievement redounded to Marcos's credit. But soon his administration was adrift. By 1969, his agrarian reform had distributed land to only three thousand tenants. Violence was as rampant as ever, partly through his own encouragement. Under the guise of fighting remnant Huks in central Luzon, he approved the formation of vigilante groups known as the "Monkees," after the popular rock group of the time, and he employed them to intimidate and even murder his rivals. Denouncing corruption, he claimed to have put his entire assets of $30,000 into a "blind trust" devoted to "scientific research for the public welfare." In fact, he was then starting to amass his colossal fortune, largely by requiring his cronies to pay him kickbacks in exchange for lucrative government contracts and other privileges. In March 1968, according to subsequent disclosures, he deposited a total of $950,000 in four accounts at the Credit Suisse in Zurich, two in his name and the others in the names of Jane Ryan and William Saunders.

Neither Marcos nor American Embassy officials in Manila were then aware of an event that portended a grave crisis for the Philippines. On December 26, 1968, in a remote village of Pangasinan province in northern Luzon, eleven young Filipinos met to found a new Communist party. They had chosen that day, Mao Zedong's seventy-fifth birthday, out of respect for the Chinese Communist leader, whose strategy of guerrilla warfare they intended to pursue. Their organizer, José Marie Sison, barely thirty at the time, was a slim figure with a scraggly mustache. The son of a wealthy landowning family, he had until recently been a lecturer in English literature at the University of the Philippines. In Manila, as elsewhere in the world, the academic community was erupting in radical protests during the 1960s. Sison, caught up in the ferment, had joined the old Communist party—only to find himself at odds with its veteran leaders, who opposed Mao's doctrine of "armed struggle." They were "weekend warriors," he told William Chapman, an American journalist, in 1986. He quit and, under an appropriate nom de guerre, Amado Guerrero, established his own party with seventy-five disciples, most of them students.

Sison soon encountered Bernabe Buscayno, alias Commander Dante, a Huk guerrilla chief. The original Huks, defeated in the 1950s, had since deteriorated into racketeers who managed prostitution, gambling and bars around Clark Field, the U.S. air base in central Luzon—usually with the tolerance of the American authorities. Buscayno, the son of a poor peasant, idealistically hoped to revive the revolution. In March 1969, he and Sison formed the New People's Army with an arsenal of seventy weapons. Though they never received Chinese aid, they taught their followers to recite Mao's aphorisms, among them "A single spark can ignite a prairie fire." It proved to be apt. Both Sison and Buscayno were later captured—but, over the next twenty years, the Communist rebellion spread to nearly every province in the archipelago as the insurgents won support in reaction to Marcos's corruption and abuses.

Meanwhile, a kinky episode that reflected the licentious flavor of the Philippines unfolded late in 1968 with the arrival in Manila of Dovie Beams, an overage American starlet who had supposedly been hired to act in a film about Marcos's wartime exploits. She began a liaison with Marcos that lasted for nearly two years, and the movie, a sham from the start, was never made. Marcos dropped her without severance pay, and the scandal broke. As a precaution, Dovie had hidden a tape recorder under the bed to acquire electronic evidence of their trysts. She convened the press and played the tapes, which student radio stations promptly broadcast—giving the public a heavy dose of Marcos grunting, breathing obscenities, crooning love songs and revealing Imelda's sexual inadequacies. Menaced by Marcos's thugs, Dovie fled to the U.S. Embassy for protection, and CIA men rushed her onto a flight to Hong Kong. Marcos ordered a Manila magazine to publish a piece defaming her as a slut, illustrated with pornographic photographs of her that he himself had snapped. Relegated to obscurity after that, Dovie resurfaced in 1988, when she was sentenced by a California court to eight years in prison for bank fraud.

Like other Filipino wives whose husbands maintained *queridas,* Imelda asked only that Marcos exercise discretion. But he had violated the rules of the game, humiliating her in the eyes of the Manila socialites whose acceptance she sought. He knew it and, to atone, catered to her every whim from then on. "It was a turning point," one of their friends later told me. "He could no longer control her, and she went crazy with power and greed."

Marcos understood, however, that his private capers were irrelevant to the politicians, who themselves kept mistresses and, in any case, admired *machismo*. The key to gaining and preserving authority, he had long before grasped, was through *utang na loob*—putting the entire political structure, from local officials to national legislators, into his debt. The means to that end was the money to dispense patronage to the provincial bosses who guaranteed the vote. Marcos displayed his mastery of the system in 1969, when he easily beat Sergio Osmeña, Jr., the lackluster son of the former president, and won an unprecedented second term. He spent the equivalent of $50 million on the campaign, part of it on a pair of American advisers, Lawrence F. O'Brien and Joseph Napolitan, longtime Democratic party professionals. His own political skills notwithstanding, Marcos somehow felt compelled to seek American counsel—he even hoped in his final days that a Washington public relations firm would save him from collapse.

Hardly had he been reelected president than he began pondering ways to retain power. A new constitution, he reckoned, would permit him to run for a third term. He entrusted his palace guard to Colonel Fabian Ver, an enigmatic cousin with vague military credentials. Concerned with possible betrayal, he tightened his circle of cronies. None of this eluded Manila's keen journalists. In February 1970, not long after his second inauguration, the *Philippine Free Press* prophetically observed that Marcos "might become a megalomaniac, drunk with his own importance [and] even consider enthroning himself as lifetime president or dictator." The publication was remarkably perceptive. Just about that time, Marcos confided to his diary: "I have that feeling of certainty that I will end up with dictatorial powers."

Though the possibility of martial law worried ambassador Henry Byroade, some of his staff saw the prospect as salutary. Francis T. Underhill, the chief political officer, subsequently reconstructed his feelings during that period for Raymond Bonner, an American writer: "This place is a hopeless mess. Power is so dispersed that nothing can be done. Graft and corruption are rife. The streets are unsafe. The Philippines needs a strong man, a man on horseback to get the country organized and going again."

Manila was roiled by student, labor and peasant protests, several provoked by the Communists. Marcos welcomed their demonstrations as justification for the eventual repression he envisioned—as his diary entries for the period indicate. "We should allow them to gather strength, but not such strength that we cannot overcome them," he wrote on February 17, 1970. However, he himself was behind much of the unrest. "The disorders must now be induced into a crisis so that stricter measures can be taken," he wrote on March 3—adding soon afterward: "A little more destruction and vandalism, and I can do anything." Nevertheless, he was typically cautious, calculating that he might not be able to muster public backing if he launched his crackdown prematurely. "I must continue to restrain myself," he wrote in his diary, "lest we lose the support of the people by a stance of tyranny."

Late in January 1971, after a day of turmoil, Marcos directed his army commander and Chief of Staff to prepare for martial law. They refused, and he subsequently relieved them. On the night of August 21, an ugly incident occurred that gave him another excuse to clamp down. Legislative elections were approaching, and the rival Liberal candidates had gathered before a crowd of ten thousand at the Plaza Miranda, a Manila square frequented by soapbox orators. Suddenly grenades and explosives tore through the rally, killing at least ten people and injuring more than a hundred others. Marcos immediately suspended the writ of *habeas corpus* and blamed the Communists, further alleging that Ninoy Aquino, who had arrived at the meeting suspiciously late from a dinner, was abetting them. But, again prudent, Marcos recoiled from imposing martial law then. The culprits were never apprehended. Years afterward, the Communists denied responsibility for the attack, confirming a CIA analysis that concluded at the time that they were too weak and disorganized to have staged such an assault.

Marcos was beginning to alarm the old oligarchy, which threw much of its weight behind the Liberals. They won six of the eight senate seats in the 1971 election, even scoring overwhelmingly in Marcos's native province. Shocked by the results, Marcos realized more vividly than ever that he would have to move decisively—and soon—to perpetuate his power.

He later claimed that several plots to liquidate him had accelerated his plan to impose martial law. One, conceived by Sergio Osmeña, Jr., was indeed genuine and, like much of the Philippines itself, surrealistic.

Early in 1972, Osmeña hired Larry Tractman, Robert Pincus and August McCormick Lehman, three American hit men with U.S. police records. He also engaged a Scotsman named Albert Brian Borthwick, the Singapore representative for Interarms, a firm owned by Sam Cummings, a former CIA man and one of the world's leading weapons dealers, who had headquarters in Alexandria, Virginia, resided in Monte Carlo and traveled on British and Irish passports—and does to this day. According to a former Interarms employee, Borthwick and Cummings agreed to cooperate with Osmeña in exchange for an exclusive arms contract once Marcos had been removed. Borthwick flew to Osmeña's hometown of Cebu to demonstrate his weapons for the American killers. One, a high-powered Belgian rifle with a cyclops scope, would be fired from a hole in a Volkswagen van at Marcos while he was playing golf. Borthwick also devised a radio-controlled toy airplane packed with explosives to dive-bomb Marcos on the golf course. A third alternative was to blow up Marcos with limpet mines hidden under the dock he used to board his yacht. After additional testing, the equipment was to be shipped to Osmeña through the police chief of Cebu.

The Singapore authorities, detecting the radio signals being tested by Borthwick, arrested and later deported him to Scotland, where he died shortly afterward of cancer. When Marcos learned of the plot from informers, he put out the dragnet. Osmeña, Tractman and Pincus escaped to the United States. Lehman, captured, went to jail—where, to make the story even more baroque, he married the warden's daughter with General Ver serving as their sponsor.

For motives that are still unclear, Marcos refrained from revealing the plot until after he had imposed martial law. He first divulged it late in 1972 to James Lowenstein and Richard Moose, staff members of the U.S. Senate Committee on Foreign Relations, who happened to be visiting Manila. The threat had been his "real reason" for seizing power, Marcos explained, adding cryptically that he had kept it secret until then to avoid "undermining public confidence." Oddly enough, the U.S. Embassy knew nothing. Lowenstein and Moose went home baffled.

★ ★ ★

Ninoy Aquino had been warning for at least a year that Marcos intended to establish a "garrison state." Confined to a military prison by Marcos in the early hours of September 22, 1972, he expected to awake to the uproar of angry crowds manning the barricades in protest against martial law. Seven years later, still in jail, Aquino sadly confided to a friend, "I judged Marcos correctly, but I misjudged the people."

Aside from Marcos opponents like Aquino, most Filipinos seemed to welcome martial law—at least during its first few years. Virtually nobody mourned the closed legislature, whose endlessly empty debates had become a joke. Nor was there much indignation over censorship of the press, which had formerly been sensational to the point of licentiousness. Overnight, city streets were clean, and garbage was collected. The public applauded the wholesale confiscation of private firearms, an army effort that eventually netted more than a half-million weapons. Crime dropped sharply, prompting a peasant near the town of Zamboanga to tell an American reporter, "Thieves no longer steal our coconuts or take clothes from our house." Businessmen were reassured by the promise of a crackdown, or at least reduction, of bribery and corruption. The prospect of sound, honest government suffused citizens with a new sense of civic virtue. Years later, a banker who by then detested Marcos, illustrated his initial attitude toward martial law: "I used to drive my sports car at top speed until, one day, a cop gave me a ticket. I was furious when he refused my bribe. But, thinking it over, I realized that I was wrong. We did need law and order to have stability and prosperity."

Marcos announced that he was pioneering a "third world approach to democracy" through his "New Society" and his new political party, the *Kilusan Bagong Lipunan,* or New Society Movement. He pledged land reform and the creation of citizen assemblies to "restore power to the people." As a gesture of nationalism, he dropped the Spanish term *barrio* and renamed villages *barangays,* after the boats that carried the early Malays to the islands. Similarly, he replaced the bicameral congress, named for its Washington parent, with a new body, the *Batasang Pambansa,* or National Assembly. He also traded the constitution, promulgated in 1935 under American auspices, for a charter that he heralded as more suited to the Philippines. And he spoke of his "rendezvous with Asia," as if he sought to break out of the American mold. Parroting his rhetoric, his foreign secretary, Carlos Romulo, onetime Pulitzer Prize winner for foreign reporting and aide to General MacArthur, decried Western-style democracy as "an alien seed" in Asian societies accustomed to authoritarian rule. Civil liberties were a "remote ideal" for poor and hungry people, Romulo said, forecasting that martial law would "achieve what democratic institutions stand for: the greatest good of the greatest number." Late in 1985, on his deathbed, Romulo recanted in a talk with Richard Holbrooke, a former assistant secretary of state, saying that the Marcoses were "robbing us blind."

But it was plain from the beginning that Marcos's lofty principles, plummy statements and contrived legalisms were merely cosmetic devices to mask his absolute power. He spent a fortune bribing convention delegates to approve a new constitution that assured him full authority, especially the right to govern by decree. Though he denied his intention to impose a military regime, he tripled the size of the army to some two hundred thousand men within a decade—increasing its annual budget tenfold to seven billion pesos in addition to more than a billion dollars in various forms of American military aid. Obsessed by loyalty, he chose his top officers from his home province, tolerating their smuggling and giving them illegal logging concessions in the regions under their command. His New Society Movement, instead of carrying out reforms, became a nationwide machine for dispensing patronage. He named Imelda to his cabinet as "Minister of Human Settlements," supposedly to promote community development—in reality to pay off his provincial supporters.

"I did not demolish the old oligarchy only to establish a new breed of oligarchs," Marcos proclaimed after declaring martial law, but he did exactly that. Contending that their feudalism blocked progress, he dispossessed the old landed and entrepreneurial clans. Yet he created his own plutocracy of relatives and cronies whose cupidity made the entrenched dynasties look selfless by comparison. In 1979, when Roy Rowan of *Fortune* asked Imelda how their family and friends had become so rich, she replied earnestly: "My dear, there are always people who are just a little faster, more brilliant and more aggressive."

Marcos resorted to blatant extortion to crush the Lopez family, whose empire of sugar estates, newspapers, mines and public utilities he coveted. The family had subsidized his election campaigns in 1965 and 1969, and Fernando Lopez served as his vice president, but Marcos was ruthless. He jailed a younger Lopez on flimsy charges of murder, pledging to release him on condition that the family sell its controlling share of the Manila Electric Company to Imelda's brother Kokoy. Marcos reneged on the promise, and the young man later escaped, possibly with Marcos's acquiescence. By then Kokoy, for a down payment of less than $2,000 to make the deal seem legal, had captured a company worth $400 million. Kokoy, later nominal ambassador to Washington, swiftly took over other hotels, factories and shopping centers with loans from government banks.

Marcos disowned other families to provide his brother Pacifico with insurance, banking and real estate firms, and steered his sister Fortuna into shipping. He even helped his elderly mother gain control of timber, tobacco and food processing companies. But his most lucrative privileges went to a group of trusted businessmen who knew how to make money—and furnish him with enormous kickbacks. To favor them, and himself, he effectively created a heavily regulated corporate state that was quickly dubbed "crony capitalism."

One of them, Herminio Disini, husband of Imelda's cousin and personal doctor, was an accountant who had gone into the cigarette filter business. He cornered the market in 1975, when Marcos exempted him from a special levy on the imported material used to manufacture filters. With government loans and other breaks, he was soon into everything from plastics and textiles to electronics and oil exploration. He reached his peak, however, in a dubious nuclear energy project that may have benefited from the complicity of both U.S. government officials and corporation executives.

Marcos decided on the showcase project in 1973—despite advice that it would be too costly and that the site selected for the plant was near a geological fault. He was encouraged by William J. Casey, a Marcos enthusiast, then chairman of the Export-Import Bank and later CIA director. Overruling several of his experts, Casey offered Marcos more than $600 million in loans and guarantees. Bids for the contract were opened, and General Electric seemed to have won. At that stage, Disini proposed his services to Westinghouse. A long and complicated battle followed, and in the end Disini prevailed. Marcos arbitrarily vetoed General Electric and chose Westinghouse, whose bid by then had climbed to more than $1 billion—far higher than its original submission. What turned the trick was a Westinghouse commission to Disini of nearly $80 million, camouflaged as a fee to his construction company for its involvement in the project. A fat slice of the money of course went to Marcos. By 1988, the nuclear plant was still unbuilt, but interest on the loans had doubled its original cost. Disini's enterprises had meanwhile crumbled in debt, and he absconded to a castle in Austria.

One of Marcos's golfing partners, Rodolfo Cuenca, thrived on government construction jobs, building roads with the army battalions financed by U.S. aid. Bending import regulations, Marcos allowed another friend, Ricardo Silverío, to become the sole Toyota distributor and leading car dealer. He gave Antonio Floriendo a penal colony on Mindanao on which to grow bananas and awarded José Campos, his son's godfather and owner of a drug firm, the exclusive contract to sell pharmaceuticals to public clinics. His two biggest protégés, Roberto Benedicto and Eduardo Cojuangco, Jr., amassed incalculable fortunes from the country's largest businesses: sugar and coconuts.

Marcos and Benedicto, old and close *compadres,* had been law school classmates and fraternity brothers. Benedicto went into banking and became an early Marcos political supporter. The Laurel-Langley Act, a commercial agreement between the United States and the Philippines, expired in 1974, ending the virtually free American market for Philippine sugar. The new quota system gave Marcos the opportunity to control the sugar industry. He put Benedicto in charge of boards to supervise production and trade, with the authority to determine prices, approve sales, extend or deny loans to planters and, among other powers, expropriate any mills and refineries deemed inefficient. Thus mandated, Benedicto required producers to borrow from his banks, buy equipment from his firms and ship their sugar aboard his trucks and vessels. He vaulted from his sugar monopoly into hotels and real estate, radio and television networks, a Los Angeles bank and a holding company in the Netherlands Antilles. A confidential U.S. Embassy study, calling him "one of the most notorious" of Marcos's cronies, noted that in 1983 his eleven largest companies paid taxes of only $100,000 on revenues of $100 million. The World Bank, which was engaged in several projects in the Philippines, urged Marcos to dismantle the Benedicto monopoly—as did the U.S. ambassador, Michael Armacost. Marcos, profiting from the scheme, did nothing.

Even more powerful among Marcos's intimates was Cojuangco, boss of the coconut business, which employs more people and earns more from exports than any industry in the country. Marcos derived a special satisfaction from his ties to Cojuangco, who was related to Cory Aquino and had broken with her side of the family in a political vendetta in their native Tarlac province. As Marcos saw it, building up Cojuangco was an indirect way to subvert Ninoy.

Cojuangco had backed Marcos in Tarlac during the 1960s. In 1974, seeing vast sums to be earned from coconuts, Marcos granted him surrogate authority to manage the industry, until then the purview of Juan Ponce Enrile, his defense secretary. On Enrile's advice, Cojuangco imposed a levy on the planters, using the money to found a bank—with Enrile as chairman. He then plowed the bank's funds into the purchase of nearly all the country's coconut-oil mills, and also acquired virtually an entire island on which to grow seedlings. Thus his monopoly reached from planting new trees to harvesting the coconuts to pressing the oil and selling the final product. He forced rivals out of business and dictated terms to giant firms like Procter and Gamble, for whom coconut oil was vital in making soap. To denounce him could be risky, as former Vice President Emmanuel Pelaez learned in 1982, when his car was mysteriously ambushed and his driver killed. Cojuangco's control of exports gave him leverage over world coconut prices—and, had Marcos not made him an ambassador with diplomatic immunity, he might have been prosecuted by the U.S. Justice Department for restraint of trade. Coconuts catapulted Cojuangco into radio stations, real estate, cement and the largest Philippine corporation, San Miguel, which besides brewing beer held both the Coca-Cola and Pepsi-Cola bottling franchises. Politically ambitious, he was chairman of Marcos's New Society Movement, and maintained a private army trained by Israeli military advisers disguised as agricultural experts. By 1985, a Manila banker reckoned, his assets were roughly $4 billion.

Cojuangco fled Manila with the Marcoses in February 1986, ending up in Los Angeles and barred by the U.S. authorities from leaving America. When I met him for the first time late in 1988, he was subdued and soft-spoken—along with Marcos one of the world's wealthiest exiles.

Through joint ventures, kickbacks and outright gifts, their cronies helped the Marcoses to accumulate a fortune that CIA analysts put as high as $10 billion. The real figure will probably never be known despite valiant efforts by Cory Aquino's investigators to uncover their "ill-gotten gains." The Marcoses operated in a baffling maze of intermediaries, dummies and phony names, and apart from their purchases of Manhattan and California real estate, they evidently preferred to remain liquid, keeping huge sums in secret Swiss and Hong Kong bank accounts. But when Marcos did involve himself in a transaction, he paid attention to the smallest detail. As one of his former aides observed, he was an Ilocano, as austere and thrifty as a Scotsman. Another of his associates later told me: "Remember, he was a lawyer. He would take apart a contract clause by clause, line by line, word by word, often for hours on an overseas telephone call."

The worldwide hunger for commodities had boosted the Philippine economy during the early days under martial law, buttressing Marcos's claim to be improving conditions, but the prosperity was transient. The Middle East oil producers hiked the price of petroleum following the Yom Kippur War of 1973, the Western industrial nations went into a slump and, as their demand for raw materials dropped, the commodities boom busted. Sugar, for example, plummeted from sixty-five cents a pound in 1974 to eight cents a pound in 1976. The Philippines, a petroleum importer, also suffered grievously from the soaring cost of oil—a blow to truckers, motorists and especially peasants who relied on kerosene lamps. The balance of payments, the measure of foreign trade, slid deep into deficit, and Marcos reached abroad for assistance.

"Countries don't go bankrupt," proclaimed Walter Wriston, chairman of Citicorp, and his fatuous remark sparked a global lending splurge. Western and Japanese bankers, desperate to earn interest from their colossal deposits of Middle East oil dollars, begged needy governments to borrow without examining their ledgers too closely. Marcos was pleased to accommodate. By 1980, his foreign debt had risen to more than $10 billion, up fourfold in five years. The Philippines owed more to the International Monetary Fund than any developing country in the world, and close to twenty percent of its faltering export earnings were going to cover the interest on the loans. The debt was to triple over the next five years, leaving the world financial community no recourse except to meet, moan and hope for even partial payments. John Maynard Keynes, the celebrated British economist of the 1930s, had neatly summed up the dilemma: "If you owe the bank a thousand dollars and default, you're in trouble. If you owe the bank a million dollars and default, the bank is in trouble."

Marcos might have survived the crisis, as other nations of Asia did, had his finances not been so precarious. He had granted favors to a local Chinese banker named Dewey Dee, who evaporated in 1981, leaving $100 million in debts from stock market and gambling losses. The Manila banks, in a panic, refused to roll over short-term loans, and several of Marcos's cronies were caught in the crunch, among them Disini and Cuenca. Disini fled the country, but Marcos bailed out Cuenca, who owed $60 million. As his other friends collapsed, Marcos also sought to rescue them in an attempt to retrieve the eroding international confidence in his regime. By 1983 he had spent some $3 billion in the effort—money that should have been devoted to economic development. Worse yet, Imelda continued her profligate shopping binges and publicity sprees. She squandered $31 million on a grotesque guesthouse made entirely of coconuts, and $21 million on a film center. The proximity of her luxurious bayside cultural center to Manila's fetid slums dramatized a "challenging transition from a traditional order to a progressive humanist society," she intoned at a fancy party there. "The contrast of shrine and shanty symbolizes the shining future against our impoverished past."

But the impoverished past was the present in urban as well as rural areas. A World Bank study estimated that the proportion of people living below the poverty line in cities had risen from twenty-four percent in 1974 to forty percent in 1980. The countryside was no better. Many sugar planters on the island of Negros, crippled by the sharp drop in world prices, simply stopped paying their workers. Reporting from that island in September 1979, Ross Munro of *Time* described the malnutrition ward of a local hospital: "The young patients seem to have been transplanted from the famines in Bangladesh and the sub-Sahara earlier in the decade. Big eyes staring from skeletal heads, matchstick limbs, bloated bellies." The number of deaths increased after the hospital director absconded with half a million dollars in medicines.

The Communists, promising change, predictably won growing support. Their armed guerrillas numbered about three thousand by 1980, and they had learned a lesson from the failure of the Huks twenty-five years before. Instead of concentrating in a single area, a vulnerable strategy, they had organized pockets across the archipelago. They also formed fronts composed of doctors, lawyers, teachers and students, many conscientious, others attracted by radical chic. Their command structure was decentralized, so that new leaders emerged after the capture of José Marie Sison, their founder, in 1977. At times they joined with the Muslim separatist movement, which dominated large parts of Mindanao. Scarcely Robin Hoods, they murdered, plundered and frequently feuded among themselves. But they were far better disciplined than the police and the army, whose abuses drove numbers of normally passive peasants into the Communist ranks, either as recruits or active sympathizers.

As he hurtled ahead with his military buildup, Marcos neglected to indoctrinate, train and equip his troops to understand the roots of the rebellion or face it properly. Ignorant, ragged, underpaid and frequently led by corrupt officers, soldiers would arrest, torture and shoot suspects, sometimes promiscuously, often looting or acting on behalf of local landowners and officials seeking revenge against rivals. They coined a euphemism, *salvaging,* to signify the arbitrary detention of villagers, many of whom disappeared after being held for interrogation. I once visited a private funeral parlor that had been improvised to serve as the public morgue of Davao, the capital of Mindanao. The proprietor, a rotund Chinese in pajamas, sat silently in a corner of the stifling, dimly lighted room as families filed through to identify the corpses of relatives found in the jungle or fished out of the river, several mutilated beyond recognition. Someone would occasionally gasp and sob at the sight of a husband, father, brother, cousin. Seldom were questions asked.

Persecuted peasants, fearful of army or police reprisals, could not complain. The violations of human rights alarmed some Filipino politicians, lawyers and professors, and a few protested. The Catholic Church, meanwhile, gradually became the most articulate and influential critic of the regime.

Reactionary and progressive currents had clashed within the Catholic establishment since the nineteenth century, when Filipino priests had struggled for recognition against the Spanish friars. During and after the U.S. colonial period, American Jesuits championed enlightened labor laws and land reform, often defying the conservative Catholic hierarchy. Encouraged by the doctrines of John XXIII, the liberal pope elected in 1958, a group of Filipino bishops banded together to advocate social justice, and they were supported by other religious and lay associations. Their sense of outrage grew as they observed the egregious waste, corruption, inequities and repression of the Marcos government. Cardinal Jaime Sin recalled his evolution to me during a talk in 1987. "We were told to stay out of politics, but politics is a human activity, with its moral aspect. If a priest could not tell his people to be clean and honest, who could?" James Reuter, a Jesuit from New Jersey who spent his life in the Philippines, perceived a graver challenge. "Under Marcos we saw graft, the country being looted, hunger, misery and the bodies of peasants killed by the army. The Communists were gaining ground. It was a race between violent revolution and peaceful change. We had to do something urgently."

Some priests and nuns rallied to the rebels, inspired by books like *The Theology of Liberation,* by Gustavo Gutierrez, a Cuban radical. Luis Jalandoni, the scion of a wealthy Negros sugar family, had been a promising young clergyman when he joined the Communists in the late 1960s, declaring that their approach was "the Christian answer" to the Philippine problem. Captured in 1973, he was acclaimed by a number of priests, who wrote that they had shared his "anguish and frustration" as he tried to help exploited peasants through legal means. Later released, Jalandoni moved to Europe to raise funds for the Communists. Another radical priest, Edicio de la Torre, expressed doubt that the Catholic Church could ever succeed. "Many Christians are subconsciously seeking martyrdom," he told an interviewer in 1973. "They are willing to give their lives to make a moral protest. I'm not sold on that idea. I want to win." Fifteen years afterward, when I saw de la Torre in Manila, he had served two or three jail terms and his body bore the scars of torture.

Priests like Jalandoni and de la Torre were exceptions, but Marcos committed a major blunder by presuming the fourteen thousand members of the Philippine clergy to be his enemies. He did nothing to deter his troops from raiding seminaries and convents, and arresting, torturing and even murdering priests and nuns. Early in 1981, to herald the arrival in Manila of Pope John Paul II, he lifted martial law—a hollow gesture, since he retained the right to rule by decree. The visit, on which Imelda spent more than a million dollars, proved to be a disappointment. Instead of blessing his regime, as Marcos had hoped, the pope decried "the violation of the fundamental dignity of the human person," adding that "social organization exists only for the service of man . . . and cannot claim to serve the common good where human rights are not safeguarded." The pope flew on to Negros, where he denounced as "injustice" a system under which "the vast majority are excluded from the benefits that the land yields." His homilies strengthened Cardinal Sin, who from then on spearheaded the opposition to Marcos, sometimes in zigzag fashion.

A jovial Chinese *mestizo* with a round, pearly face, Sin enjoyed quips and anecdotes. Once, chatting at his palatial villa, which he called the "house of sin," he sang "Twinkle, Twinkle, Little Star" to me in recollection of his early American schooling. He embraced Marcos in public and visited Ninoy Aquino in jail, thus opening himself to charges of duplicity. But while he claimed to be playing pastor to "all my flock," he bluntly admonished Marcos. As early as 1979, he warned that Marcos was driving the Philippines into civil war— "the greatest punishment that God could give any country." Four years later, he stated that Marcos had "lost the respect of the people" and ought to resign, prompting one of Marcos's aides to retort that Sin was bucking to become the "Filipino Khomeini." Imelda lobbied hopelessly through the Philippine ambassador to the Vatican to have Sin removed from Manila. Marcos kept silent in public, though he privately referred to Sin as a "meddlesome friar." Knowledgeable Filipinos regarded Sin as the pivotal figure in the Manila political swirl of the early 1980s. "The cardinal is the key to everything," one of them said. "He's the only man in the country whom Marcos fears, the only man he'll listen to because he carries the full weight of the Catholic Church." Still, it was to take more than Sin's divine message to alter the situation.

During Marcos's state visit to Washington in September 1982, President Reagan hailed him as "a respected voice for reason and moderation." Reagan, an admirer of Marcos to the end, no doubt believed his own rhetoric. Among professional practitioners of U.S. foreign policy, however, the prevailing view of Marcos had long been closer to Franklin D. Roosevelt's remark about Anastasio Somoza, the Nicaraguan dictator of the 1930s: "He may be a son of a bitch, but he's *our* son of a bitch." Successive administrations in Washington, primarily focused on the future of the Philippine bases, had flinched at exerting pressure on Marcos that might complicate new negotiations. Their concern was realistic. Fourth of July oratory notwithstanding, morality has never been the test for America's diplomatic ties to other nations, and to hold Marcos to American standards of behavior would be tantamount to breaking relations with the Russians unless they shut down the Gulag. Writing in *Foreign Affairs* in 1948, George Kennan cautioned against imposing American values on the world: "The day is not far off when we are going to have to deal in straight power concepts. The less we are then hampered by idealistic slogans, the better."

But U.S. foreign policy experts also perceived that the longer Marcos's excesses continued, the faster the Communist insurgency would spread, and increasingly threaten the bases. So his profligacy, corruption and repression represented a potential danger to America's strategic interests.

Marcos would have to be made to reform—and, if he refused, what? It was a challenge that the United States had faced with other clients. This time the answer unfolded through the extraordinary martyrdom of Ninoy Aquino, who by the spring of 1980 had been languishing in prison for more than seven years.

14. MARTYR AND MADONNA

★ ★ ★

I'm going back," Ninoy Aquino announced to me over the telephone one day early in July of 1983. He was calling from the Boston suburb where he had lived with his wife, Cory, and their children since Ferdinand Marcos had released him from prison to go to the United States three years before.

As garrulous as ever, he launched into a long analysis of the situation in the Philippines. The country was on the verge of collapse from mismanagement, corruption, foreign debt and insurgencies, and only he could persuade Marcos to reform to avert disaster. His return might be dangerous, he said dramatically, revealing that he had received several assassination threats, but he had no choice: "If I stay here, I'll just be another forgotten politician in exile."

His decision did not surprise me. He had repeated during our occasional talks in Boston that he would eventually return home. But, it seemed to me, he was deluding himself to think that he could change Marcos. I also dismissed his mention of assassination plots as characteristically theatrical. Though violence and politics were synonymous in the Philippines, the bigwigs usually spared one another, leaving the killing to their hired goons. As Ninoy rambled on, I realized that he was not seeking my advice as much as fishing for confirmation of his resolve to return—just as he had similarly canvased other friends.

On the afternoon of August 21, a Sunday, he lay dead on the tarmac of the Manila airport, presumably murdered by Marcos's henchmen. The sensational sequence was televised—from his arrest aboard the plane to the shots minutes later and the gruesome sight of his corpse. The spectacle shocked a world that, for the most part, had never heard of him.

The next morning, Cory and I appeared together on the CBS television news anchored by Diane Sawyer—Cory from Boston and I in New York. Cory broke into sobs as we talked by telephone before the broadcast, and I felt uncomfortable, as if the media were exploiting her grief. But as soon as the program began, she controlled herself and spoke in measured cadence, offering banal answers to Sawyer's banal questions. Did she plan to assume Ninoy's mantle and play a strong role in the resistance to Marcos? "I don't think so. I've only been involved in politics because of my husband. Now that he's gone maybe I will help the opposition to fulfill his dreams to restore freedom to our country. That's all." Could she explain her remarkable composure? Referring to Ninoy in the present tense, as she often would for years to come, she replied: "He and I are fatalistic. There's an appointed time in our lives, and when that time comes there is nothing to do except to pray to the Lord."

Her words sounded stereotyped, but what was extraordinary was her appearance at all in this moment of her anguish. Not until then, after knowing her for twenty years, did I grasp the dimensions of her spirit and depth of her faith. For the first time, too, I sensed that she was not the mousy housewife who had quietly served coffee during Ninoy's monologues.

Three years later in Manila, following her election as president, I recalled to her my astonishment at her poise and serenity on that horrible morning. Looking back with curious detachment, she recollected that she had prayed to prepare herself for what she considered to be her duty. "When I'm convinced that nobody else can do the job, then I give it everything I've got. I tell myself, 'Cory, you have to do this, and do the best you can.' With Ninoy dead, I knew that only I could deliver his message, and tell America and the world what happened. I gathered all my courage and strength, and did it—I hope well."

★　★　★

Journalists should not befriend politicians, but I bent the rule for Ninoy. We first met late in 1967, soon after his election to the Philippine senate. At thirty-five, he was touted as the brightest young star in the country's political firmament. I admired him instantly. Despite his cockiness, he was candid, charming, stimulating and, above all, fun. Even after the agony of prison had tempered him, he remained bouncy and optimistic, always serious yet never solemn.

A swaggering figure despite his stocky frame, Ninoy, in his horn-rimmed glasses and brushcut, struck me initially as a college freshman out of the 1930s. He often sounded like a Filipino version of Andy Hardy, punctuating his remarks with such quaint exclamations as "okey doke" and "holy moly," and he was as unleavened as an adolescent when he displayed his dubious erudition. During one of our early encounters, he reeled off odd facts and obscure statistics mixed with a hodgepodge of quotations from Jefferson, Marx, Bernard Shaw and Bertrand Russell, as if he had memorized epigrams from *Reader's Digest*. As a paradigm for the Philippines he had somehow dredged up Kemal Ataturk, the autocratic Turkish reformer of the 1920s and 1930s. Years later he cited as models Prime Minister Lee Kuan Yew of Singapore and General Park Chung Hee of South Korea, both rigid rulers. "You can be authoritarian in Asia," he held, "provided there is an economic tradeoff." Marcos, he maintained, would have been a "great president" had he produced an "economic miracle" in exchange for muting democracy. "But if you go from bicycles to bare feet and take away people's rights at the same time," he subsequently told Sandra Burton of *Time* magazine, "then the whole place goes bust."

Indeed, reviewing my notes of our talks during the late 1960s, I am astounded by the extent to which Ninoy shared Marcos's concepts. Ninoy, however, did not fog his notions in phony legalisms. He was convinced that he would become president one day. "And then," he said, "we'll have spartan leadership and no nonsense. I'll call in the politicians and tell them, 'You guys have plundered for years. Now it's going to change. You follow me—or else.' " He would smash the old oligarchs by expropriating their property, introduce agrarian reforms and stimulate industry by creating state corporations. To eliminate crime, he would confiscate private weapons and impose life sentences on persistent offenders. His formula for curbing corruption and preserving law and order: "Make examples by jailing a few, and the rest will behave." He could hardly have foreseen that, in Marcos's grab for power in 1972, he was to be the first victim of the same prescription.

Nevertheless, I could scarcely imagine Ninoy conforming to an austere regime, even his own. Despite their enormous wealth, he and Cory were not opulent in the manner of upper-class Filipinos. They lived in a modest ranch-style house in suburban Quezon City rather than in one of Manila's fancy residential enclaves and seldom attended lavish parties. Cory eschewed ostentatious dresses and jewelry, nor was Ninoy a conspicuous consumer of personal luxuries. He usually wore a sports shirt or bush jacket and khaki trousers and ate too rapidly to notice his food. But, like Marcos, he was a practical politician who knew the importance of money as an instrument to gain and hold power. I had not known him long before he revealed his assets to me. Aside from Cory's huge family fortune, he himself had roughly $3 million—though, he estimated, he had recently invested more than half a million dollars in his election. He had won a place on the Liberal ticket, he disclosed, only by allowing the party to use his two private Beechcrafts and helicopter to ferry its candidates around the country. His bulletproof Cadillac Fleetwood was another professional outlay, and he had just purchased a new Lincoln Continental, also armored. As far as I could tell, his only expensive frivolity were two nine-hole golf courses for guests on Cory's family plantation in Tarlac province north of Manila, designed by Robert Trent Jones, the noted American golf course landscaper.

Constantly posturing, Ninoy observed the tradition of *palabas,* the Tagalog term for showiness, another resemblance to Marcos. Ian Buruma of the *Far Eastern Economic Review* once asked the Marcoses for their opinion of Ninoy. "All sauce and no substance," snapped Imelda—to which Marcos interjected, "Sweetheart, that is the essence of Filipino politics." Ninoy's mother, Aurora, a formidable lady, gave the same point a different twist during a chat with me in 1987, when she was seventy-six. "As a little boy, Ninoy loved to beat the drum with the band at our town fiestas. He wanted to be a drummer when he grew up, he would say. I never expected my drummer boy to die fifty years later still beating his drum, but he did and awakened the people."

But I soon discovered that Ninoy, for all his bluster, towered over the midgets on the Manila political stage. His energy was prodigious. A study in perpetual motion, he would bolt at breakneck speed from breakfast meetings and legislative sessions to luncheon speeches, baptisms, weddings and funerals, fly to a provincial town to support a local candidate and return to tour Manila's raunchy nightclubs into the early morning. His present halo notwithstanding, he was a relentless womanizer, largely to sustain his macho image. With similar bravura, he once alarmed an American ambassador by saying "I've killed for power, and I'll kill again." He had a natural magnetism, perhaps the result of his tremendous self-confidence, and a charismatic touch that stemmed from his adaptability. I saw him mingle with peasants and housewives as easily as he hobnobbed with bankers and businessmen. In 1971, while I was on a fellowship at Harvard, he telephoned to wangle an invitation to Cambridge. I arranged for him to address a faculty group, then began to worry that he might be too coarse for the cloistered professors. To my amazement and relief, he wowed them with his eloquence—just as, during his three years of exile in the early 1980s, he fit into Harvard and the Massachusetts Institute of Technology.

Ninoy acquired his political instincts from the Aquino family. A typical Malay, Chinese and Spanish amalgam, his forebears had prospered as landed gentry in Tarlac during the nineteenth century. His grandfather Servillan, a craggy character with drooping mustaches, joined Emilio Aguinaldo's nationalist army in the war with Spain and rose to the rank of general during the struggle against the American conquest. Captured by the U.S. forces, he was condemned to death for summarily shooting prisoners because, Ninoy told me, "they ate too much." But his sentence was commuted, and he won a pardon after four years in jail. He had himself photographed in his striped prison garb and hung the picture prominently. To symbolize his resistance to the United States, he refused to learn English, and spoke only Tagalog or Spanish until the end of his life.

Ninoy's father, Benigno, was equally rambunctious. As the story goes, he burned down the parish church in order to destroy his baptismal record so that he could run for the Philippine legislature at twenty-three, two years below the legal age. Eventually becoming speaker of the lower house, he championed immediate independence from the United States during the 1930s and urged close ties between the Philippines and Asia. That conviction, coupled with opportunism, led him to serve the Japanese during World War II. After the war, one of the few Filipinos indicted for aiding the enemy, he was freed on bail and died of a heart attack while watching a boxing match. Ninoy was then fourteen and, out of filial respect, he repeatedly pleaded his father's case thereafter. "Why should he have been judged for working with the Japanese when others were praised for cooperating with the Americans?" he would say. "After all, they were both foreigners." He shared neither his father's admiration for the Japanese nor his animosity toward the Americans, but he was worried by both Japan's economic expansion and Philippine subservience to the United States.

Born Benigno Simeon Aquino, Jr., on November 27, 1932, in the Tarlac town of Concepcion, he grew up in Manila after his father's election to the legislature. His father had been married before, and the family eventually comprised nine children and stepchildren, with Ninoy the oldest son of the second brood. "You could tell he was headed for politics even at the age of five," his mother recalled. "He was an extrovert, always talking to visitors or delivering speeches to the servants." His younger sister, Lupita Kashiwahara, theorized to me that Ninoy "was never really a child." His two older half-brothers had left home and married by the time their father died, and though their mother was a dynamic woman, Ninoy became the man of the house as a teenager. He was then and thereafter a "male chauvinist," Lupita said, "continually nagging me and my sisters that our lipstick was too red or our dresses too tight." But, she added, "you felt that he was gearing his life for something big, something great."

In contrast to Marcos, he was an indifferent student. He graduated from the University of the Philippines and attended law school, but classes bored him. As a lark he became a part-time copy boy on the *Manila Times* at the age of fifteen, and quickly rose to reporter. The Korean War erupted in June 1950, and adventure beckoned when the Philippines committed a unit to the United Nations forces. Ninoy, not yet eighteen, volunteered to go along as a correspondent. The American war correspondents, many of them grizzled veterans of World War II, included journalistic luminaries like Homer Bigart and Marguerite Higgins of the *New York Herald Tribune* and Hal Boyle of the Associated Press. Raised on the American press, Ninoy basked in the reflection of their reputations. He ran their errands, and they adopted him as their mascot, editing his dispatches and teasing his teetotaling by dubbing him "Aquino the milk boy." It was an interlude he never forgot, and he revered American reporters forever after. He was also impressed by Syngman Rhee, then president of South Korea, whom he interviewed. Rhee was an intense authoritarian and nationalist, and to Ninoy he symbolized the kind of order, discipline and purpose that the Philippines sorely needed—the same attributes that his father had seen in Japan.

Ninoy returned home in 1951 to his dreary law studies but, the next year, the *Manila Times* handed him another plum: a three-month reporting tour of Southeast Asia. He went to Indonesia, which had recently cast off Dutch rule, and visited Burma, freed not long before by the British. In Malaya he observed the British fight against a Communist insurgency and saw the French in a similar war in Vietnam. Concluding that America's anti-Communist crusade in the area was misguided, he wrote that "many Asians would prefer Communism to Western oppression." Typically, his opinions zigzagged. Back in Manila, he subscribed to the official anti-Communist line and later shifted again. When I first met him, he argued that the Philippines ought to defy U.S. policy and recognize Communist China—then a bold view.

Filipino journalists frequently work for politicians, and Ninoy performed jobs for President Ramón Magsaysay—one of which won him fame. In May 1954, after three months of talks, he persuaded Luis Taruc, the Huk leader, to surrender. The exploit earned him headlines in Manila and a full-page article in *Time* magazine. But he was furious when Magsaysay, breaking a promise to amnesty Taruc, instead imprisoned the insurgent. Magsaysay cooled Ninoy off by sending him to the United States for four months to "observe" CIA training programs.

From then on Ninoy was tagged a CIA agent, and he himself boasted for years of the link to prove his intimacy with the Americans. He claimed to have informed the agency of the activities of the Communists in Tarlac, the site of Clark Field. In 1958, he said, the CIA flew him to Sumatra as part of a clandestine operation to overthrow President Sukarno of Indonesia, and he babbled about other covert connections. Several senior agency officials later assured me, however, that Ninoy was never on the CIA payroll. "We didn't trust him," one said. "He talked too much." Ninoy subsequently shaded his original story, explaining that he had worked "with" rather than "for" the agency. But the confused issue continued to nag him, and Marcos confounded it further in 1978, when he held Ninoy in prison, by accusing him of working simultaneously for the CIA and the Communists.

Ninoy turned his mission to the CIA training program in America into a honeymoon by taking along Corazon Cojuangco, whom he had wed in October 1954, when he was a month short of his twenty-second birthday. Three months younger, she was reserved and gentle—just his opposite. Their marriage was as much a dynastic union as the Marcos match. But Ninoy, in contrast to Marcos, had not chosen his bride to advance his career. And unlike Imelda, whose childhood misery motivated her to flaunt her corrupt riches, Cory had the innate sense of equanimity and security that stems from old family wealth.

The Cojuangcos were Hakkas, an ethnic minority of south China whose members emigrated in large numbers to Southeast Asia and the United States to escape the hatred of the Han Chinese. Cory's great-grandfather landed in Manila in the 1890s from coastal Fujien province, cut off his pigtail, converted to Catholicism and Hispanicized his name to José. Siring a family, he moved to the Tarlac town of Paniqui, where he prospered as a rice merchant and moneylender. The oldest of his four grandsons was Cory's father, José, and another the father of Eduardo, to whom Marcos later gave the coconut monopoly. Expanding the family business, they soon owned rice and sugar lands in addition to a bank. José, who managed the sugar mill and bank, married Demetria Sumulong, the daughter of a powerful local politician. The sixth of their eight children, María Corazon, was born on January 25, 1933, the festival of the conversion of Saint Paul.

Going into politics, José won a seat in the Philippine commonwealth legislature and installed his family in Manila, remaining there through World War II. Cory led a sheltered life, going to convent schools and spending her time with her sisters. Her father naturally knew Benigno Aquino, his Tarlac political colleague, and Cory first met Ninoy at a family party when they were both nine years old. She recalled him as a cheeky boy who "kept bragging that he was a year ahead of me in school." But she was not ready for boys and, in any case, she left the country in 1946, when her father, fleeing the ruins of the war, moved his family to the United States.

Cory attended Catholic high schools in Philadelphia and New York, then entered the College of Mount Saint Vincent in Riverdale, an affluent section of the Bronx. She majored in English and mathematics and never missed daily mass. Despite their religious tone, the schools seemed permissively American to Cory. "I was stunned," she recalled, "that the students argued with teachers, something unthinkable back home. They didn't always obey their parents, another shock for me." But she acquired some American habits. "I learned to be punctual, an unheard-of practice in the Philippines, and I began to speak frankly, which annoys Filipinos." She also ventured into American politics by joining the Junior Republicans and going to rallies for Governor Thomas E. Dewey of New York, who was running for president against Harry Truman in 1948. "I guess I was mostly excited by seeing the movie stars at the rallies," she said.

She met Ninoy again during her vacations to Manila, and they occasionally corresponded after she went back to New York. In 1953, then twenty-one, she returned home to stay, enrolling in law school to discipline herself. By now Ninoy had been a war correspondent in Korea and was a dashing young celebrity about town. Cory admired his intelligence, dynamism and gift of gab, and given his distinguished family, he was a prize suitor. He had other girl-friends, but soon he discarded them to date Cory regularly—chaperoned, of course. Finally he proposed in his blunt, unromantic fashion. "As a lover," Cory confided to a friend, "he's not an emotional person." President Mag-saysay was one of the sponsors at their wedding, and within a year, Cory bore a daughter, the first of their five children.

On an impulse, Ninoy bought a farm near Concepcion, his hometown in Tarlac. No sooner had he cleared the property than he ran for mayor and won, becoming at twenty-two the youngest mayor in the Philippines. Governing a town, with all its problems and rivalries and maneuvers, thrilled him. In particular, he wanted to prove to himself that he could mix with the peasants despite his upper-class background. The adjustment for Cory was difficult after New York. They lived in a rambling old house, with constituents wandering through at all hours. Bored, Cory listened to soap operas on her transistor radio and never complained, accepting the roles she had been taught from girlhood: loyal wife and mother.

Determined to build a redoubtable power base in Tarlac, Ninoy pulled every political and family string to achieve that goal. Through Magsaysay he pro-cured a government loan of $3 million to enable Cory's father to purchase Hacienda Luisita, a former Spanish sugar estate of eighteen thousand acres covering three townships. Cory's uncle was cut out of the deal, thus igniting a family feud that later prompted his son, Eduardo, to side with Marcos. Ninoy took over the management of the plantation, moved there with Cory and constructed a new refinery, nearly tripling production in a decade. Dubbing himself a "radical rich guy," he provided the laborers with free housing, schooling and medical care, increased their incomes and encouraged them to form a union. When he became president, he pledged, he would give them the estate—a promise, if sincere, that Cory has not fulfilled.

In 1959, at the age of twenty-eight, Ninoy was elected provincial governor, again the youngest in the archipelago. He ran the province as he did the plantation, like a modern, progressive feudal lord. Flying around in his private plane, he would swoop into towns to discuss problems with officials and drive through muddy roads to visit remote villages. He built clinics, irrigation projects and schools. Indulging his taste for gadgets, he set up a sophisticated radio network to contact local chiefs and tabulated public-opinion surveys on a computer. No choirboy, he also played rough. Violence in Tarlac, as else-where in the Philippines, was endemic, and he used his private army to dispense crude justice to rapists, cattle rustlers and other criminals. He pre-served the peace by dealing with the remnant Huk gangs that roamed the region. "I don't care if you're commies or not, but no killing," he told them. "Come here, deliver all the speeches you want, bring your families, enjoy the province, but no killing. Otherwise I'll draw the line, and back it up with force." His *modus vivendi* with the Huks later fueled Marcos's charge that he was a "Communist coddler."

Ninoy's next goal was the senate, and he narrowly won a seat in the 1967 election—becoming, at thirty-five, the youngest member of the house. Marcos was counting on another term starting in 1969, and the consensus in Manila held that Ninoy had the connections and the charisma to beat him, but would be below the legal age to run. So the focus year was 1973, when Marcos would presumably seek an unprecedented third term and Ninoy would be old enough to challenge him. Ninoy's problem, as he told it to me, was to "stay alive politically" until then. Candidly outlining his strategy, he said: "I'm going to attack Marcos again and again, and goad him into denouncing me as much as possible in retaliation. That's the only way I can keep my name in print." Faithful to his plan, he assailed Marcos in his first senate address for plotting to create a "garrison state" by building up the army. He continued his fiery rhetorical offensive over the following years, maligning Marcos for "unalloyed ruthlessness" and "calculated perfidy" and nearly every other outrage, and Marcos matched his invective, calling him an "incorrigible liar" and a "dangerous fanatic." It all seemed to be a classic Filipino war of words—until the night of September 22, 1972, when Marcos proclaimed martial law, arrested Ninoy and later charged him with subversion, murder and illegal possession of weapons.

★ ★ ★

Other Filipinos less celebrated than Ninoy suffered a worse fate than he. The police, army and vigilantes jailed, tortured and killed hundreds if not thousands—in many cases using martial law as a pretext to liquidate local rivals or bilk innocent peasants. But Ninoy, during his seven and a half years of imprisonment, came to personify the prototypical Marcos victim. At first forgotten, he grew into a symbol of resistance through his tenacity, conscience and courage, like Andrei Sakharov and Nelson Mandela. Stubborn, almost foolhardy, he compelled Marcos to deal with him on his terms, and the excruciating ordeal was his passage to maturity. He ultimately defeated Marcos, at a cost he never quite anticipated—his martyrdom.

Preoccupied with world and especially American opinion, Marcos yearned to be seen as fair. At the same time, however, he sought to crush Ninoy. He was prepared to pardon Ninoy, but only on condition that Ninoy submit to a court-martial and probable conviction. The scenario fit his penchant for legal mummery as well as his desire to demean Ninoy by first declaring him guilty and then showing him generosity. Ninoy, perceiving the charade, refused. To face a panel of army officers named by Marcos, he felt, was tantamount to being tried by Marcos himself. In any case, he had no intention of accepting Marcos's benevolence. He might consider a civilian trial, if truly honest and independent judges could be found. Marcos rejected the proposal, and Ninoy stuck to his demands, enduring an internment that included moments of terror.

Ninoy buoyantly assured his cellmates at the beginning of their incarceration that "we'll be out in six months." Most were soon freed, but Marcos reserved a frightful agony for Ninoy and José Diokno, a former secretary of justice. In February 1973, they were handcuffed, blindfolded and flown by helicopter from their prison in Manila to a military camp in central Luzon. There, stripped of their clothes, they were held incommunicado for forty-three days in stifling rooms lighted around the clock by harsh neon tubes. Fearful of poison, Ninoy would only eat crackers, and his weight fell precipitously. Cory, finally allowed to visit him, was stunned. "He had always been so confident, so sure of himself," she told me later. "Now he was lost, never knowing what the next day held in store for him. Marcos had also chosen exactly the right punishment for him, denying him the company of his family and friends, suffocating him in unbearable loneliness. Seeing Ninoy like that was one of the traumas of my life." She underestimated Ninoy's resilience, however. Never devout, he began to pray and, he recalled afterward, Christ appeared in a dream, rebuking him for forsaking religion in his quest for power. His "conversion," as he called it, led him to realize that despair and indignation would not help him. He had to fight through reason, eloquence and pleas for support in the Philippines and elsewhere—especially America.

Marcos had slammed Ninoy into solitary confinement in hopes of breaking his spirit for the court-martial that opened in August 1973. But Ninoy boycotted the proceedings as an "unconscionable mockery," and again insisted on a civilian trial. Marcos was trapped. He could not drag a protesting Ninoy before a military tribunal without appearing to be a tyrant. Nor could he meet Ninoy's demands without admitting that his powers were limited. He shelved the case for lack of a better idea. Ninoy settled into a Manila army camp, where he read voraciously and kept in touch with sympathizers by smuggling messages out through Cory during her visits.

But Marcos knew that to hold Ninoy indefinitely without a trial would shatter his legalistic façade, and in March 1975 he reconvened the court-martial. Ninoy began a hunger strike, gambling that Marcos could not afford to let him die. The episode became a test of wills between two obdurate men who at times seemed, as an American observer in Manila put it, "as if they were playing a game."

Ninoy rapidly lost forty pounds, and Marcos had him transferred to a hospital. Oddly, though, Marcos allowed him visitors like Representative Donald Fraser of Minneapolis, a liberal Democrat and ardent human rights activist. Calling Marcos a "bastard," Ninoy told Fraser that he would "rather die than grovel." But Cory became increasingly worried that his brain might be damaged even if he survived. She sent out desperate appeals, including one to me dated April 7, 1975: "Please help! Do write about the *injustice* being committed against Ninoy. Also please ask your friends in the U.S. government to send Marcos telegrams of protest against his *humiliation* and *dehumanization.*" Marcos began to fret. When William Butler of the International Commission of Jurists arrived in Manila to obtain information on Ninoy's condition, Marcos said to him, "Get your ass over to the hospital—that guy may be serious." At the same time, Marcos ordered Ninoy to be force-fed. Cory enlisted Ninoy's mother, brothers and sisters to urge him to end his fast—and, after forty days, he relented. With that, both sides hastened to save face. Marcos assured William Sullivan, the U.S. ambassador, that Ninoy's hunger strike was "phony." Parrying radicals who hoped for Ninoy's martyrdom,

Cory said, "He can best serve his country and his cause by regaining his strength."

Marcos's abuses scarcely stirred presidents Richard Nixon and Gerald Ford, much less Henry Kissinger, their secretary of state. They were chiefly interested in reaching a new accord with Marcos to preserve the U.S. bases in the Philippines, and that focus became urgent in 1975, after the Communist victory in Vietnam. Kissinger, who normally ignored the Philippines as an area outside his big power focus, took an unusual step as a lame duck late in 1976. Without consulting members of the incoming Carter administration or anyone else, he offered Marcos $1 billion for the bases in the guise of various aid programs over a period of five years. Marcos rebuffed the sum as insufficient, and President Jimmy Carter inherited the problem of concluding a new bases agreement. Signaling his aim to infuse American foreign policy with high moral standards, Carter affirmed in his inaugural address his "clear-cut preference for those societies that share with us an abiding respect for individual human rights." It fell to Richard Holbrooke, the assistant secretary of state for east Asia, to handle the tricky task of negotiating a bases pact with Marcos while persuading him to restore civil liberties.

Though only thirty-five, Holbrooke was uniquely suited for the job. Having spent years in Vietnam, he understood the futility of hustling Asians. He also knew, as a shrewd Washington bureaucrat, that he would be judged by results. His critics complained that he did not push Marcos hard enough on human rights, but he did make progress on the issue and managed as well to reach a bases agreement.

In April 1977, when Holbrooke first visited Manila in his new assignment, Marcos gave him the opulent welcome he routinely reserved for important guests, entertaining him aboard the presidential yacht with one of Imelda's lavish dinners and a night of songs. The next day, after a brief review of the bases negotiations, Holbrooke urged Marcos to release Ninoy and allow him to move to the United States, where he might retire quietly to a university fellowship. It was the first time that a senior American official had pleaded on Ninoy's behalf, and both Marcos and Imelda reacted coolly. As obsessed as ever with their image in the United States, they voiced alarm that the Carter administration, Congress and the American press would "lionize" Ninoy. Holbrooke assured them that Ninoy would be a "quick story" for the news media and then fade away, and that neither the White House nor the State Department would make a "big deal of him." Though Holbrooke dented him, Marcos typically shifted back and forth, alternately treating Ninoy leniently, rudely, gently, always striving to retain the upper hand.

Convinced that he could bring Marcos around in a personal talk, Ninoy suggested that they meet. Suddenly, on June 21, 1977, a helicopter flew him from detention to the Malacañang palace. Marcos warmly greeted him as "brod," as fraternity brothers of Upsilon Sigma Phi called each other, and wryly complimented him on his svelte figure. They bantered, Ninoy boasting that his long imprisonment had transformed him into a hero. "You know damned well," Marcos riposted, "that you would have arrested me if you had been in my place." Ninoy nodded—then, turning to the main topic, repeated his demand for a civilian trial. Marcos dangled various options, one calculated to put Ninoy into his debt: "If you're convicted, would you ask for a pardon?"

Ninoy answered flatly: "No, sir, because I am not guilty." With that the session ended.

Marcos stiffened the following November, instructing a court-martial to sentence Ninoy to death. Holbrooke advised David Newsom, the U.S. ambassador in Manila, that the verdict would have a "devastating effect" in Washington, and directed him to "make clear" to Marcos that President Carter was personally distressed. Shortly afterward, one of Marcos's close aides confidentially guaranteed Newsom that Ninoy would be spared. Marcos had backed away, satisfied that he had dramatized his power of life and death over Ninoy.

His absolute authority thus displayed, Marcos scheduled legislative elections for April 1978, the first since he had imposed martial law five years before. He hoped to impress upon Vice President Walter Mondale, who planned to stop in Manila during a tour of Asia the next month, that he was not the ogre portrayed by his opponents. Realizing that Mondale would look ludicrous arriving there after a rigged election, Holbrooke advised Newsom to urge Marcos to release Ninoy and allow him to run in a "truly free" contest. Marcos, as a token concession, permitted Ninoy to campaign—from jail.

Ninoy, chided by some backers for accommodating Marcos, affiliated with a party called Strength of the Country, or *Lakas ng Bayan,* whose acronym, Laban, means "fight." He also entered a television debate with Marcos's defense minister, Juan Ponce Enrile, showing his ardor to be undiminished. On election eve, thousands acclaimed him by honking horns, blowing whistles and ringing church bells across Manila. The election was blatantly fake. Marcos's New Society Movement swept the vote, with Imelda predictably topping the ticket in Manila. Mondale came and went, and Ninoy remained in jail. Early in 1979, Marcos acceded to the urging of his friend Senator Daniel K. Inouye of Hawaii, and signed a bases pact promising a five-year aid package amounting to $500 million—half of the Kissinger offer he had spurned.

Marcos loosened Ninoy's leash further in 1979, first granting him two hours at home to celebrate his daughter's graduation from college, later furloughing him for a day and a half for his twenty-fifth wedding anniversary and finally giving him three weeks with his family at Christmas. Aside from advertising his humanity to the Carter administration, Marcos hoped to soften Ninoy and, in the process, split the opposition. He succeeded. Fearful of being driven into the radical camp, which would isolate him from the liberal Manila elite and especially the moderate Catholic hierarchy, Ninoy spoke vaguely of compromise. His drift troubled hard-liners, but it reassured Cardinal Jaime Sin, who informed him that Pope John Paul II had told Marcos that he would visit the Philippines as scheduled in 1981 only if he could see Ninoy in prison. Sin honored Ninoy at a mass and circulated a homily extolling him: "He embodies what is best, what is good and true and courageous. . . . With all my heart and soul, I look up to him in admiration and pride."

As he pondered Ninoy's fate at the start of 1980, Marcos considered sending him into exile or naming him to a toothless "council of leaders." Ninoy flinched at being co-opted, but to remove himself from the political scene by going abroad was equally onerous. The choice was forced on him on May 5, when an escort rushed him to the Philippine Heart Center, one of Imelda's pet projects, with a heart attack. The doctors recommended bypass surgery, which could have been performed there. Intervening, Imelda prevailed on Marcos to allow Ninoy to leave the country. It would look like "monkey business" if Ninoy died during an operation in Manila, she explained—and, besides, they could now get rid of him while appearing altruistic. Marcos agreed on condition that Ninoy abstain from criticizing him in America. Complying, Ninoy pledged in writing to return and "desist from commenting on our domestic political situation" or engaging in "any partisan political activity." He also praised Imelda in a note to the head of the Manila hospital, saying: "Now that I see what she has done here . . . I take back all my hard words—hoping I do not choke." Imelda visited his room, and like old chums, they joked and gossiped. Before departing for Dallas, where he would have his operation, Ninoy gave her a gold crucifix he had worn in jail. She hung it around the neck of a statue of the Infant Jesus that sat in a hall of the Malacañang palace.

★ ★ ★

His operation over, Ninoy faced a dilemma in the summer of 1980. The Carter administration had helped to secure his release, but he feared he would be ignored if Ronald Reagan, now the Republican presidential candidate, triumphed in November. Having promised Marcos to return, how could he stall until after the election without dishonoring his pledge? Various friends, myself included, figured that Marcos would cede if Harvard offered Ninoy a fellowship. Samuel Huntington, the head of the Center for International Affairs, came through. The Aquinos settled in a large house in Newton, Massachusetts, to start what Cory later called "the three happiest years of our life." They visited the tourist sights in Boston, New York and Washington, and Ninoy's children at last began to know him as they shopped or went to the movies together.

But Ninoy was too committed to retire. On August 4, 1980, addressing the Asia Society in New York, he blasted Marcos—declaring that "a pact with the devil is no pact at all," and he no longer felt bound by his vow of silence. Unless Marcos lifted martial law, he warned, there would be "an escalation of rural insurgency" as well as "massive urban guerrilla warfare"—and he would join in the fight. "Is the Filipino worth dying for?" he asked, coining the phrase that became one of his slogans. "Mr. Marcos," he asserted, "believe me when I tell you that, like the average Filipino, I will face death in the struggle for freedom if you do not heed the voice of conscience and moderation." And, of course, he evoked General MacArthur's famous motto: *I shall return.*

Ninoy's threat was empty bombast. Over the next year, he flew to places as diverse as Nicaragua and Saudi Arabia to seek financial support, but all he received was rhetorical encouragement. Nor were his prospects for ousting Marcos by political means much better. Marcos ended martial law in January 1981 and announced plans to run for reelection in June. Both gestures were hollow, since he retained the power to rule by decree, and the election would as usual be rigged. He hoped to impress Pope John Paul II during his visit in February and also to sway Ronald Reagan, who had just been elected president. The pope, advised by Cardinal Sin, was skeptical. By contrast, Reagan did not need convincing.

Reagan had found confirmation of his conservative credo in the thesis evolved by Jeane Kirkpatrick, then a Georgetown University professor, which distinguished "authoritarian" from "totalitarian" regimes. Stripped of its aca-

demic jargon, it exorcised morality from foreign policy and favored support
for any autocracy that served America's interests. Marcos fit the category, and
Kirkpatrick was to cling to him to the end—as Reagan did all along.

Soon after his election, Reagan demonstrated his esteem for Imelda by
visiting her at the Waldorf-Astoria during one of her New York sprees. The
symbolic encounter, following Carter's pious meddling, elated the Marcoses.
Vice President George Bush boosted their morale even higher during his trip
to Manila in June 1981, when he praised Marcos's "adherence to democratic
principles." His extravagant remark was no slip of the tongue. Walter Stoessel,
the undersecretary of state, had advised him to "reassure Marcos that the
Reagan administration regards him as a friend" to allay his concerns about
criticism in Congress and the American press. Reagan went further in September 1982, when he and Nancy entertained the Marcoses in Washington, a
tribute that Carter had denied them. Later he nearly doubled Carter's aid
package for the bases, granting Marcos $900 million over a five-year period.
But State Department specialists stressed the importance of remaining on
"good terms" with Ninoy. As one of them emphasized in a secret memorandum: "He may yet achieve his supreme ambition to be Philippine president.
He is basically moderate, free enterprise–oriented and not hostile to U.S.
interests."

During her New York sojourn in late 1980, Imelda invited Ninoy to her hotel
room to caution him against counting on the Reagan administration. "You
must behave yourself," she said. "This is a different government and you could
be picked up." Their meeting, one of several during his exile, illustrated the
odd, often inexplicable, coziness of their relationship. Ninoy confided to me
that once, in New York, he responded to a summons from her at midnight to
come to party at her Waldorf suite—where, clearly, she wanted to show her
hold over him to her glitzy guests. Presumably he felt indebted to her for his
surgery, but another time she urged him to come to terms with Marcos, saying,
"You can be his heir." Demurring, he explained that he had suffered for his
principles and would compromise only if Marcos reformed. After Ninoy's
murder, Marcos similarly disclosed that he had often called him from Manila.
"He was the only opponent I really respected," Marcos said somewhat mawk-
ishly, leaving me to wonder whether he was sincere or putting on one of his
acts.

Though Cory hoped to remain in America, by early 1982 Ninoy was thinking
about going home. Most of the moderate opposition factions had grouped in
a loose coalition called the United Democratic Nationalist Organization,
headed by Salvador "Doy" Laurel, who until recently had sided with Marcos.
Without his leadership, Ninoy reckoned, they would be crushed by the Communists, whose strength was growing. The increasingly polarized political
situation was also being exacerbated by the crippled economy, a huge foreign
debt and massive corruption. Still, Ninoy believed, Marcos was the key. "The
tragedy of tragedies," he told an interviewer, "is that only Marcos can bring
us back to democracy . . . the *only* man today who can decree a clean and
honest election." By implication, only he could persuade Marcos to reform.

Time also pressed Ninoy, who had heard that Marcos was gravely ill. The
rumor was real. Marcos's debilitating yet not fatal disease was lupus ery-
thematosus, which can affect the kidneys and requires regular dialysis. During

his visit to Washington in 1982, he was tested at Walter Reed Hospital. He later underwent two kidney transplants, one on August 7, 1983, which aborted, and another, successful, in November 1984. The donor in the first is said to have been his son Bong Bong, in the second, his illegitimate son. Attributing his increasingly frequent absences to old war wounds, Marcos vehemently denied that he was sick. Indeed, he kept his condition so concealed that he stymied even the CIA, and a Filipino surgeon who discussed it with an American reporter was mysteriously murdered. His secrecy had a purpose. He had refused to appoint a successor, and any hint that he was near death would trigger a scramble for power. Speculating, Ninoy foresaw Imelda seizing the presidency with General Ver behind her as chief of a military junta. The vision infused him with a sense of urgency to return.

As usual, Ninoy talked too much, and a shower of warnings deluged him—most of them orchestrated by Marcos. On May 21, 1983, Imelda was again in New York and, speaking for Marcos, implored him "as a mother and wife" to postpone his journey until "the area is sanitized." As an inducement to stay, she offered to loan him $10 million and recruit such experts as David Rockefeller and Felix Rohatyn to manage the money. Back home shortly afterward, she told friends that Ninoy would be dead in "just one hour" if he returned. Enrile later cabled Ninoy that he was "convinced beyond a reasonable doubt that there are plots against your life," and exhorted him to wait "for at least a month."

Though worried, Ninoy refused to cancel. As he saw it, Marcos was trying to keep him away for two possible reasons: His presence might be embarrassing during Reagan's planned visit to Manila in the fall or would foul up the legislative elections scheduled for 1984. Or maybe Imelda and Ver knew that Marcos was dying and did not want him back to obstruct their takeover. Whatever, Ninoy was certain that Marcos "won't shoot me," as he told a reporter. A secret State Department prognosis was more prescient: "Assassination is not Marcos's style . . . but it is not beyond the capability of some of his operatives."

Heeding Enrile's advice to delay, Ninoy did not leave Boston until August 12. He flew to Singapore and drove to nearby Malaysia, where he met with a few Southeast Asian officials to explain his mission. Then he doubled back to Taipei, the capital of Taiwan, his springboard for Manila. There, hoping that a press escort would protect him, he picked up several correspondents, among them Sandra Burton of *Time* and his sister Lupita's husband, Ken Kashiwahara, an ABC television reporter based in San Francisco. As Kashiwahara recalled, Ninoy was on an "awful emotional rollercoaster," joking, talking, telephoning. Late on the morning of August 21, they embarked for Manila, an hour away.

Ninoy's mood varied on the flight. He chatted with the correspondents until the plane began its descent. Then he went to the toilet to slip a bulletproof vest under his tan bush jacket and, returning to his seat, he fingered a rosary and prayed. As the wheels hit the runway, he yelled with typical bravado to the television crews: "Get your cameras out." A welcoming crowd, alerted by his supporters, jammed the terminal. The plane taxied to a berth, where a blue van stood, flanked by troops. Three soldiers came aboard, holding back the reporters and passengers as they steered Ninoy into the boarding tube and down a service stairway. A jumble of voices echoed from the stairway, one in Tagalog shouting, "Here he comes, I'll do it," another in Cebuano, the Visayan language, barking, "Let me shoot." Suddenly there were five pops, strangely followed by a salvo. Killed by a single shot in the back of his head, Ninoy lay at the foot of the stairs, not far from a bullet-riddled body in mechanic's clothes, later identified as Rolando Galman.

★ ★ ★

The quintessential martyred hero, Ninoy now ranks with José Rizal as the Philippine national messiah. And his assassination, like Rizal's execution, accelerated rather than changed the country's history. By 1896, when Rizal was shot, Filipinos had already turned against Spanish rule, and his death sparked open rebellion. Similarly, Filipinos had lost confidence in Marcos by 1983, and Ninoy's murder crystallized their opposition. Both men thus kindled explosions that were awaiting a spark. In both instances, the fuse burned slowly.

Though the outrage against Ninoy spelled the beginning of his end, Marcos managed to retard his collapse for two and a half years. In part he outmaneuvered his Filipino foes until, finally, they unified behind Cory. He also benefited from America's amorphous approach as his friend President Reagan resisted pressures from the State Department, the Pentagon and Congress to act firmly. Events following Ninoy's death stumbled along two tracks: one in Manila, the other in Washington. Ultimately they converged through a series of unpredictable circumstances, again illustrating Rudyard Kipling's aphorism "A policy is the blackmail levied on the fool by the unforeseen."

Imelda was lunching with her courtiers at a chic Chinese restaurant when an urgent call summoned her to the Malacañang palace. She rushed to see Marcos, who was in bed, recovering from his kidney transplant of two weeks before. He told her that Ninoy had been shot, but had no idea whether Ninoy was dead or alive. Her friends had accompanied her, and she gave them the news, lamenting, "Now they're going to blame us." Uncertain of Ninoy's condition, she prayed to the crucifix still adorning the statue of the Infant Jesus, which he had given her before going to Dallas three years earlier. She and her group sat in the gloomy palace foyer through the afternoon as visitors shuffled in and out—Enrile, Ver, General Fidel Ramos, then commander of the constabulary. Finally someone arrived to announce that Ninoy was dead. Imelda hurried to Marcos's room and returned to report that he was vomiting, as he did in moments of stress.

Propped up, his face puffy and his voice somber, Marcos spoke on television the next day. Through Imelda and others, he said, he had "practically begged" Ninoy not to return. Then, without a shred of evidence, he blamed the "heinous" crime on the Communists, alleging that Galman had been their agent. In fact, Galman was a two-bit thug and member of the "Monkees," terrorists organized by the army to counter Communist hit squads. He had formerly worked for Cory's cousin Eduardo Cojuangco, who maintained a private security force, and had served time in jail for assault and robbery. Two days before Ninoy's murder, an air force officer treated him to a pair of whores—his unexpected last fling. The prostitutes later vanished after being abducted by a couple of armed men and, obviously murdered, their remains were finally discovered in November 1988. The scheme was crystal clear. Ninoy had been assassinated by his military escorts, who simultaneously killed the hapless Galman to make him appear to be the murderer. The audacity of the operation, conducted on a sunny day before thousands at the Manila airport, seemed incredible. Equally incomprehensible in the years ahead was the futile quest for the brains behind the plot. Was it Marcos, Imelda, Ver, Eduardo Cojuangco or a combination thereof? To this day the truth has not emerged—and perhaps it never will.

Representative Stephen Solarz of Brooklyn, a liberal Democrat and early Marcos critic, threatened to promote a cut in U.S. military aid to the Philippines unless the culprits were speedily prosecuted. Michael Armacost, the American ambassador in Manila, also pressed Marcos to act quickly. Marcos ordered a "thorough" investigation, and a spastic succession of panels and probes followed over the next two years, yielding millions of words and tons of paper—without unraveling the riddle of who ordered Ninoy's assassination.

The task was virtually impossible under a judiciary that Marcos had corrupted for years. After his first commission of jurists crumbled for lack of credibility, he named a board headed by Corazon Juliano-Agrava, a reputedly independent retired judge. But he secretly warned her against implicating Ver, claiming that the army would react violently. Complying, she said elliptically at the start of the inquiry that her aim was to promote "peace and harmony." Her four colleagues on the panel nevertheless insisted that twenty-six soldiers, including Ver, stand trial. Finally, with Agrava dissenting, the group recommended an indictment. Under U.S. pressure, Marcos reluctantly conceded. However, he covertly instructed the chief judge and prosecutor assigned to the case to acquit Ver. "Put on a show. I know how to reciprocate," he said—an implicit warning that he also knew how to retaliate.

Marcos, confident that the fix was in, promised as the trial opened late in January 1985 that Ver would be reinstated as chief of staff if acquitted. But the prosecutor, defying him, summoned Rebecca Quijano, a handsome businesswoman of thirty-two who had been aboard the plane with Ninoy and seen him shot. Observed sobbing hysterically at the airport, she was dubbed "the crying lady" by the Manila press. In court she pointed at the gunman, but the defense discredited her by revealing that she had once been jailed in Hong Kong for fraud. The accommodating judge dismissed other testimony on a technicality, and Ver and his comrades were acquitted in December. The verdict was predictable. Marcos could not permit the conviction of Ver, his *compadre*—an obligation that superseded the pursuit of justice. Still, the legal farce had a significant impact. It buttressed the U.S. officials who by now were striving to persuade President Reagan that Marcos could not be reformed. Equally important, it stoked the hostility to Marcos that had inflamed masses of Filipinos since Ninoy's assassination.

Ninoy's aged mother, Aurora, had been a political wife and mother, and she herself had keen political instincts. Hardly had Ninoy been murdered on August 21, 1983, than she turned the tragedy into political theater. Ordering his bloody face and clothes left uncleaned, she said, "I want people to see what they did to my son." His body, put on display in a Manila church, began to bloat in the tropical heat, and women fainted at the sight after waiting for hours to pay their respects. The exploitation of Ninoy's death disturbed Cory, who had returned with her children, but the effect was phenomenal.

Ninoy's funeral, a memorable event in Philippine history, took place at a baroque Manila church under the auspices of Cardinal Sin, attired in the gold and purple vestments of his station. Despite the pomp and pageantry of the mass, the atmosphere was familial. A toastmaster, sounding like an uncle at a wedding anniversary, introduced Cory as Ninoy's "better half" and, in her nasal tone, she thanked the weeping mourners for their "display of love and devotion." Sin struck a political note, decrying the climate of "oppression and corruption, fear and anguish" created by the Marcos regime. Addressing a final farewell to Ninoy, he intoned, "May the martyrs welcome you."

The funeral cortege, which brought out a million or more people, snaked through Manila for eleven hours from the church to the cemetery, covering nearly twenty miles. Bedecked with yellow chrysanthemums, Ninoy's casket rode atop a huge trailer truck that inched through the crowd as spectators looked down from windows and rooftops. The Aquinos had adopted yellow as their color, and everyone wore a touch of yellow: ribbons, caps, T-shirts. The marchers formed the letter *L* with their fingers to signify Laban, the opposition political party, and they sang "Ang Bayan Ko," or "My Country," a haunting old nationalist melody. A few, indignant at the record of American support for Marcos, booed as they passed the U.S. Embassy, but most restrained themselves to avoid offending the American news media. The American connection was still intact in the mind of one participant, who proudly remarked to Sandra Burton of *Time,* "You can compare this to the deaths of JFK and Elvis." Undaunted by a rainstorm, the mourners continued after dark, somehow producing candles that sparkled like fireflies as they reached the cemetery. The interment, in a vault, was fast, efficient and, except for a brief prayer, silent.

The procession was the first in a series of parades, demonstrations and riots that intermittently paralyzed Manila until Marcos finally fled the country. The nation faced its worst crisis since World War II, but Filipinos, inspired by Ninoy's death, released their emotions in a zany eruption of pop culture. Yellow banners festooned taxis, jeepneys and cars, and their passengers sported yellow ribbons, sold in the streets by cigarette vendors. The celebration enthralled ordinary folk, constantly in need of distraction, and it also captured the imagination of the upper classes, always ready for a new trend. Young businessmen jogged for Ninoy, society matrons gave teas for Ninoy, fashion models strutted in tight T-shirts emblazoned with Ninoy's portrait, and a punk rock star named Joey "Pepe" Smith honored Ninoy with a "musical tribute" of frenzied rhythms.

Overnight, Ninoy became an object of religious reverence. Sound trucks blaring prayers for his soul cruised the city, and worshipers packed churches to evoke his memory. Cory heralded him as a redeemer, suggesting that his soul lived in her. His mother attended a mass at which a figure of Christ on the cross bore a black heart inscribed with Ninoy's name in blood-red letters, and she spoke of his "crucifixion" at the Manila airport and his present "resurrection" in the eyes of the people. Priests repeated the same theme, one of them terming his murder a "reenactment of the death of Jesus." No less an authority than one of President Nixon's convicted aides, Charles Colson, who like Ninoy was "born again" behind bars, wrote a testimonial to him in a Manila magazine: "I consider Benigno Aquino a Christian martyr." By contrast, the Reverend Jerry Falwell of the Moral Majority visited Manila in November 1985 and reproached the U.S. press for its "unfair" view of Marcos, who had made the Philippines "a paradise."

Filipino intellectuals fit Ninoy into the Philippine tradition of the martyred nationalist. They traced his antecedents back to such self-styled messiahs as Apolinario de la Cruz, who was executed by the Spanish for his abortive peasant revolt in the nineteenth century—and, of course, to Rizal. "Our people had to be renewed in spirit," observed the Filipino writer Nick Joaquin. "The nationalist movement could reach them only in the guise of religion, a magical nature religion, but with Christian forms." Cardinal Sin also hailed Ninoy as a symbol of salvation, and his endorsement encouraged militant Filipino priests and nuns to mix piety and politics.

The ferment further eroded the confidence of the Manila business community in the ability of the regime to improve the economy. Within a month of Ninoy's death, rich Filipinos fearful of instability transferred half a billion dollars to safe havens in the United States, Hong Kong and Switzerland. The staggering capital flight shattered the Philippine peso, forcing Marcos to devalue the currency. The cost of oil and other imported necessities rose, and soaring prices rekindled the unrest. International bankers, who had loaned enormous sums to Marcos, were jittery. By October 1983, the foreign debt had reached nearly $25 billion, up $6 billion over the previous month. Investigating, the bankers found that Marcos had doctored the ledgers to show reserves of $1 billion more than he actually had—and that his regime was nearly bankrupt. Their only recourse was to reschedule the debt, but from then on their trust in him was gone. They would have been appalled had they realized the extent to which, amid all this, he was secretly squirreling millions abroad.

Inflation, unemployment and other symptoms of the sick economy were meanwhile spurring the Communist insurrection, which by late 1984 had spread to sixty-two of the country's seventy-three provinces. Marcos, to hide his inadequacies, continually minimized the threat. But in June 1984, James Nach, a U.S. Embassy political officer, sent a troubling report to Washington. A studious official who had served in Vietnam, he was familiar with insurgencies. He had traveled widely in the Philippine countryside keeping track of the Communists, and now he estimated their strength at eight or ten thousand regulars and perhaps half a million supporters—dramatic growth from the handful of teachers and students of a decade earlier. Unlike the Vietnamese guerrillas, they were not receiving arms or funds from the Soviet Union, China or any other foreign source. Plainly, Marcos was at fault. Nach doubted that Marcos was "capable of turning the situation around." And without "new directions from the top," he predicted, the "continued deterioration" could lead to "ultimate defeat and a Communist takeover."

★　★　★

Opening hearings on the Philippines in September 1984, Congressman Solarz took Nach's analysis further. A Communist victory, he said, would mean the loss of America's bases and cripple "our ability to preserve . . . the balance of power in Asia." Richard Armitage, an assistant secretary of defense, revealed at the time that the United States had leased land on the Pacific islands of Guam and Tinian for a possible "redeployment" of the bases. Other U.S. officials, equally anxious, pondered ways to avert a Philippine disaster. All agreed, as Nach had written, that Marcos was the problem.

Michael Armacost, the U.S. ambassador in Manila, shared the view. A scholarly professional, he was unsentimental, disciplined and realistic. Assigned to renegotiate the bases accord, he had hobnobbed with the Marcoses as an expedient, earning jibes from some of his staff. He switched after Ninoy's death. One of the few foreign diplomats to attend the funeral, he soon blamed Marcos publicly for the tottering economy. Irked by his shift, Imelda alleged to me that he was really a spy for his brother Samuel, then head of the Bank of America, a major Philippine creditor. He left Manila early in 1984 to become undersecretary of state, the number-three State Department job, which put him in a pivotal policy spot in Washington. His successor as ambassador, Stephen Bosworth, also a career diplomat, had no experience in Asia. But despite his placid exterior, he became one of Marcos's fervent foes. Others in the State Department included the assistant secretary for Asian affairs, Paul Wolfowitz, and John Maisto, the Philippine desk officer, who had served in Manila and had married into a prominent Filipino family. Morton Abramowitz, the intelligence chief, was a particularly blunt critic of Marcos. They were all immensely strengthened by Admiral William Crowe, the navy commander for the Pacific and later Chairman of the Joint Chiefs of Staff.

Senior officers usually defend the status quo, but Crowe, a big, bluff, bald Kentuckian, was an unusual officer. An Annapolis graduate with a Ph.D. in international affairs from Princeton, he was bold, outspoken and iconoclastic. As Pacific commander he had watched the Philippines from his Honolulu headquarters, and he was aware of the crisis there when he revisited Manila in June 1984, just before moving to Washington. He studied the situation and talked with Marcos, reaching a conclusion that he later summed up for me in his Pentagon office: "Things had to change. Marcos was not making the decisions that had to be made, primarily because of personal vanity. His health was a serious problem. He was concerned about his survival, his affluence and his well-being, and the country was sliding downhill. So, I felt, he had to go." Crowe then took two extraordinary steps for an officer trained to stay out of politics. He wrote a long letter to Marcos, proposing urgent reforms. At the same time, though certain that Marcos would not comply, he sent a report to Reagan in which he strongly suggested that "we start right now to develop a policy to persuade Marcos to leave office." Crowe was "very uneasy," he recollected: "It's not comfortable to recommend to your own government that a head of state be deposed or encouraged to step down. That is a momentous step."

Few top U.S. officials were prepared for so drastic a measure. Secretary of State George Shultz, who later favored dumping Marcos, was still undecided—though, Crowe recalled, "he listened to me." By contrast, Defense Secretary Caspar Weinberger was, in Crowe's words, "a conservative, reluctant to make changes . . . a tough man to persuade." William Casey, the CIA director, was a Marcos fan. In any case, how could Marcos be eliminated? The question evoked haunting memories of the coup against South Vietnamese

President Ngo Dinh Diem, the ouster of the shah of Iran and acquiescence to the Sandinista takeover in Nicaragua—all subsequent disasters. Reforming Marcos seemed to be the only option, but Reagan had to be convinced even of that imperative.

Marcos desperately awaited Reagan's scheduled stopover in Manila in November 1983, three months after Ninoy's murder, figuring that it would signify U.S. approval of his regime. For the same reason, his official American critics sought to annul the visit. They succeeded by reminding Nancy of the assassination attempt against Reagan in Washington in 1981, stressing that Manila was a security nightmare. Marcos was disappointed, but Reagan reassured him in a personal letter of their "warm and firm" friendship, and added, "I've always had confidence in your ability to handle things."

In January 1984, the State Department drafted a policy palatable to Reagan. While Marcos "is part of the problem," the secret document said, "he is also necessarily part of the solution." The United States did not intend to "remove" or "destabilize" him, but would persuade him to reform through a carrot-and-stick process of easing or tightening his foreign-debt burden. Admiral Crowe, Congressman Solarz, Morton Abramowitz and others were skeptical—as were, privately, even some of the State Department authors of the policy. Marcos, they expected, would make cosmetic gestures and do nothing to streamline the army, dismantle the monopolies or introduce other real changes. He did just that in May 1984 by holding legislative elections, then stiffening again when, despite the usual fraud, opposition candidates won heavily in Manila.

Gulled by Marcos's deceptive liberality, Reagan could not see the need to press him to reform. In his second debate with former Vice President Walter Mondale during the 1984 presidential campaign, he admitted that "there are things that do not look good to us" in the Philippines. To throw Marcos "to the wolves," however, would leave America "facing a Communist power in the Pacific." Reagan had swallowed the line that Marcos regularly fed U.S. presidents. But portraying Marcos as the sole barrier to Communism, as Reagan had, subverted the State Department's hopes of encouraging the emergence of a cohesive opposition that would, along with American pressure, push Marcos toward at least modest reform. Instead, Reagan had dismissed Marcos's rivals as irrelevant.

Secretary of State Shultz, though now inching into the anti-Marcos group, was temperamentally cautious. Late in 1984, when Ambassador Bosworth was back in Washington on consultation, Shultz urged him to exercise restraint. "This is no time for homers," he said. "Let's try to score a run or two, maybe get a single or a base on balls or a sacrifice bunt." But Shultz was also trying to chip away at Reagan's unalloyed devotion to Marcos. Under his influence, Reagan backtracked from his campaign remark in an interview with *The New York Times* in February 1985 and conceded the existence of a Filipino opposition that was "also pledged to democracy."

By the middle of 1985, the Philippines topped the CIA's fever chart and, Reagan's reticence notwithstanding, a growing consensus in Washington advocated amending policy to read "Marcos is the problem"—excluding him from the solution. That conclusion was reached by Frederick Brown, a member of the Senate Foreign Relations Committee staff, who toured the Philippines in August. Marcos's "prime objective is to stay in power, not to promote change," he reported, and reforms ran "diametrically counter" to his interests. The report made an impact on Senator Richard Lugar, a Republican from Indiana and chairman of the committee, as well as others on Capitol Hill. In Manila, meanwhile, Bosworth tightened the controls on Marcos's use of U.S. aid. Bosworth also exhorted Marcos to "revitalize democratic institutions"— though, Bosworth later recalled, "I could see his eyes glaze over as he heard this once more from an American ambassador."

The State Department professionals, figuring that one of Reagan's close friends might sway Marcos, recruited Senator Paul Laxalt, a conservative Republican from Nevada. As he prepared to leave for Manila in October 1985, Admiral Crowe startled him by saying, "Get rid of Marcos." Reagan, who still regarded Marcos as redeemable, entrusted Laxalt with a personal letter for Marcos that rehashed the same reforms Bosworth had proposed. Marcos defended himself in a windy monologue, digressing into complaints about his unfavorable image in the American press. Agreeing, Laxalt recommended a Washington public relations agency, Black, Manafort, Stone and Kelly, which usually handled Republicans—and which eventually charged Marcos nearly a million dollars.

Marcos had been considering a stratagem since the start of 1985. By holding a "snap" presidential election instead of awaiting the end of his present term in 1987, he could gain another six years in office. He would rig the count to win by a slim margin, thereby creating an illusion of honesty to silence his American critics. To deflect them further, he disguised the election as an American initiative by leaking to *Newsweek* that William Casey had suggested it during talks in Manila in May 1985. In fact, Casey never mentioned the subject. But subsequently, when Marcos did schedule the election, Casey claimed credit in order to gild his own role. Laxalt similarly wrote later that he had "briefly discussed" the idea with Marcos at their meetings in October. Bosworth, who was present at their two sessions, recalled differently. "At no time," Bosworth told me, "did they raise the possibility of advancing the election date." Afterward, though, Marcos did hint to Laxalt over the telephone that he was pondering an election—which he then proceeded to announce with his usual theatrical flair on November 3, 1985.

He chose for the performance David Brinkley's Sunday morning television show on ABC. Replying to George Will, the commentator, he said that he would hold an election "perhaps in three months or less." American congressmen and the news media, he added lavishly, were "all invited to come."

The spontaneity had been contrived. Marcos had advised the Manila press to prepare for an "important announcement" and slated a news conference to follow the program. Laxalt, after his telephone conversation with Marcos the night before, had planted the election question with George Will.

Marcos had used American television in hopes of conveying to the U.S. public that he was not the despot depicted by the press but truly devoted to democracy, as befit a Filipino who had grown up under America's benign tutelage. He also sought to arm his conservative claque in Washington with ammunition to fend off his State Department foes. So, once again, he saw the United States as a more crucial political battlefield than the Philippines—a perception shared by his Filipino rivals.

His Washington critics reacted variously: pessimists certain that he would fake the results and remain in office, optimists sure of his being deterred from fraud by the outside observers and thus doomed. In 1987, at his Honolulu exile, Marcos confided to me that the snap election was the "biggest mistake" he ever made. "I didn't realize that the U.S. government was going to intervene and that massive black propaganda and conspiracy by the American press would defame and libel me. Had I been alert, I would not have fallen into the trap. But it was my doing, and I accept the blame."

Conspicuously absent from his historical perspective was Cory Aquino's role in his collapse. No American effort to topple him would have succeeded had she not, by mobilizing the opposition, pushed him to the edge.

15. REVOLUTION AND RESTORATION

★ ★ ★

Dear God, let it not be me," Cory pleaded in the summer of 1985, flinching at the challenge when she was increasingly cited as the only person who could mend the split opposition to Marcos. "I didn't want to be the candidate," she recalled to me later. "I'm very private and wasn't meant to be at center stage." But she canvased family members and friends—and, begging for divine guidance, she prayed "as I'd never prayed before." The pressure on her intensified after Marcos scheduled the election. If she abstained, she knew, the likely contender would be Salvador Laurel, a routine politician of dubious repute. A priest, couching the issue in moral terms she grasped, was decisive. In this struggle between good and evil, he said, she alone embodied the values of "truth, freedom and justice" that could beat Marcos. She agreed to run on condition that her supporters compile a draft petition containing a million signatures. They did—and, after a day of meditation at a convent near Manila, she declared.

Now, in need of political counsel, she consulted the country's shrewdest politician: Cardinal Sin. He advised her to work with Laurel, but she would have him only as her vice president. Sin then urged Laurel, who had presidential hopes, to accept the number-two slot. "Cory is more popular than you are," Sin flatly told him. "Make the sacrifice, or Marcos will win." After waffling for weeks, Laurel conceded.

Cory had showed herself to be tougher than she appeared. But she was ingenuous in an interview with *The New York Times* in December 1985. The newspaper's Manila correspondent, Seth Mydans, brought along the hard-nosed executive editor, A. M. "Abe" Rosenthal, who happened to be in town. Untutored, Cory nattered away, occasionally asking the amiable Mydans how to answer the questions, or replying as though she were thinking aloud. If elected, she would "probably" try Marcos for Ninoy's murder. She favored the "removal" of the U.S. bases at some future date, preferring instead to bring the Philippines into a "zone of neutrality," and would open a "dialogue" with the Communists, many of whom merely "want justice." As for her presidential program: "The only thing I can really offer the Filipino people is my sincerity."

The Washington conservatives cackled at her naïveté. Worse yet, Rosenthal returned home to decry her incompetence. His judgment strengthened Reagan's bias against her and even left an imprint on Shultz, whose faith in Marcos had by then faded. Two months later, when Cory was the only alternative to the crumbling Marcos regime, Shultz still recalled at a key meeting that Rosenthal had pictured her as "vacant." But her flop in *The New York Times* prompted her American friends to pitch in to repair the damage.

Cory's entourage sneered at Marcos for hiring an American public relations firm. But Robert Trent Jones, the designer of the golf courses at the Aquino estate, quietly engaged D. H. Sawyer and Associates, a New York public relations firm that usually handled Democrats. At Jones's expense, Sawyer assigned Mark Malloch Brown, a rumpled Englishman, to teach Cory to cope with irreverent American reporters and to shade her remarks to appeal to U.S. audiences. Brown, formerly an editor of the London *Economist,* posed as a journalist, and Cory's aides pointed to his nationality as evidence that Americans were not involved in her campaign.

The claim was phony. William Overholt, an American banker based in Hong Kong, was a vital player. Married to the daughter of a retired Filipino general, he had extensive connections in Manila and elsewhere, which he used on Cory's behalf. He worked with Jaime Ongpin, the president of the Benguet mining company, to raise money for her. To protect her he brought in two security specialists, one formerly with Australian intelligence and the other a British secret service agent disguised as a journalist. Another important American was James Reuter, a Jesuit priest from New Jersey, whose Radio Veritas circumvented the government network to broadcast news of opposition activities along with Cory's messages. Reuter's nineteen stations received a grant from the U.S. Agency for International Development filtered through the Asia Foundation, whose Manila representative, Edith Coliver, proudly advertised her pro-Cory sentiments. Senator Lugar helped her as well by observing the election with his group of twenty American congressmen, state officials, clergymen and others. Superficially it all seemed reminiscent of Colonel Edward Lansdale's management of Ramón Magsaysay, but in fact no American was that close to Cory.

The U.S. Embassy also lent her subtle support, such as advice on how to focus on American public opinion. The U.S. aid agency partly financed NAMFREL, the National Committee for Free Elections, which was to help her by signaling Marcos's skulduggery at the polls. Her sympathizers were bolstered, too, by the real or illusory belief that Ambassador Bosworth would ultimately defend her. A tactful diplomat, he was restrained in public, but Manila's flourishing rumor mill quoted him as having pledged privately, "If Marcos tries to stay in power, we'll disintegrate him in thirty days."

For the U.S. news media the event was irresistible: a morality play in an Americanized setting with the principal characters speaking English. The major American television networks each fielded several crews along with such stars as Tom Brokaw and Peter Jennings, and they could have been back home.

The candidates knew all about prime time and ratings—so much so that Marcos insisted on being interviewed on CBS only by Dan Rather. He and Cory craved attention in the United States in the realization that American validation made them credible to the Filipinos, who distrusted their own news media. Many Filipinos suspected that Marcos had faked his war record, for example, but the story only became true after it appeared in *The New York Times*—and was reprinted by Manila's opposition newspapers. The correspondents also served as witnesses, particularly for Cory, whose staff directed them to areas where Marcos's goons might disrupt the voting. To Marcos, conversely, journalists were snooping nuisances, yet he too needed them to deliver his message.

As the campaign gathered momentum, it was plain that much of the old oligarchy dispossessed by Marcos had swung to Cory. Rich Manila matrons garbed in tailored yellow blouses answered telephones and served as typists at her headquarters or put their chauffeured cars at her disposal. Despite threats from Marcos, companies loaned her their private aircraft to tour the provinces and poured a total of some $6 million into her coffers. The clergy openly backed her. One Sunday morning, at a church on Negros, the parish priest informed me that she would receive the collection plate. I sensed, traveling with her, that she was altering the pattern of Philippine politics. Elections had traditionally been races between rival clans, with voters obedient to their patrons. Now, it seemed, Cory was in direct communion with the people, projecting an aura of sanctity that almost mesmerized devout Filipinos. Her Joan of Arc image, though a tired stereotype, was nevertheless real.

One night in the Mindanao capital of Davao, she delivered a tedious speech drafted by a professor. The audience, packed onto a school basketball court, could not have caught much of her English—and even less the academic jargon. Even so, I felt, her mere presence was electrifying. Another day I drove with her into Cavite, a heavily populated province south of Manila. Yellow banners and bunting adorned every town, and crowds hugged the road, waving the *L* sign as she inched along in her van, smiling and waving back. Her brief speeches at one spot or another were again platitudes, and again it made no difference. She exuded an air of buoyant piety attuned to the garish mysticism of Filipino religion. Marcos's few campaign outings, by contrast, were lugubrious. Visibly ill, he had to be lifted bodily onto platforms, and his cracked voice was slurred and often inaudible. He was incontinent, a grim task for his handlers.

Having witnessed other Philippine elections, I knew that crowds, speeches and cheers were less important than control of the final tally. I guessed, consequently, that Cory would lose even if she won—which was what nearly happened.

Election day, February 7, 1986, was marred by the usual cases of stolen ballot boxes, intimidation and even killings, almost all of it by Marcos's thugs. The serious cheating, though, came in adding the votes. Under U.S. pressure, Marcos had allowed NAMFREL, the independent monitor, to tabulate the results in tandem with COMELEC, the official Commission on Elections. Marcos wanted a credibly slim margin of victory, not a suspicious landslide. So, while NAMFREL reported Cory ahead, COMELEC delayed the count to enable Marcos to tailor the total. Lugar's observers immediately smelled fraud, as did the platoons of State Department and CIA men brought in especially to track the race. A night after the polls closed, thirty computer technicians tallying the vote dramatized Marcos's sham by fleeing the COMELEC headquarters for the refuge of a church—contending that the figures showing Cory in the lead were being discarded.

A State Department task force in Washington, keeping an around-the-clock watch on the Philippines, provided Reagan with massive evidence of Marcos's abuses, but Reagan preferred his own eccentric sources: Nancy fed him information that she was receiving by telephone from Imelda. Donald Regan, his chief of staff, who knew nothing about the Philippines, nevertheless pressed him to stick with Marcos. Their bias was shared by William Casey, despite the messages of his men in the field. Intuitively, too, Reagan felt attached to Marcos—as if Marcos were "a hero on a bubble gum card he had collected as a kid," as a senior State Department official mused later. He was not even keen to hear Lugar, who landed in Washington from Manila early on February 11. Sensing that Reagan was spinning out of control, Shultz had urged Lugar to return directly to the capital and drive straight to the White House.

Lugar, perceiving that Reagan was prepared to recognize a Marcos victory, warned him that Marcos was "cooking the results." Reagan replied by mentioning a television segment he had seen of Filipinos destroying ballots and identified them as Cory's campaigners—when, as it later turned out, they were Marcos supporters. Lugar persisted, relating his own accounts of Marcos's chicanery. Reagan was not listening. Speaking for him, Larry Speakes, his press secretary, implied that Cory had lost and should "get on the team" with Marcos to "form a government." That evening, at a rare news conference, Reagan admitted that violence had been "evident" and conceded to the "possibility of fraud" in the election, but he suggested that "it could have been . . . occurring on both sides." His primary concern in the Philippines were the bases, not political liberty. "I don't know of anything more important than those bases," he emphasized.

Flabbergasted, Lugar took an unusual step for a loyal Republican. He refuted Reagan, his party leader, telling an audience in Indianapolis, "The president was misinformed." Other politicians, Republicans and Democrats alike, echoed his dismay. They were largely reacting to constituents who had seen the faraway campaign on television, fallen in love with Cory and shared her passion to make good prevail over evil. Americans were rediscovering that the Philippines had once been a U.S. colony and, infused with renewed missionary zeal, they felt it their duty to extend their benevolence to their former protégés.

Cory was furious that Reagan equated her with the wicked Marcos. She vented her anger on Bosworth—who himself was devastated. He and his embassy staff had bombarded Washington with proof of Marcos's fraud, only to be shattered by Reagan's disregard. "It was probably the single worst day of my life," Bosworth later told me. He called Cory, who at first refused to see him, saying, "What for, if I'm being accused of cheating." Finally she relented and, Bosworth recalled, entering her office was "like walking into a freezer." She gave him "the full benefit of one of her icier moments"—and, in a rare gesture for an ambassador, the president's personal representative, he disavowed Reagan. "That wasn't the full U.S. position you heard," he told

Cory. "It sometimes takes us a while to reach the right conclusion, but I'm convinced that we will soon. Please be patient."

Frustrated, Bosworth shouted over the telephone to his colleagues at the State Department. "But they were just as horrified," he recollected, "and I was like the minister preaching to the choir." Shultz soon called him and, in his bland voice, said: "Okay, you've made your point. Now relax. We'll try to fix it." He did. Reagan had gone to his Santa Barbara ranch, and Shultz dunned him by telephone with details of Marcos's deceit. On February 15, Reagan finally acknowledged publicly that the "widespread fraud and violence" had been "perpetrated largely" by Marcos's side. A few hours later, Marcos announced victory—and the first foreign envoy to congratulate him was the Soviet ambassador. Cory promptly claimed success—credibly, according to the CIA's estimates.

Philip Habib, the diplomatic troubleshooter, now plunged into the confusion. A Brooklynite of Lebanese origin, he was a veteran of nearly forty years in the State Department—an ethnic rarity in the patrician corps. He had risen to become ambassador to South Korea and later undersecretary of state before a severe heart attack retired him. Still energetic, he undertook special missions. He had always prided himself on his candor and was even blunter in retirement—figuring, as he put it, that he had "paid his dues."

On February 9, two days after the Philippine election, Shultz interrupted Habib's golf game in Florida to ask him to go to Manila. Habib detested the Marcoses, but he accepted the job—which, as he subsequently described it to me, was "simply to assess the situation." Shultz's real purpose in sending him was to gain time to enable the administration to resolve the deadlock. Habib, however, was too dynamic to play a passive role.

Landing in Manila on February 15, he found himself in a swirl. More than a hundred Catholic bishops had just declared that Marcos's "fraudulent" attempt to retain power "has no moral basis." Then Cory staged a huge rally in the Luneta, appealing for civil disobedience to unseat Marcos. Habib calmed her jitters by reassuring her that he had not come to urge her to compromise. Marcos, whom he saw, claimed to have won the election. For six days Habib interviewed more than a hundred politicians, priests, educators, businessmen—and two journalists, Robert Shaplen of *The New Yorker* and me. He was particularly impressed by Enrile, who seemed to be distancing himself from Marcos and, Habib felt, might soon "reveal his hand." By February 22, as he prepared to depart, Habib had concluded: "Cory had won the election and deserved our support. Marcos was finished, and we ought to offer him asylum in the United States."

Before boarding his U.S. Air Force plane for the flight home, Habib intuitively told an American embassy officer to tell Bosworth, "Something's going to break."

★ ★ ★

Lean and leathery at sixty-two, Juan Ponce Enrile owed his wealth and status to a nimble mind, a sense of timing and patronage. He had been born illegitimate in the mountains of north Luzon and was later adopted by his father, a noted Manila attorney, who sent him to Harvard Law School. Enrile joined

Marcos in 1965 and became his defense minister five years afterward, meanwhile piling up a fortune as Eduardo Cojuangco's associate in the coconut monopoly. But he felt increasingly estranged as Marcos placed the armed forces under General Ver. Soon Enrile discovered that Ver was planning to have him murdered—a fate he escaped when his bodyguards located and liquidated the suspected killer. Enrile's fears also mounted when he learned that Cojuangco, possibly working with Ver, was gunning for him as well. In 1984, Cojuangco hired three Israeli mercenaries to train his private army of nearly two thousand men. Ninoy's death had alarmed Enrile. Until then, he told me later, assassinating a "man of any consequence" was simply not done. Now "nobody was safe."

Enrile formed his own force with a core of some thirty young officers. Starting in late 1983, he secretly imported crates of Israeli weapons along with two retired British commandos to teach his men deceptive tactics. The young Filipino officers, many of them trained in the United States, were serious soldiers—though one, Colonel Gregorio "Gringo" Honasan, was a showman whose stunts included parachute jumping while encoiled by his pet python. As professionals, they lamented the favoritism, incompetence and corruption that pervaded the armed forces, crippling their ability to check the Communist insurgents. Rex Robles, a navy captain, wept as he later described conditions to me: "Our men were fighting in shorts and rubber sandals, without uniforms, boots, even canteens. They were dying for lack of doctors, nurses, medicines—while Marcos's generals stole millions."

In March 1985, the young officers organized the Reform the Armed Forces Movement, or RAM, and soon began to plot. They outlined options ranging from the "benign," like urging Marcos to change, to the "naughty," such as abducting him and forcing him to quit. Eventually they agreed on a "naughty" plan: to oust him and set up a committee including Enrile, Cory, Cardinal Sin and Lieutenant General Fidel Ramos, the constabulary chief, as a transition back to constitutional rule. But Marcos's election announcement in November 1985 jolted them. They could not move without appearing to be thwarting the democratic process. Delaying their plot, they vowed to act should Marcos cheat. Whatever the outcome, their choice for eventual president was Enrile, not Cory.

Like boys on a lark, they noisily conspired over beer in the vast lobby of the Peninsula Hotel, and soon all Manila, including Ver and Bosworth, were in the know. Bosworth reckoned that Ver could easily crush an attempted coup or might preempt it. In either event, Marcos would reimpose martial law under the guise of restoring order, and Reagan would probably approve the action. Bosworth warned both Ver and the RAM officers to do nothing. So the two sides played "bluff" during the early weeks of 1985, as Robles recalled. "We leaked to the press that we were about to move, and they did the same. It was a matter of who blinked first."

Marcos's election chicanery finally spurred the plotters to schedule a coup for the early hours of Sunday, February 23, the feast of Saint Lazarus. Their plan was to attack the Malacañang and seize Marcos—but, above all, not kill him. They alerted Ramos, whose men were vital. Cardinal Sin, obliquely informed, obliquely blessed them. Cory, in the dark, was going with her brother to Cebu to campaign for civil disobedience, and they advised him to keep her there.

Suddenly there was a hitch. On February 20, Marcos had arrested four rebel confederates in his entourage, and they talked. The RAM officers heard of the arrest two days later, when they also learned that other comrades had been picked up. It was now the day before the coup, and Colonel Honasan warned Enrile that an attack against the palace would be suicide. He had also been told that they were about to be arrested. Hastily revising plans, they decided to retreat to Camp Aguinaldo, a large Manila military compound and site of Enrile's defense ministry, and appeal to other army elements for support.

At six o'clock on the evening of February 22, Enrile arrived at the camp, a bulletproof vest under his olive drab windbreaker. He was joined by Ramos, an undemonstrative West Point graduate. They initially had only two hundred men—no match for Marcos's legions. Enrile first telephoned Bosworth to tell him of their move. Bosworth informed Washington, then began a series of calls to Marcos, urging him not to employ force. Enrile also called Cardinal Sin to say, "I'll be dead in an hour." Soon, mobbed by correspondents, Enrile held a televised news conference in which he recognized Cory as the election winner—revealing that he himself faked nearly four hundred thousand votes for Marcos in his own region. He went on to confess to other duplicity, including the phony ambush in 1972 that gave Marcos the pretext to declare martial law.

Other soldiers drifted into the camp. Within hours, too, thousands of people swarmed around Epifanio de los Santos Avenue, known as Edsa, a broad boulevard running past the compound. Hawkers quickly poured in to peddle food, drinks, cigarettes and Ninoy souvenirs. More disaffected troops arrived, and the crowd swelled. Ramos shifted to Camp Crame, a more defensible installation across the boulevard, where Enrile later joined him. At nine o'-clock that night, the irrepressible Cardinal Sin spoke on Radio Veritas, appealing for support of "our two good friends," Enrile and Ramos. Cory, hearing news of the revolt in Cebu, was convinced that Marcos would swiftly wipe it out. The U.S. consul offered her refuge aboard an American navy frigate anchored in the port. Instead she went to a nearby convent to wait, watch and pray. She telephoned Cardinal Sin, who optimistically told her, "This may be the miracle we've been expecting."

If so, providence was assisted by clandestine American intervention. Rebel helicopters were allowed to refuel and rearm at Clark Field, the U.S. commander noting afterward that technically the base belonged to the Philippines. Defense Secretary Weinberger maintained later that the choppers were helping to "avert bloodshed," though one fired rockets at the Malacañang palace. The American military mission in Manila intercepted messages between the two sides, ostensibly to "make sure that they understood each other," but also to slip intelligence to the rebels. A team of U.S. experts tapped into Ver's secret radio net and furnished the dissidents with his orders to his men. On Sunday morning, when Marcos's troops smashed the Radio Veritas transmitter, CIA specialists provided an alternative system. Usually posing as reporters, CIA men assisted the mutineers in a disinformation campaign to spread phony news about Marcos's intentions.

Marcos could have routed the rebels at the start, when they were weak. Instead he waffled, later claiming that he was being humane. Actually he distrusted his own troops to obey his orders, and he also feared the opprobrium of American opinion. By Sunday afternoon, Manila was delirious. The boulevard between the army camps was a human sea, the crowd surging and receding like a tide as government forces arrived and retreated and returned. Demonstrators carried banners demanding Marcos's resignation. Rebel soldiers, their flag patches inverted, mingled with the throng. One of several climaxes came when loyalist tanks lumbered into the area. As people chanted hymns, priests and nuns knelt in prayer before the machines, and children pressed flowers on the crews. The tanks retired, the people advanced and the tanks withdrew. The tension continued through the day, the crowd cheering each small victory. The Edsa Revolution subsequently became a legend, encapsulated in Cory's escutcheon: People Power.

A surreal electronic battle was also going on as Marcos, Ver, Enrile, Ramos and various intermediaries haggled and bargained over the telephone. Nor was television forgotten. Ramos appeared on *Meet the Press,* vowing to defeat Marcos "by sheer numbers," while Marcos, on the same program, threatened revenge: "We will bide our time, disperse the civilians and then handle Enrile and Ramos." He had been legally elected and would not resign, Marcos insisted—adding, "I don't believe President Reagan would ask me to step down."

Washington is thirteen hours behind Manila, and reports from the U.S. Embassy were swamping the State Department on Saturday morning. At three o'clock that afternoon, Shultz assembled a few of his staff in his elegant seventh-floor office. They were dressed casually, the weekend custom. Among them were Michael Armacost, former U.S. ambassador in Manila and now undersecretary of state; Paul Wolfowitz, the assistant secretary for Asia; and Charles Hill, Shultz's close aide and alter ego, a diligent professional with a razor-sharp mind. Even at this late stage, they were struggling to shape a firm Philippine policy—proof again that policies are often forged in the heat of crisis rather than in cool contemplation.

Slow, laconic and deliberate, Shultz had watched the problem ripen into a crisis, awaiting the moment to act. Seeing that moment, he said: "Marcos is unraveling. At some point we have to tell him it's over, and offer him asylum in the United States." Armacost observed that the picture was still a blur as assorted Filipino factions jockeyed for position. "Once they see a major swing," Shultz replied, "they'll try to save themselves." Hill pleaded for a quick U.S. decision. "Don't underestimate Marcos," he stressed. "If his opponents don't move fast, he'll bring in forces from the provinces and roll over them. We could see Enrile begging for his life and house arrest, and we'll end up with the Marcos dictatorship versus the Communists." Shultz, agreeing, proposed that a statement be drafted for Reagan, pledging a "safe haven" for Marcos and his family. Even so, Shultz was not sanguine.

Marcos was not "going to bend," he went on—and nothing would embarrass Reagan more than being rebuffed by him. Besides, Shultz added, Reagan "isn't the guy to pull the plug on Marcos." So, the staff concluded, the only approach for the moment was to warn Marcos against using force—as Bosworth was doing in Manila. But the crisis still begged for action, and Shultz decided on a meeting the next morning of the National Security Planning Group, the senior policy-making committee.

At nine o'clock the group gathered around the dining room table of his house in suburban Bethesda as his wife, Helena, served coffee and homemade blueberry muffins. Those present included Weinberger, Armacost, Vice Admiral John Poindexter, the president's national security adviser, and Robert Gates, the deputy CIA director, pinch-hitting for William Casey. Habib was there, having arrived the night before from Manila. Shultz had just received a message from Bosworth: "Marcos will not draw the conclusion that he must leave unless President Reagan puts it to him directly. Go for a dignified transition out." The problem now was plain if difficult: how to persuade Reagan to tell Marcos to quit.

Leading off, Habib reported that Marcos was isolated, looked "horrible" and refused "to realize that he faces a widespread movement to dump him." When Shultz cited A. M. Rosenthal's description of Cory as "vacant," Habib dismissed Rosenthal as "a bird of passage [who] flies, perches and then flies away." If Marcos crushed the Enrile mutiny, Habib went on, he would move against Cory next. Shultz concurred: A Marcos police state would polarize the situation and benefit the Communists. He reflected on the damage caused the United States by these "total shifts," like the chaos that followed the falls of Diem and the shah. "We pay a heavy price for our past," he said. Pursuing the point, Weinberger asked, "What happens in the Philippines after Marcos goes?" Habib replied: "It's not Iran. There is a democratic opposition backed by the Catholic Church." When Shultz interposed, "We have a great store of goodwill," Habib pressed on: "If we want to have some control over the situation, we must move fast to a transition." After a brief silence, Shultz declared: "Our conclusion is unanimous. Now we need scenarios."

"Forget reconciliation," Habib began. Cory would not deal with Marcos. The group then offered proposals, one by Weinberger for a new election. "Without a new election I have trouble," he said. "You have trouble with everything," Shultz retorted. "A new election is a must," Weinberger insisted. Gates interceded: "Let's be realistic, not legalistic. The public view is that Aquino won. So we have to think of a way to install her in power and give Marcos a fig leaf to depart. Aquino in, Marcos out." Again Weinberger objected, submitting that Reagan would be distressed if he "publicly appeared" to be dumping Marcos. Poindexter agreed. Someone suggested doing nothing, to which Shultz answered, "There's a lot to to be said for that." Habib thundered: "Give Marcos a chance to stay, and he'll hang on. He has to go!" Shultz, alarmed by the danger of bloodshed if Marcos dug in, discursively recalled his experiences as a marine in a bloody battle against the Japanese during World War II. Then, back on track, he recommended public statements aimed at Marcos, coupled with an emissary to him, perhaps Laxalt again. He called another session at the State Department after lunch, in case Reagan convened a meeting for that day. As he rose from the table, Habib said, "Don't assume a quick solution."

The same cast met in Shultz's office at two o'clock, now with an acute sense of urgency. It was one o'clock on Monday morning in Manila, and Bosworth reported that Marcos might attack the rebels at daybreak. A decision by Reagan was vital before then. Charles Hill, who had attended the morning session at Shultz's house, had taken notes in his spidery handwriting: *Marcos can't govern . . . Forces favors left, bad for us . . . We have more options now than later . . . Do right by Marcos, departure in safety and dignity . . . Presidential phone call . . . Broker transition . . . Public call for no force.* Using the notes, Shultz personally wrote a step-by-step script for Reagan, proposing that Laxalt fly to Manila with a presidential message urging Marcos to resign, with Habib accompanying him to broker the transition.

At three o'clock, the group gathered in the White House Situation Room for a formal National Security Council meeting. Vice President George Bush and Treasury Secretary James Baker were there along with Casey, who had missed the discussions until then. As Reagan listened, the session rapidly became a verbal brawl between Don Regan, his chief of staff, and Habib. Regan, as one participant recalled, "didn't understand or care to understand" the issue, but "thought that he was conveying Reagan's thoughts." Evoking the Iran analogy, he vehemently opposed scuttling Marcos, called Cory an unknown quantity and warned against "opening the door to Communism." Habib, after repeating his case, concluded, "The Marcos era has ended." Endorsing Habib's assessment, Shultz said: "Nobody believes that Marcos can remain in power. He's had it." As the debate droned on, Reagan's attention waned—except when new reports arrived of imminent violence in Manila. He appeared to the anti-Marcos faction to be turning around when, at one point, he remarked that Marcos had to be "approached carefully" and "asked rather than told" to depart. He declined to telephone Marcos and tell him to go, nor would he send him a personal message. Nor would he countenance a replay of Jimmy Carter's refusal to allow the shah to enter the United States until he was near death. Marcos, he affirmed, could have asylum in America. So, as the ninety-minute meeting closed, Reagan had acquiesced to deposing his "old friend."

Two potential catastrophes haunted Reagan and his staff. One was the danger that Marcos, in a final desperate attempt to prevail, might attack the rebel camps, slaughtering masses of civilians—on world television. Equally horrible was the possibility that the mutineers might capture and murder Marcos and his family, thus reenacting the assassination of Diem in the South Vietnamese coup encouraged by the United States. To avert either disaster, Reagan approved a public statement warning Marcos that he "would cause untold damage to the relationship between our two governments" if he used force, and threatened to suspend his military aid unless he obeyed. But Reagan's decision to tell Marcos to leave was kept secret for the moment in the hope that, through private persuasion, he might go voluntarily and thus be spared the embarrassment of having been removed under U.S. pressure.

Three channels were operating. Nancy, constantly being telephoned by Imelda, told her that she and Ferdinand would "certainly" be welcomed in America. Marcos's labor minister, Blas Ople, had come to Washington to lobby for him, and Shultz advised him to urge his boss to depart gracefully. Shultz also called Bosworth, reaching him at about four o'clock on Monday morning, Manila time. He ordered him to inform Marcos that his "time was up," and that "we will make the transition as peaceful as possible." Marcos angrily rejected Bosworth and, going on television, claimed to be in control.

"I will fight to the last breath," he intoned, "even though my family cowers in terror in the palace."

Reagan afterward said with admiration that Marcos "did not want bloodshed or civil strife" and had shown restraint as a result. In reality, Marcos knew, as his troops defected to the rebels in droves, that a military response was too late. He tried to bargain. Calling Enrile, he proposed a coalition excluding Cory. Enrile, wary of Marcos's wiles, refused and urged Cory to legitimize herself quickly in an inauguration—and she did the next day. Equally obsessed with legitimacy, Marcos set his own inauguration for the following day. On Monday afternoon in Washington, while still pursuing the private conduits, Reagan approved a public plea to Marcos to quit: "Attempts to prolong the life of the present regime by violence are futile. A solution to this crisis can only be achieved through a peaceful transition to a new government." Marcos received the message at three o'clock on the morning of Tuesday, February 25, Manila time, and immediately called Laxalt in Washington, hoping through him to reach Reagan.

There, on Monday afternoon, Shultz, Habib and Armacost were in the Capitol building, secretly briefing thirty key members of Congress, including Laxalt. The telephone call from Marcos to Laxalt interrupted the session. Marcos wanted the word straight from Reagan: Was the statement about a "transition" real or another State Department plot? With Shultz, Habib and Armacost hovering over him, Laxalt confirmed it. The conversation lasted twenty minutes, Marcos's raspy voice betraying his exhaustion. He essayed alternatives, like a "power sharing" deal with Cory. After all, he said, he was a veteran at fighting Communists and negotiating with foreign creditors. Floating another idea, he might serve as Cory's "senior adviser" while remaining president until the end of his original term in 1987. Laxalt promised to consult Reagan and call him back.

The briefing finished, Laxalt accompanied Shultz to the State Department to drop off Habib and Armacost. As they drove through a snow flurry, Laxalt asked whether Marcos's proposals for a "power sharing" or "advisory" deal might work. Armacost, recoiling from the ingenuous question, explained that Marcos would eventually rally his loyalists and "you would have civil war." Laxalt then went with Shultz to the White House to confer with Reagan, Poindexter and Regan in the Oval Office. The meeting lasted thirteen minutes. Laxalt recounted his talk with Marcos, and again raised the proposal for an accommodation with Cory. "Impractical," said Shultz. Reagan, nodding assent, added that Marcos would be welcome in the United States "if he saw fit."

Laxalt moved to Poindexter's office and, fulfilling his promise, telephoned Marcos—who at five o'clock in the morning in Manila awaited the call. With Shultz guiding him, Laxalt told Marcos that Reagan had vetoed a deal with Cory but offered him asylum in America. Marcos, still angling for the Olympian word, asked if Reagan wanted him to resign. Laxalt ducked the question. "Senator," Marcos pressed, "what do you think? Should I step down?" Laxalt responded without hesitation: "I think you should cut and cut cleanly. I think the time has come." There was a silence so long that Laxalt, wondering whether they had been disconnected, asked, "Mr. President, are you there?" "Yes," responded Marcos in a thin voice. "I am so very, very disappointed."

Bosworth, who had been planning Marcos's departure for two days, decided on the advice of his military aides that a helicopter lift would be safest. He arranged to take the Marcoses from the Malacañang palace across the Pasig River by barge, then fly them to Clark Field and from there to the United States. The project, ready on Tuesday morning, was soon delayed. Marcos wanted to hold his inauguration ritual. There was packing, dawdling, telephoning friends, attempts at last-ditch deals. Finally, in the late afternoon, the Marcos family and its retinue of sixty were braced to depart. Show biz to the end, Marcos and Imelda stepped out onto a palace balcony, peered at a crowd of supporters and hecklers, and sang a farewell duet: "Because of You."

The helicopters flew the Marcoses to Clark Field, where they were to board a U.S. Air Force transport for the United States. But Marcos balked, asking instead to spend "a couple of days" with his family and friends in Ilocos Norte, his home province. His escort, Major General Theodore Allen, the chief American military aid adviser in the Philippines, telephoned Bosworth, who called Washington, which suggested that he contact Cory. She was torn between her gratitude to Marcos for releasing Ninoy to have heart surgery and her fear that he might stir his native region to revolt. After consulting her advisers, who favored a quick exit, she asked Bosworth: "Is he really ill?" "Aside from being exhausted, I don't know," Bosworth replied. "Well," she said; "let him stay the night at Clark and after that he must leave the country." Soon afterward, the Clark commander reported to Bosworth that loyalist Marcos troops were nearing the base, saying, "I want that guy out of here now." Bosworth agreed. Allen told Marcos, "You can go anywhere you want as long as it's out of the country." That night, the Marcoses and their children took off for Guam, their ultimate destination Hawaii. Once aloft, Imelda began to sing "New York, New York."

The Reagan administration reveled in the neat, bloodless change, as did even its fiercest press critics. "It is a long time since Americans of all political views have felt so good in a transforming event abroad," wrote Anthony Lewis, the liberal *New York Times* columnist, extolling Reagan's "great skill and impeccable timing." Morton Abramowitz, one of the senior State Department officials who had labored to remove Marcos, termed the conjuncture of events "luck, sheer luck."

Reagan never forgave Cory for denying Marcos a visit to his native region, but his faith in Marcos sank as the proof of plunder emerged. The loot found in the Malacañang was shocking enough. Worse yet was the evidence of racketeering by Marcos during his rule and even after his exile in Hawaii. Nearly a hundred civil suits were filed against him in the Philippines, seeking a total of nearly $100 billion. Meanwhile, a grand jury in Honolulu began to probe his attempts to buy weapons to stage a comeback, a breach of the Neutrality Act, and another in Pittsburgh started to look into alleged kickbacks in the Westinghouse nuclear project. Marcos refused to face a panel in Alexandria, Virginia, which formally charged one of General Ver's cronies with fraud in connection with official arms purchases. The big sensation, however, was the indictment on October 21, 1988, by a New York grand jury. The Marcoses and eight others, including the Saudi Arabian fixer Adnan Khashoggi, were accused of embezzling more than $100 million from the Philippine government to acquire three Manhattan buildings, defrauding American banks to finance the deal. The investigation also revealed twenty secret Marcos accounts in a Swiss bank and other clandestine deposits elsewhere. With Marcos too sick to travel, Imelda appeared in court to post $5 million bail, lent by one of her few remaining chums—the aged tobacco heiress Doris Duke. George Bush was then campaigning for president, and for Reagan to defend the Marcoses would have tarnished the Republican ticket. Nor could Reagan afford to alienate Cory, who had just signed an interim bases agreement with the United States. Reagan did nothing—though he was "pained," a senior administration official confided to me, by the final degradation of his old friend.

★ ★ ★

In the summer of 1983, the eve of his fatal return home, Ninoy told an interviewer: "If you made me president of the Philippines today, my friend, in six months I would be smelling like horseshit. Because there's nothing I can do. I cannot provide employment. I cannot bring prices down. I cannot stop the criminality spawned by economic difficulties. I mean, let's face it. When people are hungry, you can bring Saint Peter down, and you won't get a stable government." Had he rather than Cory toppled Marcos, he might have also observed that revolutions invariably raise expectations that cannot be easily fulfilled. Cory ran into that reality soon after Marcos's collapse.

The miracle of her victory inspired in Filipinos—and in many of her American admirers—the dream that she would now perform economic, social and political miracles. The end of tyranny and the revival of democracy euphorically signaled a new era of peace and prosperity. As Cory began to pick up the pieces of her shattered country, however, she faced an array of staggering problems that no individual, even with divine guidance, could resolve rapidly. Nor was she inclined to promote drastic measures. Though she labeled her overthrow of Marcos a revolution, it was really a restoration.

Cory was not a revolutionary determined to renovate the society from top to bottom. Essentially conservative, as befit a member of her class, she sought to resurrect the institutions dismantled by Marcos rather than construct a new system. In the process, she revived the old dynasties he had dispossessed, including her own family, and they jockeyed to regain their former positions of privilege. She also lacked experience and confidence in her ability to govern, and at first surrounded herself with a cacophony of advisers, each tugging in different directions. Prudent and uncertain, she was reluctant to take advantage of her immense popularity to impose her leadership, preferring instead to rule by moral example. She gradually began to assert herself and showed in instances that she had the right stuff, but she squandered her initial momentum, thereby losing a unique opportunity to introduce reforms. Into the vacuum poured a multiplicity of undisciplined, selfish, querulous factions eager to advance their own ambitions. Revisiting the Philippines during the years following Cory's takeover, I was reminded of the 1960s, with its disorder, drift and doubt. Now, as then, there appeared to be little prospect for the profound and pervasive changes vital to deter the spread of the Communist insurgency or perhaps even the return of a Marcos in different guise.

Particularly dramatic was the skepticism, disappointment and apprehension of the groups that had vaulted Cory into power: the intellectuals, businessmen, clergy and army. They clamored for stability, yet they carped at her incessantly, their behavior seeming to mirror two antithetical ingredients in the Philippine heritage: an Asian reverence for authority and a Latin penchant for hypercriticism. The uncomfortable mixture did not make Cory's task any easier as she wrestled with a job she had never wanted, and she responded to their taunts by saying, "What is your alternative?"

A foremost Filipino writer, F. Sionil José, originally an ardent supporter, unleashed a tirade in the summer of 1987, faulting her for failing to "translate her massive popularity into action" and warning that "unless she changes quickly she will bring this country to ruin." Jaime Ongpin, her able finance secretary, who had rallied the business community to her side, committed suicide in despair after a series of squabbles inside her cabinet. Father Joaquín Bernas, a Jesuit scholar and one of her closest campaign advisers, vented his frustration publicly. Her "revolution" had been "perfect," he said in an interview—"a 360-degree turn back to where we were before . . . still no social justice, still corruption and economic deprivation. . . . The people," he added, "are not getting the president they voted for." Amando Doronila, the studious editor of the *Manila Chronicle,* echoed the same theme: "There has been no national agenda, no initiatives. Cory is a passive president who follows, not leads." The army manifested its dissatisfaction in five coup attempts during her first year and a half in office—the most serious of them staged in August 1986 by Colonel "Gringo" Honasan, who had led the mutiny against Marcos. The surprise revolt nearly succeeded. "Until it was over," a Pentagon official remarked later, "we didn't realize how dicey the situation was." Cory showed unique courage and serenity during the coup, in which her son was injured. "I am fatalistic," she again told me afterward, candidly admitting her belief in predestination.

Most of the criticism of Cory was centered in Manila, a city that flourishes on political gossip. Out in the rural areas, her capacity for survival gave her an aura of sanctity that reinforced her popular appeal. Early in 1987, she held a referendum to approve her new constitution, a thick, turgid document that defied easy comprehension. It won overwhelming endorsement—actually overwhelming endorsement for Cory. Her legislative elections in May 1987 and local contests a year later both drew big turnouts, even though she had declined to create a political party. Still the malaise continued.

Striving to reconcile the disparate elements that had backed her crusade, Cory at first cobbled together a coalition cabinet. It was a basket of crabs. She chose as her chief of staff a leftist lawyer improbably named Joker Arroyo, to whom she was grateful for his defense of Ninoy. A schemer who bore an uncanny resemblance to the young Bonaparte, he was anathema to the army for his past battles over human rights violations, while his administrative incompetence appalled technocrats like Jaime Ongpin. Enrile, her defense secretary, was meanwhile plotting against her, and Salvador Laurel, the vice president who doubled as foreign secretary, had his own priorities in mind. She dumped Enrile and later fired Arroyo and Ongpin, and Laurel subsequently quit the cabinet to remain, incongruously, vice president in opposition. Cory was hailed for firmness, but two precious years had been wasted.

She blundered, her critics claimed, by refusing to decree agrarian reforms under her revolutionary powers, and instead passed the buck to the new legislature. Her virtuous purpose was to respect democratic procedure. Predictably, the debate over reforms dragged on until June 1988, when representatives for the landed interests finally voted a law riddled with loopholes. Enforcement was delegated to local councils usually controlled by landowners, who in addition won the right to challenge decisions in court—an endless process. One of the clauses, evidently sponsored by Cory's brother, José Cojuangco, would exempt their family sugar plantation by instituting a "profit sharing" arrangement for the workers—with the proprietors determining the profit. Cory's own secretary of agriculture, Carlos "Sonny" Domínguez, who had drafted a comprehensive plan, was dismayed. "More than anything," he said, "we needed radical land reform, but Cory was too cautious. She had an opportunity and she blew it."

A curious trace of nostalgia for authority emerged in observers like *Chronicle* editor Amando Doronila, who spent the Marcos years in exile in Australia. He saw in the legislature a "circus of atomized members, each acting on behalf of individual or at best limited interests" to block reforms. The "impasse," he wrote, might tempt Cory to become another Marcos or perhaps spur a military junta "to seize power in the name of national development."

But agrarian reform of any kind faced an immense obstacle: money. Aside from paying landowners for their property, the program had to furnish farmers with credit, seeds, tools and above all training. One estimate put the cost at more than $7 billion for a ten-year period, a sum the Philippines could not even begin to contemplate, given the crippled economy Cory inherited in the aftermath of Marcos's egregious profligacy. Attempts to raise funds from the sale of government companies had bogged down, and the prospects for foreign aid looked bleak.

Cory rosily declared in July 1988 that she had overcome the Marcos legacy, and that "the economy has taken off." A growth rate of about six percent in the gross national product for the previous year seemed to prove her point. So too did the appearance of Manila during my visits. I saw new houses going up in residential suburbs and a booming stock exchange. Restaurants, nightclubs and discos were packed, and shopping centers thronged with buyers of furniture, refrigerators, air conditioners and other big-tag items. The picture was both true and false. The urban middle classes were thriving, due in part to higher salaries for government employees, but the prosperity touched neither the sprawling city slums nor the countryside. A confidential World Bank study completed in the summer of 1988 observed that "there are more poor people in the Philippines today than at any time in recent history," adding that their plight "has worsened during the past three decades." Of the population of fifty-six million Filipinos, the report said, more than half lived in "absolute poverty"—meaning that their income "did not enable them to satisfy basic needs." The survey repeated a familiar litany: the government's neglect of rural areas, widespread tax evasion by the rich, a grossly inequitable land ownership pattern. Even with an unusually high growth rate of six percent, the study concluded, the Philippines would return to its 1982 economic level only by 1992—and at that barring a crisis in the world market for sugar, copra and other commodities.

A major impediment to economic growth was servicing the foreign debt of nearly $28 billion contracted by Marcos, which drained the country of forty percent of its earnings from exports. Another plague was corruption, which in 1988 cost the Philippine treasury $2.5 billion, or about one third of the national budget. As Cardinal Sin quipped, "Ali Baba Marcos fled, leaving behind the forty thieves." It differed from Marcos's plundering, a state enterprise directed from his palace. Nobody could fault Cory for personal dishonesty, but despite her campaign promise to promote integrity, she was confronted by an endemic problem.

Returning to Manila during her years in office, I again listened to the same old tales of corruption: customs agents engaged in smuggling, kickbacks on government contracts, fake licenses, payoffs to cops. A commission created by Cory to recover Marcos's "ill-gotten gains" was revamped after the revelation that its members had stolen some of those gains. One of Cory's early backers, newspaper publisher Joaquín Roces, whom Marcos had jailed, startled her at a public meeting by saying that her regime was guilty of "self-aggrandizement and service to vested interests, relatives and friends." He was transparently referring to her brother José, known as "Peping," and his wife, Margarita, or "Tingting," the reputed bosses of enterprises ranging from a gambling monopoly to the illicit barter trade in the south. A brother-in-law, Ricardo "Baby" Lopa, was denounced by the Manila press for having acquired for a pittance the companies that Imelda's brother "Kokoy" had acquired for a pittance. The petty graft by minor bureaucrats reflected their struggle to survive amid dire poverty. The reluctance to pursue offenders mirrored age-old kinship loyalties. Cory told a reporter that she had warned members of her family against abusing their position. "Short of ordering them to hibernate or go into exile," she said, "I don't know what else I can do."

The economy has also been stunted by the spiraling population, which is bound to intensify into an unmanageable problem in the years ahead. But the Catholic hierarchy has denounced birth control as "dehumanizing and immoral," and Cory has evaded the issue out of religious piety. When I first visited the Philippines in the late 1950s, there were about twenty-five million Filipinos. The population has doubled since then and is expected to double again by the year 2010, and the implications of that projection are horrendous. To keep pace with the explosion, according to a study in the *Far Eastern Economic Review,* the Philippines will have to increase food production by forty percent by the end of the century in addition to providing for thousands of schools and clinics and millions of jobs. "The pressure of people on land," a World Bank report declared in 1988, "has brought about the impoverishment of a large part of the rural sector." It is that impoverishment, probably more than any other single factor, that has fueled the spread of the Communist insurgency—a war that plainly cannot be won by battalions and bullets.

Cory announced in July 1988 that "this may be remembered as the year the insurgency was broken." But her optimistic forecast was soon punctured by a leak to a Manila newspaper of a secret military study stating that the rebels had gained "the tactical initiative in major engagements." As usual, the truth was somewhere in between. The Communists made a grave error by boycotting the election that lifted Cory into power. Their chief spokesman, Satur Ocampo, candidly admitted the mistake to me, saying, "We failed to benefit from the popular sentiment against Marcos." The movement was further weakened by disputes between advocates of a political approach and champions of armed struggle. In many places, local revolts against the government were proliferating, eluding the control of the Communists. Still, the New People's Army, as the Communist guerrillas called their force, remained dynamic, organized and menacing. By contrast, the Philippine military establishment continued to be nagged by shortages of supplies, command rivalries and other difficulties—though its morale had risen since the Marcos era. Honasan's abortive coup ironically helped by alerting Cory to the need to raise the wages of soldiers and improve their conditions.

An effective check to the Communists have been a variety of vigilante groups, like one in the Mindanao capital of Davao known as *Alsa Masa,* or "Up with the Masses"—its commander, Lieutenant Colonel Franco Calida, advertised himself to the press from an office decorated with a big poster of Sylvester Stallone as Rambo. In 1986, when I visited Davao, the Communists controlled a slum district called Agdao. Calida cleaned out the area within two years with his three thousand men, numbers of them Communist defectors. But his and other groups, acting without official supervision, summarily killed suspects and settled old feuds. Some, like the Tadtad, which means "chop," were mystical, cannibalistic cults that beheaded victims and ate their livers. Cory originally applauded the vigilantes as prototypes of "people power," but their abuses tarnished her name with human rights activists. The Lawyers Committee for Human Rights, a New York organization, concluded in June 1988 after months of research that "the human rights of Filipinos have suffered grave violations on a wide scale." Criticism from such movements, which had pleaded for Ninoy during his imprisonment, grated a raw nerve in Cory, and she angrily refuted the charge. The director of her human rights commission indirectly confirmed the complaint, however, saying that "in an environment of war . . . it is most difficult, if not impossible, to prevent brutality."

★　★　★

Revisiting the countryside has always been an opportunity for me to gain a sense of perspective outside the narrow, incestuous confines of Manila. No place in the archipelago is typical, given its diversity, but the island of Negros in the Visayas has always been a microcosm of the nation's most critical problems.

One of the poorest islands, Negros had been among the richest until the collapse of the world price for sugar, its main crop. Nearly all of its two million people are involved in the sugar industry, and the slump spared nobody. Worst hit were the three hundred thousand sugar workers and their families, whose existence has always been precarious. The government hospital in Bacolod, the province capital, treats about fifty children a day for malnutrition, and countless numbers who never reach the hospital die of starvation. They suffer from the pressure of population as well as an archaic social and economic system.

The sugar workers live on the plantations, often miles from towns. One day I accompanied a planter to a *barrio* on one of his properties, about an hour from Bacolod. We bumped in a four-wheeler over a dirt road that, he told me, turned into an impassable mire in rainy weather. Sheltered in a grove of palms, the village was a cluster of a dozen or so bamboo huts and a thatch-roofed barracks for migrant laborers—none, of course, with running water or electricity. The women, some fat and others stringy, seemed old beyond their years from childbearing, and the men were small and gnarled, their faces leathery from the sun. Families work together, planting, cutting, drying and hauling cane, earning $500 or $600 for the six-month season. Lacking crafts like basketry or weaving, they have no other income. The planter leases them a tiny plot to grow vegetables and rice. They can never afford to pay the rent, he can never collect it and they have nothing for him to dispossess. The debt had accumulated until they were indentured to him.

Their servitude ought to have made them sullen, but that day they were gaily celebrating their patron saint—and the planter, in feudal fashion, had come for the occasion. He explained to me that he was fulfilling his responsibility as a landowner, and to have failed to appear would have been taken as a snub. The laborers mixed familiarly with him, chatting and joking and betting on the cockfights, the main event. As we returned to town, he remarked almost casually: "They're mostly Communist sympathizers. I know it, and they know I know it." He left to me to deduce that he, like landowners throughout the country, had accommodated the insurgents, perhaps paying them taxes or giving them medical care.

Not long afterward, I joined a few colleagues on a trip into an insurgent "zone" on Negros. The journey was arranged by a Communist intermediary, who sauntered into the hotel one afternoon, wearing a Lacoste tennis shirt, smoking Marlboros and speaking fluent English. That night we climbed into a van, drove to the edge of a sugar field, then trekked single file by moonlight to a hamlet of five or six huts.

It was not Mao Zedong's base in the mountains of Yenan. The *barrio* was about half an hour from town, close enough to send out for a cold beer. But government troops and police seldom entered the area, either because they tolerated the rebels or were simply too lazy. Many of the guerrillas were sugar workers. Counterinsurgency experts who maintained that the peasants needed protection from the rebels misunderstood the reality: The peasants *were* the rebels.

We had hardly arrived before a band of guerrillas swept in, looking as if they had come out of central casting. They wore blue jeans and T-shirts, and a few sported bandannas à la Che Guevara. They carried American-made Armalite rifles and Uzi automatics manufactured in Israel. One brandished a Soviet AK-47, the worldwide insurgent symbol. Over beer and cigarettes, two or three of them treated me to a session of rote propaganda. They quoted Marx and Mao, decried the U.S. military bases in the Philippines and excoriated American corporations for "exploiting the masses." Their pitch to the villagers was more concrete.

"Organizing people is slow," one of them explained to me. "We study conditions on a plantation in order to know the problem—whether, for example, the workers are underpaid or abused. Then we approach them indirectly, maybe through a comrade who belongs to their family, because they naturally trust their relatives. We don't rush them. Some fear arrest, or they haven't figured out how we can help. If they refuse us, we move on and return later. Or we try to show them that we can get the landowners to meet their demands." Recently, he told me proudly, they had persuaded a planter to raise the daily wage for sugar workers from twenty pesos to thirty pesos—from a

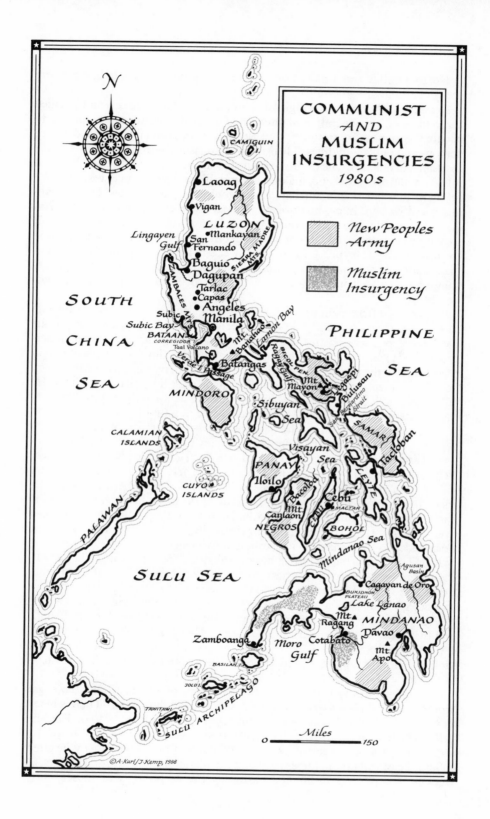

dollar to a dollar and a half. The Communists were clearly a long way from the revolution.

But they were not just benign labor organizers. They burned and pillaged the estates of uncooperative planters, and ambushed army units, mainly to acquire weapons. To show their muscle, they occasionally attacked police stations and public buildings. Their urban terrorists, so-called sparrow squads, assassinated officials. One of them recalled to me how he and his comrades had killed a reputedly cruel cop, making it sound like a scene from a western. "We followed him into a café, his regular hangout. The place cleared out immediately, and we shot him—point-blank. He never knew what hit him." Informers, another told me, were given a "people's trial" and speedy execution. "If they try to hide in the city, the sparrows get them." My interlocutor had talked to correspondents before. Like everybody else in the Philippines, the Communists cultivate the press. Late one afternoon, two insurgent commanders showed up to welcome us—and, of course, to be interviewed and photographed.

The senior of the pair was Nemasio Demafelis, a stocky figure in his late thirties whose various noms de guerre included "Iko." Of peasant origin, he had been a political science student at a local college when he went underground in 1972, caught up in the ferment of the time. A year before, in retaliation for the massacre of civilians by a paramilitary unit in a nearby town, he had planned a raid against an army garrison, killing twelve soldiers. He talked at length about the necessity for violence as the only way to "liberate the masses from oppression." By chance, some months afterward, I met him in the Bacolod jail. Evading the question of whether he had defected or been captured, he denounced the Communist policy of "all-out violence." He supported armed struggle, he said, but he also favored a flexible political approach. "The situation is polarizing," he explained. "There will be more and more killing, and more and more people will suffer." Remembering our earlier encounter in the insurgent hamlet, he recalled the other insurgent leader who had accompanied him that day, revealing to me that they subsequently clashed over strategy. He identified his comrade as Francisco Fernandez, whom he described as a proponent of indiscriminate violence.

A sinewy, taciturn man also in his late thirties, a forty-five tucked in his belt, the other rebel chief was a priest whom the villagers addressed as "Father Frank." He related his conversion to Communism as a logical process. "I went to work with the poor after completing the seminary, but soon I saw that real change required political action. I began to support the demands of the people, and that angered the planters and the army. They put me under surveillance. I was in danger of arrest, so I joined the movement." How did he square violence with his religious faith? "My conscience is clear," he replied predictably. "Our cause is just."

Priests on Negros had been in the vanguard of efforts to aid the sugar workers since the early 1970s, when a Jesuit devised the slogan "There's blood in your cup of coffee." They were encouraged by the bishop, Antonio Fortich, a large man with a furrowed face and earnest voice.

The son of a rich sugar planter, he told me that he was originally inspired to join the priesthood in hopes of easing the plight of the workers. He stressed the need for reforms in his first pastoral letter as bishop and subsequently pressed for labor unions, higher wages and improved working conditions. When the landowners protested, he warned them, "Make concessions now or you will lose everything later." But they resisted and, he said, "The social volcano is no longer just rumbling, it is already exploding." The answer was "land, land, land—what the masses want more than above all else." Skeptical toward Cory's land-reform program, he guessed that it would "determine her success or failure."

Fortich was the target of a misfired grenade in early 1987. The local military commander, Lieutenant Colonel Miguel Coronel, later accused him of shielding thirty-five Communist priests—a charge dismissed by Fortich as "false, malicious and preposterous." Several landowners also circulated the allegation. Fortich's position was nuanced. He had excluded insurgent clergymen like Francisco Fernandez from the church organization, but he would not recommend their excommunication—since, as he explained to me, "I am not the keeper of their conscience." In any case, Negros seemed to me to resemble Mississippi during the 1960s, with the rednecks pitted against the civil rights activists—with one difference: There was no Supreme Court to impose a judgment.

As in Mississippi, the controversy was not simple. The planters clung to their land less for its value, which had dropped with sugar prices, than because it symbolized the authority that their families had enjoyed for generations. They also continued to grow sugar, often at a loss, for lack of an alternative. Several of the army officers I saw had attended counterinsurgency schools in the United States and read books on Vietnam, and they understood that the struggle against the Communists was not merely a military effort. But the economic, social and political components of a progressive program were missing—partly because of resistance from the Negros landowners and also because of Cory's reticence to promote dynamic reforms.

The army, as an expedient, had created a home defense force called the "forward command." It was financed by the planters, who recruited the volunteers from among their sugar workers. These militiamen were supposed to protect their villages and furnish intelligence on rebels in their areas. A local priest dismissed the project as a scheme to preserve the privileges of the landowners. "They wouldn't be paying if they weren't getting something in exchange," he said.

Given the choice between guarding a village or laboring in the fields, volunteers were plentiful. But those I saw being trained at a makeshift camp one day were unimpressive. They were scrawny, awkward teenagers in shorts and sandals, and many, barely literate, could not easily learn the English-language signals system borrowed from the American army. It occurred to me, recalling similar units in Vietnam, that many might be Communist infiltrators. Agreeing, the captain in charge said, "That's a risk we have to take." Later, over a beer, he voiced his disillusionment. Trained at Fort Benning, Georgia, he had returned home with aspirations that had since been shattered. "We are a poor man's army."

The man in the middle on Negros was Daniel Lacson, the governor, a former businessmen educated in the United States. Bubbling with ideas, he believed in leaving the sugar estates intact while developing local industry to manufacture toys, garments and simple electronic equipment. He had already begun to promote potentially lucrative shrimp farms. What worried him was the tendency in the Philippines to launch promising programs that soon fade into bureaucratic confusion and ineptitude. The cultural affliction is known in Tagalog as *ningas cogon,* which literally means a sudden brushfire that burns out quickly—and connotes grand plans announced with great fanfare that stall for lack of follow-up. "We are urging people to hold on, to be patient, to hope," Lacson said of his design for Negros, "but something must be done fast. The time bomb is ticking."

His phrase described the challenge to the Philippines as a whole. And it also raised the question posed repeatedly since Cory was catapulted into office: "Can she make it?"

Stephen Bosworth, writing in *The Washington Post* late in 1987, had a judicious reply. "The question itself requires definition. If 'making it' means turning the Philippines into a stable, prosperous, self-confident model of democracy in a developing country, the answer is clearly no. The problems are too difficult, the Filipino sense of nationhood too weak and the time given to Aquino until the end of her term in 1992 too short. On the other hand, if the question is whether her government can survive and she can continue to make gradual but important progress, then my answer is yes." Whatever happened, Bosworth emphasized, the future of the Philippines hinged on the Filipinos themselves.

But not without the Americans.

★ ★ ★

In the aftermath of Marcos's downfall, the Filipinos faced obstacles that they could not conceivably hurdle alone. Their economy was burdened by a foreign debt that had put them at the mercy of their foreign creditors. They needed foreign investment and foreign aid. Only the United States could carry them through the crisis—and, even then, the going would be precarious.

Yet a vocal faction of Manila politicians, journalists, professors and others, determined to assert their nationalism, championed a tougher stance toward the Americans out of a complexity of motives. Some contended that the United States was not being generous enough toward one of its oldest allies, while others advocated a clean break with the Americans as an affirmation of Philippine sovereignty. In large measure, the ferment was stimulated by the permissiveness of Cory Aquino's administration. Unshackled from the fetters of the Marcos autocracy, Filipinos were indulging themselves in a feast of freedom. To denounce the United States had always been one of their favorite sports, but they realized that it was a tricky game. And, in the end, they displayed caution.

A turning point came in October 1988, with the agreement signed in Washington to ensure the operation of the U.S. bases in the Philippines until 1991, when a longer-term pact would have to be concluded. Both sides had postured during the bargaining. Cory's foreign secretary, Raul Manglapus, called America's presence in the archipelago a violation of national independence, claiming that the moment had arrived to end the residual colonial relationship. Secretary of State Shultz and other senior U.S. officials threatened to transfer the bases elsewhere, and bolstered their warning by disclosing that the cost of moving would be less than at first anticipated.

Money, not principles, ultimately concluded the dispute. After seven months of negotiations, the Filipinos settled for an American aid package of $481 million a year in exchange for the bases—one third of Manglapus's original demand. The deal sparked an outburst from Filipino nationalists, who contended that, once again, U.S. pressure had prevailed.

The compromise was a prelude to fresh discussions to prolong the life of the bases beyond 1991. But the interim accord represented an indirect admission by Filipinos that they desperately needed American assistance—and would for years to come. Also implicit in the agreement was an understanding on the part of both Americans and Filipinos that, however lopsided, thorny and at times frustrating their "special relationship" might be, it reflected a century of shared experience. Dewey, Taft, MacArthur, Edward Lansdale and Ronald Reagan, Aguinaldo, Quezon, Magsaysay, the Marcoses and the Aquinos had marched together through history along with millions of other Americans and Filipinos, and their common past had ordained both their present and their future.

CHRONOLOGY

PRE-HISTORY   Settlers cross "land bridge" from Asian mainland to Philippines 20–30,000 years ago.

10TH–12TH CENTURY   Chinese trading posts established along coast of Philippines. Vietnam, Cambodia and Thailand begin to trade with islands.

14TH CENTURY   Arab traders spread Islam to Malaya. Arabian scholar Mudum arrives in Malay Peninsula, proceeds to Sulu archipelago.

1385   Prince Henry of Portugal founds world's first maritime academy.

15TH CENTURY   Muslim missionaries reach Philippines from Indonesia and Malaya.

1402–30   Ming emperor Yung Lo sends expeditions to Philippines, establishes Chinese trading posts.

1460   Pope Nicholas V grants Portugal privilege of Christian Crusade, considered holy writ to exploration.

1493   Pope Alexander VI issues *Inter Cetera,* granting Spain rights to explore lands west of Europe, and Portugal to explore lands east.

1497   Vasco da Gama sails to India, around Horn of Africa, suppressing Muslims and claiming Indian Ocean for Portugal.

1519   Ferdinand Magellan sails from Spain in search of westward passage to Orient through America.

1521   Magellan arrives in Philippines in March, claims region for Spain.

1543   Ruy de Villalobos sails from Mexico and lands south of Mindanao, names region Philippines after Spanish crown prince, Philip II.

1565   King Philip II commissions Miguel Lopez de Legazpi to colonize Philippines. Augustinian missionaries arrive with him, later followed by Franciscans, Jesuits, Dominicans and Recollects.

1571   Legazpi's expedition lands in Manila Bay, co-opts local Muslim sultan Suleiman and establishes settlement.

1574   British, Dutch and Portuguese marauders challenge Spanish authority, raiding coastal villages. Chinese pirate Limahong attacks Manila.

1601   First university, Santo Tomás, founded in Manila by Dominicans.

1762–64   British forces occupy Manila during Seven Years' War.

1767   Charles III, the "benevolent despot," expels Jesuits from all Spanish possessions as part of his effort to curb power of monastic orders.

LATE 18TH CENTURY   Reformist governor José de Basco y Vargas introduces tobacco and sugarcane as cash crops.

1796   First American trading vessel makes Manila its scheduled port of call.

1802   Napoleonic wars halt flow of young friars from Spain, creating vacancies for Filipino priests.

1815   Galleon trade between Philippines and Mexico ends after two centuries.

1826   Conservative Spanish king, Ferdinand VII, removes Filipino priests from their parishes and reinstalls monastic orders.

1834   Spain opens Manila to world trade and foreign investment.

1841   Filipino mystic Apolinario de la Cruz founds lay brotherhood, fights Spanish, is captured and executed.

1863　Pedro Palaez, progressive Spanish prelate who supported rights of Filipino priests, dies in Manila earthquake.

1872　Mutiny at Cavite arsenal repressed by Spanish. José Burgos, Mariano Gomez and Jacinto Zamoro, liberal priests, executed by Spanish for alleged complicity.

1887　José Rizal's polemical novel *Noli Me Tangere* smuggled into Manila, creates sensation among Filipino elite.

1892　Rizal returns to Philippines from abroad, banished to Mindanao. Andrés Bonifacio founds *Katipunan,* Filipino nationalist brotherhood.

1895　Cuban rebels declare war against Spain.

1896　Governor Ramón Blanco banishes four hundred suspected Filipino insurgents. Spanish vigilantes imprison and kill hundreds of Filipinos in Manila. Bonifacio declares war on Spain, August 29. Emilio Aguinaldo and Filipino forces capture Cavite. Queen María Cristina of Spain recalls Blanco, replacing him with General Camilio García de Polavieja. Rizal executed by Spanish.

1897　Cavite recaptured by Spanish. Polavieja replaced as Spanish governor by General Fernando Primo de Rivera. Filipino officers vote to abolish *Katipunan* and establish republic with Aguinaldo as president. Bonifacio establishes rival regime and is captured and executed by Aguinaldo. Aguinaldo goes to Hong Kong after signing armistice with Spanish.

1898　The *Maine* blown up in Havana Harbor, February 15. Congress passes resolution authorizing President William McKinley to use force to end Spanish rule in Cuba, April 11. Theodore Roosevelt, assistant secretary of navy, orders Commodore George Dewey to Philippines.

　　　Dewey's fleet sinks antiquated Spanish armada in Manila Bay, May 1. Aguinaldo returns from exile, hoping to fight with Americans against Spain, declares independence, June 12.

　　　General Elwell S. Otis takes over from General Wesley Merritt as U.S. military governor of Philippines, July 25. U.S. forces enter Manila, August 13. United States and Spain sign Treaty of Paris, granting United States sovereignty over islands. McKinley calls U.S. policy in Philippines "benevolent assimilation," December 21.

1899　Aguinaldo inaugurated as first president of Philippine republic at Malolos, January 23. Willy Grayson, Nebraska volunteer, kills Filipino soldier on night of February 4, igniting war between Americans and Filipinos.

　　　Dewey returns home in September, given hero's welcome. Aguinaldo begins guerrilla warfare, retreating to northern Luzon. Colonel Henry Lawton dies in battle, December 19.

1900　General Arthur MacArthur replaces Otis as U.S. military commander. William Howard Taft arrives as first civilian governor in June. Conservative Filipinos establish *Federalista* party in December, advocating statehood for Philippines.

1901　Aguinaldo captured by Frederick Funston, March 23, pledges allegiance to United States. Taft establishes completely civilian administration, July 4. American teachers arrive aboard U.S. transport *Thomas,* August 23.

　　　McKinley dies from assassin's bullet, September 14; Vice President Theodore Roosevelt succeeds him as president.

1902　President Theodore Roosevelt declares end of Philippine war, July 4. Congress passes "organic act," law governing Philippines.

1907　Manuel Quezon and Sergio Osmeña establish *Nacionalista* party. Election founds Philippine assembly, first freely elected legislature in Asia.

1909　W. Cameron Forbes begins term as U.S. governor of Philippines, serving until 1913 and concentrating on economic development.

1913   Francis Burton Harrison chosen U.S. governor of Philippines. A liberal, he fills bureaucracy with Filipinos.

1916   Legislation sponsored by Representative William Atkinson Jones of Virginia pledges eventual independence to Philippines.

1922   Quezon defeats Osmeña as president of upper house of Philippine legislature, becomes preeminent Filipino political leader.

1930   Philippine Communist party founded.

1931   In December, mission composed of Osmeña and Manuel Roxas leaves Manila to negotiate independence bill sponsored principally by Representative Harry Hawes of Missouri.

1932   Independence bill passes U.S. Congress. Arrest of labor leader Cristano Evangelista results in ban of Communist party.

1933   Congress overrides lame-duck President Herbert Hoover's veto of independence bill in January, but Philippine legislature rejects law at instigation of Quezon, who goes to Washington to negotiate his own act.

1934   Congress passes Tydings-McDuffie Act in March, mandating ten-year transition to independence.

1935   *Sakdalista* rebellion breaks out in May.

     On September 17, Quezon elected president of Philippine commonwealth with Osmeña as vice president. Inauguration of Philippine commonwealth, November 15.

     General Douglas MacArthur arrives as military adviser to Philippine army, with rank of field marshal.

1938   Paul McNutt, U.S. high commissioner in Manila, proposes "reexamination" of American policy, suggesting postponement of Philippine independence.

1941   President Franklin Roosevelt appoints MacArthur commander of armed forces in Far East in July.

     Japanese attack Pearl Harbor and Clark Field, December 7, land main forces at Lingayen Gulf, December 22. MacArthur calls for retreat to Bataan and Corregidor. He declares Manila an "open" city, December 24.

1942   Japanese forces invade Manila, January 2. Japanese form Philippine executive commission headed by Jorge Vargas, January 23. Roosevelt rejects Quezon proposal of surrender and neutralization, February 8–9. On March 17, promising "I shall return" to Filipinos, MacArthur arrives in Australia. *Hukbalahap* guerrilla forces are formed March 29 with Luis Taruc as military commander. Bataan falls to Japanese under General Masarahu Homma, April 9. Quezon and Osmeña depart for United States, set up government in exile in May. General Jonathan Wainwright surrenders Corregidor, May 6. Inauguration of puppet republic on October 14, with José Laurel as president.

1944   Quezon dies at Saranac Lake, New York, August 1. MacArthur lands in Leyte, October 20.

1945   Japanese in last-ditch fight for Manila in February. MacArthur heralds Philippine liberation, July 5.

1946   Roxas defeats Osmeña for presidency. Roxas is inaugurated as first president of sovereign Philippines, with Elpidio Quirino as vice president, July 4.

1947   On March 17, conclusion of military bases agreement grants United States leases on bases in Philippines for ninety-nine years.

1948   Roxas outlaws *Hukbalahap* movement, March 6. He dies of heart attack while visiting Clark Field, April 15. Quirino sworn in, grants amnesty to members of *Hukbalahap,* June 21, but few accept offer. Negotiations with Luis Taruc, Huk leader, break down.

1949   During meeting with Quirino in August, President Harry Truman urges Philippine president to end corruption and mismanagement.

1950   Truman sends economic survey mission to Philippines, June 29; team urges drastic reforms. *Hukbalahap* guerrillas rename movement "Army for the Liberation of the People," November 10.

1951   Colonel Edward Lansdale arrives in Manila as adviser to Secretary of Defense Ramón Magsaysay in struggle against Huks. Lansdale secretly begins to groom Magsaysay as future president with help of Gabriel Kaplan, covert CIA agent.

1953   Magsaysay elected president of Philippines in November, defeating Quirino.

1954   On February 17, Manila newsman Benigno Aquino, Jr., meets with Taruc, who surrenders to Philippine government in May. Vice President Nixon visits Philippines to commemorate tenth anniversary of independence, July 3–4.

1957   Carlos García sworn in as president, March 18, after Magsaysay dies in plane crash. García reelected, with Diosdado Macapagal as vice president, November 12.

1958   Taruc sentenced to life imprisonment for Huk insurgent activities, June 11.

1960   President Eisenhower visits Manila in June.

1961   General MacArthur pays final visit to Philippines in July.
        Macapagal defeats García, December 14, with Emmanuel Pelaez as vice president. Macapagal proposes "era of the common man."

1963   Macapagal signs Land Reform Code into law, August 8. On November 22, Kennedy assassinated in Dallas, succeeded by Lyndon Johnson.

1964   On February 6, Aguinaldo dies at the age of ninety-four. Lyndon Johnson defeats Barry Goldwater for the presidency on November 3.

1965   Ferdinand Marcos defeats Macapagal for presidency of Philippines on November 9. Vice President Hubert Humphrey attends Marcos inauguration.

1966   In September Marcos meets with President Johnson in Washington; agreements include reduction of U.S. lease on bases from ninety-nine to twenty-five years and $45 million economic-aid package.
        Johnson arrives in Manila for seven-nation conference on Vietnam in October.

1967   Philippines join Association of Southeast Asian Nations in August, formed to "promote active collaboration and mutual assistance on matters of common interest."

1968   Marcos pardons 166 prisoners, including Taruc, September 11.
        Richard M. Nixon defeats Hubert Humphrey for the presidency on November 5.
        New Communist party of the Philippines founded on December 26, birthday of Chinese Communist leader Mao Zedong; pledges to follow Mao's principles.

1969   In January 27 State of the Union address, Marcos says Philippines will reassess foreign policy, calling U.S. economic ties a "mixed blessing." Nixon visits Manila, July 26, emphasizes Asian responsibility for its own security.
        Governor Ronald Reagan of California and wife Nancy represent the Nixons at September 10 inaugural concert at cultural center, a major project of Imelda Marcos. Campaigning on "rice and roads," Marcos defeats Sergio Osmeña, Jr., in overwhelming victory, November 11, becoming first president to be reelected. On November 18, testimony before U.S. Senate Foreign Relations Committee reveals $39 million spent on Philippine battalion to Vietnam. Marcos wants testimony kept quiet.

1970   At February 2 news conference, Marcos says he won't run for third term, claims "violence must stop [and] communism can escalate into serious threat."
        Nearly three thousand youths attack U.S. Embassy in Manila, February 18. Riot police in Manila stop one thousand from marching on U.S. Embassy following "people's protest march," March 3. Students demonstrate against United States, stage mock trial of Marcos and his wife and U.S., March 13.

Senators Stuart Symington and J. William Fulbright charge in March that Philippine contingent in Vietnam received and "misused" cash assistance.

In April 4 television interview, Marcos threatens martial law if "Communists resort to sabotage on massive scale."

Radical "patriot youth" lead violent anti-American riots, April 5. Following three days of rioting, general strike begins on April 7 to protest increased oil prices and transportation costs. Students and workers demand Marcos's resignation, burn U.S. flag during rally, May 24. Assassination attempt on Pope Paul VII upon his November 27 arrival in Manila for three-day visit.

1971   Terrorist grenades explode in Manila at August 21 preelection rally by opposition Liberal party. Marcos charges that terrorists plotting to overthrow government. Marcos suspends writ of *habeas corpus,* attributing attack to Communists. In August 24 nationwide address, Marcos vows to impose martial law to "liquidate Communist apparatus," accuses Benigno Aquino of aiding Communist subversives. Aquino denies charge and assails suspension of constitutional rights. Marcos claims emergency measures invoked three days earlier prevented Communists from imposing reign of terror. Study by Philippine legislative committee published September 6 reports that "no clear and present danger of Communist insurgency or rebellion exists in central Luzon," as charged by Marcos. In November 7 elections marked with bloody violence, opposition Liberal party wins six of eight contested Senate seats.

1972   On January 12, Marcos restores *habeas corpus* for all except those in detention. Philippines establish trade relations with Communist and Socialist countries, including Soviet Union and China, February 12.

Libyan Colonel Muammar el-Qaddafi announces support for Muslims fighting Philippine government, June 11.

Constitutional convention on July 7 votes to change form of government from presidential rule to parliamentary system.

Marcos proclaims state of emergency on August 13 after six weeks of persistent rains and devastating floods. On September 8, Defense Secretary Juan Ponce Enrile warns that Communists are threatening open rebellion against Manila "twenty-four hours a day." Three days later, two explosions hit main office of Manila electric company, blamed on Communists. Marcos threatens emergency rule to contend with increasing Communist terror raids.

Sham assassination attempt on Defense Secretary Enrile on September 22 used by Marcos to declare martial law; he imposes curfew, bans public demonstrations, closes newspapers and radio and television stations and arrests opposition politicians, including Benigno Aquino. Beginning September 27, scope of arrests broadens. On October 2, Marcos imposes death penalty for use of unauthorized firearms. On October 17, government announces arrest of four persons in connection with alleged Marcos assassination plot.

Convention approves constitution on October 20, opening way for Marcos to stay in power indefinitely.

By November 16, more than six thousand persons arrested under martial law. Nine days later, Philippine government announces arrest of three Americans allegedly involved in September assassination plot against Marcos. Imelda Marcos stabbed and seriously wounded, December 7. Marcos charges attack is part of conspiracy to kill him and his wife.

1973   Marcos signs two decrees extending martial law on January 17. He offers amnesty to all Communists, deadline set at March 15, but only two hundred respond. More political detainees released but about eight thousand still being held.

Vice President Spiro Agnew meets with Marcos in Manila, February 9.

On July 23, Marcos lifts curfews and eases restrictions on free speech. National referendum overwhelmingly approves Marcos remaining in office beyond December 31. On August 27, Benigno Aquino refuses to defend himself in trial for murder, illegal arms possession and subversion charges.

1974   Nixon resigns on August 9, replaced by Vice President Ford.

Catholic bishops petition Marcos to end martial law, Bishop Jaime Sin offers public prayer, September 1. On September 5, Islamic conference representative proposes Muslim peace plan to create autonomous Muslim state under Philippine jurisdiction. Supreme Court decision upholds legality of martial law, September 17.

1975   Catholic leaders voice doubts over possibility of honest referendum, January 12. Benigno Aquino and eight Catholic bishops file petition to block referendum. In response to Roman Catholic call for boycott, five thousand protest in first antigovernment demonstration since imposition of martial law.

Benigno Aquino begins forty-day hunger strike protesting order for his appearance before military tribunal, April 4.

1976   On January 21, citing 1973 opinion poll showing opposition to elections until 1980, Marcos postpones all national elections in the immediate future.

Aquino trial begins, August 3. Aquino boycotts trial, claiming it cannot be fair. With opponents calling for boycott, 91 percent vote to continue martial law in referendum marked by violence, October 16–17.

Jimmy Carter defeats Gerald Ford for presidency on November 2.

1977   Marcos announces measures to ease martial law, but retains power to rule by decree, August 22. Report on November 7 estimates fifty thousand civilians dead in five years of fighting between Marcos government and Muslim rebels.

Military tribunal sentences Aquino to death, November 25. Following worldwide protests, Marcos reopens trial.

1978   In April 7 nationwide elections, Marcos's New Society Movement wins control of legislature. Opposition charges fraud.

During week-long Asia visit beginning May 2, Vice President Walter Mondale urges Marcos to promote liberty and democracy.

Inaugurating legislature on June 12, Marcos sworn in as first Philippine premier in addition to post as president. He appoints Imelda to cabinet.

1979   Cardinal Sin speaks out against martial law and military abuses, appeals for Aquino's release. Marcos rejects him.

1980   Marcos's party wins January 30 local elections. Salvador Laurel breaks with Marcos, charging widespread use of "guns, goons and gold."

Benigno Aquino flies to Texas for heart treatment, May 8. Aquino warns on August 4 of possible guerrilla bombing attacks in Philippines and increase in violence unless Marcos reinstates democracy.

Eight opposition groups form coalition to unseat Marcos.

On September 20, after Washington meeting between Assistant Secretary of State Richard Holbrooke and Benigno Aquino, Marcos decries U.S. involvement in Philippine politics.

Ronald Reagan elected president, November 4.

1981   Marcos tells newsmen on January 10 that he will hold office until elections scheduled for 1984. On January 17, Marcos ends nine years of martial law because "country's economy is at least in a healthy state," retaining power to impose decrees. Marcos reelected to another six-year term, June 16.

At June 30 inauguration, Vice President George Bush praises Marcos for "adherence to democracy."

1982   Marcos appoints Imelda to his executive council, August 7. He assigns presidential powers to executive council in the event of his death.

President Reagan welcomes Marcos to United States for thirteen-day visit in September, his first in sixteen years.

1983 Aquino decides in spring to return to Manila, cautioned by Imelda and Enrile against assassination plots, but discounts warnings. Minutes after his August 21 return, Aquino is shot to death at Manila airport on returning from self-imposed exile. Alleged assassin immediately shot dead. Marcos appoints five judges to prove assassination, denying government involvement. Nearly two million join Aquino's funeral procession, August 31. Denouncing Marcos as a terrorist, five thousand students march in Manila, September 15, burning effigies of Ferdinand and Imelda Marcos and Reagan.

Peaceful rally led by Corazon Aquino a week later ends in violence as protesters break off and hurl rocks at police. Appearing on television on September 21, Marcos expresses fear of economic instability.

Preliminary hearings on Aquino's assassination begin on November 3.

1984 Legislative elections held on May 14. Marcos's New Society Movement wins 89 of 143 seats but opposition gains 41 seats over previous assembly, beats Marcos in Manila. On August 21, 450,000 march to commemorate anniversary of Aquino's death.

U.S. Senate staff study published September 29 reports that Marcos regime is in jeopardy under current political and economic crisis.

Rejecting military's contention that Aquino was killed by Communist hired gunman, investigatory panel concludes on October 23 that assassination was planned by Philippine military.

1985 On January 23, government formally charges armed forces chief of staff General Fabian C. Ver and twenty-five others in slaying of Aquino. Marcos promises to reinstate Ver if he is acquitted.

On October 12, Reagan sends Senator Paul Laxalt to Manila to urge Marcos to make political and economic reforms. Laxalt and Marcos meet on October 16 and 17. On November 3, Marcos announces plan to hold "snap elections," inviting U.S. observers to attend.

By unanimous verdict on December 2, three-member civilian court acquits General Ver and others on charges of Benigno Aquino's assassination. Prosecution witnesses disappear before or after giving testimony. Cardinal Sin denounces verdict. United States strongly opposes Marcos's reinstatement of Ver. Representative Stephen Solarz of New York calls trial "a mockery of justice," urging halt of military funds as long as Ver remains in post.

On December 3, presented with list of 1.2 million signatures, Corazon Aquino announces intention to run for president with Laurel as vice presidential candidate. Despite rumors of his ill health, Marcos claims intention of landslide victory, ridiculing Aquino for lack of political experience, inability to deal with nation's economic and security problems. During campaign, Marcos signs executive orders cutting housing and utility costs and setting housing priority zones. He promises to build schools, raise government salaries and make tax concessions.

1986 According to New York Times report on January 23, U.S. Army rejected Marcos's claims of leading anti-Japanese guerrilla unit during World War II. Marcos dismisses article as "smear campaign."

In January 23 speech to Rotarians in Manila, Aquino outlines eight-point political program to dismantle Marcos's dictatorship. Marcos pledges on January 30 to reorganize government and review constitution, economic policies and his decree-making powers, if reelected.

On February 5, Cardinal Sin warns that Catholics may follow civil disobedience if election found fraudulent, virtually endorsing Aquino.

At least thirty killed in election-day violence, February 7.

Marcos claims early win; widespread fraud reported; Aquino ahead on February 8. Aquino, claiming victory, charges massive fraud by Marcos supporters and requests meeting with Marcos to ensure smooth transition.

Marcos charges committee on free elections with vote manipulation, calling election "most peaceful" and disclaiming possibility of tampering.

Reagan urges Marcos to cooperate with opponents to reform political system. Congressman Solarz accuses administration of supporting corruption in Philippines, says Reagan response is "evidence that the White House has been transformed into an opium den . . . they've clearly lost touch with reality."

Secretary of State George Shultz convenes top U.S. government figures at his home in Washington, February 23, and drafts plan to dump Marcos. He takes plan to President Reagan that afternoon, wins his acquiescence. On February 24, Reagan administration offers Marcos asylum in United States, warning him against military action. Marcos calls for state of emergency, says his family "cowers in terror in the palace" and vows to fight "to the last breath . . . last drop of our blood."

On February 26, urged by Senator Laxalt to resign, Marcos, his family, relatives and staff are flown out of country to Hawaii aboard U.S. aircraft. Aquino government resolves to recover over $6 billion in assets Marcos gained through illegally amassed wealth; Marcos denies U.S. property holdings. Documents found on March 13 link Marcos to bank accounts and records of major expenditures.

On March 25, Aquino abolishes legislature, revokes 1973 constitution and claims all legislative powers for herself.

In unprecedented move, Switzerland freezes all Marcos accounts.

Beginning April 12, Marcos supporters demanding his return stage protests in Manila. In largest demonstration to date, twenty thousand demonstrate for Marcos.

Aquino arrives in United States, September 15, for nine-day visit, meets with Reagan and addresses Congress. Visits New York and Boston amid enthusiasm.

Draft constitution approved, October 12, providing for single six-year presidency term and granting legislature a voice in fate of U.S. bases.

1987   In crucial show of support for Aquino government, voters approve draft constitution, February 2.

Cease-fire ends after Communist rule out extension, February 8. Aquino tells military cadets on March 23 that victory, not compromise, will end rebellion. Legislative elections on May 11 give Aquino backers majorities in both chambers. On August 28, military coup against Aquino staged by Colonel Gregorio "Gringo" Honasan, officer who originally helped her to gain power. Coup fails, and Honasan arrested.

Three U.S. servicemen killed near Clark Field, October 28. Communists claim responsibility.

1988   Voters go to polls in local elections in sixty-two of seventy-three provinces, January 18; Aquino hails transition to democracy.

On February 4, several top Communist leaders arrested, including two members of central committee. Three more senior Communists seized in March.

On October 17, after seven months of negotiations, Secretary of State Shultz and Philippine Foreign Secretary Manglapus sign interim bases agreement under which the United States will pay $481 million for two years.

On October 21, Marcoses indicted by New York grand jury for fraud and embezzlement, Imelda flies to Manhattan for arraignment.

CAST OF PRINCIPAL CHARACTERS

THE FILIPINOS

EMILIO AGUINALDO: Leader of nationalist forces, first against Spain in 1896; later fought against the United States beginning in 1899. Declared independence of Philippines in June 1898; proclaimed president of first Philippine republic in January 1899. Courageous but naïve, believed that United States would back his cause. Captured by Americans in March 1901 after fighting for two years, pledged allegiance to United States. Died in 1964 at age of ninety-four.

BENIGNO AQUINO, SR.: Intense nationalist. Collaborated with Japanese during World War II, directing their puppet political party. Arrested after the war, he died before he could stand trial.

BENIGNO AQUINO, JR.: Foremost Marcos opponent whose assassination in August 1983 sparked widespread resistance to Marcos regime and eventually led to its downfall. Widely known as "Ninoy," born in 1932, began career as journalist, first gained fame by negotiating surrender of Luis Taruc, leader of *Hukbalahap* insurgency; later entered politics and successively elected mayor, province governor and senator. Rambunctious, articulate and ambitious. Arrested when Marcos declared martial law in September 1972, spent nearly eight years in jail before going into exile in United States.

CORAZON AQUINO: Elected president of Philippines in February 1986, but entered office only after army mutiny led to overthrow of Marcos. Gained world-wide renown for her performance, especially acclaimed in United States during visit in September 1986. Deeply religious and politically inexperienced, agreed to run for president as only way to unify anti-Marcos forces, campaigned vigorously with help of Catholic Church. Serene, poised, outwardly gentle, but strong-willed. Promulgated new constitution and conducted legislative and local elections after taking office, tried unsuccessfully to negotiate with Communist insurgents. Of part-Chinese origin, came from prominent landowning family. Critics claimed that she failed to deal with basic social and economic problems of Philippines, accused her of violating human rights in struggle against rebels.

ANDRÉS BONIFACIO: One of few nationalists during late nineteenth century from working-class background, espoused radical change. Founded *Katipunan,* clandestine movement, sparked insurrection against Spain in 1896. Challenged by Aguinaldo, who had him executed.

JOSÉ BURGOS: Spanish priest, born in Philippines, ran afoul of Catholic hierarchy for championing cause of Filipino clergy. Implicated in army mutiny in 1872 and executed after farcical trial; inspired early nationalists.

VENACIO CONCEPCIÓN: Former Aguinaldo general, named president of Philippine National Bank as part of program by U.S. governor Frances Burton Harrison to put more Filipinos into bureaucracy. Tried and convicted of fraud in 1920. Misconduct provided American foes of Philippine independence with ammunition.

ISABEL ROSARIO COOPER: Beautiful entertainer brought by General Douglas MacArthur to Washington in 1930 and secretly installed as his mistress. They eventually broke up, and she committed suicide in Hollywood in 1960.

APOLINARIO DE LA CRUZ: Messianic leader who launched peasant revolt against Spanish in 1841, was captured and executed. He and followers exemplified tendency of Filipinos to identify with suffering of Christ.

JUAN PONCE ENRILE: Lawyer and businessman, minister of defense under Marcos. In February 1986 staged army mutiny against Marcos, helping to bring Corazon Aquino into office. Became secretary of defense in her cabinet, but challenged her authority and was dismissed. Elected senator in 1987 legislative elections.

CRISTANO EVANGELISTA: Early labor leader; founder of Philippine Communist party in 1930, helped to organize movement by American Communist agent.

CARLOS GARCÍA: President from 1957 to 1961, took office on death of Ramón Magsaysay; was notoriously corrupt.

MARIANO GOMEZ: Priest executed with Burgos in 1872.

GREGORIO HONASAN: Colonel who led troops in mutiny against Marcos in February 1986. Known as "Gringo," later attempted coup against Corazon Aquino in 1987 and arrested, but escaped. Represented group of aggrieved army officers.

HUMABON: Tribal chief in Cebu who welcomed Ferdinand Magellan in 1521, converted to Christianity, but later turned against Spanish. He was indirectly responsible for Magellan's death, having persuaded him to fight his rival, Lapu Lapu.

LAPU LAPU: Tribal chief on island of Mactan who killed Magellan in skirmish. Since immortalized by Filipinos as first national hero.

JOSÉ LAUREL: Distinguished lawyer who served as puppet president under Japanese during World War I. Subsequently exonerated, he was elected to Philippine legislature.

SALVADOR LAUREL: Politician who broke with Marcos in 1980, ran as vice president on Corazon Aquino's ticket in 1986. Later opposed her, but remained vice president.

VICENTE LAVA: Communist leader prior to World War II, merged with Socialists to form *Hukbalahap* movement. Later the party was headed by his brothers José and Jesus, who favored premature escalation of rebellion, caused splits in movement that contributed to its collapse.

BENITO LEGARDA: A founder of *Federalista* party early in twentieth century, typical of upper-class Filipino who cooperated with United States.

FERNANDO LOPEZ: Vice president under President Elpidio Quirino and later under Marcos, scion of wealthy family and brother of powerful Manila publisher Eugenio Lopez. Family opposed Marcos, lost most its holdings, which it regained following Corazon Aquino's takeover.

VICENTE LUKBAN: Filipino nationalist general, ordered massacre of American troops at town of Balangiga in 1901.

ANTONIO LUNA: Field commander of nationalist forces, murdered by Aguinaldo in June 1899.

APOLINARIO MABINI: Adviser to Aguinaldo, called "brains of the revolution." Captured by Americans late in 1899 and exiled to Guam.

DIOSDADO MACAPAGAL: President from 1961 through 1965; mild and ineffectual, was on CIA payroll.

RAMÓN MAGSAYSAY: President from 1953 until his death in airplane crash in 1957. Former secretary of defense, he had defeated Huk rebellion, owed his success to Colonel Edward Lansdale, secret American agent.

MIGUEL MALVAR: Nationalist general, held out against the Americans until April 1902.

RAUL MANGLAPUS: Secretary of foreign affairs in Corazon Aquino's cabinet, negotiated U.S. bases agreement.

FERDINAND MARCOS: President from 1965 until 1986; ruled under martial law after 1972. Estimated to have amassed $10 billion from corrupt activities. Born in northern Luzon in 1917; was brilliant law student. Claims to have been most decorated guerrilla during World War II later disputed. Cool and calculating but misruled badly, piled up huge foreign debt through lavish spending—yet consistently supported by United States. Blundered badly by calling election in 1986, underestimating appeal of his opposition. Flown aboard U.S. aircraft to exile in Hawaii.

IMELDA MARCOS: First lady, as she liked to be known. A flamboyant exhibitionist, considered herself figure of great international importance. Marcos used her as global diplomat, also named her governor of Manila. Born in Leyte in 1929, poor relation of distinguished political family. She fled with Marcos in 1986.

SERGIO OSMEÑA: With Manuel Quezon, one of two most prominent politicians of U.S. colonial period. Disciplined and hardworking, but overshadowed by Quezon. Served as vice president of commonwealth government, became president following Quezon's death in 1944. Born in 1878 in Cebu, the illegitimate son of Chinese *mestizo,* he owed his early career to American patronage.

PEDRO PALAEZ: Catholic priest of Spanish origin, favored rights for Filipino clergy during nineteenth century. Died in Manila earthquake in 1863.

TRINIDAD PARDO DE TAVERA: Rich conservative intellectual who quit Aguinaldo to side with Americans, helped to found the *Federalista* party in 1900, advocated statehood.

EMMANUEL PELAEZ: Vice president under Macapagal, later Corazon Aquino's ambassador to Washington.

GREGORIO DEL PILAR: Aguinaldo's romantic "boy general," died in 1899 delaying Americans at battle of Tirad Pass.

MANUEL QUEZON: Preeminent political figure throughout most of U.S. colonial rule. Born in 1878, elected to first Philippine national assembly. Sent to Washington as Filipino representative, drafted American legislation that pledged eventual independence for Philippines. Negotiated final independence act in 1935, became president of interim commonwealth. Handsome, mercurial and autocratic, escaped to Corregidor when Japanese invaded; died in the United States in 1944.

ELPIDIO QUIRINO: President from 1948 through 1953, his corrupt, inept administration slid into bankruptcy.

FIDEL RAMOS: Senior general under Marcos; with Enrile staged 1986 mutiny that propelled Cory Aquino into office, later became armed-forces commander.

JOSÉ RIZAL: Most venerated of national heroes. Oculist, writer, painter, born in 1861 to well-to-do family, educated in Spain. His polemical novel *Noli Me Tangere* was Filipino equivalent of *Uncle Tom's Cabin,* stimulated opposition to Spanish rule. Though championed assimilation with Spain, convicted of treason in 1896, and executed.

BENJAMIN ROMAULDEZ: Brother of Imelda; made fortune in business under Marcos. Known as "Kokoy," was ambassador to Washington, but spent most of time in Manila.

CARLOS ROMULO: Journalist, politician and diplomat, a durable public figure. Born in 1899, won Pulitzer Prize in 1942, served as aide to MacArthur, ambassador to Washington, foreign secretary under Marcos.

MANUEL ROXAS: First president of the independent Philippine republic, elected in 1946 with MacArthur's help. Declared war against Huks in 1948, just before his death.

PEDRO ABAD SANTOS: Founder of Philippine Socialist party during 1930s. Collaborated with Communists to form Huk movement to fight Japanese during World War II.

JAIME SIN: Cardinal and archibishop of Manila, played vital role in Corazon Aquino's election in 1986.

JOSÉ MARIE SISON: Founded new Communist party in 1968, later formed New People's Army. Captured by Marcos regime, released by Cory Aquino in 1986.

SULEIMAN: Muslim chief of Manila, ceded city to Spanish governor Miguel Lopez de Legazpi in 1571.

LUIS TARUC: Military commander of Huks. Of peasant origin, born in 1913, joined Socialist party; was anti-Japanese guerrilla leader during World War II. Elected to legislature in 1946 but disbarred, led rebellion against government. Surrendered in 1954 to Ninoy Aquino, sentenced to life term by President Magsaysay, later released by Marcos.

JORGE VARGAS: Quezon's private secretary, cooperated with Japanese to protect population during World War II.

FABIAN VER: General, armed-forces chief under Marcos. Charged and acquitted of assassination of Ninoy Aquino.

JACINTO ZAMORA: Priest executed with José Burgos and Mariano Gomez by Spanish in 1872.

THE SPANISH

BASILIO AUGUSTÍN: Governor of Philippines at outbreak of Spanish-American war in 1898. Surrendered Manila to the Americans in August.

JOSÉ BASCO: Governor of Philippines, appointed in 1778, opened country to foreign trade, spurred economic growth.

RAMÓN BLANCO: Governor of Philippines, tried to save Rizal from execution in 1896. Commanded Spanish army in war against Filipino rebels, later served in Cuba.

JUAN SEBASTIÁN DEL CANO: Commanded Magellan's surviving ship, completing circumnavigation of world in 1522.

ANTONIO CANOVAS: Conservative prime minister of Spain, championed firm rule in Philippines, assassinated in 1897.

CHARLES I: King of Spain, crowned in 1517, ordained Magellan's expedition.

CHARLES III: King of Spain from 1759 to 1788, hailed as "benevolent despot," advocated liberal colonial policies.

EULOGIO DESPUJOL: Governor of Philippines in late nineteenth century. Initially liberal, became reactionary, banished Rizal to Mindanao.

ENRIQUE DUPUY DE LOME: Spanish ambassador to Washington, he defamed President McKinley, added to American imperialist clamor for war with Spain.

FERDINAND VII: King of Spain, crowned in 1814, favored conservative colonial policies.

JUAN DE FONESCA: Bishop and chairman of Council of the Indies; promoted Magellan's expedition.

RAFAEL DE IZQUIERDO: Governor of Philippines, his harsh policies provoked army mutiny in 1872.

MANUEL DE LEGAZPI: Father of Spanish colony in the Philippines. Negotiated peace with Muslims and founded Manila as capital in 1871.

FERDINAND MAGELLAN: Discoverer of Philippines in 1521. Portuguese by birth, switched allegiance to Spain. Skilled seaman, he died in tribal dispute in Philippines.

MARÍA CRISTINA: Queen of Spain, sought to protect throne for her son, but could not cope with domestic political pressures, went to war with United States in 1898.

PATRICIO MONTOJO: Commander of Spanish fleet in the Philippines, defeated by Commodore George Dewey in battle of Manila Bay on May 1, 1898.

PHILIP II: King of Spain from 1556 to 1598, presided over country from peak of power to beginning of decline as empire. Gave his name to the Philippines.

CAMILIO DE POLAVIEJA: Governor of Philippines, arrived 1897, failed to deal with Filipino rebellion.

FERNANDO PRIMO DE RIVERA: Governor of Philippines, negotiated truce with Filipino rebels in 1898.

PRÁXEDES MATEO SAGASTA: Liberal Spanish prime minister, tried to avert war with United States by promoting reforms in Cuba, but driven into conflict.

CARLOS DE LA TORRE: Governor of Philippines from 1869 to 1871. At first liberal, came under sway of reactionaries.

ANDRÉS DE URDANETA: Navigator, conceived of eastward route across Pacific. Accompanied Legazpi's expedition to Philippines in 1564.

RUY LOPEZ DE VILLALOBOS: Explorer, named islands the Philippines in 1543.

VALERIANO WEYLER: Commander in Cuba, called "butcher" for his harsh repression, recalled in 1897.

THE AMERICANS

MORTON ABRAMOWITZ: State Department official, early critic of Marcos regime.

JAMES ALLEN: American Communist agent, alias Sol Auerbach; persuaded Philippine Communist and Socialist parties to merge as Huk movement in late 1930s.

MICHAEL ARMACOST: Ambassador to Philippines from 1982 to 1984, later undersecretary of state, became a leading State Department critic of Marcos.

FRED ATKINSON: Director of education for Philippines from 1900 to 1902, emphasized vocational training.

HARRY BANDHOLTZ: Army captain in Philippines in early 1900s, early patron of Quezon.

DAVID BARROWS: Director of education in Philippines from 1902 to 1908, stressed academic curriculum.

C. JASPER BELL: Democratic congressman from Missouri, sponsored important trade act in 1946.

J. FRANKLIN BELL: General, waged brutal campaign against Filipino nationalists in 1901.

ALBERT BEVERIDGE: Republican senator from Indiana from 1899 to 1911, and eloquent imperialist.

STEPHEN BOSWORTH: Ambassador to Philippines from 1964 to 1987, played key role during 1986 elections, removed Marcos from Manila.

NATHANIEL BOWDITCH: First American ship captain to make Manila a scheduled port of call in late eighteenth century.

LEWIS BRERETON: U.S. Army Air Corps commander, lost his planes to Japanese at Clark Field on December 8, 1941.

WILLIAM JENNINGS BRYAN: Democratic party leader, defeated by McKinley in presidential elections of 1896 and 1900. Eloquent speaker, equivocal on issue of imperialism.

DANIEL BURNHAM: Famous architect and city planner at turn of century, redesigned Manila and created Baguio resort.

GEORGE BUSH: Vice president during the Reagan administration, criticized for praise of Marcos during 1981 visit to Manila. Elected president in 1988.

CLAUDE BUSS: U.S. official in Manila at time of Japanese occupation.

HENRY BYROADE: Ambassador from 1969 to 1973, failed to dissuade Marcos from declaring martial law in 1972.

ANDREW CARNEGIE: Industrialist and philanthropist, vocal anti-imperialist around turn of the century.

JIMMY CARTER: President from 1977 to 1981, rhetorical champion of human rights.

ADNA ROMANZA CHAFFEE: Army commander in 1901, supervised final offensives against Filipino guerrillas.

GROVER CLEVELAND: President of United States from 1885 to 1889 and from 1893 to 1897. Democrat, resisted imperialists.

MYRON COWEN: Ambassador from 1950 to 1952, proposed covert action to oust President Elipidio Quirino.

WILLIAM CROWE: Admiral, naval commander in Pacific from 1983 to 1985, later Chairman, Joint Chiefs of Staff. An early critic of Marcos regime.

WILLIAM DAY: Secretary of state under McKinley, cool to idea of annexation of Philippines, headed delegation to peace conference with Spain in 1898.

GEORGE DEWEY: Admiral, defeated Spanish fleet in Manila Bay on May 1, 1898, returned home to huge ovation. Born in Vermont in 1837, chosen by Theodore Roosevelt, assistant secretary of navy, to head Asia squadron. May have led Aguinaldo to believe that America backed Filipino cause.

FINLEY PETER DUNNE: Humorist around turn of century, mocked imperialism through his fictitious Mr. Dooley.

DWIGHT EISENHOWER: President of United States from 1953 to 1961, supreme Allied commander in Europe during World War II. Chief aide to MacArthur in Philippines in late 1930s, later supervised Asia strategy in War Department.

W. CAMERON FORBES: Governor of Philippines from 1909 to 1913, concentrated on economic development.

FREDERICK FUNSTON: Brigadier general, won fame for bold capture of Aguinaldo in 1901.

SAMUEL GRASHIO: Pilot at outbreak of World War II, captured at Bataan, survived death march.

WILLIAM WALTER GRAYSON: Nebraska Volunteer, fired first shot in war between Americans and Filipinos in 1899.

PHILIP HABIB: Diplomat, sent to Manila in February 1986, returned to Washington to recommend U.S. censure of Marcos.

WILLIAM HALSEY: Admiral, U.S. naval commander at battle of Leyte Gulf in 1944.

MARK HANNA: Senator and businessman, managed McKinley's presidential campaign in 1896, opposed war with Spain.

JAMES HARBORD: Constabulary officer in 1905 and early patron of Manuel Quezon.

FRANCIS BURTON HARRISON: Governor of Philippines from 1913 to 1920, appointed by President Wilson. A Democrat, he favored large political role for Filipinos to prepare them for independence, remains a major American hero to Filipinos.

THOMAS HART: Fleet commander in east Asia at outbreak of World War II, often disagreed with MacArthur.

JOHN HAUSSERMANN: Rich and influential businessman and lawyer during U.S. colonial periods.

HARRY HAWES: Democratic congressman from Missouri, drafted legislation in 1931 to grant independence to Philippines.

JOHN HAY: Secretary of state under presidents McKinley and Theodore Roosevelt, from 1898 to 1905. Novelist and poet, author of Open Door policy to guarantee free trade in China, proponent of larger U.S. role in Asia.

WILLIAM RANDOLPH HEARST: Newspaper publisher and a foremost imperialist of turn of the century, flamboyantly agitated for war with Spain.

GEORGE HOAR: Republican Senator from Massachusetts and vocal opponent of imperialism in 1898.

RICHARD HOLBROOKE: Assistant secretary of state during Carter administration from 1977 to 1981, instrumental in persuading Marcos to release Ninoy Aquino from prison.

CORDELL HULL: Franklin Roosevelt's secretary of state, negotiated with Japanese in effort to avert war in 1941.

HAROLD ICKES: Secretary of interior from 1933 to 1946, fought with MacArthur over Philippine policy.

WILLIAM JANEQUETTE: Alias Harrison George, Communist agent, went to Manila in 1924 to help found Communist party.

LYNDON JOHNSON: President of United States from 1963 to 1969, urged Marcos to commit Filipino troops to Vietnam.

WILLIAM ATKINSON JONES: Virginia congressman, sponsored act in 1916 that pledged eventual Philippines independence.

GABRIEL KAPLAN: CIA man in Manila during 1950s, played key role in promoting Ramón Magsaysay.

EDWARD KING: General, commander of American and Filipino forces on Bataan, surrendered to Japanese in April 1942.

EDWARD LANSDALE: Air force colonel and CIA agent, helped Magsaysay to fight the Huks, secretly managed his campaign for president of Philippines in 1953.

HENRY WARE LAWTON: General, killed in 1899 by Filipino sniper, given hero's funeral in Washington.

PAUL LAXALT: Republican senator from Nevada, sent by Reagan to Manila late in 1985 to urge Marcos to reform. In February 1986, at Reagan's behest, urged Marcos to resign.

FITZHUGH LEE: Consul in Havana in 1898, advised McKinley to send *Maine* there to protect Americans after riots.

PAUL LINEBARGER: American judge in Tayabas province in 1902, early promoter of Quezon's career.

HENRY CABOT LODGE: Republican senator from Massachusetts from 1893 to 1925. Passionate imperialist, joined Theodore Roosevelt in advocating Spanish-American war. Became equally fervent isolationist after World War I.

JOHN LONG: McKinley's secretary of navy, could not control Theodore Roosevelt, his assistant secretary.

RICHARD LUGAR: Republican senator from Indiana, led observers to Philippines during 1986 election, reported fraud by Marcos.

ARTHUR MACARTHUR: General, appointed military governor in 1900, had led main column against Filipino nationalists. He resented Taft's arrival, and career suffered after Taft became secretary of war and president. Father of Douglas MacArthur.

DOUGLAS MACARTHUR: General; American most admired by Filipinos. Born in 1880 in Little Rock, Arkansas, first went to Philippines with army engineers in 1904, returned as garrison commander from 1922 to 1925, back there again from 1928 to 1930 as commander for archipelago. Returned in 1935 as military adviser to Quezon, appointed supreme commander for Pacific in 1941. Fled Philippines after Japanese invasion, liberated islands in 1945, instrumental in restoring prewar political structure. Died in 1964.

JEAN MARIE FAIRCLOTH MACARTHUR: Douglas MacArthur's second wife, whom he married in 1936 after shipboard romance.

LOUISE CROMWELL BROOKS MACARTHUR: Douglas MacArthur's first wife, whom he married in 1922. A Jazz Age flapper, she disliked his rigorous military life.

MARY PINCKNEY MACARTHUR: Douglas MacArthur's mother and strong influence on him until her death in 1935.

FRANK MCINTYRE: Chief of Bureau of Insular Affairs, agency responsible for Philippines, named to job in 1913.

WILLIAM MCKINLEY: President of United States, elected 1896, assassinated 1901. Born in Ohio, served in Congress, was eloquent speaker and respected politician, but weak and indecisive, entered war with Spain with misgivings. Also drifted into annexation of Philippines.

PAUL MCNUTT: High commissioner to commonwealth government from 1936 to 1939, returned as ambassador after independence, later represented American firms in Manila. Former Democratic governor of Indiana, had presidential ambitions.

ALFRED THAYER MAHAN: Naval strategist and champion of American global role, inspired Theodore Roosevelt.

WESLEY MERRITT: General and commander of first U.S. Army expedition to Philippines in 1898.

NELSON MILES: General and U.S. Army commander at outbreak of Spanish-American war.

FRANK MURPHY: Governor of Philippines from 1933 to 1935, first high commissioner under commonwealth. New Deal liberal, former governor of Michigan, later Supreme Court justice.

CARL MYDANS: Photojournalist, covered Japanese arrival in Manila in 1942, liberation of Philippines in 1945.

CHESTER NIMITZ: Naval commander for Pacific during World War II.

ELWELL OTIS: American army commander in Philippines in 1898, in charge when war with Filipinos broke out in 1899.

DREW PEARSON: Newspaper columnist during 1930s, revealed existence of MacArthur's Filipino mistress.

JOHN J. PERSHING: General, as young captain fought against Moros in Mindanao in 1904, later governor of region, commanded American expeditionary force in France from 1917 to 1918.

WILLIAM POMEROY: American Communist, joined Huks in 1950, captured two years later, imprisoned and deported to America.

E. SPENCER PRATT: American consul in Singapore in 1898, urged Aguinaldo to join Americans in war with Spain, pledged U.S. support for Philippine independence.

PHILINDA RAND: American teacher in Philippines, arrived in 1901 after graduation from Radcliffe.

RONALD REAGAN: President of the United States from 1981 to 1989, sympathetic to Marcos. First visited Manila in 1969, when as governor of California attended opening of Imelda's cultural center.

FRANKLIN DELANO ROOSEVELT: President of the United States from 1933 to 1945, signed law in 1935 pledging independence to Philippines.

THEODORE ROOSEVELT: President from 1901 to 1908. Born in 1858, joined McKinley cabinet in 1897 as assistant secretary of navy, championed war with Spain. Elected vice president, became president on McKinley's assassination. Later favored early independence for Philippines, died in 1919.

ELIHU ROOT: Secretary of war under McKinley and Roosevelt from 1899 to 1904, Roosevelt's secretary of state until 1909. Formulated U.S. policy for Philippines, died in 1937.

CARL SHURZ: Leading anti-imperialist at turn of century. Born in Germany, was editor, diplomat, general, senator.

GEORGE SHULTZ: Reagan's secretary of state, played key role in 1986 in persuading Reagan to support Cory Aquino.

JACOB SMITH: General, in 1902 ordered harsh repression on island of Samar after massacre of American troops. Tried and convicted for brutality, forced to retire.

JOSEPH BURKHOLDER SMITH: CIA agent, arrived in Manila in 1958, paid Filipino politicians to organize new party.

STEPHEN SOLARZ: Congressman from New York, early critic of Marcos regime and supporter of Corazon Aquino.

HENRY STIMSON: Governor of Philippines from 1927 to 1928. Secretary of war in Taft cabinet, secretary of state under Hoover, secretary of war under Franklin Roosevelt.

RICHARD SUTHERLAND: MacArthur's Chief of Staff during World War II.

WILLIAM HOWARD TAFT: As first civilian governor of Philippines, determined U.S. colonial policy, which he later pursued as secretary of war and president. An Ohio judge, born in 1857, appointed to Manila by McKinley in 1900. Ceded authority to Filipino elite, strengthened oligarchy, coined term "little brown brothers" to convey his hope to Americanize the natives. Named chief justice of the Supreme Court in 1921 by Harding, died in 1930.

HARRY TRUMAN: President of the United States from 1945 to 1953, committed the United States to fight Communist insurgencies.

MILLARD TYDINGS: Democratic senator from Maryland, drafted law in 1935 to create Philippine commonwealth government with independence to follow in a decade.

JONATHAN WAINWRIGHT: General left by MacArthur to command U.S. forces in 1942. Surrendered and spent war in Japanese internment.

LITTLETON WALLER TAZEWELL WALLER: Marine major ordered to crush Filipinos in 1902, indicted for committing atrocities, in turn blamed General Jacob Smith and was acquitted.

CASPAR WEINBERGER: Secretary of defense during Reagan administration, reluctant to endorse anti-Marcos policy.

FRANK WHITE: Director of education in Philippines from 1908 to 1913, emphasized vocational training.

ROUNSEVELLE WILDMAN: Consul in Hong Kong in 1898, favored use of Filipinos against Spain in Philippines and selling them arms—with share of proceeds going to himself.

OSCAR WILLIAMS: Consul in Manila in 1898, provided Dewey with intelligence, sympathetic to Filipino cause.

WOODROW WILSON: President of the United States from 1913 to 1921. At first favored U.S. rule of Philippines, but gradually acquiesced to independence policy.

LEONARD WOOD: Governor of Philippines from 1921 to 1927. Stiff and aloof, clashed with Filipino politicians.

STEWART WOODFORD: McKinley's minister to Madrid in 1898, negotiated with Spanish in effort to prevent war. Aware of internal political pressures on Spanish, pleaded for time, but momentum in Washington for war was too great.

THE JAPANESE

MASAHARU HOMMA: General, commander of Japanese invasion of Philippines in 1941. Executed for war crimes after war.

KISHISABURO NOMURA: Ambassador to Washington in 1941, negotiated with Secretary of State Hull to avert war.

HIDEKO TOJO: Prime minister during World War II, had championed war, ousted when tide turned against Japan. Executed for war crimes after war.

KIYOSHI UCHIYAMA: Consul in Manila before World War II, tried to mobilize support for Japan among Filipinos.

ISOROKU YAMAMOTO: Admiral and architect of Japanese attack against Pearl Harbor in December 1941.

TOMOYUKI YAMASHITA: General, commander of Japanese forces in Philippines during final phase of war. Withdrew troops from Manila to save city as U.S. troops approached in 1945. Executed for war crimes.

OTHERS

EDOUARD ANDRÉ: Belgian consul in Manila in 1898, used by Dewey to arrange Spanish surrender of Manila.

HENRY: Portuguese prince known as the "Navigator," founded maritime academy in fifteenth century, inspired exploration.

RUDYARD KIPLING: British poet, wrote "White Man's Burden" as exhortation to America to annex Philippines.

LEO XIII: Pope, advocated social justice in late nineteenth century. Endorsed sale of Catholic lands in Philippines.

ANTONIO PIGAFETTA: Venetian aristocrat, joined Magellan's voyage in 1519 and chronicled expedition.

NOTES ON SOURCES

This book is history related by a journalist—a narrative of past and contemporary events. As such, the material has been derived from three principal sources: my experiences as a correspondent in Asia and Washington over a period of thirty years; more recent interviews, audio and visual, conducted for *In Our Image,* the television documentary series produced in tandem with the book; and a vast body of published and unpublished literature on the subject.

The voluminous notes I had gathered as a reporter over the years were invaluable. Like a diary, they enabled me to recapture the past as I observed and felt it at the time, rather than relying on my own fading memory. They also served as a record of the remarks and attitudes of the individuals I interviewed, many of whom may have forgotten or revised their earlier views. Whenever possible, I have cited people by name in the text. In cases where people are quoted anonymously, it was my judgment that an attribution was unnecessary—or my notes may simply have been incomplete.

The Philippines is a journalist's paradise. During all my years of reporting from there, I cannot recall a single instance of being denied an interview. Meetings often turned into lunches, dinners, weekends in the country. Presidents were invariably accessible, often on brief notice, along with members of their cabinet and other officials. So were opposition politicians and a wide range of other figures—journalists, priests, businessmen, lawyers, army officers, educators, students. Renowned Filipino hospitality extends to rural areas, where even the poorest peasants insist on sharing their meager meal with a visitor. In contrast to my experience in Vietnam, where the North Vietnamese and Vietcong rarely saw correspondents during the war, the Communist insurgents in the Philippines welcome the press, and I spoke with their leaders and guerrillas both in Manila and in the countryside. A singular advantage for an American journalist is the pervasive use of English throughout the Philippines—an enduring legacy of U.S. colonial rule.

I proceeded with caution in Manila, where conversation is an industry. Gossip—*tsismis* in Tagalog—frequently passes for fact. The newspapers are among the liveliest and least credible in the world. But I had learned long before to be skeptical, one of the tools of a reporter's trade. In the Philippines I operated on the presumption that perceptions are a form of reality, and that the truth was often to be found in attitudes rather than in a futile quest for facts.

The truth can also be elusive in Washington, where the different branches of government frequently promote rival policies, and a reporter's task once again is to navigate through these shoals. I was greatly helped by White House, State Department, Defense Department and Central Intelligence Agency officials involved in Philippine affairs. I owe a special debt of gratitude to Sharon Kotok, former chief of the Information Access Branch of the State Department, who facilitated an almost endless flow of documents declassified under the Freedom of Information Act until I felt as swamped as the sorcerer's apprentice. I also benefited from the cooperation of members of Congress and their staffs—in particular Stanley Roth of the Subcommittee on Asian and Pacific Affairs of the House of Representatives' Committee on Foreign Affairs.

A legacy of the American colonial era are the staggering collections of documents available in U.S. archives. The National Archives and the Library of Congress, both in Washington, are treasure troves. I located useful material at the Lyndon Johnson Library at the University of Texas, and at the Nixon Presidential Materials Project of the National Archives, where I was helped by Joan Howard, a curator. Equally important were the archives at Cornell University, the East-West Center of the University of Hawaii, the University of Michigan, Harvard and Yale. The U.S. Army Military History Research Center at Carlisle Barracks, Pennsylvania, and the U.S. Army installation at the Presidio in San Francisco are filled with documents and photographs of the early American military intervention in the Philippines. Many Americans whose grandparents, parents or other relatives served as soldiers, teachers, officials, businessmen and missionaries in the Philippines graciously loaned me personal letters, journals and other mementos. The list of sources in the United States would not be complete without mentioning the extraordinary Cellar Book Shop in Detroit, with its thousands of books on the Philippines. Its proprietor, Morton Nestorg, is an American born and raised in Manila, and his wife, Petra, is a human catalog.

Much of the archival material in Manila was destroyed during World War II. However, two valuable sources remain—the Ayala Museum and the Lopez Foundation, whose curators cooperated in this effort. But the most useful archive in Manila is the U.S. Historical Collection, which is located in the U.S. Information Service and directed by Lewis Gleeck, Jr., a retired American consul. The *Bulletin* published by the collection is a rich source of material on the American experience in the Philippines. The Solidaridad Book Store in Manila, run by the writer F. Sionil José and his wife, Tessa, furnished me with books and journals, including *Solidarity,* their scholarly periodical.

Many excellent books deal with specific periods and issues, but there are few general works on the Philippines. The most thorough is Fred Eggan, *The Philippines,* 4 Vols. (New Haven: Human Relations Area Files, Yale, 1955). A brief but eloquent introduction is David Joel Steinberg's *The Philippines: A Singular and Plural Place* (Boulder, Col.: Westview Press, 1982). Useful primers are Albert Ravenholt, *The Philippines: A Young Republic on the Move* (Princeton: D. Van Nostrand, 1962); Keith Lightfoot, *The Philippines* (New York: Praeger, 1973); and Emily Hahn, *The Islands: America's Imperialist Adventures in the Philippines* (New York: Coward, McCann & Geoghegan, 1981). A work crammed with material is Lewis Gleeck, Jr., *General History of the Philippines: The American Half-Century* (Quezon City: R. P. García, 1984). I also relied on Teodoro Agoncillo, *A Short History of the Philippines* (New York: New American Library, 1975); Agoncillo and Milagros Guerrero, *History of the Philippine People* (Quezon City: R. P. García, 1977); and Onofre Corpuz, *The Philippines* (Englewood Cliffs, N.J.: Prentice-Hall, 1965). A Filipino nationalist overview is Renato Constantino, *The Philippines: A Past Revisited* (Manila: Renato Constantino, 1975). Daniel Schirmer and Stephen Rosskamm Shalom have put together a useful collection of documents in *The Philippines Reader* (Boston: South End Press, 1987). A handy tool is *Philippine Almanac* (Manila: Aurora, 1986), a statistical compilation.

Finally, in the category of general views, I recommend the very insightful articles by Ian Buruma in the *Far Eastern Economic Review* and the *New York Review of Books;* articles by Theodore Friend in *Orbis* and other publications; essays by Adrian Cristobal in *Occasional Prose* (Manila: Vessel Books, 1984); and Carmen Nakpil Guerrero's book of essays entitled *A Question of Identity* (Manila: Vessel Books, 1973). James Fallow's essay "A Damaged Culture," *The Atlantic Monthly,* January 1987, is provocative. The Filipino author F. Sionil José's novels and short stories offer penetrating glimpses into life in the Philippines.

1. ALL IN THE FAMILY

Much of the material in this chapter comes from my direct observation. I attended the State Department banquet for President Corazon Aquino held on September 17, 1986, and also interviewed her on her impressions of her visit to the United States. Her aides Teodoro Locsin, Jr., Teodoro Benigno and Mark Malloch Brown provided me with information, and I interviewed Secretary of State George Shultz as well. I relied on *The New York Times* and *The Washington Post* for further details of Cory's visit.

The historical introduction in this chapter is fleshed out in later chapters, for which references will be found below. The descriptive passages on the American cultural influence on Filipinos are based on my own observations as well as on talks with Alejandro Roces, Carmen Nakpil Guerrero, Adrian Cristobal, David Joel Steinberg and especially Doreen Fernandez, a cultural anthropologist. Raul Manglapus, the foreign secretary and an avid jazz musician, treated me to an exuberant rehearsal of his band, the Executive Combo. The classic analysis of the interaction between colonizer and colonized is O. Mannoni, *Prospero and Caliban,* trans. Pamela Powseland (New York: Praeger, 1968).

Bishop Francisco Claver, Father Jaime Bulatão, Father John Carroll and Patricia Licuanan, among others, provided me with explanations of Filipino social customs and values. Published works on the subject include Bulatão, "Hiya" (Quezon City: *Philippine Studies,* July 1964); Carroll, "Philippine Social Organization and National Development" (Quezon City: *Philippine Studies,* October 1966); essays in Frank Lynch, ed., *Four Readings on Philippine Values* (Quezon City: Institute of Philippine Studies, Ateneo, 1964); essays by Fred Eggan and George Guthrie in Guthrie, ed., *Six Perspectives on the Philippines* (Manila: Bookmark, 1968); Guthrie and Fortunata Azores, "Philippine Interpersonal Behavior Patterns" in *Modernization: Its Impact in the Philippines* (Quezon City: Institute of Philippine Culture, Ateneo, 1968); Emma Porio, Frank Lynch and Mary Hollnsteiner, *The Filipino Family, Communist and Nation: The Same Yesterday, Today and Tomorrow* (Quezon City, Institute of Philippine Culture, Ateneo, 1975); George Forster, "Cofradia and Compradrazgo" in the *Southwestern Journal of Anthropology* (Albuquerque: University of New Mexico, 1953); Tomas Andrés and Pilar Ilada-Andrés, *Understanding the Filipino* (Quezon City: New Day, 1987) and Chester Hunt et al., *Sociology in the Philippine Setting* (Quezon City, Pheonix, 1954). Excellent analyses of the impact of social values on politics are in Carl Lande's monograph "Leaders, Factions and Parties: the Structure of Philippine Politics" (New Haven: Southeast Asia Studies Program, Yale, 1964) and Lucian Pye, *Asian Power and Politics* (Cambridge: Harvard University Press, 1985).

The passage on the U.S. bases in the Philippines is derived from interviews with Secretary of State Shultz; Admiral William Crowe, Chairman of the Joint Chiefs of Staff; Nicholas Platt, U.S. ambassador to the Philippines; and Raul Manglapus. I was a member of a study group on the bases at the Council on Foreign Relations, which resulted in a monograph by Fred Greene entitled *The Philippine Bases: Negotiating for the Future.* I am indebted to William Berry for his Cornell doctoral dissertation on the bases as well as to Carolina Hernandez for her study of the subject.

As the narrative indicates, the article entitled "What's Wrong with the Philippines?" by Benigno Aquino, Jr., appeared in the July 1968 issue of *Foreign Affairs.* I discussed the gist of the article with Aquino at the time.

2. IN SEARCH OF SPICES AND SOULS

Magellan's voyage to the Philippines fits into the context of the age of discovery, a subject covered in several fine histories. The most recent is Daniel Boorstin's popular *The Discoverers* (New York: Random House, 1983), which contains an exhaustive bibliography. A very readable history is Michael Edwardes, *Asia in the European Age* (London: Thames and Hudson, 1961). Introductions for the general reader are Brian Harrison, *Southeast Asia: A Short History* (London: Macmillan, 1964) and Stanley Karnow, *Southeast Asia* (New York: Life World Library, 1963, 1965). An interesting Asian analysis by an Indian diplomat is K. M. Pannikar, *Asia and Western Dominance* (New York: John Day, undated). Father Martin Noone, a Columban missionary, has written a lively account entitled *The Islands Saw It: The Discovery and Conquest of the Philippines, 1521–81* (Dublin: Helicon Press, 1983), which reaches beyond Magellan's voyage to describe the Spanish colonization of the archipelago by Miguel de Legazpi. Noone includes a large bibliography of Spanish documents. The standard biography of Magellan is Francis Guillemard, *Life of Magellan* (London: Hakluyt Society, 1890).

Among the many original accounts of the period are the classic Armando Cortesão, ed., *Suma Oriental of Tome Pires* (London: Hakluyt Society, 1944) and *Commentaries of the Great Alfonso de Albuquerque,* trans. W. Gray Birsh (London: Hakluyt Society, 1975). The most comprehensive single collection of documents on the Spanish period in the Philippines, from the discovery and settlement to the arrival of the United States, is Emma Helen Blair and James Alexander Robertson, eds., *The Philippine Islands: 1493–1898,* 55 Vols. (Cleveland: A. H. Clark, 1903; reprinted by Cachos Hermanos, Mandaluyong, Rizal, 1973). Blair and Robertson were American scholars who went to the Philippines at the turn of the century and amassed their documents there and in Spain, only to encounter difficulties in finding a publisher. Their work not only revealed to the American imperialists the history of the Spaniards who had preceded them, but it is the only history that the Filipinos have of the Spanish colonial period. I will refer to Blair and Robertson in the notes for the next chapter. For the purposes of this chapter, their set contains the papal bulls dividing the world between Spain and Portugal, and much of the Spanish official nattering prior to Magellan's voyage. It also includes the eyewitness story of Magellan's voyage, Antonio Pigafetta's famous *Il Primo Viaggio Intorno Al Mondo,* which has been translated more recently by R. A. Skelton (New Haven: Yale University Press, 1969). Blair and Robertson contains accounts of later Spanish exploration of the Philippines, and the start of colonization under Legazpi, including his correspondence with his superiors in Mexico.

The basic geographies are Frederick Wernstedt and Joseph Spencer, *The Philippine Island World: A Physical, Cultural and Regional Geography* (Berkeley: University of California Press, 1967); T. M. Burley, *The Philippines: An Economic and Social Geography* (London: G. Bell, 1973); Charles Robequain, *Malaya, Indonesia, Borneo and the Philippines,* trans. E. D. Laborde (London: Longmans, Green, 1954); Norton Ginsburg, ed., *The Pattern of Asia* (Englewood Cliffs, N.J.: Prentice-Hall, undated); George Cressey, *Asia's Lands and People* (New York: McGraw-Hill, undated); and E.H.G. Dobby, *Monsoon Asia* (London: University of London Press, 1961). D. H. Grist, *Rice* (London: Longmans, Green, 1958) is as basic as its title.

As is mentioned in the narrative, the pre-Hispanic Filipinos had an oral tradition and left virtually no record of their culture. The best descriptions are those of early Spanish explorers and priests, many of whom had insatiable curiosities. One of the most thorough, entitled *Labor Evangelica,* is by Francisco Colin, a Jesuit, and was first published in Madrid in 1663 and appears in Vol. 40 of Blair and Robertson. Another early reportage, by Miguel de Loarca, is also translated in Blair and Robertson. F. Landa Jocano, a Filipino anthropologist, advanced his theory that Filipinos originated in the islands in *Questions and Challenges in Philippine Prehistory* (Quezon City: University of the Philippines, 1975).

3. THE SPANISH BOND

Blair and Robertson, cited above, contains a wealth of material on the Spanish colonial era. Especially interesting are the documents on official Spanish colonial policy and the role of the Catholic Church. Basic histories of the Spanish period are John Leddy Phelan, *The Hispanization of the Philippines: Spanish Aims and Filipino Responses, 1565–1700* (Madison: University of Wisconsin Press, 1959); John Foreman, *The Philippine Islands* (New York: Scribners, 1899); Nicholas Cushner, *Spain in the Philippines* (Rutland, Vt: Tuttle, 1972); and Dean Worcester, *The Philippine Islands and Their People* (New York: Macmillan, 1898). The aforementioned history by Agoncillo and Guerrero also deals with the period. An excellent brief analysis of the Spanish period is contained in the opening chapters of Peter Stanley, *A Nation in the Making: The Philippines and the United States, 1899–1921* (Cambridge: Harvard University Press, 1974).

Descriptions by visitors to the Philippines include *Travel Accounts of the Islands* (by various European explorers from the sixteenth to the nineteenth century), 2 Vols. (Manila: Filipiniana Book Guild, 1968, 1971); and John Bowring, *A Visit to the Philippine Islands* (Manila: Filipiniana Book Guild, 1963). Life during the Spanish colonial period is contained in James E. Leroy, *Philippine Life in Town and Country* (New York: Putnam, 1905); Robert MacMicking, *Recollections of Manila and the Philippines During 1848, 1849 and 1850* (Manila: Filipiniana Book Guild, 1967); and William Henry Scott, *Cracks in the Parchment Curtain* (Manila: Limited Editions, 1968). Manila in the late eighteenth century is described by Nathaniel Bowditch in Thomas and Mary McHale, eds., *Early Philippine-American Trade: The Journal of Nathaniel Bowditch, 1796* (New Haven: Southeast Asia Studies, Yale, 1962). A readable memoir of a wealthy Filipino's life in the late nineteenth century is Felix Roxas, *The World of Felix Roxas* (Manila: Filipiniana Book Guild, 1970).

The British occupation of Manila in the late eighteenth century, the opening of the Philippines to foreign trade and the evolution of Spanish economic policy in the nineteenth century are described in documents in Blair and Robertson. A standard work on the subject is William Lyle Schurz, *The Manila Galleon* (New York: Dutton, 1939). Economic development and its political and social impact is vividly described in the chapter entitled "Turmoil of Change" in Stanley's *Nation in the Making*. Other authoritative books are Alfred McCoy and Ed. C. de Jesus, *Philippine Social History: Global Trade and Local Transformations* (Quezon City: Anteneo, 1982) and Conrado Benítez and Austin Craig, *Philippine Progress Prior to 1898* (Manila: Filipiniana Book Guild, 1969). The development of sugar cultivation in the nineteenth century is described by the British consul in Iloilo at the time: Nicholas Loney, *A Britisher in the Philippines* (Manila: Filipiniana Book Guild, 1969).

Several books and articles deal with the Chinese: Edgar Wickberg, *The Chinese in Philippine Life, 1850–98* (New Haven: Yale University Press, 1965) and "The Chinese Mestizo in Philippine History," *Journal of Southeast Asian Studies* (March 1964); Alfonso Felix, Jr., ed., *The Chinese in the Philippines 1770–1898* (Manila: Solidaridad, 1969); Shubert Liao, ed., *Chinese Participation in Philippine Culture and Economy* (Manila: Bookman, 1964); and Virginia Benítez Licuanan, *Money in the Bank: The Story of Money and Banking in the Philippines* (Manila: PCIbank Human Resources Development Foundation, 1985). For a comparison with other countries in the area, a basic work is Victor Purcell, *The Chinese in Southeast Asia* (London: Oxford, 1965). George Weightman of Lehman College, New York, shared his expertise on the subject with me.

The link between mysticism and peasant unrest is described in one of the most remarkable books on the Philippines: Reynaldo Clemena Ileto, *Payson and Revolution: Popular Movements in the Philippines* (Quezon City: Anteneo, 1979). Ileto, whom I interviewed, also helped me to understand the importance of mysticism and dissent to this day. Another sound book on the subject is David Sturtevant, *Popular Uprisings in the Philippines 1840–1940* (Ithaca: Cornell, 1976).

Two books by Father John Schumacher are vital to an understanding of religion and the rise of nationalism in the Philippines: *Father José Burgos: Priest and Nationalist* (Quezon City: Ateneo, 1972) and *Revolutionary Clergy: The Filipino Clergy and the Nationalist Movement 1850–1903* (Quezon City: Ateneo, 1981). Also valuable is Gerald Anderson, ed., *Studies in Philippine Church History* (Ithaca: Cornell University Press, 1969).

Father Schumacher has also traced the development of Philippine nationalism in the nineteenth century in *The Propaganda Movement, 1880–1895: The Creators of a Filipino Consciousness* (Manila: Solidaridad, 1973). The subject is also covered in Agoncillo's history. The story of Andrés Bonifacio and the rise of the Katipunan is told by Agoncillo in *The Revolt of the Masses: The Story of Bonifacio and the Katipunan* (Quezon City: University of the Philippines Press, 1956) and in his *Writings and Trial of Andrés Bonifacio* (Manila: Bonifacio Centennial Commission, 1963). The relevant documents are contained in Horacio de la Costa, *Readings in Philippine History* (Manila: Bookmark, 1965). A narrative account of the early nationalist movement is contained in John R.M. Taylor, *The Philippine Insurrection Against the United States,* 5 Vols. (Pasay City: Eugenio Lopez Foundation, 1971). The Taylor series had an unusual history. Taylor, a U.S. Army captain, collected and translated more than twelve thousand Filipino nationalist documents between 1902 and 1906. William Howard Taft, by then president, blocked their publication, presuming them to be sensitive. They remained in the National Archives in Washington until 1957, when they were published in Manila. I refer to them in subsequent chapters.

José Rizal has inspired a massive literature. His two principal novels, *The Lost Eden (Noli Me Tangere)* and *The Subversive (El Filibusterismo),* were published in English translation in 1968 by the Indiana University Press, Bloomington, Ind. I have referred to three biographies: Austin Coates, *Rizal: Philippine Nationalist and Martyr* (London: Oxford University Press, 1968); Rafael Palma, *The Pride of the Malay Race,* trans. Roman Ozaeta (New York: Prentice-Hall, 1949); and Bernard Reines, *A People's Hero* (New York: Praeger, 1971). An interesting essay is Leon Ma. Guerrero, "Rizal as Liberal, Bonifacio as Democrat," in *We Filipinos* (Manila: Daily Star, 1984).

Emilio Aguinaldo has also spawned a vast literature. He related his early life in Aguinaldo, *Memoirs of the Revolution,* trans. Luz Colendrino-Bucu (Manila: privately printed, 1967). The story is retold by Carlos Quirion, *The Young Aguinaldo* (Manila: Aguinaldo Centennial Year, 1969) and by David Haward Bain, *Sitting in Darkness: Americans in the Philippines* (Boston: Houghton Mifflin, 1984). A hagiography is Alfredo Saulo, *Emilio Aguinaldo* (Manila: Quezon City, 1983). Aguinaldo's early activities, his expedient pact with the Spanish and move to Hong Kong are in his memoirs and in Agoncillo, Taylor and other sources.

A useful book on prominent Filipinos of the late nineteenth and early twentieth centuries is Arsenio Manuel, *Dictionary of Philippine Biography* (Quezon City: Filipiniana Book Guild, 1955).

4. AMERICA GOES GLOBAL

The battle of Manila Bay, one of the great legends of American history, has been told and retold in hundreds of publications. A fine contemporaneous account is contained in Marrion Wilcox, ed., *Harper's History of the War in the Philippines* (New York: Harper & Brothers, 1900), a compilation of reports from *Harper's* magazines and an invaluable source on the time. Other good accounts are in Ronald Spector, *Admiral of the New Empire: The Life and Career of George Dewey* (Baton Rouge: Louisiana

State University Press, 1974) and G.J.A. O'Toole, *The Spanish War: An American Epic 1898* (New York: Norton, 1984). Dewey's *Autobiography* (New York: Scribner's, 1913) also describes the battle. The U.S.S. *Olympia* has been preserved and can be seen at Penn's Landing in Philadelphia.

A highly readable history of the period is Margaret Leech, *In the Days of McKinley* (New York: Harper, 1959). Another is H. Wayne Morgan, *William McKinley and His America,* (Syracuse: Syracuse University Press, 1963). The standard biography of McKinley is Charles Olcott, *The Life of William McKinley,* 2 Vols. (Boston: Houghton Mifflin, 1916). A superb biography of Roosevelt is Edmund Morris, *The Rise of Theodore Roosevelt* (New York: Coward, McCann, 1979). More of Roosevelt at the time is described in Howard Beale, *Theodore Roosevelt and the Rise of America to World Power* (Baltimore: Johns Hopkins University Press, 1956) and in Henry C. Lodge, ed., *Selections from the Correspondence of Theodore Roosevelt and Henry Cabot Lodge, 1884–1918* (New York: Scribner's, 1925). Henry Cabot Lodge's biography is Karl Schriftgiesser, *The Gentleman from Massachusetts* (Boston: Little, Brown, 1944). The experience of the secretary of navy can be seen in Margaret Long, *The Journal of John Long* (Rindge, N.H.: Richard Smith, 1956). Alfred Mahan's principal books are *The Influence of Sea Power upon History, 1660–1783* and *The Interest of America in Sea Power, Past and Future* (Boston: Little, Brown, 1898). His biography is Charles Taylor, *The Life of Admiral Mahan: Naval Philosopher* (London: John Murray, 1920). Among the many studies on the U.S. Navy is Harold and Margaret Sprouse, *The Rise of American Power* (Princeton: Princeton University Press, 1939). A superb, concise essay, with original documents, is John Grenville, "American Naval Preparations for War with Spain, 1896–1898, in *Journal of American Studies,* April 1968.

Many excellent books relate America's drift into war with Spain. One of the best, which analyzes the Spanish as well as the U.S. side of the story, is Ernest May, *Imperial Democracy: The Emergence of America as a Great Power* (New York: Harcourt Brace Jovanovich, 1961). Others include Walter Lafeber, *The New Empire, An Interpretation of American Expansion 1860–1898* (Ithaca: Cornell University Press, 1963); John Grenville and George Young, *Politics, Strategy and American Diplomacy: Studies in Foreign Policy, 1873–1917* (New Haven: Yale University Press, 1966); Frederick Merck, *Manifest Destiny and Mission in American History: A New Interpretation* (New York: Knopf, 1963); Frank Freidel, *The Splendid Little War* (Boston: Little, Brown, 1958); Daniel Schirmer, *Republic or Empire* (Cambridge: Schenkman, 1972); Richard Hofstadter, "Manifest Destiny and the Philippines" in *America in Crisis,* ed. Daniel Aron (New York: Knopf, 1952); and George Kennan, *American Diplomacy, 1900–1950* (London: Secker and Warburg, 1952).

The background to the events in Cuba is in Hugh Thomas, *Cuba* (New York: Harper & Row, 1971) and also in José Martí, *Our America: Writings on Latin America and the Struggle for Cuban Independence,* ed. Philip Foner (New York: Monthly Review Press, 1977).

The story of the *Maine* is told in O'Toole and in John Edward Weems, *The Fate of the Maine* (New York: Holt, 1958). The postmortem on the incident by Admiral Hyman Rickover is *How the Battleship Maine Was Destroyed* (Washington, D.C.: Government Printing Office, 1976). William Randolph Hearst's role is vividly told in W. A. Swanberg, *Citizen Hearst* (New York: Scribner's, 1961), and also in J. E. Wisan, *The Cuban Crisis as Reflected in the New York Press* (New York: Columbia University Press, 1934). In a similar vein there is Marcus Wilkerson, *Public Opinion and the Spanish-American War* (Baton Rouge: Louisiana State University Press, 1932).

5. IMPERIAL DEMOCRACY

The debate in Washington over whether to retain the Philippines is well told in Leech and May. A brilliant essay on the subject is Louis Halle, *The United States Acquires the Philippines: Consensus vs. Reality* (Lanham, N.Y.: University Press of America, 1985). Leech contains excellent sketches of Henry Cabot Lodge and Albert Beveridge, key imperialists. Beveridge tells his own story in *The Meaning of the Times* (Indianapolis: Bobbs-Merrill, 1908). Edmund Morris vividly describes Theodore Roosevelt. The anti-imperialist material is massive: E. Berkeley Tompkins, *Anti-Imperialism in the United States: The Great Debate, 1890–1920* (Philadelphia: University of Pennsylvania Press, 1970); Moorfield Storey and Marcial Lichauco, *The Conquest of the Philippines* (New York: Putnam, 1920); Robert Beisner, *Twelve Against Empire: The Anti-Imperialists, 1898–1900* (Chicago: University of Chicago Press, 1968); Henry Stoddard, *Mark Twain in Eruption,* ed. Bernard DeVoto (New York: Harper and Brothers, 1940); Carl Shurz, *Speeches, Correspondence and Political Papers* (New York: Putnam, 1913); William Jennings Bryan, *Republic or Empire: The Philippine Question* (Chicago: Conkey, 1900); George Hoar, *An Autobiography of Seventy Years* (New York: Scribner's, 1903); and, above all, Finley Peter Dunne, *Mr. Dooley at His Best* (New York: Scribner's, 1938). The atmosphere of the period is reflected in Mark Sullivan's lively chronicle *In Our Times* (New York: Scribner's, 1926).

The description of U.S. troops preparing to embark is derived from a visit to the Presidio and also from reports in the Nebraska press provided to me by the Nebraska State Historical Society.

Dewey described his early days in Manila in hearings before the U.S. Senate Committee on the Philippines that began late in January 1902. The testimony is included in Henry Graff, ed., *American Imperialism and the Philippine Insurrection* (Boston: Little, Brown, 1969). Dewey at the time is also described in Spector and by H. L. Williams, *Taking Manila: In the Philippines with Dewey* (New York: Hurst, 1899). Acid portraits of Generals Merritt and Otis appear in Stuart Creighton Miller, *"Benevolent Assimilation": The American Conquest of the Philippines 1899–1903* (New Haven: Yale University Press, 1982) and in Leon Wolff, *Little Brown Brother* (Garden City N.Y.: Doubleday, 1961). The documents regarding the involvement of Pratt and Wildman, the U.S. consuls in Singapore and Hong Kong, are in the Taylor collection. The phony battle for Manila in August 1898 is described in Taylor, O'Toole, Spector and in the reports of the *Harper's* correspondents in the *Harper's* history of the war.

I visited Aguinaldo's family home in Cavite, where the independence ceremony was held. Agoncillo has described Apolinario Mabini, whose correspondence is in the Taylor collection and also in his *Letters* (Manila: National Heroes Commission, 1965). A sketch of Mabini is in Nick Joaquin, *A Question of Heroes* (Manila: National Book Store, 1981). The story of the Philippine republic is told by Agoncillo, *Malolos: The Crisis of the Republic* (Quezon City: University of the Philippines Press, 1956). I also visited Malolos, where a decrepit museum commemorates the republic. An interesting contemporary plea for an understanding of the Filipinos is by a British observer, Richard Brinsley Sheridan, first published in New York and London in 1900, and reprinted as *The Filipino Martyrs* (Manila: Malaya Books, 1970).

The debate over the treaty with Spain is described in Leech and May. Rudyard Kipling's "White Man's Burden" is in *A Choice of Kipling's Verses,* ed. T. S. Eliot (London: Faber and Faber, 1941).

6. CIVILIZING WITH A KRAG

The best single body of war reporting from the American side is the *Harper's* history of the war, whose stars included John Bass, Oskar Davis, William Dinwiddie and Frank

Millet. Davis also wrote *Our Conquests in the Pacific* (New York: Stokes, 1899) and Millet published *Expedition to the Philippines* (New York: Harper, 1899). Accounts of the war from the Filipino side are contained in the documents in the Taylor collection. The buildup of tensions that led to the outbreak of the war between the Americans and Filipinos is described in detail in Taylor, with supporting documents. An eyewitness American account of the outbreak is William Irwin, "The First Fight with the Insurgents," *The Independent,* March 30, 1899, and the descriptions in Taylor, Wolff, Creighton Miller and Agoncillo are equally vivid. The Taylor collection contains the Filipino version. I am indebted to the Nebraska State Historical Society for providing me with material on Willie Grayson as well as John Johnson, "The Saga of the First Nebraska in the Philippines, *Nebraska History,* June 1949 and, by the same author in the magazine in winter 1969, "Colonel John Miller Stotsenburg: Man of Valor." Other state historical societies, notably in Kansas and Oregon, have also been helpful. In 1986 my colleague Andrew Pearson interviewed Harry Embree, then aged 104, the last surviving U.S. veteran of the war in the Philippines, at his home in Lawrenceville, Kansas. The U.S. Army Military History Collection at Carlisle Barracks called on the families of Spanish-American war veterans, and amassed an archive of letters, diaries and photographs. I am grateful to the curators, Richard Sommers and John Slonacker, for their help.

Contemporary accounts of the war include Needom Freeman, *A Soldier in the Philippines* (New York: Neely, 1901) and Frank Neely, *Fighting in the Philippines* (New York: Neely, 1899.) Apart from Wolff, Miller and Bains, already cited, two excellent histories are John Gates, *Schoolbooks and Krags: The U.S. Army in the Philippines, 1898–1902* (Westport, Conn.: Greenwood Press, 1973); Russell Roth, *Muddy Glory: America's "Indian Wars" in the Philippines 1899–1935* (West Hanover, Mass.: Christopher Publishing House, 1981); and William Sexton, *Soldiers in the Sun* (Harrisburg, Pa.: Military Service Publishing Company, 1939). Glenn May compared the experiences of an American and a Filipino soldier in "Private Presher and Sergeant Vergara: The Underside of the Philippine-American War," in Peter Stanley, ed., *Reappraising an Empire: New Perspectives on Philippine-American History* (Cambridge: Harvard University Press, 1984).

Rivalries in the Filipino camp are described in Taylor and in Joaquin's *A Question of Heroes.* The death of Gregorio del Pilar is romantically told in the *Harper's* history as well as in Joaquin.

Jacob Gould Schurman's deliberations are included in the *Report of the Philippine Commission to the President,* Vol. 2 (Washington, D.C.: Government Printing Office, 1900). A good analysis is in Stanley, *Nation in the Making.* Philip Jessup has written the definitive *Elihu Root* (New York: Dodd, Mead, 1938) and William Thayer the *Life and Letters of John Hay* (Boston: Houghton Mifflin, 1908).

7. LITTLE BROWN BROTHERS

President McKinley's decision to appoint William Howard Taft governor of the Philippines is described in Leech. How Root evolved a policy for Taft is told in Stanley, *Nation in the Making.* The authoritative biography of Taft is Henry Pringle, *The Life and Times of William Howard Taft* (New York: Farrar and Rinehart, 1939). Stephen Hess has insights into the Taft family in *America's Political Dynasties from Adams to Kennedy* (New York: Doubleday, 1966). The life of the Tafts in Manila is told in Mrs. William Howard Taft, *Recollections of Full Years* (New York: Dodd, Mead, 1914). Taft as governor is analyzed by Lewis Gleeck, Jr., in *The American Governors-General and High Commissioners in the Philippines* (Quezon City: New Day, 1986). Taft's private feelings about the Filipinos are contained in his private letters, which are on file at the Library of Congress.

A brief account of General Arthur MacArthur's background is contained in the splendid biography of his son Douglas by D. Clayton James, *The Years of MacArthur, Vol. 1, 1880–1941* (Boston: Houghton Mifflin, 1970). Arthur MacArthur's disputes with Taft are in Wolff, Miller and other histories.

The best analysis of Taft's support for the *Federalistas* is in Stanley's *Nation in the Making.* Another fine account, which describes the genesis of the Filipino upper class, is Charles Farkas, "Partido Federal: The Policy of Attraction," in the *Bulletin of the American Historical Collection,* October–December 1978. The report of the Schurman commission, cited earlier, contains the testimony of the elite Filipinos who founded the *Federalista* party. Pardo de Tavera's background is in the *Dictionary of Philippine Biography* and in Father Schumacher's book on the propaganda movement, both of which are also mentioned earlier.

The continuing war is described in the *Harper's* history and in Wolff, Miller, Gates, Roth and other histories. The accounts of atrocities are also in those histories as well as in the testimony of American soldiers before the U.S. Senate Committee on the Philippines in early 1902. The Filipino side of the story, including Aguinaldo's switch to guerrilla warfare, is in the Taylor collection of documents.

President McKinley's reelection campaign in 1900 is told in Leech and Morris. Frederick Funston made a career of relating his capture of Aguinaldo, and his speeches are reported at length in the American press of the period. He wrote several accounts, e.g., "How Aguinaldo Was Captured," *Army and Navy Journal,* July 20, 1901. His Spanish guide, Lázaro Segovia, also wrote a memoir, *The Full Story of Aguinaldo's Capture,* trans. Frank de Thoma (Manila: Amigos de País, 1902). Simeon Villa's eyewitness tale of Aguinaldo's flight across Luzon and eventual capture is in Vol. 5 of the Taylor collection. David Haward Bain has pulled all the stories together in his excellent *Sitting in Darkness.* Wolff and Miller describe the Batangas campaign.

The Balangiga massacre and the American reprisals on Samar produced a voluminous literature. The situation on Samar as seen by the Filipino nationalists, including the plan to slaughter the Americans, is in the Taylor documents. Sergeant James O. Taylor (no relation), a U.S. Army historian, compiled eyewitness accounts of the survivors, *The Massacre of Balangiga* (Joplin, Mo.: Camp Henry Lawton, 1931). The contemporary report made after the incident by Captain Edwin Bookmiller is in the National Archives. Major Waller's report and the transcripts of both his trial and the trial of General Jacob are in the National Archives. A later account is Joseph Schott, *The Ordeal of Samar* (Indianapolis: Howard Sams and Company, 1964). Debate over the episode continues to this day, e.g., Kenneth Ray Young, "Guerrilla Warfare: Balangiga Revisited," in *Leyte-Samar Studies* (Tacloban: Divine Word University, 1964); Stuart Creighton Miller, "Our Mylai of 1900," *Transaction,* September 1970; and John Gates, "The Philippines and Vietnam: Another False Analogy," *Asian Studies,* April 1972. I am indebted to my colleague Eric Neudel, who interviewed Filipinos at Balangiga in 1987.

The comparison between the Philippine-American war and Vietnam is largely based on my experiences as a correspondent in Vietnam. A perceptive analysis is Glenn May, "Why the United States Won the Philippine-American War 1899–1902," in the *Bulletin of the American Historical Collection,* January–March 1985. Milagros Camayon Guerrero detailed Aguinaldo's failure to mobilize peasant support, a main reason for his defeat, in *Luzon at War: Contradictions in Philippine Society, 1898–1902* (Ann Arbor: University of Michigan doctoral dissertation, 1977).

8. AMERICA EXPORTS ITSELF

The best accounts of the early U.S. colonial effort are Peter Stanley's aforementioned *Nation in the Making* and Glenn May, *Social Engineering in the Philippines: The Aims, Execution and Impact of American Colonial Policy, 1900–1913* (Westport, Conn.: Greenwood Press, 1980).

The atmosphere of the period is captured by Lewis Gleeck, Jr., in *American Institutions in the Philippines, 1898–1941* (Manila: Historical Conservation Society, 1976); *The Manila Americans, 1901–1964* (Manila: Carmelo and Bauermann, 1977); *Americans on the Philippine Frontiers* (Manila: Carmelo and Baurmann, 1977); and *Laguna in American Times: Coconuts and Revolucionarios* (Manila: Historical Conservation Society, 1981). The *Bulletin of the American Historical Collection*, which Gleeck directs, is valuable for its reminiscences both by Americans and Filipinos of the U.S. colonial era. Gleeck, who generously shares his time and knowledge with visitors, deserves to be anointed the chronicler of the American experience in the Philippines.

Tom Carter, an American resident of Manila, has compiled anecdotes in *The Way It Was* (Quezon City: García, 1985) and in *Then and Now* (Manila: Historical Conservation Society, 1983). Mary Fee, *A Woman's Impressions of the Philippines* (Chicago: McClurg, 1910) and Joshena Ingersoll, *Golden Years in the Philippines* (Palo Alto: Pacific Books, 1971) are among other interesting personal accounts. Florence Horn's lively *Orphans of the Pacific* (New York: Reynal & Hitchcock, 1941) caused a controversy at the time because of its irreverent portraits of Filipinos and Americans. I also consulted the *Manila Times* for the early years of the century. Much of the material in this chapter comes from interviews with Filipinos and Americans who remembered the period before World War II.

Glenn May's description of American educational policy and practice is masterful. A succinct analysis of the subject is Clodualdo Leocadio, "Philippine Education," in the *Bulletin of the American Historical Collection*, July 1975. As its title suggests, Gates's *Schools and Krags* describes the role of early American soldiers as teachers. Other books are Morton Nestorg, *Backward, Turn Backward: A Study of Books for Children in the Philippines* (Manila: National Book Store, 1985); Geronima Pecson and Maria Racelis, *Tales of the American Teachers in the Philippines* (Manila: Carmelo and Bauermann, 1959) and Arthur Pier, *American Apostles to the Philippines* (Boston: Beacon Press, 1950). Carlos Romulo recalled his early American schooling in *I Walked with Heroes* (New York: Holt, Rinehart and Winston, 1961).

I am grateful to Katharine and Mary Anglemyer for the letters and journals of their mother, Philinda Rand, which have since been contributed to the Schlesinger Library at Radcliffe. I also owe a debt of gratitude to Mrs. E. L. Burmaster of Niagara Falls, New York, for the diary of her father, Benjamin Neal, a teacher in the Philippines from 1901 to 1904. I obtained many original letters from the University of Michigan Library. Frederick Marquardt, later an Arizona editor, recalled his boyhood in Leyte in *Before Bataan—and After* (Indianapolis: Bobbs Merrill, 1943), and he later told me the story in an interview. In nearly every interview I conducted with Filipinos, from Cory Aquino and the Marcoses to peasants in the countryside, I asked about their memories of American education. Virginia Benítez Licuanan loaned me her mother's letters, recounted her father's experience as a student in America and reminisced on her own college days in Missouri. Doreen Fernandez discussed America's cultural influence with me. The subject is covered at length in her publication *International Popular Culture*.

The story of the construction of Baguio is told by Florence Horn, who described the resort during the period before World War II, and by Virginia Benítez Licuanan in *Filipinos and Americans: A Love-Hate Relationship* (Manila: Baguio Country Club, 1982). Beth Day tells the story of the Manila Hotel in *The Manila Hotel: The Heart and Memory of a City* (Manila: Manila Hotel, undated). Horn antagonized the American community in Manila when she wrote about its racial biases and narrowness. Gleeck, who has described American club life in his books, is more benign in his unpublished study "American Life Styles in the Colonial Philippines."

The subject of economic development is a major section of W. Cameron Forbes, *The Philippine Islands* (Cambridge: Harvard University Press, 1945). Stanley and May describe Forbes's economic policies at length, and Gleeck quotes from Forbes's journals in the books on the governors cited earlier. A good short account is Norman Owen, "Philippine Economic Development and American Policy: A Reappraisal," in *Compadre Colonialism* (Manila: Solidaridad, undated). Shirley Jenkins describes early trade and economic policy in *American Economic Policy Toward the Philippines* (Palo Alto: Stanford University Press, 1954), a book that mainly deals with economics after World War II. Other important works on economics are James Ralston Hayden, *The Philippines: A Study in National Development* (New York: Macmillan, 1942) and A.V.H. Hartendorp, *History of Industry and Trade of the Philippines* (Manila: American Chamber of Commerce, 1958). A Filipino view is Pedro Salgado, *The Philippine Economy* (Quezon City: García, 1985).

9. STUMBLING TOWARD SELF-RULE

America's early political tutelage in the Philippines is described and analyzed in Stanley's *Nation in the Making,* May's *Social Engineering,* the Agoncillo and Corpuz histories and a superb book, Theodore Friend, *Between Two Empires* (New Haven: Yale University Press, 1965). Gleeck also covers the period in his history of the U.S. governors. I referred as well to three essays in the collection entitled *Compadre Colonialism*—Michael Cullinane, "Implementing the 'New Order': The Structure and Supervision of Local Government During the Taft Era"; Norman Owen, "Philippine Society and American Colonialism"; and Frank Jenista, Jr., "Conflict in the Philippine Legislature: The Commission and the Assembly from 1907 to 1913." The period seen from the Filipino viewpoint is summed up in Bonifacio Salamanca, *The Filipino Reaction to American Rule, 1901–1913* (Quezon City: New Day, 1984) and Rawlein Soberano, *The Politics of Independence: The American Colonial Experience in the Philippines* (New Orleans: Alive Associates, 1983). A graphic look at the response of the Filipinos to the Americans throughout the period prior to World War II can be seen in Alfred McCoy and Alfredo Roces, *Philippine Cartoons: Political Caricature of the American Era 1900–1941* (Quezon City: Vera-Reyes, 1985).

The standard biography of Sergio Osmeña is Vicente Albano Pacis, *President Sergio Osmeña: A Fully Documented Biography* (Quezon City: Phoenix, 1971). I am indebted to Michael Cullinane for "Playing the Game with the Americans: Sergio Osmeña and the Rise of the Provincial Politicos, 1898–1907," from his unpublished University of Michigan doctoral dissertation "*Ilustrado* Politics and the Rise of the Partido Nacionalista." Cullinane also provided me with additional information in telephone interviews.

The literature on Manuel Quezon is massive. His own pallid autobiography, written without notes during his exile in the United States during World War II, is *The Good Fight* (New York: Appleton, 1946). More detailed is Carlos Quirino's reverent *Quezon: Paladin of Philippine Freedom* (Manila: Filipiniana Book Guild, 1971). Quezon's beginnings as an American protégé are described by Cullinane, "The Politics of Collaboration in Taybas Province: The Early Political Career of Manuel Luis Quezon, 1903–1906," in Stanley's *Reappraising an Empire.* Dean Worcester's warnings against Quezon are in the Worcester papers at the University of Michigan Library, along with the transcript of Quezon's trial for rape. A contemporary look at Quezon is Teodoro Kalaw, *Aide-de-Camp to Freedom,* trans. Maria Kalaw Katigbak (Manila: Teodoro

Kalaw Society, 1965). Florence Horn caustically described Quezon in her book, as did John Gunther in *Inside Asia* (New York: Harper, 1942). Theodore Friend's analysis of Quezon is especially perceptive, and in interviews Friend provided me with an interesting comparison of Quezon and Ferdinand Marcos. Miguel Bernad, a Jesuit priest, compared the two most popular Philippine presidents in "Quezon and Magsaysay" in his book of essays *Tradition and Discontinuity* (Manila: National Book Store, 1983). Buss, who knew Quezon well during the late 1930s, offered me his personal recollections.

For Worcester's influence during the early period of U.S. rule, a vivid account is Peter Stanley, " 'The Voice of Worcester is the Voice of God': How One American Found Fulfillment in the Philippines" in Stanley, *Reappraising an Empire*. The Worcester papers at the University of Michigan Library describe his activities. The flavor of the period is colorfully evoked in Reynaldo C. Ileto, "Orators and the Crowd: Philippine Independence Politics," in *Reappraising an Empire*. The quality of Philippine provincial politics, then and later, is analyzed in Mary Hollnsteiner, *The Dynamics of Power in a Philippine Municipality* (Quezon City: University of the Philippines, 1963), in Quirino's biography of Quezon, the Manila newspapers of the time and in Landé's monograph cited earlier.

Stanley describes the change in U.S. policy with the advent of the Wilson administration in *Nation in the Making*. Francis Burton Harrison's memoir is *The Cornerstone of Philippine Independence* (New York: Century, 1922), but more interesting details are in *Extracts from the Harrison Diaries* (Ithaca: Cornell University Press, 1947). Passages from the debate in the U.S. Congress are quoted in Soberano, cited earlier. Gleeck describes Harrison in his history of the governors. The Philippine National Bank scandal is explained in Stanley, *Nation in the Making,* and in Virginia Benítez Licuanan's history of banking in the Philippines. A staggering collection of documents on the case is available in the National Archives in Washington.

The best single account of the jockeying for independence is Friend's *Between Two Empires.* Leonard Wood's tenure as governor is related by Gleeck in his history of the American governors and also in Hermann Hagedorn, *Leonard Wood: A Biography* (New York: Harper, 1931). Wood's quarrels with Quezon are told in Quirino's biography of Quezon. The classic biography of Stimson is Elting Morrison's *Turmoil and Tradition: The Life and Times of Henry L. Stimson* (Boston: Houghton Mifflin, 1960). An important essay is Friend's "The Philippine Sugar Industry and the Politics of Independence" in *The Journal of Asian Studies,* February 1963. Frank Murphy is described by Gleeck in his portraits of the governors.

Economic conditions before World War II are analyzed in Shirley Jenkins's economic history and in Frank Golay, *The Philippines: Public Policy and National Economic Development* (Ithaca: Cornell University Press, 1961). Florence Horn portrays the rich Filipino families and the effect of the pattern of trade with the United States.

10. MacARTHUR'S MANDATE

The authoritative biography of Douglas MacArthur is D. Clayton James, cited earlier. Much of the material for this chapter is culled from the first of the three volumes. The popular biography, William Manchester's *American Caesar: Douglas MacArthur, 1880–1964* (Boston: Little, Brown, 1978), is lively reading but is riddled with small errors. Of special interest for this book was Carol Morris Petillo, *Douglas MacArthur: The Philippine Years* (Bloomington, Ind.: Indiana University Press, 1981). Petillo first revealed the story of Quezon's gift of $500,000 to MacArthur in *Pacific Review,* February 1980, thereby sparking protests from MacArthur's admirers. Petillo also did considerable research on MacArthur's love affair with Isabel Rosario Cooper, alias "Dimples."

The story is also told in detail in Oliver Pilat, *Drew Pearson* (New York: *Harper's Magazine Press*, 1973), though Pilat wrongly identifies Isabel as Helen Robinson. Tom Carter, a longtime American resident of Manila, whose Filipino wife was related to Isabel, has furnished me with details. As mentioned in the text, I observed MacArthur in the Philippine context as a *Time* correspondent in 1961. I am indebted to Claude Buss for his recollections of MacArthur in Manila before World War II.

Peasant unrest in the Philippines leading up to the Sakdal revolt is described in Sturtevant, cited earlier.

Quezon's appointment of MacArthur as his military adviser is related in James and Friend as well as in Quirino's biography of Quezon. The evolution of the Orange and Rainbow plans is described and analyzed in several histories, most notably Ronald Spector, *Eagle Against the Sun: The American War with Japan* (New York: Macmillan, 1985) and Louis Morton, "Germany First: The Basic Concept of Allied Strategy in World War II," in *Command Decisions,* ed., Kent Roberts Greenfield (Washington, D.C.: Office of the Chief of Military History, Department of the Army, 1960). The efforts to create a Philippine army are in James and Friend. MacArthur's buoyant appraisal is *Report on National Defense in the Philippines* (Manila: Bureau of Printing, 1936). Eisenhower's disputes with MacArthur are contained in Robert Ferrell, ed., *The Eisenhower Diaries* (New York: Norton, 1981) and in Stephen Ambrose, *Eisenhower: Soldier, General of the Army, President-Elect, 1890–1952* (New York: Simon and Schuster, 1983). Further perceptions of Eisenhower are in Merle Miller, *Ike the Soldier as They Knew Him* (New York: Putnam, 1987) and Fred Greenstein, *The Hidden-Hand President: Eisenhower as Leader* (New York: Basic Books, 1982).

The best short account of Quezon's mercurial attitudes toward the Japanese is in Friend's *Between Two Empires*. More details are in James Eyre, *The Roosevelt-MacArthur Conflict* (Chambersburg, Pa.: Craft Press, 1950). I interviewed Claude Buss for his memories of the period. The Japanese presence in the Philippines is described in Friend and Florence Horn, and a good analysis is Grant Goodman, *Four Aspects of Philippine-Japanese Relations, 1930–1940* (New Haven: Southeast Asia Studies program monograph, Yale, 1967).

Japan's war plans dating back to the early years of the century are in Spector's *Eagle Against the Sun* and Louis Morton, "Japan's Decision for War" in *Command Decisions,* both cited earlier, and in F. C. Jones, *Japan's New Order in East Asia, 1937–45* (London: Oxford University Press, 1954); Samuel Eliot Morison, *The Rising Sun in the Pacific, 1931–1942* (Boston: Little, Brown, 1948); and Saburo Ienaga, *The Pacific War 1931–1945* (New York: Pantheon, 1978). Spector and others tell the story of the breakdown of negotiations in Washington. A Japanese view is Masuo Kato, *The Lost War: A Japanese Reporter's Inside Story* (New York: Knopf, 1946). The atmosphere in Manila on the eve of the war is described by Manchester; Carl Mydans, *More Than Meets the Eye* (New York: Harper, 1959); and Clark Lee, *They Call it Pacific: An Eyewitness Story of Our War Against Japan from Bataan to the Solomons* (New York: Viking, 1943). Claude Buss provided me with his recollections of those days, as did John Horton, a young U.S. Navy officer, and Samuel Grashio, an American army air corps pilot at the time.

11. WAR AND REDEMPTION

The literature on World War II in the Philippines is massive, as reflected in the 222 pages of books and articles that comprise Morton Nestorg, *The Philippines in World War II and to Independence (December 8, 1941–July 4, 1946: An Annotated Bibliography* (Ithaca: Cornell Southeast Asia Program, 1977). An essential road map for tracking the war is Peter Young, *The World Almanac of World War II* (New York: Pharos Books, 1981).

The three basic histories are Louis Morton, *The War in the Pacific: The Fall of the Philippines* (Washington, D.C.: Office of the Chief of Military History, U.S. Army, 1953); M. Hamlin Cannon, *The War in the Pacific: Leyte—the Return to the Philippines* (Washington, D.C.: Office of the Chief of Military History, U.S. Army, 1954); and Robert Ross Smith, *The War in the Pacific: Triumph in the Philippines* (Washington, D.C.: Center of Military History, 1984). Also required reading are volumes two and three of D. Clayton James, *The Years of MacArthur* (Boston: Houghton Mifflin, 1975, 1985); Manchester and Spector; Samuel Eliot Morison, *Leyte, June 1944–June 1945* (Boston: Little, Brown, 1958) and *The Liberation of the Philippines: Luzon, Mindanao, the Visayas, 1944–1945* (Boston: Little Brown, 1959); and Hanson Baldwin, *Great Mistakes of the War* (New York: Harper, 1950) and *Battles Lost and Won: Great Campaigns of World War II* (New York: Avon, 1968). The U.S. decision to retake Luzon is told in James, Spector and in Robert Ross Smith, "Luzon Versus Formosa," in *Command Decisions,* cited earlier. MacArthur's own story is told rather limply in *Reminiscences* (Greenwich, Conn.: Fawcette, 1965). General Lewis Brereton's account of the outbreak of the war in the Philippines is *The Brereton Diaries* (New York: Morrow, 1946). The naval war is told in William Halsey and Joseph Bryan III, *Admiral Halsey's Story* (New York: McGraw Hill, 1947) and in a speech by Thomas Hart, "What Our Navy Learned in the Pacific," *U.S. Naval Institute Proceedings, January 1943.* Clark Lee is tough on MacArthur in *One Last Look Around* (New York: Duell, Sloane and Pearce, 1947). A solid narrative is William Breuer, *Retaking the Philippines* (New York: St. Martin's, 1986).

A luminous history of the war seen from the Japanese viewpoint is John Toland, *The Rising Sun: The Decline and Fall of the Japanese Empire, 1936–1945* (New York: Random House, 1970). The Japanese view is also related in David Bergamini, *Japan's Imperial Conspiracy,* 2 Vols. (New York: Morrow, 1971) and in Saburo Ienaga, cited earlier. Personal accounts by Japanese include Shohei Ooka, *Fires on the Plain* (New York: Knopf, 1957); Tetsuro Ogawa, *Terraced Hell* (Rutland, Vt.: Tuttle, 1972); and Tadashi Moriya, *No Requiem* (Tokyo: Hokuseido Press, 1968).

There are dozens of personal accounts by Americans. A very vivid one is Samuel Grashio and Bernard Norling, *Return to Freedom: The War Memoirs of Colonel Samuel Grashio* (Tulsa, Okla.: MCN Press, 1982). Another is Paul Ashton, *Bataan Diary* (privately printed, 1984). I interviewed Grashio and Blair Robinette, another American veteran of the war. I also interviewed Carl Mydans, whose *More than Meets the Eye* is excellent, and Claude Buss recalled to me the entry of the Japanese into Manila. Studs Terkel has collected war stories in *The Good War: An Oral History of World War Two* (New York: Ballantine, 1984). Other accounts include Carol Petillo, ed., *The Ordeal of Elizabeth Vaughn: A Wartime Diary of the Philippines* (Athens, Ga.: University of Georgia Press, 1985); Forbes Monaghan, *Under the Red Sun: A Letter from Manila* (New York: McMullen, 1946); Shelley Mydans, *The Open City* (Garden City, N.Y.: Doubleday, 1945); and Ernest Miller, *Bataan Uncensored* (Long Prairie, Minn.: Hart, 1949).

The official American history of the guerrilla movement is Charles Willoughby, *The Guerrilla Resistance Movement in the Philippines 1941–1945* (New York: Vantage Press, 1972). Individual accounts include Russell Volckmann, *We Remained: Three Years Behind the Enemy Lines in the Philippines* (New York: Norton, 1954); Carlos Quirino, *Chick Parsons, America's Master Spy in the Philippines* (Quezon City: New Day, 1984); and Clair Phillips and Myron Goldsmith, *Manila Espionage* (Portland, Ore.: Binfords & Mort, 1947). I interviewed Lee Telesco, an American officer with the Filipino guerrillas on Leyte. Among the best Filipino guerrilla accounts are Jesus Villamor, as told to Gerald Snyder, *They Never Surrendered* (Quezon City: Vera-Reyes, 1982) and Uldarico Baclagon, *They Served with Honor: Filipino War Heroes of World War II* (Quezon City: DM Press, 1968). The role of the *Hukbalahap* during the war is told in

Eduardo Lachica, *Huk: Philippine Agrarian Society in Revolt* (Manila: Solidaridad, 1977); Benedict Kerkvliet, *The Huk Rebellion: A Study of Peasant Revolt in the Philippines* (Berkeley: University of California Press, 1977); and Luis Taruc, *Born of the People* (New York: International Publishers, 1953). I interviewed Taruc at length on the subject.

I cite Carl Mydans on his prison camp experience in the narrative. Among other accounts of prison are Ashton's *Bataan Diary* mentioned earlier; A.V.H. Hartendorp's *The Japanese Occupation of the Philippines,* 2 Vols. (Manila: Bookmark, 1967); and Renton Hind, *Spirits Unbroken* (San Francisco: Howell, 1947).

The foremost American expert on Filipino collaboration with the Japanese is David Joel Steinberg, whom I consulted. His main works are *Philippine Collaboration in World War II* (Ann Arbor: University of Michigan Press, 1967; "José P. Laurel: A Collaborator Misunderstood" in *Journal of Asian Studies,* August 1965; "An Ambiguous Legacy, Years at War in the Philippines" in *Pacific Affairs,* summer 1972; and "The Philippine 'Collaborators': Survival of an Oligarchy" in *Southeast Asia in World War II: Four Studies,* ed. Joseph Silverstein (New Haven: Southeast Asia Studies, Yale, 1966). An excellent comparison of the Japanese occupation in the Philippines and in Indonesia is Theodore Friend, *The Blue-Eyed Enemy: Japan Against the West in Java and Luzon, 1942–1945* (Princeton: Princeton University Press, 1988). A readable book is Teodoro Agoncillo, *The Fateful Years: Japan's Adventure in the Philippines,* 2 Vols. (Quezon City: García, 1965). Agoncillo discusses the collaboration issue in *The Burden of Proof: The Vargas-Laurel Collaboration Case* (Manila: University of the Philippines Press, 1984). Benigno Aquino's pro-Japanese views are explained in "The Role of the Kalibapi" in *Free Philippines,* October 1943. Laurel's apologia is his *War Memoirs* (Manila: José Laurel Foundation, 1962). Vicente Alvarez has done the same for Vargas in "Ambassador Vargas: A Patriot" in *Philippine Review,* December 1943. I am indebted to Claude Buss for his recollections of Vargas.

12. DEPENDENT INDEPENDENCE

The Philippine independence ceremony is described in the Manila press of the time. Manuel Roxas was extolled in a cover story in *Time,* July 8, 1946. MacArthur's postwar policy was excoriated by Harold Ickes, *Secret Diary* (New York: Simon and Schuster, 1953); in Stephen Rosskamm Shalom, *The United States and the Philippines: A Study in Neocolonialism* (Philadelphia: Institute for the Study of Human Issues, 1981); and in two books by Hernando Abaya, *Betrayal in the Philippines* (New York: A. A. Wyn, 1946) and *The Untold Philippine Story* (Quezon City: Malaya, 1967). I interviewed Abaya in Manila in 1987. Clayton James and Manchester both discuss MacArthur's involvement in Philippine politics, as does David Bernstein, *The Philippine Story* (New York: Farrar, Straus, 1947). The collaboration controversy is covered by Steinberg, Agoncillo and others in the books and articles cited earlier.

The history of the U.S. bases is described in detail in the doctoral dissertation by William Berry mentioned earlier and by Ronald Spector in *Admiral of the New Empire,* his biography of George Dewey, also cited earlier. The bases issue is further discussed in George Taylor, *The Philippines and the United States: Problems of Partnership* (New York: Praeger, 1964); Taylor, "The Challenge of Mutual Security," in Frank Golay, ed., *Philippine-American Relations* (Englewood Cliffs, N.J.: Prentice-Hall); Claude Buss, *The United States and the Philippines: Background for Policy* (Washington, D.C.: American Enterprise Institute, 1977); Roland Simbulan, *The Bases of Our Insecurity* (Manila: Balai, 1983); Shalom; and Fred Greene's study for the Council on Foreign Relations mentioned earlier.

The best account of U.S. economic and trade policy is Shirley Jenkins, cited earlier.

Shalom covers the subject, as does Frank Golay in his economic study and in "Economic Collaboration: The Role of American Investment" in *Philippine-American Relations*, mentioned earlier. Abaya shows how MacArthur and Roxas engineered the 1946 election to assure the ratification of the "parity" arrangement. A sound study is Vivian Tan, "Unequal Partners: United States Policy Toward the Philippines and the Philippine Trade Act of 1946," *Pilipinas*, Spring 1987.

The origins of Communism in the Philippines is told in Charles McLane, *Soviet Strategies in Southeast Asia* (Princeton: Princeton University Press, 1966) and Malcolm Kennedy, *A Short History of Communism in Asia* (London: Weidenfeld and Nicolson, 1957). James Allen, the American Communist agent, described his organizing effort in a short, readable monograph, *The Radical Left on the Eve of the War* (Quezon City: Foundation for Nationalist Studies, 1983). The conditions that spawned the *Hukbalahap* movement are described in Kerkvliet, cited above, as well as in Erich Jacoby, *Agrarian Unrest in Southeast Asia* (London: Asia Publishing House, 1949) and Robert Hardie's unpublished *Philippine Land Tenure Reform: Analysis and Recommendations* (Manila: U.S. Mutual Security Agency, 1952). Lachica tells the story of the Huks, mentioned earlier, and Luis Taruc relates his personal experiences in *Born of the People*, also mentioned earlier, and in *He Who Rides the Tiger* (New York: Praeger, 1967). Taruc granted me several interviews, and I also talked with Alberto Saulo and Jesus Lava, both former Huks.

The best single book on the Huk rebellion itself is Kerkvliet. With Kerkvliet's guidance, I visited the areas of central Luzon where he had done his research and interviewed many of the same peasants. The authoritative work on Magsaysay is José Veloso Abueva, *Ramón Magsaysay: A Political Biography* (Manila: Solidaridad, 1971). The Magsaysay myth in the U.S. press, promoted by Edward Lansdale, is exemplified by the cover story in *Time*, November 26, 1951. A sounder appraisal of Magsaysay is John Osborne, "Magsaysay Faces His Opposition," *Time*, June 21, 1954. Lansdale was admiringly caricatured in William Lederer and Eugene Burdick, *The Ugly American* (New York: Norton, 1958) and cruelly drawn in Graham Greene, *The Quiet American* (New York: Penguin, 1974). Lansdale's own feeble account is *In the Midst of Wars* (New York: Harper and Row, 1972). A far better biography of him is Cecil Currey, *Shadows: The Story of Edward Geary Lansdale* (Boston: Houghton Mifflin, 1988). Among the many technical books on the Huk uprising are Douglas Blaufarb, *The Counterinsurgency Era: U.S. Doctrine and Performance* (New York: The Free Press, 1977); Napoleon Valeriano and Charles Bohannan, *Counterguerrilla Operations: The Philippine Experience* (London: Paul Mass Press, 1962); Uldarico Baclagon, *Lessons from the Huk Campaign* (Manila: M. Colcol & Co., 1956); Robert Ross Smith's unpublished *The Hukbalahap Insurgency: Economic, Political and Military Factors* (Washington, D.C.: Office of the Chief of Military History, Department of the Army, 1963); and D. Michael Shafer, *Deadly Paradigms: The Failure of U.S. Counterinsurgency Policy* (Princeton: Princeton University Press, 1988). An eloquent personal account of the Huk defeat is William Pomeroy, *The Forest* (New York: International Publishers, 1974). My colleague Andrew Pearson interviewed Pomeroy, who lives in London. Aquino's capture of Taruc was reported in the Manila press at the time, and he also told me the story. I interviewed Manuel Manahan, a Magsaysay aide who was involved in planning Taruc's capture, and General Jesus Vargas, then a senior officer and later defense secretary.

13. CONJUGAL AUTOCRACY

I visited the Philippines often from my base in Hong Kong between 1959 and 1970, and much of the material for that period is derived from my reporting for *Time, The*

Saturday Evening Post and *The Washington Post.* I returned in 1984 to research this book and its companion television documentary, and frequently revisited the Philippines between then and 1988. Besides my own observations, I have benefited from a mass of State Department documents declassified under the Freedom of Information Act. I also relied on press reports, notably by Tillman Durdin, Henry Kamm, Joseph Lelyveld and Fox Butterfield in *The New York Times;* Lee Lescaze and Jay Mathews in *The Washington Post;* Peter Kann in *The Wall Street Journal;* Phil Bronstein in the *San Francisco Examiner;* Melinda Liu in *Newsweek;* and Ian Buruma and Guy Sacerdoti in the *Far Eastern Economic Review.*

Henry Byroade's account of the martial-law declaration is based on interviews with him, Richard Usher and CIA sources that have requested anonymity. Raymond Bonner has related in his extremely detailed *Waltzing with a Dictator* (New York: Times Books, 1987) that President Nixon gave Marcos the green light in a telephone conversation. But no record of any such call is recorded in the White House logs of the time, which are available in the Nixon archives. Nixon issued a denial of the Bonner story. I also checked with Alexander Haig and John Holdridge, members of the National Security Council staff at the time. Thus my conclusion that the U.S. role in Marcos's imposition of martial law was one of acquiescence rather than complicity. Francis Tatu's recollection that he might have planted the idea with Imelda's brother comes from an interview with Tatu. Enrile told me that his ambush was a sham in an interview in Manila in 1988. The reports of violence in Manila are from the Manila press and from Reuben Canoy, *The Counterfeit Revolution* (Manila: Philippine Editions, 1981), an excellent book. Marshall Green's reaction to martial law comes from Green and from his congressional testimony.

As my narrative indicates, my account of the period before the Marcos presidency is based on my own observations. I have used the Manila press of the time, especially the *Philippines Free Press,* and such publications as *Asia Survey* and the *Far Eastern Economic Review.* Albert Ravenholt turned out several excellent reports for the American Universities Field Staff and also shared his knowledge with me. A solid journalistic account of the period is in Robert Shaplen, *Time out of Hand* (London: Andre Deutsch, 1969). Academic studies include David Wurfel's section on the Philippines in George Kahin, ed., *Government and Politics of Southeast Asia* (Ithaca: Cornell University Press, 1964); Willard Elsbree's perceptive essay "The Philippines" in Rupert Emerson, *Representative Government in Southeast Asia* (Cambridge: Harvard University Press, 1955); and the essays in Gabriel Almond and James Colemen, eds., *The Politics of the Developing Areas* (Princeton: Princeton University Press, 1960). I was helped during those days by Filipino friends, notably Sixto Roxas and Max Soliven, as well as by numbers of U.S. officials—ambassadors Charles Bohlen and William McCormick Blair, Francis Underhill, William Hamilton and Frazer Meade. David Sternberg, unbeknown to me a CIA man, was always a stimulating source of ideas and information.

Joseph Burckholder Smith's experiences are told in his *Portrait of a Cold Warrior* (New York: Putnam, 1976). I also interviewed Smith at length in Washington in 1987 and over the telephone. As I say in the narrative, Emmanuel Pelaez confirmed his connection with the CIA, but Diosdado Macapagal, Jaime Ferrer, Manuel Manahan and Raul Manglapus, all mentioned by Smith, ran for cover.

I interviewed Macapagal frequently during his presidency and as late as 1985. His commissioned biography, by Quentin Reynolds and Geoffrey Bocca, is *Macapagal the Incorruptible* (New York: David McKay, 1965) and his speeches are in *Diosdado Macapagal, The Common Man* (Manila: privately printed, 1961). He was sketched by Willard Hanna, *Eight Nation Makers: Southeast Asia's Charismatic Leaders* (New York: St. Martin's, 1964) and by Vera Micheles Dean, *Builders of Emerging Nations* (New York: Holt, Rinehart and Winston, 1961).

I covered the 1965 election campaign and met Marcos at the time and thereafter, including a final visit in Hawaii. So my impressions of him come from firsthand observations, I have discussed him with several of his aides, including Adrian Cristobal, his speech writer; Francisco Tatad, his former press secretary; and his business associates, among them Eduardo Cojuangco; and I have relied on numerous other accounts as well. His official biography, by Hartzell Spence, is *For Every Tear a Victory* (New York: McGraw-Hill, 1964). His own pretentious notions about himself filter through his own books, ghost written by the talented Adrian Cristobal—examples being *Notes on the New Society of the Philippines* (published by Ferdinand Marcos, 1973) and *The Democratic Revolution in the Philippines* (Englewood Cliffs, N.J.: Prentice-Hall, 1979). His interview with Ina Ginsburg in *Interview* in 1984 is a good example of his self-created mythology. He even lied about himself to himself in his private diaries, which were found in the Malacañang palace after the Marcoses fled in 1986. Extracts from the diaries were published by William Rempel of the *Los Angeles Times* in October 1988. I acquired the entire set of documents on Marcos's fake war records from the National Archives in Washington; an abbreviated version appeared in *The New York Times,* January 23, 1986. A scholarly study of the declining Philippine economy prior to martial law is H. A. Averch, F. H. Denton and J. E. Koehler, *A Crisis of Ambiguity: Political and Economic Development in the Philippines* (Santa Monica, Calif.: The Rand Corporation, January 1970). The story of the aborted assassination plot against Marcos by three American hit men was told to me by James Lowenstein and Richard Moose, then staff members of the U.S. Senate Foreign Relations Committee; additional details were provided by Edward Ezell, curator of armed forces history at the Smithsonian Institution, who was then employed by Sam Cummings in Singapore.

My impressions of Imelda are also based on firsthand observations in several meetings over the period from 1965 to 1987, when I visited the Marcoses in Hawaii. An irreverent biography of her is Carmen Navarro Pedrosa's *The Untold Story of Imelda Marcos* (Rizal: Tandem, 1969). A brilliant essay in the form of a review of the book is Ian Buruma's "St. Cory and the Evil Rose," in *The New York Review of Books,* June 11, 1987. Another book is Katherine Ellison, *Imelda: Steel Butterfly of the Philippines* (New York: McGraw-Hill, 1988). Ina Ginsburg's interview with Imelda in *Interview* is revealing. Imelda's "cosmic vision" of the universe is foggily described in her picture book *The New Human Order* (privately printed, undated). I am indebted to Carmen Nakpil Guerrero and Adrian Cristobal, former aides to the Marcoses, for their analysis of Imelda.

The Marcoses have generated a tidal wave of literature, especially following Aquino's assassination and their own collapse. Aside from Bonner and Canoy, cited earlier, the books include: Primitivo Mijares, *The Conjugal Dictatorship* (San Francisco: Union Square Publications, 1976); David Rosenberg, ed., *Marcos and Martial Law in the Philippines* (Ithaca: Cornell University Press, 1979); Robert Pringle, *Indonesia and the Philippines: American Interests in Island Southeast Asia* (New York: Columbia University Press, 1980); Larry Niksch, *The Internal Situation in the Philippines: Factors Affecting Future Trends* (Washington, D.C.: Library of Congress, Congressional Research Service, February 1980); Niksch and Marjorie Niehaus, *The Internal Situation in the Philippines: Current Trends and Future Prospects* (Washington, D.C.: Library of Congress, January 1981); Alfred McCoy, *Priests on Trial* (Ringwood, Australia: Penguin, 1984); Hermie Rotea, *Marcos's Lovey Dovie* (Los Angeles: Liberty Publishing, 1983); Steve Psinakas, *Two Terrorists Meet* (San Francisco: Alchemy Books, 1981); José Lacaba, *Days of Disquiet, Nights of Rage* (Manila: Salinlahi Publishing House, 1982); Fred Poole and Max Vanzi, *Revolution in the Philippines: The United States in a Hall of Cracked Mirrors* (New York: McGraw-Hill, 1984); William Sullivan, *Obbligato, 1939–1979: Notes on a Foreign Service Career* (New York: Norton, 1984); Filomen Rodriguez, *The Marcos Regime: Rape of a Nation* (New York: Vantage Press, 1985); John Bresnan, ed., *Crisis in the Philippines: The Marcos Era and Beyond* (Princeton:

Princeton University Press, 1986); Lewis Gleeck, Jr., *President Marcos and the Philippine Political Culture* (Manila: unidentified publisher, 1987); Beth Day Romulo, *Inside the Marcos Palace* (New York: Putnam, 1987); Charles McDougald, *The Marcos File* (San Francisco: San Francisco Publishers, 1987); and Sterling Seagrave, *The Marcos Dynasty* (New York: Harper and Row, 1988).

Robert Shaplen's pieces in *The New Yorker* during the Marcos era were consistently informative. Two excellent analyses of Marcos stand out—Ian Buruma, "Marcos and Morality," *The New York Review of Books*, August 13, 1987, and Ross Marley, "Is Ferdinand Marcos a Political Genius?" in *Pilipinas*, Fall 1985. I am indebted to William Overholt of the Banker's Trust Company for his reports on the Philippine economy. Details on the Marcos cronies are exhaustively described and analyzed in confidential reports of the U.S. Embassy in Manila. I gained valuable insights into the growth of the Communist insurgency under Marcos from James Nach of the U.S. Embassy; Tim Wright, an analyst at the U.S. naval command in Hawaii; and Francisco Nemenzo of the University of the Philippines. A sound book on the rebels is William Chapman, *Inside the Philippine Revolution* (New York: Norton, 1987). Colonel Galen Radke, former U.S. Army attaché at the U.S. Embassy in Manila, furnished me with details on the Philippine military establishment, as did General Rafael Ileto, later defense secretary under Cory Aquino. Human rights abuses under Marcos are contained in Amnesty International reports from 1975 onward and in the reports of the Lawyers Committee for Human Rights. The human rights issue was raised at hearings of the U.S. Senate Foreign Relations Committee and its House equivalent during the period, and also in State Department reports.

Many Filipino sources furnished me with information on the Marcos period, among them: Vicente Chuidian, José Diokno, Juan Ponce Enrile, Antonio Gatmaitan, Salvador Laurel, Ramon Mitra, paul Manglapus, Jaime Ongpin, Joan Orendain, Emmanuel Pelaez, José Romero, Carlos Romulo and Cardinal Jaime Sin. The current and former U.S. officials I interviewed included Morton Abramowitz, Michael Armacost, Stephen Bosworth, Richard Holbrooke, Paul Kattenburg, John Maisto, James Nach and John Negroponte of the State Department, and Richard Armitage of the Defense Department. Father John Carroll and Father James Reuter, Jesuit residents in Manila, were both helpful. I owe a debt of gratitude to Lewis Burridge, then president of the American Chamber of Commerce in Manila, for his assistance.

14. MARTYR AND MADONNA

To say that I bent the journalistic rules by befriending Ninoy Aquino does not mean that my dispatches about him were uncritical. I called the shots as I saw them and he, having been a newspaperman, understood my loyalty to my professional standards. He was also a seasoned politician who realized that he had to take the bitter with the sweet. By contrast, Cory has not been entirely comfortable with the press, a sign, perhaps, of her political inexperience. Nevertheless, I interviewed her before and after her rise to the presidency.

As the narrative makes clear, my conversations with Ninoy and subsequent talks with Cory have provided me with much of the material for this chapter. Many of the books cited earlier cover this period. The biographies of Ninoy, all reverential, are Nick Joaquin, *The Aquinos of Tarlac* (Manila: Cacho Hermanos, 1983); Asunción David Maramba, *Ninoy Aquino: The Man, The Legend* (Manila: Cacho Hermanos, 1984); and Alfonso Policarpio, Jr., *Ninoy the Willing Martyr* (Manila: Isaiah Books, 1986). Cory's biographies are Lucy Komisar, *Corazon Aquino: The Story of a Revolution* (New York: George Braziller, 1987); and Isabelo Crisostomo, *Cory: Profile of a President* (Quezon

City: Kriz, 1986). Guy Pauker, a friend of the Aquinos, canonized Cory in "President Corazon Aquino: A Political and Personal Assessment," in Carl Landé, ed., *Rebuilding a Nation* (Washington, D.C.: Washington Institute Press, 1987). Pauker also shared his knowledge with me, as did Claude Buss, who knew the Aquinos as well. I am indebted to Sandra Burton of *Time*, who loaned me the manuscript of her forthcoming book, *Impossible Dream: The Marcoses, The Aquinos and the Unfinished Revolution*, to be published by Warner.

Ninoy was great copy during his political heyday, and I have found voluminous details on him in the Manila newspapers, notably the weekly *Philippine Free Press*. His mother, Aurora, and his sister Lupita Kashiwahara recalled his childhood to me. He had hundreds of friends, acquaintances and rivals, numbers of whom spoke of him to me over the years; one of those closest to him was Heherson Alvarez, later a senator. Ninoy's disclosures of his CIA connection, real or inflated, were made in talks with me and subsequently in his televised debate with Enrile during the 1978 election campaign. Cory has reminisced to me on their life in Boston. Professor Sam Huntington of Harvard and Professor Lucian Pye of MIT have also recollected that period. I occasionally saw the Aquinos in Boston.

The assassination of Ninoy has been related frequently. Before his departure for Manila, he gave a very quotable interview to *Mother Jones;* I have quoted passages from the piece, which appeared in January 1984. The attempts to dissuade Ninoy from returning were told to me by him at the time, and are also in Burton and Lewis Simon, *Worth Dying For* (New York: Morrow, 1987). Ken Kashiwahara and Burton, who were aboard Ninoy's plane, have described the experience to me. Imelda recollected her reaction to the news to me in an interview; Carmen Nakpil Guerrero, who was with her during that day, recalled the scene for me. Ninoy's funeral filled the Manila press at the time. I gathered the pop culture and religious mood from interviews as well as from a contemporary piece by Ian Buruma in the *Far Eastern Economic Review*.

The various official investigations are recounted in a speculative book by Gerald Hill and Kathleen Thompson Hill mistitled *The True Story and Analysis of the Aquino Assassination* (Sonoma, Calif.: Hilltop, 1983). The Agrava Commission testimony and conclusions are in *Reports of the Fact-Finding Board of the Assassination of Senator Benigno Aquino, Jr.* (Manila: Mr. & Ms. Publishing Company, 1984). Accounts of the investigation were reported at length in cables to Washington from the U.S. Embassy in Manila.

The mounting economic problems of the Marcos regime are described in William Overholt's reports cited earlier. Marcos's decline is pictured by Robert Manning in "The Philippines in Crisis," in *Foreign Affairs*, Winter 1984. Nach's report on the growing Communist insurgency is among the declassified U.S. Embassy documents I acquired. The rising anti-Marcos sentiment in Washington comes from interviews with the American officials cited. Admiral William Crowe was especially candid. I am grateful to Nayan Chanda, the Washington correspondent of the *Far Eastern Economic Review*, who obtained a copy of the State Department policy drafted in January 1984. Frederick Brown of the Senate Foreign Relations Committee staff discussed his report with me. Paul Laxalt recalled his mission to Manila in "My Conversations with Ferdinand Marcos: A Lesson in Personal Diplomacy," in *Policy Review*, Summer 1986. His account was contradicted by former Ambassador Bosworth in an interview, as well as by other State Department officials. The story of Marcos's appearance on the David Brinkley show was clarified for me by U.S. Embassy sources in Manila and by Tom Loranger, a Laxalt aide.

15. REVOLUTION AND RESTORATION

Cory expressed her reservations about running for president to me, as she did to others, in the summer of 1985. The story of Laurel's acquiescence to the vice presidential slot was told to me by Laurel and by Cardinal Sin. The sidelights on Cory's interview with *The New York Times* were related to me by Seth Mydans. Robert Trent Jones and Mark Malloch Brown provided me with information on Cory's public relations effort.

I spent about seven weeks in the Philippines in early 1986, covering the elections that took place in February. My information on the Americans who helped Cory comes from those mentioned in the narrative. I interviewed Allen Weinstein of the Center for Democracy in Washington, who helped to organize the Lugar mission. I also interviewed Lugar and read his book *Letters to the Next President* (New York: Simon and Schuster, 1988), which describes his trip and his return to Washington. Bosworth provided me with the details of "the worst single day of my life." Philip Habib and I are *compadres* as fellow alumni of Seth Low Junior High School in Bensonhurst, Brooklyn, and he related his role to me during that period.

Captain Rex Robles of the Philippine navy was one of my main sources for the story of the reform movement in the armed forces. I was given other details by Enrile and Bosworth. Sandra Burton and Lewis Simon have researched the episode, which has been recounted in a flood of books published since Cory's takeover. The events of February 1986 are in Monina Allery Mercado, ed., *People Power: An Eyewitness History of the Philippine Revolution of 1986* (Manila: Reuter Foundation, 1986); *Bayan Ko! Images of the Philippine Revolution of 1986* (Hong Kong: Project 28 Days, 1986); Patricio Mamot, *People Power* (Quezon City: New Day, 1986); Cecilo Arillo, *Breakaway* (Manila: CTA Associates, 1986); Ninotchka Rosca, *Endgame: The Fall of Marcos* (New York: Franklin Watts, 1987); James Fenton, "Snap Revolution" in *Granta* (Cambridge, England), 1986; Quijano de Manila (pseudonym of Nick Joaquin), *The Quartet of the Tiger Moon: Scenes from the People Power Apocalypse* (Manila: Book Stop, 1986); and Donald Alan Jagoe's unpublished thesis, *Turmoil, Transition . . . Triumph? The Democratic Revolution in the Philippines* (Monterey, Calif.: Naval Postgraduate School, 1986).

The early effort in Washington to turn Reagan against Marcos was reported by Leslie Gelb in *The New York Times,* January 26, 1986. State Department sources furnished me with an authoritative blow-by-blow account of the events in Washington beginning on Saturday, February 22—including notes on the meeting at Secretary of State Shultz's house on Sunday morning. The same sources provided me with notes of the White House meeting on Sunday afternoon, and Marcos's telephone conversations with Laxalt that followed.

I should mention for the record that Marcos denied to me in a conversation in Hawaii that he had spoken to Laxalt on the telephone. When I asked why he decided to leave his palace, he replied that Bosworth had threatened to send in U.S. Marines to oust him and that an American gunboat was headed up the Pasig River to blast him out. Bosworth has denied these stories as preposterous, and I believe him. I omitted Marcos's version from the narrative as another figment of his imagination. Bosworth gave me the details of Marcos's departure, including his telephone conversation with Cory— which she confirmed in an interview with me.

The indictment of the Marcoses for fraud was reported in the press. Reagan's disappointment was conveyed to me by an administration official.

The appraisal of Cory as president is based on my two reporting trips to the Philippines in 1987 and 1988. Claude Buss was buoyant in *Cory Aquino and the People of the Philippines* (Stanford, Calif.: Stanford Alumni Association, 1987), but subsequently tempered his optimism. Similar caution was expressed at a conference I attended in June 1986, the text of which is in Mark Nelson, ed., *The Philippines and the United States* (New York: Asia Society, 1986). Carl Landé et al. outlined the problems faced by Cory in *Rebuilding a Nation,* cited earlier. Landé, a scholar at the University of Kansas, expressed his disappointment with her performance in subsequent telephone interviews. A left-wing Filipino critique of Cory is Renato Constantino, *The Aquino Watch* (Quezon City: Karrel, 1987). By contrast, Patricio Mamot takes a favorable view of her early months in office in *The Aquino Administration's Baptism of Fire* (Manila: National Book Store, 1987). A balanced if not very rosy assessment is Robert Shaplen's two-part series "The Thin Edge," *The New Yorker,* September 21 and September 28, 1987. A thorough and equally doubtful look at the Philippines under Cory is the survey entitled "A Question of Faith," which appeared in *The Economist,* May 7, 1988.

The agrarian reform law has been analyzed in the Manila press and in the *Far Eastern Economic Review,* which also published the rather pessimistic World Bank report. The *Review* has also carried several studies on the population problem. The human rights issue under Cory has been raised by Amnesty International and by the Lawyers Committee for Human Rights.

I interviewed the Communist leaders in Manila, and saw insurgents in the field in Negros. The accounts of my observations of Negros need no elaboration. Two useful works elucidate the economic and social problems of the sugar industry—Filomeno Aguilar, Jr., *The Making of Sugar: Poverty, Crisis and Change in Negros Occidental* (Bacolod: La Salle Social Research Center, 1984) and Niall O'Brien, *Revolution from the Heart: The Extraordinary Record of a Priest's Life and Work Among the Poor of the Philippine Sugarlands* (New York: Oxford University Press, 1987).

INDEX

STANLEY KARNOW began his journalistic career in Paris in 1950 as a *Time* correspondent. After covering Europe, Africa and the Middle East, he went to Asia for *Time* and *Life* in 1959, and subsequently reported from there for the London *Observer, The Saturday Evening Post, The Washington Post* and NBC News. He was an editor of *The New Republic* and a columnist for King Features. His books include *Southeast Asia; Mao and China: From Revolution to Revolution;* and *Vietnam: A History.* He won six Emmys as well as Dupont, Peabody and Polk awards as chief correspondent for *Vietnam: A Television History,* and is the recipient of two Overseas Press Club awards for newspaper reporting.

Born in New York City, Mr. Karnow graduated from Harvard and attended the Sorbonne and the Ecole des Sciences Politiques in Paris. He has been a Nieman Fellow, Kennedy Fellow and East Asia Research Center Fellow at Harvard, and a Poynter Fellow at Yale. He lives in Potomac, Maryland, with his wife, Annette, a painter, and has three children and a grandchild.